Montreal Museum of Fine Arts, formerly Art Association of Montreal

Spring Exhibitions 1880–1970

In 1880 the Art Association of Montreal established the Spring Exhibitions, an annual event which played a critical role in establishing a widespread appreciation of Canadian art. When the Association became the Montreal Museum of Fine Arts in 1948, it continued to sponsor the event for more than twenty years. Open to all artists, the exhibitions frequently received from 1,500 to 2,000 submissions, with many of the exhibitions having between 400 and 500 works. In its ninety-year history it presented 23,201 paintings, sculptures, etchings, engravings, stained glass and tapestry designs; from 1885 to 1947 architecture was included, and 1,292 pieces of painted china were exhibited between 1894 and 1926. In all the Spring Exhibitions represented the work of 3,163 artists from across Canada, with approximately 100 from the United States, Britain, or Europe.

In compiling a catalogue of these exhibitions Evelyn McMann has produced a comprehensive record of Canadian art during nine decades of tremendous development. Her work refers the reader to biographical information about the majority of the artists, and makes available for the first time information on hundreds of lesser-known artists. The many cross-references make it possible to locate artists who exhibited under two or more names, and the record of more than 150 prizes awarded through the exhibitions adds another useful resource. For researchers and art historians this volume provides an invaluable point of access to a vast body of Canadian art.

Evelyn de R. McMann is retired from the staff of the Vancouver Public Library, where she was responsible for the indexing of Canadian art for the Fine Arts and Music Division. She also compiled Royal Canadian Academy of Arts / Académie royale des arts du Canada: Exhibitions and Members 1880-1979, published 1981.

EVELYN de R. McMANN

Montreal Museum of Fine Arts, formerly Art Association of Montreal

SPRING EXHIBITIONS 1880-1970

UNIVERSITY OF TORONTO PRESS
TORONTO BUFFALO LONDON

Toronto Buffalo London
Printed in Canada
Reprinted in 2018
ISBN 0-8020-2650-8
ISBN 978-1-4875-7708-7 (paper)

Canadian Cataloguing in Publication Data

McMann, Evelyn de R. (Evelyn de Rostaing), 1913-
Montreal Museum of Fine Arts, formerly Art Association of Montreal; spring exhibitions 1880-1970

ISBN 0-8020-2650-8

1. Art, Canadian - Exhibitions - Indexes.
2. Art, Modern - 20th Century - Exhibitions - Indexes.
3. Art, Modern - 19th century - Exhibitions - Indexes.
4. Montreal Museum of Fine Arts - Exhibitions - Indexes.
I. Title.

N6545.M25 1987 709'.71'0740114281 C87-094767-2

Contents

Preface

The Art Association of Montreal was incorporated as a private society 23 April 1860, and is the oldest Canadian art institution still active. The majority of members were collectors, with a few artists from the Montreal Society of Artists, founded 1847, and other local artists. For a number of years the Association rented space for an annual exhibition, mainly of paintings from the members' collections, with some paintings by member and guest artists.

When the Association received a bequest from Benaiah Gibb in 1877 of land on Phillips Square, $8,000 towards a building fund, and his collection of ninety paintings, predominantly by Dutch and Flemish artists, and several bronzes, a gallery was built with space for art classes and a library. The Phillips Square gallery was officially opened 26 May 1879 by the Governor General, the Marquis of Lorne, and his wife H.R.H. Princess Louise. The gallery at the present location on Sherbrooke Street West was opened 9 December 1912, by the Governor General, H.R.H. the Duke of Connaught, the Duchess of Connaught, and their daughter H.R.H. Princess Patricia, who had been one of the artists in the 1912 Spring Exhibition. The architects of the new gallery, Edward and William S. Maxwell, exhibited details of their plans in the 1911 Spring Exhibition.

The Association changed its name to the Montreal Museum of Fine Arts in 1948 to indicate that the collections of paintings and sculpture had been extended to include the decorative arts. The Museum is now known under the name Musée des beaux-arts de Montréal. Over the years a number of paintings and sculpture from the Spring Exhibitions were added to the permanent collection.

After establishing Canada's first permanent art gallery, the Association decided in 1880 to emphasize the high merit and importance of Canadian art by making its annual exhibition a show-case for Canadian artists. In so doing it was also the first and only gallery to organize and maintain for ninety years an annual exhibition of works by Canadian artists from coast to coast.

The first 'Special exhibition of works of Canadian artists, including Diploma Pictures, etc, from the recent exhibition of the Canadian Academy of Arts, Ottawa,' was organized and funded by the Association, not, as is sometimes presumed, by the new Academy (the prefix Royal was granted 22 June 1880). Although the Diploma Works were loaned by Canada's equally new National Gallery, some artists entered works not shown in the Academy's inaugural exhibition, 6 March 1880, and there were also works by artists who had not exhibited with the Academy.

The Spring Exhibitions suffered a confused numbering in the early years when the annual spring exhibition of the Royal Canadian Academy replaced them each second or third year until 1907, after which the Academy changed its annual to autumn, in 1909 (see p 415). The title 'Annual Spring Exhibition' first appeared on the 1883 catalogue. The 'Fifteenth Annual Spring Exhibition,' 1894, was the first to be numbered, and confirms 1880 as the first. The numbering remained consistent to 1965, except that 1911 was numbered the twenty-seventh, and 1912 was numbered the twenty-ninth. To add to the confusion a note in the 1942 and 1943 catalogues had two errors, 'The Spring Exhibition has been an annual event since 1881.'

In 1967, on the occasion of the centennial of Confederation, a retrospective exhibition was organized to honour over one hundred artists who had won the famous Jessie Dow prize, 1908 to 1965, and five other prizes. The prizes are described on pp xii-xiii.

From 1968 to 1970 the tradition of spring exhibitions was carried on by 'Survey,' in which the exhibitors were chosen and invited by a jury.

During the years 1880 to 1970 the 3,162 exhibitors included artists from across Canada, with about one hundred American, British, or European artists. The 23,201 works are a comprehensive record of nine decades of art in Canada as represented by painters, sculptors, engravers, etchers, graphic artists, stained glass designers, tapestry weavers and photographers. Architecture was included from 1885 to 1947, and 1,292 pieces of painted china were exhibited between 1894 and 1926. The exhibitions were open and artists were eager to participate, resulting in peak years of approximately two thousand submissions. The space was generous, allowing for more than four or five hundred works to be displayed in nearly one-third of the annuals.

The many references to the Spring Exhibitions in books and periodicals testify to the important place they occupy in Canada's art history, and their inestimable value to artists. In recognition of their significant contribution the exhibitions were held under the distinguished patronage of the

Governors General. The altruistic commitment of the Association to encourage young artists, advance the careers of the better-known artists, and induce the public to appreciate and collect Canadian art was achieved in full measure.

This book was compiled at the request of Miss Juanita Toupin, Chief Librarian of the Museum. The considerable assistance of Miss Toupin, and her staff, has been much appreciated, and it was of particular help to have available the extensive resources of the library, opened in 1882.

Robert G. Hill, who is writing a biographical dictionary of architects in Canada, 1800-1950, has most generously supplied the birth and death dates of the architects. Without his kind assistance most architects would have joined the many other exhibitors who, in spite of more than two years of searching, were never born and never died.

Miss Jacqueline Hunter, Chief Librarian, and Charles C. Hill, Curator of Canadian Art, National Gallery of Canada, have been a constant source of aid and encouragement throughout the compiling of this record.

The library files of the Musée des beaux-arts de Montréal, Musée d'art contemporain, National Gallery of Canada, Art Gallery of Ontario, and the Vancouver Public Library, Fine Arts and Music Division, have made it possible to find biographical information that is not otherwise available. The staff of each library has my sincere thanks for its assistance, and interest in this project.

Miss Joan A. Bulger, Associate Editor, William Rueter, RCA, Senior Designer, and Peter B. Scaggs, Production Manager, have answered a deluge of letters and questions in preparing the pages for publication. Their kindness and patience have been most gratefully received.

As a born Montrealer, and having seen the Spring Exhibitions over many years, I have found the time spent on this project as enjoyable as a visit home, meeting old friends. It has been a happy task, and I am deeply indebted to Miss Toupin for having made her request.

Evelyn de Rostaing McMann
Vancouver
September 1987

Guide to Entries

Works exhibited are listed by the name of the artist. The entries contain the following information:

DOE, JOHN
23 Feb 1873, Ottawa 19 May 1947,
Halifax. B CWW36 M NGC Juror
addr: Ottawa: 62 McLaren St, 1890-2;
90 Sparks St, 1910-16. Halifax, 1601
Barrington St, 1928-44
1890 45 Mountain stream
1892 61-3 Seashore wc $35 each
1910 35 Birches $225 (MBAM)
1916 59 Blue Lake wc $45 (listed
1967, Jessie Dow prize)
1928 72 Evening (Mr K.W. Morris)
1944 205 Themes nm $30
1894-7 Assoc prize, landscape, 1892
port: by Alan Ross, 1936-302

Name of artist

Biographical data
Date and place of birth and death, when obtainable. The initials indicate biographical sources, pp xv-xviii.

Juror
The catalogues listed the jurors in 1938-41, 1943, and 1945-7. List of jurors and the years they served, pp 413-14.

Address
Catalogues had the full address 1891-1965; the city only, 1880, 1967-70; no address 1881-9.

Works exhibited

Catalogue numbers are in the second column. 61-3 indicates three works with precisely the same title and medium.

Titles are entered as listed in the catalogues.

Medium. Painting without medium is oil. No medium, nm, has been used when the catalogue had a section for 'Drawing, water colour, pastel, etc,' without identification of each work. List of abbreviations, p xix.

Size was not noted in the catalogues until 1967.

Illus. Catalogues were not illustrated until 1960.

Price. All prices in the catalogues are noted.

(Mr K.W. Morris). Name of lender.

(MBAM). Indicates the work is in the permanent collection of the gallery noted. List of galleries, pp xix-xx.

Because of title changes during the years between the exhibition of a work and when it was acquired by a gallery, and the omission of size in the catalogues until 1967, it was not possible to identify with certainty all the exhibited works now in public galleries.

Port. A portrait of the artist, the name of the exhibitor, and the year it was exhibited.

Prize awards

The Association awarded prizes in 1891-4, and the catalogues of 1892-7 noted the winners by the category of the prize, not by the title of the work. All artists residing in Canada or Canadian artists studying or residing abroad were eligible to compete.

There were first and second prizes for paintings in oil: figure ($200/$100), marine or landscape ($200/$100), artist now an Association student or had been within three years ($75/$50), painting by an artist under thirty not a member of the RCA ($100/$50). Water colour ($100/$50). One prize for portrait in oil ($100), and still life in oil ($100). There was a special $200 prize for the picture obtaining the most votes by exhibition visitors; each admission ticket had one vote, single Association membership, two votes, each family membership, three votes.

The award longest in duration was the Jessie Dow prize, for oil and water colour, sustained by Miss Dow from 1908 through 1950, and continued by Dr J.W.A. Hickson to 1956, by Mrs M.E. Allan, CBE, and Mr R.N. Hickson to 1960, and from 1961 to 1965 by Mrs M.E. Allan, CBE, and Mrs R.N. Hickson.

From 1944 to 1953 there was a two-jury system: Jury I

awarded the two Jessie Dow prizes, Jury II selected the avant-garde works to receive the Association prizes for oil and water colour. After 1953 a single jury was reinstated to award all prizes.

In 1957 the Ladies' Committee of the Museum established a sculpture prize.

A Centenary grand prize, in memory of Ronald T. Riley, for a work in any medium was awarded in 1960, the centenary of the Museum.

The Canada Council from 1961 to 1963 made available funds on a matching basis, for purchase awards, and seventeen works thus entered the Museum's collection.

The Albert H. Robinson Grand Award was inaugurated 1963, from funds from a bequest of Mrs Mary E. Davis.

The catalogue of 'Prize Award Winners, 1908-1965, Spring Exhibitions,' 1967, recorded the 108 artists, the years, and titles of 147 works that received an award. The exhibition included 53 prize-winning works, and 22 substitutes, by living artists.

Not included

The Councillors of the Museum were listed in some of the catalogues; and there was unreliable indication of artists' and architects' memberships in various associations.

Biographical Sources

AAA American art annual. Washington, DC, American Federation of Arts. Checked 1900-33

AGO Art Gallery of Ontario. The Canadian collection. Toronto, McGraw-Hill Company of Canada, Limited, 1970

B Bénézit, Emmanuel. Dictionnaire critique et documentaire des peintres, sculpteurs, dessinateurs et graveurs. Paris, Librarie Grund, 1976 edition

CC1 CC2 Creative Canada: a biographical dictionary of twentieth-century creative and performing arts. Compiled by the Reference Division, McPherson Library, University of Victoria. Toronto, University of Toronto Press, Vol 1, 1971, Vol 2, 1972

CE Canadian encyclopedia. Edmonton, Hurtig Publishers, 1985

CNS Canadian Newspaper Service Reg'd. Reference book: biographical reference data and other general information. Montreal, Canadian Newspaper Service Reg'd. Checked 1927 and later editions

Co Colombo, John Robert. Colombo's Canadian references. Toronto, Oxford University Press, 1976

CWW Canadian who's who, Kieran Simpson, editor. Toronto, University of Toronto Press, 1979 to date. Previous editions: The Times, London. Toronto, Musson Book Co, 1910; Arthur L. Tunnell, editor, 1936-75. Toronto, Trans Canada Press, 1936-8 to 1964-6; Toronto, Who's Who Canadian Publications, 1967-9 to 1973-5

DBA Dictionary of British artists 1880-1940. Compiled by Jane Johnson and A. Greutzner. Woodbridge, Suffolk, Antique Collectors Club, 1976

DBW Dictionary of British watercolour artists up to 1920, H. L. Mallallieu. Woodbridge, Suffolk, Antique Collectors Club, 2nd revised edition 1986

DCB Dictionary of Canadian biography. Toronto, University of Toronto Press, 1966, in progress

DIA Dictionary of Irish artists, Walter George Strickland. Shannon, Irish University Press, 1969

DMS New dictionary of modern sculptors, Robert Maillard, general editor. New York, Tudor Publishing Co, 1970. Original edition, Nouveau dictionnaire de la sculpture moderne. Paris, Fernan Hazen, 1970

DVP Dictionary of Victorian painters, Christopher Wood; revised 2nd edition, research by Christopher Newell. Woodbridge, Suffolk, Antique Collectors Club, 1978

EC Encyclopedia Canadiana. Toronto, Grolier Society of Canada, 1972 edition

ED Dictionary of Eskimo artists in sculpture and prints, Philip Howard Gray. Roseman, Mont, University of Montana, c 1974

F Fielding's dictionary of American painters, sculptors and engravers, Mantle Fielding; new, completely revised, enlarged and updated, editor Glenn B. Opitz. Poughkeepsie, N Y, Apollo Book, 1978

G Graves, Algernon. The Royal Academy of Arts: a complete dictionary of contributors and their work from its foundation in 1769 to 1904. London, Henry Graves & Co Limited, and George Bell & Sons, 1905

Gr Groce, George C., and Wallace, David H., editors. New York Historical Society's dictionary of artists in America 1564-1860. New Haven, Conn, Yale Univesity Press, 1957

H Harper, J. Russell. Early painters and engravers in Canada. Toronto, University of Toronto Press, 1970

IO Index of Ontario artists, Hennie Wolff, editor. Toronto, Visual Arts of Ontario and Ontario Association of Art Galleries, 1978

L Larousse. Dictionary of painters. New York, Larousse & Co, Inc, 1981. Original edition, Le Larousse: des grands peintres. Paris, Larousse, 1976

M MacDonald, Colin S. Dictionary of Canadian artists. Ottawa, Canadian Paperbacks, 1967-82, Adams to Rakine, in progress

MO98 MO12 Morgan, Henry James. Canadian men and women of the time. Toronto, Briggs, 1898 and 1912 editions

NGC National Gallery of Canada. Catalogue of paintings and sculpture. Vol 3, Canadian school, R.H. Hubbard. Ottawa and Toronto, published for the Trustees by University of Toronto Press, 1960

PMC Prominent men of Canada, 1931-2, Ross Hamilton, editor. Montreal, National Publishing, 1932

R1 R2 Roberts, Charles G.D., and Tunnell, Arthur L., editors. A standard dictionary of Canadian biography; the Canadian who was who. Toronto, Trans Canada Press, Vol 1, 1875-1933, 1934; Vol 2, 1875-1937, 1938

RA Royal Academy. A dictionary of artists and their works in the annual summer exhibitions of the Royal Academy of Arts, 1905-70. East Ardsley, Wakefield, Yorkshire, E.P. Publishing Limited, 1973-82

RSA Royal Scottish Academy. A complete list of the exhibited works by Raeburn and by Academicians, Associates and Honorable Members, 1826-1916, giving details of those works in public galleries. Compiled under the direction of Frank Rinder. Glasgow, James Maclehose & Sons, 1917. Bath, Kingsmead Reprints, 1975

RSBA Royal Society of British Artists. Members exhibiting 1824-1962, Maurice Bradshaw. Leigh-on-Sea, F. Lewis Publishers, 1973-7

TB TB2 TB3 Thieme, Ulrich, und Becker, Felix. Allgemeines Lexikon der bildenden Kunstler von der Antike bis zur Gegenwart. 37 vols, 1907-50. (2) Vollmer, Hans. Allgemeines Lexikon der bildenden Kunstler der XX Jahrhunderts. Vols 1-5, 1953-61. (3) Vollmer, Hans. Vols 5-6, 1961-2. Leipzig, E.A. Seeman, 1907-62

W78 Wallace, W. Stewart, editor. Macmillan dictionary of Canadian biography. Toronto, Macmillan of Canada, 1978

Previous editions, 1945 and 1963, also checked

WBA Walters, Grant G. Dictionary of British artists working 1900-50. Eastbourne, Eastbourne Fine Arts, 1975

WHC W.H. Coverdale collection of Canadiana: paintings, water colours and drawings. Manoir Richelieu collection. W. Martha E. Cooke. Ottawa, Public Archives of Canada, 1983

WWA Who's who in American art. Washington, D C, American Federation of Arts, 1936-47; New York, R.R. Bowker, 1953 to date

WWB Who's who in art: being a series of alphabetically arranged biographies of the leading men and women in the world of art to-day. London, Art Trade Press Limited, 1927 to date

WWC Who's who in Canada, B.M. Greene, editor. Toronto, International Press Limited, 1922 to date

WWW Who was who in American art: compiled from the original thirty-four volumes of the American Art Annual, and Who's who in art: biographies of American artists, from 1898 to 1947, edited by Peter Hastings Falk. Madison, Conn, Sound View Press, 1985

Y Young, William. Dictionary of American artists, sculptors, and engravers from the beginnings through the turn of the twentieth century. Cambridge, Mass, William Young Company, 1968

Abbreviations

ABBREVIATIONS

acry	acrylic	m tech	mixed technique
alum	aluminium	maq	maquette
aqua	aquatint	medln	medallion
archi	architecture	mezz	mezzotint
b&w	black and white	min	miniature
call	calligraphy	mispr	misprint
cart	cartoon	mm	mixed media
carv	carving	monoc	monochrome
cer	ceramic	monog	monograph
charc	charcoal	monot	monotype
col	colour	nfs	not for sale
coll	collage	nm	no medium
conc	concrete	np	no price
d	diameter	port	portrait
dec	decorative	pr	print
des	design	pyro	pyrography
drwg	drawing	rel	relief
dry pt	dry point	sculp	sculpture
engr	engraving	sergph	seragraph
etch	etching	st gl	stained glass
gr	graphic	tap	tapestry
h	high	temp	tempera
illum	illumination	ter cot	terra cotta
illus	illustration	text	textile
jwlry	jewellery	unfr	unframed
lacq	lacquer	wc	water colour
lino	linoleum	wd	wood
litho	lithograph	wld	welded

GALLERIES

AE	Agnes Etherington Art Centre, Queen's University
AGH	Art Gallery of Hamilton
AGO	Art Gallery of Ontario

LPL	London Public Library and Art Museum
MBAM	Musée des beaux-arts de Montréal
MQ	Musée du Québec
NGC	National Gallery of Canada
RM	Robert McLaughlin Art Gallery
SPL	Sarnia Public Library and Art Gallery
UG	University of Guelph

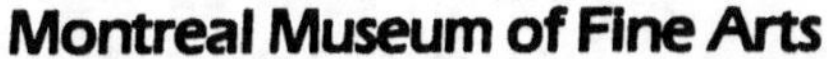

Montreal Museum of Fine Arts

Exhibitions

A

ABBOTT, HARRIET A.
addr: Montreal, 419 Guy St
1901 103 Through the bracken, Ste Agathe wc $10
104 Among the hills, Ste Agathe wc $10

ABBOTT, ISABELLA MARY
23 Dec 1890, Montreal
addr: Montreal: 1919; 299 Pine Ave W, 1921-5
1919 1 Sketch in the Laurentians wc $15
2 A Laurentian lake wc $10
1921 1 Autumn day wc $20
1922 1 November sun and shadow wc $30
1923 1 The edge of a wood, Senneville wc $25
2 High water, Senneville wc $25
3 Late August wc $25
4 Le Mont Brulé wc $25
1924 1 Early morning mist $45
2 Sketch $20
1925 6 Rampikes $40
7 Late afternoon sunshine wc

ABBOTT, JOHN BETHUNE
23 Dec 1882 - 1919, Montreal B H Mo12
addr: Montreal: 419 Guy St, 1901-3; 1018 Sherbrooke St, 1905-6; Montreal, 1908; c/o Art Assoc, 1909; 299 Pine Ave W, 1910; Art Assoc, 1911-15; 679 Sherbrooke St W, 1917; Art Gallery, 1918-19
1901 105 Old Selworthy Church, Somerset wc $25
106 A Belgian windmill wc $10
1903 124 South Tower, Senneville wc $25
125 Dunster, from the dykes wc $25
126 Sunset and snow wc $25
127 The pond, Braeside links wc $25
1905 124 Early June wc $40
125 Evening wc $35
126 Misty morning, October wc $30
127 An October evening wc $40
1906 168 Clearing weather wc $35
169 The last of the snow wc $40
170 Dawn, St Andrews wc $30
171 A still autumn day wc $25
1908 157 Once upon a time wc $35
158 Last rays wc $30
159 On the edge of the wood wc $30
160 A cloudy afternoon wc $40
1909 7 Misty spring $35
8 Summer by the sea $60
9 Autumn haze $25
10 Grey winter $25
1910 8 Sunny glade $50
9 Law's cottage $25
10 Birches $30
1911 1 Three birches $40
2 Clearing weather, St Andrews $50
3 Early autumn $25
1912 7 The last rays $60
8 After the shower $30
9 The three oaks $20
1913 1 Moonlight, early evening $30
2 A break in the clouds $30
3 Sea mist and glistening sands $60
1914 1 Moonrise $25
2 A quiet pool $40
1915 1 Early winter $60
1916 1 A freshing breeze $40
2 A bit of the factory district $30
1917 1 Moonlight $40
2 Rocks near Métis $75
3 Our garden $30
1918 1 Low tide, St Andrews $35
2 On the edge of the links $25
1919 3 A freshening breeze, St Andrews $40
4 Dawn $35

ABBOTT, PHYLLIS C.
addr: Montreal: 299 Pine Ave W, 1922-9; 505 Pine Ave W, 1934-5
1922 2 Late autumn, sketch $20
1923 5 Owl's Head, Lake Memphremagog $40
6 Autumn colouring $35

1924 3 Rising mist $40
4 October morn $30
1925 1 A bend in Les Hurons River $40
2 Clear day, early autumn $40
3 Over the city $40
4-5 Sketch wc $15 each
1929 1 Snow storm wc $10
2 House tops $35
1934 1 North beach, Percé, Que $75
1935 1 Cliffs, Bonaventure Island $100

ABBOTT, ROBERT
addr: Montreal, 2005 Favard St
1947 1 Freighter and tugs $150

ABBOTT-SMITH, R. B.
addr: Westmount, 10 Bellevue Ave, 1920-2
1920 1 A British outpost in Macedonia wc
2 In the Laurentian foothills wc $20
1921 2 The market place, Salonika wc $35
1922 3 Ruse Kassandra, Salonika wc $30

ABRAHAM, MARY B.
addr: Chatham, Ont, 356 Victoria Ave, 1934-7
1934 2 Lombardy poplars $75
1935 2 A midland valley $125
1936 1 Thunder in the air
1937 1 A bit of the Wye Valley $60

ABRAHAMSON, UNA STELLA (m Roy A. Abrahamson)
6 Aug 1922, London, Eng
addr: Ottawa, 7 Dunvegan Rd, 1951-4
1951 74 Gourds and pewter $40
1954 1 Asters $50

ABRAMSON, AÑITA see ELKIN, ANITA

ACER, ANNE LOUISE (m Peter Burgess)
11 Dec 1928, Montreal
addr: Ste Anne de Bellevue, Que, Macdonald College, P O Box 104
1954 2 Summer poppies $50

ADAMS, BARBARA see WILKES, BARBARA

ADAMS, CYRIL
14 Feb 1921, Montreal
addr: Montreal, 555 Richards St
1945 1 Haile Selassie wc

ADAMS, GEORGE C.
addr: Montreal: 1501 St Catherine St W, 1932; 1642 Lincoln Ave, 1936; 2010 Union Ave, 1946-7
1932 1 Benoit Street, Montreal wc $50
1936 2 The visitor $250
3 Still life $50
1946 1 The green smock $200
1947 2 A glimpse of Christ Church Cathedral $200

ADAMSON, ANNA HATFIELD (m James S.C. Adamson)
addr: Ottawa: 194 Cobourg St, 1915; 128 Powell Ave, 1917-24
1915 412 Chocolate set 12 pieces
413 Orange set 7 pieces
414 Tea set 6 pieces
415 Lemonade pitcher $3-
416 Marmalade jar $10
417 Satsuma box $10
418 Satsuma rose jar $9
419 Satsuma plaque
420 Fruit bowl
1917 396 Belleek jardinière
397 Belleek vase
398 Biscuit jar
399 Bread plate
400 Bonbon box
1918 410 Belleek jardinière $20
411 Bread plate, French $10
412 Chop dish, French $18
413 Belleek tea pot
414 Fruit bowl, 6 small bowls $50
415 Marmalade jar $10
1920 325 Lamp vase, Belleek china, and shade $150
1924 348 Satsuma caserole
349 Canadian vetch plate
350 Satsuma plate

ADNEY, EDWIN TAPPAN Amer
13/23 Jul 1868, Athens, Ohio 10 Oct 1950, Woodstock, N.B. B F M TB
addr: Montreal: 14 Phillips Sq, 1923; 364 Dorchester St W, 1924; 364 Sherbrooke St W, 1925; 62 Drummond St, 1927; 1220 Drummond St, 1930
1923 222 Armorial glass, Bolton des
223 Armorial panel, Griswold des
224 Arms, McLean dec panel
225 Arms dec panel
1924 269 The Earl of Crawford and Lord Welles joust before King Richard II carved panel $400

1925 8 A river in New Brunswick wc $35
9 North canoes at a portage wc
1927 1 Montreal Express on Lake Superior wc
1930 251 Panel of arms, Norton $200
252 Panel of Arms, Peabody $200

ADSHEAD, IRENE LOUISE
addr: Montreal, 5324 4th Ave, Rosemount, 1941-3; St Eustache, Que, Elmsgrove, Box 7, 1945
1941 277 Head of a man plaster
1942 227 Mrs A. Adshead plaster
1943 250 Study of a Negress sculp
1945 2 Miss Joan Cleasby

AHIER, CHARLES
fl 1900-12. H
addr: Montreal, 284 Bourgeois St
1912 10 Hunting caribou, Labrador

AHOLA, ANNE JOSEPHINE
27 Feb 1896, Hiintelys Vaara, Finland
addr: Aurora, Ont, RR2
1962 54 Cradle of immortality nm $500

AHRENS, CARL HENRY VON
15 Feb 1863, Winfield Ont, 27 Feb 1936, Toronto. B CC1 H M Mo12 NGC TB3
addr: Toronto, 48 Caroline Ave, 1892. Doon, Ont, 1894-8. Galt, Ont, Big Trees, 1931-3
1892 1 Cradled in the net $250
2 A modern cherub $200
3 Little mother $50
1894 1 Goose girl
2 Building the fleet
3 A grey evening
4 Dutchman and sheep
5 Dutch rag pickers $300
6 The widow $100
1895 1 After rain
2 Ripe corn time $250
3 A wet evening at the village $150
4 Moon and meadow $150
5 Evening $30
6 One day $30
1898 1 The coming storm $250
2 Smoky weather $150
3 Wet evening $150
4 The lane $75
5 A lone shore $100
1931 1 Summer $250
2 The lane $1,500
1932 2 Broken meadows $350
3 Changing seasons $300
1933 1 Trees and meadows $500
2 The mill $550
435 The road to town etch
436 Woodland etch $15
1894-5 Assoc hon mention 1892 figure

AIKINS, LOUIE A.
1889 1 Grapes $35

AIKMAN, GEORGE W. Scot
1830 - 8 Jan 1906, Edinburgh. B DBA DBW DVP TB
1883 115 Evening hour

AIROLA, PAAVO OLAVIA
15 Apr 1915/14 Jun 1918, Karelia, Finland. CWW83 M TB3 WWA82
addr: Vernonville, Ont, RR1, 1954-7. Colborne, Ont, 1959. Toronto, c/o Roberts Gallery, 759 Yonge St
1954 3 Tulips $400
4 Still life with black bottle $350
1955 1 Collaboration $400
1956 1 Fishing huts $300
1957 1 Three boats $350
2 Quietude $400
1959 1 Still life with black bottle $350
1960 1 My daughter Anni $400
2 Still life with black bottle $350

AITCHISON-WALKER, JESSIE
addr: Fontenay aux Roses, France, 4 ave Bourg la Reine, 1914; Fontenay aux Roses, 1915
1914 Walker
413 The white night etch
414 When the day is done etch
415 After mass etch
416 Street corner etch
1915 2 An old French church etch $10
3 the willow etch $7
4 Vulture etch $7

AITKEN, JAMES ALFRED Scot
1846, Edinburgh. 21 Dec 1897, Glasgow. B DBA DBW DVP G H TB
1884 124 On the berwickshire coast wc $100

AITKEN, MELITA (m R.J. Aitken)

1866, Drumbo, Ont. 28 Aug 1945, Vancouver. B DBA H
addr: Victoria: 316 Cook St, 1932; 424 Linden Ave, 1933-37. Vancouver, 1550 W 15th Ave, 1941-3
1932 4 A full bowl wc $300
5 Basket of pansies wc $150
6 The crimson rose wc $100
7 From a Victoria, B.C. garden wc $100
1933 3 Peonies from Victoria wc $500
4 The jug from Normandy wc $250
5 Oriental poppies wc $300
6 Vase of roses wc $100
1935 3 Single and double peonies of 'Little Oaks', Victoria wc $300
4 Hibiscus of Hanula, Hawaii wc $300
5 Yellow hibiscus of Hanula, Hawaii wc $150
1936 4 Oriental poppies in a Chinese wine bottle wc $50
5 Alamanda of Hawaii wc $40
1937 2 Torch ginger of Hawaii, native of Java wc $150
1941 1 The golden banded lily of Japan wc $150
2 A rare magnolia bloom wc $75
1943 2 Too well known wc $30

AKSTINAS, JOSEPH
18 Dec 1922, Ukmerge, Lithuania
addr: Montreal, 5165 Walkley Ave, Apt 3
1954 5 Autumn landscape $150

ALBINSON, DEWEY Amer
9 Mar 1898, Minneapolis. AAA33 TB2 WWA40
addr: Quebec, 75 Ste Ursule
1939 1 Cap Diamant $400
2 Habitant house $400
3 Frost and snow $350
4 Mountain Hill $300

ALEXANDER, CHARLES (b Charles Alexander Smith)
2 Nov 1864, Galt, Hamburg or London, Ont. June 1915, London, Eng. B H Mo12 TB2
addr: Paris, c/o Drexel Harjis & Co, 31 Boul Haussmann, 1891
1888 Smith, C. Alexander
26 Atrappé $125
1891 1 Les gamins s'amusent $1,000
2 Notre Dame de Moret $300
3 Sunset on the Seine $400
4 Port de Menton $400

ALEXANDER, HAROLD RUPERT LEOFRIC GEORGE, Earl of Tunis, Governor General of Canada, 1946-52
10 Dec 1891, London, Eng. 16 Jun 1969, Windsor Forest, Berks, Eng
addr: Ottawa
1947 3 The Norfolk Broads, England
4 Twin Isles, B.C.

ALEXANDER, WILHEMINA (MINA) (m L.H. Alexander)
2 Jul 1871 - 1962, Hamilton, Ont
addr: Hamilton, 176 Hughson St S, 1931-6
1931 3 Blue and pink $75
4 Zinnias $100
1932 8 Physalis and bittersweet $125
9 Summer flowers $90
1933 7 Regal lilies $100
8 Peonies $100
1934 3 Iris $100
4 Goldfish $75
5 Zinnias $150
1935 6 Peonies $100
7 Tiger lilies $90
8 Wild crab apples $35
1936 6 September bouquet $100

ALEXANDER, WILLIAM WALKER
9 Aug 1870 - 3 Apr 1948, Toronto. AGO M
addr: Montreal, 116 King St W
1929 295 Traffic on the Thames etch $10
296 Melting snow etch $10

ALFORD, FRANK
addr: London, Eng
1923 7 Boy in second-hand shop $600

ALFRED, PAUL (b Paul Alfred Ernest Meister)
10 Apr 1892, Hanley, Staffs, Eng, 6 May 1959, Ottawa. M NGC WWA62
addr: Ottawa, 144 Concord St, 1922-4
1922 4 Winter sunset wc $75
5 Sunshine and shadow wc $50
6 Winter wc $50
1923 8 Summer landscape wc $30
9 The level crossing wc $30
1924 5 A Laurentian village wc $150
6 Winter landscape wc $150
270 The Tower, Parliament Bldgs,

Ottawa, drwg $50

ALLAN, ANN LOW
addr: Montreal, 4095 Côte des Neiges Rd
1935 9 Tulips $75

ALLAN, MARGUERITE I. see BULLER, MARGUERITE I.

ALLAN, MARJORIE L.
addr: Montreal; 386 Sherbrooke St W, 1922-8; 900 Sherbrooke St W, 1930-1
1922 7-9 Still life wc $7 each
1923 11-12 Still life wc $16.50, $15
13 Still life wc
1924 7-8 Still life wc $15, $25
1925 10 The pink house $15
11 The boat house $15
12 Still life wc $20
1926 179 Lucille charcl $7
1928 1 Coat of arms wc
1930 1 Still life $50
2 Portrait
1931 5 Coloured girl $50

ALLARDICE, E. A. (Mrs)
addr: Montreal, 607 University St
1923 10 Head of girl b&w $25

ALLEN, NEWSTEAD ADAMS
fl 1913-37
addr: Westmount, 79 Columbia Ave
1937 324 Suburban residence

ALLEN, RALPH
6 Dec 1926, Raunds, Northants, Eng
AGO CC1 M WWA62
addr: Kingston, Ont; 55L Alfred St, 1959-67; Kingston, 1968
1959 2 Edge of the lake, No 3. $200
Jessie Dow prize, 1967-1, 26 x 40 (R. Bruce Sloane, M.D, Philadelphia, Penn)
1968 1 Orange pressure copolymer plastic 35 x 60 $500
2 Two forms 60 x 36 $500

ALLEN, THOMAS Amer
19 Oct 1894, St Louis. 24 Aug 1924, Boston. B F TB1/3
1889 2 At the end of the lane $375
3 Night cometh on $125

ALLEN, WILLIAM R.
addr: Westmount: 229 Westmount Blvd, 1929; 4707 Westmount Blvd, 1935-6. Montreal, 6545 Sherbrooke St W, Apt 3, 1955
1929 3 Evening wc
1935 10 York Minster wc
1936 7 Tugs, St John, N.B.
1955 2 Sugar bush in October $100

ALLER, ROBERT C.
1922, Dauphin, Man
addr: Montreal: 1429 Stanley St, Apt 14, 1948-9; 1935 Tupper St, Apt 2, 1951
1948 95 Totems dry pt
1949 1 Montreal, 1948 temp $80
153 Portrait with hands aqua $25
1951 121 Capital punishment temp $150

ALLEYN, GEORGE EDMUND
9 Jun 1931, Quebec. AGO CC2 M NGC
addr: Quebec, 58 Laurier Ave, 1954-6; 430 Laurier Ave, 1960. Montreal, c/o Galerie Dresdnère, 2170 Crescent St
1954 6 Landscape, Baie St Paul
1956 2 Rocks $200
1960 3 Marine $500
131 November nm $75
1962 40 Corrosion nm $250
41 Paspebiac nm $225

ALLISON, FRANK DRUMMOND
29 Mar 1883 - 1951, Saint John N.B.
addr: Montreal, Joyce's Chambers, Phillips Sq, 1916. St John, 43 Carleton St, 1928-39
1916 3 Twin pines, Rothesay $50
1928 2 The old Château Espalion wc $250
1932 10 Gerona $250
11 The bridge at Mende $250
1933 9 Château de Calmont wc $60
10 Bab Djedid, Fez wc $100 (listed 1967, Jessie Dow prize)
1934 6 Knaresborough $400
1939 5 Saddle Rock $175
6 Incoming tide wc $75

ALLISON, LOUISE MUIR (m William Gordon Stockwell)
b Rothesay, N.B. CNS40
addr: Montreal, 1019 Sherbrooke St W, 1937-8
1937 3 Ebony, ivory and rose $50
1938 1 Beach, Nova Scotia $35

ALSTON, T. HAMILTON
addr: Montreal, 800 Shuter St
1915 10 The rising moon $35

AMESS, ELIZABETH (m Frederick Arthur Amess)
addr: Vancouver, 2375 Oak St
1947 5 Evening study wc $75

AMOS, LOUIS AUGUSTE
18 Aur 1869 - 20 Aug 1948, Montreal
addr: Montreal: 175 Mansfield St, 1927; 1414 Crescent St, 1933
1927 Amos, Saxe & Cormier
179 Montreal Court House, bronze doors model
1933 Amos, L.A. & Amos, P.C.
339 Quebec Liquor Commission store, Montreal photo
340-1 Residence, Upper Belmont, Westmount 2 photos
342 Notre Dame Hospital, Montreal, power house and laundry building 2 photos
see also Cox, Alfred A, 1895

AMOS, PIERRE CHARLES
23 Mar 1897 - 26 Nov 1976, Montreal
see Amos, Louis Auguste, 1933

ANDERS, FREDERICK
addr: Montreal, 7776 Champagneur Ave
1935 11 Grey wc $5
384 Study drwg $15

ANDERSON, HELEN VIOLET
1882, Brockville, Ont Mo12
addr: Ottawa, 46 Wellington St, 1906-9. Paris, 18 rue Boissonande, 1910. Montreal, 154 Drummond St, 1910-11
1906 1 A model $50
2 A Suffolk common $25
3 Haycocks $15
4 Clouds $15
5 In Hampshire $25
172 Reflections wc $15
1908 1 Wood interior $30
2 Landscape $50
1909 1 The village street wc $75
2 The green door wc $60
3 A country road wc $60
1910 5 Our house, Givernay $40
6 Sentinal trees $75
7 Landscape $75
1911 6 Landscape $150

ANDERSON, LOUELLA H.
addr: Sydney, N.S, 96 S. Bentinck St
1935 8 Low Point, Cape Breton $75

ANDERSON, MABEL GARFIELD FENDER
28 Dec 1896, Baddeck, N.S.
addr: Montreal, 5 Holton Ave, 1912-13. Moncton, N.B, 109 John St, 1935
1912 18 Gertrude $15
1913 4 Sugar camp $10
5-6 Sketch b&w $8 each
1935 12 Geese at wayside trough wc $10
385 Rocky bay drwg $10

ANDERSON, MARGUERITE see DOERNBACH, MARGUERITE ELIZABETH (PEGGY)

ANDERSON, MARJORIE W.
addr: Montreal, 3794 Côte des Neiges Rd, 1942-3. Westmount, 4484 Western Ave, 1944-6
1942 1 Hills in winter $20
1943 3 An autumn afternoon, Woodlands $25
1944 1 In the Bahamas $50
1945 3 Dominion Square $75
1946 2 Lake Orford $75

ANDERSON, MILLICENT GORE (m P.H. Anderson) fl 1893-1930 DBA G RA
addr: Ottawa: 1908; 121 Sparks St, 1909
1908 161 One of the unemployed wc $35
162 Old hulk, Gaspé wc $50
163 Study of a child wc $50 (listed 1967, Jessie Dow prize)
1909 4 The bank of the stream wc $25
5 Soap bubbles wc $40
6 Gaspé wharves wc $40

ANDERSON, RONALD TRENT
10 Oct 1938, Madison, Wis WWA73
addr: Halifax
1968 3 Thunder Rock transparent wc 22 x 30 $400

ANDRE, FRANCOISE MARISE SYLVIANE (m Charles Stegeman)
13 Aug 1926, Les Sables d'Olenne, France M
addr: Skokie, Ill, 9527 Leclaire Ave, 1963-4
1963 1 The shield $800

1964 1 The guardians $1,100

ANDREW, ISA BELLE
addr; Westmount 428 Metcalfe Ave
1915 421 Jug $15
422 Candlestick $6.50
423 Vase $4

ANDREW, PAUL SINCLAIR
16 Feb 1908, Antigonish, N.S.
addr: Montreal: 1445 Bishop St, 1931-3; 1158 Beaver Hall Sq, 1934-6; 3531 Ste Famille St, 1937-40; 3050 Kirkfield Dr, 1947-54
1931 359 Reclining figure drwg $25
1933 11 Grey day $50
1934 Andrews, mispr
7 Still life $40
1935 13 Still life $50
14 Escalators $50
15 A.J.A, portrait sketch
1936 9 Arthur
10 The cast $50
1937 4 Tulips $100
5 Fruit $100
1938 2 Street scene $30
1939 7 Janet $200
8 Interior $100
9 Still life $50
10 Self portrait $40
1940 1, 3, 4 Still life $60 each
2 Studio view $30
1947 6 Still life $100
1949 2 Still life $300
1953 1 Still life $100
1954 7 Still life $150

ANDREWS, A. S. (Miss)
addr: Montreal, 2274 St Catherine St
1892 150 Study of a duck wc $25

ANGUS, MAUD see CHIPMAN, MAUD

ANTIGNA, MARC
b Paris fl 1890-1910 B H
addr: Montreal, 2714A St Catherine St, 1901-3
1901 1 Mlle B.G.
2 Monsieur M.A.
3 Case of 6 miniatures
1903 1 Mdme R.A. framed by artist
2 Mdme Cornu framed by artist

APTER, SONIA
28 Nov 1906, New York
addr: Montreal: 3647 Durocher St, 1932; 1154 Beaver Hall Sq, 1933
1932 plaster, 1932-33
454 Kathleen
1933 504 Bernard M. Bloomfield bust
505 Head of a young woman $200

ARBUCKLE, FRANCES see JOHNSTON, FRANCES

ARBUCKLE, GEORGE FRANKLIN
17 Feb 1909, Toronto AGO CC2 CWW82 M NGC TB2/3 WWA82
addr: Montreal, 4100 Côte des Neiges Rd, 1946-52. Toronto: 52 Lascelles Blvd, 1960; Toronto, 1967
1946 3 Spring $600 (listed 1967, Jessie Dow prize)
1947 7 March break-up $850 (listed 1967, Jessie Dow prize)
8 Sunday afternoon $600
1948 1 Spring rain $800
1951 1 Barn with hay press $1,000
1952 1 Sunday $1,000
1960 4 Catalpa cat $1,000
1967 2 Rara avis. 1966 mm 48 x 36

ARCHAMBAULT, FRANCOISE
addr: Montreal, 1485 Fort St, 1940-3
1940 5 Mon studio $65
6 Cabane à sucre $30
1941 3 L'écluse $50
1942 2 Le village dans la vallée $75
1943 4 Le quai $85
5 Pivoines $100

ARCHAMBAULT, LOUIS DE GONZAGUE PASCAL
4 Apr 1915, Montreal AGO CC1 CE CWW84 M NGC TB3 WWA84
addr: Montreal, 8248 Henri Julien At, 1946-9
1946 4 Composition No 302B $150
1949 167 Oiseau lyre bronze, ter cot galet naturel
168 Nuit et jour ter cot $150 (AGO)

ARCHIBALD, EDITH THURSTON (m John Smith Archibald)
addr: Westmount, 4278 Dorchester St
1916 360 Jardinière lustre $10

ARCHIBALD, IAN THURSTON
23 Mar 1897 - 26 Nov 1976, Montreal
addr: Montreal, 514 Keefer Bldg, 1936-40
1936 460 Proposed high school, Notre Dame de Grace

461-3 Residence (3)
1940 Archibald & Illesley
308 Macy's Reg'd, drug store and restaurant pencil
309 Residence, Westmount pencil
310 Montreal Convalescent Hospital photo

ARCHIBALD, JOHN SMITH
14 Dec 1872, Tobermory, Scot 2 Mar 1934, Montreal CNS27 Mo12
addr: Montreal: 314 Dorchester St W, 1917; 326 Beaver Hall Hill, 1925; 1134 Beaver Hall Hill, 1927-8; 514 Keefer Bldg, 1440 St Catherine St W, 1929-33
1917 371 School, Outremont Protestant School Trustees
1925 291-2 House, Kingston, Ont, lake front, street front perspective
293 Forum Bldg, Montreal, perspective, by James Crockart
1927 180 Proposed residence, Westmount
181 Queen's Hotel
182 Montreal West school
183 Terrace houses, Redpath St
184 Tramways Terminus Bldg, Craig St, David Shennan architect
1928 210, 212 Château Laurier, Ottawa, extension, Totem Tea Room
211 Masonic Memorial Temple
1929 223 New Manoir Richelieu, Murray Bay, Canada Steamship Lines
224 Queen's University, Kingston, new gymnasium
225 CNR hotel and station, Halifax assoc John Schofield
1930 208 Manoir Richelieu photo assoc John Schofield, 209-10
209 CNR, Château Laurier Hotel, Ottawa, new banquet room
210 CNR hotel, Saskatoon
1931 250-1 Montreal Masonic Memorial Temple, Sherbrooke St front, St Mark St front assoc John Schofield, 252-3
252 CNR, Hotel Vancouver model
253 Château Laurier, addition, 1930. Original building, by Ross & Macfarlane photo
1933 343 CNR, Hotel Vancouver
344 Montreal Convalescent Home Archibald & Turcotte, 345
345 St Mary's Memorial Hospital

ARISS, HERBERT JOSHUA
29 Sep 1918, Guelph, Ont AGO CWW84 M WWA84
addr: London, Ont
1968 The Somme series
4 The German soldier mm 40 x 30 $300
5 The German General Staff mm 48 x 38 $550
6 The casualty mm 38 x 26 $250

ARKAUSKAS, STAN
addr: Montreal, 6685 10th Ave
1961 68 Night ride into Durango nm $90
69 Aristocracy of Angul nm $110

ARMINGTON, CAROLINE HELENA WILKINSON (m Franklin Milton Armington)
11 Sep 1875, Brampton, Ont 25 Oct 1939, New York AGO CWW36 WWW
addr: Paris, France
1910 11A Marché aux Pommes etch $10
11B Le Seine et Notre Dame etch $9
11C Quai Vert, Bruges etch $9

ARMINGTON, FRANKLIN MILTON
28 Jul 1876, Fordwich, Ont 23 Sep 1941, New York AGO CWW36 WWW
addr: Paris, France, 8 rue de la Grande Chaumière
1910 etching
12A Canal, Amsterdam $9
12B Val-de-Grace, Paris $9
12C Moulin à vent, Holland $10
12D Place du Bourg, Bruges $12
12E Rue Wallonne, Bruges $12
12F Intérieur, Beguinage, Bruges $10
12G Cour des maisons Dieu, Bruges $12
12H Halle du Beurre $12
12I Quai des Dominican $12

ARMOUR, PHYLLIS (Mrs Hertzberg)
c 1885, Toronto d 1975
addr: Bowmanville, Ont, Willow Haven, RR 4, 1937-9
1937 404 The old pine tree dry pt $15
1939 Herkberg, mispr
406 The cedar grove dry pt $12

ARMSTRONG, FREDA (Mrs)
addr: Montreal, 16 Parkside Pl
1939 11 Peonies $100

ARMSTRONG, THOMAS WILLIAM
11 Feb 1908, Ovington-on-Tyne, Eng
addr: Verdun, Que, 6999 Woodland Ave
1946 5 St Joseph Oratory $100

ARMSTRONG, WILLIAM WALTON
9 Nov 1916, Toronto M NGC
addr: Montreal: 1494 Mackay St, 1944; 1102 Elgin Terrace, 1945-8; 3427 Ontario Ave, 1949-50; 1600 Selkirk Ave, 1953
1944 2 Portrait of a girl $200
1945 4 Portrait
5 Figure in a room $100
1946 6 Portrait head $85
7 Landscape, Ste Anne de Bellevue $85
1947 9 Seated girl $100. 1967-3, 35 x 36 Jury II prize (Eric McLean, Montreal)
1948 2 Landscape, Whitefield, N.H. $100
1949 3 Still life with oranges and decanter $100
4 Portrait of a woman in striped shawl $100
1950 94 Seated woman with mandolin $300
95 Still life $250
1953 67 Olive trees and barn $125

ARO, PAUL
addr: Toronto, 93 Carlton St, 1945-7
1945 6 Mandolin $60
1946 8 Street scene $100
1947 10 Wash day $100
11 Vegetables $100
295 Refugees ink drwg $10

ARONSON, MARION
6 Jan 1913, Montreal
addr: Montreal, 2234 Girouard Ave, 1942-3. Westmount, 1375 Greene Ave, 1944-58. Montreal, 5128 Westbury Ave, 1962
1942 3 Lilacs $35
4 Still life $35
1943 6 Landscape with trees $30
1944 3 The hill, Ivry $100
1945 7 Windy Hill $100
8 Landscape with rocks $50
9 Roof tops $50
1946 9 Landscape, St Sauveur des Monts $75
10 Bright morning, St Sauveur des Monts $50
1947 12 Composition $50
1949 5 The fantastic mountain $100
6 Landscape, St Sauveur des Monts $100
1950 96 Landscape in blue $100
1951 75 Fall $100
1953 66 Summer day $80
1955 3 Bride $100
1957 3 Gray day $150
1958 46 Blue landscape nm $50
1962 42 Song of the earth nm

ARY, SYLVIA BERCOVITCH (m Sol Ary)
15 Apr 1923, Moscow
addr: Montreal: 4278 City Hall Ave, 1941; 4264 St Dominique St, 1949; 4849 Hutchison St, 1955-7
1941 4 From the window wc $15
1949 154 Head pastel
1955 4 Cowboy $100
1957 4 Portrait of the artist $150

ASHBY, G. S.
addr: Montreal, 6 Lorne Ave
1913 7 Still life $125
8 Life study b&w $25

ASHBY, HERBERT WILLIAM
addr; Montreal, 6 Lorne Ave, 1911-13; 12 Highland Ave, 1922-5
1911 7 The dead canary $50
8 Sidney Carter, Esq $100
9 Portrait $10
1913 9 Mrs Ashby
1922 10 Portrait of a lady
11 Zinnias
1923 14 Arundel Road, Laurentians $100
15 Portrait of a child
1924 9 A Laurentian road
10 Sweet peas
1925 13 Peter McCrimmon, Esq, Lost River, Que
14 Laurentian road, Lakeview, Que $100

ASHFORD, A. B.
addr: Montreal: 1117 St André St, 1926; 2041 Kimberley St, 1929
1926 180 God's Providence House, Chester, Eng drwg $15
1929 297 Old Germany b&w $25
298 Whitby, England b&w $30

ASHFORD, WALTER R.
addr: Montreal, 4149 Beaconsfield Ave
1945 10 Gladiolus wc

ASIMAKOS, JOHN
24 Apr 1935, Boston
addr: Halifax
1968 7 Water roulette mm 18 1/2 x 24 $300
8 Wind thicket 25 x 30 $300

ASLIN, HARRY R.
addr: Montreal: 6525 Sherbrooke St W, 1960; 4861 Grosvenor Ave, 1962
1960 132 Winter garden nm $75
1962 55 Figure nm $90

ASSELIN, BEATRICE TOBIN
addr: Montreal: 4544 Harvard Ave, 1935; 4520 Wilson Ave, 1937
1935 11 Red tulips $15
1937 6 Mary McCort

ATKINS, CAVEN ERNEST
25 Feb 1907, London, Ont AGO M NGC WWA53
addr: Toronto, 16 Howland Ave
1939 12 From my window

ATKINSON, FLORENCE
addr: Montreal, 118 St Famille St, 1897-8 B H WWW
1897 243 Brush, comb tray
244 Cologne bottle
245-6 Vase (2)
247 Marmalade jar
1898 235 Jar
236 Calendar
237 Ink bottle
238 Cup & saucer
239 Vase

ATKINSON, SOPHIA M.
Nov 1876, Newcastle, Eng fl 1965
addr: Montreal, 679 Sherbrooke St W
1928 3 At San Buenaventure Mission, Cal wc
4 In the foothills of Alberta wc $45
5 A trail through the woods, Jasper Park wc $45

ATKINSON, WILLIAM EDWIN
22 Mar 1862, Islington 31 Jul 1926, Toronto AGO B CWW10 H M Mo12 NGC TB
addr: Toronto: 203 Crawford St, 1897; 207 Crawford St, 1905-6; Toronto Junction, 1908; 207 Crawford St, 1926
1897 1 Cloudy moonlight $200
2 Old grist mill below Quebec $40
3 Woodland $35
1903 3 Threatening weather, Holland $40
4 After the rain, Holland $50
128 The shelter wc $50
1908 3 The sand cart $150
167 A Dutch farm wc $100
1926 1 The hillcrest $300
2 Black Creek $150
3 Homewards wc $175
4 Fall day, Dartmoor,Devon wc $75

ATRILL, ANNEKE (m Verne Atrill)
12 Feb 1924, Haarlem, Holland
addr: Montreal, 2477 W Broadway Ave, 1958. Montreal West, 14 Wolesley Ave S, 1960
1958 47 Taking the rail nm $125
1960 133 King Lear nm

AUBIN, J. B. ERNEST
addr: Montreal: 459 Dorchester St E, 1915-24; 5136 Papineau Ave, 1926-36
1915 11 Study $10
1919 5 Un jour d'éclipse étude $20
6 Etude $20
1920 3 La Croix du chemin $75
4 Vieille maison pochade $25
294 Tête de Bébé étude plâtre
1921 288 Le rêve plâtre
1922 12 Etude b&w $10
331-2 Etude plâtre
1924 305 Retour de champ sculp
1926 5 Nos veilles maisons $200
1929 4 Lever de soleil $125
299 Ancien magasin, Marché Bonsecours pen & ink $15
300 Ancien restaurant pen & ink $15
1930 3 Old candy store $50
1935 445 Nu plâtre
1936 508 Le rêve drwg

AUERBACH, MALCA ROSE
fl 1891-1913 AAA1900 B
addr: Montreal: 2284 St Catherine St, 1891-4; 2291 St Catherine St, 1895; 151 Hutchison St, 1897-1900
1891 5 Field flowers $30
6 Marguerites and buttercups $30
1894 7 Mes pensées $35
8 Romeo et Juliet $30
1895 7 Violets $15
1897 4 Apples $60
1900 1 Roses $60

AULD, GEORGE E. B.
17 Apr 1908 - 17 May 1940, Montreal
see Wilson, George E, 1936-40

AULD, JEAN M.
addr: Montreal, 417 Mackay St
1924 11 White birches, P.E.I. wc $25

AUSTIN, B.
1886 128 Music evening at Rivière du Loup
134 Laval University, Quebec

AUSTIN, DOROTHY see STEVENS, DOROTHY

AUSTIN, ESTHER (Mrs)
addr: Westmount, 130 Clandeboye Ave
1905 128 Côte St Luc Road wc $20

AYKROYD, WOODRUFF KERR
3 May 1940, Toronto
addr: Toronto, 40 Concord Ave, 1935-6
1935 386 Rouen, France etch
387 The mill, Canoe Lake, Ont etch $10
388 Westminster Bridge, London etch $15
1936 509 Noon hour at the waterfront dry pt $12.50
510 Wash day in old Quebec dry pt $12.50

AYOTTE, LEO
10 Oct 1909, Ste Flore, Que 21 Dec 1976, St Hyacinthe, Que M
addr: Montreal: 3442 Ste Famille St, 1943; 4076 St Crhistophe St, 1946-9
1943 7 Self portrait $75
1946 11 Rue St Christophe $90
1947 13 Futur Lacordaire $75
14 Paul
1949 7 Reflets

B

BABINSKI, MACIEJ ANTONI
c 1931, Poland
addr: Montreal, 3541 Lorne Ave
1950 146 Massacre of the innocents etch & aqua $12

BAGLEY, D. MARY (m Geoffrey Spink Bagley)
addr: Montreal: 1456 St Mark St, 1931; 4982 Queen Mary Rd, 1932; 5245 Côte St Luc Rd, 1933-6. Beloeil, Que, 1937-8
1931 6 The Ottawa River wc $45
7 A Tudor inn, Kent wc $75
1932 12 A mountain shack wc $30
13 Old house in sunshine wc $50
1933 12 Mount St Pierre, Gulf of St Lawrence wc $45
13 Petite Rivière aux Renards wc $35
1934 8 After the snowfall wc $35
9 February sunshine wc $35
1935 16 The derelict, Tadousac wc $30
17 The pilot house wc $50
1936 12 The Saguenay cliffs wc $50
13 Snow laden roofs wc $60
14 Fall, Sault au Recollet wc $50
15 Winter shadows $150
1937 7 Flowers in winter wc $50
8 Early morning, Beloeil wc $35
1938 3 Trente de Beloeil wc $50

BAGLEY, GEOFFREY SPINK
3 Nov 1901, Pontefract, Eng
addr: Montreal: 1456 St Mark St, 1931; 4982 Queen Mary Rd, 1932; 5245 Côte St Luc Rd, 1933-6
1931 8 The Green Mountains wc $100
9 In west Flanders wc $80
10 Notre Dame, Bruges wc $100
1932 14 The little canyon $350
15 A Laurentian road $200
16 Kentish 13th century bridge wc $75
1933 14 Petite Rivière aux Renards $200
437 Chapel of our Lady of Beaumont wd engr unfr $6
1935 18 Labrador shore $350
1936 16 Prévost, winter wc $125
17 Summer nude $150
18 Beaumont shore $175

BAIG, DAISY
10 Oct 1916, Amherst, N.S.
addr: Halifax: YWCA, 1940; 28 Vernon St, 1941; 253 Oxford St, 1942; 58 Bland St, 1943-44
1940 7 Still life, musical friends $75
1941 5 Assorted fruits $35
1942 190 Giraffes lino cut $10
1943 8 Still life study $20
1944 133 Design for crest pen & ink

BAIGENT, ROBERT RICHARD

1830, Winchester, Eng 1890, Toronto
H
1881 69,78 Landscape wc

BAILEY, LAURESTINE M.
b Fredericton, N.B.
addr: St Anne de Bellevue, Macdonald College, 1918-19
1918 3-4 Rhododendrons, Jamaica Plains, sketch
380 Window, Christ Church Cathedral, Fredericton, N.B.
381 Renaissance ceiling des
382 End of library des
383 Box cover des
384 Cover for address of welcome, and wallpaper des
385 To imitate tapestry
386 Cactus
387-8 Conventional flower forms
443 Silver ring, 3 stones
444 Silver chain with stones
1919 Wallpaper designs
375 Naturalistic
376 Conventional flower forms
377 Brown, gold and blue

BAILEY, MARGARET MURPHY (m William Taylor Bailey)
addr: Montreal, 106 St Luke St
1900 188 Large tray, roses
189 Desert plates, 6
190 Plate, head
191 Framed head

BAILLARGEON, GERARD (signs Loudigny)
addr: Montreal, 3003 Cedar Ave
1964 Londigny mispr
98 Bloturue nm $150

BAILLY, EVERN EARL
8 Jul 1903 - 1 Jul 1977, Lunenburg, N.S.
M NGC (Bailey, Bailley, Earle mispr)
addr: Lunenburg, N.S.
1923 16 Dashing waters wc $10
1924 12 Under the clear February sky wc $20
13 January reflections wc $20
1925 15 Winter clouds wc $35
16 On the coast of Lunenburg wc $35
1933 15 From a Lunenburg window wc $35
16 Lunenburg harbour
1934 10 Little Harbour, N.S, wc $75
11 My memory of Quebec wc $65

BAIN, SOPHIA JOYCE
10 Mar 1908, Winnipeg
addr: Toronto, 402 Huron St
1942 5 Sketch wc
191 Study of a head, No 2 chalk

BAKER, EDWIN D.
addr: Montreal, 3851 University St
1947 15 Night snow wc $45

BAKER, J. HYATT
addr: Montreal West, 2 Strathearn Ave S
1944 155 Heather at two years rel plaster

BAKER, WILLIAM ROBERT
2 Feb 1919, London, Eng IO
addr: St Catharines, Ont
1968 9 Laus 47 1/2 x 39 1/2 $500
10 Cano 47 1/2 x 39 3/4 $500

BALBONI, CARLO
addr: Montreal: 316 Notre Dame St E, 1909-10; 566 Dorchester St E, 1928; 1120 Dorchester St E, 1929; 1173 St Timothée St, 1935; 1167 St Timothée St, 1944
1909 383 Bust plaster
384 Bust, portrait
1910 354 Mrs C. sculp
1928 336 Signor Grimaldi bronze $200
337 Signor Carrillo bronze $200
1929 357 M. Ernest Decary bronze
1935 446 Madame Balboni plaster
447 Rev Curé Maltempi plaster
1944 156 Carlo Balboni, artiste plaster

BALDWIN, A.
addr: Montreal, Art Emporium, 2255 St Catherine St
1906 6 Winter on the mountain $100

BALHARRIE, JAMES WATSON
6 Jun 1910, Ottawa CNS60
addr: Ottawa, 334 Bronson Ave
1944 4 Old house in autumn wc $40

BALL, ARTHUR
3 Feb 1929, Leeds, Eng
addr: St Laurent, Que, 1365 Ouimet St
1959 41 Golgotha wd $150

BALLON, IRIS SHKLAR

11 May 1931, Montreal
addr: Montreal; 3647 Durocher St, Apt 11, 1953-4; 4687 Bonavista Ave, 1955; 3320 Côte Ste Catherine Rd, 1958
1953 93 Nick's gouache $40
1954 86 Three wise men gouache $35
87 Mogambo cafe gouache $35
1955 84 Flemish king and queen in church nm $55
1958 48 Girl with flowers nm $75

BANTING, BEATRICE ALINE MYLES (m J. Maitland Banting) (signs Myles)
29 Jul 1911, Hamilton Ont M
addr: Hamilton: 178 McNab St S, 1939-41; 21 Augusta, Apt 1, 1943-6; 132 Herkimer St, 1947-8
1939 13 Flower piece $60
14 Portrait of a little boy
1940 8 Self portrait
9 Portrait of a Polish girl $100
1941 6 Ukrainian Canadian $35
1943 9 Sergeant Ruth Gill $150
1944 5 Corporal Jimmy Morrow $140
1945 11 Sketch $60
1946 12 Young girl $150
13 Carolyn $90
1947 16 Girl in white blouse $150
17 Young woman, sketch $80
1948 3 Portrait of Patty $250

BARBAUD, KATIE see FRANCOIS-BARBAUD, KATIE

BARBEAU, CHRISTIAN MARCEL
18 Feb 1925, Montreal CC2 CE CWW84 M
addr: Montreal, 4541 rue St Hubert, 1945. Verdun, 3185 Evelyn St, 1949. Rouville, Que, St Mathias, 1952. Montreal: 4700 Boyer St, 1954; Galerie du Siècle, 1494 rue Sherbrooke, 1965
1945 12 Convoitise $40
1949 8 Soupir dans le trébuchard pittoresque des alentours poudres $350
9 Une maîtresse cajole un arc-ec-ciel $150
1952 116 Les combustions originelles wc $35
1954 8 La torture des esprits lucides $450
1965 1 Mion-Mion $1,200

BARBEAU, NAPOLEON
addr: Montreal, 388 St Lawrence St
1903 5 Raisin et noix $30

BARBEAU, SUZANNE see MELOCHE, SUZANNE

BARKER, ERNEST CONYERS
18 Mar 1909, Toronto IO WWA53
addr: King, Ont, Jarvis Estate
1939 15 Flower piece $60
16 Small town landscape $60
17 Variations of a curve $50

BARKER, HERBERT JACKSON
addr: Montreal, 5987 Esplanade Ave, 1933. Verdun: 512 Gordon Ave, 1934; 535 Osborne St, 1935-6; 989 Melrose Ave, 1940
1933 17 Head of a girl pastel $20
18 Along the shore at Caughnawaga wc $20
1934 12 Study $30
13 Farm on Queen Mary Rd wc $35
1935 19 Winding road $20
20 Autumn, farm at St Michel $20
1936 19 The blue vase $125
1940 10 Waterfront, Verdun wc $50

BARNARD, JULIA BINGHAM (m H.J. Barnard)
1900, London, Eng M
addr: Winnipeg, 1674 Portage Ave, 1944-7
1944 134 Sparrow's pen & ink $5
1947 20 Horse radish leaves $75

BARNES, MADELINE L.
addr: Ottawa, 850 Wellington St, 1939-40
1939 18 Spring buds $25
19 Spring blossoms $25
20 Autumn, upper Ottawa $25
21 Tulips $25
1940 11 Summer shadows wc $20

BARNES, WILFRED MOLSON
10 Oct 1882 - 14 Feb 1955, Montreal CC1 CNS36 M NGC PMC TB3
addr: Montreal: 14 Lorne Ave, 1905-9; 637 Grosvenor Ave, 1910; 571 St Catherine St W, 1911-15; 747 St Catherine St W, 1916-28; 1501 St Catherine St W, 1929-47
1905 220 Fairyland dec wc $10
221 1492 dec wc $10
222 The coming storm nm $10
223 Alone nm $10

224 Adoration nm $10
225 The dancer nm $10
226 On duty nm $10
227 In a hurry nm $10
1906 176 The enchanted isle wc $5
297 Moonlight b&w $5
298 The reflection b&w $5
299 The curve b&w $5
300 Idleness b&w $5
1908 168 The aristocrat pencil $25
169 D'Artagan wc $25
170 G.C. Fox, Esq wc
1909 11, 13 Decoration wc $20, $12
12 Sketch wc $12
1910 13 Illustration b&w $15
14 Dr W.S. Barnes
15 H.H. Keller, Esq
16 Signor E.C. Barbièri
1911 10 Old barn, N.H. $35
11 Dam, N.H. $35
12 A touch of autumn $25
1912 19 Decorative landscape wc $40
1913 420 The dancer
1914 4 Straits of Belle Isle $150
5 Decorative figure wc $75
1915 12 The Ascutney Valley, N.H. $125
13 The pond $75
1916 4 Solitude $200
5-6 Wood interior $75 each
7 Rhythm wc $75
1917 6 Rising mists $350
7 A summer evening $250
8 Motif found on a cross-road $250
1918 5 Hay field $300
6 The woodland pool $250
7 The old red barn $125
1919 7 The wings of night $500
8 The spot of sun $175
9 Dawn $175
10 Afterglow $100
11 Sketch $35
1920 5 The hooded clouds $500
6 The golden hour $300
7 The west yet glimmers $300
8 The meadow $35
1921 3 Night's magic mantle o'er the countryside $100
4 Sunny spots of greenery
5 When common ways are dressed in twilight's charm $350
1922 13 Where the river dreams $600
14 The lure of the morning $500
15 Then came still evening on $500
16 Motif from a deserted village $40
1923 17 From a deserted village $200
18 As evening shuts the gates of day $175
19 Early morning $40
20 Morning gold $40
1924 16 The glowing bow that smiled the clouds away $250
17 When evening shuts the gates of day $500
18 The pool $40
19 Opening in the woods $40
1925 17 The last glow of day $500
18 Iceberg
1926 6 Golden morning $500
7 The meadow after rain $40
1927 2 The Connecticut Valley, evening $300
3 Twillingate, Newfoundland $65
4 Iceberg, Notre Dame Bay, Newfoundland $65
1928 6 The red barn $200
7 The little white house $65
8 Noonday $65
1929 5 The west wind's burden $70
6 Light and shadow $70
7 The stream $70
8 Cloud shadows $300
1930 4 Sunrise off Labrador $110
5 Sunrise, the Arctic current $150
6 The wake of the Uvira $175
7 Morning shadow $300
1931 11 Fall meadow pastel $300
12 When magic is abroad $140
13 The golden gates of morning $140
1932 17 The embankment pastel $250
18 The iceberg pastel $140
19 Summer storm $70
1933 19 The edge of the woods $50
20 Hill at sunset $125
1934 14 The lake $300
15 A summer day pastel $250
1935 21 Yellow house $140
22 Over the valley $140
23 Summer shower $140
24 Summer sunset $140
1936 20 The hilltop $500
21 Summer sunset $150
1937 9 Heavy weather pastel $250
10 The valley $125
1938 5 New England village $250
1939 22 The hill beyond $125
1940 12 Meadow, afternoon $250
1941 7 Where the river dreams $100
8 The valley $100

1943 10 The brook $100
1945 13 Cloud pattern pastel $200
1947 21 Shadow in the valley $150

BARNHOUSE, DOROTHY PAUL (m D.P. Barnhouse)
1914, Burin, Nfld M
addr: Edmonton, 10233 123rd St
1940 13 Nanki Poo, study of a Pekinese wc $15
14 Powell Street, Vancouver wc $25
15 Saskatchewan valley wc $30

BARNJUM, VIOLET
addr: Montreal, 113 Tupper St
1906 7 A Dutch child $25
8 Portrait of a child
9 Portrait sketch

BARNSLEY, JAMES MACDONALD
20 Feb 1861, West Flamboro, n Dundas, Ont 25 Feb 1929, Verdun, Que B EC H M Mo12 NGC TB2
addr: New York, The Holbein, 145 W 55th St, 1891. Montreal, c/o Art Assoc of Montreal, 1892, 1894-5, 1897-8, 1900-1, 1903, 1905-6, 1912, 1914. Hudson, Que, 1908. Montreal: 219 Bleury St, 1909; c/o Scott & Sons, 99 Notre Dame St W, 1911, 1913, 1915-21
1886 99 Dieppe harbour (MBAM)
1888 21 After the rain $500. Exhibited at Paris Salon, hon mention, 2nd class medal; Versailles Exposition, 1st class medal
29 A breezy day $120
126 Spring time wc $100
1889 4 Fishing boats off Newhaven $120
97 Beating to windward wc $75
98 In the month of May wc $75
99 Afternoon in August wc $35
178 No 99 with a fair wind etch $15
1891 7 Misty moonlight $150
8 Autumn evening $75
9 Evening light $75
142 In twilight wc $35
143 A break in the clouds wc $30
144 A gray day in Holland wc $30
145 Twilight on Mount Royal wc $30
146 Afterglow wc $30
1892 4 The last rays $1,000 (MBAM)
5 Marine $250
6 A wreck $125
7 Bass Rocks, Gloucester, Mass $75 (NGC)
151 Marine wc $50
1894 9 Dieppe $400 (NGC)
10 Windmill $50 (MBAM)
11 East Gloucester, Mass $100
12 A sandy road, Thury, France $125
167 Gretz, in France wc $100
168 Twilight wc $40
169 A marine wc $40
170 Bridge at Glengariff wc $35
171 At sea wc $30
1895 8 Landscape, near Mouie, France $125
9 Windmill in Holland $100
10 Near Hontonville, France $50
11 Woods at Fontainebleau $40
143 Marine wc $50
144 Windmill near Dordrecht wc $40
145 Moonrise wc $35
146 Winter at East Gloucester, Mass wc $30
1897 5 Landscape in Holland, autumn $100
6 French landscape $100
7 Seascape $30
131 Landscape near Bameudo, France wc $35
132 Winter in Central Park, New York wc $75
133 Landscape, Otsaga, N.Y. wc $35
134 Marine wc $35
135 On the Richelieu River wc $30
1898 6 Landscape in Holland $70
7 Thury, France $70
8 Dieppe $65
9 Winter in Central Parl $65
119 Gathering wild flowers wc $35
120 Mending the nets wc $35
121 A misty day wc $35
122 Evening wc $25
1900 2 Fishing nets, East Gloucester $75
3 Basin de la Bastille $75
4 Sunset $75
5 Snow at Aniers, near Paris $45
116 Boats at Gloucester wc $25
117 In New York state wc $25
118 Rocky Neck wc $25
1901 4 The Bass Rocks, Mass $80
5 Lighthouse, St Malo $80
6 Landscape, near Paris $70
7 Bridge at Gréz, near Paris $60

8 Evening, Affaurgy $60
9 Landscape near Thury, France $55
107 By the river wc $35
1903 6 Landscape in Brittany $200
7 At Thury $100
8 Cliffs, French coast $125
9 Landscape, Holland $125
10 Percé Rock $100
11 The phantom ship $55
129 Landscape in France wc $30
130 Fish house, Gloucester wc $30
131 Coming squall wc $20
132 Ships at sea $20
133 Sunset wc $20
134 In Brittany wc $20
135 Landscape wc $20
1905 1 A Normandy farm $300
2 Sunset in Brittany $150
3 St Malo Fort $125
4 Wharf, St Malo $125
129 Muckross Abbey wc $75
130 Cochno, Scotland wc $75
1906 10 Dieppe $75
11 On the Seine $100
12 Near Hauntanville $125
13 Eastern Point lighthouse $200
14 Rocky Point, Gloucester $200
1908 4 On the Seine, Paris $100
5 Wheat stacks $80
6 The Trocadero $70
7 At Sceaux, France $125
8 In the fields, Holland $150
9 On the French coast $150
10 On the Seine $70
11 Sunset in France $125
171 Haystacks wc $100
1909 14 Canal St Martin, Paris $175
15 Russcarp, near Whitby $125
16 Dieppe $200
17 Landscape, France $100
18 Village, Percé $125
19 Evening wc $125 (NGC)
1910 17 French landscape $100
18 On the Seine $150
19 Autumn, France $150
20 On the Seine, below Paris $80
21 Autumn, Canada $80
1911 13 Dieppe, Jetéé des Poulets (sold to National Gallery, Ottawa)
14 Landscape, Thury $225
15 Rothesay Castle $80
16 Landscape, Holland $200
17 Low tide $75
18 Bass Rocks wc $60
1912 20 Sunset in France $250
21 French landscape $350
22 Dieppe $250
23 Dutch landscape $200
24 Rocky Point, Gloucester $200
25 Haystacks wc $125
26-7 Seascape etch $30, $25
28-9 Seascape pen & ink $20, $15
1913 10 French farm, Fleury $200
11 On the Seine $200
12 Sunset in France $200
13 Milking time $250
14 Seascape b&w $25
15 French landscape wc $100
16 Original study for picture b&w $75
1914 6 Mont St Michel $150
7 Fishing boats $600
8 Farm at Hauntonville (sic) $200
9 Farmyard $250
10 Muckross Abbey wc $100
11 The gallery god wc $100
12 Baie des Chaleurs wc $60
13 Haystacks wc $125
1915 14 In the fields, Holland $175
15 The farm, Fleury, France $175
16 The farm, Hontville (sic) $225
17 Springtime in France $200
18 Moonlight on the Seine $150
19 Mont St Michel $150
10 In the orchard $50
21 The flock, Holland b&w $35
22 Laren, Holland b&w $50
23-4 Sketch b&w $50 each
1916 8 Dieppe $250
9 St Servan $150
10 Farm at Thury S200
11 Evening wc $100
1917 9 Autumn $150
10 Sunset in France $200
11 Dieppe $250
12 Sunset $100
13 The last rays $100
14 Marine with boat $100
1918 8 Haystacks $200
9 The farm $200
10 Fields in Holland (sold to National Gallery, Ottawa)
11 Sunset in France $200
12 Three sketches (sold to National Gallery, Ottawa)
13 Seascape b&w $25
14 Design for picture b&w $75

1919 12 Winter wc $25
13 River and boats wc $75
14 Night scene in Holland $150
15 French landscape, sunset $200
16 The old farm, Thiery $200
17 The barn yard $200
1920 9 French landscape $250
10 The rainbos $200
1921 6 Dieppe pier, 1884 $275
7 Sieppe docks, 1884 $275
8 Paris docks, 1884 $275
1894-7 Assoc 1st prize 1892, landscape

BAROTT, ERNEST ISBELL
25 Mar 1884, Canastota, N.Y. 15 May 1966, Montreal CNS36 CWW64 NGC
addr: Montreal: New Birks Bldg, 1915; 1019 Canada Cement Bldg, 1928-34
1915 Barott, Blackader & Webster
385-6 St Denis Theatre, interior, exterior
387 St George's Church
1928 Barott & Blackader, to 1934
213 Bell Telephone Bldg, Montreal
1931 254 Bank of Montreal, Ottawa head office
255 Aldred Bldg, Place d'Armes
1933 346-50 Bank of Montreal, Ottawa, north front, south entrance, banking room, details, sculpture details
1934 367-9 Two proposed houses, Pine Ave, view from south, and north, plans, garden layout. Landscape archi Charles Perrochet, assoc to T.G. Todd

BARR, RUTH L.
addr: Montreal
1908 172 Sketch pastel $10

BARRE, RAOUL
29 Jan 1874 - 21 May 1932, Montreal W63
addr: Montreal, 947 St Urbain St, 1901. New York, 7 W 108th St, 1905. Montreal: 346 St Catherine St E, 1928; 990 Cherrier St, 1929-30; 648 Sherbrooke St W, 1931
1901 189 Six subjects for illustration b&w
1905 228 Jeanne d'Arc nm $100
229 Le jeune acrobate nm $100
1928 9 Grand'mère $275
1929 9 Mrs Elzear Roy
1930 8 Fille du Céleste Empire $350
1931 14 Vieux colon de St Faustin

BARRETT, DONALD
addr: Montreal, 1446 St Mark, Apt 3
1950 97 Still life $75
142 Mountain and hills wc $45

BARRETT, HUGN JOHN
2 May 1935, Ahuntsic, Que
addr: Montreal: 621 Prince Arthur St, 1959; 981 Rockland Ave, 1960
1959 26 One day in the fall of the year nm $100
1960 Barret, mispr
134 From time to present nm $150

BARRON, BELLE BLAIR
addr: Hamilton, 32 Inverness Ave
1935 25 Bittersweet wc $50

BARRY, JOHN JOSEPH
21 Jun 1885, Hamilton, Ont d 1952
AAA29 CWW52 WWA53
addr: Toronto: 18 Grenville St, 1932-8; 1677 Bathurst St, 1939-47;49 Montrose Ave, 1950
1932 366 The pine tree etch $15
367 Spanish cart etch $15
368 In the harbour etch $12
1933 438 Farm house etch $6
439 Low tide etch $6
1934 422-3 New England scene, Nos 1,2 etch $12 each
424 Old apple tree etch $15
425 From my window, Rome etch $12
1936 511 House on the hill etch $10
512 Hill top etch $10
513 Docked etch $10
1937 384 Early morning etch $9
385 Dawn etch $9
386 In the slip etch $5
387 Chartres, France etch $7
1938 149 The farm etch $12
1939 380 Hilltop etch $10
1941 216 Old building, Rouen chalk $15
217 Peaceful harbour etch $10
1943 11 The barn pastel $20
12 Corner grocery pastel $20
219 Hilltop etch $12
220 Along McCaul Street pencil $10
1944 135 The barn dry pt $10
136 New England scene etch $15

1945 249 Chartres etch & dry pt $15
250 Hawkestone etch $10
251 Farm house etch $8
1946 249 Head of old lady lino block $5
250 Douarnenez, Brittany col drg $12
251 Study for etching pencil $10
1947 296 The Seine boat etch $12
297 The peddler etch $15
298 Rome, from my window etch $10
1950 81 Market, Assisi pen study for lino block $7

BARRY, LILY EMILY FRANCES
3 Aug 1863, Montreal, d 1955 CNS36 Mo12
addr: Montreal: 702 Sherbrooke St, 1906; The Richmond, 1911; 86 Union Ave, 1912-13; 580 Union Ave, 1917; 2010 Union Ave, 1929
1906 15 Portrait
1911 19 The stream $20
1912 30 Early June, Beaupré $25
1913 17 The living room, Kilmarth
1917 15 Nocturne $20
16 Ste Agathe $25
1929 10 Looking down $40
11 May morning, Ardintoul $20

BARRY, MONA (Mrs)
addr: Montreal, 3500 Vendome Ave, 1943. Lachine, 5 36th Ave, 1946. Montreal, 2273 Melrose Ave, 1947
1943 13 Laurentian spring $150
1946 15 Year's at the spring wc $40
1947 22 Laurentian farm $150

BARTH, NATHAN
addr: Montreal, 4437 Colonial Ave
1927 185 Rose window, Beth Jehuda Synagogue $25

BARTLETT, JOHN LAWRENCE
9 May 1907, Toronto
addr: Toronto, 122 Fallingbrook Rd
1951 2 Paris, Ont $300

BARTMAN, JANET SHELSY
addr: Montreal, 3420 Hutchison St
1932 20 Palestrina, Italy wc $100
455 Fragment ter cot $90

BARTOLINI, MARIO
22 Aug 1930, Montreal
addr: Montréal, 8390 rue St Urbain
1961 108 Séquence concave steel

BARTON, DOROTHY S.
addr: Longueuil, Que
1913 450 Cocoa set $25

BARTON, GEORGIE see READ, GEORGIE

BARWICK, JOHN ALFRED
22 Dec 1912, Toronto
addr: Lachine, Que, 825 40th Ave, 1953-60
1953 2 Reflections $150
1956 3 Yacht and winter canvas $150
1960 5 Portugese Harbour, Gloucester, Mass $300

BASTIEN, PAUL
addr: Montreal, St Denis Bldg
1933 351 Bain Quintal

BASTIN, MICHELE
26 Jul 1944, Brussels
addr: Montreal, 5685 Gatineau Ave, Apt 15
1961 1 Les pénitents $475

BATES, KENNETH
addr: Grand'mère, Que, 1923-5
1923 21 The hills of Pennsylvania $400
22 The St Maurice
1925 19 Laurentian landscape $500
20 Laurentian twilight $500
21 Au bord du lac $500

BATES, MAXWELL BENNETT
14 Dec 1906, Calgary 14Sep 1980, Victoria AGO CC2 CE CWW80 M NGC TB3 WWA59
addr: Calgary, 1411 7th St W, 1954-8; Victoria, 1968
1954 9 Two girls $185
1955 5 Green still life $165
1957 104 Puppets nm $100 hon mention
1958 1 Spring snow $400
1968 11 Parrot 24 x 20 $100
12 Exhibition 20 x 24 $125

BATES, PATRICIA MARTIN (m C.A. Bates)
5 Jun 1927, Saint John B CE M
addr: Wainwright, Alta, Denwood P O, 1963. Victoria, 1968
1963 2 Green and gold bathers $300
73 Offrande à une ombre nm $75

1968 13 Mandalas for love and peace etch 32 x 32 $100
14 Mandala for love encircled etch with relief 19 x 23 $50
15 Empery of the black mandalas perforated etch 26 x 18 $75
16 Mandalas for a glass wall 24 x 24 nm $75

BATES, ROY ELLIOTT
20 Jan 1882, Connecticut Mo12
Montreal, 626 Dorchester St
1914 14 The wealth of Longpré, France $250
15 Marsh and mountain, north Wales $50

BAXTER, JOSEPH WILSON IAIN (N.E. Thing Co)
16 Nov 1936, Middlesborough, Eng CE CWW82 M WWA76
addr: Calgary, 1209 20th St NW, 1961. Vancouver: UBC Fine Arts Dept, 1965; Vancouver, 1968-9
1961 70 Colony No 1 nm $100
1964 2 The mover $600
1965 2 Still life, handbag & hat box No 3 $250 (MBAM)
1968 17 Bagged landscape with boat vinyl, air, water, boats 24 x 26 $800
18 Tubes vinyl & air 180h $1,000
19 Cirrus cloud, with blue carrying case vinyl, air & cloth 108 x 15 $750
20 Inflated inflated vinyl 48 x 15 $750
1969 N.E.Thing Co, to 1970
8 Talk nm
1970 film transparencies, metal, light 19 1/2 x 13 1/2 x 5
53 Still life, three orange cans
54 Landscape with tree
55 Community hall, 20 miles east of Regina, Sask
56 Prairie landscape, 1968, mid-Saskatchewan, west of Regina
57 Nude, 1968

BAXTER, RICHARD
addr: St Lambert, Que: 52 Mortlake Ave, Southward, 1914-24; 136 Sanford Ave, 1925; 300 Curzon, 1926-39
1914 16 Design, playing card backs wc $30
17 Rivière des Prairies wc $15
18 Evening in the quarry wc $15
19 Evening wc $15
1915 25 A September afternoon $75
26 Lengthening shadows $75
27 A Laurentian cottage wc $10
28 Across the river wc $10
1916 12 After the storm $100
13 Winter fuel $100
1917 17 A grey day $100
18 September sunshine $80
19 Early spring $80
20 Willows $15
1919 18 July sunshine $20
19 Summer afternoon $20
20 Late afternoon $20
21 Chambly Fort $20
1920 11 A summer day $75
12 Autumn $20
1921 9 Early spring $20
10 Winter evening $20
11 Summer $20
1922 17 October $75
18 Autumn afternoon $30
1923 23 A Quebec farm $200
1924 14 Poplars $25
15 Quietude $25
1925 22 Indian summer $20
23 October $20
1926 8 Near St Constance, Que $30
1927 5 Near Kennebunk Port $50
1928 10 Kennebunk River, Maine $80
1930 9 Pier, Cape Porpoise, Maine $30
10 Turbots Creek, Maine $30
11 Cape Porpoise Light, Maine $25
12 Mid-day, Fortunes Rocks, Maine $25
1931 15 Autumn morning, Piedmont $25
1932 21 Goat Island, Maine wc $15
22 Spring snow wc $15
1939 23 Gale House $40

BAYLEY, EMMA UNIACHE/UNIACKE
addr: Montreal: 1908; 45 Tupper St, 1909
1908 12 Her first born
1909 20 Meditation $40 (Uniacke)

BAYNE, FRANCES see FORBES, FRANCES

BEAMENT, THOMAS HAROLD
23 Jul 1898, Ottawa AGO CC2 CWW84 M NGC TB3 WHC WWA84 Juror
addr: Ottawa, 26 Nepean St, 1925.

Montreal: 725 St Catherine St W, 1926; 1475 St Catherine St W, 1930-2; 3419 Drummond St, 1934-5; 1494 Mackay St, 1936-9;c/o Watson Art Gallery, 1940-2. Rosemere, Que, 1947. Montreal, c/o Watson Art Gallery, 1948-9; 1551 Bishop St, 1950-3; Montreal, 1967
1925 24 Silent winter $75
1926 9 Autumn tapestry $250
1930 13 Laurentian winter $100
1931 16 Growth and demolition $500
17 The octagnal barn $75
1932 23 H.M.S.Danae $450
24 Thaw $100
1934 16 Coastal rhythm $100
17 Late afternoon, winter $100
18 The grey barn $100
1935 26 West Indian laundry $1,000
27 Covered bridge (listed 1967 Jessie Dow prize)
28 Portrait study
29 Late summer, Laurentians $175
1936 22 Mowers on the hillside $1,000
23 Laurentian valley $350
24 Return from school, near St Hyacinthe $200
25 Laurentian home $200
1937 11 Barbadian sugar mill $500
12 Porto Rican landscape $350
13 Thaw up the Ottawa River $250
14 View from Gordon Reed's, St Sauveur $150
1938 6 Departure for the hunt $750
1939 24 Ice cutters $750
1940 16 Silent northland $500
1942 6 Submarines and mother ships $250
1947 23 Orphanage in the hills $300
24 Entrance to St John's
25 Showery day, Londonderry
1948 4 South Shore, St John's, Nfld
1949 10 Still water $800
1950 1 On the headland $850
1952 2 Gossips $750
1953 3 Greece, 1944 $450
1967 4 West Indian washerwomen, 1934. 36 1/4 x 45 1/4 (MBAM, 1935) (may be 1935-26)

BEAMENT, THOMAS HAROLD (TIB)
17 Feb 1941, Montreal CWW84 M WWA84
addr: Westmount, 4709 The Boulevard, 1961-3
1961 71 Composition No 20 nm $50
1963 3 Fickle $400 (MBAM)

BEARD, ELEANORA
addr: Montreal, 707 Pine Ave, 1901-6
1901 108 Day closing in, Montreal harbour wc $10
1903 136 A misty morning wc $10
137 Reclaimed wc $6
1906 177 Old buildings, Grey Nuns Street wc $20

BEARDMORE, HELEN LOUISE
addr: Montreal, 605 Pine Ave
1920 13 Washing day wc $35

BEATTIE, DOROTHY (Mrs)
addr: Westmount, 443 Elm Ave
1940 17 White peony wc $10

BEATTIE, J. JESSIE I.
addr: Montreal; 309 Stanley St, 1920-5; 3483 Stanley St, 1929-35
1920 14 Portrait, sketch
1921 12 Loch Moidard, Scotland $50
1922 19 Cap à l'Aigle, sketch wc
1923 24 Kennebunk Beach, Me, sketch wc
1924 20 Orkney, sketch wc $15
1925 25 Looking up Côte des Neiges Road wc $25
26 Old houses, Lachine Canal wc $25
1929 12 St James the Apostle Church pastel $25
1930 14 From my studio window wc $10
1931 18 From my studio window wc $20
1933 21 Mutton Bay, Labrador $75
1934 19 Jamaica landscape $75
20 Percé, Que $75
1935 30 Montego Bay $100

BEATTIE, W. W.
addr: Montreal; 309 Stanley St, 1924-5; 3483 Stanley St, 1930
1924 21 Cap à l'Aigle, sketch wc
22 Chambly, sketch wc
1925 27 Old houses, St Agnes, Que wc
28 Old house, Wading River, Long Island, USA wc
1930 15 The Richelieu, early spring wc
16 Chambly, sketch wc

BEATTY, JOHN WILLIAM
30 May 1869 - 4 Oct 1941, Toronto AGO B CC1 CWW36 EC M NGC TB2/3 W78
addr: Toronto, 336 Jarvis St
1909 21 Blaricum, north Holland nm $100

22 The beach, Katwyke nm $50
23 Old church, Dordrecht nm $50
port: bust, by Joan Sloan, 1941-60

BEATTY, MARGARET see FRAME, MARGARET

BEAU, HENRI
27 Jun 1863, Montreal 15 May 1949, Paris B CE H Mo12
addr: Paris, 22 ave St Ouen, 1894. Montreal: 20 Park Ave, 1897; Fraser Hall, 9 University St, 1901; 2484 St Catherine St, 1905-6; 622 St Catherine St W, 1909; 291 Mountain St, 1914; 814 Cherrier St, 1946
1894 13 Dr de Martigny, sketch
1897 8 La liseuse $100
1901 10 Spring $200
11 Heather at sunset $100
12 Heather at dawn $100
13 In the fields $75
14 Geese herder $75
15 Forest at Fontainebleau $100
16 Autumn $75
1905 5 The picnic $150
6 The pond $80
7 Lady in black
8 Mrs B.
9 Mr P.B.
10 Miss B.
1906 16 Idyll
17 Study in red
18 Landscape
19 Lamp effect
1909 24 Woman in pink $110
25 Jardin potager $85
26-7 Paysage $45, np
1914 20 The Seine, near Conflans
21 St Maria dei Servi, Siena
22 Morning in Brittany
23 Sunset in Brittany
1946 16 Portrait, the red scarf

BEAU, PAUL
1 Nov 1871 - 7 Jul 1949, Montreal
addr: Montreal: 2484 St Catherine St, 1905; 936 St Catherine St W, 1909: 291 Mountain St, 1913
1905 268 Brass clock, 1/4 strike $100
1909 385 Vase copper flammé $15
386 Card receiver bronze and copper $15
387 Book holders $10
1913 421 Writing set iron and brass, 8 pieces $75
422 Umbrella holder copper and brass $55

BEAUCAGE, LEOPOLD
addr: Montreal, 5414 Côtes des Neiges Rd
1957 5 Bouquet de fleurs $50
6 Portrait de jeune fille $60

BEAUCHAMP, ALPHONSINE
addr: Montreal, 2170 St André St
1922 375 Chocolate set, jug, 12 cups & saucers $75
376 Large jug $25
377 Small jug $20
378 Jewel case $18

BEAUDOIN, ARMANDE
addr: Montreal, 5214 De Lorimier Ave
1951 76 Trouées de soleil $75

BEAUDOIN, SUZANNE see DUMOUCHEL, SUZANNE

BEAULAC, W. GOSSELIN
addr: Trois Rivières, Qué, 642 rue Ste Angèle
1955 6 Soir d'hiver $200

BEAULIEU, FLORENT
4 Sep 1933, Montreal
addr: Montreal, 7764 De Gaspé Ave
1957 105 Les sapins nm $30

BEAULIEU, LOUIS JACQUES see JAQUE, LOUIS

BEAULIEU, PAUL VANIER
24 Mar 1910, Montreal B M TB3
addr: Montreal: 6210 Somerled Ave, 1943; 3679 Laval Ave, 1950; 3157 Lacombe Ave, 1951-63
1943 15 Olga
1950 98 Tête de Savoyard $175
1951 77 Nature morte $125
1952 85 Still life $150 (MBAM)
128 Head dry pt $15
1953 102 Landscape with figure etch $15
1956 4 Nature morte au vase de fleurs $400
1960 6 Cinétique murale I $525
1963 4 Costa Brava $1,200

BEAULIEU, SIMONE AUBRY
5 Aug 1917, Montreal M

addr: Outremont, 36 Roskilde Ave
1951 78 Nature morte à la carafe $150
79 Fleurs et poires $180

BEAUPRE, ALFRED
addr: Montreal: 1908; 75 Desery St, 1909-10; YMCA, Drummond St, 1914
1908 13 Premier romance $500
1909 28 La jeunesse de la terre $300 (MBAM)
1910 22 Nature morte $50
1914 24 Conquest of a cavern, Stone Age $300 (MBAM)

BECHMAN, FREDERICKA
addr: Montreal, 3465 Jeanne Mance St, 1932. Westmount: 4862 Sherbrooke St W, 1935; 516 Grosvenor Ave, 1936
1932 25 Baby's head pastel $25
1935 31 June
1936 26 Duncan Carter pastel
27 Maris Bishop pastel

BECK, GERTRUDE E.
addr: Montreal, 91 Clanrandal Ave
1922 20 Autumn, Kawartha Lakes

BECK, IDA
b Montreal
addr: Westmount, 432 Metcalfe Ave, 1934-6
1934 21 A young Chinese woman pastel $30
1935 32 Nuns' farm, Westmount, wc $18
1936 28 Peonies and still life pastel $20
29 Portrait study pastel $25

BECKWITH, JAMES E. Amer
21 Dec 1907, Mount Pleasant, Iowa
WWA38
addr: Montreal: 4134 Dorchester St W, 1934; 4864 Côte des Neiges Rd, 1935-6
1934 22 Spring at the yards wc $65
23 Across the river wc $65
24 Drying nets wc $65
25 Factories wc $65
370 A sanitorium cottage
371 A little theatre, proscenium arch
371 A world's fair information building
1935 33 The bather wc $100
34 The mountain wc $75
35 Farm wc $75
389 Industrial charcl $40
1936 30 Highway wc $40
31 City scene wc $50
32 The Square wc $100
33 Energy and vacuum wc $50

BEDARD, PAUL
b ca 1904 19 May 1931, Quebec
addr: Quebec, 15 St Sauveur St
1930 17 Jeune fille lisant $30
18 Vieilles maisons à Québec $30

BEDER, JACK
14 Mar 1910, Opatow, Poland Juror
addr: Montreal: 72 Duluth Ave W, 1932; 3942 St Urbain, 1935; 74 Prince Arthur St E, 1936-40; 140 Evans St, 1941-2; 432 Rigaud St, 1945-8: 1089 Beaver Hall Hill, 1950; 5996 Somerland Ave, 1952-7; 7522 Guelph Rd, Côte St Luc, 1959-60
1932 26 Stonecutter's place, St Lawrence Blvd $75
1935 36 And by night they resume their existence
37 Tramway pastel $50
1936 34 Woman at table pastel $100
35 The drunk wc $100
36 Old dwellings $75
1936 15 After the rain $75
16 Rooftops $50
17 View from a roof $50
1938 7 Cabaret temp
8 Girl in pajamas pastel $50
1939 25 Roofs temp $125
26 Milton Street, Montreal $125
27 Interior $85
28 Still life temp $85
1940 18 Ste Famille Street, Montreal $100
19 Birches, Mount Royal $65
20 Winter afternoon $75
1941 11 Autumn morning $125
1942 7 Autumn rain $75
8 Morning light $60
1945 14 Interior with chair temp $45
1948 69 Country road, Laurentians gouache $60
1950 143 Calm bay wc $50
1952 86 Littered beach, N.B. $350
1955 85 Backroofs nm $30
1957 7 Lakeshore, Laurentians $175
106 In the woods nm $225

1959 42 Plant forms wc sculp
1960 7 The old Massey house $175

BEECH, ARTHUR
8 Sep 1875, Oldham, Lancs, Eng 1948, Winnipeg
addr: Winnipeg, 602 Rathgar Ave
1930 253 The breakwater wd block $25
254 Autumn wd block $14
255 Peace wd block $10

BEEVOR, A. F.
fl 1882-1908 H
addr: Montreal, 1908
1888 T.F, mispr
67 A wet day, Prout's Neck wc $20
100 On the sands, Prout's Neck wc $20
133 Spouting Rock, Prout's Neck wc $15
1908 14 Lumber camp, Restigouche

BELANGER, LOUIS JOSEPH OCTAVE
20 Jun 1886 - 1972, Montreal B CNS36
addr: Montreal, 1117 St Hubert St, 1919-26. Outremont, 53 St Catherine Rd, 1928. Montreal, 4440 Kent Ave, 1951-2
1919 22 Windmill Point, 50 years ago
23 Sketch on river, Ste Rose $15
24 Mr W.B, sketch b&w
1920 19 Les bouleaux du Mont Royal $175
1921 13 On Mount Royal $50
1925 29 Notre Dame de Paris $125
334 Port Louis, Bretagne drwg $15
1926 10 L'automne au Luxembourg $250
11 Les vieux livres pastel $40
1928 11 Crossing St Lawrence River $80
12 First snow, Ste Adèle $125
13-14 Autumn, Piedmont $125 each
1951 3 Portrait $100
1952 3 Père et fils $350

BELISLE, HENRI
addr: Montreal, 3450 St Urbain St
1934 426 La menuiserie etch $8
427 Rue des Carrières etch $7.50
428 Le cerisier etch $7.50

BELIVEAU, RENE CHARLES
20 Nov 1872, Montreal H
addr: Montreal: 720 St Urbain St, 1900; 348A Sanguinet St, 1903; 726 Berri St, 1906; Montreal, 1908; 1074 St Urbain St, 1909-10
1900 6 Effet de matin, pres Versailles $75
7 Nature morte, légumes $35
8 Nature morte, pommes $25
1903 12 Portrait of the artist
1906 20 Cour de Ferne, Fontainebleau $75
178 Sous-bois wc $15
301 Chanteuse des cours b&w $20
322-3 Music dec panel nm $50 each
1908 15 Enfant au repos $150
16 Basse-cour $60
1909 29 Dans les champs $100
30 Dans l'attente $100
31 Le petit moulin $75
32 M.L. portrait
1910 23 Le petit pécheur $50
24 Sous-bois $75

BELL, ALISTAIR MACREADY
21 Oct 1913, Darlington, Eng CC2 CE CWW84 M TB3 WWA84
addr: West Vancouver, 2566 Marine Dr
1955 86 Tidal marsh No 3 nm $75

BELL, MARY see EASTLAKE, MARY

BELL, OLGA (m John Outram)
addr: Ottawa, 136 Maclaren St, 1932, 1936. Montreal, 1202 Seymour Ave, 1934
1932 27 Petunias and grapes $45
1934 26 A March day $25
1936 Outram
333 Willie's home $20

BELL, PETER ALAN
21 Apr 1918, Grantham, Eng WWA80
addr: St John's, Nfld
1968 25 Fourth view from my window 36 x 48 $400
26 Fifth view from my window 36 x 48 $400
27 Adel sergph 26 1/2 x 19 1/2 $50
28 Ancestor, version 2 sergph 27 1/4 x 19 1/2 $50

BELL, RUTH O.
addr: Montreal West, 185 Eaton Ave, 1932-3
1932 illumination
369 King Robert of Sicily $30
370 Influence $25
371 Text $7
1933 440 The arrow and the song $35

441 Pater Noster $25

BELL-SMITH, FREDERIC MARLETT
26 Sep 1846, London, Eng 23 Jun 1923, Toronto AGO CC2 CE CWW10 EC H M Mo98/12 NGC R2 TB3 W78
addr: Hamilton, 1880. Toronto, 1891. Paris, 203 Blvd Raspail, 1892. Toronto, 336 Jarvis St, 1894-1923
1880 115 Tobogganing, on the way up wc
119 Tobogganing, clear the track wc
139 Tobogganing, at the foot of the hill wc
144 Niagara winter wc
163 Shinny on the ice wc
189 Tobogganing, the start wc
190 Summer wc
1883 8 Frenchman's Bay, Maine wc
9 Rocks in the Thousand Islands wc
12 Duck Brook, Mount Desert wc
18 Foggy morning, Casco Bay wc
26 Eagle Lake, Mount Desert, Me wc
46 Great Head, Mount Desert, Me wc
58 Noon, North Gonway, N.H. wc
62 Regatta, Toronto Bay wc
1885 110 A rainy day on the St John River wc
118 A warm day on Mount Washington wc
120 On the Bay shore, St John wc
121 A freshet on the St John River wc
129 A river road wc
136 Fog clearing, Bay of Fundy wc
1886 60 The beached margent of the sea
78 The late Col Dyde, ADC
1888 68 Valley of the Ottertail, B.C. wc $350
83 Roger's Pass, B.C. wc $250
99 Sunrise in the Selkirks wc $200
111 Hazy day, summit of the Rockies, B.C. wc $200
119 The Hermit Range wc $150
131 A sunny day in the Illecillewaet Valley, B.C. wc $150
1889 174c Canyon of the Fraser River wc $175
1891 147 A snow clad monarch of the Rockies wc
148 Gorge on the Illecillewaet wc $200
149 In the Fraser Canyon wc $150
150 A Rocky Mountain valley wc $150
151 A breezy day, Bay of Fundy wc $65
152 A valley in gloom wc $65
1892 13 Le soir $350
152 Canyon, Rocky Mountains wc $200
153 Paris, street scene near Notre Dame wc $25
154 Paris, street scene near Place St Michel wc $25
155 Paris, street scene, St Germain des Pres wc $25
156 Au jardin du Luxembourg, Paris wc $50
157 Avenue in the Luxembourg Gardens wc
158 In St James' Park, London wc $25 (crossed out, On the coast of Cornwall written in, np)
1894 18 Landscape $20
19 M. Matthews
20 Dutch interior, making wooden shoes $175
172 Pont Neuf, Paris wc $250
173 Westminster wc $250
1895 147 St Paul's from Ludgate Hill wc $100
148 Jardin du Luxembourg, Paris wc $35
1897 12 Rainy day on Westminster Bridge $125
13 Island Park, Toronto $150
14 On London Bridge $200
15 Grey day on the Thames $50
16 Evening, Holland $50
17 A forgotten melody $75
1898 123 On the Saguenay wc $25
124 Piccadilly wc $20
125 The Row, Hyde Park wc $20
126 On the Thames wc $35
1900 10 Hyde Park Corner $40
119 A cloud girt peak in the Selkirks wc $100
120 A rainy day in the Selkirks wc $100
1903 138 Ludgate Hill wc $75
139 The day is done, Melrose Abbey wc $75
140 Saint Dunstan's, Fleet Street wc $75
141 Statue of Charles I, Charing Cross wc $75
1905 131 Westminster Abbey, evening after rain wc $200

132 Canadian fishing boat at sea wc $100
133 Stormy weather, Cape Breton wc $65
134 Pont Royale, Paris wc $30
1906 21 A glacier tarn in the Rockies $500
22 The pigeons of St Paul's $35
23 A street in London $50
179 London, Ludgate Hill wc $200
180 A murky day, Yoho Valley wc $200
181 Near Notre Dame, Paris wc $35
182 Siwash Indian catching salmon, Fraser River wc $35
1908 17 Sunrise $300
18 Sunrise, eastern entrance to Rockies $75
19 The Chancellor $30
20 A bit near Glacier $30
175 Mountain solitude wc $300
176 Evening, Luxembourg Gardens wc $75
177 The Row, Hyde Park wc $40
178 Rainy day, St Paul's wc $40
1909 33 The heart of the Empire wc $400 (listed 1967, Jessie Dow prize)
34 St Paul's from the river wc $200
35 Rainy day, Piccadilly wc $50
36 Summer sunshine wc $50
37 Approaching Tower Bridge wc $40
38 Early morning, Moraine Lake wc $30
39 Arch, Constitution Hill wc $15
40 Lyceum Theatre wc $15
1910 25 The bird of prey ("Vide our mutual friend") $500
26 Misty morning on the Thames wc $200
27 A sunlit shore, Sandown $400
1911 20 A September afternoon $250
21 A hazy day, Lake Louise $175
22 The open sea wc $100
23 Westminster wc $30
24 Near Hyde Park Corner wc $30
25 King William Street wc $25
26 St Paul's at day break wc $25
27 Broad Sanctuary, Westminster wc $30
1912 31 Morning mists wc $300
32 St Martin's in the Field wc $35
33 Near St Paul's wc $30
34 Twilight, near St Martin's Lane wc $25
35 St Mary's in the Strand wc $30
36 St Clement's Danes wc $35
37 Wet day, Westminster $25
38 The Strand, near Somerset House wc $50
1913 18 The Great Divide $500
19 Lake O'Hara $500
20 Waterloo Place $25
21 Near Waterloo Bridge $25
22 Canyon of the Fraser River wc $50
23 Gracechurch Street wc $50
1914 25 Evening, Hyde Park Corner $35
26 Children's fête, Rotterdam wc $200
27 Solomon's Porch, Westminster wc $200
28 Gad's Hill Place wc $30
1915 29 The heart of the Selkirks $600
30 Albion's rocky coast $100
31 A veteran of the Crimea $400
32 King George V's coronation $30
1916 14 The path over the hill $300
15 Sunny afternoon, Hyde Park $125
16 Village, Mal Baie, Que $75
17 Gracechurch St, London wc $40
18 The Old Curiosity Shop (Dickens) wc $20
19 Evening, Rochester, Kent wc $20
1917 21 Trafalgar Square $200
22 An old shepherd $125
23 The blue haze of England wc $100 (listed 1967, Jessie Dow prize)
24 Dick Swiveller and the Marchioness $50
25 Oliver Twist asking for more $50
26 Mr Micawber and David Copperfield $30
1918 15 Waterloo Bridge $125
from Dickens, 16-18
16 The Pickwick Club
17 Bob Cratchit's dinner $75
18 Mrs Leo Hunter's garden party $75
19 Hyde Park Corner, after rain wc $100
20 Sunny afternoon in Hyde Park $100
1919 31 Hyde Park Corner wc $75
32 Golden sunlight, Lake Louise $200
33 Twilight, London Royal Exchange $100
34 Canadian pasture $200
35 Grey day on the Thames $65
36 The morning paper $50

1920 15 The friendly waiter (David Copperfield) $50
16 Holborn, Staple Inn at night wc $100
17 Victoria Embankment, London wc $100
18 Mount Temple, Paradise Valley wc $75
1921 14 Fleet Street, London, St Paul's in distance $125
15 Solitude, evening in the Selkirks $100
16 The meeting of the waters, Glacier, B.C. $50
1922 22 Parting day, Canadian Rockies $400
23 The theatre hour, Leicester Square $400
1923 25 Sunrise in the Selkirks $300
26 The day's decline, Canadian Rockies $125
1894-5 Association 1st prize 1892 wc
port: by Sherwood, William A. 1891-128

BELLE, CHARLES ERNEST DE
17 May 1873, Budapest 3 Sep 1939, Montreal AGO CWW36 M NGC PMC TB2/3
addr: Montreal: 705 St Hubert St, 1913; Scott & Sons, 1914; 1129 Decarie Blvd, 1916-18; 202 Dupuis Ave, 1919-26; 1538 Sherbrooke St W, Medical Arts Bldg, 1929-32; 3602 Northcliffe Ave, 1933-6
1913 101 Spring pastel $100
102 Babes in the wood pastel $180
103 Alone pastel $120
104 A summer day pastel $120
105 Wonderland $800
106 Meditation, a study $800
1914 93 The maiden's prayer $300
94 Jesus, the man $400
1916 73 Spiritual Christ $400
74 The young settlers $250
75 Symphony in snow pastel $100
76 The rising pastel $150
77 The little princess $60
78 Homeless pastel $50
79 Children pastel $60
1917 95 Peace wc $200
96 Lonely road pastel $120
97 The children's day pastel $150
98 The window pastel $150
99 The waifs pastel $150
100 The highest creation pastel $250
1918 78 Little Nora $75
79 Refugees $75
80 Ye have forgotten $250
81 A bleak day $180 (NGC)
82 There is a happier land far away pastel $200
83 Recollection wc $120
1919 25 Symphony
26 Into the light pastel $250
27 Meditation pastel $450
28 Youth pastel $200
29 In Flanders fields where poppies grow pastel $180
30 Playmates $180
1920 56 Sunshine of life $1,000
57 Last of winter $250
58 Poetry pastel $500
59 The dancers pastel $250
1922 71 The evening bell pastel $300
72 The orchard pastel $350
73 The child garden pastel $800
74 The babes in the wood pastel $450
1923 60 Young Canada $1,500
61 The Nun's wood pastel $500
62 Homeless $250
63 When winter comes $500
1924 58 Re-united $1,000
59 Three of seven $1,500
60 March pastel $300
61 The little fairies $500
1926 34 When nature sleeps pastel $350
35 Melodie in pastel $1,200
36 The daisy pastel $700
37 The heavenly garden pastel $1,000
1929 52 The age of joy pastel $2,000
53 Children of Mr and Mrs Fred Peverley pastel
54 A hymn pastel $500
55 Evening pastel $500
1930 49 Children of Mr and Mrs Eric Millar
50 The twins pastel $350
51 Madonna and Child
52 The nightingale pastel $250
1931 69 A quartette pastel $600
70 Baby of Dr and Mrs J. Jekill pastel
71 Heavenly pastel $700
1932 75 Forgotten $2,000
76 Lonely road $400
77 Purity $2,000
78 The future pastel $600

1933 68 The quartette pastel $600
69 Christianity pastel
70 Wonderland pastel $400
71 Trinity pastel $500
1934 78 Heavenly $1,800
79 Spiritual pastel $450
1936 110 The sisters pastel $500
111 The little maids pastel $450
112 Our pal pastel $450

BELLE, WILLIAM GEORGE DE
20 Sep 1906, Glasgow 17 Feb 1975, Montreal
addr: Westmount, 227 Kensington Ave
1940 311 Residence, Chicago, Ill

BELLEFEUILLE, ANNETTE SENECAL DE (m Lionel de Bellefeuille)
addr: Ottawa: 243 Chapel St, 1917; 187 Springfield Rd, 1936-49
1917 Senécal
326 Printemps, cushiontop wc $25
1936 113 Deux roses wc
114 Le bocal devant la fenêtre wc
115 Bouquet de roses wc
116 Lis wc
1937 70 Narcissus wc $60
71 Fleurs légères wc $40
1939 98 Cactus
1943 16 Roses jaunes wc $20
1949 11 Jeune fille $50

BELLEFLEUR, LEON
8 Feb 1910, Montreal AGO CCI M NGC TB3 WWA76
addr: Montreal: 10437 De La Roche St, 1945-7; 11151 Drapeau Ave, 1949-51; 4906 St Catherine St E, 1952; 1440 Bernard Ave W, 1956-8; Montreal, 1967
1945 15 Le cheval rouge $35
1947 26 Polichinelle à la lune $150
1949 12 Volupté aux cheveux roux $50
13 Poissons aux seins bleus $75
1950 99 Souvenir des bêtes enchantées $25
1951 80 Faune en délire $300
81 Nocturne aux oiseaux $100
Jury II prize, $150. 1967-5, 24 x 26 (Albert Dumouchel, Montreal)
1952 117 Maisons d'oiseaux gouache $50
1956 5 Aux Illinois $90
6 Lueurs d'encens $90
1957 8 Les diaprées $200
107 Les oiseaux parasols nm $75
1958 49 Septenaire nm $150
50 Fortuna major nm $150

BELLEMARE, JEAN PIERRE (signs Belmar)
addr: Longueuil, Que, 397 Guilbault, Ave
1964 Belmar
3 "SEDI" $300

BELLERIVE, MARCEL
24 Jul 1934, Grand'Mère, Qué
addr: Montréal, 3830 rue St Christophe
1959 27 Blanc distrait nm $50

BELLIS, DAISY MAUD
16 Feb 1887, Waltham, Mass WWA47
addr: Ste Anne de Bellevue, Que, Macdonald College, 1924-30
1924 351 Teapot enamel
352 Sugar bowl enamel
1925 30 Faithful housekeeper
31 Leonore pastel
1926 181 Bedcover batik
182 Curtains batik
1930 19 Sunset wc $25

BELMAR see BELLEMARE, JEAN PIERRE

BENEY, GABRIEL DE
addr: Outremont, 756 ave Bloomfield
1964 20 Sortie du port $300

BENISON, ROSS
addr: Lachine, Que, 625 44th Ave
1951 135 Wheat stacks b&w wash

BENJAMIN, GERSHON
addr: Montreal: 25 Drolet St, 1916; 906A City Hall Ave, 1917-19; 628 St Catherine St W, 1920-3
1916 20 Awaiting b&w
1917 27 Head of a boy b&w
28 Head of a girl b&w
29 An Oriental b&w $5
1918 21 Autumn $20
22 Sunlight $15
23 Pumpkins $20
24 Winter $15
1919 37 Autumn sun $15
37A Mr E. Dyonnet, RCA, sketch
1920 20 Zylda b&w $20
1922 21, 23A Landscape $40 each
1923 27 Portrait b&w
28 Portrait, sketch b&w

BENN, ROBERT LAWRENCE
addr: Montreal: 2181 Prud'homme Ave, 1954; 4994 Queen Mary Rd, Apt 4, 1956
1954 10 Mood study $65
1956 7 Non-objective study $100

BENNETT, ERNEST
addr: St Hilaire, Que, 1943. Montreal, 3042 Trafalgar Ave, 1954
1943 17 The Atlantic coast
1954 11 Mullion Cove, Cornwall $350

BENNETT, JOHN ALFRED EVEREST
29 Mar 1919, Diss, Eng AGO IO M
addr: Toronto, 152 Mildenhall Rd, 1954-7. Don Mills, Ont, 18 Brian Cliffe Dr, 1964. Toronto, 1967
1954 12 Vista $150. Jessie Dow prize 1967-6, 24 x 36 (Loretto College, Toronto)
1955 87 The bridge of silence nm
1957 9 Snifters $150
1964 4 Sun temple $500

BENOIT, MARIE ANTONIA
24 Sep 1927, Margate, Eng
addr: Ottawa, 554 Driveway
1954 13 Vermilion

BENSKIN, GERALD R.
addr: Sabrevois, Que
1939 29 California sand dunes wc $50

BENSON, D. F.
addr: Montreal, 12 Tower Ave
1918 25 Situation in Russia b&w

BENSON, G. W.
addr: Montreal, 12 Tower Ave
1919 378-80 Heraldic work wc

BENTLEY, DOROTHY see WILLIAMS, DOROTHY

BENTLEY, WINIFRED K.
addr: Ottawa: 29 Robert St, 1930; 3 Hartington Pl, 1931
1930 256 The Sabbath rest etch $15
257 Signora etch $12.50
258 A pioneer's barns etch $12.50
1931 360 Summer breezes dry pt $10
361 La fileuse dry pt $6
362 William dry pt $15

BENY, WILFRED ROY <u>ROLOFF</u>
7 Jan 1924, Medicine Hat, Alta 16 Mar 1984, Rome AGO CC2 CE CWW83 M NGC TB3 WWA84
addr: Toronto, Trinity College
1945 16 The soil $300
17 Prairie cathedral, Medicine Hat, Alta pastel $100

BERCOVITCH, ALEKSANDRE
15 Mar 1893, Cherson, Russia 7 Jan 1951, Montreal AGO TB3 (Alexander, Alexandre, Alexsander mispr)
addr: Montreal: 88 Colonial Ave, 1927; 2110 Clarke St, 1928-9; 109 Laurier Ave, 1932-3; 4480 De Bullion St, 1934; 4264 St Dominique St, 1935-42; 78 Prince Arthur St, 1950
1927 6 Turkoman Chechana wc $100
1928 15 Turkoman $25
16-19 Sketch wc $25 each
1929 13 Bokhara temp $200
14 Composition $200
1932 28 Sketch wc $200
1933 22 L'hiver wc $150
23 Summer wc $150
1934 27 Still life $100
28 Sade Shapiro, pianist
29 Landscape, Canadian motif
30 De Bullion Street $75
1935 38 The negro girl (AGO)
39 Ninel, the little grandmother
40 The srtist's family
1936 37 The girl with the shell, Percé pastel $400
38 My son pastel
1937 18 Les fleurs
19 Winter in the Laurentians
20 Cliffs, Bonaventure Island wc
21 The beach of Mr Major, on Bonaventure Island temp
1938 9 Ninel pastel
1939 30 Composition temp $400
1940 21 Mr and Mrs Abraham Klein
1941 12 Portrait of a girl $100
1942 9 Girl with red hair $150
10 Nude pastel $350
1950 100 Negress $600

BERCOVITCH, SYLVIA see ARY, SYLVIA

BERENDS, HANS
addr: Montreal 2381 St Antoine St, 1930-40; 2124 Tupper St, 1942-3
1930 20 Barns, St Helen's Island $30

1932 29 Studio corner $25
1934 31 Side show $175
1936 39 Cedar Lodge, Magog
1940 22 The wayside Cross, St Calixte, Que $45
23 Chez Madame Paget, St Calixte, Que $45
1942 11 La paroisse
1943 18 Manoeuvres Brockville, Ont $75

BERG, HELENA (m Victor Fritjof Berg)
21 Jul 1917, Zakopane, Poland
addr: Dorval, Que: 95 Petunia Ave, 1951; 95 Cloverdale Ave, 1954-55
1951 4 Matilda and Dalia
1954 14 Seashore $150
1955 7 Wheatfield

BERG, VICTOR FRITJOF
3 Jan 1917, Tallinn, Estonia
addr: Dorval, Que, 95 Cloverdale Ave, 1954-5
1954 88 Chateau Ramezay, Montreal temp $100
1955 88 Sleeping cat nm $50

BERGER, ANTOINE
addr: Montreal, 1047 Berri St
1939 31 Antoine by himself pastel
32 Portrait of a child pastel $75
33 Small St Peter Church, Montmartre pastel $50
34 Place du Tertre, Montmartre pastel $50

BERGERON, GERMAIN, Frère
18 Dec 1933, Ste Perpétue de Nicolet, Que
addr: Montreal, 3791 Queen Mary Rd, 1963-4
1963 94 Junon-Paon metal $250
1964 114 Fétiche metal $230

BERGERON, PAUL EMILE
Addr: Montreal, 6581 Hamilton St, 1945-51
1945 18 Near St Tite des Caps, Que $100
1946 17 Evening in the Laurentians $100
1949 14 Sunday morning, Ste Adele $100
1951 5 Le printemps à St Tite des Caps $75

BERGERON, SUZANNE (m Jean-Claude Suhit)
23 Jun 1930, Causapscal, Que AGO CC1 M NGC TB3
addr: Montreal, Galerie Agnes Lefort, 1504 Sherbrooke St W
1964 5 Forêt lumineuse $800 (MBAM)

BERGMAN, HENRY ERIC
10 Nov 1893, Dresden, Germ 8 Feb 1958, Winnipeg AGO CC2 M TB2/3
addr: Winnipeg, 368 Baltimore Rd, 1931-4
wood engravings, unframed
1931 363 White-caps $8
364 Northern phenomena $5
365 Light $5
366 Night quarters $5
1934 429 The first drops $10
430 Iris $10
431 The stump $12
432 Oaks and wind $10

BERNSTEIN, ALAN L. see MAYEROVITCH, HARRY, 1937

BERTRAND, NOEMI
addr: Montreal, 804 Sherbrooke St W
1926 183 Globe daisy, table centre batik $30
184 Solar impression, scarf batik $25
185 Berries, scarf batik $25
186 Mimosas, centre piece batik $8

BETHUNE, HENRY NORMAN
3 Mar 1890, Gravenhurst, Ont 12 Nov 1939, Huang-shih-K'ou, China CE EC
addr: Montreal, 3437 Peel St
1935 41 Night emergency
port: by Richard S Eve, 1941-223; by Rita Briansky, 1953-7

BETHUNE, MAY MANLEY
1888 19 A study of roses $25
23 The king apple $75

BETTS, M. D. (Miss)
addr: London, Ont, 536 Queen's Ave
1914 29 Case of miniatures $300

BETTS, RANDOLPH COTGRAVE
20 Dec 1902, Montreal

addr: Montreal, 2175 Prud'homme Ave, 1934-5. Town of Mount Royal, 230 Lazard Ave, 1940-4
1934 373 Proposed house, Montreal West
433 Bookplate pen & ink
1935 349 Proposed residence, Outremont
390 Bookplate drwg
1940 312 Residence, Thurlow Rd, Hampstead
313 Residence, Laird Blvd, Town of Mount Royal
314 Residence, Surrey Gardens, Westmount, under construction
1942 192 Christmas card drwg
223 Cottage, Town of Mount Royal drwg
224 Cottage, Hampstead drwg
225 Cottage, Montreal West drwg
1943 221 Old houses, Edinburgh drwg
244-5 Cottage, Town of Mount Royal
246 Laboratory building
1944 151 Residence, Town of Mount Royal

BETTS, SARAH A. (m Georges Betts)
addr: Ottawa, 236 Lisgar St
1951 82 Boat house $50

BEVERIDGE, KARL JOHN
7 Nov 1945, Ottawa CWW80 WWA84
addr: Toronto
1969 1 B-693 polyethylene, steel rods 96 x 86 x 1

BICE, CLARE
24 Jan 1909, Durham, Ont 18 May 1976, St John's CWW73 M WWA78 WWB76
addr: London, Ont, 1010 Wellington St, 1952-60
1952 4 Setting for a sea piece $250
1960 8 Canadian wilderness $650

BIDER, F. A.
addr: Montreal, 448A Guy St
1926 187 Fish st gl $25
188 Fox st gl $20

BIELANSKL, GINO
addr: Rosemount, Que, 5240 10e ave
1964 82 Petits dessins nm $180

BIELER, ANDRE CHARLES
8 Oct 1896, Lausanne AGO CC2 CE CWW84 EC IO M WWA84 WWB76 Juror
addr: Montreal, 223 Milton St, 1924, 1929. St Famile, Isle d'Orleans, 1928. Montreal: 2039 Peel St, 1932-3; 3745 ave de l'Oratoire, 1934-5. Kingston, Ont: 12 Dundas St, 1937; Queen's University, 1939, 1948, 1955; 33 Hill St, 1944, 1953, 1956-9. Glenburnie, Ont, 1968
1924 23 La maison peinte
24 St Saphorin et les Alpes
25 Le départ
1928 20 Les berlines, Québec $75
21 Les bûcheron $75
1929 15 St Sauveur $100
1932 30 Pêcheur, gaspesien $300
1933 24 Le printemps $135
1934 32 La tabac $380
33 L'arrosoir wc $42
1935 42 The pink wood $325
1937 22 Rivière du Nord $200
1939 35 Before the auction $400
36 Wet earth temp $225
1944 6 Les draveurs au repos oil temp $200
1948 5 Allant au baptême temp & oil $180
1953 94 The green stall temp $135
1955 8 Tout en cherchant $350
1956 8 Lady patroness of the old peoples' home $375
1957 10 Le repas de famille $300
1959 3 Sous-bois $325
1968 intaglio prints
21 Blue spruce 26 x 20 $70
22 Dawn 26 x 20 $70
23 Bodoni 26 x 20 $70
24 Figure two 40 x 26 $140
port: sculp, by Marjorie S. Winslow 1944-170

BIELER, ANDRE CHARLES THEODORE (TED)
23 Jul 1938, Kingston, Ont B CC1 CWW84 IO M WWA84
addr: Kingston, 33 Hill St, 1957-9. Toronto, Isaacs Gallery, 832 Yonge St, 1965
1957 11 Au vieux moulin $60
1959 28 Dollar Bill's place, after prohibition nm $55
1965 31 Seven pillars concrete $300

BILL, EDWARD B.
fl 1885-1903 H
1885 84 Christmas on the Welsh moors

BILLAUX, MARY JANE HELENE (m Hugh Clifford)
24 Sep 1903, London, Eng
addr: West Vancouver, 2264 Marine Dr, 1947; 931 22nd St, 1957
1947 27 Seated girl $175
1957 12 Boy with recorder $150

BILLMEIER, RICHARD
1921, Bavaria
addr: Montreal: 2340 Lincoln Ave, Apt 15, 1960; 12 Oldfield Ave, Apt 15, 1961
1960 9 Winterland $350
1961 2 Landscape illus (purchase award MBAM)

BIRCH, EMILY L.
addr: Montreal, 26 Crescent St
1895 15 Still life
16 Marsh mallows

BIRD, ERNEST EARL
1869, London, Eng
addr: Morin Heights, Que, The Bungalow, Campbell's Farm, 1935-7
1935 43 Lunch, the skiers' hill, Morin Heights wc $20
1936 40 My gateway, Morin Heights wc $45
41 A clump of trees, Piedmont Hills in the distance wc $25
1937 23 An old Laurentian barn in the autumn wc $35

BIRD, JOHN ALEXANDER HARRINGTON Eng
23 May 1846, England 3 Jan 1936, Hammersmith, London B DBA DVP G H TB1/3 WBA
addr: Montreal, 1880
1880 65 Cattle
166 Going to market wc
174 Feeding the sacred ibis chalk
175 View in Portland harbour wc
1881 16 Peasants attacked by wolves
1883 2 York River, Maine wc

BIRKS, ROBERT MORRIS
1848/68 Jan 1938, St Anne de Bellevue, Que H
addr: StAnne de Bellevue, 1912. Montreal, 485 St James St, 1917. St Anne de Bellevue, 1921
1885 9 A Canadian wood barge
19 Half-way Rock lighthouse
88 Fishing smack
1912 39 Fogbound vessel
1917 30 Soudanese
1921 17 The sea
18 Landscape
289 Elizabeth plaster

BISHOP, JOHN HAROLD GILBERT
18 Sep 1908, Bathurst, N.B.
addr: St John: 147 Prince William St, 1936-8; 72 1/2 Prince William St, 1945
1936 42 Still life pastel $15
43 Fog wc $15
44 Wharf at St Martins wc $15
45 Summer wc $15
1938 10 Summer playtime wc $20
1945 19 Spring freshet wc $75

BISHOP, OLIVE
addr: Montreal, 4147 Dorchester St
1901 211 Poster heads china
212 Portrait, Mme Viger Le Brun

BISSET, JAMES
addr: Montreal, 616 Union Ave
1926 143-4 War cenotaph, perspective view, elevations, block plan
145 Suburban residence, a study

BISSON, HENRI
b Ste Marie, Beauce Co, Que CNS36
addr: Montreal: 4146 Adam St, 1934-7; 4596 De Lorimier Ave, 1942-3
1934 480 Désir plaster $250
1935 448 Innocence plaster $300
449 Le repos de modèle plaster $60
1936 582 Obsession plaster $150
583 Misère et pauvreté plaster $250
1937 445 Nuit d'été plaster $75
446 Jeunesse plaster $100
1942 228 Eve plaster $800
1943 251 RCAF plaster $200

BISSON, YVETTE
18 Mar 1926, Montreal
addr: Montreal, 6613 rue de Normanville
1961 109 Joy, trio stone $150

BLACHFORD, BERNICE MABEL

31 Aug 1923, Montreal
addrL Lachine, 670 47th Ave
1958 2 Mother and child $100

BLACHFORD, MAUDE B.
addr: Montreal: 31 Draper Ave, 1930; 3791 Draper Ave, 1932-8
1930 259 Iris in conventional design b&w $10
1931 367 Mountain ash in conventional design wc $25
1932 372 Decorative rose des wc $20
373-4 Conventional design b&w $15 each
1935 44 Decorative rose des wc $10
1936 514 Frontispiece des b&w $10
515 Iron work des wc $25
516 Conventional design wc $10
1937 24 Mountain ash design wc $25
25 Metal work design wc $25
388 Frostispiece des b&w $15
1938 11 Metal work design $25

BLACK, LOUISE BARBARA see FLOOD, LOUISE BARBARA

BLACKADER, GORDON HOME
12 Aug 1885, Montreal 10 Aug 1916, France
addr: Montreal, 236 Mountain St
1912 Blackader & Howe
412 Le Pavilion de Clos Payen
see also Barott, Ernest Isbell, 1915

BLADEN, GEORGE WILLIAM LOUIS
11 May 1888, London, Eng
addr: Montreal: 5 Selkirk Ave, 1920; 84 St François Xavier St, 1922
1920 21 Summer $50
1922 24 The Japanese parasol $150

BLAKE, E. (Miss)
addr: Montreal: 1908; 580 Sherbrooke St W, 1909; 738 Sherbrooke St W, 1912-13. Westmount, 622 Grosvenor Ave, 1914-18
1908 343 Tankard, orange
344 Vase, jonquils
345 Loving cup
346 Vase, narcissus $4
347 Vase, peacock des $10
348 Cup & saucer, lustre and gold $2
349 Vase, pink wild roses $5
350 Vase, lustre and matt $2
351 Punch cup
352 Tea set, pink roses, 3 pieces $7
1909 1 Two plates, Irish scenery
2 Vase, field daisies
3 Vase, hollyhocks
4 Vase, chrysanthemums
5 Tea set, 3 pieces
1912 426 Vase, narcissus
427 Box, dragon fly
428 Plate, sweet pea
1913 Blaikie, mispr
451 Bowl $10
452 Vase $7
453 Plate $5
454 Cream & sugar set $5 each piece
455 Chipped ice tub $6
1914 477 Plaque $6
478 Chocolate pot $7
479 Cream & sugar $6
480 Teapot tile $3
481 Pair candlesticks $5
1915 424 Fern dish $7
425 Radish dish $3
426 Hot water jug $3
427 Plaque, Japanese motives $10
428 Almond dish, flat enamels $2.50
429 Cologne bottle $2.50
1916 361 Vase, blue and silver $10
362 Plate, snowdrop design $5
363 Small bowl, blue and gold $3
1917 401 Coffee pot $10
402 Plate $7
403 Butter tub $5
404 Marmalade jar $5
1918 416 Plate, blue and silver $6

BLAND, JAMES ALFRED ANTHONY
1856, n Ilkley, Yorks, Eng 1928, Ottawa H
addr: Pembroke, Ont
1894 17 A quiet day on Lake Allumette $20

BLASER, HERMAN
25 Jul 1900, Thun, Switz
addr: Montreal: 902 Burnside Pl, 1934-5; 2102 University St, 1937; 710 Confederation Bldg, 1939; 1325 Dorchester St W, Apt 6, 1940-1; 2015 University St, Apt 27, 1942-57

1934 34 Harbour at Bremen wc
1935 45 St Faustin, Que wc $35
1937 26 The red roof wc $75
27 Sunday afternoon wc $50
1939 37 Mount Royal through a clothes-line wc $35
38 Leisure hours wc $35
39 Old ferry wharf wc $20
1940 24 The connoisseur wc $60
25 Trees wc $30
1941 13 Sailor recruits wc $75
14 Sightseers, McGill Campus wc $75
15 Fishers in the anchorage wc $50
16 Boating club wc $50
1942 12 Windy day $250
13 A rainy day wc
1943 20 Home on leave wc $75
1945 20 At Belmont Park wc $150
1946 18 Grey sky wc $85
1950 101 Woman peeling apples $125
1954 121 Street scene nm $50
1955 9 Girl with gladioli $250
1957 13 Fish market $500

BLATCHLY, WILLIAM DANIEL
1838, Bristol, Eng 1903, Toronto H
addr: Toronto, 119 Rose Ave
1897 136 The spring on the hill wc $50

BLAUER, RONALD
addr: Montreal West, 157 Percival Ave
1960 10 Still life $175

BLIER, JEAN-MARC
24 Jul 1921, St Eleutrere, Que
addr: Montreal, 600 Fulford St
1950 2 Pentes ensoleillées $125

BLOCH, AASE
21 Dec 1917, Oslo, Norway
addr: Haileybury, Ont, 86 Browning St
1954 15 Rock garden $200

BLONDHEIM, ADOLPHE WIERNER Amer
16 Oct 1888, Baltimore, Md B F TB2 WWA62
addr: New Hope, Pa, 1931-3
1931 19 Michael S. Jacobs pastel
368 Two old women etch $50
369 Old man etch $35
1933 25 S.W. Jacobs, KC MP
442 Old lady of Provence etch $35
443 Provence etch $35

BLOOMFIELD, EDGAR
addr: Vancouver, 850 Hastings St W, 1919-23
1919 38 A corner at Canterbury wc $100
39 Notre Dame de Paris wc $100
1923 29 Sunset on Fraser, B.C. $150

BLOORE, RONALD LANGLEY
29 May 1925, Brampton, Ont AGO CC2 CE IO M WWA76 Juror
addr: Toronto, Cameron Gallery, 840 Yonge St
1963 5 White painting No 8 $800

BOBAK, BRUNO JOSEPH (Bronislaw)
23 Dec 1923, Wawelowski, Poland AGO CC1 CE M NGC WWA84
addr: Ottawa, Hogs Back, Rideau View, 1947. North Vancouver: 1795 Peters Rd, 1954; 1191 Wellington Dr, 1955-6. Fredericton, 1967-8
1947 28 Cleve, Germany wc $50
1954 89 Eclipse wc $80 (listed 1967, Jessie Dow prize)
1955 89 Root and rocks nm $75
1956 79 Death of a season nm $200
1967 7 Solace. 1966. 48 x 40
1968 29 Envoy 40 x 60 $900
30 Wheel of life triptych 40 x 30 side panels, 60 x 40 centre panel $2,000
31 Widow consoling herself 40 x 60 $900

BOBAK, MOLLY JOAN LAMB (m Bruno Joseph Bobak)
25 Feb 1922, Vancouver AGO CC2 CE M NGC WWA59
addr: North Vancouver: 1795 Peters Rd, 1954; 1191 Wellington Dr, 1955
1954 16 Canterbury bells $125
1955 10 Composition of a park $150

BOILARD, K.
addr: Montreal
1908 275 Hand carved wooden clock case, style Louis XV $50

BOILARD, RAPHAEL
1881 - 13 Oct 1935, Montreal
addr: Montreal: 4469 Delorimier Ave, 1931; 4222 Delorimier Ave, 1932
1931 256 Salon Louis XV
257 Residence, Miami, Fla

258 Art Association building
259 Bird's-eye view of new city hall and business centre
1932 330-1 Hotel Luxor Inn, Lachine pencil des and photo
332 Bird's-eye view new Bonsecours market and surroundings pencil des

BOISSEAU, ALFRED
28 Feb 1823, Paris 1901, Buffalo NY
B Gr H
1881 6, 14 Portrait of a gentleman
32 Portrait of a lady
1883 90 The late Miss Tessier
95 Salut, a study from life of a Montreal carter
114 J.A. Beauvais, President CSSC
143 The late Dean, Faculty of Medicine, McGill University
1885 52 Mr T.W. DeWolf
82 A poor old man, a study
86 Italian selling plaster figures
91 Mdlle Louise Beaudet
1886 59 A dying artist, last look at an unfinished work
92 H. Beaugrand, Mayor of Montreal
111 Portrait

BOISVERT, GILLES
16 Feb 1940, Montreal
addr: Montreal, 2059 Kimberley Ave
1961 3 Peinture II $250

BOISVERT, MARC
1939, Sherbrooke, Que
addr: Montreal, 3498 St Domonique
1964 115 Sentinelle fer soudé $250

BOIVIN, JEAN-PIERRE
6 Aug 1926, St Hyacinthe, Que
addr: St Hyacinthe, 2220 rue Cartier
1955 140 Famille wd $75

BOLDUC, ROBERT
addr: Montreal, 3545 McTavish Ave
1946 273 N. Harper plaster, in bronze $250

BOLTE, HILDE KLARA
18 Jul 1922, Hamburg, Germany
addr: Montreal, 4025 Maplewood Ave, Apt 2, 1952-60
terra cotta 1952-60
1952 78 Tango notturno $50
1953 62 Mother bear $65
63 Drinking tiger $50
1954 131 St Francis $85
132 Bird $50
1955 141 Madonna $250
142 Fountain des model
1956 142 Mother $100
1959 43 Rooster $85
1960 228 Fish $50
229 Bird $35

BOLTON, ADA Eng
fl 1891-1903 DBA G
addr: London, Eng, 1 Osborne Terrace, Clapham
1895 18 The Sanctuary, Westminster Abbey $65

BOLTON, RICHARD ERNEST
18 Mar 1907, Montreal CNS40 CWW84
addr: Montreal: 1178 Phillips Place, 1938-40
1937 325 House, Mr J.P. Aston
326 Design, 7 room house
1938 Bolton & Fellowes
129 Laird House, Town of Mount Royal
1940 315 House, Town of Mount Royal
316 Proposed house, Montreal
see also Fetherstonhaugh, Harold Lea, 1947

BOND, MARION
b Antigonish, N.S. M
addr: Halifax, 32 Kent St, 1933-46
1933 26 Negro $100
1934 35 Biddy $25
1935 46 Old lifting wheel $15
1936 46 Boats at anchor, Peggy's Cove $25
47 Rocky coast, Prospect, N.S. $60
1937 28 The loitering brook $100
29 Spring on the North West Arm $100
1939 40 Modesty Cove $75
41 Repairs $100
1940 26 Sandy Cove, N.S. $50
27 Evening falls $50
28 Cliff at Deep Cove $25
29 Boats at Peggy's $25
1943 21 Five and ten $50
1945 21 St Margaret's Bay $100
1946 19 Coast near Peggy's Cove $150

BONE, CHARLES RICHARD
9 Apr 1899, Belleville, Ont d 1974 M
addr: Montreal: 506 Old Orchard Ave, 1930; 4118 Old Orchard Ave, 1932; 1507 Bishop St, 1935-7; 1671 Sherbrooke St W, 1939; 1486 Chomedy St, Apt 4, 1940
1930 21 Kenton, Devonshire wc $35
1932 31 Portrait wc $15
1935 47 Village church, Lower Winchendon wc $50
1936 48 St Mary's Church, Cartmel wc $25
1937 30 Anstruther wc $50
1939 42 Winchester Cathedral wc $50
1940 30 In the Canadian Rockies wc $50
31 Laurentian snow wc $25

BONET, JORDI
7 May 1932, Barcelona 25 Dec 1979, Montreal M TB3 WWA82
addr: Montreal: 1625 Henri Bourassa Blvd, 1959; 10550 Olympia Blvd, 1960; Montreal, 1967
1959 29 Buste d'homme ink drwg (listed 1967, Jessie Dow Prize)
1960 11 Couple $175
1967 8 Couple. 1963 col ink 30 x 40

BONHAM, DONALD
9 Nov 1940, Oklahoma City
addr: London, Ont
1970 1 Canadian invasion machine fibreglass 126 x 66

BONHAM, MARY ELIZABETH
b 1878
addr: Quebec: 1908; 46 d'Artigny St, 1910-15. Montreal, 836 Oxenden Ave, 1917-20. Westmount, 34 Burton Ave, 1921. Montreal, 8 Oldfield Ave, 1922. Westmount, 225 Melville Ave, 1927
1908 179 On the Jacques Cartier wc $15
1910 28 A peasant cottage, Youghal wc $20
29 Voorstraatshaven, Dordrecht wc $35
1911 28 Aber Falls, north Wales wc $50
29 The first snowfall wc $25
30 St Paul's, from Waterloo Bridge $25
1912 40 Early spring wc $30
1913 24 Old Quebec, beneath the cliffs wc $30
25 Spencer Grange woods wc $25
1914 30 Ste Anne Mountain, Beaupré wc $25
31 Quebec in fog wc $10
1915 33 After the storm, old Quebec wc $30
1916 21 And the winter shall come wc $35
22 The last ray, Cape Diamond wc $35
23 The ancient capital wc $35
24 A showery day, Levis wc $25
1917 31 Jacques Cartier River at Val Cartier Camp wc $25
32 Old bread oven, Beaupré wc $25
33 A corner of old Quebec wc $15
34 Early morning, Quebec wc $25
1918 26 Valcartier Church wc $25
27 Cape Diamond wc $30
28 A Dutch canal
1920 22 A rainy day drwg
23 Fairies drwg
1921 19 Mary had a little lamb wc
20 Bobbed wc
21 The owl and I wc
22 Pussy's lost breakfast wc
1922 24A Little Bo-Peep wc $30
24B Shadows wc $25
24C Pussy willows wc $20
24D The bed time fairy wc $25
1927 7 Beneath the cliffs of old Quebec wc $75
8 Percé Rock, Que wc $15

BONIN, FERNAND
addr: Verdun, Que, 4159 Blvd Lascalle, 1945-6
1945 22 Gouache $35
1946 20 Forêt $150
21-2 Gouache $25 each

BONLI, HENRY THOMAS
8 Aug 1927, Lashburn, Sask
addr: Saskatoon, 434 Hilliard St E, 1963-4
1963 6 White field No 1 $200
1964 6 River No 1 $300

BOOK, FLORA
addr: Montreal, 1725 Kenelworth Rd
1964 83 Still life nm

BOOTE, ARTHUR J.
addr: Calgary, 26 South Hill, Ogden, 1936-9

1936 49 Columbia Valley, near Golden, B.C. $35
1937 31 Mount Wapta, Yoho Valley, B.C. $25
1939 43 Early morning, Morraine Lake, Alta $45
44 Near Waterton Lakes, Alta $40

BOOTH, HAROLD H.
addr: Ottawa, Chateau Laurier
1919 40 Parliament Buildings, Ottawa, looking west wc $25
41 A promise of rain off Yorkshire coast wc $35
42 The home pasture wc $35
43 Ayrshire cattle, sketch wc $30

BORDEN, MARJORIE MARY
13 Feb 1911, Montreal
addr: Ottawa, 8 Tormey St, 1932-5
1932 32 Landing stage $50
1935 391 Portrait drwg $25

BORDUAS, PAUL-EMILE
1 Nov 1905, St Hilaire, Que 22 Feb 1960, Paris AGO B CC1 CE CWW58 M NGC TB3 WWA62 Juror
addr: Montreal, 953 Napoleon St, 1938. St Hilaire, RR 2, 1947-51
1938 12 Adolescente
1947 29 Parachutes végétaux $350
30 Les carquois fleuris $350 (MBAM)
1949 15 Réunions des trophées $350 (Jury II $150 prize, Listed 1967)
1950 102 Mes pauvres petits soldats $175
1951 83 L'eruption imprévue $500

BORENSTEIN, SAMUEL
15 Jan 1908, Suwalkie, Poland 15 Dec 1969, Montreal W78
addr: Montreal; 3543 Ste Famille St, Apt 4, 1937-9; 1215 Greene Ave, 1940; 5322 Clark St, 1941-6; 4407 Carlton Ave, 1952-3; 5777 Rand Ave, Cote St Luc, 1957
1937 389 A Montreal scene drwg
1939 45 Mount Royal Avenue wc $50
1940 32 Old Montreal $200
1941 17 Winter in Canada wc $100
1942 14 View from Bonaventure Island
1944 7 St Jacques Church
8 Night scene
1946 23 Street in Piedmont
252 Drawing sanguine
1952 87 View of Montreal $300
1953 68 Mont Rolland $200
1957 14 Street scene $400

BORNSTEIN, ELI
28 Dec 1922, Milwaukee, Wis CC2 CE M WWA84
addr: Saksatoon, University of Saskatchewan, Dept of Art, 1955-6. Chicago, 1968
1955 90 Downtown bridge nm $60
1956 80 The tower nm $60
1968 Borenstein, mispr
Structurist relief painted alum
32 No 3. 1965. 24 X 34 x 5 3/4 $4,000-US
33 No 4. 1965. 24 x 34 x 4 3/4 $4,000-US

BOSCH, LODEWYK
addr: Victoria, 639 Yates St
1931 20 Zinnias $350
21 Carnations $350

BOSTROM, ROBERT ERNEST
25 Aug 1883, Newman, Ga 12 Dec 1963, Montreal CNS51
addr: Montreal: 211 McGill St, 1927; 24 McGill St, 1928; 660 St Catherine St W, 1934
1927 186 Residence, Westmount
187 Residence, Carleton Ave, Westmount
1928 214 Proposed residence, Westmount
215 Residence, E.S. Frosst, Esq, Westmount
1934 374-5 Country house, Lac Brulé, Que photos

BOSWELL, HAZEL MAY
19 Apr 1882, Quebec
addr: Paris, 3 rue Leopold-Robert, 1910-11. Quebec, 19 St Genevieve Ave, The Cape, 1925
1910 30 Le dernier point wc $30
1911 31 Street study wc $25
32 Croquis du Marché des Fleurs wc $10
1925 32 The orchard path wc

BOTTOMLEY, H
addr: Montreal, 92 St Mark St

1912 41 In an Anglesey village wc $25
42 On the Welsh coast wc $25
43 Where once a garden smiled $20

BOUCHARD, EDITH MARIE
13 Mar 1924, Baie St Paul, Que M
addr: Baie St Paul, Moulin César, 1950-2. Montreal, Dominion Galleries, 1438 Sherbrooke St W, 1954-5
1950 103 Intérieur $20
1952 88 Intérieur lilas au banc de seau et baquet
89 S'amusant seul $60
1954 17 Le printemps, Baie St Paul $175
1955 11 Les noces au printemps au 2ième rang à Baie St Paul $195

BOUCHARD, GEORGE LORNE HOLLAND
19 Mar 1913 - 26 Apr 1978, Montreal M WWA78
addr: Montreal, 1472 Sherbrooke St W, 1931. L'Abord à Plouffe, 7 Laurier Blvd, 1932. Montreal, 1486 Mackay St, 1934-6, 1938, 1947-9. Drummondville, Que: c/o Dennison Mfg Co, 1937, 1939; 123 Lowring St, 1940-2; 19A Holmes St, 1944-6. Verdun, Que, 1182 Moffat Ave, 1950-4. Montreal, 4070 Jauron St, 1955-61
1931 22 McGill College cab stand, Sherbrooke St W $200
1932 33 De bonheur dimanche matin, l'Eglise Bonsecours wc $50
1934 36 Chute au Diable, Labelle, Que, wc $35
37 Floating cofferdam crib into place, northern Ontario wc $35
1935 48 Second Range, Douglastown, Gaspé wc $100
1936 50 Looking downstream, St Francis River, Drummondville, Que $35
1937 32 From the Third Range, Douglastown, Gaspé $175
390 Portrait charcl
1938 13 In at Willie Grant's, Douglastown $125
1939 46 Winter, Point St Peters, Que $175
1940 33 De la grande visite $350
34 L'heure du crépuscule $200
35 Un coin canadien $200
1941 18 March at Mechins, lower St Lawrence $400
1942 15 Midwife $500
1944 9 The St Lawrence from Les Eboulements $500
1945 23 Sunny afternoon, Baie St Paul $175
24 March day, Rivière au Gouffre $175
1946 24 L'anse à Brilliant $300
25 View from the Barachois, Douglastown $350
26 Fair and mild $300
1947 31 Shipbuilding, lower St Lawrence $500
32 Gaul's place, Gaspé coast wc $125
1948 70 Boyhood days, Gaspé coast wc $150
1949 16 December, St Francis River $200
1950 3 Interior, maple sugar cabin $600
1951 6 Street scene, Montreal $500
50 The ice house wc $150
1952 5 Wolfe's Cove, Quebec $900
1953 4 La traversée de Lévis $500
5 View from the Citadel $300
1954 18 Cobalt, Ont $500
1955 12 Quebec street at night $125
1956 61 Côte de la Montagne, Québec nm $100
1957 15 Le dégel $600
1958 3 Commuters shortcut $800
1960 12 Approach of spring $600
13 Les traverses $600
1961 4 Return from school $750

BOUCHARD, MARIE
addr: Montreal: 248 St Hubert St, 1922; 326 St Denis St, 1924
1922 333 Tête de jeune fille plaster
334 Madame G. plaster
1924 306 Jeune fille, 1924 sculp $90

BOUCHARD, MARIE CECILE
1920, Baie St Paul, Que d 1973 CCI M
addr: Baie St Paul, Que, Moulin César, 1945-8
1945 25 Scène d'été, le retour à la ferme $25
1947 33 Nature sombre, veillée intérieur $30
34 Nature morte sur fleurs sauvages $25
1948 6 Intérieur au plafond jaune $45

BOUCHARD, SIMONE MARIE (S. MARY)
11 Jun 1912, Baie St Paul, Que d 1945 CCI M

addr: Baie St Paul, Que
1945 S. Mary
26 Scène d'hiver, les voitures $25
27 Nature morte $25
28 Bouquet de fleurs $25

BOUCHER, JEAN
addr: Ottawa, 459 Besserer St
1945 29 Hockey game

BOULTBEE, ALFRED ERNEST
26 Mar 1864, Newmarket, Ont 1 Dec 1928, Toronto H WHC
addr: Toronto, 35 Crescent Rd
1897 137 The Pont Neuf, Paris wc $50
138 Morning on the Thames, near Kew wc $40
139 The fountain of Villeneuve, Switzerland wc $40

BOULTBEE, CONSTANCE MARY
addr: Toronto, 35 Crescent Rd
1897 18 Portrait
140 Penzance, Cornwall wc $20
141 Carrisbrook Castle, Isle of Wight wc $15

BOULTBEE, HESILL MALLOCK (m Paul N. Boultbee)
17 Nov 1913, Kennilworth, Eng 28 May 1966, Montreal
addr: Montreal: 1477 Sherbrooke St W, 1944; 1488 Crescent St, 1945. St Jerome, Que, Hotel Lapointe, 1946. Montreal, Rockhill Apts, 4864 Côte des Neiges Rd, 1947-53. Westmount, 605 Roslyn Ave, 1957
1944 10 Summer in Bic $75
1945 30 Low tide, Bic $75
1946 27 Anchorage, Port au Persil $75
1947 35 Rainy day, Greene Avenue $75
1950 4 Port au Persil $100
1953 6 Winter's morning, St Adele $185
1957 16 Rock concept $85
108 Summertime, St Adele nm $85

BOULTER, IDA
addr: Montreal, 219 Peel St
1901 213 Blue bonbon box
214 Malachite bonbon box

BOULTON, MURIEL CAMERON WELSH
13 Feb 1881, Charlottetown d 1957, England M NGC TB3
addr: Quebec: 1908; 18 Ann St, 1909; 44 St Genevieve Ave, 1910; 130 St Augustin St, 1912
1908 21 The chess problem $300 (NGC)
22 The little model $100
1909 41 In the New Forest $50
42 Beverley
1910 31 Lago di Lecco $25
32 Near San Trovaso, Venice b&w $25
33 The Dee, north Wales $40
34 Bellagio $25
1912 44 In my studio $40
45 After tea, in my studio $50

BOURBEAU, LOUISE
addr: Québec
1968 34 Bios pierre calcaire 30h $450

BOVEY, JEAN
addr: Montreal, Grosvenor Apts
1909 43 The lodge wc

BOWLES, NEWTON ROWELL
4 Dec 1916, Chengtu, China M
addr: New York, 867 W 181 St, 1960-4
1960 14 Lost souls $500
1961 5 Ecce homo $550
1962 1 Hartebeest $450
1963 7 Blood wedding $750
1964 7 Figure $500

BOWMAN, RICHARD IRVING Amer
15 Mar 1918, Rockford, Ill
addr: Winnipeg, University of Manitoba, School of Art, 1951-2. Redwood City, Cal, 1967
1951 84 Chaos in mechanics $60
85 Flight $400
1952 90 Kinetograph 20 $450. Jury II prize. 1967-9, oil & fluorescent lacquer 40 x 41 (Robert C. Dickenman, M.D, Detroit)
129 Kinetograph wc col etch $50

BOYD, EDWARD FINLEY
1878, Montreal 1964, Westport, Conn
addr: Montreal: 247 Mountain St, 1901; Montreal, 1908; 255 Bleury St, 1909-10; 247 Mountain St, 1920
1901 109 The brook wc $20
1908 23 Morning mist, France $100
24 Old street, Pont de l'Arche $50

25 Luxembourg Gardens, morning $25
26 Sunny afternoon below Quebec $35
1909 44 Going to the bull fight $700
45 Autumn afternoon $75
46 Smoky afternoon $40
47 The autumn harvest $225
48 First snow, lower St Lawrence $40
1910 35 Red autumn $200
1920 24 Winter, Connecticut $125

BOYD, JAMES HENDERSON
16 Dec 1928, Ottawa AGO CWW84 M WWA84
addr: Ottawa, 484 Roosevelt Ave, 1963. London, Ont, 1968
1963 74 Lapis philosphorum nm $80
1968 metal collage, relief prints, all 24 x 28, $150
35 Reconstruction
36 Western's stockings and mini skirts
37 Ship from Western
38 The vice-president (finance)

BOYD, MARGARET M.
addr: Montreal, 247 Mountain St, 1900-21
1900 192 Vase
193 Desert plate
194 Claret jug & tumblers $15
195 Flower bowl $6
1901 215-16 Plaque
217 Tankard $55
218 Panel $20
1903 277 Vase
278 Photo frame $6
1906 363 Flower dish
364-5 Vase
366 Fern bowl $3.50
367 Tray $2
368 Hair box, powder box
1909 6 Tea set $35
7-8 Stein $8.50 each
9 Vase $7
10 Plaque
11 Punch bowl $55
1912 429 Satsuma bowl enamel $4
430 Satsuma box enamel $2.75
431 Fern pot $3
432 Vase $9
433 Child's plate $2.50
434 Candlestick $3
1914 482 Gossip set, Vanity fair $75
483 Gossip set, Moonlight $50
484 Sandwich tray $12
485 Sandwich basket $6
486 Cup & saucer $4.50
487 Vase, emperor moth $15
488 Fruit bowl $10
489 Satsuma box $8
1915 430 Blue plate under glaze $15
431 Blue vase under glaze $20
432 Vase $8
1917 405 Pitcher $4
406 Bonbon
407 Ornamental piece $10
408 Box $10
409 Jar
410 Stein $6.50
1919 409 Vase, landscape lustre dec $20
410 Vase, fir trees lustre dec $20
411 Hot water pot $8 (Highly commended)
1921 325 Covered dish lustre
326 Stein $8
327 Plate enamel & lustre $7
328 Dish lustre $10
329 Strainer box enamel & gold $4.50

BOYER, M. JEAN
addr: Westmount, 551 Argyle Ave
1921 23 Study of a head

BOYER, MARTHE
addr: Westmount, 492 Strathcona Ave
1930 22 Hadrian $50
260 Design lino cut $10

BOYLE, JOHN BERNARD
23 Sep 1941, London, Ont CE
addr: St. Catharines, Ont, 1968-70
1968 Rebel series, oil on wood
39 Totem 84 x 24 $600
40 Bear and Brendan 63 1/2 x 24 $400
41 Lois and Greg 44 x 24 $300
1970 2 St Paul West 54 x 90
3 Thomson in my back yard 24 x 48 (MBAM)

BRADFORD, JOHN LOCKE
1 Apr 1897, Windsor, N.S.
addr: Hunt's Point, N.S, 1950-55
1950 87 Toadstools red cedar $20
88 Sea floor cottonwood bark $25

1955 143 Fern fiddleheads wd carv

BRAIS, SIMEON
1886 - 31 Jul 1963, Montreal
addr: Montreal: 294 St Catherine St E, 1928; St Denis Bldg, 354 St Catherine St E, 1929-33
1928 Brais & Parent, 1928-9
216 Apartment house
1929 226 Arsenal, Regiment de Châteauguay
1933 352 City Hall, addition

BRAITSTEIN, MARCEL
11 Jul 1935, Charleroi, Belg AGO CC2 CWW84 M WWA84
addr: Montreal: c/o Agnes Lefort Gallery, 1504 Sherbrooke St W, 1961; 911 Jarry St W, 1963; Montreal, 1967
1961 110 Envol wld steel illus. Ladies Comm prize, $250. 1967-10 27 1/2h (MBAM)
1963 Metamorphosis II steel $550

BRAND, PAMELA
London, Eng
addr: Montreal, 4999 Marmier Ave
1953 69 Group 2 $45
103 Print I dry pt $5

BRANDTNER, FRITZ
28 Jul 1896, Danzig 7 Nov 1969, Montreal AGO CC2 M NGC W78 WWA70 Juror
addr: Winnipeg, 707 Sherbrook St, 1931. Montreal: 1255 Fort St, 1934; 1154 Beaver Hall Sq, 1939-50; 5545 Côte St Luc Rd, 1951-3; 4840 Plamondon, Ave, 1955-7; Montreal, 1967
1931 23 Mountains III wc $150 unfr
370 Skeena River lino cut $15 unfr
1934 38 Sunflower $200
1939 47 Men and horses $250
1941 19 Trees $200
20 City at night $75
1942 16 War $50
193 Nude drwg $50
1943 22 Sixteen Island Lake No 3 wc $75
1945 31 Spy Rock $150
32 Still life $150
1946 28 Ghosts of the woods $150
29 Sixteen Island Lake wc $125 (Jury II prize, 1967-11 20 x 24) (H.E. Shister, M.D, Montreal)
1947 36 On the beach $150
1950 104 Gay camp-table $250
1951 86 Vestibule $250
1952 118 Summer No 3 wc $150
1953 70 Yacht club $250
1955 13 After the storm $800
1956 82 City at night nm $250
1957 109 The last light nm $175

BRANGERS, ERNEST MAURICE
23 Dec 1928, Toronto
addr: Toronto, 1576 Queen St E
1949 17 The pool $100

BRANTON, WINONA YOUNG
addr: Calgary, Acadia Apts, No 11
1949 18 Pattern from rock crystal $75

BRASSARD, SYLVIO
addr: Quebec, Château Champlain, R.334
1933 Brassart, mispr
353 La reconstitution du village canadian-français du XVIII siècle, au Jardin Zoologique de Québec photo

BREEZE, CLAUDE HERBERT
9 Oct 1938, Nelson, B.C. AGO CE IO M
addr: Vancouver
1968 Control Centre series cling & aborite on hard board, acrylic on canvas 48 x 18 $600 each
42 No 1: Southern tourist
43 No 2: Black power

BREHN, CHARLES G.
addr: Montreal: 236 Hogan St, 1925; 4891 Orleans St, 1927-9
1925 335 Church of St Stanilas drwg $15
388 Medallion Americain copper bas-rel $25
1927 259 Royal Victoria Hospital, Montreal chalk $10
1929 301 Church of Infant Jesus, Mile End chalk $10

BREITMAN, SAMUEL
addr: Montreal, 5692 Esplanade Ave, 1939-40
1939 48 The flood wc $50
1940 30 High Street

BREMNER, DOUGLAS
21 May 1893, Montreal CWW38
addr: Westmount, 3769 The Boulevard

1945 33 Vermont in summer pastel

BRETT, KATHERINE see MAW, KATHERINE BEATRICE (BETTY)

BRETZLOFF, GILBERT EMILE
23 Sep 1914, Otter Lake, Que
addr: Aylmer East, Que, 60 Charles St
1955 144 Mother and child stone $75

BRIANSKY, RITA (m Joseph Prezament)
25 Aug 1925, Grajewa, Poland M WWA84
addr: Montreal: 4611 Park Ave, 1944-51; 5823 Jeanne Mance St, 1952; 4850 Plamondon Ave, 1953-4; 2970 Goyer St, 1955; 2650 Goyer St, 1957-8; 4903 Westhill Ave, 1960
1944 11 Self portrait
1945 34 Jasora
35 Shirley
1946 30 Adolescence $150
1947 37 Sorrow
1949 19 Ida $150
1951 7 Backyard hockey $85
1952 6 Man reading a newspaper $75
130 Sleeping baby brush & ink
1953 7 Dr Bethune $700
8 Self portrait
1954 19 Early spring $100
1955 91 Sleeping child nm
1957 17 Convalescent $75
1958 4 Late afternoon $125
1960 135 Alone nm $20

BRICKUS, CLAIRE see SHONIKER, CLAIRE

BRICKUS, VIKTORAS
1924, Lithuania
addr: Toronto, 105 Isabella St
1960 136 North brush nm $120

BRIGDEN, CORRY WILLIAM
29 Sep 1912, Toronto AGO
addr: Hamilton, 77 Paisley Ave S
1940 346 For the old is the mending of nets $15

BRIGDEN, FREDERICK HENRY
9 Apr 1871, London, Eng 24 Mar 1956, Bolton, Ont AGO CC1 CNS40 CWW52 EC M NGC PMC TB2 WWA59
addr: Toronto: 92 Bay St, 1903-6; Toronto, 1908; 103 Rose Ave, 1909; 92 Bay St, 1910-12; 160 Richmond St, 1918-27; 188 Glencairn Ave, 1947; Newtonbrook, Ont, 1952
1903 142 Still waters wc $35
143 The rippling brook wc $40
144 Harvest on the hill wc $50
1906 183 The sun's last look into the valley wc $75
184 A passing shower wc $30
185 In the valley of the Kennebecasis wc $75
186 A grey day, Nova Scotia wc $50
1908 27 In eastern Canada $200
180 Kakabeka Falls wc $100
181 The silver stream wc $75
182 Autumn on the hills wc $75
183 On the Nipegon River wc $50
1909 49 Morning on the lake wc $35
50 Morning mists wc $35
51 Northern woods wc $75
52 A port on the lake wc $35
53 Along the lake shore wc $35
54 The coast of Lake Superior wc $75
1910 36 The road by the sea $50
1912 46 A Quebec pastoral wc $75
47 In the north country wc $100
48 The golden hour wc $200
1918 29 Summer clouds wc $100
1927 9 Northern waters wc $125
10 Down to Lake Superior wc $150 (AGO)
1947 38 Wonder Pass wc $200
1952 7 Snow in the hills, Eastern Townships, Que $375
port: by Kenneth Keith Forbes 1945-89

BRISSET, LEO
26 Oct 1926, Montreal
addr: Montreal, 2418 Châteauguay St
1950 105 Madone $150

BRISSET, LEO (Mrs)
addr: Montreal, 2418 Châteauguay St
1947 39 Jeune homme $40

BRISSOT, FRANK Eng
fl 1879-83 B DBA G H
1883 125 A stable interior

BRITTAIN, MILLER GORE
12 Nov 1912 - Jan 1968, Saint John, N.B. CC2 CE M NGC WWA60
addr: Saint John: 206 Winslow St W,

1938; 108 Prince William St, 1939; 102 Prince William St, 1942; 42 Prince William St, 1949
1938 14 Warehouse pastel $25
150 Little theatre rehearsal drwg $50
1939 49 Promenade $125
50 Master McCullough $110
381 D'ye ken John Peel? drwg $50 (copyrt Toronto Saturday Night)
1942 17 Leaving the clothing depot oil & temp $125
194 Three longshoremen drwg $50
1949 112 When the morning stars sang together gouache, pastel, wc $125

BRITTON, HARRY
23 Sep 1878, Cambridge, Eng 23 Jul 1958, Toronto AGO CC1 CWW55 M NGC TB2 WWA53
addr: Toronto: 390 Bloor St, 1909; 340 Bay St, 1910-12; 67 Wellesley St, 1919
1909 55 The goatherd $150
56 Marguerite $100 (NGC)
1910 37 St Paul's in winter $150
1912 49 Cornish fisherman $100
1919 44 Low tide, St Ives $40
45 Sunset, Amsterdam $40
46 Sorrento, Italy $40
47 Houses in Normandy $60
48 Dutch boats $40
49 On the Thames

BRITTON, HENRIETTA HANCOCK (m Harry Britton)
20 May 1874, Ealing West, Eng 27 Jul 1963, Toronto
addr: Toronto, 836 Dovercourt Rd, 1945-6
1945 36 Incoming tide pastel $300
1946 31 An old mill pond, Nova Scotia $175

BROCK, GUY N.
addr: Montreal, 219 Milton St, 1905. Westmount, 4282 Sherbrooke St W, 1913-22. Montreal, 1501 St Catherine St W, 1932
1905 14 Harbour in winter $15
1913 26 Willows $25
1914 32 St Luc $50
33 Barges $25
1917 35 The tow boat $75
36 Fall morning, Sault au Recollet $75
1918 30 Winter quarters $100
31 Market day $75
1919 50 Beside the dock $35
51 Knife grinder $35
1922 25 Reflections, Norfolk, Va $40
26 From city park, Norfolk $40
27 Hampton Roads, evening $40
28 September, Beaupré $40
1932 34 The Beaupre road $100

BRODEUR, ALBERT SAMUEL
1862, Montreal H
addr: Montreal: 8 Cuthbert St, 1903-5; 141 Cherrier St, 1906-28
1903 145 The harbour, Montreal wc $20
146 The Montford, at her wharf wc $25
1905 135 La Chapelle de l'Hôtel Dieu wc $40
1906 187 Autumn wc $20
188 In the woods wc $15
1908 184 Soleil d'automne wc $20
1910 38 Interior, Eglise du Gesu $25
39 Landscape wc $15
1915 34 Landscape, autumn effect wc $30
1917 37 Landscape wc $50
38 On St Helen's Island wc $20
39 Winter
1918 32 Harbour scene, Montreal wc $25
33 Woodland in October wc $25
34 In my yard wc
1928 22 Dans la parc Mont Royal wc $25
23 Le vieux moulin, Lachine wc $25

BRODEUR, JEAN
b 1939
addr: St Polycarpe, Que, RR1
1965 22 Tweed on the menu nm $125

BRODIE, HUGH (Mrs)
addr: Montreal: Côte St Antoine, 1894; 4223 Dorchester St, 1895
1894 245 Plate
1895 233 Jardiniere

BRODIE, HUGH JOHN
addr: Montreal, 5726 Sherbrooke St W
1947 7 Mai Ruth $100

BRODIE, KATE S. (Mrs)
fl 1891-1933 DBA
addr: Montreal: 315 Prince Arthur St, 1929; 1839 Lincoln Ave, 1932-3
1929 16 Highland village near Aban, Scotland $1,200
17 The Pike Pool, near Granton-on-Sprey, Scotland $990
18 Highland homes, near Dalmally Scotland $950
1932 35 The Highland Clachan, Glen Finlas, Scotland
1933 27 Farmyard near Abenakis Springs, Que $500

BROECK, CLEMENCE VAN DEN Belg
25 Nov 1843, Molenbeck-St Jean, Brussels 3 Feb 1922, Uccle, Brussels B TB1/3
addr: Samois-sur-Seine, France
1905 11 The tiff $150
12 Provision d'hiver $150
13 Arab chief $125

BROKENSHAW, L.
addr: Montreal, 3469 Jeanne Mance St
1941 21 The violinist
22 Portrait of a young man pastel $30

BRONFMAN, PHYLLIS (m Jean Lambert)
24 Jan 1927, Montreal CWW84 WWA84
addr: Westmount, 15 Belvedere Rd, 1940-5
1940 399 Kids plaster
1941 278 Five and a half plaster
1942 229 Missing the bus plaster $25
1943 252 Miss Helen MacDonald sculp
1944 157 Oenone plaster
1945 273 Lindy Lou plaster
274 Composition plaster $50

BROOKER, BERTRAM RICHARD (pseuds Richard Surrey, Huxley Hearne)
31 Mar 1888, Croydon, Eng 21 Mar 1955, Toronto AGO CC1 CE CWW52 EC M TB3 WWA53
addr: Toronto, 107 Glenview Ave
1931 24 Figures in landscape $450

BROOKS, CAROL ELIZABETH
16 Dec 1919, Winnipeg
addr: Westmount, 623 Victoria Ave
1940 347 Drawing-room, Roosevelt House wc

BROOKS, FRANK LEONARD
7 Nov 1911, Enfield, London, Eng AGO CWW84 M WWA82
addr: Toronto, 67 Douglas Cr, Apt 15
1941 23 Winter willows $200
24 Main Street, Gore Bay wc $50

BROOKS, MARIA Eng
1837, Staines Eng 16 Nov 1913 B DBA DVP G H RSBA TB WWW
addr: New York, Sherwood Studio, 58 W 57th St, 1891-2
1883 142 Whither?
1885 12 An old, old story
25 Lilies
29 Mrs Abbott Brown
33 Ready for a bowl
39 Edith
46 Far, far away
48 Rev Henry Wilkes, DD LLD
49 Ready for bed
53 Rev Abbot Brown
1885 54 Down Piccadilly, returning from Covent Garden Market
56 Ready for a tramp
68 Wayfarers
1886 74 Laura
77 Missionaries explaining the doctrines of Christianity to a pagan British family
81 Cottage near Falls of Montmorency
82 Little Fatty
84 Azaless
1886 101 Beauport cottages
104 Our nurse
1891 11 Polly! Polly! Polly! $300
12 Forty winks $250
1892 14 A B C D $150

BROOMFIELD, ADOLPHUS GEORGE
26 Aug 1906, Toronto CWW84 M WWA84
addr: Hamilton, 930 King St E, 1938; Mimico, Ont, 58 Hillside Ave, 1939
1938 etchings 1938-9
1938 151 Loan shark $10
152 Gossip $10
153 Pickup $10
154 Cafe $10
1939 382 Covered bridge near Kitchener, Ont $10
383 Last call $10
384 Water sleigh, Kearney, Ont $10
385 Northern Ontario School $10

BROUCHON, S.
H
1880 75 At liberty

BROUSSEAU, DELPHIS
addr: Montreal, 6738 St Lawrence Blvd
1932 333 Je suis le chemin medln

BROWN, ANNORA
1899, n Red Deer, Alta Feb 1987, B.C.
addr: Fort Macleod, 1931-45
1931 25 Winter moonlight temp $50
1935 49 The gap $50
50 House by the roadside $25
1936 51 Indian farm Brocket, Alta $25
52 Cloudy day, Alberta $25
1937 33 Otter and elk tepees wc $60
34 Travois wc $60
1939 51 Fire weed wc $40
52 Mountain columbine wc $40
1941 25 Fire weed wc $40
1945 37 Western wild flower, mountain lily wc $55

BROWN, DANIEL PRICE ERICKSEN
21 Aug 1939, Forrestville, Ont IO
addr: Toronto
1970 4 The wedding tray temp 24 x 30
5 Portrait of a young Canadian girl temp 14 x 18

BROWN, DAVID ROBERTSON
28 Aug 1869 - 28 Mar 1946, Montreal
CNS27 CWW55 Mo12 PMC
addr: Montreal: Canada Life Bldg, 1897-1910; 1111 Beaver Hall Hill, 1927; 980 St Catherine St W, 1933; 1010 St Catherine St W, 1934
1897 Brown, MacVicar & Heriot, 97-8
229 Royal St Lawrence Yacht Club des
1898 213 St Matthias Church, Westmount des
1909 403 Children's Memorial Hospital
404-5 McGill Medical Bldg, from University st, hospital grounds
1910 Brown & Vallance
380 Saskatchewan University, development plans
381 Agricultural College, Saskatchewan
382 Live stock pavilion, Saskatchewan
383 Proposed building, St James St
1927 188 Masonic Peace Memorial, London, England
189 Memorial Gates, University of Saskatchewan
190 Study for an hotel
1933 354 Entrance doorway to T.M. Hutchison residence, Westmount
355-6 Grace Dart Home Hospital, Montreal, entrance, doorway
357 University of Saskatchewan Saskatoon, Arts Bldg. preliminary studies
1934 376-7 Residence, Mr Hugh Paton, interior photos 2

BROWN, DOROTHY J.
addr: Westmount, 533 Victoria Ave
1940 37 Fish pond, Westmount Conservatory wc $30

BROWN, FRANK ERICHSEN see ERICHSEN-BROWN, FRANK

BROWN, G. WINNIFRED
addr: St Lambert, Que
1915 468 Brooch, turquoise matrix $10
469 Brooch $8
470 Brooch, lapis lazuli $8
471 Brooch, sapphire doublet $9
472 Scarf pin, black opal $8
473 Pendant, amethyst doublet $9
474 Ring, pearl $10
475 Ring, turquoise $10
476 Ring, turquoise matrix $7

BROWN, HELEN M.
addr: St Anne de Bellevue, Military Hospital
1919 412 Centre flower bowl $35
413 Rose bowl, small
Honorable mention

BROWN, JEAN
addr: Pekisko, Alta
1913 27 A country hillside $20

BROWN, JESSIE E.
addr: Montreal, 164 Crescent St, 1911-15
1911 33 Sketch
1912 50 Sketch $15
51 The mill $15
52 Sketch pencil $10
1913 28 The sugar bush $20
29 Lachine Canal b&w $10

30 Bonsecours Market b&w $10
1914 34 Spring
35 La rue $20
36 M.L. b&w $10
37 Sketch
38 Sketch b&w $10
1915 35 Sketch b&w $10

BROWN, JESSIE TOPHAM
1882, England 1974, Vernon, B.C.
addr: Vancouver, 3318 1st Ave W
1914 39 A rift in the clouds wc $25

BROWN, LILY MCENTEE (Mrs)
fl 1887-91 H
addr: Montreal, The Sherbrooke, 1891
1888 27 August day $20
28 Summer afternoon $20
66 Sketch wc $7
86 Spring wc $35
97 Late summer wc $15
1889 96A Rainy day $25
96B Camp at Trout Lake $18
96C Hillside $45
100 The pool wc $15
101 Sunset wc $15
102 Edge of the orchard wc $20
103 Road to Binnewater wc $25
1891 13 The burne-side $40
153 The road to Nonquitt wc $35
154 A summer day wc $20

BROWN, NORMAN (Mrs)
addr: Montreal: 20 Durocher St, 1913; 55 Bishop St, 1914; 114 Crescent St, 1916
1913 456 Vase, peacock des $20
1914 490 Sample of dinner set $400
1916 364 Vase $20

BROWN, ROBERT
addr: Montreal, The Cavendish
1913 31 Stirling Castle wc $500
32 The Abbey Church, Dumfermline wc $50
33 Old Quebec wc $25
426 Church des
427 Bungalow des

BROWN, UNA
addr: Toronto, 175 Indian Rd
1917 40 The old beech road $50
41 A Sketch $45

BROWN, W. W.
1881 34 A match safe
36 Atlantic House beach
50 Bounding Cave, coast of Maine

BROWN, WINNIFRED E.
addr: Montreal: 4887 Sherbrooke St W, 1911-13; c/o Art Association Montreal, 1914; 262 Regent Ave, 1915; 284 Clifton Ave, 1916
1911 34 Spring
1913 34 Winter $20
35 The dam, Beaupré $20
1914 40 Rue du Lac $50
41 Sybil, a sketch b&w $10
1915 36 Monday morning $75
37 Frog pond $25
1916 25 The willow $15
26 Old doorway, Bellevue $15

BROWNE, ARCHIBALD see BROWNE, JOSEPH ARCHIBALD

BROWNE, FITZJAMES E. see BROWN, JOHN JAMES & SON

BROWNE, GEORGE W. (Mrs)
addr: St Lambert, Que, 1901-13
1901 219 Figure panel $15
220 Card box $4
1903 147 On the mountain wc $10
1905 269 The wave
270 The bather
271 Mary Magdalene $10
272 A study from life $8
273 Girlhood
274 Plate $5
1906 369 The birth of the pearl plaque
370, 372 Fancy head plaque
371 Love's dream panel
373 Miniature
374 Sunset panel $2.50
375 Evening panel $2.50
376 Apple trees panel $2.50
377 Vase, lilies $10
378 Blue conventional plate $3
379 Stein, moonlight $15
380 Stein, nasturtium $10
381 Stein, silver conventional $6
382 Stein, currant $5
383 Stein, apple $6
384 Stein, landscape $6

385 Bowl, currants $5
386 Nut bowl lustre $6
387 Small bowl lustre $5
388 Small vase, black & silver $4
1908 353 The sunbeam $85
354 Sleep $60
355 A cool retreat $85
356 Salad bowl $13.50
357 Stein, gold $12
358 Stein luatre $9
359 Vase, gold & lustre $9
360 Teapot enamel $7
361 Card receiver lustre $6
362 Vase, moonlight $4
363 Chocolate pot lustre $10
364 Plate, green & gold $6
365 Plate, peacock motive $3
366 Plate, bees lustre $4
367 Plate, nasturtium leaves $3
1909 12 Vase, peacock $15
13 Chop plate $10
14 Chocolate pot $13.50
15 Tea set, blue & gold $15
16 Vase, fish $8
17 Plate, conventional peacock feather $7
18 Plate, blue & gold $4
19 Cylinder vase, peacock $10
20 Candlestick $5
21 Vase, lustre & gold $6
22 Coffee pot, black $7
23 Tea set, lustre & gold $13.50
24 Vase $7
25 Stein $4
26 Ink bottle $3.50
27 Small round vase $4
28 Tea steeper $2.50
1910 415 Vase, Japanese $10
416 Plate, conventional peacock $8
417 Card plate, Persian $3
418 Plate $3
419 Vase, parrot $10
420 Vase, peacock feather $8
421 Cylinder base, Japanese $8
422 Vase, small $5
423 Rose jar $7
424 Hot water pot $7
425 Vase, bronze & gold $9
426 Bowl $3
427 Candlestick $6
1911 312 Satsuma plate $6
313 Satsuma bowl $5
314-15 Plate $, $4.50
316-17 Bowl $4.50, $4
1912 435 Plate, red & gold $4
436 Bowl, black & silver $7
437 Card receiver $6
438 Bowl, green $7
439 Satsuma plate $8
440 Satsuma bowl $5
441 Satsuma vase $6
1913 457 Cylinder vase $10
458 Small box $3.50
459 Bowl $7

BROWNE, JOHN JAMES & SON
John James, d 1893. Fitzjames E, son
addr: Montreal, 207 St James St
1909 407 Catholic College, front elevation

BROWNE, JOSEPH ARCHIBALD
28 Feb 1862, Liverpool, Eng 7 Nov 1948, Cornwall, Ont AGO CWW48 H M Mo12 NGC PMC
addr: Toronto, 423 1/2 Yonge St, 1898. Montreal, 1903. Toronto, 5 King St W, 1906. Montréal: 781 University St, 1924; 815 University St, 1925; 679 St Catherine St W (Watson Gallery), 1927. Lancaster, Ont, 1928-36
1898 10 Moonrise $400
1903 13 Summer evening $300
1906 24 The Pollards
1924 26 Winter in the Adirondacks
1925 33 After the shower $1,000
34 The silver cloud $500
35 Night fall $500
36 Winter in the Adirondacks pastel $100
1927 11 Slumbering waters, Toronto (Thousand, 1967) Islands $1,000 (listed 1967, Jessie Dow prize)
1928 24 Frost and snow $450
25 The mountain farm $450
1932 36 Evensong
1933 28 The cloud
29 The hidden moon
30 The blue door
1934 39-40 Tone poem IV, VII
1935 51 The golden cloud $1,500
1936 53 The spirit of winter $2,000

BROWNELL, PELEG FRANKLIN
27 Jul 1857, New Bedford, Mass 13 Mar 1946, Ottawa AGO CC2 CE CWW36 H M Mo98/12 NGC PMC TB3 W78
addr: Ottawa: c/o J. Wilson & Co

1892-4; 660 Rideau St, 1895; Ottawa, 1903; 124 Wellington St, 1906-9; 307 Wilbrod St, 1913; Ottawa, 1914; 177 Sparks St, 1917
1889 7 A village notary $100
1892 15 The step-child $100
1894 21 Wilfred Campbell
22 A June Day $50
23 Landscape
1895 19 Dr H. H.
20 Autumn dec panel $150
21 Snow, thawing $25
1903 14 Childhood $100
15 Log cabin, evening $100
16 Autumn landscape $50
1906 25 Sweet Violet $150
1908 28 Idling $75
29 Head, young girl $75
30 The spinner $200
31 The seamstress $100
1909 57 Fishwife of Calvados $200
58 Moraine Lake, Valley of the Ten Peaks $250
59 Autumn hillside $150
1913 36 The Marina, San Juan $250
37 Market at Basseterre, St Kitts $150
1914 42 Market, Basseterre, St Kitts, $300
43 On the beach, St Kitts $175
44 Percé Rock and pier $250
45 Pier and fishing boats, Percé $150
1917 42 Strawberry time, Percé $200
43 Mt Misère, St Kitts, BWI
1895 Assoc prize, 1894, portrait

BRUCE, MARY LISETTE
11 Mar 1913, Montreal
addr: Montreal, 1746 Cedar Ave, 1954-5
1954 20 Bottles
1955 14 Bottles and fruit $115

BRUENECH, GEORGE ROBERT
1851, St Malo, France 22 Jul 1916, Toronto B H Mo12
addr: Toronto: 32 Bismark Ave, 1892-94; Toronto, 1897-1908
1883 15 Ile à Massacre, near Bic wc
41 Evening in Muskoka wc
42 Quebec, from Pointe Levis wc
48 A mountain road in Lower Canada wc
49 Caught in the rain wc
1889 104 Veblungsnaes, Romsdal Fjord, Norway wc $75
105 Mousehole Harbour, Cornwall wc $75
106 Ofoten Fjord, Norway wc $75
107 Leer-Foss, near Trandhjem wc $75
1892 159 In Amsterdam, Holland wc $50
160 Summer afternoon, Vermont wc $40
1894 174 Before sunrise, near North Cape, Norway wc $35
1897 142 The North Cape, Norway wc $35
1908 185 Mount Wyndham, Straits of Magellan wc $100

BRULERIE, BERNARD DE LA
addr: Montreal, 624 St Catherine St W
1913 38 Etude $100

BRUNEAU, KITTIE (m Serge Gilbert)
12 Oct 1929, Montreal CC1 M WWA84
addr: Montreal: 2151 Lincoln Ave, Apt 4, 1958; 3421 Drummond St, Apt 79, 1960-1; Galerie Libre, 2100 Crescent St, 1963
1958 5 La famille $150
1960 15 Roi sur fond rouge $125
137 Tête blanche nm $75
1961 6 Nouveaux mariés d'Odanak $300
1963 8 Fond de la mer $350

BRUNET, JEAN EMILE
18 Mar 1899, Huntington, Que 11 Jan 1977, Montreal B M
addr: Montreal, 654 Côte des Neiges Rd
1916 309 Louis Siméon, memorial rel bust

BRUNI, UMBERTO
24 Nov 1914, Montreal M
addr: Montreal: 6572 Fabre St, 1946-51; 9945 ave Delorimier, 1955-8
1946 32 Bateaux de pêche
1951 8 Old tree $75
1955 15 La montagne aux Bleuets $125
1958 51 Detail of a mural project nm $150

BRUNTON, ALICE
addr: Montreal, 3600 McTavish St, 1937-41

1937 35 Roots and rocks wc
1939 53 Wild iris wc
1940 38 Wild flowers wc $10
39 Ferns and violets wc $25
1941 26 Porcelain ginger, Hawaii wc
27 Alamander, Hawaii wc

BRUYERE, C. H.
addr: Montreal, 2024 McGill College Ave
1934 41 Birches and shadows, at Rockcliffe Park, Ottawa, Ont $175

BRYAN, ALFRED THOMAS GEORGE
20 Nov 1907, Toronto
addr: Toronto, 250 Heath St W
1940 40 A day at the fair $200

BRYAN, VIOLET EDEN (m A.I. Bryan)
1908, Ramsgate, Eng
addr: Hudson Heights, Que
1955 16 Planting rice

BRYCE, WILLIAM C.
addr: Westmount, 77 Holton Ave
1936 54 Sunrise, Fox River pastel $35

BRYDONE-JACK, KATHARINE SYBIL RYAN (m H.D. Brydone-Jack)
1 Dec 1895, Sackville, N.B. 29 Nov 1945, Montreal
addr: Montreal, 3488 Côte des Neiges Rd, Apt 12A, 1936-40
1936 55 Cynthia pastel
56 Elizabeth Anne pastel
57 Flowers pastel $90
1937 36 Tulips pastel
37 Hughie pastel
1940 41 Primulas pastel $90
42 The skier, portrait

BRYMNER, WILLIAM
14 Dec 1855, Greenoch, Scot 18 Jun 1925, Wallasey, Ches, Eng AGO B CC2 CE CNS36 CO CWW10 EC H M Mo12 NGC R2 TB1/3 W78
addr: Montreal: c/o Art Association, 1891-7; 67 St James St, 1898-1906; Montreal, 1908; 255 Bleury St, 1909-18; 16 Lorne Ave, 1919-21
1883 83 A country store, on the Ottawa
89 Sketch on the Ottawa
1885 8 One summer day
27 A wreath of flowers (NGC)
42 The lonely orphans taken to her heart
1888 3 Early spring $50
8 Le jour de fête $125
17 Par derrièr chez mon père $250
30 Study of a head $50
48 The young squaw $25
52 At the window $50
1889 8 The swing $750
9 The smithy $150
10 A summer morning $200
11 Low tide, Baie St Paul
12 Where the road dips to the valley $35
13 The spinning wheel $75
14 Spring, Baie st Paul $100
1891 14 Waste lands $200
15 At the mouth of the Gouffre $75
16 Stranded schooner $75
17 The oven $75
18 Haying time, Valois $90
19 September afternoon $75
20 Clearing weather, lower St Lawrence $80
21 Low tide, Baie St Paul $150
1892 16 In County Cork, Ireland $400
17 Champ de Mars, Montreal $250 (MBAM)
18 The carpenter's shop $75
19 Near Killarney, Ireland $75
20 Summer skies $90
21 Entr'acte $120
1894 24 Reverie $367
25 Hell's Gate, Rocky Mountains $105
26 The Illecillewaet Glacier at sunset $80
1895 22 Isabella $200
23 Winter $75
149 Dort wc $30
150 Chateau Landon wc $25
151 The Loing at Nemours wc $25
152 Old street, Nemours wc $25
1897 143 William Hope, Esq wc
144 A grey girl wc $300
145 Le jardin des Soeurs wc $40
146 The carrier's horse wc $75
147 Showery weather wc $75
148 Oats wc $40
1898 11 The lode star $100
12 Robertine $100
127 The picture book wc $200 (NGC)
128 Old canal, Bruges, Belgium wc $35
129 In County Kerry, Ireland wc $35
130 An Irish cottage wc $35

131 London Bridge wc $35
132 London Bridge, Surrey side wc $35
133 At Killarney wc $35
134 On the Laune, Kerry, Ireland wc $35
1900 11 Clearing weather, Beaupré $200
12 At sunset $100
13 Setting moon: impression $40
14 Cedars $60
15 Part of decoration, dining room in country house
121 July weather, Cap Tourment wc $75
122 Summer, Beaupré wc $75
1901 17 The brooklet $100
18-19 Haymaking, sketch $30 each
20 Sunset at Dort $30
110 July, lower St Lawrence wc $100
111 A corner of the farm wc $75
112 A sheep pasture wc $75
113 Thunder clouds wc $75
114 September, old Canada wc $80
115 Clover wc $35
116 At the spring wc $25
117 Habitant wc $20
1903 17 Summer morning $150
18 Woods in June $150
19 Road to the church, evening $150
20 Old wharf at low tide, evening $150
148 The horse of all work wc $80
149 Florence wc $80
150 An out of the way corner, Venice wc $50
151 Sheep pasture wc $50
152 Girl's head wc
1905 15 The seiners, lower St Lawrence $250
16 Italian fortune teller $125
17 A July day $200
18 Potato digging $30
19 September sunlight $150
20 A grey day by the sea $40
136 Un vieux wc $150
137 Master Fisher, portrait wc
1906 26 Little girl in red $250
27 Prelude $200
28 Head of an Indian $75
29 Lower St Lawrence $100
30 Early morning $125
189 Cool glades wc $200
190 Le petit moulin, St Eustache wc $50
1908 32 In the sunlight $150
1909 60 The letter $1,000
61 Evening $500 (NGC)
62 K.R. MacPherson, K.C. (MBAM)
63 Miss Buller
64 Sketch wc
65 The cours, Martigues wc $75
66 Last sunlight wc $35
67 A grey day $35
1910 40 A deserted dwelling $500
41 Carita $300 (AGO)
42 At Martigues wc $75
43 The red wall wc $75
1911 35 Summer evening $500
36 Quebec
37 Louisburg
38-43 Small sketch $25 each
1912 53 Autumn leaves $600
54 Elm trees, late September $250
55 William Hope, Esq, in costume of 1815
56 Small sketches (4) $25 each
404A Feeding chickens $500 (MBAM)
1913 39 Old cottage $500
40 Elms, evening in July $250
41 The Law house
42 Indian summer wc $150
1914 46 October $800 (MQ)
47 A road in autumn $300
48 Girl's head $75
49 By the light of the lantern $250
1915 38 Fog on the coast $250 (NGC)
39 Incoming tide $250 (listed 1967, Jessie Dow prize)
1916 27 The trinket $350 (MQ)
28 Elms at sunset $250
29 Midday, le cours, Martigues $200
1917 44 October, lower St Lawrence $250
45 Afternoon in October $250
1918 35 Coast at Louisburg wc $30
36 Outside the ruined fortifications, Louisburg $30
37 Incoming tide $30
38 A rough little bay, Louisburg $30
39 The pond, October wc $150
40 Givernay, France wc $100 (listed 1967, Jessie Dow prize)

41 A stream in County Kerry, Ireland wc $50
1919 52 Somber day $500
53 A young girl $100
1920 25 The Oise, St Leu d'Esserent $350 (listed 1967, Jessie Dow prize)
26 St Leu d'Esserent $300
27 St François, Ile d'Orleans wc $150
1921 24 Evening, Ste Famille $350
25 Incoming tide, Louisburg $350 (AGH)
26 Coast at Louisburg $350 (NGC)
1929 The late William Brymner, CMG
19 The St Francis valley $750
20 The lower St Lawrence $750
1894-5 Assoc 2nd prize, 1892, Figure. Hon mention, 1892, landscape
port: sketch by Mary Marguerite (Rita) Daly, 1919-90

BRYSON, FLORENCE ADELAIDE
addr: Outremont, 7 Peronne Ave, 1936-9. Montreal, 1430 Sherbrooke St W, 1940
1936 58 Ryoko-San $40
1937 38 Joan pastel
39 Chinese boy, study $40
1939 54 Pepper tree $25
386 Chita etch $12
1940 43 Joan Bryson
44 Jeanne Laberge

BRYSON, MARY
addr: Ormstown, Que
1918 417 Candlestick $5
418 Teapot stand, round bas-rel $2.50
419 Teapot stand, square bas-rel $2.50
420 Jardinière bas-rel $5

BUCHANAN, JAMES MICHAEL
addr: Montreal, 5890 Côte St Antoine Rd
1942 18 Grand Banks fisherman $150
19 Backwater wc $50

BUCHANAN, MINDA
b Canada B
addr: Paris, France
1910 44 Le soir à la rivière

BUCK, MARGARET E. (Mrs)
addr: Montreal, 3520 McTavish St
1944 12 Jamaica girl

BUCKHAM, ROBERT MARSHALL
16 Aug 1918, Toronto
addr: Bais d'Urfée, Que, 15 Apple Hill
1955 17 Clowns $150

BUISSET, CAROLE
addr: Montreal, 5685 Gatineau Ave,
1960 16 La mort des heures $250

BUKAUSKAS, ROMUALDAS
1 Jan 1929, Pakruojus, Lithuania M
addr: Ville LaSalle, Que, 732 5th Ave
1957 18 Quebec $80

BULLER, AUDREY D. (Mrs Parsons)
addr: Montreal, 729 Sherbrooke St W, 1922-3
1922 29 Doreen
1923 30 Miss Bee Warner
port: by Randolph Hewton, 1921-116

BULLER, CECIL TREMAYNE (m John Joseph Aloysius Murphy)
1888 - 29 Sep 1973, Montreal M NGC WWA62
addr: New York, Art Students' League 1910. Montreal: 111 Drummond St, 1912; 154 Drummond St, 1916; 147 Bishop St, 1917-18; Montreal, 1919. New York, 21 Greenwich Ave, 1920
1910 43 Study of a head pastel $20
1912 57 A serene afternoon $35
58 Study, child's head pastel $15
1916 30 La Ville Close wc $45
31 Grey day in Brittany wc $45
1917 46 Fantasie b&w $15
1918 Murphy, 1918, 1920
263 Summer sky, lower St Lawrence $40
1919 54 Three women etch $20
1920 188 French Canadian oven lino cut $20

BULLER, GLADYS see COLTHURST, GLADYS

BULLER, MARGUERITE I. (Mrs Allan)
addr: Montreal: 111 Drummond St, 1905-6. 1911; Montreal, 1908; Bishop's Court Apts, 147 Bishop St, 1910, 1912, 1917. Brookline, 50 Stirling Rd, 1914. Montreal, 154 Drummond St, 1915

1905 230 Panel des $10
231 Le repos nm $7
232 Punch and Judy nm $7
1906 191 In the Tuileries wc $15
192 Story of a brigand wc $15
193 Audrey wc
194 Street scene wc $15
1908 33 The mother $35
34 Audrey
186 Design wc $15
187 Lost, five cents wc $25
1910 Allan, 1910-17
1 Emma $25
2 In winter pastel $20
3 Sketch pastel $15
4 Evening pen & ink $15
1911 4 The blue vase $20
5 Winter day $20
1912 11 Study of a head $75
12 Spring time $50
13 Late afternoon $35
14 The bird shop $50
15 Sketch $35
16 Here, as last year, the fields begin pen & ink $25
17 Miniatures (2)
1914 3 Young woman $100
1915 5 The cyclamen $150
6 The young girl $150
7 Daffodils $125
8 Sketch $25
9 Still life $150
1917 4 Flowers $125
5 Portrait of a lady $200

BUNNETT, HENRY RICHARD SHARLAND Eng
b England, fl 1881-9 H WHC
1885 7 Grey dawn
1886 76 Bonsecours, the old City Hall
97 Entering Montreal harbour
1888 2 View on the Richelieu, villages of St Antoine and St Denis $50
4 Citadel of Quebec, from the old market $250
41 Isle aux Cerfs, St Charles, Richelieu River
1889 15 Hector $125

BURGE, THOMAS see SPENCE, D. JEROME, 1940

BURGESS, ANNE LOUISE see ACER, ANNE LOUISE

BURGOYNE, GERTRUDE M. (Mrs)
addr: Montreal, Royal George Apts, 1452 Bishop St, 1937-8
1937 40 Roses wc
41 Euphorbia and budleia
1938 15 Clematis and butterflies, on ivory $35

BURGOYNE, LORNA HEYWOOD (m L. Von Ritschl)
25 Oct 1894, Plympton, Devon, Eng 3 Apr 1961, Toronto B DBA RA WBA
addr: Port Perry, Ont, RR2, 1937-8. Toronto, 312 Pacific Ave, 1954
1937 miniatures, 1937-54
42 Spring posy $23
43 Shirley poppy $22
44 Tiger lily $20
45 Primula $18
1938 16 Moss roses $27
17 Lady nicotine $27
18 Begonias in a rose bowl $30
19 Autumn glory $35
1954 90 Posy with clematis - Two yellow roses - Posy with scabious wc $25 each

BURGOYNE, SAINT GEORGE
7 Aug 1882, England Nov 1964, Montreal M NGC
addr: Montreal: P O Box 103, 1911. P O Box 212, 1912-13; 2588 Park Ave, 1914-16; 2584 Park Ave, 1917-20; 2198 B St Denis St, 1921-4; 6636 St Denis St, 1925-49
1911 44 Lumber shanties, night wc $10
45 Souvenir of Cape Breton wc $15
1912 59 Across the roofs $75
60 The old bridge wc $15
61 Evening pastel $15
1913 43 Autumn landscape $100
44 Autumn afternoon wc $10
1914 50 Rocks and breaking waves $50
51 The settlement, winter wc $10
52 The shadowed mount pastel $10
1915 40 Over the shallows, Orrs Island, Me $100
1916 32 Winter landscape pastel $25
33 The mountain brook wc $10
34 Spring wc $10
1917 47 Falls, Devil River, Laurentians pastel $10
48 White water, dusk pastel $15
49 Winter afternoon pastel $10
50 Where trout lurk wc $15

51 Seascape wc $10
1918 42 Falls, Boulé River, Laurentians wc $15
43 Autumn afternoon wc $10
44 A Laurentian brook wc $15
45 Winter landscape wc $10
1919 55 Where brook joins river $15
56 On Boulé River, Laurentians $25
57 A Laurentian river $10
58 Gray day, Orrs Island, Maine $10
59 At Orrs Island, Maine $15
60 Spring, Sault au Recollet $10
1920 28 Lumber mill, Boule River $50
29 Sunset, Sault au Recollet wc $20
30 A mountain brook pastel $35
1921 27 Old house, Back River wc $20
28 Spring $35
29 A Laurentian brook $50
1922 30 Reflections wc $10
31 Shadows on the snow wc $15
32 Hillside under snow wc $25
33 Autumn afternoon wc $40
1923 31 Late afternoon wc $50 (NGC)
32 Sunshine and shadow wc $25
33 The alder screen wc $25
1924 27 A road, Lac Supérieur, Que $50
28 Winter landscape wc $50
29 Outlet, Lac 'Tit Gris, Que wc $25
30 Hilly road, Lac Supérieur, Que wc $35
31 Glimpse of the lake wc
1925 37 Mont Tremblant, from Lac Supérieur, Que wc $50
38 Outlet, Lac Supérieur, Que wc $50
39 Spring freshet, Devil River, Que wc $35
1926 12 On Archambault Creek $100
13 Grey day, Laurentians wc $50
14 Outlet of Lac Supérieur, Que pastel $50
1927 12 A grey day wc $35
1928 26 Open water, Archambault Creek $100
1929 21 At the base of the Tuque, Devil River, Que $150
1930 23 Road to Lac Supérieur wc $100
1931 26 Spring, North River, Cape Breton wc $30
27 Mountain stream, C.B. wc $40
1932 37 Lumberman's Bridge, Archambault Creek, Laurentians $100
38 Fast water, Boulé River, Que $50
39 February day, Archambault Creek, Laurentians wc $40
40 Laurentian hillside wc $40
1933 31 February, Archambault Creek wc $35
32 Spring, Boulé River, Lac Supérieur wc $35
1934 42 The last loads $50
43 Edge of a lake wc $25
44 Laurentian landscape wc $25
1935 52 A Laurentian farm $100
53 Autumn in the Laurentians wc $25
54 A Laurentian lake, winter wc $35
1936 59 The log-team, Laurentians
60 Path through the bush wc $35
1937 46 A Laurentian settlement $150
1938 20 The barn, winter wc $35
1939 55 Laurentian bush, winter wc $35
56 Road beneath cliff, Lac Supérieur, Que wc $35
1940 45 Laurentian landscape wc $35
1941 28 Sundown, Bear Lake wc $35
1942 20 Below the dam, Bear Lake wc $50
1943 23 Hillside clearing, Bear Lake wc $35
1944 13 Hills and a clearing, Laurentians wc $35
1945 38 Clearing near a ridge, Laurentians wc $35
1946 33 Shack in the Laurentians wc $50
1947 40 Bear Creek, Lac Supérieur, Que, early March $150
1949 20 Bridge, autumn sundown $75

BURNETT, ARTHUR S.
addr: Montreal, 392 Bleury St
1915 41 Autumn tints $25

BURTON, DENNIS EUGENE NORMAN
6 Dec 1933, Lethbridge, Alta AGO B CE CWW84 IO M
addr: Toronto: 206 St George St, Apt 605, 1958; 18 Austin Terrace, 1959; 45 Wellesley St E (rear), 1961-2; 229 Erskine Ave, 1963; 846 Yonge St, 1964; Toronto, 1970
1958 6 Alberta sky $180
7 For Edward B. $200

1959 44 Monument for Ed metal $125
1961 7 Round the world $400
1962 2 Cassiopeia (A) 1703
1963 9 Speak
10 Fovea $250
1964 8 Untitled $800
1970 God damm the pusher man felt markers & mm 69 x 60 illus

BURTON, EDLEY ALLEN
11 Jan 1901, Walnut Cove, N Carolina M
addr: Ottawa: 437 Booth St, 1944-7; Ottawa, 1967
1944 14 Blue water $80
1945 39 Farm Point $100 (Jury II prize. 1967-12 30 x 35)
1946 34 Blue Lake $100
1947 41 River workers $75

BUSH, CHARLES ROBERT (signs Charles Robb)
28 Jun 1938, Toronto IO WWA84
addr: Toronto, David Mirvish Gallery, 596 Markham St
1965 Robb
16 Untitled $600

BUSH, JOHN HAMILTON (JACK)
20 Mar 1909 - 23 Jan 1977, Toronto AGO B CC1 CE CWW73 M TB3 WWA76 Juror
addr: Toronto: 1 Eastview Cr, 1959-65; Toronto, 1967
1959 4 Red vision $600
1963 11 Paris No 3 $800
1964 9 Blue spot on green $800 (LPL)
1965 3 Colour coat illus $1,200. Albert H. Robinson prize, $500. 1967-13 90 x 54 (David Mirvish Gallery)

BUTLER, BERYL
addr: Westmount: 369 Clarke Ave, 1925-9; 699 Aberdeen Ave, 1934-43
1925 40 Old China wc
1929 22 Near Knowlton, Que wc $25
1934 45 Celery fields $25
1936 61 At work on the farm $35
62 Mrs M.
1942 21 Ailsa, portrait wc
1943 24 A wayside shrine $50

BUTLER, CHARLES HENRY OSBERT
15 Feb 1908, Mewborough, Eng Aug 1980, Montreal
addr: St Hubert, Que, 3430 Côte Noir, 1964; Montreal, 1967
1964 116 Eve and the apple wd illus $600. Ladies Comm prize, 1967-14

BUTLER, DOUGLAS
addr: Niagara Falls, Ont, 2629 Lundy's Lane
1949 113 The elements wc $15

BUTLER, KENNETH JOHN (JACK)
23 Apr 1937, Pittsburgh, Pa M
addr: Winnipeg, 326 Broadway Ave
1964 84 Touch nm $60

BUYLE, FERDINAND
addr: Brussels, Belg
1906 195 Master Raphael de Sola pastel

BYRD, ERIC
b 1905
addr: Montreal, 4779 Meridian Ave
1955 18 The Chinese duck $300

BYERS, JOHN ROBERT MONK
2 Apr 1905, Brockville, Ont M
addr: Toronto, 113 Roncesvalles Ave, 1931. Town of Mount Royal, 121 Trenton Ave, 1946-9. Montreal West, 313 Westminster Ave N, 1952
1931 416 Frank Sperry, Esq plaster $400
1946 274 Freedom from fear (fragment) plaster bronze $1,000
1948 113 Swimmer plaster $75
1949 169 Little Dot plaster $250
1952 79 The reader bronze $300

C

CADET, CLAIRE HAGGAR (Mrs)
15 Aug 1931, France
addr: Montreal, 3932 McKenzie St
1959 45 Jeu d'échecs ter cot $250
46 Distraction ter cot $150

CAIN, DOROTHY GERTRUDE MASON (DOLLY) (m Charles P. Cain)
25 May 1914, Belleville, Ont
addr: Belleville, 58 Charlotte St, 1963-4
1963 12 Farm, Prince Edward County $200
1964 10 Cattle barn, Cannifton Rd $300

CAIRNIE, JEAN FISKEN

addr: Westmount, 14 Windsor Ave, 1913-18
1913 461 Fern pot
1914 491 Bread tray
1916 365 Orange bowl
1917 411 Vase
412 Tea caddy
1918 421 Fruit dish

CAIRNS, J.
1883 120 Old mill at Arbilot, Forfarshire

CAISERMAN, GHITTA (m Alfred Pinsky. m Maxwell W. Roth)
2 Mar 1923, Montreal AGO CC1 CE CWW84 M NGC TB3 WWA84 Juror
addr: Montreal: 4223 Esplanade Ave, 1936-9; 433 St Joseph Blvd W, 1943-5; 3504 Colonial Ave, 1946; 643 Milton St, 1947-55. Westmount, 353 Kensington Ave, 1956-63
1936 63 From my window pastel
1938 21 Roof tops pastel
1939 57 Still life pastel
1943 222 Night shift etch $10
1945 40 Loading $100
41 Work scene $150
1946 35 Alleyway $125
36 Gossiping $150
1947 42 Button game $100
43 Portrait $60
1949 114 Pyramids gouache $100
1950 147 Still life with mushrooms pastel $100
1951 87 Recorder player $200
1952 91 Interior $200
92 Resting $200
1954 91 Actress wc $85
1955 19 Bathers $225
1956 83 Child nm $100
1957 19 Studio windows $400 (MBAM)
20 Child painting $300 Hon mention
1958 8 Studio still life $350
1960 17 Spring $600 (LPL)
1961 8 Stairways $600
1963 13 George loves Mary $600

CALDWELL, ALTHA HAYDOCK (m William Caldwell)
1872, Cincinnati, Ohio
addr: Montreal: 82 Victoria St, 1905-6; 51 Shuter St, 1910-11; 737 Shuter St, 1921
1905 21 The shepherd
22 Portrait
23 Japanese shadows
138 Miniature wc
1906 31 A peasant woman
32 Study of calves
33 Early spring
1910 46 Portrait
47 Milking time pastel $75
48 The deserted house $30
49 The river bank $50
50 Street in Seville $25
1911 46 A memory of Japan $350
47 Portrait of the artist
48 A study
1921 42-3 Portrait study

CALDWELL, ELIZABETH A. (Mrs)
fl 1894-04 H
addr: Montreal: 17 Lorne Ave, 1894; 70 St Matthew St, 1897; 211 Peel St, 1898; 213 Peel St, 1900-3
1894 27 A bit of the harbour, Montreal $15
175 Low tide, Scarboro, Maine wc $35
1897 248 Tray $16
249 Fruit plate $5
250 Small bonboniere $3
251 Cake plate $5
252 Bread and butter plate $1.50
253 Cup & saucer $2.25
254 Bonbon dish
255 Tea caddy
1898 135 A bit of Montreal harbour wc $30
136 A gloomy thought wc $12
240 Jardinière and stand $40
241 Vase, lilacs $25
242 Vase, roses $18
243 Vase, chryanthemums $12
244 Tray, roses $10
245 Vase $7
246 Jewelled bonbon box $2
247 Jewelled match box $2
1900 196 Jardinière, roses (Royal Victoria College)
197 After dinner coffee pot (Mrs Robert Mackay)
198 Chocolate pot
199 Chocolate cup & saucer (Mrs Edwin Hanson)
200 Biscuit jar
201 Turquoise blue cup & saucer
202 Chocolate cup & saucer

(Miss Murray)
203 Chocolate cup & Saucer
(Miss Coverton)
204 Jardinière, chrysanthemums $50
205 Chocolate pot malachite tints $25
206 After dinner coffee pot $20
207 Small chocolate pot, violets $8
208 Small vase, Belique (sic) $8
1902 221 Ideal head porcelain medln
222 Vase, roses and lilacs
223 Underglaze blue plate
224 Cup & saucer
1903 153 Early morning, Scarboro Beach wc $20
154 Low tide, evening, Scarboro Beach wc $20
155 Evening sketch wc $10

CALL, FRANK OLIVER
11 Apr 1878, West Brome, Que 7 Sep 1956. CWW52
addr: Lennoxville, Que: Bishop's College, 1933-41; Lennoxville, 1943. Knowlton, Que, 1945-6
1933 33 March evening, Orford Mountain $60
1934 46 March morning $30
47 Ebb tide $25
1935 55 Japanese peonies $50
1936 64 June Morning, Gaspé Bay $75
65 Early morning, Magog River $40
1937 47 Japanese peonies $65
1938 22 Phlox $60
1939 58 Japanese peonies $65
1941 29 Iris $25
1943 25 Summer flowers $50
1945 42 Delphiniums $75
1946 37 Phlox $75

CALLAHAN, HOWARD D.
addr: Halifax, 133 Morris St, 1940-1
1940 348 Unpainted wood drypt $5
1941 30 Last winter $75

CALLOW, EDWARD
addr: Montreal, 550 Milton St
1940 46 Still life $45

CAMARERO, JORGE LEON (GEORGE L.)
19 Mar 1908, Quito, Ecuador
addr: Montreal: 1231 St Catherine St W, 1931; 4669 Park Ave, 1932
1931 Camerro, mispr (Jorgen Leon)
28 Before the concert $1,200
1932 George L.
41 Impromptu: impression $75

CAMERON, ALLAN ARCHIBALD
19 Feb 1905, Chicago 13 Oct 1938, Montreal
addr: St Lambert, Que, 561 Victoria Ave
1933 506 Aro bronze $25

CAMERON, LILIAN T.
fl 1897-1920 DBA H
addr: Montreal, 6 Phillips Place
1897 19 A Portsmouth lane $15

CAMERON, LOIS
addr: Montreal, 4040 Harvard Ave, 1939-40
1939 59 Spring flowers $50
1940 47 White roses $25
48 Lady with flowers $25

CAMERON, OLIVE S.
addr: Westmount, 4467 Montrose Ave
1939 387 Mother drwg

CAMPBELL, DUNCAN (Mrs)
addr: Westmount, 66 Aberdeen Ave
1925 314 Satsuma vase

CAMPBELL, F. ELIZABETH
addr: Ste Anne de Bellevue, Que, Box 295, Macdonald College
1956 10 San Miguel de Allende, Mexico $30

CAMPBELL. MARY WALKER
addr: Toronto, 574 Sherbourne St, 1905. Winnipeg, Stelle Block, Portage Ave, 1906
1905 275 Blue vase, butterfly $65
276 Green vase, primrose
277 Tea set, waxberry 3 pieces $45
278 Small vase, snake $15
279 Small vase, wild tansey $25
280 Tray, pitcher plant
281 Large plaque $20
282 Small plaque $5
283 Red and brown vase $20
284 Brown and white vase $6
285 Green jug $10

286 Small green & gold vase $7
1906 389 Plaque, gold fish $35
390 Plaque, mermaid $40
391 Tray, evening primrose
392 Platter, game $24
393 Plate, peacock feather $17
394 Bowl, thimbleberry $40

CAMPBELL, ROBERT
1883, Dumbarton, Scot d 1967
addr: Edmonton, 10452 86th Ave
1931 29 Indian paint brush wc $25

CAMPBELL, ROBERT G.
addr: Montreal: 584 St Catherine St W, 1928; 1224 St Catherine St W, 1929-32; 1188 Phillips Pl, 1935-6
1928 27 In a western city $150
1929 23 After the rain $200
24 The little mill, Laurentian Mountains wc $75
227 Proposed rose garden, Summerlea Golf Club
1930 211 Formal gardens, D.S. McMaster, Esq, St Genevieve, Que
1931 260 Garden, H.C. Flood, Esq, Montreal
1932 42 Laurentian winter wc $50
334-5 Garden, S. Stuart Molson, Esq, Montreal photos (2)
1935 56 Sunday in the Townships wc $65
1936 66 Golden morn, Eastern Townships wc $50
464 Flower garden, John B. Pangman, Esq, Westmount
465 Formal garden, residence Redpath Cr, Montreal

CANN, ELIZABETH LOVITT
6 Oct 1901, Yarmouth, N.S. M
addr: Yarmouth, N.S, 13 Vancouver St, 1936-47
1936 67 Falmer (sic) $125
1940 49 Artie in red dress $40
1941 31 A country girl $125
1942 195 Girl's head contédrwg $15
1943 26 A soldier's wife $125
1945 43 The farmer's son $150
252 The kerchief drwg $10
1946 253 Fishing village, late autumn litho $7.50
1947 299 Rummage sale in mission school litho pencil drwg $10

CANTIN, A. N.
addr: Montreal
1908 308 Studies for U.S. Senate dining-room

CANTLIE, BEATRICE MARY see HAMPSON, BEATRICE MARY

CAPEL, AUDREY, see DORAY,AUDREY

CAPELLO, LUIGI G. (or CAPPELO)
b Italy fl 1874-88 H
addr: Montreal, 1880
1880 68 Greek dwelling, time of Sapho
1883 162 A shady nook
163 St Michale, near Montreal

CARETTE, CLAUDE
1935, Québec
addr: Québec, c.o. 462 Haute Ville, 1956. Sillery, Qué, 2430 Ch de Foulons, 1960
1956 84 Cimetière à Québec nm $35
1960 138 Paysage No 1 nm $65

CAREY, ALICE INGLIS
addr: Westmount, 3660 The Boulevard
1934 48 Betty

CARLESS, WILLIAM
addr: Montreal, McGill University
1927 191 A country house
192 Chapel, Grand Seminary, Quebec
see also Turner, John Philip, 1914-470-2

CARLI, ALEXANDER
addr: Montreal, 1466 Notre Dame St, 1891-2
1891 215 L.O. David, bust $100
216 Edmont Dyonnet bust $75
1892 228 Mgr L.F. Laflèche bust
229 Charles Carli bust
230 Il Signor Pietro Santi bust

CARLILE, DAVID M.
addr: Montreal: 360 Beaver Hall Sq, 1944; 650 Haig, Ave, Longue Pointe, 1944; 6378 Mondland Ave, 1947
1923 34 Nibt St Eloy, from Vimy Ridge wc $20
1924 32 Log cabin, Laurentians wc $25
33 Lac L'Achigan, Laurentians wc $25

1925 41 Farm house, Laurentians wc $20
42 Lake L'Achigan, Que wc $20
43 End of the lake, L'Achigan, Que wc $20
44 Old house, corner of Ontario and Papineau Streets, Montreal wc $20
294 Concrete arch bridge for Montmorency Falls, Que des
1944 15 Champlain Street, Quebec wc
1947 44 Beebee's Cove, Port Daniel, Gaspé wc $40

CARLISLE, MARY HELEN Eng
1869 Grahamstown, S. Africa 19 Mar 1925, New York AAA28 B DBA DVP G RA TB1/2
addr: Montreal, 99 Notre Dame St W
1919 61 The Church of Notre Dame, Montreal pastel $500
62 The Chapel of the Sacred Heart, Montreal pastel $500

CARLYLE, FLORENCE
1864, Galt, Ont 7 May 1923, Crowborough Eng B CC2 DBA DVP G H M Mo98/12 NGC R2 TB3 W78
addr: Paris, France, 1892-5; Woodstock, Ont, 1898-1911; Wimbledon, Eng, The Grange, 1913. London, Eng, 1915
1892 22 A Bretagne peasant $200
23 An interior in Bretagne $75
1895 24 La vielle Victorine $200
1898 13 Road through the fields
1901 21 A summer day $30
22 Coming tide, Portuguese girl at Cape Cod $30
1903 21 The story book $85
22 The ship builder $75
23 Grey day $75
24 Poppy sprite $50
25 The garden $50
1910 51 Grey and gold $400 (AGO)
52 The moth $250
53 The patio $300
54 The joy of living $250
1911 49 Young girl $150
50 Edition de luxe $250
51 Pippa Passes $350
1913 45 The spring song $300
1915 62 April $150
63 The son and heir $110
64 Under my window $50

CARMAN, ELIZABETH THOMPSON
addr: Montreal, 276 Pine Ave W
1925 45 Betty pastel

CARMICHAEL, ADELE MILLER
addr: Coaticook, Que, 1931. Whitby, Ont, Gilbert & Centre Sts, 1933
1931 30 Midsummer day in the Catskills
1933 34 Still life $60

CARON, J. M.
addr: Montreal, 406 St Denis St
1923 35 The old corner pastel $15

CARON, PAUL ARCHIBALD OCTAVE
4 Sep 1874 - 14 Feb 1941, Montreal CC1 CNS36 M NGC TB3
addr: Montreal: 723 Sherbrooke St, 1905; 12 Prince Arthur St, 1906; Montreal, 1908; 124 Prince Arthur St, 1909; 49 Durocher St, 1910; 104 Bishop St, 1913. Ste Anne de Bellevue, Que. 1914-23. Montreal: 161 Beaver Hall Hill, 1924-8; 1117 St Matthew St, 1929-40
1905 233, 236 Study of a child nm
234 Burning of Str. Montreal nm
235 Mde C. nm
1906 302 Girl's head chalk $25
303 Child's head chalk $15
1908 188 Boy with drum crayon
189 Study of a child crayon
1909 68 Child study sanguine
1910 55 Lyndall sanguine
56 Nurse, portrait study sanguine
1913 46 Abdul Baha, portrait pastel $75
47 Study of a child pastel $40
48 Nursery rhyme, poster for cocoa wc $100
1914 53 Autumn study
54 Poplars
55 Study, early morning
1915 42 Barges
43 Old French house, Lachine, Que
44 Cement workers
45 A collier
1916 35 Cement workers $150
36 Maurice, portrait study b&w
37 Gwendolyn F, portrait study b&w
38 Infant b&w $30

1917 52 Painting the boats in early spring $250
53 Infant daughter of Rev C.F. Lancaster b&w
54 Infant son of J.H. Gordon, Esq b&w
55 Cicely, portrait study b&w $50
1918 46 A winter sketch $35
1919 63 Gladioli $60
64 In winter quarters wc $60
65 Boat building docks wc $40
66 Bonsecours wc $40
67 St Anns on the Ottawa wc $40
68 A winter morning wc $40
1920 31 Pickens wc $100
32 The river road wc $75
33 In winter quarters wc $75
34 The Lake of Two Mountains wc $50
1921 30 The Oka road $250
31 A December morning $100
32 Ste Anne's Islands pastel $150
33 Sun-break wc $100
1922 34 Hollyhocks $300
35, 36 Portrait study b&w $50 each
1923 36 Je me souviens $250
37 Cicely $300
38 Old shops, Notre Dame Street wc $70 (NGC)
39 Child study b&w $40
1924 34 Old French hotel $300
35 Hollyhocks $250
36 Old courtyard, St Vincent St, Montreal wc $70
271 Market day chalk $50
1925 46 Les coins du Palais de Justice, Montréal $300
47 Rue St Amable, Montréal $200
48 Market day wc $150
49 Caughnawaga village street wc $100
1926 15 Old book shop, Montreal wc $100
189 Courtyard, Bonsecours wd block pr $10
190 Montreal snow box wd block pr $10
1927 13 Autumn afternoon wc $40
wd block pr $20 each, 260-2
260 Old shops, Place Viger, Montreal
261 Chinese shop, Montreal
262 Gateway, Silver Dollar Inn, Montreal
1928 28 Old courtyard in Quenec wc
29 Mitoyen wall in Quebec wc
290 Intendant Bigot's residence, Quebec wd block
1929 25 Les habitants wc $100
1930 24 Mitoyen wall, Quebec wc $150
25 Old French residence, St Paul St, Montreal wc $150
26 Jacques Cartier Square, Montreal wc $200
1931 31 At Bonsecours Market $200
32 Old courtyard, Montreal $200 (listed 1967, Jessie Dow prize)
33 La Rivière du Gouffre, Baie St Paul $200
34 Gipsy camp at Maisonneuve, Hochelaga $200
1932 43 Midi wc $200
44 Rue Champlain, Québec wc $200
45 Rouelle St Eloi, Montréal wc $200
46 A hill farm, Baie St Paul wc $200
1933 35 La rue de Laval, Québec wc $200
36 The road to Les Eboulements wc $200
1934 49 Côte à Coton, Québec wc $100
50 La rue St Eustache, Québec wc $100
51 Lower Town, Quebec wc $100
52 The Ramparts, Quebec wc $100
1935 57 Early spring, Baie St Paul wc $200
58 The St Jovite road, Laurentians wc $200
59 Champlain Street, Quebec wc $100
60 Old courts, Craig East, Montreal wc $100
1936 68 February, Baie St Paul wc $300 (listed 1967, Jessiw Dow prize)
69 A hillside, Baie St Paul wc $200
70 Courtyard, Montreal wc $200
71 A Quebec doorway wc $100
1937 48 Les copains wc $300
49 In the Laurentides wc $250
50 A Quebec corner wc $150
51 Brushwood burners, Mount Royal wc $150
1938 23 Portrait study wc
24 Upper Seigneurs Street, Montreal wc $350
1939 60 In the Chinese quarter $200
61 Chinese shops, Montreal $200
1940 50 The hills of Ste Adèle wc $300
51 Ste Adèle, Què wc $200

1941 deceased
32 A Laurentian village road
port: by Oscar De Lall, 1932-379

CARRICK, MARGARET L.
addr: Calgary, Mount Royal College, 1931-6
1931 35 At the setting of the sun $35
1935 61 February 1935, Exshaw, Alberta $20
1936 72 Age $25

CARRIER, MARCEL LUCIEN
13 Feb 1923, St Henri, Montréal
addr: Ste Agathe des Monts, Qué.
c p 714
1964 11 Entreprise privée $500

CARRINGTON, CHARLES KEMP
20 Nov 1914, Fort William, Ont
addr: Sault Ste Marie, Ont, 65 Lansdowne Ave, 1952-3
1952 flomaster pen, 1952-3
69 Haunted bandstand $35
1953 57 Old French square $40

CARRUTHERS, ELEANOR ROTHWELL
29 Nov 1908, Peterborough, Ont
addr: St Catharines, Ont, 5 Woodruff Ave, 1955-7
1955 20 Barn yard activities
92 Three gables nm $65
1956 85 Notre Dame des Victoires nm $75
1957 21 Growth $75

CARSON, ANITA PAULINE JENNER (Mrs Carson)
25 May 1920, Ottawa M
addr: Ottawa, 191 McLeod St
1962 3 Composition 12 $500

CARSWELL, KATHLEEN W.B.(m W.R. Simpson)
addr: Westmount, 710 Roslyn Ave, 1937-40. Montreal: 5620 Decelles Ave, 1942-6; 4684 Van Horne Ave, 1947
1937 52 Mrs E.E. Tedford pastel
53 Hughie wc
1938 25 Self portrait
1940 53 Wet pavements wc
54 October still life wc
1942 22 Out of the fog wc
1943 27 Old farmhouse wc
28 Sunday down south wc
1944 16 Quebec farm wc $25
1945 44 Rain clouds wc $35
45 The saw mill wc $35
46 Tumbling water wc $35
1946 38 Provincetown wharf wc $35
39 Sand dunes, Provincetown, Mass wc
40 Mending the nets wc
1947 45 Black and rose $150
46 Low tide wc $35
47 Between piers wc $35

CARTER, DOROTHY FRANCES COLLEY (m A. M.W. Carter)
31 Aug 1903, Stevenage, Herts, Eng
addr: Ottawa, 173 Daly Ave, 1947-53
1947 48 Lunch hour shower wc $75
49 Quebec design No 4 wc $70
1952 56 Evanescene wc
1953 52 Lilac time wc $55

CARTER, E. (Miss)
fl 1888-9 H
1889 108 Flowers wc $10

CARTER, HENRY THOMAS
1850 Belfast, Ire 19 Dec 1931, Falmouth, Eng B H
addr: Montreal: 136 Metcalfe St, 1891-8; 186 Peel St, 1900-3; 916 Dorchester St. 1905; Montreal, 1908; 392 Dorchester St, 1909-14; 303 St James St, 1915-23
1888 91 Elaine wc $25
128 Châteauguay wc $15
1891 155 Old windmill, Lachine wc $35
156 Cascades of the St Lawrence wc $15
1892 161 Montmorency Falls wc $40
162 Old Point Claire wc $20
1894 176 Return of Ulysses wc $100
1897 149 The land of the lotus eaters wc $100
1898 137 St Eustache wc $30
1900 123 Montmorency Falls wc
1901 118 Little Métis wc $25
1903 156 Three silent pinnacles of aged snow wc $100
157 Past work wc $40
1905 139 The factory wc $20
140 Cascades of the St Lawrence wc $20
1908 190 St Eustache wc $25
191 St François de Salles, from

Terrebonne wc $15
1909 69 The city of God wc $40
70 Chambly wc $40
1910 57 From Outremont Golf Grounds wc $25
58 Lac Supérieur wc $15
1911 52 Old haunted Château, La Tortue wc $25
53 At Hudson, Quebec wc $15
54 St Laurent, from Mount Royal wc $15
1912 62 At Highlands station wc $25
63 St Simeon stylites wc $15
1913 49 Manitou, Horseshoe Lake wc $60
50 Chambly wc $35
51 Côte des Neiges, from Westmount Golf Links wc $35
52 Chambly, old church wc $15
1914 56 Côte des Neiges, from Little Mountain wc $15
57 Côte St Luc wc $10
58 Outremont wc $10
59 Chambly wc $15
1915 46 Lake St Joseph wc $15
47 St Adolphe de Howard wc $15
48 The Flying Dutchman wc $50
1916 39 Vanderdecken wc $12
40 Roslyn Avenue, Westmount wc $15
1917 56 Falls of Little Metis wc $25
57 Mount Royal heights wc $40
58 Côte des Neiges wc $15
59 Outremont Golf Grounds wc $15
1918 47 In the trail of the submarine $40
48 Drop down cold rivulet to the sea $12
1919 69 At St Eustache 20
1920 35 Come autumn, sae pensive in yellow and grey wc $15
36 Woodland glade wc $15
1923 40 Drop down cold rivulat to the sea wc

CARTER, J. V.
addr: Montreal, 600 Sherbrooke St E
1921 57 Portrait b&w

CARTER, THELMA M.
addr: Montreal: 2314 Oxford Ave, 1938; 4406 Earnscliffe Ave, 1940
1938 26 Portrait $100
1940 52 Gloria $75

CARTIER, MARCELLE MONTREUIL (m Roland Cartier)
18 Jun 1907, Quebec
addr: Quebec, 41 Laurentide Ave
1953 9 Nu $75

CASINI, GUIDO
b Castelfiorentino, Italy
addr: Montreal: 1048 Sherbrooke St E, 1928; 3649 Dorion St, 1929-30; 4237B Chapleau St, 1934; 1274 Papineau Ave, 1935
1928 338 Monument aux morts de la Guerre, érigé à Firenzuola, Italie photo
1929 26 The Arch of Druso, Rome wc $30
358 Rt Hon W.L. Mackenzie King plaster
359 Self portrait plaster
1930 302 Self portrait marble
303 Late Curé Baillairgé of Verchères plaster
1934 481 Self portrait plaster $200
482 My girl, Flora plaster $150
483 Mr S. Brais, architect plaster $30
484 Mr Guiseppe Baldecchi plaster $30
1935 450 Mr Louis Caron, Pres, La Lux Gold Mining Corp plaster $200
451 Miss Pia Brigidi, daughter of Italian consul plaster $200
452 Mr Teodoro Pizzagalli plaster $40

CASS, LOUISE
b 1930
addr: Montreal: 3750 Coronet Rd, Apt 5, 1950-1; 1600 Selkirk Ave, 1952
1950 144 Landscape, Ste Adolphe de Howard wc $35
1951 88 Still life $65
1952 119 Orchard, St Hilaire wc $60

CASSILS, EDITH M.
addr: Montreal, 209 University St
1901 225 Poster placque
226 Bonbonière, Maud Muller
227 Ink bottle

CASTEL, MADELINE
addr: Outremont, 1027 Laurier Ave, 1913.

Montreal, 25 Labadie St, 1915
1913 53 Sunset $15
54 Le Petit Cap $15
1915 49 Norman b&w
50 Sketch b&w

CASTLE & SON
fl 1879-1906 H
addr: Montreal: 1901; 2446 St Catherine St, 1906
1885 158a Hall window des st gl
158b Memorial window, St John des st gl
1889 190 Courtship of Gabriel, Longfellow's 'Evangeline' st gl
1901 192-5 Memorial window des
1906 324-5 Dining room des
326 Lounging room des

CASTLE, MONTAGUE
b Montreal 11 Apr 1939 F H WWW
addr: Montreal, 3 Lorne Ave
1888 designs 1888-91
138 Arabesque ceiling
Room in white and gold
Memorial window
Stained glass fanlight
139 Stained glass skylight
1891 210 Stained glass windows

CATHERWOOD, CATHARINE
addr: Montreal, 5400 Queen Mary Rd
1951 9 March $75

CAVERHILL, HAZEL M.
addr: Montreal, 386 Sherbrooke St W, 1923. Westmount: 48 The Boulevard, 1925-9; 3090 The Boulevard, 1931-6
1923 41 Still life wc
1925 50 Sketch wc $15
1926 16 Still life wc $20
1929 27 Still life $75
1931 36 Cyclamen $75
37 The porcelain madonna $175
1932 47 Calla lillies $75
1935 62 Galja
63 Tulips from Kay's garden $100
1936 73 White tulips, glass bubles $50
74 Egypt

CHABAUTY, CHARLES E.
addr: Montreal, 126 St Charles Barromee
1901 71 Paysage du Dauphine b&w $100

CHADWICK, RICHARD VAUX
20 May 1916, Montreal
see Fetherstonhaugh, Harold Lea, 1947

CHALLENER, FREDERICK SPROSTON
7 Jul 1869, Whetstone Eng 30 Sep 1959, Toronto AGO B CCI CWW55 M Mo12 NGC PMC TB W78 WWA59
addr: Toronto: 87 Garden Ave, 1891-5; 43 Adelaide St, 1900-3; 57 Adelaide St, 1905; Toronto, 1908-9. Conestogo, Ont, 1910. Toronto, 115 King St E, 1916. Conestogo, Ont, 1917. Toronto: 112 Roehampton Ave, 1925; 1158 Bay St, 1927
1891 22 A dreamy day $35
23 A lake-side pasture $15
24 Harvest time $15
1894 28 Golden October $500
29 The hay field $160
30 The morning lunch $80
31 A boys bathing place $35
32 Head
177 A grey autumn day wc $15
178 An autumn reverie wc
1895 25 A sunny morning $75
1900 16 A singing lesson $100
17 Where the lake and river meet $40
1905 24 Pagan dancer $50
25 Haymakers $50
26 Spirit of the woods $50
203 An allegory of summer pastel $100
1908 34a The old pioneer $35
1909 72 Greek girls bathing $25
73 Girl in blue drapery $25
74 Feeding her pet $50
1910 59 Mother love $200
60 A classic idyll $20
1916 41 The purple butterfly $1,000
1917 60 In the orchard $50
1925 51 First contingent leaving Gaspé, October 3rd 1914 $750
52 A riverside cottage $75
1927 14 Blossom time $50
15 The scout's story $175

CHALMERS, ROLAND JOHN ANDERSON
12 Nov 1884, Rochester, Kent, Eng
addr: Montreal, 159 Villeneuve St, 1922-3. Lachine, 106 51st St, 1924-7
1922 37 Old Quebec Hotel courtyard, Bonsecours Market b&w

38 Old houses, rue des Carrières b&w
39 Old courtyard, St Vincent St, Montreal, b&w
40 Nelson's Monument, Notre Dame St, Montreal b&w
1923 42 'Dicken's' leather bottle b&w
43 'Dicken's' Jaspers gate b&w
44 Rue Sur le Fort, Québec b&w
1924 272 Old Hudson Bay Trading Post, Montreal b&w
273 Bonsecours Church, Montreal b&w
274 Old house, Lakeshore Road, Montreal b&w
329 Memorial competition, Ottawa, accepted des
1925 336 Lower Town, Quebec drwg $35
337 St Vincent St, Montreal drwg $15
338 Office of L.J. Papineau, Chief of Rebellion, 1837-8 drwg $25
339 Courtyard, Quebec Hotel, Bonsecours Market, Montreal drwg $15
1927 263 Rue des Carrières, Montreal etch $30
264 Victory Tower, Ottawa etch $30
265 Old Quebec Hotel, Montreal etch $30

CHALUT, DENISE
2 Oct 1928, Montreal
addr: Montreal, 5968 Cartier St
1959 47 Le movement mosaic $75

CHAMBERS, FRANK PENTLAND Eng
Nov 1900, England B DBA RA TB2 WWB29
addr: Montreal, McGill University
1932 456 Portrait rel bronze
457 Pugilist plaster

CHAMBERS, JOHN RICHARD (JACK)
25 Mar 1931 - 13 Apr 1978, London, Ont
AGO CC2 CE CWW70 IO M WWA78
addr: Toronto, 36 Cathcart St, Apt 4, 1964. London, Ont, 1968-70
1964 12 Olga near Arva $1,100 (MBAM)
1968 44 Tap 84 x 84 $1.700
1970 7 Dresser tinted graphite, paper on wood 48 x 40

CHAMPAGNE, ARISTIDE BEAUGRAND
17 Nov 1876 - 16 Dec 1950, Montreal
addr: Montreal
1908 309 Eglise, style Roman Byzantine plan

CHAMPNEY, BENJAMIN Amer
20 Nov 1817, Ipswich, N.H. 11 Dec 1907, Woburn, Mass B F Gr TB WWW
1885 67 Mote Mountain and Ledges, N Conway

CHAPDELAINE, FLAVIEN NORBERT
1859 St François du Lac, Que 1926, Montreal H
addr: Nicolet, Que
1894 33 Un essai $75

CHAPLIN, A. M. (Mrs)
fl 1882-91 H
addr: Montreal, 23 Luke St, 1891
1886 118 A view from Montreal mountain
121 A portrait in crayon
124 Snowball and lilac
129 A quiet nook at Beloeil Mountain
130 View at Cap à L'Aigle
1891 157 Sunset, Metis

CHAPMAN, F. M. (Miss)
addr: Montreal, 23 Bishop St
1914 60 Fig trees, Cairo
61 Volosca

CHAPPELLE, MARGARET MORGAN (m G.F. Chappelle)
1919, Winnipeg M
addr: Edmonton, 12525 104 Ave, 1943-5
1943 29 Still life wc
1945 47 In bloom wc $100

CHAPUT, OLIVIER
addr: Tetreaultville, Que, 2288 St Emile St
1936 584 Music Hall of Fame, d'après dessin de C. Schwennerp plaster
585 Ma famille plaster

CHARAD, WILLIE LAZARUS (BILL)
24 July 1924, Montreal
addr: Montreal: 113 Villeneuve St W,

1954-5; 4585 Dupuis Ave, Apt 4, 1957; 4800 Côte St Catherine Rd, 1960
1954 22 Prefontaine, Que $150
23 Still life with potatoes $100
1955 93 Trees nm $25
1957 22 Landscape $100
1960 18 Rustico, P.E.I. $125

CHARBONNEAU, MONIQUE
25 Jun 1928, Montreal
addr: Montréal: 1552 rue Viel, 1952; 1556 rue Viel, 1960-1; 12042 rue Valmont, 1864
1952 93 Jeu de cartes $80
1960 19 Peinture $110
1961 9 No 6 $300
72 No 27 nm $100
1963 75 Mersoleil nm $50
1964 13 Sans titre $375

CHAREST, THERESE
addr: Outremont, 505 Stuart Ave
1936 75 Rocher Percé wc $15
76 Baie St Paul wc $10

CHARLEBOIS, JOSEPH CHARLES THEOPHILE
1872 - 21 Oct 1935, Montreal
addr: Montreal: 1178 Phillips Place, 1931; 1220 Drummont St, 1932-4; 157 Milton St, 1935
1931 38 Paternoster, late XIV century gouache $500
39 Ave Maria, late XIV century gouache $200
40 Auld lang syne gouache $200
41 Coat of arms gouache
1932 48 Pater, XIII century gouache
49 Motif of XIV century gouache
1933 37 Canada, a poem illum gouache
38 Paternoster illum gouache
1934 53 Oath Hippocrater illum
54 Poem illum $200
55 Pasternoster illum
1935 64 Lettre de Sir Wilfred Laurier à M. L.O. David illum
65 Enluminure $400

CHARMOY, COZETTE DE (m Albert A. Shea)
1939, London, Eng
addr: Montreal, 4095 Côte des Neiges, Apt 28
1964 21 Le fusil $400

CHARNEY, HYMAN
22 Jul 1907, Poland
addr: Montreal, 6292 De Vimy Ave, 1954-7
1954 24 Three Yeshiva boys
1957 23 Early autumn

CHARNEY, MELVIN
28 Aug 1935, Montreal CE
addr: Montreal, 3295 Ridgewood Ave
1965 23 Mr Smith's icon nm $100

CHARTERS, GEORGE A.
addr: Montreal: 434 St Antoine St, 1919; 7766 Querbes Ave, Apt 4, 1936
1919 70 In their winter haven $100
1936 77 Winter haven $125
78 Vermont, autumn $100

CHASE, RONALD
29 Dec 1934, Seminole, Okla
addr: Montreal, Galerie Libre, 2100 Crescent St
1962 43 The Bodega nm $135

CHATFIELD, EDITH L. (m Stevenson Milne Gossage)
1906, New Haven, Conn
addr: Toronto, 82 Hillsdale Ave W, 1945. Como, Que, Apple Tree Shott, 1953
1945 Gossage
104 The front porch $125
1953 10 Prickly pears on a green plate $150

CHAUSSE, JOSEPH ALCIDE HAN
7 Jan 1868, St Sulpice l'Assumption, Que 7 Oct 1944, Montreal CNS 27 CWW38 Mo12
addr: Montreal, 30 St James St W
1929 228-31 Empress Theatre, Montreal, front elevation, proscenium arch, fountain, organ screen, west wall from balcony, restroom

CHAVIGNAUD, GEORGES
24 Sep 1965, Finistère, France 3 May 1944, Meadowvale, Ont AGO H M Mo12 NGC TB3
addr: Montreal, c/o Henry Morgan & Co, 1903-5. Meadowvale, 1906-9. Toronto, Mackenzie & Co, 1912. Halifax, 292 South St, 1913. Meadowvale, 1931

1903 26 A rainy day in Holland $300
158 Old canal of Sluis wc $250
159 A Flemish village wc $200
1905 141 The canal boat wc $125
142 Moonlight wc $125
143 Grey morning wc $165
144 Fishing boats wc $65
1906 34 The pond, morning $400
196 Le matin wc
197 Petit Pierre wc $200
198 Le soir wc $150
199 La chaumière wc $200
1908 35 Summer idyll $200
192 Woodland wc $300
1909 75 Windy day $100
1912 64 Heyst wc $400
1913 55 Souvernir of Holland $350
1931 42 Old church of St François, Isle of Orleans wc

CHENEY, ANNA GERTRUDE LAWSON (NAN)
(m Hill Harrison Cheney)
22 Jun 1897, Windsor, N.S. 3 Nov 1985, Vancouver NGC
addr: Montreal, 604 Union Ave, 1925; Ottawa, 55 Sunset Blvd, 1927-31. Montreal, 3610 Lorne Cr, 1936. Vancouver, 1282 Connaught Dr, 1939. Capilano, B.C, 3065 Capilano Rd, 1947
1925 53 Old apple tree, Robinson's Point
54 Wild grape vine
1927 16 The clothes line $40
1928 30 Fishermen's houses $50
1929 28 Gloucester $85
29 Early evening snow $75
1930 27 French village, N.S. $50
28 The Lindy, Herring Cove, N.S. $50
29 Fish wharf, Halifax, N.S. $50
30 Herring Cove, N.S.
1931 43 Consolidated Smelters, Trail, B.C. $200
44 Black Bear Gold Mine, Rossland, B.C. $200
1936 517 Zeta Psi Fraternigh charcl & wash $35
1939 62 Nikolai Seminoff $75
63 Tina Teminoff $75
1947 50 Lumber Mill, Nelson, B.C. $200

CHERRY, AILEEN ALMA
4 Sep 1895 - 27 Aug 1958, Belleville, Ont
addr: Belleville, 83 Hyland Ave, 1922-50
1922 41 A tranquil by-way $75
1932 50 Autumn $35
1943 30 The Murray Hills $100
1944 17 An old village street $175
1945 48 Beyond the village $150
49 Shannonville $85
1946 41 At the top of the hill $85
42 Sunshine and rain $175
1950 5 Old settlement $150

CHESHIRE, LORNA DEAN
7 Apr 1931, Montreal
addr: Pointe Claire, Que, 4 Wavesley Rd, 1957. Paris, 9 rue Sébastien Bottin, 1958
1957 110 Fantasy and the moon nm $10
1958 52 Lines on aquatine. 1957 nm $12
Hon mention

CHESTERTON, WALTER
1845, London, Eng 13 Nov 1931, Ottawa
H
addr: Montreal, 225 Sherbrooke St W, 1909-16
1909 76 Sunset near the Gatineau wc $30
1910 61 Old sawmill, Cartierville wc $50
62 A Westmount sunset wc $30
1911 55 The old blockhouse $50
56 When daylight wanes, Vaudreuil $50
57 Springtime, Fletcher's Field wc $20
1912 65 Fog at Bic $60
66 Private practice $35
67 The Gorge, Bic River $35
1913 56 The willows, Scarborough Beach $85
57 Summer haze, Rio $35
58 Moonlight, Scarborough Beach $25
1914 62 Creeping in through snow and mist $80
63 Rocks, Scarborough, Maine $40
64 Rocks, Prout's Neck, Maine $100
1915 51 A summer day, southern Manitoba $100
1916 42 The Red man's burden $50

CHICOINE, OWEN ALEXANDER
4 Jul 1916, Belle Anse, Gaspé, Que 23 Dec 1982, Mont St Hilaire, Que
addr: Belle Anse, Gaspé
1955 21 Fruit $150

CHICOINE, RENE
1905 - 10 Aug 1981, Montreal WWA78
addr: Montreal, 6617 St Vallier St, 1940-4
1940 55 Clouds $50
1941 33 Coq d'or $150
34 Night effect $50
35 Mrs M. V.
1942 24 Green eyes $150
25 One of the nine $100
1944 18 Study $200

CHIPMAN, M. ISABEL PRADOS (m L.C. Chipman)
addr: Montreal, 522 Pine Ave W, Apt 6, 1955-8
1955 94 Path in the forest nm $60
1956 11 Cityscape
1958 9 Through the looking glass $75

CHIPMAN, MAUD M. ANGUS (m Walter William Chipman)
addr: Montreal: 240 Drummond St, 1906; Montreal, 1908; 284 Mountain St, 1910-18
1906 173 Venice wc
174 The poplars wc
175 A woodland path wc
1908 164 The mill, Jacques Cartier River wc
165 Late afternoon, Senneville wc
165 October landscape wc
1910 63 Autumn, Pine Bluff wc
64 Village, lower St Lawrence wc
65 Salzburg wc
1913 59 Landscape, lower St Lawrence wc
60 Cornfield wc
61 Foggy day, Pointe au Pic wc
1914 65 The stubble field
66 The garden wc
1916 43 A garden, Senneville wc
44 A cottage, Senneville wc
1918 49 Jacques Cartier River

CHIPMAN, NOEL INGERSOLL
14 Oct 1890, Montreal CWW36
addr: New York, 324 W 56th St, 1922. Montreal: 45 Lincoln Ave, 1927-8; 1827 Lincoln Ave, 1929; 2058 Victoria St, 1931-3; 1536 Bishop St, 1936; 1474 Drummond St, 1937-9
1922 42 Mariana
1927 193 Residence, Grant Johnston, Esq
194 Residence, B.M. Hallward, Esq
195 Alterations for W.C. Wonham, Esq
1928 217 Ironwork
218 House, Cartierville
219 Sun porch, The Boulevard
1929 232-3 Cottage, garage, P. A. Thomson, Esq, Como, Que
234 Residence, C.G. Bronson, Esq, Clarke Cr, Westmount
235 Cottage, J.N. Laing, Esq, Metis Beach, Que
1931 261 Parish house and rectory, Church of St John the Evangelist
262 W. Scott & Sons, main picture gallery
263 Alterations, residence, P.A. Thomson, Esq, Como photo
264 Library and residence, W.A. Wonham, Esq photo
1933 358 Miscellaneous interiors
359 Church of St John the Evangelist, lighting
1936 466 Cottage alterations, Mrs Hope Scott, Ste Agathe
467 Summer residence, E.E. Kenyon, Esq, Como
468-9 Residence, Lady Drummond, copper lighting fixtures, entrance hall, drawing room
1937 327 Garden view, residence, V.M. Lynch-Staunton, Esq
328 Christ Church Cathedral, lighting photo
329 Alterations, basement space, A.T. Henderson, M.D. photo
1938 130 Library alterations, R. E. Thorne, Esq
131 Cottage, B.M. Hallward, Esq, Ste Agathe
132 Residence, C.G. Bronson, Esq
1939 346 Proposed store front to existing building wc
347 Residence, Westmount wc
348 Cottage, Como, Que wc

CHOQUETTE, MARCEL
addr: Montreal, 1110 St Laurent, 1940. St Paul, l'Ermite, Que, 1941. Montreal, 971 Coté St, 1941-5. St Lambert, 20 Argyle St, 1947
1940 400 Infame plaster $75
401 Chagrin plaster $10
1941 279 Shy plaster $100

1942 23 Chiffon pastel $35
230 Roger Gill, Esq plaster
1943 31 Nature morte pastel $25
223 Gardien de nuit charcl
1944 158 Study plaster $100
159 A. R. D, Esq plaster
1945 253 Etude drwg $25
275 Frère Marie Victorin plaster
1947 332 Dr Camille Bernier, Médécin, fondateur Hôspital des Incurables plaster

CHOWNE, GERARD, Capt
addr: Montreal, 43B McGill College Ave., 1925 late Capt Gerard Chowne
55 Roses $750
56 Ronda wc $150
57 Grasse, A.M, evening wc $100
58 Dieppe wc $100

CHRISTENSEN, ETHEL MADILL (m Clifford Christensen)
28 Feb 1926, Glendive, Mont
addr: Edmonton, 6515 123rd St E
1964 14 No 1004 $300

CHRISTENSEN, HENRY T.
addr: Calgary, 333 Commercial Bldg
1931 45 The silvery Bow $75

CHRISTOPHER, ANNA H.
addr: Montreal, 1656 Jeanne Mance St, 1926. Ste Agathe des Mont, Que, 1927. Montreal, 219 Harvard Ave, 1929
1926 238 Jeanne plaster
1927 305 Old man plaster $25
306 Florin plaster $25
1929 360 Miss M. Millward plaster $50
361 Mrs M. plaster $50
362 Master Billy Fischer plaster $25

CICCIMARA, RICHARD MATTHEW
12 Jul 1924, Vienna 19 Jun 1973, Greece
addr: Victoria
1968 45 Four figures, withdrawn/retiré wc & wax 48 x 60 $500

CINQ-MARS, ALONZO
14 Apr 1881, St Edouard de Lotbinière, Que
addr: Longueuil, Que; 16 Charlotte St, 1931; 16 1st Ave, 1932; Longueuil, 1933; 2 Grant St, 1933-41
1931 417 Un jeune héros canadien buste plâtre
418 Emile Nelligan medln plâtre
419 Octave Crémazie medln plâtre
420 Louis Fréchette medln plâtre
1931 458 Sir Henry Thornton medln $10
459 Le petit chanteur à la croix de bois plâtre
1933 507 Faucher de St Maurice medln
508 Ernest Lavigne medln
1934 485 Calixa Lavallée medln bronze
486 Charles Gill medln bronze $10
487 Samuel Genest medln bronze $10
488 Joseph-Edmond Roy plâtre
1935 453 Leon Gerin medln bronze
454 Emile Nelligan medln bisque $1.25
455 Charles Gill medln bisque $1.25
456 Pamphile LeMay medln bisque $1.25
1936 586 Rév Frère Grégoire bronze
587 Stanislas Coté porcelain
1937 447 H.M. King George V plâtre
448 H.M. King George VI plâtre
449 Benjamin Sulté bronze
1938 189 Phillip Aubert de Gaspé buste bisque
1939 449 Samuel Genest buste plâtre
1940 402 Etienne Parent, journaliste bronze $15
403 Suzanne L. bronze
1941 280 Jean Dansereau, pianiste medln bronze $25

CLAPP, WILLIAM HENRY
29 Oct 1879, Montreal 21 Apr 1954, Oakland, Cal AAA31 B F M NGC TB2/3 WWA47
addr: Montreal: 1908; 255 Bleury St, 1909-10; 33 Bank of Toronto Bldg, 1911; 255 Bleury St, 1912-14. Isle of Pines, Cuba, 1915. no address 1918
1908 36 Autumn morning, France $250
37 Church of San Antonio, Spain $260
38 Morning in Spain $260 (listed 1967, Jessie Dow prize; illus 29 x 36 1/2) (National Gallery)
39 A warm morning, Spain $60
40 A study in vibration $35
41 Bathers $110
41a Noon, Cuenca, Spain $250
1909 77 The captive $300

78 Waders $300
79 Le bas noir $80
80 Village of Cuenca, Spain $300
81 Breaking wave $40
1910 66 Lumber boats $300
67 The new church $300
68 Bird nesting $300
69 Afternoon $300
70 Autumn $35
1911 58 Waders, No 2 $300
59 Miss Williamson
60 Children bathing $300
61 Memory of a visit behind the scenes $300
62 Sunset $300
1912 68 Under the arbor $300
69 A rainy day $300
70 Nude pastel $30
71-2 Landscape wc $18 each
73 Landscape wc $12
1913 62 Landscape $125
63 Morning $300
64 Old house, Berthier $125
1914 67 Landscape, France $300
68 Landscape, Canada $125
1915 52 Sunset, St Sulpice $125
53 High water, St Sulpice $125
54 Gertrude $125
55 The bridge at St Suplice $35
57 First love wc $30
1918 50 A garden flirtation
51 A Cuban Inca

CLARE, BEATRICE
addr: Westmount, 716 Roslyn Ave
1934 434 The Van Horne barn, Ministers Island, N.B. pen & ink

CLARE, MARGARET
addr: Westmount, 716 Roslyn Ave
1935 66 Trilliums wc

CLARK, A.J.
addr: Toronto: 189 Springhurst Ave, 1915-20; 435 Spadina Ave, 1921
1915 358 HRH Duchess of Connaught bas rel $25
359 E. Pauline Johnson bas rel $20
360 General William Booth bas rel $10
1916 310 Lord Strathcona sculp
1917 Clarke, 1917-19
357 Sir Edmund Walker sculp
1919 360 Gen Sir Arthur Currie bas rel art bronze copies $50
361 Sir Charles Tupper bas rel art bronze copies $25
362 Memorial plaque bas rel des
1920 295 Sir James Whitney bas rel, min bronze $25
296 Over the top bas rel panel (actual size of original model)
297 A Scottish pioneer bas rel min
1921 290 Cherry Street Harbour Bridge, Toronto presentation plaque bas rel
291 Crest, memorial detail actual size of model sculp

CLARK, BARRY FERGUSON
6 Oct 1937, Lethbridge, Alta
addr: Montreal, 3851 University St
1958 10 Coastal landscape No 1 $350

CLARK, HELENE
addr: Montreal, 3501 Addington Ave
1950 106 Smoked fish $25

CLARK, JAMES RONALD
7 Dec 1904, Hamilton
addr: Montreal: 648 Sherbrooke St W, 1936; 3610 Lorne Cr, 1937; 3484 Shuter St, 1938; 3610 Oxenden Ave, 1939; 3010 Oxenden Ave, 1940
1936 79 Shafts and sheds $75
1937 J.P. Clark mispr
54 Fall $75
1938 27 Fletchers Field $35
28 Fishing $25
1939 64 Fishing sheds $50
65 Thaw $30
1940 58 Tracks wc $40
59 Main Street $50
60 Market

CLARK, L.
addr: Preston, Ont, White Cottage, Concession Rd, 1934-9
1934 435 The broken mill etch $10
436 The Basilica of Christ the King, Hamilton, Ont etch $7.50
437 Mill ruin, Doon, Ont etch $5
1935 392 Coles Mills, Hespeler, Ont etch $750
393 Cedars and sunlight etch $7.50

394 Evening etch $5
1936 518 Ontario stump fence etch aqua $10
519 Construction head office building, Gore Fire Insurance Co etch aqua
520 Muskoka birches etch aqua $7.50
521 Still life col etch $10
1937 391 Georgian Bay aqua $12.50
392 Speed Mills, Hespeler, Ont aqua $12.50
393 Young elms, Muskoka aqua $7.50
1939 388 Summer storm etch aqua $10
389 Pioneer hearth, Waterloo County etch aqua $10

CLARK, PARASKEVA PLISTIK (m Orestes Allegre. m Philip Clark)
28 Oct 1898, St Petersburg 10 Aug 1986, Toronto AGO CC1 CE IO M NGC TB3 WWA80
Juror
addr: Toronto: 315 Lonsdale Rd, 1933; 145 Briar Hill Ave, 1939-40; 256 Roxborough St E, 1943-7; 56 Roxborough Dr, 1954-60
1933 39 Still life $75
1939 66 Lake in the morning $100
67 Wooden bridge in Quebec $100
1940 56 Bathing the horse $175
57 Landscape with church wc $60
1943 32 View from Stewarts Rock, Muskoka $225
1947 51 Reflections, 2nd version temp $100
52 Public bath in Leningrad temp $100
1954 92 November roses, 1st version wc $100
1955 95 Old Muskoka supply boat nm $125
1956 86 Old bridge, Algonquin nm $100
1957 111 Grey day, Muskoka nm $75
1960 20 Ice bound street $200

CLARK, RONALD see CLARK, JAMES RONALD

CLARKE, ALMA
addr: Westmount, 334 Elm Ave, 1921. Montreal, 445 Côte des Neiges Rd, 1929
1921 34-7 Miniatures
1929 Clark
30 Three miniatures

CLARKE, B. STANLEY
fl 1897-1902 H
addr: Toronto, 72 Admiral Rd
1898 138 Shoreham, Sussex, England wc

CLARKE, EARL EDWARD WINTON
1879, Woodstock, Ont 20 Feb 1954, Victoria
addr: Victoria, 1461 Pembrooke St
1932 460 Boy with glider bronze

CLARKE, EDITH GRAEME
addr: Toronto, 15 Winchester St
1914 69 Pines, Eglington, Toronto $35

CLARKE, EMMA
d 31 Dec 1946, Belleville, Ont
addr: Belleville, Ont
1912 74 Black bass $75

CLARKE, KATHERINE A.
b Toronto
addr: Toronto, 15 Winchester St
1913 65 At the old fort, Toronto $40

CLARKE, M. LILLIAN
addr: Saint John, 34 Paddock St
1936 80 Silver dollars wc $25
81 Green jug wc $20
522 Banana boat des $50
523 Home cooking des $15

CLARKE, PEGGY
addr: Toronto: 268 Manor Rd E, 1935; 56 Manor Rd, 1936; 64 Oakwood Ave, 1938-40
1935 395 Four and twenty tailors dry pt $10
396 Lyman Hatfield dry pt $7
397 Seashore wash drwg $25
398 Bunty dry pt $7
1936 82 Isobel's new doll wc $20
470 Nursery for little boy four elevations pen & ink with wash
524 Jimmie pencil $15
1938 brush drwg, anniline dyes 155-6
155 Pink harlequins
156 Harlequin with blue nose $15
157 Boy angel pen drwg $12
1939 390 Shetland colt charcl $20
391 Miguel, horseman brush drwg $15
1940 61 Jane's room
349 In the park pen & ink $15

350 John Street pen & ink $15
351 Sebastian brush drwg

CLARKES, GERARD LUTHER
1934, Winnipeg
addr: Toronto, 1315 Bay St
1963 14 The wedding $390 (MBAM)

CLEGHORN, WILLIAM HENRY EDWARD
1902 - 25 Mar 1962, Montreal
addr: Westmount; 474 Mount Pleasant Ave, 1937-9; 511 Lansdowne Ave, 1941
1937 55 Pasture gate
1939 68 Autumn landscape $20
69 Murray Park wc $20
1941 36 Bill's underwear $45
port: by Oscar DeLall, 1957-14

CLELAND, MARY ALBERTA
20 Aug 1876, Montreal d 1960 M NGC TB3
addr: Montreal: 244 Guy St, 1897-1903; 15 Souvenir St, 1905-29; 2211 Souvenir St, 1930-43
1897 20 Old windmill, Lachine $15
236 A sketch in clay sculp
1898 14 In port $15
229 Study of a head sculp
1900 18 Evening, Métis $25
19 Low tide, Métis $25
1901 23 Evening $20
1903 27 An August morning $15
28 A country wood $25
1905 27 Haying $25
28 Study of ducks $30
29 Portrait
1906 200 Miss Elsie Michaels pastel
201 Helen Mostyn Lloyd and her Goidie sketch
202 Mother and child wc
353 Bust sculp
1908 42 Rio di San Barbara, Venice $30
43 Sketch, Naples and Vesuvius $35
44 Sketch, via Sistina, Rome $25
192a Wilhelmina pastel $75
1909 82 Waiting pastel $65
83 Portrait pastel
84 A June day $20
1910 71 Portrait pastel
72 Pierre pastel
73 Study of a child pastel $40
74 Mother and child pastel $50
1911 63 Madeleine pastel $75
1912 75 Barbara pastel $100
76 Near Beaupré $35
77 A sketch $15
78 A winter sketch $15
1913 66 The school, Cartierville $25
67 Autumn sketch $20
68 Venetian sketch $25
69 Ste Cécile Street $20
1914 70 A sketch $20
71 March day, Commissioners Street, $35
72 Peggy, daughter of Mr and Mrs N.M. Yuile pastel
73 A study pastel $50
1915 58 Old St Anne's Market wc $100
59 Sketch, St Andrews E, Que wc $35
60 Sketch, a corn field $25
61 Sketch, Hampton Beach, N.H. $15
1916 45 In the Laurentian wood $100
46 Sketch $35
47 Drawing pastel $25
311 Betty and Mary sculp $50
1917 61 Good Harbour beach Gloucester, Mass $35
62 Near Gloucester, Mass $75
63 Gloucester, Mass, sketch $20
1918 52 Feeding time wc $75
53 In the glades, Cushing Me $25
54 Cab stand, Uptown 6647 $35
1919 71 Cutting ice, Greece's Point, Que $125
72 An October day, Cushing, Que $75
1920 37 An interior wc $75
38 In the Laurentians, sketch $50
39 On the beach, sketch $50
1921 38 A winter's day $400
39 The mill stream, St Andrews E, $125
40 Early spring $75
41 Study of a head pastel $75 (NGC)
1922 43 Leba pastel $200
44 Colin Campbell, son of Mr and Mrs R.H. Dumbrille pastel
45 Cold storage $350
1923 45 Evening, Beaupré, Que $175
46 The sheep pen pastel $65
247 The new baby sculp $20
1924 37 Selby pastel $250
38 In the woods $60
39 A hillside garden $50
40 Evening wc $60
1925 59 CPR right-of-way $35

60 On the beach $50
61 Valeri pastel $250
1926 17 Late afternoon, Bonsecours Market $75
18 Logging team wc $75
19 An anxious moment pastel $250
1927 17 St Gabriel farm house, built 1698 $200
18 Phlox $50
19 Zinnias $40
1928 31 Venetian canal $50
32 St Paul Street $50
1929 31 On the way to Carillon $200
32 Les bûches $200
33 Peonies $100
34 Zinnias $100
1930 31 The market place wc $75
32 In the Laurentians pastel $40
33 Ste Cécile Street $60
1931 46 Japanese peonies $75
47 At Rawdon, Que wc $75
1932 51 Phlox
52 Peonies, Solange $85
1933 40 At the bird bath $350
41 A winter sketch $40
1934 56 White frost $225
47 Winter sunlight, Mascouche, Que $50
1935 67 The cathedral $65
1936 83-5 Winter sketch $50, $40, $30
1937 56 Lilabet pastel $150
1938 29 Group of flowers $75
1939 70 Susan pastel
1940 62 Noon, Mascouche, Que $250
1941 37 Woodland brook $110
1943 33 An interior wc $75

CLEVELAND, EDWARD T.
addr: Montreal, 311 Birks Building
1920 40 The meadow

CLIFFORD, MARY see BILLAUX, MARY

CLOUTIER, ALBERT EDWARD
12 Jun 1902, Leominster, Mass 9 Jun 1965, St Hilaire, Que CC2 CNS40 CWW64 M NGC W78 WWA62 Juror
addr: Montreal: 1801 University Tower Bldg, 1933-6; 522 Pine Ave W, 1937-8. Ottawa, 84 Carling Ave, 1948. Montreal, 522 Pine Ave W, 1949-57. St Hilaire Station, 109 rue Michel, 1960
1933 42 Moulin de Gaspé, near l'Islet wc $50
43 At Percé wc $50
44 The beath, Little Fox River, Que wc $50
1934 58 In La Malbaie village $350
59 May Woo $175
1935 68 In the Laurentians, from Ste Agnes $300
69 Midday, winter, near Ste Adèle $250
70 Little white cottage, La Malbaie wc $45
1936 86 March winds, Cacouna wc $85
87 Maple woods, Mebec wc $85
1937 57 The tannery by the clay bank $650
1938 30 Cap à l'Orignal, winter $300
1948 8 Winter Hill Road, St Faustin $200
1949 115 Fishing cove, Blue Rocks, N.S. wc $100 (listed 1967, Jessie Dow prize)
116 Port-aux-Basques, Newfoundland gouache $200
1952 8 Spruce country, northern Quebec $600 (listed 1967, Jessie Dow prize)
1953 11 Ste Adèle, winter $800
1954 25 Winter afternoon, downtown Montreal $500
1957 24 La Montagne, Tremblante $600
1960 21 La clairière $550

CLUSE, ZILLAH MARY
7 Jun 1916, Toronto
addr: Montreal West, 239 Percival Ave, 1935-7
1935 457 Mona plaster
458 Nude sketch plaster
1936 588 Elizabeth plaster
589 Tranquility plaster
1937 450 Eskimo plaster $60
451 Dawn plaster $45

CLYMER, JOHN FORD
29 Jan 1907, Ellenburgh, Wash M
addr: York Mills, Ont, 69 Donwoods Dr
1934 60 Caribou country $100
61 Little brother $65
62 Javanese dancing girls $250

COBBETT, EDWARD JOHN Eng
Apr 1815, London, Eng d 1899 B DBA DVP G TB
1885 59 Art

COBURN, FREDERICK SIMPSON
18 Mar 1871 - 26 May 1960, Upper Melbourne, Que AGO CC2 CE CNS36 CWW58 M Mo12 NGC TB3 W78 WWA53 Juror
addr: Montreal, c/o Scott & Sons, 1906. Upper Melbourne, Que, 1910. Antwerp, 39 Rempart des Béguines, 1913. Upper Melbourne, 1917-19; Montreal: 14 Phillips Sq, No 201, 1920; 79 Mansfield St, 1921-2; 146 Mansfield St, 1923; 52 St Matthew St, 1924. Upper Melbourne, 1925. c/o Art Association, 1926; 52 St Matthew St, 1927; 1258 St Matthew St, 1928-44

1906 203 Spring wc $100
204 The plague pastel $100
205 Spring pastel $125
1910 75 The green gown $125
76 Landscape at Moll $110
77 Milking wc $60
1913 70 Snow in the air $600
1917 64 Logging, the Creek Road $250
65 The lonely road $250
66 The wood road $300
67 Trotting on the ice $250
68 Second-growth, scrub pine $100
69 Danville roses $100
1918 55 Elms at Melbourne $155
56 Wind in March $125
57 On the St Francis $125
58 Still life $135
59 Logging $135
60 Winter effect
1919 73 Logging $200
74 The red cariole $200 (MBAM)
75 Sunlight in the woods $200
76 Frosty morning $200
77 Ploughing $200
78 Gray morning $200
1920 41 Winter morning in the woods $300
42 Wind and wintery weather $350
43 Evening glow, winter $300
44 Wood cutter $300
1921 44 A heavy load uphill $400
45 L'habitant $450
46 Oxen and sunlight in the woods $500
47 Hauling cordwood, grey day $550
1922 46 Road through the woods $400
47 L'habitant $165
48 Spring morning at Melbourne, Que $450
49 The watering trough $350
1923 47 Drawing logs, winter $275
47a At Coress $300
48 Winter landscape $400
49 Coloured etching $75
1924 41 Cloud shadows, St Francis valley $700 (NGC)
42 Habitant winter sports $350
43 The coming of spring $350
44 Logging at Gore $350
1925 62 The silent woods $450
63 The last load $450
64 The golden valley $450
65 The edge of the woods $250
1926 20 Green and gold, Quebec $350
21 Logging, a heavy load $400
22 Logging, a March morning $150
1927 20 Un brin de causette $450
21 The hired man $450
22 Winter sun $450
23 Winter mist $250
1928 33 Hauling cordwood $500
1929 35 March morning $650 (listed 1967, Jessie Dow prize)
36 Road at Melbourne $450
1930 34 Near Baie St Paul $750
35 Wood interior $700
1931 48 Winter evening at Melbourne $750
49 Mud Brook bridge $400
50 Cloud shadows $750
1932 53 The rollway $700
54 A fine winter morning $550
55 The fortunate skier $450
56 Cross country $400
1933 45 Winter sun $600
46 Rollway $500
47 Noon $300
48 The edge of the wood $300
1934 63 Mademoiselle Y. J.
64 Road at Stukley $400
65-6 Nude study $300 each
1935 71 La danseuse Carlotta
72 March snow $500
73 Nude study $500
74 Blueberry Mountain, Melbourne $500
1936 Three studies of the dancer Carlotta 88-90
88 Balero
89 Rumba de Cuba
90 Cake walk
91 Shell flowers and porcelain $350
1937 58 Grey winter $500

59 Sunny winter $750
1938 31 Portrait of a dancer
1939 71 Nude study $500
72 The old cariole $500
1940 63 The road to Bedard's mill
64 Salmon Creek and Blueberry Mountain $500
65 Nude study $350
1941 38 Morin's barns $500
39 The pasture road $500
40 Gladioli $250
41 Petunias $250
1942 26 Winter evening at Gore $650
27 Firewood $500
28 Pulpwood $500
1943 34 Somewhere in Quebec $750
35 The sunlit valley $500
1944 19 Cordwood $500

COBURN, MALVINA SCHEEPERS (m Frederick Simpson Coburn)
b Belgium d 1933
addr: Richmond, Que, 1918. Upper Melbourne, Que, 1919-21; Montreal, 79 Mansfield St, 1922. Upper Melbourne, 1925. Montreal, c/o Edlington's Ltd, 146 Mansfield St, 1926
1918 Scheepers 1919-21
326 Chaumiere en Flanders $30
327 Roses $15
1919 306 Canal en Flanders $60
307 Shrine in Flanders $50
308 Footbridge in Holland $50
309 Chaumiere en Flanders $50
310 Petite maison en Flanders $30
311 Milking time, Flanders $50
1920 242 Intérieur Flamand $75
243 Sheepfold $100
244-5 Landscape, Holland $8 each
1921 247 Old Flemish interior $125
248 The sheepfold, Belgian camp $725
249 Winter in Flanders $125
250 Milking time, Flanders $125
1922 50 Red roofs, Walchren $125
51 Bergerie, Flanders $125
52 Crepuscule $75
53 Rentree du troupeau $175
1925 66 Blue evening $100
67 Derniers rayons $125
68 Startled $100
69 Potato gathering $100
1926 23 The mill $150

COCHAND, PIERRE-HENRI
27 Apr 1924, Ste Marguerite, Que NGC
addr: Ste Marguerite , Que, 1949-52
1949 117 Sand dunes, Agunquit, Me wc $50
1950 57 On dry land wc $60
58 The Alvan T. Fuller wc $60
1951 51 Spring thaw wc $60
52 Rivière aux Mulets wc $75
1952 57 Rue Champlain wc $60

COCHRANE, BERTHA L.
fl 1891-1915 AAA1900 H
addr: Hillhurst, Que, 1891-1903. Montreal: 37 Metcalfe St, 1905; 74 Hutchison St, 1906; Montreal, 1908; 265 University St, 1909; 59 Park Ave, 1910; 83 Sherbrooke St W, 1912-14; 22 Sherbrooke St W, 1915
1891 25 Study of daffodils $12
1892 24 Sweet violets $15
25 Roses $10
1894 34 Roses $10
1895 26 Still life $10
1897 150 Interior wc $15
151 Iceland poppies wc
1898 139 A dull day, North Hatley wc $10
1900 124 October wc $5
125 Across Lake Massawippi wc $6
1901 119 A corner wc $5
120 A quiet spot wc $5
1903 160 On the road to Mt Mansfield wc $20
161 My neighbour's back door wc $20
1905 30 Sketch of pasture
31 Towards evening
1906 35 Little French Street, St Andrews $20
36 At St Andrews $15
37 On the North River, St Andrews $15
Church of St John the Evangelist pastels 206-9
206 Interior $20
207 The lecturn $20
208 Side aisle $15
1908 45 Frances $40
46 Near the Salute, Venice
1909 85 Amy $40
86 Resting $45
1910 78 A morning walk $25

79 The little green house on the hill $50
80 At Phillipsburgh etch $5
81 Venetian canal etch $5
1912 79 Three sketches at Beaupré $5 each
1913 71 Summer $20
72 Interior St Matthew's Church, Quebec $30
73 Sketch at Senneville $10
74 Sketch $10
1914 74-5 Cottage at Runswick, Yorkshire $40 each
76 At Runswick, Yorkshire $30
77 View from the Palatine Hill, Rome $30
1915 65 Sketch
66 Runswick Bay, Yorkshire, Eng

COCHRANE, JOSEPHINE G. Amer
B WWA40
addr: Baltimore, Md, 213 W Monument St, 1912-16
1912 80 Evening $35
1915 67 The Blue Madonna, Bruges $25
68 Our windmill
1916 48 The Quebec Bridge $15

COCHRANE, K. (Miss)
addr: Montreal, 88 Crescent St, 1910. Brockville, Ont, 32 St Andrew St, 1913. Westmount, 4 Windsor Ave, 1922
1910 82 General store, Hudson wc $8
1913 75 Old courtyard, Saint Servan, Brittany wc $10
1922 54 Corner of Beaver Hall Hill and Dorchester Street wc $25

COCKBURN, JEAN see MUNRO, JEAN

COGENHOPE, P. DE GRAAF
addr: Montreal, 1441 Mackay St
1945 50 Zagreb market $100

COLBECK, ELVA
addr: Montreal, 249 Girouard Ave, 1924-5
1924 353 Cake plate enamels
354 Olive dish
1925 315 China bowl $35

COLDREY, CHARLES C.
addr: Montreal: 1908; 62A City Councillors St, 1909; 84 Cathcart St, 1910; 14 Cathcart St, 1911; 44 Victoria St, 1915-16
1908 47 The work shop $15
1909 87 Study of a head $10
88 Girl reading $20
1910 83 Portrait of a man
1911 64 Study of a child
1915 69 Study of an old man
1916 49 Boat in ice $75
50 The market $125

COLE, FLORENCE see TRENHOLME, FLORENCE

COLEMAN, ARTHUR PHILEMON
4 Apr 1852, Lachute, Que 26 Feb 1939, Toronto CWW38 H Mo98/12
1881 67 Study of rocks, Tadousac wc
70 A grey evening on the Otonabee wc
84 Des Arables Rapids, upper Ottawa wc

COLES, DOROTHY RHYNAS
addr: Montreal, 174 Jeanne Mance St, 1916-27; 3466 Mance St, 1928-37
1916 51 Joan and Macgregor b&w
52 Phyllis b&w
53 Sketch b&w
54 My old friend b&w
1917 70 A Brittany peasant $35
71 Mistress Joan $30
72 J.C.A. Heriot, Esq b&w $10
73 La grand'mère
74-5 Portrait sketch $5 each
1918 61 The quay $15
62 Lake Memphremagog $15
63 Sergt Blair Bell, sketch b&w $10
64 A V.A.D, sketch b&w $10
1919 79 Mrs Clement Coles
80 Frank Houghton, Esq, sketch b&w
81 W. Chase Thompson, Esq b&w
82 Mrs Thomas R. Jones b&w
1921 48 Lorna
292 Phyllis plaster
1923 248 Alice bust
1925 70 Portrait
71 Athol Brae, Port Credit
72 Pine tree, Port Credit
1926 24 Portrait
1927 24 Brittany net menders
25 Low tide, Concarneau

26 Forio d'Ischia, Italy
27 Forio d'Ischia, sketch
1928 34 Portrait
35 Mary
36 The three sisters, Percé $35
1929 37 Elizabeth pastel
1930 36 Mary and Bingo pastel
37 Peter pastel
261 Forio, d'Ischia wd cut $7
262 Ivry wd cut $6
263 A snowy day lino cut $5
264 Wood fairies lino cut $5
304 Clement Coles, Esq plaster
1931 371-2 Church of St Andrew and St Paul, interior I and II charcl
1932 375 Christmas messengers wd cut $5
376 Sea-horse lino cut $3
461 Gordon plaster
1933 509 Colin plaster
1934 489 Rev F. Scott Mackenzie, MA DD plaster
1936 525 Swan pool Falmouth, Eng col wd cut $10
1937 60 Ivry North

COLLETTE, CLAUDE ROBERT
28 Mar 1919, Montreal
addr: Montreal, 1871 Fleury St
1954 26 Le reniement de Pierre $250

COLLEY, DOROTHY see CARTER, DOROTHY

COLLIER, ALAN CASWELL
19 Mar 1911, Toronto ACO CC1 CWW84 IO M NGC TB3 WWA84
addr: Toronto, 115 Brooke Ave, 1954-60
1954 27 Ore car on the 2875, Delnite Mine $300 (NGC)
1955 22 Winter mood, Lake Ontario $250
1960 22 Navigation markers, Dingwall, Cape Breton $450

COLLINS, JOHN ALTON
7 Oct 1917, Washington, D.C. CWW82
addr: Hampstead, Que, 5629 Queen Mary Rd, 1940-50. Valois, Que, 63 Elmwood Ave, 1951-55; Valois, 1967
1940 66 Dredging the channel wc $25
1941 42 Rain at Snowdon wc $35
43 Westmount Station wc $35
1942 29 Grandstand managers wc $35
30 Street car stop wc $35
1943 36 On leave wc $50
37 Scattered showers wc $50
38 Between rounds wc $50
1944 20 Under the bridge wc $50
21 Barber shop wc $50
1945 51 St James Cathedral wc $75
52 The car stop wc $75
1946 43 Early snow wc $75
44 January thaw wc $75 (1967-15 29 x 20 Jessie Dow prize. coll Ronalds-Reynolds & Co, Montreal)
1947 53 Training ship, Almirante, Saldanha wc $75
54 September shadows, Terrebonne, Que wc $75
1948 71 Morning at the market wc $75
1949 118 Snow on St Antoine St wc $75
1950 59 November freeze-up wc $75
60 Rainy road, Tadousac wc $75
1951 53 Evening rush wc $75
1952 58 In the locks wc $75
1953 53 Suburban station wc $75
1954 93 Snow on Victoria Square wc $75
1955 96 Empty house nm $75

COLLYER, NORA FRANCES ELIZABETH
7 Jun 1898, Montreal d 1979 M
addr: Montreal: 4029 Dorchester St W, 1919-46; 3400 Ridgewood Ave, Apt 29, 1949. Westmount, 442 Elm Ave, 1953-5
1919 83 Rollie
84 Sketch b&w
1920 45 Ethel $10
46 Playtime $15
1921 49 Illustration for 'The ancient mariner' $20
50 North Hatley, Que
51 Jean
52 Recess $50
1922 55 The yellow balloon $100
56 Daisy $150
1923 50 Kate $100
51 Portrait $75
1924 45 Village, Eastern Townships $200
46 After the first snow
1925 73 Foster, Que, sketch $20
74 Old house, Montreal $60
1927 28 Lisieux $100
266 Old church, Normandy red chalk $20
1930 265 Bermuda, sketch pen & ink $12
1931 51 Village $100

52 Katevale $20
53 Old church, Island of Orleans $20
1933 49 December thaw, Eastern Townships $125
50 The wooden bridge $100
51 Farm near Bolton Pass $20
1934 67 The North River $200
68 Eastern Townships farm $200
1935 75 Lake Massiwippi, Que $150
76 Brill church $20
1936 92 Back yards $75
93 June, Eastern Townships $150
94 Autumn, Eastern Townships $150
1937 61 White tulips $20
62-3 Cap à l'Aigle, Que $20, nfs
1938 33 Cyclamen $25
1939 73 The round barn $125
74 Lilies
1940 67 Lilies $35
68 St Etienne de Bolton, Que $100
69 Farm house, Cap à l'Aigle $100
1941 44 Farm near St Fidèle, Que $100
1942 31 Foster, Que $150
1943 39 Trafalgar Day $35
1946 45 The creek $50
1949 21 The window $150
1953 12 Golden apples $100
1955 23 Poppies $75

COLONNA, EDWARD (b Klonne, aka Eugène, and Edmond)
27 May 1862, Mulheim-am-Rhein, Germ
14 Oct 1948, Nice, France B H TB
addr: Montreal, 2464 St Catherine St, 1891
1889 Edward, 1889-91
109 A day's thaw wc $25
110 A green sky wc $25
111 Quebec wc $50
112 A clear sky wc $25
113 View in Quebec wc $30
114 Sunset effect wc $30
1891 26-34 Landscape
211 Smoking room interior des
212 Mosaic des
213 Mosaic glass window des

COLSON, FREDERICK
23 Jul 1854, Shedfield, Eng d 1924
CWW10 H
addr: Ottawa: 1905-16; 466 Besserer St, 1922
1905 146 October afternoon, Green Mountains wc $20
147 Cloudy day, Beaupré wc $15
1906 209 September evening after rain wc $30
210 The village mill, St Eustache wc $30
211 A mère wc $20
212 Habitant farm, St Eustache wc $30
1908 193 In old New England wc $30
194 A winding road wc $20
1909 90 A golden hilltop wc $25
91 Elmdale farm wc $25
1910 84 Crooked Willow farm wc
85 A distant shower wc
86 An old bridge wc
1911 65 Great Fontley Farm, Hampshire wc $15
66 Street corner, Bishop's Waltham wc $15
67 Old English inn yars wc $15
1912 81 A Vermont hillside wc $35
82 An old English mill wc $15
83 On the Little River, St Eustache wc $15
1913 76 In the Gatineau country wc $35
77 October, Rockcliffe Park, Ottawa wc $35
78 Droxford church, Hampshire, Eng wc $35
79 A bridge in Winchester wc $35
1914 78 On the Rideau River wc $15
79 Winter sketch, Ottawa wc $15
80 A country road wc $15
1915 70 The close of day wc $35
71 Evening in the Vermont hills wc $35
1916 55 A little garden in the city wc $35
1922 57 November afternoon, near Ottawa pastel $40

COLTHURST, GLADYS A. BULLER
addr: Montreal West
1915 72 Portrait study
73 Richard, son of R. Moffatt, Esq
74 Mother
75 Peter, son of P.S. Renford, Esq
76 Barbara, daughter of H. Maurice Esq
77 Playmate
78 Mrs John Richardson
79 Annie, daughter of F.S. Quick, Esq

COLVILLE, DAVID ALEXANDER
24 Aug 1920, Toronto AGO B CC1 CE
CWW84 L M NGC TB3 WWA84 Juror
addr: Sackville, N.B: Owens Museum of Fine Arts, 1940-1; Mount Allison University, 1942; Sackville, 1947; Sackville, P.O.Box 253, 1954-7
1940 70 The Atlantic coast $50
71 Weaving room $100
72 Still life $110
1941 45 Coastline $50
218 Head of a youth drwg $25
1942 32 Old woman $40
33 Art gallery $40
1947 55 Landscape with horses $175
56 Rocks at low tide wc $60
1954 94 Soldier and girl at station glazed temp $350
95 Man on veranda glazed temp $300
1956 87 Family and rain storm nm $600
88 Horse and train nm $450 (AGH)
1957 112 Cat on fence nm $45

COMBER, SYDNEY
29 Jan 1887, Brighton Eng 20 Oct 1961, Montreal CNS47
Montreal, 515-7 New Birks Bldg
1929 236 Elmhurst Dairy, Montreal $500
237 Ideal Bread Co, Hamilton $300

COMFORT, CHARLES FRASER
22 Jul 1900, Edinburgh AGO B CC2 CE
CWW82 EC M NGC TB3 WWA66 WWB72
addr: Toronto: 87 St Clair Ave E, 1927; 48 Cheritan Ave, 1931; 25 Severn St, 1939
1927 29 Quebec landscape $300
1931 54 Dreamer $600 (AGH)
1939 75 Pioneer survival $600 (NGC)

COMINES, C.
addr: Montreal, G.P.O.Box 34, 1956-8
1956 89 Journey nm
1958 53 The harbour nm

CONDE, KENT L. DE
addr: Outremont, 864 Bloomfield Ave, 1935-48
1935 77 Early snow wc $40
78 Late afternoon, Morin Heights wc $50
79 Farm house, Lachute wc $75
1936 117 Snow clad wc $100
118 Sunlit hills, Morin Heights wc $100
119 Evening shadows wc $75
120 The habitant house wc $45
1937 72 The pine grove, Rouge River wc $100
73 Farm house, Laurentian Mountains wc $35
1938 36 Laurentian Mountains, Huberdeau wc $85
37 Late afternoon near Lost River wc $35
1939 76 Zero weather near Huberdeau wc $100
77 Mid-afternoon, Huberdeau wc $100
1940 73 Summer days, Otter Lake wc $100
1943 40 Fall, Channeville wc $40
41 Après l'incendie, Lachute wc $40
42 The alley-way, Montreal wc $60
1945 53 Otter Lake wc $125
1946 46 Spring, Pointe-aux-Chênes wc $50
47 Old barn wc $50
48 The barn yard wc $50
1947 57 Winter vigil wc $150
1948 72 Morning mist wc $100

CONDER, STANLEY NESBITT
22 Jan 1924, Winnipeg
addr: Port Credit, Ont, 1580 Winterhaven Rd
1958 11 Still life, abstract $150

CONNAUGHTON, ALICE
addr: Montreal, 929 St Urbain St
1906 213 Still life wc $10

CONNELL, DOROTHY (m Herbert Connell)
addr: Montreal, 3821 Ridgevale Ave
1956 90 Peter nm

CONNER, RALPH
1895, Birkenhead, Eng 10 May 1951, Toronto
addr: Waterloo, Ont, c/o Deluxe Upholstery Co, Ltd, 1949-51
1949 22 Antiques $100
1951 54 Back yard wc $40

CONSIGLIO, FRANCO
15 May 1902 5 Dec 1970, Montreal
addr: Hampstead, Que, 68 Stratford Rd

1937 330-2 Residence, Hampstead (3)

CONSTANTINEAU, T.L. FLEURIMOND
27 Aug 1905, St Leonard de Port Maurice, Que 15 Mar 1981, Montreal
addr: Montreal: 2090 St Hubert St, 1932; 204 Jarry St, Apt 3, 1933-6; 6596 St Denis St, 1939-46
1932 T.L. Eurimond, 1932
57 Chantier $100
58 La coupe du bois $50
1933 52 Eglise Bonsecours $50
1934 69 La Croix du chemin $50
1935 80 Eglise St Jacques, ruines $25
1936 95 Le vieux traineau $25
96 Scène d'hiver $25
1939 78 Les champs dorés $75
79 Rue Craig, Montréal $75
1940 74 Champ de Mars, Montréal $150
75 Rue Berri, Montréal $75
1941 46 Duel aérien $100
1942 34 Rue Sherbrooke Ouest $75
1943 43 Labour d'automne $400
1945 54 Vielle maison Sault-aux-Récollets $125
55 Boulevard Lévesque, Pont Viau $125
1946 49 Scène d'hiver $75
50 Paysage de Rawdon $75

CONTANT, EDGAR
addr: Montreal, 1922 St Denis St
1922 62 M. B.

CONTANT, GABRIEL YVES GERARD
4 Jan 1931, Joliette, Qué
addr: Montréal: 1617 rue Cartier, 1953-4; 1809 est rue Sherbrooke, 1960
1953 13 Paysage, St Donat $25
1954 28 Jeune fille dans un intérieur $75
1960 23 Carnaval chinois $75

CONTENT, RENE
addr: Montreal, 6762 Somerled Ave
1951 10 Le vieux Montmartre $75

COOK, ANNE
addr: Westmount, 438 Strathcona Ave
1957 113 The sea nm

COOKE, ARTHUR J.
addr: Montreal, 8 Lincoln Ave, 1903
1888 65 Kittens $30
1903 deceased (Mrs Arthur J. Cook)
162 Beyond bonds wc

COOKE, EDWY FRANCIS
10 Mar 1926, Toronto AGO IO M WWA80
addr: Toronto, 190 Howard Ave, 1948-52
1948 73 Organization with light gouache $90
1950 61 Ogdensburg Junction, N.Y. wc $125
1951 55 Trains, tracks and tower wc $75
122 Polyphemus gouache $150
1952 94 Urban landscape $250

COOMBS, EDITH GRACE (m James Sharp Lawson)
22 Dec 1890, Hamilton, Ont CCI CNS36 CWW73 M WWA66
addr: Toronto: 648 Ontario St, 1931; 64 Grenville St, Studio 3, 1935-41
1931 55 The sky woman, from Wyandot myths of creation $750
56 Dogwood and trilliums wc $75
57 Cardinal flowers wc $75
373 Head of a doe drwg $20
1935 81 My garden gate wc $60
82 On the Magnetawan River wc $45
1940 76 May morning wc $60
1941 47 Jacks wc $70

COONAN, GERALDINE EMILY
30 May 1885 - 23 Jun 1971, Montreal NGC
addr: Montreal: 1908; 13 Farm St, 1909-26; 627 Farm St, 1930-3
1908 195 A sketch crayon
1909 89 Sketch $30
1910 87 Evelina, 1830 $50
88 Study $25
89 The duck pond $25
90 Play $25
1911 68, 72 Sketch $15 each
69 Leaving the vestry $35
70 The communicants $35
71 The study $15
1912 84 The boat
85 Wading
86 First communion (MBAM)
87 Shell gatherers
88 Children and goats
89 Portrait
90 Children on seashore
1913 80 Summer day $100
81 Portrait $75

1914 81 La marquise #200
82 The communicant $200
83 The old gown $200
84 Girl with a fan $150
1915 80 Two Spanish girls $200
81 The dance $225
1916 56 Italian girls $175
57 The circus $125
58 Sketch $25
1917 76 The concert $300
77 The procession $250
78 Sketch $20
1918 65 Popcorn seller $150
1919 85 The red basket $150
86 The wharf $150
87 The fair $150
88 The island wharf $30
1920 47 Spanish dancer $150
48 Woman knitting $250
49 Girl and cat $150
50 Sault-au-Récollet $150
1922 58 Ponte Vecchio, Florence $300 (NGC)
59 Gate in Florence $65
60 Square in Venice $40
61 Gate in Rome $65
1923 52 Portrait $250
53 Girl in dotted dress $300
1924 47 Carmelita $300
48 Old bridge in Florence $45
1926 25 Santa Croce, Florence $350
1930 38 The blue armchair $300
1933 53 The Chinese kimono $300

COOPER, ALICE
addr: Hamilton, Ont, 51 Fairleigh Ave N, 1942-3
1942 35 Little drum major qc $75
1943 44 In my mirror wc

COOPER, ALICE MARY CHARLTON (Mrs)
1870, Durham, Eng
addr: Toronto, 15 Avenue Rd, 1910-18
1910 91 In Perthshire $40
92 Autumn trees, Toronto $40
1918 66 Peonies $50

COOPER, ANTHONY
addr: Hamilton, Ont, 156 Edgemont St S
1934 70 Chinese girl $115

COOPER, JEAN JACQUES
17 May 1924, Nancy, France
addr: Toronto, 40 Avenue Rd
1951 11 Bouquet printemps $50

COOPER, W. C.
addr: Montreal, 91 Ontario St W
1924 49 Weston Church, Norfolk wc $15
50 Tolland, Cornwall wc $15

COPE, DOROTHY WALPOLE STEVENS (m Clive A. Cope)
5 Sep 1915, Vancouver CWW73 M WWA76
addr: West Vancouver, 840 Evelyn Dr, 1958-60
1958 54 Objects in a vertical pink space nm $35
55 Harsh orange at varying depths nm $75
1960 139 Three groups in warm colours nm $90

COPPOLD, LESLIE GEORGE MURRAY
22 Jun 1914, Montreal
addr: Montreal: 3405 Grand Blve, 1939; 4309 Beaconsfield Ave, 1943-7; 4877 Patricia Ave, 1949-52
1939 80 Wagon wc
81 Trees wc
1943 45 Tree wc
46 Shrine wc $200
47 Village wc $200
48 Wagon wc $200
1944 22 Road wc $200
23 Girl wc
24 Birch wc $60
1945 56 Caughnawaga wc $300
57 St Remi $250
58 Oven wc $200
1946 51 Bridge wc $175
52 Well $250
1947 58 Barrel wc $175
59 Wagons wc $275
60 Rain wc
1949 119 Log, Mont Tremblant wc $200
120 Ste Lucie de Doncaster wc $300
1950 62 Tree and silo wc $350
63 Mountain wc $225
1952 9 The Asia $300

CORBEIL, WILFRED, Père, Clerc de St Viateur
20 Mar 1893, St Lin, Que d 1979
addr: Joliette, Que, Séminaire, 1920-22. Outremont, 1145 St Viateur St, 1926-7. Joliette, Séminaire, 1933-46

1920 51 L'Acropole drwg
1922 361 Direction Provinciale des Clerc de Saint Viateur wc
362 La salle d'entrée, 'hall' wc
1926 26 L'enfant à l'album pastel
1927 267 La vieille maison drwg
1933 54 La cour au Séminaire de Joliette gouache
55 La chapelle, Joliette gouache
1935 83 La tribune de l'orgue gouache
1936 97 Le vieux clocher, Séminaire de Joliette gouache
98 Le pavilion du S. Coeur Séminaire de Joliette gouache
1940 317 Le Noviciat des Clercs de St Viateur, à Joliette
1941 262 Le Noviciat de Joliette 3 photos, architecture
1943 49 Cours enneigées gouache
1945 59 La cabane à sucre wc
60 Rue sous la neige wc $60
1946 53 Cabane à sucre gouache $150
54 Grange rouge gouache $100

CORBETT, HELENA MAE
6 Sep 1885, Windsor, N Dakota
addr: Toronto, 666 Spadina Ave
1928 37 Marine $40

CORBOLD, CAROLINE (Mrs)
addr: Montreal, 264 Hospital St
1933 56 Blue hyacinthe $35

CORMIER, ERNEST
5 Dec 1885 - 1 Jan 1980, Montreal
CE CNS36 CWW73 NGC Juror
addr: Montreal: 1908; 52 Sherbrooke St W, 1923-4; 630 St Urbain St, 1925; 175 Mansfield St, 1927; 2039 Mansfield St, 1928-33; Montreal, 1967
1908 48 Panneau dec
49 Stil life
1923 54 Fontaine à la Villa Madama, Rome
249 Reveil wax
1924 51-2 Barques de pêche à Pescara wc
307 Etude de tête sculp
1925 75 Colonnade de Trianon à Versailles, sketches A,B,C wc
1927 30 Pergole à Ravello wc
31 Vieux pont à Torcello wc
32 Fontaine à Viterbe wc
33 Fontaine du Jardin Borghese à Rome wc (1967-16, Jessie Dow prize)
1928 220 Université de Montréal photo de la maquette
221 Le Temple de Pestum wc
222 La Piazetta à Venise wc
223 St Marc à Venise wc
1929 38 Chioggia wc
39 Albano wc
40 Ravello wc (listed 1967, Jessie Dow prize)
238 Eglise St Ambroise
239 Ecole Ste Julienne Falconieri
1930 39-40 Jardin de l'Alhambra à Grenade 39 wc, 40 oil
41 Pont en Espagne wc
1931 58 Interieur Chapelle Chigi à Santa Maria del Popolo à Rome wc
59 Piazza del Popolo à Rome wc
60-1 Tolède wc
1932 59 Fontaine à Naples wc
60 Jardine Boboli à Florence wc
61 Generalife à Viterbe wc
62 Fontaine à Viterbe wc
1933 57 Temple of Jupiter at Pestum wc
58 La Piazetta, Venice wc
59 Monte Casino wc
60 Nemi wc
see also Amos, L.A. 1927

CORNELIUS, LOUISE
addr: Halifax, 39 Victoria Rd
1892 163 English primroses wc $12
164 Chinese primroses wc

CORNU, SOPHIE (Mde)
addr: Montreal, 670 Sherbrooke St W, 1913-17
1913 82 Vieux jardin, Nice wc
83 L'Allée de la Méditation wc
1914 85 Cyprès de St Cassien wc $30
86 Bord de la Cagne wc $35
1915 82 Au pied des Alpes, Vaudoises $20
1917 79 Environs de Nice wc
80 Une échappée sur Cannes

CORRIVEAU, JEANNE D'ARC
14 Mar 1931, Kingsey Falls, Qué
addr: Québec
1968 tapisserie, 46-7
46 Bleu, blanc, rouge 48 x 48 $1,000

47 Terre des hommes 72 x 96 $1,800
cartons de tapisseries 48-9
48 Abstraction No 2 19 3/4 x 16 7/8
$200
49 Abstraction No 1 20 x 25 3/4 $200

COSGROVE, STANLEY MOREL
23 Dec 1911, Montreal AGO CC2 CE M NGC WWA84 Juror
addr: Montreal: 5194 Mountain Sights Ave, 1936-9; c/o Dominion Gallery, Sherbrooke St W, 1949: 4994 Queen Mary Rd, Apt 10, 1950; Dominion Gallery, 1956; 2075 Crescent St, 1960; 1438 Sherbrooke St W, 1964
1936 99 Eileen
1937 64 Winter, near Montreal $45
65 Gaspé coast
66 On the beach, St Georges, Gaspé $45
1939 82 Trees $50
83 Leo
1949 23 Head
1950 107 Winter 1950 oil on gesso
108 Woman with brown dress
1956 12 Nature morte au pot $900
1960 140 Mother and child n, $300
1964 15 Chemin de halage $750 (hallage mispr)

COSTICO, G. B.
addr: Montreal, 255 Bleury St
1917 81 Portrait $350
82 Unprotected $500

COTE, THERESE TARDIF
13 May 1926, Lachine
addr: Longueuil, Qué, 74 ave Leopold
1959 48 Les oiseaux soapstone $200
49 Torso soapstone $100

COTTINGHAM, MURIEL HARTLEY (m W. Randolph Cottingham)
15 Jun 1889, Winnipeg
addr: Winnipeg, 220 Wellington Cr
1932 63 Maryland bridge wc $40
64 St Andrews pastel $25

COTTON, JOHN WESLEY
29 Oct 1869, n Dundas, Ont 24 Nov 1931, Toronto AAA29 AGO
addr: Toronto, 327 Huron St
1913 John N mispr
88 On Hampstead Heath aqua $20
89 Harbor, St Ives, Cornwall etch $15
90 The Belfry, Bruges etch $8
91 Old bridge, Chester etch $15

COUGHTRY, JOHN GRAHAM
8 Jun 1931, St Lambert, Que AGO CCI CE IO M NGC WWA84
addr: Toronto: 235 Spadina Ave, 1957; 7 Sultan St, 1958; Isaacs Galleries, 832 Yonge St, 1963-5. Ibiza, Spain, Santa Eulalia del Rio, 1964. Toronto, Isaacs Galleries, 1965; Toronto, 1967
1957 25 Daffodils
1958 12 Afternoon interior (listed 1967, Jessie Dow prize)
1963 15 Two figures $1,500
16 Drawing for myth series V $350
1964 16 Two figures XIV $1,700
1965 4 Two figure series XVIII $1,700
1967 17 Dark room 72 x 48 (Canadian Industries Ltd, Montreal)

COULOURIDES, DEMETRIUS
addr: Montreal, 10 St James St W
1946 275 Etude plaster

COULSON, HARRY A.
addr: Montreal, 64A City Councillors St (Harry W. in catalogue addr list)
1894 246-7 Decorated vase
248 Rose plate
1897 deceased (R.B. Coulson, 394 Lansdowne Ave, Westmount)
25 Portrait, on porcelain

COULSON, SAMUEL E. (Mrs)
addr: Montreal, 81 Mansfield St
1895 234 Tea caddy
235 Photo frame

COURTENAY, LYSLE CAMERON
addr: Ottawa, 189 Metcalfe St
1923 55 A hill at Wakefield, Que $35
56 Winter day in the Gatineau, Que $35

COURTICE, RODY KENNY HAMMOND (m Andrew Roy Courtice)
30 Aug 1895, Renfrew, Ont 6 Dec 1973, Toronto AGO CWW70 M WWA73
addr: Markham, Ont, RR1
1939 84 Grandiflora blanca $50

392 Paul drwg

COUSINEAU, ALFRED
addr: Montreal, 2438 St Andre St
1913 92 Portrait de l'auteur

COUTU, GILLES ULRIC HUBERT
3 Nov 1933, Montreal
addr: Montreal, 6514 Drolet St
1963 96 Tête bronze $400

COUTURIER, PHILIBERT LEON French
26 May 1823, Chalon sur Sâone, France
26/29 Nov 1901, St Quentin, France B TB
addr: Paris, France
1898 19 Ducks and ducklings $60
20 Corner of a farm yard $60

COVERLY-PRICE, A. VICTOR Eng
31 Jan 1901, Winchester, Eng DBA RA WBA WWB82
addr: Ottawa, Earnscliffe, office of United Kingdom High Commissioner
1935 84 In an Andean village, Peru wc $100
85 Mosque by moonlight, Egypt wc $100

COVICY, SYBIL
addr: Montreal, 4841 Hutchison St
1938 34 Ski boots pastel $10

COWAN, ELEANOR L.
addr: Westmount, 1 Bellevue Ave
1919 414 Jardiniere
415 Nut bowl
416 Vase
417 Pair of candlesticks
418 Compote
Hon mention

COX, ALFRED ARTHUR
23 Feb 1860, Oxford, Eng 28 Nov 1944, Souldern, Eng
addr: Montreal: office, 61 Temple Bldg, St James St, 1891-5, 1898-1901; 112 Mansfield St, 1909; residence, 83 Union Ave, 1897; 118 Union Ave, 1898-1900; 48 Union Ave, 1903; 118 Union Ave, 1905-9
1894 179 The old Westgate, Conterbury wc
1895 153 The bell tower, Canterbury Cathedral wc $25
154 On the north shore, Lake Superior wc $20
155 A bit of Mount Royal wc $20
1897 152 A view from King's Bridge, Canterbury wc
153 A view from Castel des Monts, St Agathe wc
1898 140 Après une bourrasque de neige wc
1900 126 The Citabel, Quebec, from the St Lawrence wc $10
127 Kent Gate, Quebec wc $10
128 The cupola, Hotel Dieu, Montreal wc $10
1903 163 St John's Gate wc $15
164 St Lawrence, near Verchères wc $15
1905 32 The River Swale, Yorkshire $75
33 The River Wye, near Ross $100
34 Kings Mills, Castle Donington, Leicester $75
35 Muskoka sunset $50
148 Allan Wharf, Quebec wc $30
1906 38 The ravine pool $150
39 After rain, Swaledale $100
40 A Derbushire grouse moor $150
41 Song of the surf $100
42 A very dry breakfast $50
214 Montmorency Falls, from below wc $25
215 Radcliffe Library, Oxford wc $45
1908 50 Expectancy $30
1909 92 On the alert $40
93 A bit of Burrard Inlet wc $20
94 On the south shore, Bermuda wc $25
1895 Cox & Amos
216 Block of stores and dwellings, St Catherine St and Greene Ave
217 Block of residences, Hillside Ave
218 Interior, new baptistery, Church of St John the Evangelist prelim sketch
1898 214 St Luke's Church, Waterloo Que, new tower and spire
215 Club house, Montreal Hunt Club des
216 St Matthias Church, Westmount selected des
1900 179 Church of the Advent, Westmount, reredos des
1901 196 St Peter's Church, Sherbrooke reredos, altar table sketch

1909 408 New Eastern Townships Bank building

COX, ARTHUR W.
1840, England Aug 1917, Nottingham, Eng H TB W78
addr: Toronto, 170 Roxborough Ave, 1891-2; 39 Huntley St, 1894
1881 5 After the storm, Muskoka
1883 99 Departing day
101 There is a rapture on the lonely shore
150 Where the deer drink
1885 5 A Canadian valley, near Ancaster
28 Father's boat
41 The trysting tree, head of Drummond Street
43 A Muskoka solitude
81 Peace
87 Sunset, Long Lake, Muskoka
89 Dawn
92 Twilight, Mount Orford, Que
108 Lake St Louis from the pines, Mount Royal wc
137 A cottage home of Canada wc
1888 54 The ford, Androscoggin River, West Bathel $75
1891 35 The Silurian Gates of Elora $500
1892 31 The Vale of Gilead $50
1894 41 When the tide is out

COX, DIANA W.
addr: Westmount, 530 Mount Pleasant Ave
1936 100 Study of zinnias $25

COX, EDWIN JAMES
1850, Montreal c 1930 H
addr: Montreal: 1908-10; 114 St François Xavier St, 1913-17; Montreal, 1914-18; 10 Victoria St, 1926-8; 1420 Victoria St, 1929
1908 310 Illuminated address
311 Engrossed letter of condolence
1910 384-5 Illuminated work specimens
1913 93 Emblazoned coat of arms wc
94 Illuminated address wc
1914 443 Illuminated address
1915 388 Illuminated work
1916 326-7 Illuminated honour roll
1917 372 Illuminated work wc
1918 389 Illuminated address
1926 27-8 Illuminated address wc
29 Quebec wc
1927 34-5 Illuminated address wc
1928 38 Illuminated minutes wc
291 Bank of Montreal steel engr
292 Canadian Bank of Commerce steel engr
1929 302 Book plates engr
303 Illuminated text

COX, EDYTHE C.
addr: Montreal, 530 Mount Pleasant Ave, 1936-40
1936 101 Trilliums in white bowl wc $20
102 Gaillardias wc $20
1937 67 Old barn $30
68 The dead trees $30
1939 85 Quebec farm house $25
1940 77 Portrait
78 Nue couchée $100
79 La petite maison à la campagne $25
80 Woods at Shawinigan Falls, winter $30

COX, ELFORD BRADLEY
16 Jul 1914, Botha, Alta AGO CC2 IO M WWA62
addr: Toronto, Upper Canada College, 1948-9
1948 114 The heavenly harp walnut $350
115 Slender torso cedar $200
1949 170 Torso cedar $75

COX, FANNIE
addr: Canterbury, Hambledown, Eng
1894 42 Landscape with sheep $100
43 Landscape with cattle $100

CRABTREE, CHARLES ARCHIBALD
c 1880-1943
addr: Montreal, 415 Dorchester St, 1909. Ottawa: Rockcliffe, 1925; 53 McKinnon Rd, Rockcliffe, 1928
1909 95 The garden $50
1925 76 The old garden wc $75
1928 39 Wood fringe pastel $20
40 Old garden pastel $20

CRABTREE, ELVINA KENNEDY GREENHAM (m Charles Archibald Crabtree)
1878, London, Eng d 1943
addr: Westmount: 374 Greene Ave, 1906; 218 Greene Ave, 1909. Ottawa: 53 Mc-

McKinnon Rd, Rockcliffe, 1925-8; 95 McKinnon Rd, Rockcliffe, 1931-3
1906 Greenham, 1906-9
77 A soldier $45
308 A study b&w
1909 155 Yellow heads $50
1925 77 A jolly skier $150
1926 30 Peonies $50
31 Pensive wc $35
1928 41 A studio supper $60
1931 62 Patricia
1933 61 Farm in a valley $40

CRABTREE, GRAHAM
addr: Ottawa, 559 Langs Road
1964 17 Nude

CRABTREE, JOHN G.
b Ottawa
addr: Ottawa, 95 McKinnon Rd, Rockcliffe, 1931-2
1932 65 Still life with bottles $100
1933 62 Man in a yellow hat $50
63 Landscape $25

CRAGG, MONA
addr: Town of Mount Royal, Que, 37 Wicksteed Rd, 1933-6
1933 64 St Paul Street, Montreal $20
1934 71 Grey day, Terrebonne $50
1935 399 Christmas card des drwg $20
1936 103 Christmas paper des wc $25

CRANSTON, DULCIE BELLA (m Guy R.L. Potter)
addr: Ottawa, 21 Dalbousie St, 1925-7
1925 78 Still life $25
1927 Potter
145 Still life $30

CRANSTON, HOY
addr: Ottawa, 266 Flora St
1919 89 German kultur

CRAWFORD, ADELINE B. (m David Crawford)
addr: Montreal: 69 McGill College Ave, 1895-1906; Montreal, 1908
1895 236 Pitcher, rococo des
237 Spoon holder
238 Fruit dish, chrysanthemums
239 Pair of candlesticks
240 Vase blue underglaze
241 Bonbon dish
242 Cup & saucer
243 Fruit dish
1898 248 Plate, scene on Bow River, Rockies
249-50 Cup & saucer
1900 209 Bird plaque $20
210 Blackberry plaque $10
211 Vase $10
212 Box $5
213 Fair lady min $5
214-15 Miniature, jewelled $10 each
216 Miniature framed $7
217 Biscuit jar
1903 279 Large tankard
280 Vase lustre & gold
281 Vase lustre & bronze
1905 287 Cup & saucer green lustre & bronze
288 Vase, stork lustre & bronze
289 Vase, narcissus
290 Card receiver
291 Salad bowl, Chinese des
1906 395 Large loving cup, Dutch group
396 Cake plate
397 Tea plate
398 Cup & Saucer, part of set
399 Cup & saucer pink & green, conventional des
1908 290 Miniatures gold mounted pair, framed
368 Plaque, girl with red hair
369 Cream & sugar

CRAWFORD, EUGENIA M.
addr: Montreal: 93 Durocher St, 1891; 23A University St, 1892
1886 Crawford, Miss
135 A study from a bronze
1889 Eugenia N, 1889
115 Old barn, Baie St Paul wc $12
116 In the woods, Les Eboulements wc $25
1891 158 Where the rushes grow, Baie St Paul wc $20
1892 165 Our barn wc $10

CRAWFORD, FLORENCE A.
addr: Westmount, 4548 St Catherine St, 1911-12. Montreal, 979 Tupper St, 1913-14
1911 318 Plate
319 Vase
320 Bowl
1912 442 Bowl $6
443 Stein $8

444 Sherbet cup & saucer
445 Tea set, 3 pieces
1913 462 Blue matt vase
463 Biscuit jar
1914 492 Coffee cup & saucer

CRAWFORD, JULIA TILLEY
18 Apr 1896, Kingston, N.B. 8 Jan 1968, Saint John, N.B. AGO M WWA66
addr: Saint John: Queen Square Apts, 1936-42; 265 Charlotte St, 1943
1936 104 Just Maria wc
1941 48 On the window sill $85
1942 36 Back to the land $60
1943 50 B portrait $100

CRAWLEY, ALICE MARIAN FINNIE (Mrs)
14 Mar 1915, Peterborough, Ont
addr: St Catharines, Ont, 53 Lowell Ave
1956 13 Winter $80
14 Church $50

CRESSWELL, WILLIAM NICHOL
1822, Devon, Eng 1888, n Seaforth, Ont AGO H NGC W78
addr: Seaforth
1880 128 The last of the brig, Mount Desert, Maine wc (NGC)

CREVECOEUR, JEANNE DE
addr: Montreal: 168A Mansfield St, 1909-11 (163A, 1909, mispr); Fraser Institute, 1913-15; 9 St Matthew St, 1916-18; 857 Oxenden Ave, 1923-5
1909 96 Sketch
97 Sketch b&w
1910 103 Sketch
104 Sketch pastel $10
105 Suzanne pastel $10
106 Gretchen pastel $10
1911 78 Study pastel
79-81 Sketch pastel $15, $15, $10
1913 111 M C.E. Bonin, Consul Général de France pastel
112 Fantasie pastel $40
113 Child's head pastel $60
114 Study pastel $40
1915 83 Quaker girl pastel $40
84 Sketch pastel $25
85 Sketch pastel
1916 80 Fine feathers
1918 84 Study pastel $50
85 Miss R.G. pastel
86 Miss M, sketch pastel
87 V.A.D. pastel $25
88 Study pastel $50
1923 57 Portrait pastel
58 Cinderella pastel $50
1924 68 Study of a child, Jane
69 The sleeping beauty pastel
1925 84 Russian peasant girl $100

CRIPPS, W. H.
addr: Drummondville, Que, c/o Dennison Mfg Co, 1937-40. Montreal, No 1, Wireless School, Queen Mary Rd, 1942. St Hubert, Que, Flying Squadron, RCAF, 1943. Ulverton, Que, 1947
1937 lino cut 1937-43
394 Street singers $12
395 Skaters $12
396 Skier $10
1940 352 Saturday afternoon $8
353 2.45 on time $12
1942 L/Ac RCAF
196 Lobsterman $10
197 Spring at Lakeside $10
1943 Cpl RCAF
224 Herald of spring
1947 300 October wd cut $15

CRIST, LELA GURNEE
15 Dec 1895, Sheet Harbour, N.S.
addr: Halifax, 76 Morris St
1934 72 Madonna min $18
73 Helen Rose min
74 Lady of the 70's min

CROCKART, JAMES BISSET
19 Jul 1885, Stirling, Scot 19 Apr 1974, Huntington, Que
addr: 314 Dorchester St W
1917 83 After rain $50
84 Portrait
port: by Thomas Reid Macdonald 1936-262
see also Archibald, John Smith 1925-293

CROCKER, JAMES A. SYDNEY
d 1886 H
1881 77 Carlists skirmishing wc
80 Spanish muleteer wc

CROMBIE, MAUREEN
addr: Montreal, 1001 Sherbrooke St W
1939 393 Abdominal operation drwg

CROMPTON, MABEL ANN ELIZABETH
fl 1901-31 DBA RA TB2 WWB34
addr: Winnipeg, 315 Mountain Ave, 1929. Hebden Bridge, Yorkshire, Eng, Hollins House, 1931
1929 41 Case of miniatures A-Victory, B-Nesta, C-Jane $100 each
1931 63 Nesta min $100
64 Diana min $100
65 His first ride min $100

CROOKER, ISABELLE P.
addr: Montreal, Chateau Apts, 1321 Sherbrooke St W, 1939-40
1939 86 Junior
87 Bobbie
88 Miss Mary Hampton Lee $200
89 Old timer $150
1940 81 Dinah $25

CROOKS, EVELYN JEAN LAMONT (Mrs)
25 Sep 1904, Coalfields, Sask
addr: London, Ont, 72 Peter St
1958 13 Dos mujeres

CROSS, FREDERICK GEORGE
2 Sep 1881, Exeter, Devon, Eng 8 Sep 1941, Lethbridge, Alta M
addr: Brooks, Alta, 1932-5
1932 66 Evening on the range wc $50
1935 86 Wild geese wc $50

CROSS, HELEN see O'MANSKY, HELEN

CROSSEN, SONIA ST BARBE (m Austin U. Sargent)
8 Nov 1930, Montreal
addr: Westmount, 543 Roslyn Ave, 1952-5. Montreal, 3432 Peel St, Apt 201, 1960
1952 131 Abstraction scratch board
1955 97 Portrait $15 per print
1960 Sargent
107 Self portrait - Italy $250
108 Portrait of a man $200

CROSSLEY, T. LINSEY
c 1878 22 Apr 1973, Guelph, Ont
addr: Valleyfield, Que, c/o Defence Industries Ltd
1946 55 Changing shift, nitro wc $150

CROSTHWAIT, IRWIN LELAND (BUD)
24 Jun 1914, Creston, B.C.
addr: Dorval, Que, 11 Clement Ave, 1944. Ottawa. 185 Sparks St, 1945; Dorval, 11 Clement Ave, 1946.Menzonio (6671) Ticino, Switz, 1967
1944 25 Bonsecours Church wc (listed 1967, Jessie Dow prize)
26 April in Montreal wc
1945 61 St James Cathedral wc $100
1946 56 Provincetown wc $75
57 Provincetown harbour wc $125
1967 18 Normandy beach 30 x 36

CROWE, GEORGE KENNETH
11 Jul 1900, Guelph, Ont 2 May 1940, Montreal
addr: Montreal West, 42 Ballantyne Ave N, 1932. Montreal, c/o F.G. Robb, 1178 Phillips Place
1932 377 Temple of Castor and Pollux, Girgenti, Sicily drwg $50
378 Doorway, the Corso, Taormina, Sicily drwg $25
1933 360-1 Experiment in the technique of commercial design model

CRUIKSHANK, WILLIAM
25 Dec 1848, Broughton Ferry, Scot 19 May 1922, Kansas City AGO CE EC H M NGC R2 TB1/3 W78
addr: Toronto: 1908; Arcade T, Yonge St, 1910
1885 58 Hauling the mast
1892 32 On the field of Waterloo $100 (Cruickshank mispr)
1910 107 Pretty face $200
108 His capital wc $200 (listed 1967, Jessie Dow prize)

CULLEN, MAURICE GALBRAITH
6 Jun 1866, St John's, Nfld 28 Mar 1934, Chambly, Que AGO B CC2 CE CNS36 EC H M Mo12 NGC PMC R2 TB1/2/3 W78
addr: Montreal, 10 1/2 Phillips Sq, 1897-8. Paris, 1900. Montreal: 100 St François Xavier St, 1903; 96 St François Xavier, 1905; 3 Beaver Hall Sq, 1906-17; 360 Beaver Hall Hill, 1918; 67 St Famille St, 1920-5, 1927; c/o Watson Art Galleries, 679 St Catherine St W, 1926, 1928; 1397 St Catherine St W, 1929-32
1897 26 Quebec from Levis $75
27 In winter quarters $50
28 On the wharf, Levis $50

29 The ship's dock $50
1898 21 In winter quarters $75
22 Drawing ice $75
23 The Louise Basin, Quebec $75
1900 25 On the lower St Lawrence $40
26 Sunset, Lake of Two Mountains $25
27 Custom House, Montreal $40
1903 30 On the Seine $150
31 Winter in Brittany $200
32 A Brittany interior $150
33 On the Giudecca, Venice $150
34 Marine $100
234 On the Lagunes pastel $150
1905 36 Work $300
37 Marine $100
38 Moonlight $30
39 After the snow $75
204 Winter evening pastel $40
205 The hay barge pastel $40
1906 43 A winter sunset, Cove Fields $150
44 Côte au coton $150
45 The St Lawrence, winter $75
46 Sunglow $100
47 Twenty below zero $50
216 A Laurentian stream pastel $75
217 Petit Cap, Levis pastel $75
1908 51 The brook $300
52 On the road to the mill $150
1909 98 After the storm $500
99 Old Montreal $300 (MBAM)
100 The hay barge $150
101 Forgotten $150
102 The pond $40
1910 109 The cove $1,000
110 At the end of the river $300
111 The end of the winter $150
112 Hazy day $150
1911 82 Phillips Square $300 (listed 1967, Jessie Dow prize)
83 Dominion Square $200
84 St John's harbor, evening $100
85 Snowstorm $100
86 Winter afternoon $100
87 Evening $50
1912 95 Lifting fog, Petty Harbor, Nfld $150
96 New grain elevator $150
97 A Laurentian valley $75
98 Street scene $300
99 Torby, Newfoundland $200
100 Venice $75
101 Brittany washerwoman $300
1913 95 The first thaw $300 (listed 1967, Jessie Dow prize) (MBAM)
96 Venetian boats pastel $75
97 Winter $100
1914 87 The ice harvest $1,500 (NGC)
88 The willows $350
89 The Cache River $150
90 Frost and snow
1915 86 The saw mill $350
87 On the road to the ice fields $350
88 Winter $350
89 The gully $75
1916 59 The end of the day $1,000
60 Snowstorm, Dominion Square $400 (MQ)
61 The river $300
62 The creek $75
1917 87 An autumn afternoon $150
88 The snowstorm $200
89 On the Cache River $200
90 March $100
91 Evening $100
92 In the northland pastel $400
1918 67 Cache River
68 Lumber camp $100
69 Habitant farm pastel $100
70 The excavation pastel $150
71 Blue vetch pastel $100
72 North Mount pastel $200
73 The valley of the St Lawrence $250
1920 52 Ice harvest, Longueuil $400
53 Loading ice $300
54 Cache River pastel $500
55 Early winter pastel $200
1921 53 Spring on the Cache River $1,000
54 The muskeg $350 (NGC)
55 The northland pastel $500
56 A Laurentian river $300
1922 63 The St Lawrence $500
64 A November morning at Lac Tremblant $500
65 Evening pastel $500
66 On the Cache River pastel $200
1923 59 A March evening $800 (NGC)
1924 53 Sunrise, Lac Tremblant $600
1925 79 Winter sunrise, the Laurentians $600
1926 31A Huy on the Meuse $350 (NGC)
1927 36 Quebec from Levis $1.000
1928 42 The Valley of the Devil

43 River, near St Jovite $1,200
1929 42 Chute au Parons $2,000
43 Laurentian river
44 Last gleams, St Margaret's
1930 42 Laurentian twilight pastel $1,000
43 Hoar frost and snow, Laurentians
1931 66 Late November, Cache River pastel
67 After a snowfall in the Laurentians
1932 67 The North River $1,000 (MBAM)
68 The Cache River pastel $1,000
port bust: by Alfred Laliberté 1907-311

CUMMINS, ETHEL M.
addr: Montreal, 175 Mansfield St, 1916. Magog, Que, Pine Croft, 1917
1916 63 Farm $20
64 Sketch $10
1917 85 Sketch at Georgeville $25
86 McGill Lodge $15

CUMMINS, JANE CATHERINE
1841, Amherst Island, Ont 1893, Munich, Germ H M NGC
addr: Montreal, 26 Union Ave
1891 36 Children at play $35

CUNDILL, CONSTANCE G.
addr: Montreal, 1562 Pine Ave W, 1933-6
1933 444 The nativity wd engr $10
445 A Devonshire village wd engr $8
446 The camp in the woods wd engr
447 Côte Carrière, Cap à l'Aigle, Que wd engr
1936 105 Cape gooseberries $6

CUNNINGHAM, ADAM
addr: Kenogami, Que: 14 Lapointe St, 1934-5; 9 Oak St, 1936; 5 Oak St, 1946
1934 75 The Saguenay wc $75
76 The old wharf, Chicoutimi wc $40
1935 87 Open water wc $50
1936 106 Lady fayre wc $25
1946 58 Ebb tide, Tadousac wc

CUNNINGHAM, EVELYN M. (m Cyril Cunningham)
addr: Montreal, 3434 Harvard Ave
1939 90 Sherbrooke Street West $25

CURNOE, GREGORY RICHARD
19 Nov 1936, London, Ont AGO CCI CE M
addr: Toronto, Gallery Moos, 138 Yorkville Ave, 1964. London, Ont 1970
1964 18 The greatest profile in the world $500
1968 collages on wood with plexiglass
50 In memory of the R100 at St Hubert 10 x 36 $200
51 British arms aerostat No 2 7 1/2 x 60 $150
52 British naval aerostat No 3 10 x 23 1/2 $150
53 Control cabin and forward power car of the R34 6 x 17 $125
1970 8 Victoria Hospital, series 3, view from the most easterly window, north wall, May 5th to December 18th 1969 acry, wallpaper & marking ink on plywood, with taped casette and speaker 108 x 48 illus

CURRIE, JOHN A
addr: Montreal, 326 Beaver Hall Hill
1925 295 Roman bridge, Verona
296 Temple in Borghese Gardens, Rome

CURRY, ELIZABETH ELEANOR
1864, Russell, Ont May 1941, Hamilton H
addr: Ottawa: 132 McLeod St, 1924; 91 4th Ave, 1925; 199 2nd Ave, 1928; 62 Renfrew Ave, 1929; 62 Redfern Ave, 1932
1924 54 In the Gatineau valley wc $35
1925 80 Burning leaves wc $45
81 A breezy day wc $35
82 Hay Market, Ottawa pastel $30
1928 44 Storm at sea wc $70
45 The Lizard, Cornwall coast wc $65
46 Boats, Mousehole, Cornwall, Eng wc $60
1929 45 Cap Barré, Perce, Que wc $30
1932 69 A house by the side of the road wc $90
70 Winter in Ottawa wc $40

CURRY, PEGGY (m Stewart L. Curry)

21 Aug 1885, Gosforth, Northumb, Eng
addr: Halifax, 29 South Park St
1941 49 Drewent Inn, Derbyshire, Eng $50

CUTTLE, HARRIET MCLEOD
addr: Quebec, 709 Château St Louis, 305 Grand Allée
1942 37 Jean's wedding $35
198 Beatrice charcl $25

CUTTS, GERTRUDE E. SPURR (m William Malcolm Cutts)
1858, Scarborough, Yorks, Eng 21 Jul 1941, Port Perry, Ont AGO CWW38 DBA H M NGC TB3
addr: Toronto, 248 Gerrard St, 1894-1909 (243 Gerrard St, 1894, mispr); St Ives, Cornwall, Eng, 1912
1894 Spurr, 1894-1909
143 By the river, Mimico Creek $50
1895 122 A bright November day $35
123 After the gale $35
124 In russet mantle clad $10
196 Fish out of water wc $50
1897 209 A relic of 1820 wc $35
210 Indian summer on the Humber wc $25
211 Last days of autumn wc $25
1898 99 A dead pheasant $100
1900 96 Scarboro', old town $100
97 Reigate Heath $65 (Health, mispr)
98 Betchworth, Surrey $45
99 Drag Creek, Haliburton $20
1901 89 Mending nets, Cape Cod $50
90 A Surrey cottage $40
91 Firs, Cape Cod harbour $30
174 Beeches wc $25
1903 103 Sunny lane in a Welsh valley $45
104 Afon Las, 'Blue River,' north Wales $45
1905 110 Above the valley $75
111 A bit of old Quebec $20
112 A Welsh cottage $20
1906 152 Welsh moorland $50
153 Grist mill, Dinas Mawddwy $25
154 Grey day on the Llugwy River $25
1908 140 Sunset glow, the Beguinage, Brussels $85
141 From the Quai Verte, Bruges $20
142 The Jurusalem Church, Bruges $85
1909 341 Grey day, St Lawrence marshes $75
342 Godshues, Bruges $75
1912 102 His only companion $75

CUTTS, WILLIAM MALCOLM
1857, Allahabad, India 29 Jan 1943, Port Perry, Ont CCI CWW36 H M NGC PMC TB3 W78
addr: Toronto, 43 Adelaide St, 1897. Port Perry, Ont, 1931
1897 30 December
1931 68 Wind, rain and sunshine $250

CUVELIER, LEONCE E.
Aug, 1874, Paris
addr: Montreal: 64 Mentata St, 1912; 499 Berri St, 1913. Montreal South, Mercier Ave, 1915 (number not in cat)
1912 103 Décoration theátrale maq $60
104 Faust, 1 er acte maq $60
1913 98 Rue St Pierre, Cane, France b&w
428 L'étang du Grand Séminaire dela rue Sherbrooke maq wc
429 Un rue au Caire, Egypte maq wc
1915 90 The arrival of Christopher Columbus at San Salvador curtain des wc
91 Terrace on the heights of the Marne maq
1915 92 Salon, Louis XVI maq

CYOPIK, WILLIAM
17 Feb 1921, Welland, Ont IO M WWA70
addr: Welland, Ont
1968 acrylic, 54-7
54 Journey's end 38 x 48 1/4 $400
55 Red wing 36 x 42 $400
56 Medallion 36 x 42 $400
57 Dominant blue 36 x 42 $400

CZOTTER, MARIKA GYONGYOSSY, (Mrs)
3 Dec 1922, Mohacs, Hungary
addr: Montreal, 3550 Linton Ave
1962 56 Un soir tranquille nm

D

DAGENAIS-GOYER, DOLORES
addr: Montreal, 3238 Lacombe Ave
1937 69 Portrait of an old lady min

DAGLISH, PETER WILLIAM
1930, Gillingham, Kent, Eng M
addr: Montreal: 542 Sherbrooke St W, 1957; 673 Vitre St W, Apt 5, 1958-60; c/o Jacques Hurtubise, 8558 Waverly St, 1961; 1409 Tower St, Apt 1, 1962; c/o 7045 D'Abancourt St, 1964
1957 26 Fragment of autumn foliage $40
1958 56 Edge of Griffintown nm $40
1960 141 Backdrop nm $35
1961 10 Deuce illus purchase award (MBAM)
1962 4 Cody $300
5 Storage $300
1964 19 Red-red $100

DAGYS, JACOB (b Jokubas Dags)
16 Dec 1905, Lithuania M WWA84
1954 133 The Lithuanian folks dance sculp $650
1957 156 O Lord, forgive them wd $100
157 Her head is down wd $150
1959 50 Have an apple? wc $300

DALE, JACK
b 1928
addr: Vancouver
1970 9 Mirrored image from textures No 1 film, plexiglass, mirror 32 x 24 x 3
10 Cubed woman No 7 photosensitized glass, plexiglass, mirror 34 x 16 x 16

DALE, MARIAN see SCOTT, MARIAN

DALLAIRE, JEAN PHILIPPE
9 Jun 1916, Hull Que 26 Nov 1965, Vence, France AGO B CE M NGC TB3 WWA53
addr: Montreal: Dominion Gallery, 1438 Sherbrooke St W, 1953-4; Galeris Dresdnere, 2170 Crescent St, 1961
1953 95 Who's who in life gouach $250
1954 29 Adam et Eve
30 The cursed painter! $325
1961 73 La quatorze juillet nm $275

DALLEGRET, FRANCOIS
26 Sep 1937, Lyautey, Morocco
addr: Montréal
1968 gravures, 58-9
58 Super/super/face 31 1/4 x 25 $400
59 High/way four 28 1/2 x 28 1/2 $170
60 Abstratomic 1/16 géant billes d'acier trempé entre 2 verres 14 1/2 x 14 1/2 $370
61 Colonne cinq aluminum, bois, formica 84h $2,200

DALLEY, ERNEST R.
1908 53 The bend $25

D'ALONZO, JOSEPH
b 1932
addr: Montreal, 9695 Hochelaga St
1955 24 Modèle au repos

DALY, GERALDINE D.
addr: Montreal, 3544 Decarie Blvd
1934 77 Near Metis wc $5

DALY, KATHLEEN FRANCES (m George Douglas Pepper)
28 May 1898, Napanee, Ont AGO CE CWW84 IO M WWA84
addr: Toronto, 441 Walmer Rd, 1929. Ottawa, 16 Torrington Pl, 1930-32. Toronto: 441 Walmer Rd, 1935; 25 Severn St, 1939
1929 304 Sous le Cap, Quebec dry pt $15
305 Perugia dry pt $10
306 From the bridge, Lausanne aqua $10
307 Ponte Vecchio, Florence aqua $10
308 A street, Baie St Paul reed pen $10
309 Among the hills, Quebec reed pen $10
310 St Urbain, Que reed pen $10
311 Housetops lino cut $5
1930 44 St Urbain $50
266 Angelina aqua $15
1932 71 Blue Rocks, N.S. $60
72 Tubs of mackerel $60
73 Houses, Baie St Paul $30
1935 88 Yellow chair $175
1939 91 Montagnais Indian $40
92 Indian boy $40

DALY, MARY MARGUERITE (RITA)
28 Apr 1892, Montreal
addr: Montreal: 17 Esplanade Ave, 1911-12; 39 Fort St, 1913-15; 16 Maplewood Ave, 1916; 399 Wilson Ave, 1917-19.

Chicoutimi, Que: Box 241, 1922-9; 67 Cartier St, 1933
1911 88 Sketch
1912 105 Sketch $20
1913 99-100 Sketch $20 each
1914 91 Portrait
92 Old memories $50
1915 93 Aunt Harriet
94 Lucile
95 Portrait of my father
96 The girl in black
1916 65 Frances
66 Study in pink
67 Coney Island, New York wc $10
68 Brighton Beach, New York wc $10
69 Hudson River, New York wc $10
1917 93 A sketch
94 Claire
1918 75, 77 Portrait
76 Lucille
1919 90 Mr Brymner, sketch
91 Study of a head
1922 67 An impression of a child
1926 32 Girl's head $20
33 Old house on Long Island
1927 37 Marie Dubuc
1929 48 Winter $50
49 Autumn $50
50 Cottage, Lake Joseph $50
51 Winter on the banks of the Saguenay $20
1933 65 An old chestnut tree $30
66 On the Saguenay $25

DAMIANI, JIMMY
addr: Montreal, 7764 St Dominique St, 1945-6
1945 62 Octogenarian pastel $100
1946 59 Mr T. James pastel $100
60 Diane pastel $60

DANBY, KENNETH EDISON
5 Mar 1940, Sault Ste Marie, Ont CC2 CE CWW84 IO M NGC WWA84
addr: Toronto, 40 Park Rd, 1964. Guelph, Ont, 1967-70
1964 85 Fur & bricks nm $275 illus (listed 1967, Jessie Dow prize)
1967 19 The red wagon. 1966 temp 42 x 32 (Mr Paul Duval, Toronto)
1970 11 Pulling out temp 32 x 44 illus (A.J. Latner, Toronto)

DANDURAND, G. (Mrs)
addr: Montreal, 548 Sherbrooke St W
1910 113 Bouleaux $30
114 Rivière Mauve $40

DANIS, MAURICE
addr: Montreal, 1637 St Hubert St, 1934-5
1934 490 Description of the Canadian Pacific plaster
491 Rêverie plaster
1935 459 La Résurrection plaster $350

DANKS, HILDA MARGARET LAWRENCE (m Walter F. Danks)
1893, London, Eng 16 Aug 1969, Niagara Falls, Ont
addr: Niagara Falls, 621 Ellis St
1960 142 Small fox nm $100

DANYLEWICH, MORRIS JOHN
27 Sep 1938, Lachine, Que
addr: Lachine, 732 12th Ave
1964 86 Mike, Adam & me nm $40

DAOUST, SYLVIA MARIE EMILIENNE
24 May 1902, Montreal AGO CNS40 CWW84 M NGC WWA84
addr: Montreal, 171 Beaubien St, 1930-43. Strathmore, Que, 237 St Joseph Blvd, 1946-55
1930 305 M Leufroi Valiquette plaster
1932 462 Portrait de l'artiste par elle-même plaster
1933 520 Mon frère plaster
1934 492 Miss M. Giguère sculp
493 Mr L. Desgagné sculp
494 Baby's head sculp
1935 460 Simone Hudon, Quebec bronze
461 Tête de jeune fille plaster
1936 590 Monsieur L.F. plaster
1937 452 Bedawbenokwa, jeunne huronne plaster $75 bronze $300 (NGC br)
1938 158 Vielle maison à Caughnawaga etch
190 Madone plaster $10 bronze $75
1939 451 St Joseph plaster
1940 404 Fillette plâtre patiné $50
1942 231 St Dominique merisier wd carv
232 Madone cotonnine wd carv
1943 253 Jeune fille plâtre patiné
1946 276 Ste Cécile wd carv
1951 70 Lucie plaster $300 (NGC)

DARBY, ROBERT
26 Sep 1896, Liverpool, Eng
addr: Ottawa, 428 Rideau St, Apt 14, 1935-6
1935 89 The bathers wc $75
1936 107 The pool wc $175
108 Ottawa River wc $75

D'ARCY, BARBARA M. CONYERS
addr: Quebec: 45 Esplanade, 1929-30; 44 St Louis St, 1932-3
1929 312 Cinderella and her sisters nm $30
313 The tryst nm $25
314 Snow White and the wicked queen nm $20
315 La Fête Dieu nm $15
1930 45 The landing of Columbus, 1492 $50
46 Night idyll $30
47 Blue Beard $25
48 Après le souper $15
1932 74 Angélique des Meloisses et La Corriveau (from Chien d'Or) $15
1933 67 The little men's house in the woods $15

DARE, LAURA see PRICE, LAURA

DARLING, THOMAS (Mrs)
addr: Montreal: 99 Drummond St, 1895-1906; Montreal, 1908
1895 244 Basket, Dresden
245 Jardinière
246 Vase
247-8 Cup & saucer (2)
1900 218 Claret jug
219 Plate
1901 228 Fern dish
229 Bonbon box
1903 282 Loving cup $4
283 Plate, roses $6
1905 292 Fruit dish
1906 400 Vase, iris
401 Two salt cellars
1908 370-1 Cup & saucer (2)

DARRACH, ANNA
addr: Montreal, 107 1/2 Bleury St
1903 165 Autumn, Mount Royal wc $15
166 Hill, Cap à l'Aigle wc $15

DAUDELIN, CLAUDE
1 Oct 1920, Granby, Que CE M WWA84
addr: Pointe Claire, Que, Montée Ste Marie, 1952. Kirkland, Que, 17166 Range Ste Marie, 1963-5
1952 145 Ozia plaster
1963 97 Eurocoque bronze $250
1965 32 Hiéroglyphe bronze $450 (MBAM)

DAVENPORT, SUMNER GODFREY
6 Nov 1877, Framingham, Mass 7 Mar 1956, Montreal
addr: Georgeville, Que
1945 63 August, Shepherd's Bay wc

DAVID, CHARLES
5 Apr 1890, Montreal 23 Nov 1962, Outremont, Que CNS51 CWW61 PMC
addr: Montreal, 617 Keefer Bldg
1927 196 Ecole St Augustin de Cantorbéry

DAVID, FLORENCE MEREDITH Eng
1850, London, Eng DBA DVP G
addr: Montreal, 704 Sherbrooke St, 1891
1889 192 Portrait ter cot
193 Portrait plaster
194 Proserpine, replica sculp $300
195 Piety sculp $350
1891 217 Piety bust

DAVIDSON, C. G. (Mrs)
addr: Westmount, 50 Aberdeen Ave
1914 493 Plate
494 Small jug

DAVIDSON, FLORENCE
addr: Montreal: 466 Guy St, 1921; 288 Mackay St, 1922
1921 58 Menimsha Creek $150
59 Gay Head Cliffe $100
60 Sea and sky $100
61 L'automne $75
1922 68 At Marblehead wc $100
69 The glory of October wc $100

DAVIDSON, FRANCES
addr: Westmount, 15 Springfield Ave
1938 159 The wooden bridge etch $5

DAVIDSON, J. HERBERT (Mrs)
addr: Westmount, 50 Aberdeen Ave

1917 413 Tobacco jar $15
414 Cylinder vase $8

DAVIES, EDWARD Eng
21 Mar 1841, Aldgate, London, Eng
29 Aug 1920, Leicester B DBA DBW G
RA WBA
addr: Leicester, Eng, 131 Marlboro' Rd
1909 103 Behind the sand dunes, Sutton-on-Sea wc $50
104 On the Ayrshire coast wc $50
105 Caernarvon Castle wc $80
106 Fresh morning, Lincolnshire wc
107 Coast wc $50
108 The brook wc $50
109 Sand dunes wc $50

DAVIES, GEORGE E.
addr: Montreal: 4 Stanley Mansions, 1905; 134 Mackay St, 1906; Montreal, 1908
1905 all water colors
149 Low tide, Borthy-Gest, N. Wales $75
150 Near Lands End, Cornwall
151-3 Cottage homes of England $26 each
154 An old water mill $26
1906 218 The mill in the wood $50
219 Head of an old man
220 Newlyn, Cornwall $125
1908 196 A lady of quality

DAVIES, MARGARET ELIZABETH REGAN (Mrs)
addr: Beloeil Station, Que
1953 96 Composition pastel

DAVIES, WILLIAM HENRY
11 Oct 1872, Sedgley, Staff, Eng
addr: Montreal: 404 Birk's Bldg, 1909; 121 Bishop St, 1918; 677 St Catherine St W, 1919; 703 St Catherine St W, 1926; 1517 Drummond St, 1931; 3677 St Famille St, 1936; 11880 Pasteur St, 1937; 10844 Durham Ave, 1948
1909 409 Old houses near Lucerne and Hermance
410-11 Country house des plan, elevation
1918 Davis, mispr 1918-19
390 Country house, decorative treatment living room, perspective des
1919 381-2 Bungalow, exterior, interior wc
383 Staircase, town house wc
384 Hall, country house wc
385 Louis XVI drawing room wc
386 Swiss wayside sketches wc
1926 191 Fitted dining room des pencil
1931 265 Georgian library panelled with knotted pine wc
1936 109 Bonsecours Market wc $50
1937 333 Living-dining room, country residence wc & polychrome pencil
1948 74 Eventide, Notre Dame de Bonsecours wc $150

DAVIS, HUNTLY WARD
22 Oct 1875, Montreal 12 Oct 1952, Ste Marguerite, Que
addr: Montreal: 29 Belmont St, 1928; 647 Belmont St, 1933-4
1928 224 Proposed house pastel
1933 362 Children Hospital, Montreal
363 Block of houses
364 Private house
365 Ironwork
1934 378-9 Architectural drawing

DAVIS, JOHN CRAIG
addr: Montreal
1970 12 Untitled black sculpture 1/5 polyester resin 26h illus
13 Untitled red, white and blue polyester resin and American flag 22h
14 Untitled white sculpture 1/5 epoxy 26h

DAVIS, KIRSTANBERG
addr: Montreal, 3179 St Urbain St
1921 305 Memorial of world's greatest war inlaid wd

DAVIS, MARIE
addr: Montreal, 64 St Suplice Rd, 1938-40
1938 35 Nude $100
1939 96 Youth $100
1940 82 Violette

DAVIS, PHILIP WEIR
addr: Westmount: 4041 Dorchester St W, 1935; 533 Clarke Ave, 1939
1935 90 Grey day, Booth Bay harbour $50
91 Village church at sundown
1939 97 North River, St Marguerite's, late afternoon $65

DAWES, PRUDENCE ANN
28 Jul 1917, Montreal
addr: Senneville, Que, 1935-6. Westmount, Gleneagles Apt, 1937
1935 462 An old man plaster
1936 591 Youth plaster $50
1937 453 Mr Pilon plaster $125
454 Charles S. Saxe, Esq bronze $250

DAWSON, B.
addr: Westmount, 52 Rosemount Ave
1937 455 Study plaster

DAWSON, F. A.
fl 1880-92 H
1886 116 The Falls of Montmorency

DAWSON, GWEN
addr: Kingston, Ont, 119 Earl St, 1942-5
1942 40 Mending the nets wc $25
1944 27 Summer landscape wc
1945 64 The barhour wc $40

DAY, FANNY M.
addr: Montreal, 209 Stanley St, 1900-9
1900 220 Jardiniere
221 Tray
222 Plate
223-4 Cup & saucer $3.50, $3.00
1905 293 Plaque, roses $5
294 Plate, violets
295-6, 300-1 Cup & Saucer
297 Plate, asters $4
298, Vase, iris
299 Nut bowl $2.75
302 Head, my sweetheart
1908 372 Plate, poppies $5
373 Brown vase
374 Brown vase, large $10
375 Jardiniere, clover $12
376 Dish, violets
377 Dish, roses $12
378 Cup & saucer $5
379 Cream, sugar $12
380 Plate, Dutch figure $5
1909 29 Cup & Saucer, yellow
30 Cup & saucer blue $5
31 Cup & saucer green $5
32 Plate $5
33 Six small plates $15

DAY, FORSHAW
4 Nov 1837, London, Eng 22 Jul 1903, Kingston, Ont EC H M Mo98 NGC W78
1883 85 Winter scene near Campbellton, Quebec
86 A shady place
1888 13 Junction of Bow and Spry Rivers, NWT $50
103 Lake at Laggan, NWT wc $120
116 Mount Deville Range, NWT wc $80
134 Falls Leanchoile, Rockies, NWT wc $110

DAY, MABEL KILLAM (m Frank P. Day)
7 Jul 1884, Yarmouth, N.S. d 1961, Yarmouth, N.S. WWA62
addr: Fredericton, N.B.
1910 115 Lake Annis $50
116 Under cool birches $50

DEAN, C. W. (Mrs)
addr: Montreal, 4282 Sherbrooke St
1900 225 Bonbon box, Persian des
226 Cup & saucer, green scroll

DEAN, THOMAS G.
b 1947
addr: Montreal
1970 15 970 Market Street acry 96 x 12
16 Bleury Canada offset litho & steel 66h

DEANE, E. ELDON
addr: New York 6 W 28th St
1916 70 St Paul's Church, Sault au Récollet wc $25
71 Evening at Sault au Récollet wc $25
72 Canal, afternoon, Montreal wc $25

DEANE, ELSIE
addr: Montreal: 149 Durocher St, 1922; 326 Beaver Hall Hill, 1924
1922 70 Good night cover des wc
1924 57 Cover design wc

DECARY, LOUIS JOSEPH THEOPHILE
21 Sep 1882, St Jerome, Que 4 Jun 1952, Montreal
addr: Montreal, 313 Centre St, 1910-11

1910 117 Moments de loisir wc
386 A seminary
387 A gymnasium
388 Studies
1911 295 A seminary

DEDUAL, LUCIEN FREDERIC
addr: Montreal, 6002 Chateaubriand Ave
1948 9 Winter scene, Val David $190

DEHAHN, RETA
addr: Montreal, 3550 Ridgewood Ave
1952 80 Mr Hugh M. plaster

DE JONG, SHIRLEY see WALES, SHIRLEY

DE KERGOMMEAUX, DUNCAN see KERGOMMEAUX, DUNCAN CHASSIN DE

DELACOURT, MARJORIE V.
addr: Montreal: 578 Dorchester St W, 1920-22; 31 Chomedy St, 1926
1920 326 Rose jar $12
327 Rose bowl $15
1921 330 Butterfly bread tray
331 Acorn bowl
1922 379 Butterfly vase $30
1926 160 Flat vase, rose and black $45
161 Tall vase, green and silver lustre

DE LALL, OSCAR DANIEL
12 Sep 1903, St Petersburg 21 May 1971, Montreal CWW67 M NGC
addr: Montreal: 1620 Sherbrooke St W, 1932-4; 3652 St Urbain St, 1935; 3805 Drolet St, 1936; 1829 Lincoln Ave, Apt 3, 1937; 2031 Union Ave, 1939-40; 3456 University St, 1941-3. Westmount, 1 Sunnyside Ave, 1944-50. Montreal, 1551 Bishop St, 1951-3
1932 379 Paul Caron, Esq, portrait study charcl
380 Mrs O.J.N. Dawes, portrait study charcl
1933 448 Head of a man, study charcl $35
1934 81 In Russian head-dress $250
440 Fred A. Lallemand, Esq, portrait study charcl
1935 92 Loyola
1936 121 Elena
526 Miss Martha Allan charcl
1937 74 Mrs F. Bindoff
75 Prof J.W. Bridges, PhD
397 Dr W.W. Francis charcl
1939 102 Miss Lorna Mowat
1940 86 Miss E.K. Scott
1941 104 Self portrait
105 Mrs F.H. Sproule
1942 41 Mrs Alan Bronfman
1943 51 Miss M. MacSporran, MA
1944 28 Miss M. Heye
1945 65 My wife, portrait
1946 61 Frances
62 Sandra
1947 142 Habitant of St Mathias $600
143 Portrait of Bee
144 Mrs L. MacKay Smith
1948 20 Mrs H.J. O'Connell
1949 53 Miss Audrey Guy
1950 20 Mrs L. Lehan
1951 21 Mrs F. Sugden
1952 22 Self portrait
1953 14 Mr E. Cleghorn
port: by Max Schulz, 1938-105

DELBOS, C. EDMUND
addr: Toronto
1908 197 Landscape wc $40

DELFOSSE, MADELEINE
5 Apr 1918, Montreal CNS51
addr: Montreal, 825 St Joseph Blvd E
1939 103 Glaieuls $100

DELFOSSE, MARIE JOSEPH GEORGES
8 Dec 1869, St Henri des Mascouche, Que 24 Dec 1939, Montreal CC2 CNS36 M Mo12 NGC PMC TB3 W78
addr: Montreal: 232 St Elizabeth St, 1892; 1562 Ontario St, 1894-1905; 348 Berri St, 1906; 257 Sherbrooke St E, 1910; 259 Sherbrooke St E, 1911-12; 690 Sherbrooke St E, 1913-22; 718 Sherbrooke St E, 1926-7; 714 Sherbrooke St E, 1928; 1316 Sherbrooke St E, 1929-36
1892 33 The old Bonsecours Church $50
1894 44 Still life $80
45 Electric light effect $50
1895 30 Still life $60
1898 24 Château de Ramezay $200
1900 28 Marguerites $40
1901 24 My mother
1903 35 Château de Ramezay $500
36 M Rodolphe Girard
1905 40 Malbaie $40

1906 68 La Transfiguration $60
221 Christ Church Cathedral, evening pastel $55
304 St Eustache, episode from 'Les contes vrais' of Pamphile Lemay b&w $50
1910 118 La fée du logis
119 Mde G. D.
120 Old Bonsecours Church $150
1911 89 Musique $600
90 Old windmill, Contrecoeur, 1743 $200
91 Vielle Eglise Notre Dame, construite en 1672 $250
92 Sault au Recollet $25
1912 106 Residence of Gédeon Catalogne, projector of the earliest Lachine Canal, 1693 $300
107 Pensionnat des Dames de la Congregation Notre Dame, 1840 $200
108 Première école privée ouverte par M de Laprairie, 1683 $200
109 Entrée de Notre Dame de Pitié $100
110 Notre Dame de Pitié $150
1913 115 Vielles maisons, rue Notre Dame, 1669 $450
116 Premier moulin à vent, Montréal, 1647 $350
117 Notre Dame des Victoires, 1718 $300
118 Hôtel Dillon, coin Place d'Armes et Jacques, 1790 $450
1914 95 The two sisters
96 Pendant le sermon, St James Church
97 Notre Dame de la Pitié, le Monastère, 1840
1915 97 Petite rue St Julien le Pauvre, Paris $250
1916 81 La lettre $1,000
1917 101 Repentigny, 1680, presbytère et église $200
102 Repentigny, église $75
103 Petite rue Joly, Montréal $150
1918 89 Lecture interrompue $500
90 Collége de Montréal, fin du XVII siecle $150
91 Rawdon $100
1919 92 Le denil de la patriè $1,200
1920 68 La Vierge à la Couronne d'Epines $600
69 Le Montréal d'autrefois $500
1921 73 Sous les vieux saules $650
1922 75 Fin d'hiver $650
76 Vieille maison au bas de la montagne $350
1926 38 Le vieux séminaire $550
1927 38 Printemps $450
39 Vieille église de Nohant, France, pays de Georges Sand $200
1928 47 Vieille Eglise St Gabriel, rue St Gabriel $350
1929 56 Residence de Sir Georges Etienne Cartier, rue Notre Dame est $300
1934 82 The last two old houses of St Vincent Street, Montreal $500
83 Les bouquinistes, Paris $300
1936 122 L'ancien Hôtel du Canada à Montréal
123 Ruines du vieux moulin de la Rivière des Prairies

DELISLE, LAURENT
addr: Montreal, 3693 Hutchison St
1941 52 Après le lunch $250

DELRUE, GEORGES
26 Sep 1920, Tourcoine, France M
addr: Montréal, 1434 ave Hôtel de Ville, 1944-6
1944 30 Dimanche matin rue Bonsecours $75
1945 67 Marché Bonsecours wc $30
1946 64 Autumne wc $35

DE LUCCA, YARGO DIETER MUELLER
1 Jun 1925, Cassel, Germ M
addr: St Eustache-sur-le-Lac, Que, 1810 Oka Road, 1955-7
1955 25 Reading boy $800
1956 91 The man in the canoe nm $15
92 Men resting nm $15
1957 27 Crossing the lake $240

DENECHAUD, SIMONE
8 Oct 1905 - 11 Sep 1974, Montreal
WWA53
addr: Montreal: 5428 Hutchison St, 1935; 4096 St Denis St, 1941-6
1935 93 Madame Adrien Duranleau $250
1941 53 Cecile Chabot, poet
1943 52 Gladioli $125
1946 65 Christ mourant $100

66 Fleurs $100

DENIS, LEONIE
addr: Montreal: 790 Albert St, 1923; 846 Marie Anne St E, 1924
1923 cuir/leather 1923-4
64-5 Pochette, cuir repoussé $5 each
66 Pochette $6
67 Couvre-livre $6
1924 70 Couvre-livre cuir repoussé $25
71-3 Pochette cuire repoussé $15, $10, $6

DENNIS, CLAUDE W.
fl 1880-1911 H
addr: Montreal: 102 Hypolite St, 1901; 104 Hypolite St, 1903; 229 1/4 St Urbain St, 1905; 229A St Urbain St, 1906; Montreal, 1908: 405 St Urbain St, 1909-11
1901 121 The rocks, Cacouna wc $40
1903 167 Waiting for his master wc $60
168 The old oven wc $30
169 The path to the farm wc $30
1905 41 Cool retreat $125
155 The old trading post wc $40
156 Rev W. Barnes min wc
1906 49 Shady brook $175
50 A familiar path $30
222 Lumber barges wc $50
1908 54 A tow, Lake St Louis $60
55 Country road $125
56 Moonlight $60
1909 110 The stream that flows through Dixie $125
111 Evening wc $60
1910 121 Childhood's days wc $75
122 Lake shore wc $50
1911 93 Mountain view, Adirondacks $150

DENOVAN, PARKER
addr: Toronto, 64 Strathallan Blvd, 1939-40
1939 104 The old market square, Quebec $65
105 Winter's mantle, Ontario farm $50
1940 87 North Church, Marble Head $60
88 Gloucester yacht harbour $75

DENTON, FRANCIS WILLIAM (FRANK)
b Toronto CWW84
addr: Toronto, 16 Killarney Rd, Forest Hill Village, 1945-7
1945 68 September camp, Canoe Lake
69 Shipyard
1947 61 Gloucester pier

DE PALMA, ARMAND see PALMA, ARMAND DE

DEROCHE, BESSIE BOGART (Mrs)
addr: Ottawa, 318 Lyon St, 1918-24
1918 92 Pine woods
93 Church door, Quebec
1919 93 Fields on the Bay of Quinte $125
1920 70 Wellington Street, Ottawa $50
71 View from the new Parliament Building $150
1921 69 Sunshine and shadow $30
1923 68 Village street
69 Circus, sketch
1924 74 Flower study

DEROME, GILLES
addr: Montreal, 5821A Clanranald Ave
1960 143 Rideau de bambou nm $200
230 Boeuf ter cot

DEROUIN, RENE
1936, Montreal
addr: St Eustache-sur-le-Lac, Que, 1810C Chemin d'Oka
1960 144 Engagement nm $150
145 Mitla nm $150

DERRICK, ETHEL
addr: Montreal: 329 Mackay St, 1922; 1260 Mackay St, 1930
1922 77 Rutherford house wc $20
1930 53 A study $25

DERY, FRANCOIS
26 May 1941, Montreal
addr: Montreal
1970 19 Energie solaire mm 78 x 108

DE SAINT JUST, VIATEUR
addr: Joliette, Que
1918 94 Sous-bois $8

DESAUTELS, CHARLES-EMILE
23 Jan 1912, St Hyacinthe, Que
addr: Montreal: 2314 Letourneaux Ave, 1936-51; 6668 26th Ave (Rosemount) 1955
1936 124 Still life $20

1937 76 Still life $100
1939 106 Ananas
1941 54 Portrait
1942 42 Procession $300
1947 62 Poulpe
1951 89 Le pot aux poissons
90 Poisson
1955 26 Le condottière

DESAUTELS, G. S.
addr: Montreal, 5369 Brodeur Ave
1958 57 Nature enchêvetrée nm

DESBIENS, GUY
addr: Montreal, 3498 St Dominique St
1964 87 Ionisation nm $75

DES CLAYES, ALICE
22 Dec 1891, Aberdeen, Scot AGO DBA CNS36 NGC
addr: Montreal: 6 Beaver Hall Sq, 1915-17; 360 Beaver Hall Sq, 1918-20. London, Eng, 156 Holland Park Ave, 1921. Montreal: 360 Beaver Hall Sq, 1922-5; c/o Watson Art Galleries, 679 St Catherine St W, 1926. Chorleywood, Herts, Eng, 1928. Montreal: 1158 Beaver Hall Sq, 1929; 1340 St Catherine St W, 1931; 1158 Beaver Hall Sq, 1932-40
1915 98 Poor pastures
99 Market day $125
100 Carmen
1916 84 Midnight mass $200
1917 104 Near Kirkfield wc $125
1918 95 Carting driftwood, near Balsam Lake, Ont $200
96 Ice cutters, Ste Anne de Bellevue pastel $75
97 A winter evening pastel $20
98 Sunset at Ste Anne de Bellevue, sketch pastel $15
1919 94 St Antoine Market $200
95 The shrine $200
96 The tired workers $200
97 The stable wc $275
98 Mafeking pastel
1920 61 The sand cart $400
62 Ice cutters at St Anne de Bellevue $300
63 Bonsecours Market $200
64 Saturday wc $100
1921 62 A coach at the Crown & Thistle $275
63 The George, Wallingford wc $200
1922 78 A June evening $175
79 A French farm wc $125
80 The country home wc $60
81 A farm in Picardy wc $40
1923 73 Harvest in Picardy $350
74 The caravan $75
75 Giving the donkey a drink wc $35
76 Ploughing wc $30
1924 62 Place Jacques Cartier, vendredi $250
63 The last furrow $125
1925 85 Getting seaweed, Côte d'Emerande $50
86 Taking seaweed from the surf, St Malo $55
87 Cherbourg market, sketch wc $35
1926 39 Seaweed cart $200
40 Homewards $130
41 Carting seaweed $60
42 Rough weather wc $80
1928 48 Autumn afternoon, Buckinghamshire wc $75
49 Market day wc $75
50 A sand cart on the coast of Picardy wc $75
51 Loading up wc $85
1929 57 The huntsman returning $200
58 Two grey horses pastel $75
1931 72 Carting seaweed, St Malo $65
73 Horses grazing by lake wc $45
74 The passing cloud wc $25
1932 79 The old Berkeley Hunt at Chardeloes min $50
80 Ploughing min $40
81 The broken rein min $40
1933 72 The farm pastel $40
73 Dartmoor ponies, England $65
1934 84 Ice cutters on the St Lawrence $200
85 Across the moor to Meldon Tor $60
1935 94 Woodford, Wilts, England $50
95 North Devon pastoral pastel $50
1936 125 Loading $250
126 Upton Grey pastel $55
127 Dartmoor ponies $40
128 Woolacombe Bay wc $40
1940 83 Ponies on Dartmoor $60

DES CLAYES, BERTHE
1877, Aberdeen, Scot d 1968 AGO DBA

CNS36 NGC
addr: Montreal: 6 Beaver Hall Sq, 1912-17; 360 Beaver Hall Sq, 1918-25; c/o Watson Art Galleries, 679 St Catherine St W, 1926; 360 Beaver Hall Sq, 1927; 1158 Beaver Hall Sq, 1928-41. Devon, Eng, 1967
1912 111 Paysage, Normandie $300
112 Printemps $125
113 Sur les dunes, Etaples $250
114 Dans les jardins du Luxembourg $75
115 Pont Neuf $75
116 Vue de St Suplice $75
1913 107 Pont Neuf, Paris $75
108 Jardin du Luxembourg, Paris $75
109 The farm $250
110 The roadway $250
1914 98 At Barkmere, Que $150
99 In the woods $65
100 Evening $175
101 The lake, Barkmere $175
1915 101 Evening $300
102 Farm road, St Eustache $175
103 The pond $175
104 A Devonshire orchard $125
105 Baby MacInnes
106 Miniature
107 Portrait miniature
108 Winter $75
1916 85 Sunshine and shadow $275
86 The old oak $200
87 On the Minas Basin, N.S. $60
88 Spring time in Nova Scotia $60
89 Early spring wc $50 (listed 1967 Jessie Dow prize)
1917 105 Pour la Patrie wc $75
106 Reaping wc $50
107 In the Luxembourg Gardens, Paris $65
108 Near Etaples, France $125
109 The river, Sweetsburg $65
110 Sunny afternoon $100
1918 99 October evening $75
100 Marsh lands pastel $125
101 First primroses wc $50
102 Wintertime wc $50
103 Sundown $50
1919 99 In the Luxembourg Gardens, Paris wc $150
100 Digging potatoes $300
101 The covered bridge, Upper Melbourne, Que $200
102 The fisherman $65
103 Autumn evening $750 (listed 1967, Jessie Dow prize)
1920 65 The white house $75
66 Autumn wc $60
67 October wc $60
1921 64 Old farm, Ambleteuse, France $200
65 French peasant girl $175 (NGC)
66 Late autumn $100
67 Old cottage, Ambleteuse $75
1922 82 Winter $450
83 The load of ice $450
84 In Gloucester harbour $200
85 The little shepherd wc $100
1923 70 A sandy cove, Nova Scotia $500
71 In Blue Rocks harbour, N.S. $300 1967-20 24 x 18 (National Gallery of Canada)
72 A winding road $300
1924 64 The valley road $500
65 October, St Andrews, Que $400
66 Fishing boat, Nova Scotia $115 (NGC)
67 Early spring, Melbourne pastel $100
1925 88 The hill $450
89 Old street in Fowey, Cornwall, England $50
90 Fisherman's cottage, Nova Scotia wc $50
91 Winter night pastel $200
1926 43 Old cottages, St Andrews, Que $325
44 Fowery harbour, Cornwall $130
45 The shepherd $150
46 Evening pastel $80
47 The moor pastel $50
1927 40 On the river road $75
41 The canal, Herts $75
42 Winter $75
1928 52 Winter in Quebec pastel $75
53 Fishing boats, Blue Rocks N.S. wc $110
1929 59 The flower girl $100
60 Mending the nets $85
61 Blossom time in Normandy $45
62 Appledore Quay, Devon $85
1930 54 A river road, Melbourne pastel $125
55 Sunny lane, Cornwall $60
1931 75 Bridge at Bruges, Le Quai Vert $175

76 Paulette $100
1932 82 The little farmhouse, Quebec $300
83 Autumn ploughing, Quebec $150
84 An early snowfall $85
1933 74 Autumn, near Richmond, Que $300
75 Dominion Square, Montreal $300
76 Miss A.M. Parent
77 Irene, daughter of John Irwin, Esq pastel
1934 86 A peaceful harbour $200
87 An old courtyard in the city $100
88 Feeding the calves wc $75
1935 96 The ship $165
97 Sea urchins $100
1936 129 An October harvest $350
130 In the village, Como $325
1937 77 The St Francis River, Que $350
78 An October day, Quebec $350
1938 38 In a sugar bush, Rougemont $225
1939 99 Spring $250
100 Hauling ice on the St Francis River $200
101 Collecting sap in a sugar bush $200
1940 84 Ice cutters in the Laurentians $275
85 In the Laurentians $75
1941 55 Laurentian hills $200

DES CLAYES, GERTRUDE
1879, Aberdeen, Scot 23 Aug 1949, London, Eng B DBA CNS36 NGC
addr: Montreal: 6 Beaver Hall Sq, 1912-17; 360 Beaver Hall Sq, 1918-25; 1158 Beaver Hall Sq, 1929; 1340 St Catherine St W, 1931; 1158 Beaver Hall Sq, 1933-6
1912 117 An English girl
118 Le femme du pécheur
119 Un gentilhomme d'Espagne
120 Portrait of a man unfr
121 Autumn dec panel
122 Who killed Cock Robin?
1914 102 Joan, daughter of Professor Eve
103 Marian, daughter of Robert Dale, Esq
1915 109 Mrs A.F.C. Ross, and her daughter Meredith
110 Mrs Meredith Cape and her son
1917 111 George, son of F. Beardmore, Esq pastel
112 Miss Judy MacInnes, sketch pastel
113 Peggie, sketch pastel $75
114 Anna, daughter of R. Dale, Esq
115 Louis, son of Mrs F.G. Johnson
1918 104 Anna Dale
105 Bobbie
106 Mrs F.N. Beardmore pastel
107 Sally Gertrude pastel
1919 104 David, son of Percy Matthias, Esq
1921 68 Study of a child pastel
1922 86 Diana, daughter of Victor Drury, Esq
87 Barbara, daughter of F. Pitcher, Esq pastel
1923 77 Fisherman's home, Nova Scotia $325
78 Betty pastel
1925 92 Autumn $50
93 The old barn $35
1929 63 The blue bonnet pastel $65
64 Flowers pastel $75
1931 77 Babes in the wood $125
78 Head of a child $100
1933 78 The blue bird $1,750
79 A village belle $250
80 Rose $50
81 Yvonne $50
1935 98 The blue sunbonnet pastel $75
1936 131 Primavera pastel $100

DESMARAIS, AMANDA
addr: Montreal, 320 St Denis St
1903 37 Still life $25

DESMEULES, GABRIEL
16 Feb 1902, La Malbaie, Que CNS36
see Robitaille and Desmeules, 1929

DESROSIERS, PIERRE
addr: Montreal, 1257 Plassis St
1939 452 Tête d'enfant plaster $100

DESROSIERS, ROLLAND
addr: Montreal, 1849 Cadillac St
1942 234 Confidence plaster $30

DESQUEYROUX, A. H.
addr: Montreal: 409 St Antoine St, 1910; 336 Mackay St, 1912. Strathmore,

Quebec, 1914
1910 123 Miniature portrait
1912 123 Miniature sur ivoire
124 Roses pastel $100
1914 104 Miniatures on ivory, 6 $50 each

DESY, PAULINE
addr: Montreal, 261 Ontario St E
1926 239 Monsieur M sculp

DEVENYI, ESTER B. (m Tibor Devenyi)
1929, Budapest IO
addr: Merrickville, Ont RR4
1960 146 October nm $50

DEVLIN, MAUD
addr: Quebec, 144 Grande Allée, Apt 26
1958 14 Landscape $100

DEVLIN, MURRAY JOHN
24 Nov 1924, Vancouver
addr: New Westminster, B.C, 1121 Hamilton St
1959 7 6 p.m. December city $225

DEWEY, CHARLES MELVILLE Amer
16 Jul 1849, Lowville, N.Y. 17 Jan 1937, New York B F TB1/3 WWA36
1889 16 The early morn $275

DEZIEL, FRANCOIS
10 Jul 1914, St Mathieu, Que
addr: Montreal, 1336 St Zotique St
1946 67 Chez le Père Chopin $200

DIAMOND, HYMAN
addr; Montreal, 5341 Côte St Luc Rd, Apt 3, 1942-3
1942 199 Tjawan crayon & pencil
200 Ragamuffin crayon & pencil
201 Okluk pencil drwg
1943 225 Illuminated testimonial (Mr Alan Bronfman)
226 Illuminated testimonial (Mr J. Levinson)

DI CARLO, GEORGE ALAIN
29 Jun 1926, Belleville, Ont
addr: Montreal, 1442 Sherbrooke St W
1954 97 Henri No 1 wax encaustic $150

DICHMONT, JAMES
31 Dec 1875, Accrington, Lancs, Eng
addr: Calgary, 337 20th Ave W (sic)
1947 63 The old cottonwood tree wc $45
64 Sunshine and shadow wc $35

DICKENS, HARRY B.
addr: Ottawa, 269 Slater St
1946 68 The pilgrim $500
69 Is it nothing to you? $750

DICKINSON, SARA (m Andrew Dickinson)
c 1897, Orkney, Scot
addr: Montreal, 1434 St Catherine St W
1943 Sarah
53 From my window $25
1947 65 Mums $150

DIETRICH, RICH
addr: Verdun, Que, 822 4th Ave
1931 79 Brothers $450

DIETSCHE, RICHARD W.
addr: Montreal: 5995 Hutchison St, 1934; 5209 Sherbrooke St W, Apt 37, 1937
1934 89 At Laval des Rapides pastel $25
90 St Hilaire pastel $100
1937 79 Creek at Cote Virtue $100

DIGNAM, MARY ELLA WILLIAMS (m John Sifton Dignam)
13 Jan 1860, Port Burwell, Ont 6 Sep 1938, Toronto EC CNS36 CWW36 H Mo98/12 TB2
addr: Toronto; 101 Maitland St, 1892; 509 Markham St, 1894; 250 Rusholme Rd, 1895; 275 St George St, 1897-8; 284 St George St, 1912-13; 252 Poplar Rd, 1925-36
1886 63 Still life
M.E. Dynam
80 Bon silené and jafrans roses
1888 7 A harmony $25
31 Pansies $25
44 Niphetos roses $35
53 Head of French peasant girl $75
1889 17 Touched by frost $200
18 Where the mulleins grow $50 (mullins, mispr)
19 Dream of roses $150
20 Marigolds
21 Spring morning $100
1892 34 Mamma wants me $35

35 Marigolds $25
1894 46 A poppy garden $30
47 A memory $75
1895 31 Wild morning glory $100
1897 31 Windmill near Dort, Holland $60
1898 25 Roses $75
1912 125 Dutch interior $125
1913 119 In the Hague wood pastel $75
120 The Salute, Venice $50
1925 94 Zinnias $150
1926 48 Roses $450
1928 54 Anemones $150
55 The marsh $150
1929 65 Peonies $200
66 Red maple $125
1930 56 Poppies $75
57 Water lilies $150
58 Rocks and reflections $200
1931 80 Autumn, Muskoka $200
1936 132 On the dunes, North Sea $125
133 Boat at mouth of old Rhine $75

DINGLE, JOHN ADRIAN DARLEY
4 Feb 1911, Barmouth, Wales 22 Dec 1974, Mississauga, Ont CWW70 M WWA76
addr: Erindale, Ont, Upper Middle Rd, RR 1, 1956-60
1956 16 Genesis $550
1960 25 Fishboat fugue $500

DINGLE, RUTH MARION (m Peter Hugh Douet)
4 Dec 1908, Calgary 31 Dec 1980, Owen Sound, Ont
addr: Westmount: 582 Landsowne Ave, 1930-40; 54 Thornhill Ave, 1946-50
1930 59 The road to the lake $25
1931 81 Mount Tremblant, St Jovite $15
1933 82 September sunshine, Canoe Lake $40
1934 91 Autumn bouquet $100
1936 134 Gem of the woods, Algonquin Park $40
135 Tanamacoon River, Algonquin Park $40
1937 80 Tiger lilies $100
81 Gladioli and delphinium $100
1939 107 Algonquin colour, Algonquin Park $40
108 Cottage bouquet $50
1940 89 Maligne Lake $40
90 Mount Edith Cavell $40
1946 70 Bring in the rations wc
71 The Cariboo country, B.C. wc
1947 66 Fisherman's Cove, N.S. wc $75
1948 96 The laundry cart etch & aqua $10
1950 6 Cock $75

DION, GILBERT
addr: Montreal, 2108 Bleury St
1942 43 A toast to surrealism $500

DIONNE, THERESE
addr: Montreal, 784 Beaubien St E
1946 278 Alfred Laliberté plaster
279 Young Negro plaster
280 Canadian girl plaster

DIX, WAKEFORD G.
1888, Garden Island, Ont
addr: Toronto: 45 Kendal Ave, 1936; 71 Lombard St, 1939
1936 136 Tug $150
1939 109 Idle ships wc
110 Gray day wc $40

DOBELL, SYBIL see ROBERTSON, SYBIL

DODWELL, ISABELLE
addr: Montreal, 4065 Côte des Neiges Rd, 1932-3
1932 85 Miss Isabelle Ritchie pastel
1933 83 Miss Nancy Talmie, sketch pastel

DOERNBACH, MARGUERITE ELIZABETH (Mrs Peggy Anderson)
9 May 1917, Philadelphia
addr: Montreal: c/o Mrs. P Anderson, 1814 Dorchester St W, 1944-5; 3425 Peel St, 1946. St Sauveur des Monts, Que, 1947
1944 31 Artist $150
1945 71 Farm house garden wc $55
254 Textile Union meeting drwg $25
1946 74 Birches wc $50
1947 333 Dead soldier sculp $800

DOGGART, A. R.
see Tetley, Charles Reginald, 1914-467

DOKE, WILLIAM ROBERT NELSON
addr: Montreal, 5341 Côte St Luc Rd

1964 88 Tranquility nm $85

DOMENJOZ, MAURICE
addr: Montreal, 3512 Claude St, 1946-56
1946 281 Candeur wd
282 Goddess wd $85
283 Inca priest wd $50
1955 27 Boats & fish $125
1956 17 Still life with red fish $125

DOMINGUE, MAURICE
addr: Montreal: 1434 Le Caron St, 1946-7; 32 St James St W, 1949. Pointe aux Trembles, Que, 10 St Jean Baptiste Ave, 1951
1946 Domingue-Landriau, M.
75 Activité nautique wc $75
1947 69 The old caboose wc
1949 121 Symphony in purple wc $50
1951 56 New York after a storm wc $75

DONALD, ADELINE see WEBSTER, ADELINE

DONATO, VINANTE
addr: Montreal, 1292 de la Roche St
1919 363 La bacchanale sculp
364 Vers le nouvel horizon sculp
365 La fortune sculp $70

DONLY, EVA BROOK (m Augustine William Donly. m A. Williams)
30 Apr 1867 - 1 Jan 1941, Simcoe, Ont
H M NGC TB3 WWA40
addr: Toronto, 63 Inglewood Dr
1926 49 Guanajuato, Mexico wc $125

DONNELL, JAMES M.
1884, Edinburgh d 1957
addr: Montreal: 376 Claremont Ave, 1928-9; 3811 Prud'homme Ave, 1934; 8 Amesbury Ave, 1935; 1461 Bleury St, 1936-8
1928 56 Old sheds $75
1929 67 Côte des Neiges $60
1934 94 Evening, Rawdon, Que pastel $75
95 Quiet waterway pastel $40
1935 99 Evening, Oireau River pastel $50
1936 138 Spring thaw, Rawdon temp $50
1937 82 Sun bath wc $25
83 Reflections wc $25
1938 39 The gate at Kuwait wc $50

DONNELLY, LILLIAN E.
addr: Montreal, 18 Seymour Ave, 1909-10
1909 34 Vase, iris $35
35 Vase, conventional peacock $20
36-7 Vase, conventional mistletoe $10, $8
38 Vase, gold iris $10
39 Vase, yellow rose $7
40 Three cups & saucers $3 each
1910 428 Tray
429 Butterfly tray
430 Butterfly plate
431 Plate
432 Vase $4

DORAN, MARGARET FELICITE HENEY (m Anthony Burke Doran)
addr: Ottawa, 321 Chapel St
1940 91 August afternoon, homestead at Aylmer, Quebec

DORAN, MAUD E.
addr: Montreal, 1020 Tupper St, 1917-19
1917 116 Cliff drive, Bermuda $30
117 Cliff view, Bermuda $30
1918 108 A view on Kanawaki Links $15
109 Old bridge at Lachine $10
1919 105 Canadian scene
106 After the storm
107 Our mountains in winter

DORAY, AUDREY M. CAPEL (m Victor Doray)
4 June 1931, Montreal M
addr: Lachine, Que, 61 56th Ave, 1953-7
1953 Capel, 1953-4
71 Woodlands $45
1954 21 The smoker
1957 28 Taxco $100

DOUCET, EMMANUEL ARTHUR
16 Sep 1888, Massachusetts 11 Jun 1960, Montreal
addr: Montreal, 263 St Catherine St E 1933-4
1933 366 Bank office
1934 380-1 Residence

DOUET, PETER HUGH
addr: Montreal, 54 Thornhill Ave
1948 97 Market place etch & aqua $10

DOUET, RUTH see DINGLE, RUTH

DOUGLAS, BLOOMFIELD, Capt RNR
1832-1906 H
addr: Montreal, 26 Belmont St, 1892. Ottawa, Marine and Fisheries Dept, 1897
1892 36 Outward bound
37 Homeward bound
1897 32 A close shave $100
154 Old French fort, Annapolis, N.S. wc $15

DOUGLAS, CHRYSTIE LUDLOW
6 Apr 1900, New York 20 June 1960, Montreal
addr: Montreal: 2 Summerhill Ave, 1927; 5011 Grosvenor Ave, 1933; 4694 Grosvenor Ave, 1937; 1190 University St, 1937. Westmount, 467 Clarke Ave, 1949
1927 43 Roman theatre at Verona wc
268 Castle del'Ovo, Naples pencil
269 Ponte Fabrice, Rome pencil $30
270 Church of St Dominico, Siena pencil
271 Arena at Arles pencil $20
1933 84 Craig Street, Montreal wc $20
1937 84 Autumn trees wc
85 Early spring wc
334 Infirmary Building, Bishop's College School, Lennoxville, Que
335 House, C.S. Bradeen, Esq, Oakland Ave, Westmount
336 House, Philip D. Magor, Esq, Hampstead, Que
1949 122 Val David hills wc $50

DOUGLAS, EDWIN
addr: Winnipeg, 633 Stella St
1964 25 Nude and bedroom $850

DOUGLAS, HORTENSE P. A.
addr: Montreal, 2 Summerhill Ave
1922 88 Miss Beatrice Hill
89 Stained glass window des $25

DOWNES, LIONEL FIELDING
15 Apr 1900, Wigan, Lanc. Eng d 1972
addr: Montreal: 362 Notre Dame St W, 1936; 3494 Hutchison St, Apt 1, 1940-54
1936 139 Morning sunlight pastel $20
1940 92 Rainy day $50
1941 56 In the barn pastel $50
1943 54 Conquest $250
55 February evening $60
1944 32 January mood $125
1954 31 Averse d'été, rue de la Fabrique, Québec $225

DOWNEY, FRANK
addr: Montreal, 1131 University St, 1930. Ville St Laurent, Que, 1932
1930 60 At the Glades, Scituate, Mass $200
1932 86 Rockport, Gloucester, Mass

DOWNING, ROBERT JAMES
1 Aug 1935, Hamilton, Ont CWW84
addr: Toronto
1968 64 Crossed rectangles acry 11 1/2 x 11 3/8 $750
65 Exploding cube No 2 alum & red epoxy 36 x 36 $1,400 (MBAM)

DOYLE, KATIE
addr: Montreal, 54 Drummond St
1906 223 S.S. Fessenden wc

DRAKE, WILLIAM ALEXANDER
7 Nov 1891 - 15 Sep 1946, Toronto AGO
addr: Toronto, 284 Glenholme Ave
1929 316 Moulin Havigne, veaux Belgique etch $25
317 Journal Square Bridge, under construction etch $20

DRAPER, CHARLES F. Eng
DBA DVP G TB
addr: Montreal: 9 Highland Ave, 1923-5; 4055 Highland Ave, 1941
1923 79 Porta della Carta, Venezia b&w
226 Tiberias etch $12.50
227 Suez etch $12.50
1925 341-4 War memorial in bronze des
1941 57 Pont Sully, Paris

DREANY, EDWARD JOSEPH
29 Feb 1908, North Bay, Ont
addr: Toronto: 10 Gloucester St, 1935; 534 Carlaw Ave, 1936-8; 114 Marion St, 1939-41; 38 Glenlake Ave, 1944-5
1935 100 The cabin at '93' wc $40
1936 140 Corpus Christi Sunday $150
141 In the nickel smelter wc $35
142 Store at Copper Cliff wc $30
1937 86 The brick factory wc $35

87 Corpus Christi Sunday wc $30
88 Afternoon breeze wc $30
89 Church at Copper Cliff wc $30
1938 40 Olan's Mill wc $40
41 The brick factory III wc $50
1939 111 Temedol wc $40
112 In the sugar bush $125
1940 93 The milk house wc $50
1941 58 The picnic wc $40
59 Fishing shack wc $40
1944 33 Nocturne wc $40
1945 72 Stores at night wc $50

DREANY, FREDA JOHNSTON (m Edward Joseph Dreany)
addr: Toronto, 114 Marion St, 1939-41
1939 113 Scene in a barnyard wc $40
1941 220 Eileen chalk $25
221 Too tired to eat chalk $25

DRENTERS, ANDREAS
13 Mar 1937, Poppel, Belg
addr: Acton, Ont RR 1
1965 33 Pregnant woman iron $350

DREYFUS, RAOUL HENRI French
18 Sep 1878, London, Eng B DBA TB2
addr: Paris, Société des Artistes Français
1922 89A Portrait

DROPE, MCCLEARY HERBERT (Swami Bodhi Anando)
31 Oct 1931, Detroit
addr: Winnipeg
1968 66 From the series, Homage to Helios wld cor-ten steel 96 x 32 $5,000
67 Monument study 24 x 17 $1,200

DROUIN, JEAN CHARLES
31 Jul 1887 - 28 Feb 1951, Montreal
see Prefontaine, Alfred, 1912-17

DROUIN, MICHELINE
c 1935, Quebéc
addr: Québec, 367 rue 15ème
1956 18 Paysage immergé $60

DRUMMOND, ARTHUR ALEXANDER
28 May 1891, Toronto AAA29 WWA76
addr: Toronto, 63 Inglewood Dr, 1919-33. Orono, Ont, 1935-67
1919 108 On the coast of Victoria $100
109 Harvest $75
1920 72 Summer morning in the Adirondacks $150
73 A breezy day $50
74 Autumn in the Rockies wc $30
1921 70 On the coast of Maine $75
71 Bathers, York Beach $75
72 The buccaneer wc $50
1922 90 Incoming tide $175
91 The beach at Ogunquit $175
92 Bathers $50
93 The path to the sea wc $50
1923 80 The cooper shop $75
1926 50 Autumn in Muskoka $175
51 The Whirlpool Rapids, Niagara wc $100
52 Upland meadows wc $100
53 Autumn in the Caledon Hills wc $65
1927 44 October woods, Muskoka $175
45 Thatcher's Twin Lights, off Cape Ann $200
1928 57 Fishing boats, Rockport harbour $175
58 By Lake Ontario wc $50
1930 61 A road through the Caledon Hills wc $100
62 Bay of Quinte wc $50 (listed 1967, Jessie Dow prize)
1931 82 An Adirondack stream wc $50
83 A sunny lane, Rice Lake $150
1933 85 The north beach, Percé $150
86 Parliament Hill, from Hull wc $100 1967-22 Parliament Buildings, Ottawa, from Hull, 1932. wc 20 1/2 x 29
1934 96 A storm at Anse-aux-Gascons $150
97 Percé Rock wc $100
98 Cliffs at Percé wc $50
1935 101 After the storm, Peggy's Cove, N.S. $165
1936 143 Lake of Bays, Muskoka wc $50
144 Lumina, Lake of Bays wc $50
145 Autumn woodland wc $100
1937 90 Coast scene, Nova Scotia wc $100

DRUMMOND, BERNICE EILEEN THOMPSON (m Orville Lee Drummond)
13 Oct 1905, Picton, Ont
addr: Kingston, Ont, 110 Bagot St, Apt 2
1945 73 Corner store, Hull $45

DRUMMOND, BETTY JEAN
17 Dec 1919, Trochu, Alta
addr: Toronto, 224 St George St, Apt 509
1957 29 Ballet $150

DRUMMOND, DOUGLAS R. A.
addr: Montreal, 1008 Melrose Ave
1939 394 Retired drwg
395 Spring water drwg

DRUMMOND, JEANIE REDPATH
fl 1891-06 H
addr: Ottawa, 149 Somerset St
1891 159 Byzantine Court, Crystal Palace wc (Bazantine, mispr)

DRUMMOND, MOIRA ELIZABETH
1 Aug 1904, Montreal
addr: Montreal, 47 Draper Ave, 1926. Westmount, 235 Metcalfe Ave, 1927. Montreal: 2075 Comte St, 1929; 1455 Drummond St, 1935. Westmount, 510 Argyle Ave, 1936; 18 Thornhill Ave, 1938
1926 192 St Bruno etch $15
193 Orsanmichele, Florence etch $20
194 Old houses on the Arno etch $15
1927 272 Lac Manitou, January etch $15
273 January days etch $10
1929 318 Sunset, Port of Spain etch
1935 102 Mrs J.A.D. McCurdy
103 St Hilarion $250
104 Laurentian village $200
1936 146 Joe Smokwasett $200
147 Baie des Roches $100
148 Cowichan woman $100
1938 42 Kafir lily $60
43 First snow $40

DUBE, LOUIS THEODORE
1861 St Roch des Aulnaies, Que 1937, Paris B H
addr: Paris: ave de Saxe, 1892; 111 rue de Courcelles, 1903; 11 rue Théodore de Banville, 1913
1892 38 Madame Dubé in her studio
39 Assorted fruit
1903 38 Watering the cow $300
39 Le goûter $1,000
284 Case of miniatures
1913 121 Interior of the Musée du Louvre $500

DUBOIS, VIOLET ELIZABETH PICK (m J.H. Edward Dubois)
5 Mar 1914, Montreal
addr: Montreal, 3375 Ridgewood, Apt 8
1958 15 Late Dr Wm Dudley Woodhead $100

DUBREUIL, JEAN-PAUL
addr: Montreal, 4617 Papineau Ave
1945 74 Symphony, still life $100

DUCHARME, RAOUL
addr: St Hyacinthe, Que, 150 Girouard St
1917 118 Moonlight b&w $20

DUCLOS, GRACE GILLELAN (m Arnold W. Duclos)
addr: Ottawa, 152 James St, 1927-32
1927 46 Mrs T.J. Gillelan, Ottawa
1932 87 Self portrait
381 Kenneth drwg
382 Fun drwg

DUFF, ANN MACINTOSH
14 Jul 1925, Toronto AGO CWW84 IO M WWA84
addr: Toronto, 133 Imperial St
1960 147 Wet day nm $150

DUFF, WALTER RAYMOND
3 May 1879, Hamilton 1 Sep 1967, Toronto
addr: Toronto, 1 Breadalbane St, 1914. Montreal, 413 Dorchester St W, 1923
1914 105 Chrysanthemums wc $150
106 Hannah Bamford etch
107 Noel Marshall, Esq etch
108 Trinity University, Toronto etch $25
109 Upper Canada College, Toronto etch $25
1923 81 Zinnias wc $250

DUFFIN, HAROLD A.
addr: Weston, Ont, 24 Patika Ave
1955 99 Still life I nm $75

DUFFY, HELEN
b Zurich
addr: Montreal, 6874 Sherbrooke St W

1954 98 September, Ile Cadieux wc

DUGGAN, IVY
addr: Montreal, 4382 Delorimier Ave
1949 24-5 Children at play, No 1, No 2 $25 each

DUGGAN, KATHLEEN
addr: Montreal, 4382 Delorimier Ave
1950 7 The book stand $35

DUGUAY, RODOLPHE
27 Apr 1891 - 25 Aug 1973, Nicolet, Que CE CWW70
addr: Montreal, 710 Berri St
1920 75 Chenal, la ferme, Nicolet

DULUDE, CLAUDE
30 Mar 1931, Montreal CWW84
addr: Laval-des- Rapides, Que
1968 eaux -fortes sur cuivre 68-9
68 Pleine-lune 6 x 7 1/4 $40
69 Pleine terre 6 x 7 1/4 $40
70 Avant acry 46 x 36 $250
71 Aprés acry 46 x 36 $250

DUMOUCHEL, ALBERT
15 Apr 1916, Bellerive, n Valleyfield, Que 11 Jan 1971, St Antoine-sur-Richelieu, Que AGO B CC1 CE M NGC TB3 Juror
addr: Montreal, 1737 Gouin Blvd E, 1949-51
1949 123 L'acrobate sur les toits gouache $75
1950 109 Les Mendoles $150
1951 91 Le ciel déchiré de cris déchiré comme un alle $75
123 L'assasinat d'une huître perlière oil & wc $50

DUMOUCHEL, SUZANNE BEAUDOIN (m Albert Dumouchel)
25 Dec 1920, Montreal
addr: Montreal
1968 72 Chéops II eau-forte 23 x 26 $50
73 Les fraises litho 19 1/2 x 26 $50
74 Trilogie l'oeil litho-triptyque 19 1/2 x 26 chaque panneau $120
75 La douche acry 28 x 35 $200

DUNBAR, FREDERICK ALEXANDER TURNER
1849, Guelph, Ont d 1912
1889 196 Very Rev Dean of Quebec bust $25
197 Msgr Raquet head sculp $25

DUNCAN, ALICE MCLAREN
1879, Colborne, Ont
addr: Colborne, Ont, 1920-5
1920 76 The quaint old barn $125
1925 95 Evening sunlight $75

DUNCAN, ALMA MARY
2 Oct 1917, Paris, Ont IO
addr: Montreal: 4032 Lacombe Ave, 1937; 4936 Lacombe Ave, 1940-4. Ottawa, 131 Somerset St W, 1960
1937 91 Through the studio window wc
1940 94 Self portrait
95 Still life with book $50
96 Snowdon $25
1941 60 Self portrait
222 Nude standing at basin charcl $50
1942 44 Resting $100
1943 56 Army women in warehouse $250
57 September landscape $100
1944 137-8 Workers, Nos II, III drwg $50 each
1960 26-7 Industry, Nos 1,2 $125, $175

DUNCAN, DOROTHY (m Hugh MacLennan)
28 Jul 1903, East Orange, N.J. 22 Apr 1957, Montreal CWW55 W78
addr: Montreal: 1575 Summerhill Ave, Apt 605, 1953; 1535 Summerhill Ave, 1955-7
1953 73 Tom Tucker $175
1955 MacLennan 1955-7
56 Mushrooms $175
1956 37 Yankee façade $190
38 First flight $175
1957 62 Sailor's chapel $275 (MBAM)

DUNLOP, ALEXANDER FRANCIS
Aug 1842 - 30 Apr 1923, Montreal H Mo98/12 NGC
addr: Montreal: 61 Temple Bldg, 1894-1903; Lindsay Bldg, 1909
1889 184 Temple Building, St James Street
185 House on Edgehill Ave
1894 Dunlop & Heriot, 1894-5
259 Ice grotto
260 St George's Church, tower

261 Eker's Brewery
262 City house
263 City, or country villa
1895 219 Mr Hugh Graham's house, entrance and hall
1897 230 Standard Insurance Chambers, St James Street
231 Interior view, reception and hall, Holmwood, residence of A.F. Dunlop, Esq
1898 217 J. Auld, Esq, residence McGregor Street
1903 264 Outremont Golf Club
1909 412 Sarah Maxwell School
413 Department store building
414 Molson's Bank, Revelstoke, B.C.

DUNLOP, GLADYS
addr: Montreal, 102 Mackay St
1910 124 Baby Evelyn

DUNNING, MARY GORDON (m Fred E. Dunning)
addr: Charlemagne, Que, 1915-21. Montreal, 524 Valois Ave, 1933-6
1912 446 Plate
1915 433 Ice cream tray
434 Tea pot, sugar, cream
435 Powder box
436 Vase
1917 415 Vase $10
416 Comport $7
417 Plate $5
1918 422 Vase, conventional des
423 Salad dish
424 Sandwich plate
1921 332 Large vase
333 Plate
334 Small vase
335 Dish
1933 449 Border design, luna moth $10
450 Border design, banded purple $10
1934 441 Butterfly, red under wing des $10
442 Butterfly, Pacific tiger des $10
443 Butterfly, little sulphur des $10
1935 400 Red admiral des $10
401 Io moth des $10
402 Camberwell beauty des $10
1936 528 Hawk moth des $10
529 Io moth des $10

DUPRAS, M. PIERRE
3 Jun 1937, Montreal
addr: Montréal Nord, 12220 ave Salk
1964 26 Japon 3 $400

DUQUET, GEORGE HENRY
addr: Quebec: 1 St John St, 1909-28; 29 1/2 St Stanilas St, 1943-6
1909 112 Port Neuf, Paris $25
113 Coin d'interieur $25
1910 125 Ruined houses, Beauport, built 1651 $120
1922 94 Basilica Square, Quebec $200
1923 82 Methodist Church, Quebec $200
83 A morning in late September $200
1924 75 Louise Basin, Quebec $250
1925 96 Church of Les Eboulements with its old cemetery $150
1928 59 Le divan $500
60 Schooners au Bassin Louise, Québec $350
1943 58 Informal snack (Goûter aux huîtres) $300
1946 76 Oriental table corner $75

DUQUET, MARIE MARTHE SUZANNE
8 Nov 1917, Outrement, Que
addr: Outremont, 5852 Durocher St, 1942-50
1942 45 Nature morte $150
46 Paysage Matane $75
1950 110 La femme au tapis $300

DUQUETTE, GEORGE
addr: Montreal, 1199 Bleury St
1933 513 Ste Imelda wd
514 St Joseph and Child wd

DURAND, FERNAND
28 Dec 1939, Montreal
addr: Montreal, 4005 Melrose Ave
1962 73 Manon bronze $300

DURGIN, HARRIET THAYER Amer
fl 1889-1901 WWW
1889 117 Tea roses wc $125
118 The wild New England shore wc $125

DURNFORD, ALEXANDER TILLOCH GALT
28 Jul 1898 - 22 Mar 1973, Montreal
CNS27 CWW73
addr: Montreal: 9 Simpson St, 1921-6; 374 Beaver Hall Sq, 1927; 1110 Castle Bldg, 1928; 1410 Stanley St, 1929-30; 660 St Catherine St W, University Tower Bldg, 1931-6
1921 306 William's College, York b&w $18
307 12th C tower, Chartres Cathedral, France $15
308 Ex libris zinc cut $15
1922 363 Roof detail, Choristers Hall, Wells b&w
364 Side aisle, arcade, St Cuthbert, Wells b&w
1924 76 The Fisk Building, New York
1925 297 Zeta Psi Memorial Chapter House, University Street
1926 146 Regina cenotaph competition drwg
1927 197 Residence, 53 Forden Ave, Westmount photo
198 Residence, Shediac, N.B. pencil
1928 225 Proposed building, Ottawa
226 Residence, J.R. McDougall, Esq, Redpath Cr, Montreal
227 Residence, D.A. Wanklyn, Esq, 3600 Atwater Ave, Montreal
228 Garage, J.W. Young Smith, Esq, Shediac, N.B.
1929 240 Residence, Westmount, elevation, entrance
241-3 Residence, D.A. Wanklyn, Esq interior
1930 212 Cunard, uptown office, 1312 Sherbrooke St W photo
213 Sun room, J.M. Molson, Esq, Clarke Ave, Westmount
214 Residence, Mackay Smith, Esq, Belvedere Rd, Westmount
1931 266 Natural pine room, residence Mr & Mrs T.G. Morgan, Sunnyside Ave, Westmount photo
267 Residence, Shediac, N.B. photo
268 Residence, Dr & Mrs Campbell P. Howard, Clarke Ave, Westmount photo
269 Residence, Mr & Mrs John M. Molson, Clarke Ave, Westmount
1932 336 House, Dr E.M. Eberts, Val David, Que photo
337 An entrance hall photo
1933 367-8 Residence, Mr & Mrs C.H. MacDougall, Cartierville photos
369 White Circle Luncheonette Co, Decarie Blvd, hot dog stand pencil
1934 382 Residence, Denis Stairs, Esq, Lexington Ave, Westmount photo
383 Ski lodge, John H. Molson, Esq, Piedmont, Que pencil sketch
384 Domestic architectural types pencil sketch
1935 350 Country house, Mrs Ross Sims photo
1936 471 Interior, country house, Mrs Ross Sims, St Sauveur photo
see also Fetherstonhaugh, Harold Lee, 1934-47

DURNFORD, GEORGE
addr: Montreal: 660 Sherbrooke St W, 1916-17; 189 St James St, 1922
1916 90 The old fort at Chambly wc
1917 119 The Bull Rock, Metis Beach wc
1922 95 A pilot boat, 5th decade of 19th century

DUTTON, HAZEL I.
addr: Montreal, 373 Marlowe Ave
1919 419 Candlesticks $7
420 Coffee pot $6.50

DUVAL, LOUIS
addr: Montreal, 5201 Decarie Blvd
1956 19 Primulas $295

DYNAM, M.E. see DIGNAM, MARY ELLA

DYONNET, EDMOND
25 Jun 1859, Crest, France 8 Jul 1954, Montreal B CC2 CE CNS36 CWW52 EC H M MO12 NGC TB W78 WWA52
addr: Montreal: 81 Imperial Bldg, 1891; 1000 Dorchester St, 1892; c/o Art Association, 1894; Fraser Institute, 1895; 9 University Ave, 1897-1912; 283 University Ave, 1913; 255 Bleury St, 1920
1891 37 Portrait
38 Cloître $50
39 Statuaire $150
1892 40 Mr T. Carli
41 Mr W. Lorenz
42 The last crust $250
43 A field of beets, St Hrnei $80
44 Montreal, from the island $30

45 The wharf, foot of McGill Street $25
46 Cabbages, Lachine Road $50
1894 48 The cigarette $500
49 M Ingres
50 Yale, B.C. $50
51 The Pacific coast at Victoria $30
1895 32 Master W, Hobart Molson
33 Portrait of a lady
34 Mr C.H. Sobeski
35 Autumn tints $50
36 The old windmill $35
37 The Lower Lachine Road $28
1897 33 Sunset at Labelle $100
34 A harvest day $80
35 Approaching rain $80
36 Looking down the valley, Fontainebleau $80
37 The coast of Gaspé $55
38 A boat in Montreal harbour $40
1898 26 St Feréol Road $250
27 Les Laurentides $175
28 Cattle returning home $100
29 Le Loing, France $75
30 A yoke of oxen $50
1900 29 H.S. de Lotbinière Harwood, MP
30 W. Herrick, Esq
1901 25 O.M. Gould, Esq
26 R. Boulet, MD
27 Mrs W.L. Voigt
28 Miss A. Lorin
29 A. Macpherson, Esq
30 Charles Gill, Esq
1903 40 F.L. Wanklyn, Esq
41 Head of a girl $50
1905 42 The Laurentians
43 Italian landscape
44 Grand Rivière
45 Shore at St François
206 Man reading pastel
1906 51 Mr Alfred Brunet
52 Mr Jules Helbronner
53 Miss A.L.
54 Boy playing mandolin $200
55 Morning at St Adèle $75
56 Lac Tremblant $50
57 In the wood $50
58 Waterfall, Lac Tremblant $40
59 Afternoon on the lake $30
60 Evening on the lake $30
1909 114 R. Pinkerton, Esq
115 The picture book $300
1910 125 Mons J. Poivert
1912 126 Mrs Hayter Reid
127 The top of the hill $250
128 Girl reading $250
129 Rosine $100
1913 122 J. Hammond, Esq, RCA
123 Early morning, Berthier $300
124 A country road, Berthier $250
1920 77 A.W.P. Buchanan, Esq KC
1894-7 Assoc Hon mention, 1892, portrait, figure. Assoc prize, 1894, portrait
port: by F. Iacurto, 1949-48; A.L. Ewan, 1932-383; G. Benjamin, 1919-37A; bust, A. Carli, 1891-216

DZENIS, EDOUARDS A.
18 Apr 1907, Latvia IO M
addr: Toronto, 233 Lake Shore Dr, 1955-61
1955 100 Horses nm $100
1956 93 Horses nm $75
1960 148 Fishermen nm $200
149 On the beach nm $150
1961 74 Composition with horses nm $200

E

EARLE, AGNES C. (m Stuart C. Knox)
addr: Westmount: 172 Edgehill Rd, 1923-28; 739 Upper Belmont Ave, 1936
1923 84 Midwinter wc $50
1924 77 Les écureuils, Québec wc $20
1927 47 In the bazaars Cairo wc $50
1929 Knox, 1929=36
125 Market day in St Thérèse wc $25
1936 230 Zinnias wc $15
231 The ski trail wc $25
232 The pine tree wc $25

EARLE, PAUL (Mrs)
addr: Westmount, 530 Mount Pleasant Ave
1909 41 Bowl $50

EARLE, PAUL BARNARD
23 Sep 1872 - c 1955, Montreal M NGC OMC TB3 WWA56 Juror
addr: Westmount, 530 Mount Pleasant Ave, 1906-10, 1912-14. Montreal, Thomas & Earle, 1911. Notre Dame de Grace, 1915-16. Montreal, 149 King Edward Ave, 1917-20. Westmount: 770 Côte St Antoine Rd. 1921; 172 Edgehill Rd, 1922-34. Montreal, 1475 St Catherine St W, 1935-7

Westmount, 333 Redfern Ave, 1943-44
1906 61 Village road, St Joachim $25
1908 57 April morning $35
1909 116 Spring, Côte St Luc nm $75
1910 127 Belvedere Road $75
128 Farm house $50
1911 94 Montreal, from Mount Royal, sunset $75
1912 130 Winter, Saint John, N.B. $40
131 Winter sunlight $50
1913 125 Bend of the river $75
126 An April day $100
1914 110 Windswept hillside $300
111 Late afternoon $300
112 The last rays $250
1915 111 The old canal, Lachine $300
112 A Laurentian farm $150
113 Approaching storm $300
114 October landscape $300
1916 91 The passing of winter $250
92 Summer landscape $250
1917 120 The first snow $250 (NGC)
121 Early spring $250
1918 110 The old farmhouse $250
111 Woods in autumn $250
1919 110 The summer home $250
111 Farmlands, Côte St Luc $250
1920 78 A northern river $350
79 The end of the lake $300
1921 74 The sanctuary $350
75 Rivière des Ormes, midsummer $350
1922 96 Birch trees, autumn $350
97 Early September $300
98 A peaceful valley $450
1923 85 The last load $350
1924 78 Misty morning $250
1925 97 River farm $200
98 November $75
99 Quebec farmhouse $125
1926 54 When winter ends $200
1927 48 Dawn $200
49 Early winter $75
50 Autumn sunshine $75
1928 61 Evening, Ste Thérèse $250
1929 68 Indian summer $350
69 Passing showers $350
70 Clearing weather $150
1930 63 Midday $100
64 The north country $200
65 The edge of the bush $250
1931 84 Quebec farm $250
85 The north country $500
86 Northern Quebec $500
87 Misty day, Quebec $250
1932 88 Calm before storm $200
89 Winter afternoon $200
90 Quebec landscape $200
91 Village street $100
1933 87 Midday, Baie St Paul $450
88 The farm $450
89 Old farmhouse $250
90 Indian summer $350 (listed 1967, Jessie Dow prize)
1934 99 Snow flurries $250
100 Spring $200
101 In harbour $200
102 Autumn $200
1935 105 Point Levis $400
106 Clearing weather $350
107 Late afternoon $125
1936 149 Cloud shadows $500
150 Woods, near Magog $250
1937 92 Wharves, Château Richer $250
1943 59 The last gleam $600
60 Château Richer $250
1944 34 Winter afternoon $200

EARLE, PEGGY
addr: Westmount, 22 Chesterfield Ave, 1940-3
1940 97 Scene from the window
1943 61 Hollyhocks $30

EARNSHAW, ARTHUR
addr: Sherbrooke, Que: 215 Victoria St, 1939; 13 Montcalm St, 1946
1939 114 The St Francis valley, Sherbrooke wc $45
1946 77 Water lily $45

EASTLAKE, CHARLES HERBERT Eng
fl 1889-1940 B DBA DBW DVP G TB WBA WWB29
addr: St, Ives, Cornwall, 1897. Montreal, 900 Sherbrooke St W, 1940
1897 39 Landscape
1940 98 Street, St Sauveur wc $25
99 Brixham, trawlers, sketch wc $25

EASTLAKE, MARY ALEXANDRA BELL (m Charles Herbert Eastlake)
1864, Douglas, Ont 27 Jun 1951, Ottawa
AGO B DBA G H Mo98 NGC TB1/2/3 WWB27
addr: Paris, 9 rue Campagne Première, 1891. Montreal, 742 Sherbrooke St, 1892. Croydon, Eng, c/o Mrs Fuller,

Hollywood, Duppas Hill, 1894. St Ives, Cornwall, 1895-7. Croydon, Eng, 60 Sanfield Rd, 1900. London, Eng, 6 Clarendon St, Warwick Sq, 1901-3. London, Eng, 1908. Montreal, 72 Maxwelton Apts, 1923-4. Croydon, Eng, Hollywood, Duppas Hill, 1925. Montreal: c/o Mrs John F. Stairs, 731 Sherbrooke St W, 1926-7; 1509 Sherbrooke St W, 1930-2. Surrey, Eng, 1933. Montreal, 1509 Sherbrooke St W, 1935-7; 900 Sherbrooke St W, 1940-1. Almonte, Ont; 1943; Old Burnside Cottage, 1945-6

1888 Bell, 1888-1900
40 Decorative heads $50
57 Like some vision olden of far other time, When the age was golden in the young world's prime $40
1889 5 Old Breton peasant $25
6 La gardienne $75
1891 10 Twilight reverie $250
1892 8 Fairy tales $200
9 Study of a child reading $40
10 A little Dutch maid $40
11 A bit of moorland $25
12 A dreary outlook $50
1894 14 In the orchard $80
15 A nibble at last $100
16 Flower girl $80
17 Interior $50
1895 12 Moonrise $200
13 Treasure trove $100
14 Between the lights $40
1897 9 An idyll $75
10 Overcome by family cares $40
11 Sailing boats $40
1900 9 When spring rides through the woods $250
1901 31 Mrs John Stairs
122-4 Sketch pastel $20, $12, $12
1903 Bell, 1903-8
232 The elder sister pastel $30
233 Breton school boys pastel $30
1908 173 The green gown wc $75
174 Dutch fisher girl pastel $30
1923 86 The Ramparts, Montreuil-sur-Mer, GHQ during the war $1,000
87 Mother and child $500
1924 79 The young mother pastel $75
80 Petit bébé $40
1925 100 Hamoxen, au clair de lune wc $50
101 Ann pastel $65
102 Bluebells pastel $50
103-4 Portrait pastel
1926 55 Market day, a village in France $50
1927 51 Mobilization day, 1914, French fisherwomen watching the departure of the fleet $1,000 (NGC)
52 Winter moonrise $400
53 The little gray village $150
54 Snowy day pastel $60
1930 66-7 In Provence wc $75 each
68 Market, northern France pastel $150
69 Dark tower wc $60
1931 88 The bad tempered cat pastel $100
89 Fisherman's house, St Tropez wc $45
90 On the south coast wc $45
374 The evening star linoproff $22.50
1931 92 Gentle memory $150
93 Fisherman's houses, St Tropez $75
1933 91 Zinnias $100
92 Cotswold farm $300
93 Boy with harmonica $150
94 Fisherman's home, Cornwall
1935 108 The young mother pastel $50
1937 93 The willow tree $100
1940 100 Little shops on Guy Street $80
101 Polperro $75
1941 61 Dr Maude Abbott, LLD
62 Woodland pool $100
1943 62 Rocky stream $125
1945 75 Winter $125
1946 78 Blue jays in conference $100
1892-7 Assoc prize, 1891 Genre/figure

EASTMAN, ANTONIA (m S. Mark Eastman)
1886, Paris, France 1972, Vancouver
addr: Saskatoon, 807 17th St E, 1949. Vancouver, 2776 Pine St, Apt 203, 1951
1949 124 Saskatoon en hiver wc $75
1951 57 Red cedars, B.C. wc $100

EASTMAN, ELIZABETH M.
b 1905
addr: Kitchener, Ont, 194 Claremont Ave
1956 94 The picnic nm $35

EATON, CHARLES HARRY
13 Dec 1850, Akron, Ohio 4 Aug 1901, Leonia, N.Y. B F H TB WWW

1889 22 Wet days in October $650

EATON, MARIA
1889 119 Interior of the Jesuit Church, Montreal wc $50
120 A study wc $50

EATON, WYATT
6 May 1849, Phillipsburg, Que 7 Jun 1896, Newport R.I. AGO B CE F H NGC R2 TB W78
addr: New York, 1880, 1892
1880 38 Whittling
52 Portrait
1885 144 The gleaner wc
1886 51 Noon-day rest
64 The late Hon John Young
1892 47 Sir William Dawson painted for McGill University

ECHLIN, JOAN
addr: Ottawa: 257 Sussex St, Apt 8, 1956; 125 Sussex Dr, Apr 2, 1960
1956 20 Manotick bouquet
21 Forest light
1960 150 Vignette de Montréal nm

ECKERS, HANS
addr: Beloeil, Que
1951 124 Peace or war ink & wc
136 Feeling of spring ink

ECKHARDT, BARBARA
addr: Montreal, 1442 Stanley St, Apt 1, 1943-5
1943 63 Out of the old
1945 76 Emerging

EDE, FREDERICK CHARLES VIPONT Amer
22 Feb 1865, USA d c 1907 B H TB Y
addr: Paris, 1891. Sorques, n Paris, 1892-4
1889 121 Cows in pasture wc $45
122 Driving home the cows wc $50
1891 40 Landscape with cattle $125
41 At Marlotte, Seivre et Marne
42 Landscape with sheep $75
1892 48 Landscape and cattle $250
49 Spring $100
50 Autumn $125
1894 52 Cattle in the fields $250
53 Cattle by the river $150
54 Landscape near Sorques $125
55 Silvery birches $100
56 Landscape $100
1892-4 Assoc prize, 1891, Landscape

EDION, HENRI
16 Feb 1905, Vienna
addr: Montreal: c/o N. Timar, 528 Champagneur Ave, 1958; 3459 Drummond St, 1960-1
1958 58 The scientist nm $120
1960 151 Calling the birds nm $230
1961 75 The zoo at night nm $165

EDSON, AARON ALLAN
18 Dec 1846, Stanbridge, Que 1 May 1888, Glen Sutton, Que AGO B CE DCB EC H M NGC TB W78
addr: Montreal, 1880
1880 3 Camp in the woods
10 Autumn, near Bolton, E.T.
14 Old disused forest road
39 A trout stream in the forest
64 Mount Orford, Eastern Townships
74 Creek at Longueuil
103 Spring time wc
114 Going to school wc
118 Summer time wc
131 Harvesters wc
1881 51 Happy day, Glen Sutton wc
55 Pool by the wood wc
1883 121 A day in December, at Cernay, France
139 Old willows, at Cernay
161 Up the Seine
1885 11 Home, sweet, sweet home
93 A sketch from nature
113 Head waters of the Missisquoi wc
1886 22 Homestead of Robert Burns wc
29 Cottages near Ayr, Scotland wc
105 Ham farm house
106 Cliffords farm near Hownslow
107 Style at Ham, near Richmond Park
108 Old gate at Ham Park
109 Across the fields, near old Hampton
1888 71 Evening wc $200
130 Near Hampton Court, England wc

EDSON, ALLAN
addr: Montreal West, 123 Westminster Ave
1942 47 Dock fire, Brooklyn, New York wc $25

EDSON, WILLIAM
addr: Montreal: 140 Cherrier St, 1894; 441A St Urbain St, 1895; 428 St Charles Borromée St, 1897
1894 180 The brook wc $50
1895 156 Sketch, farm wc $10
157 Sketch, brook wc $10
1897 40 Violin study $40

EDWARDS, BURGOYNE
b c1870
addr: Montreal, c/o Canadian Trade Journal Lt, 12 Coristine Bldg
1906 224 Dawn, Cape Breton wc $25

EDWARDS, HENRIETTA MUIR (m Q.C. Edwards)
1849, Montreal 1931 Macleod, Alta H Mo12
1883 82 Roses
118 Trilliums
119 Portrait
159 Evening flower
160 Roses

EDWARDS, WILLIAM H.
addr: Toronto, 40 Norway Ave, 1924-5
1924 all etchings
275 Scarborough Bluffs $12
276 March edge $12.50
277 Up north $10
1925 343 Stoney Lake $15
344 The old camp $16

EGAN, J. HUGH
fl 1892-1929 H
addr: Montreal: 310 Laval Ave, 1892; 337 St Paul St, 1897; Montreal, 1903. Outremont: 650 Hutchison St, 1905; Outremont, 1908; 1976 Hutchison St, 1909; Outremont, 1911; 259 Durocher St, 1912; 257 Durocher St, 1913-20; 341 St Philips St, 1925; 332 St Ferdinand St, 1927; 730 Durocher St, 1929
1892 51 Study of a head
1897 41 Harbour scene $30
1903 42 On the canal $75
1905 46 The market gardener $50
1906 225 Goldenrod wc $10
226 Under the shadow of the Citadel, Quebec wc $15
1908 58 The water cart $35
1909 117 Road to the sandpit $50
1911 95 Winter, St Paul River $100
1912 132 Autumn afternoon $50
133 Village street $20
1913 127 The snow dump $60
128 The hay barge $30
1914 113 Breezy day, harbor $15
114 A cool retreat $40
1916 93 Stranded $20
1917 122 The landing $25
123 The ford $25
1920 80 November evening $25
1925 105 Below the Citadel, Quebec pastel $60
1927 55 October, Lake of Two Mountains $75
1929 71 Dismantling the wreck $80
(1906, F. Hugh, 1916, I. Hugh, mispr)

EGERTON, ROWLAND PHILIP
25 Nov 1891, Lahore, India
addr: Montreal, 1744 Mance St, 1913. Ottawa, 201 Cobourg St, 1957-8
1913 129 Miss Joan Walker b&w $25
1957 30 Rondo $100
1958 16 Rideau Lake (571) $150

EITEL, GEORGE EDWARD
25 Jan 1906, Preston, Ont 8 Nov 1961, Kitchener, Ont AGO M
addr: Kitchener, 82 Filbert St, 1951-5
1951 58 Mennonites leaving church wc $50
1952 59 A rainy day in autumn wc $35
1953 54 Trees and rocks wc
1954 99 Trout Creek wc
1955 101 New nets nm $50

ELDERKIN, E. K.
addr: Montreal, 772 Sherbrooke St W
1942 48 View from the convent pastel

ELFINGER, S.
addr: Montreal, 1550 Stanley St, Apt 37
1955 28 Harvest $250

ELIAS, ARTHUR EDWARD
11 Mar 1872, Llansadwrn, Wales
addr: Ottawa, 518 Gilmour St, 1922-3
1922 99 Circe and the Greeks wc $150

100 Tintagel in Cornwall, King Arthur's days $200
101 Scene in old London, Shakespeare, Henry 4th $150
102 The goblin city $200
1923 88 The forest of fear, from 'Croquemitaine' wc $150
89 The summons wc $75
90 Dafydd ap Siericyn, the famous Welsh (Lancastrian) outlaw leaves his cave of Carry-y-Gwalch, north Conway, to attack the Yorkists $50

ELIOT, MARY R.
addr: Ottawa, 148 Elgin St, 1936-9
1936 151 Farm on Lyn Road $35
1939 115 Leroux mills $35

ELIOT, RUTH MARY
22 Jun 1913, Ottawa AGO
addr: Ottawa, 148 Elgin St, 1934-40
1934 103 Wakefield, Quebec $15
1938 44 Somerset, Bermuda $40
1939 116 Needle's Eye light $35
1940 102 Pickanock, Quebec $40
103 Greenbush, Ontario $40

ELKIN, ANITA (m Henry S. Abramson)
addr: Montreal, 3457 Marlowe Ave, 1945-7
1945 77 Still life
1947 71 Shirley $85

ELLINGER, CARLTON D.
addr: Montreal: 1441 Drummond St, 1936; 6306 Park Ave, 1937; 2022 Union Ave, 1939; 5309 Park Ave, Apt 7, 1943-5
1936 scratchboard drawing 530-1
530 Rare old glass in Vernay collection $75
531 Ship inn $50
colour wood blocks 532-3
532 Still winter's night $10
533 February
1937 398 Japanese archer drwg $25
1939 396 Nude drwg $20
1943 64 Sugar camp on Isle Bizard wc $35
65 Spring thaw on Lake of Two Mountains wc $35
1945 255 Nude bather crayon $50

ELLIOTT, SOPHY LOUISA
1881, Montreal
addr: Montreal, 3825 Addington Ave, 1937-9
1937 94 The old school house wc $10
95 The parish church wc $15
1939 117 Zinnias wc $10

ELLISON, JOHN
24 Oct 1912, Hamilton, Ont d 1957 M
addr: Hamilton, 264 Main St, 1947. Montreal, 7455 Sherbrooke St W, 1949-51. Beaconsfield, Que, 101 Lynwood Dr, 1955
1947 70 Tower Road, St John's, Newfoundland wc $60
1949 26 Long's Hill, St John's $200
1950 64 Chinatown, Vancouver wc $100
1951 13 Gossip on Gower Street, St John's $200
1955 102 Rain, St John's, Nfld nm $150

ELLWOOD, WILLIAM JAMES HOWARD
22 Feb 1893, Cottesmore, Eng
addr: Westmount, 4709 The Boulevard
1940 104 Fisherman's hut $25

ELPHICK, JEAN see HANSON, GERTRUDE JEAN

ELROD, GLADYS F. (Mrs)
addr: Westmount, 513 Grosvenor Ave, 1934-5
1934 all miniatures, 1934-5
104 Mother wc
105 Father wc
106 David Banks wc
107 Queen Christina wc
1935 109 John Knox
110 James Knox

ELSTERMAN, RUDOLF VON
b Osnabruck, Germany
addr: Lac Supérieur, Qué
1935 111 Early nocturne, Lac Supérieur wc $50

ELWES, SIMON Eng
29 Jun 1902, Theddington, n Rugby, Eng d 1975 B DBA DVP RA TB2 WBA WWB72
addr: London, Eng
1933 95 Mrs T.H.P. Molson

EMOND, PHILIPPE
1930, Montreal

1956 95 Fugue perpétuelle nm
96 Buisson cristallin nm

ENGELBERT, ERIK
19 June 1924, Denmark
addr: Montreal, 5841 Queen Mary Rd
1957 158 K. M. plaster

EPP, WILLIAM HAROLD
1930, Glenbush, Sask
addr: Saskatoon, Sask
1968 76 Monument to night stelcoloy G steel 39 x 24 x60 $800

ERDRICH, NANCY (Mrs)
1 Jul 1920, Montreal
addr: Montreal, 4780 Côte des Neiges
1958 17 Manhattan at night $75

ERIC, E.
addr: Westmount, 516 Grosvenor Ave, 1928; 496 Mountain Ave, 1930
1928 62 Boats, St Tropez wc $125
63 Old chapel, St Tropez wc $100
64 Paysage, south of France wc $100
1930 70 Oriental girl $600
71 Safed, Palestine wc $300
267 Street in Jerusalem drwg $50
268 Walls of Jerusalem drwg $50

ERICHSEN-BROWN, FRANK
29 Aug 1878, Galt, Ont 27 Mar 1967, Toronto CWW64
addr: Toronto, 66 Dunvegan Rd,
1940 Erichson-Brown, mispr
105 North Island, Westerns, Georgian Bay

ESLER, JOHN KENNETH
11 Jan 1933, Pilot Mound, Man AGO M WWA84
addr: Winnipeg, 55 Hargrave St, Apt 15, 1963. Calgary, 1968
1963 76 Prairie winter nm $55
1968 water lift etching 77-8
77 Diary of a lost hunter 18 x 18 $75
78 Distant light. Diary of a lost hunter 25 x 25 $75
serigraphs, oil on acrylic 79-80
79 Mandala 24 x 24 $450
80 Mandala No 2 48 x 49 $750

ESSAR, GARY
addr: Kindersley, Sask, Box 10
1964 89 August 12, 1963, No 2 nm $75

ESSEX, MARGARET MARY
25 Jan 1891, Toronto
addr: Montreal, 264 Beaver Hall Hill, 1919-25
1919 116 Illustration (c/o Canadian Home Journal) b&w
1920 81 Portrait pastel
1922 103 A gay and gallant gentleman pastel $150
104 Portrait pastel $50
1925 106 G.S. Bushe, Esq pastel

ETROG, SOREL
29 Aug 1933, Jassy, Romania AGO CCI CE CWW84 IO M WWA84
addr: Montreal, Dominion Galleries, 1438 Sherbrooke St W, 1965. Toronto, 1968
1965 34 Embrace bronze $1,800
1968 81 Two acrobats bronze 55 x 31 x 15 $6,000
82 Survivors are not heroes bronze 74 1/2 x 30 1/2 x 20 $7,500

EVANS, BERNARD WALTER Eng
26 Dec 1843, Birmingham, Eng 26 Feb 1922, London, Eng B DBA DBW DVP G H TB1/3 WBA
1883 27 The mountainside, near Barmouth Junction, N. Wales wc

EVANS, BLANCHE B.
fl 1891-1906 H
addr: Montreal, 497 St Urbain St, 1891-2. New York, 8 Percy St, 1894. Montreal, 497 St Urbain St, 1895
1891 43 After toil $50
1892 52 Nancy
53 Glowing visions
166 The pines, Mount Royal wc $15
1894 57 Sweetheart $50
1895 38 Portrait
158 My lady wc $15
159 A head wash drwg
160-1 Pen and ink drwg $5 each

EVANS, DORIS E.
addr: Montreal, 791 University St, 1916-18

1916 94 Worry
1918 112 Sketch

EVANS, FREDERIC JAMES MCNAMARA Eng
b London fl1886-29 DBA DBW DVP G RA TB WBA WWB29
addr: Penzance, Eng
1908 198 Something wrong with the works wc $75
199 A fair maid's fortune wc $75
200 A Cornish fisherman wc $35

EVANS, OWEN NORTON
1864, Toronto H
addr: Montreal: 1909; 31 Bishop St, 1910-23; 1219 Bishop St, 1936
1909 118 In the heart of the wilds, Nominigue wc
119 A Laurentian meadow wc
1910 129 October, Hudson Heights
130 Path to lake, Laurentians
131 Evening
132 Trout weather, Laurentians
1911 96 Faith $125
97 First snowfall $50
98 In the Laurentians
1912 134 Chez nous $250
1913 130 Summer's lingering bloom $50
131 Morning mist, Laurentians $75
132 The merry men $150
1914 115 Ste Anne de Bellevue $50
116 Sketch $15
117 Morning mists, Laurentians $40
1915 115 November $50
116 Autumn Laurentians $50
1916 95 Sketch, winter morning $15
96 Stormy night, Laurentians $50
1917 124 Frosty morning, Laurentians $100
1918 113 Orphans, a Laurentian roadside incident $100
1919 112 Showery September day, Laurentians $75
1921 76 Winter scene, Laurentians $75
1922 105 Evening
1923 91 Late afternoon, Laurentians $50
1936 152 Sawmill, St Adolphe wc

EVE, RICHARD S.
addr: Montreal, 3646 Lorne Cr, 1939. Baie d'Urfe, 20746 Lakeshore Rd, 1940-1
1939 118 Eastern Townships wc $25
1940 106 Mount Royal temp $25
107 Nose-Dive trail, spring wc $25
354 Squirrel linoblock $5
1941 223 Dr Norman Bethune, pneumo apparatus pencil & wc $25
224 Picnic place pencil & wc $25

EVELEIGH, HENRY
26 Jul 1909, Shanghai AGO WWA70
addr: Montreal, 8 Shuter St
1939 119 Self portrait $500
120 Lea André $500

EVELEIGH, JESSIE
addr: Montreal, 137 Mackay St, 1909-10
1909 42 Vase, narcissus
43 Plate
44 Vase $9
45 Vase, stork $15
1910 433 Vase
434 Stein, Dutch
435 Stein

EVELEIGH, ROMANY
10 Dec 1934, Montreal
addr: Montreal, 5341 Earnscliffe Ave, 1954. Rosemere, Que, 218 Des Bois Cr, 1960
1954 32 Harbour $250
33 Fisherman's wharf $175
1960 152 Snowdrift nm $225

EVELY, JOHN HENRY
5 May 1918, Verdun, Que
addr: Verdun, 869 2nd Ave
1939 121 Autumn, Weir, Que wc $25

EWAN, ANNIE L.
addr: Montreal: 327 Mackay St, 1915-20; 102 Chomedy St, Apt 2, 1921; 1486 Chomedy St, 1932, 1245 St Mark St, Apt 25, 1937
1915 117 Portrait
1916 97 Portrait sketch b&w
1917 125 Sketch
126 Sketch b&w
1918 114 Portrait
115 Georgeville, Que, sketch $20
1919 113-14 St Patrick, Que $15 each
115 The Pointe, Rivière du Loup
1920 82 Captain David Ewan
1921 77 Miss Eleanor Ewan
78 Tadousac, Que
1932 383 E. Dyonnet, sketch charcl
1937 96 Farm, Georgeville, Que $20
97 Wharf at Georgeville, Que

EWART, PETER
1918, Kisbey, Sask
addr: Montreal, 4367 Mayfair Ave, 1943-9. Vancouver, 225 W 12th Ave, 1950
1943 66 Down at Baccaro
1947 72 Surf, Spider Island, B.C. $500
73 Early morning, Spider Island
1949 27 Rocks and surf $175
1950 8 Journey's end $500

EWEN, FRANCOISE see SULLIVAN, FRANCOISE

EWEN, WILLIAM PATERSON
7 Apr 1925, Montreal CC2 CWW84 IO M TB3 WWA84
addr: Montreal: 1241 Fort St, 1950; 2349 Grand Blvd, 1961; 4127 Wilson Ave, 1962-3
1950 111 Still life with bottles $110
112 Landscape
1961 12 Nuit d'été illus Purchase award (MBAM)
1962 7 Orange and orange $500
1963 21 Abstraction No 1 $750

EXARCHOU, CATHERINE see GENSONNET, CATHERINE

EYDEN, JEAN S. (m J.W. Eyden)
St Helens, Lancs, Eng
addr: Winnipeg, 52 Woodrow Pl, 1943-7
1943 67 Old barn, St Boniface wc $25
1944 35 Still life wc $30
1945 78 South from the Elgin, Ottawa wc $25
1946 70 Rue Charles Dickens wc $45
1947 74 St Flavien Street, Quebec wc $40

EYRE, IVAN KENNETH
15 Apr 1935, Tulleymet, Sask CE CWW84 WWA84
addr: Winnipeg: University of Manitoba, School of Art, 1957; 400 Assiboine Ave, 1964; Winnipeg, 1968-70
1957 31 Still life with table $250
1964 27 The horses No 2 $250
1968 83 Pink Evelyn 93 x 35 1/2 $900
84 Tulleymet plain 93 x 58 $1,500
85 Red Jack polychromed plaster & cloth 22h $1,500
86 Esoteyreic rhapsody acry 44 x 50 $900
1970 20 Deep purple acry 84 x 86
21 Black women acry 62 x 84 (MBAM)

F

FABIEN, HENRI ZOTIQUE
4 Jul 1878, St. Henri, Montreal 31 Dec 1935, Ottawa B CNS36 H M
addr: Montreal, 3169 Notre Dame St, 1897-1905. Ottawa: 18 Division St, 1912-14; 188 Booth St, 1915-19. Hull, Que, 163 Notre Dame St, 1921. Ottawa: 590 Rideau St, 1930-1; 88 5th Ave, 1934-5
1897 42 Apples $15
1898 31 Dessert $30
141 Rosina charcl
142 Mon Grand-père charcl
1901 32 L'intérieur de la maison $60
1903 43 Le grain $100
44 Côtes du Finistère $80
45 Route du Touquet Etaples $25
46 Pont Alexandre III $20
1905 47 Rough sea $40
48 Golden plover $25
1912 135 Brume du matin $100
1913 133 Moonlight on the Gatineau $150
1914 118 Near Portneuf $35
119 Benjamin Sulte b&w
120 Madame M. sanguine
121 Master Jacques F. b&w
1915 361 Portrait bust sculp
1916 98 The frozen fleet $300
99 The lime kilns $200
100 The Château, Ottawa
101 Un vieux canadien b&w $55
312 Portrait bust sculp
313 Le pensée se dégageant de la matière sculp
1918 116 The château $200
117 A little Scotch girl $75
118 The falls at Hogsback, near Ottawa $60
370 Renaissance bas-rel
1919 117 Atlanta $300
1921 79 Fleur et fruits $165
80 L'estacade $65
1930 72 An amateur
1931 375 Front arabesque, Eva drwg
1934 108 Portrait of a Spanish dancer $1,000
1935 112 Portrait

FAED, JAMES Scot

b 1857 17 Feb 1920, London, Eng B DBA DVP G RA TB1/3 WBA
addr: London, Eng, 38 Abbey Rd, 1913-14
1913 134 And the mountains bring peace $375
135 A path on the Galloway hills $210
1914 122 The passing of the crofts $1,000
123 The everlasting hills $750
124 The old drove road $400
125 A highland burn $150

FAFARD, JOSEPH YVON (JOE)
2 Sep 1942, Ste Marthe, Sask CE WWA84
addr: Regina
1970 22 Three figure arrangement, Nancy, Hettie and Ted plaster, & steel rods 60h illus

FAINMEL, CHARLES
c 1900, Russia
addr: Montreal: 818 City Hall Ave, 1923-5; 3531 St Famille St, 1928-30
1923 92 Portrait study
1924 81 Sketch pastel
278 Study of a head b&w
1925 107 Ships
108 Sketch
345 Study of a head drwg
346 Sketch in conté
1928 65 Jeanne $1,000
66 Wu Yee Hee $500
1928 293 The model charcl $150
294 Study charcl $150
295 The smoker charcl $100
296 Allouma linocut $50
1929 319 Drawing pencil $100
320 Drawing charcl $100
363 Leda sculp
364 Silence sculp
1930 306 Negro head stone

FAINMEL, MARGUERITE PAQUETTE (m Charles Fainmel)
4 Jun 1910, Montreal AGO WWA53
addr: Montreal: 1440 St Catherine St W, 1938; 5174 Côte des Neiges, Apt 19 1942
1938 Paquette
89 Ivan
1942 49 Still life
50 Ivan

FAINOS, EYAGELOS
addr: Montreal, 5153 Burret Ave
1955 29 Snow forest $650

FAIRLEY, BARKER
21 May 1887, Barnsley, Yorks, Eng
11 Oct 1986, Toronto AGO CE CO CWW84 EC
addr: Toronto, 197 Dawlish Ave, 1939-40
1939 122 Bruce
123 Edge of town $50
1940 108 Head of a man

FALCONAR, E. N. (Mrs)
addr: Montreal, 1052 Mackay St, Apt 2, 1936. Hudson Heights, Que, Box 95. 1937
1936 153 A village street in Berkshire wc $6
1937 98 The hills at Balmaclellan, Galloway wc $10

FALCONER, COLIN HARLEY
addr: Sackville, N.B, Mount Allison Art Gallery, 1940. Ottawa, c/o National Gallery of Canada, 1945
1940 109 Early morning $35
1945 79 Misty morning $75

FALES, DOUGLAS ALLAN
1929, Montreal
addr: Verdun, Que, 716 Argyle Ave
1956 22 Fish $100
97 Glassware nm $85

FALK, GATHIE
31 Jan 1928, Alexander, Man CE WWA82
addr: Vancouver
1970 23 Bird cage metal, enamel, flock, ceramic, overglaze 18 x 22 x 65 illus
ready made, enamel, roplex, polvester, resin, flock, ceramic, life size 24-26
24 Chair with coat and fish
25 Rug
26 Cabinet with flower pots

FANCOTT, EUGENE
addr: Montreal, 1191 Union Ave
1937 99 Janet
100 Herbert Whittaker
101 Betty

FANIEL, ALFRED JEAN JOSEPH
19 Apr 1879, Verviers, Belg 8 Feb 1950, Montreal
addr: Montreal: 1062 St André St, 1911; 1324 Erables St, 1912-15; 1262 Marie Anne St E, 1916-21; 642 Jeanne d'Arc St, 1922
1911 99 Nature morte, fruits et legumes $75
100 Nature morte, metaux $75
1912 136 Nature morte $175
1913 136 The pond $15
137 The old tree $25
1914 126 Landscape in winter $35
1915 118 Interior of a chapel $40
1916 102 North wind $100
103 The old walk $225
1917 127 Landscape in winter $25
128-30 Landscape in summer $25 each
1918 119 Malines, Belgium $100
120 Le vieux chemin $40
1919 118 Le Rysehmolen, Brussels $150
1920 83 Souvenir de Belgique $300
1921 81-2 Residence, M.A. Frigon, Sault aux Récollets, entrée de la residence $45 each
1922 106 Vieille ferme, Blvd Rosemount $150

FANSHAW, HUBERT VALENTINE
14 Feb 1878, Sheffield, Eng 11 Aug 1940, Winnipeg M NGC TB3
addr: Winnipeg, 161 Lyle St, Deer Lodge, 1923-35
1923 93 After rain wc $40
94 Sun fire wc $40
1927 56 San Juan Capistrano $45
57 A prairie trail $45
58 A day in spring $45
1931 91 Evening, Clear Lake, Manitoba wc $40
376 Clear Lake block pr $15
377 Windswept prairie block pr $15
1932 94 Pacific coastline $50
95 Clear Lake, Manitoba wc $40
1935 113 The bent pines of Clear Lake wc $75

FAREY, LOUIS
addr: Montreal, 25 Mackay St
1906 327 Charles, and library nm $25
328 Regency salon nm $25
329 Elizabethan hall nm $15
330 Inglenook des $12

FARNCOMB, CAROLINE
12 Jan 1858, Newcastle Ont 13 Nov 1951, London, Ont H
addr: London, Ont, 374 Central Ave, 1900; 156 Central Ave, 1901-5; Montreal, 1908. London, 1909
1900 31 Fruit $15
32 Some more, please $20
1901 33 Dorothy $20
34 Wild duck $15
35 Partridges $12
1903 47 Waiting for the sleigh $25
48 Spanish girl $35
1905 49 Lavoir $30
1908 59 Beginning the day $30
1909 120 Sketch $12

FASKEN, LAURA (Mrs)
addr: Regina, 2216 Angus St
1936 154 Ample store $35

FAUCHER, JEAN CHARLES
8 May 1907, Montreal B TB3 WWA62
addr: Montreal, 3550 Ste Famille St
1944 36 La route, Ste Pétronille, Ile d'Orléans $100
37 Vieille maison, St Pierre, Ile d'Orléans $100
38 Québec, vu de l'Ile d'Orléans $100

FAULKNER, PHILIPPA MARY BURROWS (m George U. Faulkner)
28 Feb 1917, Belleville, Ont IO
addr: Belleville, Ont, 210 Church St
1952 60 Mexican chicken sellers wc $70

FAUTEUX, HENRIETTE (m Jules T. Massé)
30 Oct 1924, Coaticook, Que M
addr: Montreal: 96 Sherbrooke St W, 1943-6; 3635 Laval Ave, 1949-50; 367 St Louis Sq, 1956-61; Galerie Camille Hébert, 2075 rue Bishop, 1964
1943 69 Paysage
1946 82 Lady in green
1949 28 Henri Hébert, RCA
29 Evening $50
1950 82 Madame Rodolphe Mathieu pastel on wd
1956 98 Bassin Louise nm $50
1959 30 Generation nm $110

1960 28 Demain brillant $175
29 Pariade $150
1961 13 Ailes solaires $300
14 Fraîcheur diurne $110
1964 28 Hérauts $275

FAUTEUX, MARIE CLAIRE CHRISTINE
23 Sep 1890, Montreal CNS36
addr: Montreal, 225 Prince Arthur St, 1912-15; 284 Mackay St, 1916-17; 100 Closse St, 1918-22. Westmount, 674 Roslyn Ave, 1929. Montreal, 853 Sherbrooke St E, 1946-7
1912 137-8 Beaupré $20, $15
1915 119 Portrait
120 Composition $15
1916 104 Portrait
105 Composition $15
1917 131 Portrait of my Grandmother
132 Composition, the bather $50
1918 121 L'arbe centenaire $75
122 Portrait
123 Sketch pastel
1919 119 Solitude wc
120 Reverie wc $20
121 Enchantment wc $20
122 Dawn wc $50
123 Marguerite min
1920 84 Portrait
Composition 85-7
85 The spirit of the lake wc $25
86 Les Rois Mages wc $25
87 Why lags the lazy worshipper outside wc $25
1921 83 Brume, nuit wc $25
84 Mirage wc $25
85 Solitaire wc $20
86 Abandon wc $30
1922 107 Forest nymphs $100
108 Midinette, portrait study $75
109 Old church of St Peter, Paris $25
1929 72 Automne doré $500
1946 80 Winter scene, Arvida, Que $150
81 Canadian flowers wc $75
1947 75 Nature morte $75

FAUTEUX, ROGER
addr: Montreal, 2200 Souvenir St, 1946-7
1946 254 Attente ink $20
255 Inertie ink $20
1947 301 Songeur ink $25
302 Promenade ink $35
303 Solitaire ink $40

FAVAL, C.
addr: Venice
1918 124 Venice, San Giorgio $125
125 Venice by moonlight $75
126 Armenian Monastery, Venice $125

FAVRE, M.
no address
1915 362 K.R. Macpherson, Esq, KC bust
363 Indian Chief Yellow Head bas-rel $50
364 Hockey group wax $400
365 Melancolie du passé ter cot $250
366 Portrait medln

FEATHERSTONE, GRACE LILLIAN
23 Dec 1888, Montreal
addr: Toronto, 111 Bedford Rd
1918 425 Coffee pot, 6 cups & saucers $50

FEDIOW, PAULINE see REDSELL, PAULINE

FEHER, GEORGES
addr: Montreal, 1423 St Matthew St
1954 34 Still life $100

FELLOWES, NORTON ALEXANDER
5 Nov 1905 - 1 Dec 1969, Montreal
addr: Montreal, 1178 Phillips Pl, 1931-6
1931 270 Residence, Redpath Cr
271 Residence, Hampstead
272 Residence, Lexington Ave, Westmount
1936 472 Residence, Westmount preliminary study
473 Residence, G.W. Nourke, Esq, Westmount
see also Bolton, Richard E, 1938

FELSEN, PHYLLIS
addr: Westmount: 4124 Dorchester St W, 1937-40; 79 Bruce Ave, 1941; 4142A Dorchester St W, 1942-3. Cowansville, Que (Ont, error), P O Box 267, 1944
1937 457 Helen plaster $75
458 Alena plaster $50
459 Head of a child plaster $75
1938 192 Marcus A. Felsen plaster
1939 453 Louis Solomon plaster $150
1940 405 Dorothy Leclair plaster
406 Negro plaster

1941 281 Sapper plaster
1942 235 Negro plaster $75
1943 255 Miss Norma Darling plaster
1944 160 Rezso, portrait plaster

FENWICK, KATHLEEN M.
17 Jun 1901, London, Eng 28 Sep 1973, Ottawa WWA70
addr: Ottawa, 152 Argyle Ave
1929 321 Old Dartmouth etch
322 St Mark's, Venice etch
323 Virgin and Child etch

FENWICK, WILLIAM ROLAND (ROLY)
4 Feb 1932, Owen Sound, Ont IO
addr: Toronto, 25 Close Ave
153 What is the creative process? nm $200
154 Supine figures nm $125

FERGIE, MARY
addr: Montreal, 1509 Sherbrooke St W, 1947-9
1947 76 Robe bleu
1948 10 Still life II $150
1949 30 Study $25

FERGUSON, ELIZABETH G.
addr: Westmount, 642 Murray Hill, 1939-41
1939 124 Portrait wc
125 Mrs Alex Ferguson wc
1941 63 Still life wc $25

FERRIER, WALTER A.
addr: Montreal, 1475 Mansfield St, 1935. Westmount, 4215 Western Ave, 1937
1935 114 Spring flowers wc $50
1937 102 The lobster trap wc
103 Repairing at low tide, Gloucester wc $40

FERRON, MARCELLE (m René Hamelin)
29 Jan 1924, Louiseville, Que CCI CE CWW84 M WWA84
addr: Montreal South, 448 Lasalle St, 1947. c/o Galerie Denyse Delrue (Montreal), or 8 Louis Dupont, Clamart, Seine, France, 1960-3
1947 Ferron-Hamelin
77 Huile No 8
1960 30 Le signal Dorset illus Purchase award (MBAM)
1963 22 On the windy bay $1,100

FETHERSTONHAUGH, HAROLD LEA
31 Mar 1887, Montreal 3 Feb 1971, Ste Anne de Bellevue, Que NGC
addr: Montreal: 340 University St, 1914; 823 Drummond Bldg, 1920; 511 St Catherine St W, 1920-1; 85 Osborne Ave, 1922-3; 374 Beaver Hall Sq, 1927; 1164 Beaver Hall Hill, 1928; 1410 Stanley St, 1930; 660 St Catherine St W, University Tower, 1931-47
1920 88 Santa Maria dei Miracoli, Venice wc
89 Square in Munich wc
1923 267 House, E.L. Pease, St Bruno
1927 199 Château St Louis, Quebec photos
200 Residence, W.C. Pitfield, Esq, Saraguay, Que photos
201 Residence, Redpath Crescent, Montreal perspective
202 Residence, W.R.G. Holt, Esq, Montreal model
1928 229 Residence, A.T. Patterson, Esq
230 Residence, W.R.G. Holt, Esq
231 Residence, Atwater Ave
232 Office building, Hanson Bros
1930 215 Cathedral Church of St Andrew and St Paul; 1933, 370-2
216 University Tower, Montreal
217 Residence, T.W. McAnulty, Esq, Westmount
1931 273 Residence, Westmount
1933 373 Laurier Clinic
1934 385 Quebec Winter Club pencil
386 National Breweries, office building pencil
1914 Fetherstonhaugh & McDougall, 1914-27
444-5 Francis McLennan, Esq, house perspective, photo of plans
1920 310-12 H. Austin Ekers, Outremont, residence view from SW, library mantel, entrance hall
313 Bovril Ltd, Montreal, new building
1921 309 J. Bowman Peck, Esq, residence, Cap St Jacques, Que, additions, alterations
310 Windsor Hotel, Montreal, alterations
311 H.R. Drummond, Esq, house, Lac Charlebois, Que
1922 365-6 W.M. Birks, Esq, St Bruno, Que, additions, remodelling

1927 Fetherstonhaugh & McDougall, associate architect, C.J. Saxe
203 Arts Building, McGill University, remodelling photos
1934 Fetherstonhaugh & Durnford, 1934-47
387 Eight-roomed house, Hampstead, Que
388 House on hilly site des pencil
1935 351 Country house, H.S. Joyce, Esq pastel
1936 474-5 Country house, Mrs Walter Molson, Ste Agathe, exterior, interior photos (2)
476 Proposed residence drwg
477 Entrance detail, residence Ramezay Rd photo
1937 337 Douglas Hall Residence, McGill University drwg
337 Living room. residence, Mr & Mrs E.J. Trott, Montreal photo
339-40 Exterior, living room, ski lodge, Mr & Mrs J.R. Timmins, St Margaret's, Que photos (2)
1938 133-4 Lighting fixtures, Douglas Hall photos (2)
135 House, St Sauveur photo
136 House, Piedmont photo
1939 349 Chancel rail, Church of St Andrew and St Paul
350 Residence, A.A. Aitken, Esq, St Margaret's, Que
351 Lighting fixture, Royal Victoria College
352 Residence, Raymond Carneux, 77 Sunnyside Ave, Westmount
1940 322 Residence, Mr & Mrs H.H. Smith, Quebec City
323 Residence, Mr & Mrs L.W. Haslett, St Margaret's, Que
324 Residence, Mr & Mrs L.W. Hampson, St Margaret's, Que
1947 330 First United Church, Town of Mount Royal model photo
331 Proposed residence, Westmount
see also Ross, George Allen, 1927-239

FETHERSTONHAUGH, P. (Mrs)
addr: Winnipeg, 801 Dorchester Ave
1913 138 In the Rockies, Laggan $15
139 Lake Louise $25
140 Lake Louise, early morning pastel

FIELD, SAUL
12 Jan 1912, Montreal IO M
addr: Montreal: 3561 Shuter St, 1941; 5262 Park Ave, 1942; 214 Prince Arthur St E, 1945-7
1941 64 European mother $100
65 Refugees $150
1942 51 See how they run! $150
1945 80 Rest period $175
1947 78 Lac Renaud wc $125
79 Parc Lafontaine wc $125

FIENNES-CLINTON, ELEANOR
1886, Cheshunt, Eng
addr: Hamilton, Ont, 122 McNab St S, 1934-6
1934 109 Back of Augusta Street, Hamilton $100
1935 115 Cadgwith, Cornwall wc $40
1936 155 Old houses, Hamilton Bay $50

FILER, MARY HARRIS (m Antonio Romo)
31 Dec 1920, Edmonton AGO
addr: Montreal, Nurses' Home, Royal Victoria Hospital, 1945-6. Dunham, Que, St Helen's School, 1947. Montreal: 4642B Park Ave, 1948; 4085 Gage Rd, 1949; 1555 Summerhill Ave, Apt 506, 1951-2
1945 81 Windy March day, Regina wc $75
1946 83 Gloxinia wc $25
84 House and trees wc $25
1947 80 McGill Campus wc $50
81 Fountain in park wc $65
1948 75 Madonna and child wc $40
98 Still life lino block pr $25
1949 125 Winter storm outside wc $50
155 Odalisque lino block pr $25
1951 125 Shallow water over rock wc $35
1952 132 Odalisque pen & ink $50

FILION, ARMAND
10 Mar 1910, Montreal M
addr: Montreal, 2949 Lévesque Blvd, 1957-64
1957 159 Femme assise stone $800
1958 78 Mère et enfant wd $500
1964 117 Chevalier bardé bois & clous $500

FILION, GABRIEL
2 Feb 1920, Montreal M
addr: Montreal, 1120 Dutrisac St
1963 23 Rouge - 63

FILION, JEAN-PAUL
24 Feb 1927, n St André Avellin, Que
CC2
addr: Montreal: 6280 Iberville St,
1951; 8431B St Denis St, 1952
1951 92 Le bateau des légendes $40
126 Escalade énchantée gouache $25
1952 133 Le poisson au cristal ink on blueprint $60

FILION, PIERETTE
4 Mar 1935, Arvida, Que
addr: Quebec, 16 La Porte St
1956 23 Nu blanc $85

FINDLAY, FRANK R.
1888, Montreal 10 Apr 1977, Montreal
see Findlay, Robert, 1928-38

FINDLAY, JEAN see NESS, JEAN

FINDLAY, ROBERT
12 May 1859, Inverness, Scot 3 Feb
1951, Montreal
addr: Montreal: 1908; 10 Phillips Pl,
1914; 1188 Phillips Pl, 1928-38
1908 312 Residence, M.D. Davis, Esq
313 Residence, Geo. Sumner, Esq
314 Residence, A.E. Ogilvie, Esq
315 Residence, G.H. Smithers, Esq
316 Old houses, Montreal, recently demolished
1914 446 T.B. Macaulay, Esq, Westmount residence perspective
447 Herbert Molson, Esq, Ontario Ave, residence perspective
448 D.C. Macarow, Esq, Peel St, residence perspective
449 Calvary Church, Westmount, interior photos
1928 Findlay, Robert & F.R. 1928-38
233 Old and new Montreal
234 Proposed residence, Lexington Ave, Westmount
235 Proposed residence, H.W. Soper, Esq
236 Country home, Mrs Charles Meredith, Senneville, Que
1929 244 Laurentian bungalow sketch
1930 218 Residence, G.L. Ogilvie, Esq, Cartierville, Que
219 Residence C.N. Sommer, Esq, Lexington Ave, Westmount
220 Residence, H.W. Soper, Esq, Avenue Rd, Westmount
1931 274 Residence, J.A. Raymond, Esq, Macgregor St, Montreal
275 Residence, W.W. Ogilvie, Esq, Saraguay, Que
276 Residence, Alexander Buchanan, Esq, Pointe au Pic, Que
277 Residence, W.C. McLeod, Esq, Westmount
1932 338 Conservatory and palm room, Residence H.W. Molson, Esq
339 Private garage, W.W. Ogilvie, Esq, Saraguay, Que
340-1 Interior views, residence C.N. Sommer, Esq
1933 374 Residence, J.A. Raymond, Esq, photo
375 Residence, A. Bronfman, Esq, Westmount photo
1934 389-90 Residence, W.W. Ogilvie, Esq, Saraguay, general exterior view, exterior detail, view into sun terrace photos
391 Residence, A. Bronfman, Esq, Westmount, exterior detail view photo
392 Proposed residence, Westmount, Chas Perrochet, Del. ink & wc
1937 Findlay, Robert & F.R. & P. Roy Wilson
341 House, Boyden Kinsey, Jr, Hampstead
1938 137-8 Pavilion, Murray Park, Westmount, SE corner view, distant view photos

FINE, PHYLLIS KURTZ
3 Aug 1924, Toronto IO
addr: Toronto, 19 Elderwood Dr
1964 118 Wedlock hydrocal bronze $1,000

FINLEY, FREDERICK JAMES
4 Jun 1894, Newcastle, Australia 14
May 1968, Toronto CWW64 M NGC W78
WWA66
addr: Toronto: 26 Osborne Ave, 1928;
63 Warland Ave, 1950
1928 297 Portobello etch $18

298 Captive etch $12
1950 9 Fijians with coral $350

FINLEY, GERALD ERIC
17 Jul 1931, Munich, Germ CWW84 WWA84
addr: Toronto, 63 Warland Ave
1960 155 First snow, Muskoka nm $800

FINLEY, SAMUEL ARNOLD
24 Jun 1874 - 18 Jun 1933, Montreal
addr: Montreal: 2 Bishop St, 1898; Temple Bldg, 1903; 160 St James St, 1906; Montreal, 1908; 1002 New Birks Bldg, 1916
1898 218 Architectural studies abroad
219 Sketches pen & ink
220 Sketch of an Italian grotto
1903 Finley & Spence, 1903-8
265 Guardian Assurance Co, new building, St James St, accepted competition desg
266 Proposed building
1906 331 Linton Apartments, Sherbrooke St
332 Molson's Bank, Toronto
333 Molson's Bank, West End Branch
334 Western Hospital
335 Federal Life Assurance Co, Hamilton
1908 317 New government building, Ottawa competition desg
318 Office building desg
1916 Finley & Gagnon
328 Post office, St Agathe
329 Post office, St Gabriel de Brandon
330 House, J.W. Domville, Esq Rosemount

FIORE, GIUSEPPE
18 Aug 1931, Mola di Bari, Italy
addr: Montreal: 7720 Bloomfield, Ave, 1954; 3834 Rachel St E, Apt 5, 1960-1
1954 35 Paysage de Québec $225
1960 31 Métamorphose $250
1961 15 Automaticité $200

FIORUCCI, VITTORIO
1932, Zara, Yugoslavia
addr: Montreal, 2115 Crescent St, Studio 8
1963 24 Sign of Cancer $250

FISHER, AGNES (m Eric Fisher)
b c 1890
addr: Westmount: 24 Holton Ave, 1938-9; 642 Victoria Ave, 1940-1
1938 193 Negro's head plaster
1939 454 Lorraine plaster
1940 407 Garden piece, St Francis d'Assisi plaster $50 stone $150
1941 282 Alexis Reford plaster

FISHER, AMY
addr: Montreal: 47 Fort St, 1892-4; The Stanley, Stanley St, 1901-6
1892 54 Shelling peas $50
1894 58 Study of a head $10
1901 125 Anchored wc $5
1903 170 October wc
1905 157 Weird sentinels wc $10
158 Beyond the city wc $8
303 A summer cloud plaster panel $5
1906 227 Low tide wc $8

FISHER, BRIAN RICHARD
10 Mar 1939, Uxbridge, Eng CC2
addr: Vancouver: 1322 Hornby St, 1965; Vancouver, 1968
1965 5 Maya No 1 $500 (MBAM)
1968 polymer acry on canvas 87-8
87 Crisis 44 x 44 $750
88 Ascension 44 x 44 $750

FISHER, ETHEL M.
addr: Montreal, The Stanley, Stanley St, 1901-6
1901 126 The meadow brook wc $3
1903 171 Gray day on the canal wc $5
1905 159 Early spring wc $8
160 Gray day, November wc $8
1906 228 A heat haze wc $10

FISHER, ORVILLE NORMAN
24 Nov 1911, Vancouver WWA62
addr: Vancouver, 1793 E 56th Ave
1955 103 Barnyard hoe-down nm $65
104 Tribal council nm $65

FISHER, RUEBEN see KALMAN, MAXWELL M.

FITZGERALD, CLARA see OSLER, CLARA

FITZGERALD, MAY
addr: Montreal: 216 Peel St, 1912;

164 Crescent St, 1914
1912 139 Sketch $20
1914 127 Portrait $35
128 Sketch b&w $5

FLANCER, LUDWIG
26 Mar 1900, Warsaw 10 Mar 1980, Florida
addr: Montreal: 5687 Park Ave, Apt 16, 1944-55; 4625 Plamondon Ave, Apt 2, 1962-4
1944 39 Flower pot $65
1945 82 Little paradise
83 Birch trees on Mount Royal
1950 113 Still life $100
1951 93 Fecundity $175
94 Spring in the Laurentians $150
1952 95 Fillion station $225
1953 74 L'idylle $150
1955 30 At the foot of Mount Royal $200
1962 57 Early spring, St Rose nm $150
1964 29 Water lilies $250

FLEMING, ALEXANDER M.
9 Sep 1878, Chatham, Ont 24 Jan 1929, Guelph, Ont
addr: Chatham, Ont
1909 121 The finger of light unfolding the day $150

FLEMING, ARCHIE G.
addr: Westmount, 476 Victoria Ave, 1937. Montreal, 214 St James St W, 1939-48
1937 104 Autumn near Aberfoyle, Scotland wc
105 Summer's dying glory wc $40
1939 126 Low tide near Kennebunkport, Maine $40
1940 110 Turbots Creek, Maine wc $25
1942 52 Morning shadows wc $30
53 The bridge, Knowlton wc $30
54 Seascape, Maine wc $30
1943 70 The house on the hill wc $30
71 Early spring, near Oka wc $90
1944 40 Fishermen's Cove, Maine wc $40
1945 84 October morning wc $45
85 Laurentian road in winter wc $45
86 Laurentian woods wc $100
1946 85 Fishing boats wc $65
1947 82 Barns in winter wc $50
1948 76 Stream in winter $55

FLEMING, GERTRUDE VANDELINDER (m P.J. A. Fleming)
b Petrolia, Ont
addr: Edmonton, 11414 100th Ave, 1935-6. Calgary, 3210 3rd St SW, 1941
1935 116 Full bloom wc $30
1936 156 Delphinium wc $50
1941 66 Delphiniums and roses wc $35

FLEMMING, H. W.
addr: Montreal, 2283 Wilson Ave, 1936-7
1936 157 Ste Cecile Street, Montreal $50
157A Morning on the Intervale $50
1937 106 Harvest time, Trent River. Ont $50

FLEURY, H. (Mme Théo Fleury)
addr: Montreal, 7058 De St Valier St, 1928-9
1928 H. Fleury
339 Mon guide plaster $50
340 Myrto plaster
1929 Mme Théo Fleury
365 M. Antoine Gerin Lajoie, auteur canadien 1824-1882 plaster

FLINN, WESLEY ROBSON
b 1906, Toronto
addr: Toronto, 101 King St W
1931 92 John

FLOOD, BARBARA see FLOOD, LOUISE BARBARA

FLOOD, EVA I.
addr: Montreal, 111 Drummond St
1920 90 Rocks, Grand Manan $10
91 On the beach, St Andrews, N.B. $15

FLOOD, LOUISE BARBARA BLACK (m Wilfred John Flood)
5 Jul 1903, Sackville, N.B.
addr: Ottawa, 451 Roxborough Rd, Rockcliffe, 1939-45
1939 127 Mr Butts, janitor $165
128 The downs, Salisbury, Eng $55
1940 111 Mrs G.S. Murphy
1945 87 Lt Col A.L. Black
88 Fall ploughing $50

FLOOD, WILFRID JOHN
17 Jan 1904, London, Eng 24 Mar 1946, Ottawa
addr: Ottawa: 24 Kenora St, 1934-5; 401 Hamilton Ave, 1939
1934 110 Lobsterman's shanty, Maine wc $45
111 Narcissus wc $35
1935 117 My friend, Henri pastel
118 Summer afternoon wc $40
119 Silo wc $35
1939 129 The Gatineau in March wc $45
130 Boiling the sap, sugar bush wc $45

FLOUD, PHYLLIS ALLEN FORD, Lady (m Sir Francis Lewis Castle Floud)
addr: Ottawa, Earnscliffe
1937 107 Farm buildings wc $15

FORBES, DONALD R.
addr: Verdun, Que, 651 Manning Ave, 1937-55
1937 108 Interior of shed wc $10
1939 131 Plant wc & temp $15
132 Spring wc $10
133 Autumn wc $25
397 Fisherman at night drwg $10
1941 67 Night wc
1955 105 The farm nm $150

FORBES, FRANCES KIRKPATRICK (m W.F. Bayne)
11 May 1911
addr: Halifax: 141 Coburg Rd, 1936; 438 Quinpool Rd, 1937; 37 South Park St, 1941-3
1936 158 Study $50
1937 109 Ferguson's Cove, N.S. $75
1941 Bayne, 1941-3
9 In the park wc $20
10 The fair wc $15
1943 14 Fish stores wc $25

FORBES, JEAN MARY EDGELL (m Kenneth Keith Forbes)
18 May 1897, Karachi, India M
addr: Toronto, 87 Alcina Ave
1940 112 Flower decoration $300

FORBES, JOHN COLIN
23 Jan 1846 - 28 Oct 1925, Toronto
B CWW10 EC H M Mo98/12 NGC R2 TB1/3 W78
addr: Ottawa, 25 Cliff St, 1891. Montreal: 998 Dorchester St, 1903; 99 Notre Dame St W, 1925
1885 35 Mount of the Holy Cross
47 Mount Stephen, on the line of the CPR
62 The village forge
1889 23 Evening on the marsh $85
1891 44 After the shower $200
45 A quiet spot $75
46 On the beach $75
47 Coast of Maine $75
1903 49 J. Colin Forbes, RCA, electric light effect
50 Sunrise, Baie de Chaleurs $400
51 Mrs W.G. Ross
52 Prof H.T. Bovey
1925 109 Dunnottar Castle, Stonehaven, Scotland $750

FORBES, KENNETH KEITH
4 Jul 1892, Toronto 25 Feb 1980, North York, Ont AGO CC2 CWW80 M NGC PMC TB2 WWA62
addr: London, Eng, 1914. No address, 1918. Montreal: 821 Lorne Cr, 1920; 660 Sherbrooke St W, 1927-8; 1374 Sherbrooke St W, 1929. Toronto: 64 Grenville St, 1930-1; 87 Alcina Ave, 1933-52
1914 129 R.P. McA. Smith
1918 Lieut K.K. Forbes
127 My cousin, from memory. Painted in the trenches
1920 95 Mushrooms in Sark $250
96 The red feather $300
97 Billets $200
98 Venus' pool $750
1927 59 Portrait of my wife $1,000
60 Early morning $450
61 Evening, Lac Oureau $150
1928 67 Mrs Hugh Heasley
1929 73 Mrs MacKenzie R. Campbell
74 Mrs John L. McSweeney
75 Birches, Mount Royal $500
76 Lazy beach $300
1930 73 Mrs Rykert McCuaig
1931 93 Mrs Ronald Graham
1933 96 Dr A.L. Lockwood
97 John B. Laidlaw, Esq
1935 120 Mrs Jules Timmins
1937 110 Mrs Walter Vaughan
1945 89 Fred Brigden, RCA
1952 10 W.B. Scott, Esq, QC

FORBES, MARY see RIORDON, MARY

FORD, HARRIET MARY
1859, Brockville, Ont 1939, England
AGO DBA H M NGC TB3 WWB29
addr: Toronto: James' Bldg, 1894-5; 378 Markham St, 1911
1894 59 A woman's story by a winter's fire $400
60 At the vintage $100
61 Study of a piping boy $50
1895 39 Portrait, E.C.H.
40 Noontide study $75
1911 101 Sunshine and shadow $40
102 Au café $40

FORD, JEAN F. (Mrs)
addr: Westmount, 449 Elm Ave
1946 86 Summer tapestry $75

FORGUES, REMI-PAUL
addr: Montreal, 5301 Trans Island Ave
1951 127 Les jouets gouache $75
128 L'été, joie et tristesse gouache $200

FORRESTALL, THOMAS DE VANY
11 Mar 1936, Middleton, N.S. CC1 CE CWW84 M WWA84
addr: Fredericton, N.B.
1968 89 The passengers egg temp 31 1/2 x 48 $900

FORSEY, FLORENCE E.
addr: Ottawa, 187 4th Ave
1934 111A Old Spanish church, Cuernavaca, Mexico wc $40
112 Courtyard in Cuernavaca, Mexico wc $25

FORSTER, JOHN WYCLIFFE LOWES
31 Dec 1850, Norval, Ont 24 Apr 1938, Toronto AGO B CC1 CE CNS36 EC H M Mo98/12 NGC TB1/3 W78
addr: Toronto: 81 King St E, 1892; 25 King St (sic) 1900; 24 King St W, 1909
1889 24 Portrait
1892 55 Miss Maude
56 Sandford Fleming
57 Artist's mother
1900 33 Theodore Harding Rand, DCL
1909 124 Miss Hanbury Williams
125 Helen Merrill

FORSTER, MICHAEL
7 May 1907, Calcutta, India AGO M WWA53 Juror
addr: Montreal, 4800 Côte des Neiges
1952 96 Complect $150

FORTIER, IVANHOE
9 Dec 1931, St Louis de Courville, Que M
addr: Montréal, 8658 blvd St Michel, 1960; 8660 blvd St Michel, 1963
1960 231 Group wd & metal $175
1963 100 Equilibristes metal $1,200

FORTIER, KATHLEEN E.
addr: Westmount, 404 Metcalfe Ave, 1912-15
1912 447 Candlestick
448 Tea caddy
449 Stein $15
1913 464 Orange bowl $30
465 Blue bowl $30
1914 495 Six-sided vase
1915 437 Plate, fresia des
438 Bowl, birds

FORTIN, MARC-AURELE
14 Mar 1888, Ste Rose, Que 2 Mar 1970, St Jean de Macamic, Abitibi, Que AGO B CC2 CE CWW61 EC M NGC TB2 W78 WWA53
addr: Montreal: 483 St Hubert St, 1911; 109 St Hubert St, 1912; 1664 Hutchison St, 1913; 232 St Hubert St, 1914; 136 St Hubert, 1915. Ste Rose, Que, 1916. Montreal: 210 Champ de Mars, 1918; 205 Berri St, 1924; 351 Notre Dame St E, 1926-8; 111 Prud'homme Ave, 1929; 351 Notre Dame St E, 1930; 1425 Pierce St, 1931; 449 Notre Dame St E, 1932; 443 Notre Dame St E, 1933. Ste Rose, Que, 246 Ste Rose Blvd, 1935-41. Montreal, 370 Laurier Ave, 1942-54. Ste Rose, Que, 1967
1911 103 Hay time $200
1912 140 The passing cloud $60
141 After sunset $15
142 Les borde de la Saskatchewan, Edmonton $125
1913 141 Old houses $40
142 Hay time $40
1914 130 November snow $40
131 Street scene, Montreal $35
132 Misty morning $15
133 The snowfall $20
1915 121 March snow $150

122 Old houses pastel $40
123 Autumn leaves pastel $30
1916 106 Etude $60
1918 128 A snow storm $120
129 Rural landscape $150
1924 82 The lonely road $80
83 Rustic landscape in Province of Quebec $40
1926 56 Opulent autumn, a lonely road wc $60
57 Opulent autumn, corner of a village wc $60
1927 62 Trees by the roadside $100
63 Opulent autumn in the hills $40
64 Roof tops $50
1928 68 Summer sunshine $90
69 Summer after rain wc $90
70 Autumn sunshine wc $80
71 An October day wc $200
72 Harbour scene, Montreal wc $50
1929 77 Landscape, Laurentians $60
78 Landscape, Westmount wc $60
79 Trees near the river wc $125
1930 74 Landscape at St Laurent wc $125
75 Old houses, Longueuil $40
1931 94 After rain $90
95 Landscape at Hochelaga $90
96 Fall landscape wc $60
97 Landscape at Hochelaga wc $75
378 La porte etch $25
1932 96 Landscape at Hochelaga $125
97 Harbour scene, Montreal pastel $90
98 Harbour scene, Montreal wc $70
384 Landscape at Hochelaga etch $70
1933 98 A late fall landscape $75
99 Landscape at Côte des Neiges wc $70
1935 121-2 Landscape at Hochelaga wc $75 each
123 Fall landscape, Ste Rose pastel $70
1936 159-60 Landscape, Ste Rose $30 each
161 Landscape, Hochelaga $50
162 Wood barges, Hochelaga wc $40
1937 111 La drague, le port Montréal $200
112 Etude d'orme, autumne $125
113 Paysage à Ste Rose $200
114 Neige de mars $150
1938 45 April shadows $150
46 Les Eboulements landscape wc $60 (Aboulements mispr) (listed 1967, Jessie Dow prize)
47-8 Landscape, Hochelaga wc $50 each
1939 137 Landscape à St Simeon wc $90
138 Landscape at St Urbain $150
139 Landscape at Hochelaga $75
1940 114-15 Landscape at Hochelaga wc $100 each
116 Landscape, St Laurent, Island of Orleans $300
117 Snow scene, Ste Rose $100
1941 69-70 Landscape, Isle of Orleans wc $150 each
1942 55 Paysage Gaspésie (Newport) $300
56 Paysage Gaspésie (bateau) $300
1943 72 Paysage de l'Ile d'Orléans wc $100
73 Vielle maison à Ste Rose $200
1944 41 Paysage de Gaspésie $600
42 Ombre d'autumne wc $50
43 Paysage près Montréal wc $50
1945 90 Vieille maison, bas de Terrebonne wc $100
1946 87 Paysage de Gaspésie, Percé wc $150
88 Vieille barque, Gaspésie wc $75
89 Paysage à Terrebonne, Québec wc $75
1947 83 Paysage, Baie St Paul wc $150
84 Old boat, Port au Persil wc $150
85 Landscape Port au Persil wc $150
1948 77 Barqies wc $75
78 Paysage de Gaspésie wc $150
1949 126 Landscape, Hochelaga wc $150
1950 10 Scène de rue Québec $200
65 Barque à Mont Louis casein $300
1951 59 Paysage à Westmount wc $60
1952 11 Maison à Ste Rose $125
1954 100 Boat in Gaspé wc $80
1967 22 Landscape at Ste Rose. 1933-4 37 3/4 x 47 1/2 (MBAM)

FOSBERY, ERNEST GEORGE
29 Dec 1874, Ottawa 6 Feb 1960, Cowansville, Que AGO B CNS36 CWW55

EC M Mo12 NGC PMC TB2 W78 WWA53 WWB52
Juror
addr: Ottawa: 479 Cooper St, 1894,1897-1900; c/o Wilson & Co, 1895. Buffalo: 62 N Norwood Ave, 1910; 62 Claremont Ave, 1911. Ottawa: 123 Sparks St, 1912; 44 Central Chambers, Elgin St, 1913-14; 108 Sparks St, 1931; 571 Manor Rd, Rockcliffe, 1945
1894 62 Head of a girl
1895 41 Golden rod in Manitoba $25
1897 43 Portrait of a lady
44 Portrait sketch
45 Landscape $25
1900 34 The pond $30
35 Beehives $25
1909 122 Supper $500
123 Portrait
1910 133 In the heat of the day $500
134 At work $500
1911 104 Kenneth, aged six $750
105 In the track of the sun
1912 143 A.F. Newlands
144 Lamplight $500
1913 143 Thomas C. Keefer, Esq, CMG
144 The sou'wester $250
145 Autumn sunlight $50
146 The housemaid $400
1914 134 Breakfast $400 (NGC)
135 At Shanty Bay $500
136 Buena Viste Station, Rockcliffe Park $250
137 Ottawa etch $20
1931 98 James Wilson, Esq (NGC)
1945 91 Sir Lyman Poore Duff, PC

FOSBERY, LIONEL GOOCH
12 Jan 1879, Ottawa 10 Feb 1956, Wakefield, Que M
addr: Ottawa, 177 Sparks St, 1916-17. Aylmer, Que, 1927. Ottawa, 1 Roseberry Ave, 1929
1916 314 Panel. Strathcona Trust competition sculp
1917 358 Master Thomas Henry Fosbery plaster, marble $250
359 Youth plaster, bronze $150
1927 307 Rt Hon Sir Robert Laird Borden plaster, bronze $375
1929 366 Late Earl Haig plaster $75 bronze $200
367 1924 bronze $300
plaster, bronze $300 each, 368-9
368 Bather, girl book end
369 Bather, youth book end

FOSS, JULIA O. (Mrs)
addr: Sherbrooke, Que, c/o S.F Morey
1892 58 The Queen's Highway $25

FOSTER, FRANCIS ROLAND (FRANK)
28 Jan 1875, London, Eng 14 Jul 1943, Montreal CNS29
addr: Montreal, 340 University St
1915 389 House, Westmount Blvd

FOSTER, LAUREL G.
addr: Montreal, 147 Bishop St
1920 enamel on Satsuma & Belleek
328 Bowl
329 Rose jar
330 Vase
Women's Art Society prize
331 Box

FOUCAR, KENNETH W.
addr: Montreal, 1172 Phillips Pl
1935 403 Prospective log cabin drwg

FOULIS, JEAN M.
addr: Saint John, N.B.
1908 201 Market slip, St John wc $12

FOURDRINIER, EMILY LOUISE
7 Jul 1870, Waterloo, Que 23 Aug 1896, Ottawa H
addr: Montreal, 12 Tupper St, 1891-4
1891 48 Students at work $25
1892 59 A windy September morning $30
60 Sketch of a lady
61 Tired out $75
1894 63 Study of a rose $15

FOURNELLE, ANDRE
16 Oct 1939, Montreal
addr: Outremont, 781 Rockland Ave
1964 119 Pays latéral, fonte $450

FOURNIER, ALEXANDER PAUL
11 Oct 1939, Simcoe, Ont IO WWA80
addr: Toronto
1968 90 Rats No 4 ink on canvas 28 3/4 x 34 3/8 $135
91 The lake set No 9 oil wash on rice paper 24 x 36 $150
92 Devon set No 3 50 x 50 $500

FOWLER, DANIEL

10 Feb 1810, Down, Kent, Eng 14 Sep 1894, Amherst Island, Ont AGO B CE EC H M NGC R2 TB
addr: Amherst Island, Ont, 1880-92;
1880 109 Dead game, Canadian wc (NGC)
134 Dead bittern, flurry of snow wc
140 Mare and foal wc
153 Hollyhocks wc
157 Wood duck wc
1886 1 Bolton Abbey wc
3 In the New Forest wc
5 A trout stream wc
14 Castle Dinas Bran, Wales wc
19 Postam wc
33 Looking out for Father's boat wc
40 Val d'Aosta wc
41 At Berncastle on the Moselle wc
1889 123 October afternoon, Morrows Bay, Amherst Island wc $50
124 Fisher boys, Sussex, England wc $30 (NGC)
125 Low water, Bay of Quinte wc $50
126 Where the wild winds have their way wc
127 Ruins of Vale Crucis Abbey, Wales wc $35
128 Very old trees at Tivoli, Italy wc $35
129 A heavy squall wc $35
1892 167 Merl on the Moselle wc $125
168 Summer afternoon wc $60
169 Mill stream near Bern Castle, on the Moselle wc $60
170 Confluence of Moselle and Rhine, Coblentz wc $50

FOX, DELLA C.
addr: Westmount, 237 Clarke Ave
1917 418 Grape tray (semi con) $25
419 Vase $20
420 Pin tray $1

FOX, GEORGE GREENFIELD
30 Jun 1870 - 11 Nov 1933, Montreal
addr: Montreal: 35 Crescent St, 1911-15; 761 Sherbrooke St W, 1921-8; 1617 Sherbrooke St W, 1929-33
1911 106 Old bridge, N.H. $35
107 Lily pads
1912 145-6 Moonlight
147 The garden
1915 124 The dunes, Ogunquit, Me $75
125 Montreal from Mount Royal $25
126 Katrina $25
1921 87 The Devil's Kitchen, Ogunquit
1922 111 Fish huts
112 Marine
1924 84 The cove
85 Ebb tide
1925 110 Fishing boats $150
111 Fishing nets $150
1926 58 Fish huts $50
1927 65 Fog, Grand Manan $200
66 Early afternoon $60
67 Headland, Grand Manan $100
1928 73 Sun and fog, Grand Manan $200
1929 80 Early winter $200
81 Late afternoon $150
1930 76 Fishing boats, Grand Manan $100
77 Surf, Grand Manan $150
1931 99 Marine, Grand Manan, N.B.
100 Full sea, Grand Manan, N.B.
1932 99 Surf $150
100 After the storm $200
101 Opalescent sea $150
102 Spirit of the sea $100
1933 100 Morning light $400
101 Silver sea $300

FOX, JOHN RICHARD
26 Jul 1927, Montreal B CCI CE M NGC WWA84 Juror
addr: Westmount, 492 Mountain Ave, 1951. Montreal: 1602 Selkirk Ave, 1960; Montreal, 1968
1951 95 The balcony $200
96 Landscape $175
1960 32 Boats, Wellfleet $750
33 Harbour, Wellfleet $700
1968 93 Le miroir acry 50 x 35 $1,100
94 Atelier vert 36 x 24
95 Atelier automne 32 x 24

FOX, LOUISE CASS (m John Richard Fox)
addr: Montreal, 1602 Selkird Ave
1955 106 Composition III nm $60

FOX, WINIFRED GRACE MCGILL (m Charles Harold Fox)
26 Nov 1909, Avondale, N.S.
addr: Kentville, N.S, 18 Caldwell Ave
1941 71 Seven times eight $35

FRAME, MARGARET JOSEPHINE GERALDINE FULTON (m H.S. Beatty)
2 Jun 1903, Oxford, N.S. M
addr: Ottawa: 430 Daly Ave, 1941; 111 Sparks St, 1945
1941 225 Lieut G. Rochereau de la Sablière drwg
1945 92 George, son of Air Vice Marshall de Niverville pastel

FRAME, STATIRA ELIZABETH WELLS (m William Frame)
15 Sep 1870, Waterloo, Que 29 Nov 1935, Vancouver
addr: Montreal, 570 Milton St
1934 113 From the fifth floor $300
114 The patchwork quilt $275
115 Japs fishing, Vancouver B.C. $125

FRANCE, EURILDA LOOMIS Amer
(m Jessie Leach France)
26 Mar 1865, Pittsburgh, Pa 15 Feb 1931, New Haven, Conn AAA31 B F H TB3
addr: Montreal, 102 St Mathew St, 1898-1901
1898 32 A disappointed call $200
143 Summer wc $60
144 Sunlight wc $50
1900 129 Old fashioned garden wc $100
1901 127 A country window wc $100

FRANCE, JESSIE LEACH Amer
8 Oct 1862, Cincinnati, Ohio 1926, New Haven, Conn AAA28 B F TB3
addr: Montreal, 102 St Mathew St, 1898-1901
1898 33 Early moonrise $150
34 Arrival of a herring boat, Holland $60
145 The road to the sea wc $50
1900 36 Moonlight $50
37 On the beach, Baie St Paul $45
130 Twilight wc $25
1901 36 Twilight, coast of Maine $300
37 Grey day, Scarboro, Maine $150
38 Moonlight, coast of Maine $75
128 Coast of Maine wc $100

FRANCHERE, JOSEPH CHARLES
4 Mar 1866 - 12 May 1921, Montreal CC2 CE H NGC TB3 W78
addr: Paris, 9 rue Des Fourneau, 1891. Montreal, 218 St Lawrence Blvd, 1894; 35 St François Xavier St, 1895; 376 Lagauchetière St, 1897-1900; 169 Peel St, 1901; 60 St Denis St, 1903-18; 6678 Ste Famille St, 1919; 67 Ste Famille St, 1920-1
1891 49 Still life $60
50 An Italian girl $100
1894 64 My friend
65 Winter in the country $40
1895 42 Monsieur V.R.
43 Madame V.R.
44-5 Landscape $30 each
1897 46 Mde P.P. Martin
47 Le printemps $125
1900 38 Place Jacques Cartier $600
39 Thinking $80
40 Study of a head $75
1901 39 Mde N.P. Boucher
40 Japonaise canadienne $125
41 Le petit gourmet $60
1903 53 Mdlle B.
54 Rivière du Loup $40
1905 50 Fortune teller $75
1906 62 After supper $600
63 Mr G. Lamothe, KC
336 Drawing for the Artisan's Society
1908 60 Les deux mères $200
61 Indiscretion $100
1909 126 Dr J.P. Rottot
127 Le Fort de Chambly $125
128 En caleche wc $35
1910 135 Hon R. Dandurand, KC
136 Retour du bal $400
1911 108 Sport canadien $180
109 Scène d'hiver $75
1912 148 Mde A. Vaillancourt
149 Prenier chagrin $150
150 Après la messe, hiver $400
1913 147 Le retour, hiver $400
148 Le fin de jour $150 (NGC)
149 Lassitude $200
1914 138 Rêverie $400
139 Grand'mère $150
140 Etude
141 Winter $150
1915 127 M F. de S.A. Bastien, CR
128 Fin de jour du hiver $200
129 Eté $150
130 Vieux canadien $150
1916 107 Mme A. Michaud
108 La poudrerie $500
109 Golden youth $400
1917 133 Honourable Joseph Bolduc

134 Etude, tête $125
135 Hiver $150
136 Fin du jour $100
1918 130 Vieux Montréal (Rivers) $400
131 Le père Pierre $175
132 Marcelle, portrait
1919 124 Aimé Geoffrion, CR
125 Hiver $250
126 Vieilles granges $125
127 En vacances $175
1920 92 Mr Isaie Préfontaine
93 Mr Alfred Laliberté, RCA
94 Les deux amis $200
298 La moissonneuse statuette plâtre $20
1921 88 La grand'mère $100

FRANCK, ALBERT JACQUES
2 Apr 1899, Middleburg, Netherlands
28 Feb 1973, Toronto AGO CE M WWA76
addr: Toronto, 90 Hazelton Ave
1960 34 Belair Street, Toronto $700

FRANCOIS-BARBAUD, KATIE
b France
addr: Montreal, 5111 Jeanne d'Arc Ave
1952 61 Carnaval en Bigorre wc & mm $100

FRANK, J. PETER
3 Jun 1903, St Gall, Switz.
addr: White Rock, B.C.
1931 101 On the Pacific coast wc $50
102 Landscape, Quebec wc $65

FRANKENBERG, EMME (Mrs)
29 Dec 1896, Dortmund, Germ.
addr: Montreal, 5154, Notre Dame de Grace Ave, 1940-54
1940 118 Castle in Naples $100
119 In the sun $150
120 Lilac $100
121 Sunflowers $125
1941 72 Autumn flowers $150
73 Lilies $100
74 Double portrait of Gloria
1942 57 Negro girl $150
58 Still life $100
1943 68 Amaryllis $225
1944 44 Med student
45 Spring in Taormina $160
1945 93 Self portrait
1946 90 My son
91 Dr R.
1947 86 Happy memories $175
1952 12 L.P., portrait
1954 36 Maria $150

FRASER, CAROL LUCILLE HOORN (m John Fraser)
5 Sep 1930, Superior, Wis CC2 WWA84
addr: Halifax: 1352 Queen St, 1963-4; Halifax, 1968
1963 25 The vineyard $750
1964 30 The winter window $1,250
1968 96 Spanish landscape ink & wash drwg 18 x 22 1/2 $125
97 Spain col ink 17 3/4 x 21 1/2 $100
98 Spring rain 50 x 60 $650
99 Garden diagram 50 x 60 $900

FRASER, FREDERICK ALEXANDER
17 Jun 1897, Toronto
addr: Toronto, 23 Albany Ave, 1926-30
1926 59 Berri Street, Montreal $75
1927 68 October snow, Alton, Ont $75
1928 74 The Bluffs of Scarboro wc $95
1929 82 A showery day, Bay of Quinte wc $100
83 October maple wc $85
1930 78 Morning, Owen Sound $100
79 The edge of the wood wc $125

FRASER, GLADYS M.
addr: Montreal, 4949 Queen Mary Rd, Apt 32
1940 122 Quelle journée sombre, East Gloucester, Mass wc $15

FRASER, JOHN ARTHUR
1838, London, Eng 1 Jan 1898, New York AGO B CE DBA EC G H M Mo98 NGC TB W78
addr: Toronto, 1880. New York: 114 W 18th St, 1891; 157 E 47th St, 1894
1880 7 Laurentian splendour (NGC)
11 In breezy October, Bay Chaleur
23 At a lobster fishery
44 Study for seaside idyl
45 Day break, low tide
46 Grey morning and dropping tide
67 A last ray
123 An autumn study wc
142 A rocky beach, Bay Chaleur wc
149 Early morning, Dalhousie, N.B. wc

1883 133 A trout pool on the Escuminue
1886 7 A gray day (Nahant) wc
8 Near the close of a stormy day wc
9 A sunny bit of lake shore wc
13 A quiet bit of river wc
16 A mountain road wc
35 Morning at Nahant after a stormy night wc(Nahaut mispr)
37 A mill race wc
38 At the mouth of a tidal river wc
43 A sunny afternoon wc
45 Late afternoon at rocky Nahant wc
1891 51 Angling in the Highlands, November morning $900
52 In the Pass of Brander $250
53 Neath threatening skies, in spring time $250
1894 181 On the Linnhe Lock from Appin wc $250
182 On a Scotch River wc $100
183 A riverside wc $100
184 At Gorrie, Arran wc $50
185 A by-path wc $50
186 A grey morning on the Thames wc $50
1894 Medal. Chicago 1893

FRASER, OLIVE HAMLEY
27 Mar 1892 d 1981
addr: Westmount, 445 Prince Albert Ave, 1912-14. Richelieu, Que, 1915. Montreal, 321 Mackay St, 1916. Richelieu, Que, 1917-20
1912 450 Brown jug $4
1913 466 Small bowl $8.50
467 Japanese vase $5
468 Large vase
1914 496 Candlestick green & silver
497 Bouillon cups, blue & gold
498 Salad bowl, orange and berries
499 Jardiniere, sea gulls $5
500 Card tray, butterflies lustre $3.50
501 Salt and pepper $300
502 Plate, Japanese enamel $10
1915 439 Satsuma vase, blue birds pair $6
440 Tiny coffee cups, six $10
441 Vase, after sundown
1916 366 Vase, futurist black matt
367 Vase, spider web $15
368 Cider pitcher, Japanese $15
369 Dresser set, green lustre
1917 421 Rose jar
422 Compote $10
423 Flower stand $50
1918 133 Collection of minature sketches $5
426 Vase, hexagonal, oriental des $15
427 Box, bats, Satsuma enamels $10
428 Tray, blue birds, conventional des $7
1919 128 Rose garden, Elizabeth Park, Hartford, Conn wc
129 Miniature sketches $5 each
1920 99 Miniature sketches $5 each (Clive H. Fraser, 1912, mispr)

FRAYDAS, STANISLAS (STANLAS)
4 Sep 1908, Betecom, Belg
addr: Montreal, 680 Laurentian Blvd
1957 32 Suburbia $500

FRAYN, CLARENCE V.
addr: Montreal, 46 Overdale Ave, 1913. Westmount: 438 Mount Stephen Ave, 1919; 4265 St Catherine St W, 1920.
1913 423 Sugar basin silver set with amethysts $50
enamelled copper 424-5
424 Candlestick $20
425 Patch boxes $14.50
1919 130 Peggy wc
131 Madame X pastel
1920 100 Still life wc $35
314-15 Aisle window, St Mathias Church, Westmount des and executed

FRECHETTE, MARIE MARGUERITE
Apr 1878, Ottawa F
addr: Vancouver, 1600 Davie St
1922 113 Le beret rouge min $100
114 A musician, poartait min
115 Landscape, Swiss
116 Interior

FREEDMAN, A. O.
addr: Montreal, 255 Sherbrooke St W
1917 360 Gassed sculp

FREEDMAN, LILLIAN

addr: Outremont, 891 Stuart Ave, 1939-41
1939 399 Mightier than man charcl $15
400 Wild bushes charcl $15
1940 356 Pathway charcl $15
1941 226 Another pathway charcl $15

FREEDMAN, NATHAN
addr: Montreal, 5679 Park Ave
1945 94 Main Street, St Sauveur

FREEMAN, D.
addr: Montreal, 900 St Catherine St W
1914 142 Mark Popkin $100

FREIMAN, LILLIAN (LILY)
22 Jun 1908, Guelph, Ont B M TB3
addr: Montreal, 567 Maplewood Ave
1922 Lily Frieman
111 Study $250

FRENCH, BETTY M. (m Lloyd O. McCaughey)
1921, London, Ont M
addr: Ottawa: 65 Bullock Ave, 1954-5; 809 Moore Ave, Britannia Heights, 1957
1954 37 Two sisters
1955 31 Kathryn
1957 114 Paula nm $40

FRENCH, REGINALD EDWARD
addr: Verdun, Que, 459 4th Ave, 1941-2
1941 75 Grain elevators, Lachine Canal
1942 59 Gloomy Sunday, St Madeline $65

FREW, GEORGE SUMNER
addr: Montreal, 3454 Peel St
1940 123 Spaniel pup pastel

FREYVOGEL, CHARLOTTE R.
addr: Montreal, 162 Villeneuve St
1921 89 Still life (crochet work) $80

FRIPP, THOMAS WILLIAM
23 Mar 1864, London, Eng 30 May 1931, Vancouver CC2 CE EC H NGC TB3
addr: Hatzic, B.C, The Studio, 1913-18
1915 131 End of autumn day, B.C. wc $100
132 Sunrise on Fraser River, Hatzic, B.C. wc $40
133 Lake McArthur, Canadian Rockies wc $25
1916 110 Asulkan Glacier, B.C. wc $25
111 The Summit Mount Aberdeen wc $25
1917 137 The shadow of a storm, Mt Sir Donald wc $150
138 Mount Lefroy from Sentinel Pass wc $150
139 Edge of the lake wc $25
1918 134 Mount Sir Donald wc $30

FRY, A. JOANNA
addr: Montreal: 83 Simpson St, 1914; 14 St Famille St, 1915
1914 143 One who looks on; a study $75
144 Husbandry mural dec $250
145 Sixteen Island Lake wc $20
146 Naomi b&w
1915 135 On Sixteen Island Lake wc $15
136 Evening, Sixteen Island Lake wc $15
136 Frontispiece for 'The mission of Victoria Wilhelmina' wc

FUGLER, GRACE (m Leonard Hutchinson)
22 Jun 1915, Hamilton, Ont AGO
addr: Hamilton, 12 Hamilton Ave, 1936-9
1936 534 Queen Anne's lace wd cut $7.50
535 From the upper road wd cut $7.50
1937 399 Travel and sound block pr $10
1938 160 Precious engr $8
1939 401 Farmer's wife pencil drwg
402 A room with a view engr $5

FUHRER, WALTER
27 Oct 1933, Zurich, Switz
addr: Montreal, 3660 Lorne Cr, Apt 11, 1963-5
1963 101 Early morning metal $250
1965 35 Venus steel $300 (MBAM)

FULLER, GWENDOLYN MARY NORRIS (m Laurance B. Fuller)
7 Jun 1896, East Farnham, Que
addr: Montreal, 4925 Piedmont Ave, 1941-6. Westmount, 16 Severn Ave, 1949
1941 works in plaster 1941-9
283 Head of St Maurice
1943 256 Head of a Negro $100
1945 277 Joyce, portrait
1946 284 Venus $150
1949 171 Frankie M. Norris

FYLES, FAITH
Cowansville, Que
addr: Ottawa: 368 Frank St, 1917-21; 336 Kent St, 1924; 51 James St, 1925-6; 340 MacLaren St, 1930; 96 Maple Lane, 1934-9
1917 140 Misty day, Lake St Louise, B.C. $35
141 In the garden wc $35
142 Montmorency Falls, Que wc $35
1918 135 The bourgainvillea, Bermuda $25
136 Misty afternoon $35
1921 90 A March morning $100
91 The city from the farm $60
1924 86 Menton Garavan, south France pastel $75
1925 112 Cagnes-sur-Mer pastel $65
113 Farm on the Gatineau pastel $30
114 Beach at Newquay pastel $35
1926 60 Menton Garavan pastel $65
1930 80 Over the hills $150
1934 116 Beside the ackee tree, Jamaica $100
1935 124 Between showers, Jamaica $35
1939 140 Oaks and maples $150
141 In my garden $150

FYSHE, AVIS SELINA
28 Apr 1886, Halifax AAA30
addr: Montreal, 1501 St Catherine St W, 1943-50
1943 illuminated testimonials
227 Sir Edward Beatty
228 Meg and Frank
1944 illuminated manuscript, 1944-5
139 Guy Drummond Memorial
1945 256 Shakespeare sonnet $50
257 Every child $75
1946 manuscript
256 Famous men
257 Lullaby
258 Christopher Plantin $35
1950 66 Country lane, Stanstead wc $75

G

GABO also GABORIAU, PIERRE see LAPALME, PIERRE GABORIAU

GADBOIS, DENYSE (Mrs Chaput)
4 Dec 1921, Montreal M WWA53
addr: Montreal, 1558 Pine Ave, 1950. Westmount, 382A Olivier Ave, 1957. Montreal, 3873 Van Horne Ave, 1960
1950 114 Still life
1957 33 Lise $125
1960 35 Etude $400
156 Etude nm $100

GADBOIS, MARIE MARGUERITE LOUISE LANDRY (m Emilien Gadbois)
27 Nov 1896, Montreal M NGC WWA53
addr: Montreal, 29 Glencoe Ave, 1936-40. Outremont, 346 St Catherine Rd, 1945-7. Montreal: 1558 Pine Ave W, 1948-9; 3423 Oxford Ave, 1953-60
1936 536 Etude drwg
537 Tête de fillette drwg
538 Portrait d'enfant drwg
1937 115 Nature morte $125
116 Paysanne
117 Portrait
1938 49 Portrait
50 Paysanne
1939 142 Madame L.
143 Portrait
403 Femme à l'éventail pastel & charcl
1940 124 Portrait de jeune fille
1945 95 Femme à la cravate bleu
1946 92 Nature morte $350
93 Nature morte au livre $150
1947 87 Femme à la fenêtre $300
88 Attentè $150
1948 11 Eve $300
1949 31 Nature morte $200
32 La lettre $250
1953 75 Nature morte No 1 $350
1960 36 Jeune fille en jaune $350

GADBOIS, ROBERT
addr: Winnipeg, University of Manitoba, School of Art
1951 97 Escaping shadow $150
98 Substance of terror $150

GAGEN, ROBERT FORD
10 May 1847, London, Eng 2 Mar 1926, Toronto AGO B CC1 EC H M NGC R1 TB1/3 W78
addr: Toronto: 1880; 79 King St W, 1892-4; 90 Yonge St, 1898-1900; 157 Bay St, 1906; Toronto, 1908; Mail Bldg, 1909-10
1880 102 Balsams wc
146 An evening study in the marsh, Toronto wc

162 Calla lillies wc
180 An interesting yarn wc
186 Early evening, coast of Maine wc
1881 65 Rhododendrons wc
1883 6 In a conservatory wc
28 Hollyhocks wc
37 On the top of White Head, Portland, Maine wc
40 Lilacs wc
147 The ocean
1892 171 Dirty weather, Peaks Island, Maine wc $35
1894 187 Lilacs wc $125
188 Under the birches wc $150
1898 146 Fine weather on Memphremagog's hills wc $50
1900 131 Sunset Rock, East Gloucester, Mass wc $25
132 A colour study, Gloucester harbour wc $25
133 A cloudy summer day wc $25
134 The willow road wc $25
1906 229 Part of the Hermit Range, Selkirks wc $50
230 At Monhegan Island, Me wc $30
231 Black Head, Monhegan Island wc $30
1908 202 A soft day in the Grampians wc $150
1909 129 On the cod banks nm $200
130 Purple gloom of evening, Selkirks nm $100
131 Morning near the Great Glacier, Selkirks nm $50
1910 137 Morning on a Scotch Loch wc $100

GAGNON, CHARLES
23 May 1934, Montreal B CC2 CE M WWA84 Juror
addr: Montreal: 2055 Lincoln Ave, Apt 10, 1962; 3510 Addington Ave, 1963-5; Montreal, 1969
1962 8 The beach $1,000
1963 26 The gap illus $1,200. Hon mention
1964 31 Le sixième jour a.m. $900 (MBAM)
1965 6 Le huitième jour 11 illus $1,000 Hon mention
1969 2 Etapes No 2 80 x 108

GAGNON, CLARENCE ALPHONSE
8 Nov 1881 - 5 Jan 1942, Montreal AGO B CC1 CE CWW38 EC M Mo12 NGC TB1/2 W78 Juror
addr: Westmount, 25 Melbourne, 1901-3. Montreal, c/o Henry Morgan & Co, 1905-6. Paris, 1908. Montreal, King's Hall, 591, St Catherine St W, 1909. Paris, 9 rue Falguière, 1910-11; 7 rue Falguière, 1912. Montreal: Johnson & Topping, 1913; Art Assoc, 1915-16; Arts Club, 51 Victoria St, 1917; Montreal, 1918-20. Baie St Paul, Que, 1923. Montreal, Art Assoc, 1925.
1901 42 Still life, duck $15
129 Head, study chalk $5
197-8 Magazine cover des $5 each
1903 55 Head of old man $80
56 Moonlight, Beaupré $50
57 Clearing weather, Beaupré $40
1905 51 Pont Neuf, Paris $50
52 Twilight, Luxembourg Gardens $45
53 Interior, Normandy $125
54 Old woman reading $125
1906 64 Old woman eating soup $350
65 A frugal meal $350 (NGC)
66 Autumn $250
67 Old trees $200
68 Venetian fishing boats $35
305 Les Jardins du Luxembourg etch $10
306 Le soir etch $10
1908 62 Japanese fantasy
63 On the sands, Dinard (MBAM)
64 The willows
65 Old street, Dinan
1909 132 Les deux Plages, Paranie et St Malo $500
133 Autumn morning, Moret on the Loing $150
134 Early winter moonrise, Baie St Paul $90
135 Château Gaillard, Normandy $75
136 The yellow dress $50
137 The Seine, Pont de l'Arche $25
etchings, 138-147
138 Mont St Michel, Brittany $12
139 Rue des Petits Degnés, St Malo $12
140 Overhauling fishing vessels, St Malo $12
141 Port de Bourgogne, Moret $12

142 L'orage $15
143 Rue des Cordeliers, Dinan $18
144 Tour de l'Horloge, Dinan $18
145 Canal de Loing, Moret $12
146 Rue à Nemours $12
147 Route de Picardie
Prints of above (138-47) have been purchased by Petit Palais of Fine Arts, South Kensington Museum, galleries of the Hague, Berlin, Dresden and Mulhausen, Art Institute, Chicago, and Walker Art Gallery, Liverpool
1910 138 Early morning mist, Normandy $200
139 St Malo $200
140 Autumn afternoon, La Selle, south Seine $200
141 Early morning, Mont Saint Michel $150
1911 110 Moret-sur-Loing, early morning
111 Early moonrise, Rivière Rance, Brittany
112 Moonlight, St Eustache $300
113 Autumn evening $125
1912 151 Winter in the Laurentians $100 (NGC)
152 St Malo, from St Briac $150
153 Monastery of St Francis, Assise $250
154 Late summer afternoon on the Seine $250
1913 150 Mrs Selkirk Cross
151 The thunder cloud, St Malo $250
152 The Campo, Sienna $400
153 Late winter afternoon, Laurentians
1915 137 Old houses, winter $300
138 Village, morning, winter $300
139 Lake of Geneva $250
149 Twilight in the Laurentians $200
1916 112 Cloud shadows, winter $350
113 Evening, winter $250
1917 143 The wayside Cross, winter $500 (listed 1967, Jessie Dow prize) (NGC)
144 Street scene, Quebec at night $300 (NGC)
145 Early October, moonrise $300
146 Winter scene in the Laurentians $150
147 Morning mist $150
1918 137 Morning mist $500
138 Sunday morning, winter $700
139 Northern woods $500
140 Twilight, winter $300
1919 132 The train, winter $300
133 Evening, lake scene, Venice $300
134 Early morning, Laurentians $300
1920 101 March in the birch woods $900 (AGO)
102 A Quebec village street, winter $700
103 A Laurentian homestead $400 (NGC)
104 Indian summer $400
1921 92 Laurentian forest and stream $500
93 Golden autumn, Laurentians $500
94 Midwinter scene in a Canadian village
1922 118 The pond in October $700
1923 95 Heating the oven, winter scene $800
1925 115 Schooner in the ice pack $600
116 Winter in the Laurentians $400
117 October moonrise $450
118 The red sleigh
1909 Hon mention, (Paris) Salon, 1906

GAGNON, WILLFORD ARTHUR
b 1878
addr: Montreal: 74 Guardian Bldg, 1909; Montreal, 1918; 175 Mansfield St, 1927; 2039 Mansfield St, 1928-33
1909 415 Proposed residence, Pine Ave
416 Proposed residence
1918 391 Architectural renderings
1927 204 Proposed country residence
1928 237 Proposed façade, art shop and galleries cardboard model
1931 278 Maison à Chicoutimi model
1933 102 The Coliseum, Rome wc
103 Base of the Campanile, Venice wc
104 The Duomo, Lucca wc
376 Proposed suburban residence model
see also Finey, Samuel A, 1916

GALARNEAU, LEOPOLD
fl 1882-92 H
Addr: Montreal, 5 Oxenden Ave, 1891
1889 25 Paddy, portrait of a hunter $50

1891 54 Norah, a hunter

GALBRAITH, ELIZABETH ROBERTA (BETTY) (m C.D. Cornell)
15 Jan 1916, Montreal M
addr: Westmount: 4340 Montrose Ave, 1939; 222 Melville Ave, 1943. Halifax, 113 South Park St, 1945. Montreal, 1227 Sherbrooke St W, 1946
1939 144 Mary Lyle Kyte pastel
1943 74 Young Canadian soldier pastel $25
75 Young sailor RCNVR pastel
1945 96 Air cadet pastel
1946 94 Jocelyn $50

GALEA, EDWARD ZARB
31 Aug 1893, Valletta, Malta CNS40
addr: Montreal: 66 Notre Dame de Lourdes, 1926; 1211 St Urbain St, 1927
1926 Galeay, mispr
240 Portrait relief
1927 205 Project, a church
206 Project, an apartment house

GALT, JOCELYN (m George Galt)
12 Mar 1927, Montreal M
addr: Westmount, 765 Lexington Ave, 1952-4
1952 62 Old stove wc
70 Floral design pen & ink
1954 122 Floral design nm $25

GAMACHE, JANINE (m Philippe Paquet)
1931, Québec M
addr: Québec, 272 rue 11è
1961 16 Le roi $100

GANDIER, JOAN ALBERTA GILMOUR (m John C.C. Gandier)
14 Feb 1925, Brockville, Ont
addr: Westmount, 10 Rosemount Ave, Apt 101
1954 101 Composition No 23 des temp $45

GARDHAM, ADDI (m Frederick J. Gardham)
26 Jun 1917, Ottawa
addr: Ottawa, 66 5th Ave, Apt 5, 1953-8
1953 97 Merry-go-round wc $40
1954 102 Trio wc $45
1955 107 Old Fort Henry, Kingston nm $60
1956 99 Boats nm $85
1957 115 Still life with pears nm $100
1958 59 Italian vase nm $100

GARDINER, A. (Miss)
addr: Paris
1910 142 La Seine etch $8
143 Day coloured etch $5
144 Le Cannet etch $7
145 Collanges etch $9
146 Meyssac etch $7

GARDINER, JOHN RAWSON
Mar 1866, London, Eng 7 Feb 1956, Montreal
addr: Montreal: Temple Bldg, 1892; 136 Metcalfe St, 1895-7; Temple Bldg, 1903; 185 St James St, 1905; 1100 Beaver Hall Hill, 1930
1892 222 Board of Trade Building, Montreal arch des
1895 220 A lakeside cottage
221 A bungalow, Beaurepaire
222 Entrance to Henry VII Chapel, Westminster Abbey $25
1897 156 A farmer's home, Sussex, England wc $25
232 A suburban residence
1903 267 St Stephen's Church, Montreal
268 A bungalow
1905 246 Managers Hove, Laprarie
1930 221 St Barnabas Church

GARNEAU, HECTOR DE SAINT DENYS
13 Jun 1912, Montreal 24 Oct 1943, Ste Catherine de Foosambault, Que CE
addr: Westmount, 353 Olivier Ave
1937 118 Ciel en automne

GARNEAU, PIERRE
b 1926
addr: Montreal: 5610 Canterbury Ave, 1944-50; 3493 Stanley St, 1958
1944 46 The orchestra pastel $50
47 Atomic storm pastel $50
1945 97 Composition organique temp $40
1946 95-6 Composition temp $45 each
97 Composition temp
1947 89 Composition $65
90 Gathering in space $100
1949 127 Composition No 1 gouache
1950 115 La chauve-souris $75
116 La fleur oil gouache, conti $100

1958 60 Nature morte nm $125
61 L'usine étiente nm $75

GARNETT, M.
1885 116 Along the Restigouche wc
122 A peep from a pullman on the Metapedia wc

GARNIER, JACQUES
M
addr: St Marc-sur-le-Richelieu, Que
1960 236 Corpus ter cot & enamel $500

GARSIDE, THOMAS HILTON
16 Jan 1906, Duckinfield, Ches. Eng
18 Jan 1980 M
addr: Montreal: 1680 Le Caron St, 1934; 6263 Briand St, 1935-6; 1682 Le Caron St, 1937; 2209 Melrose Ave, 1941-9
1934 117 Chapel of St Jean, Ile d'Orleans, Que $75
1935 125 Eglise de St Jean, Ile d'Orleans $75
1936 163 Old barns, St Patrick St, Montreal $100
1937 119 Old Canadian house, St Laurent, Montreal $200
120 Late afternoon sunlight, Ville LaSalle, Montreal $100
1941 76 The hay cart, Ville LaSalle $100
1943 76 Spring thaw $150
77 Sanguinet Street from my window $200
1944 48 The storm $350
49 When spring breaks through $300
1945 98 The Rouge Rapids $500 (MBAM)
99 March day $350
1946 98 Autumn
99 French Canadian house, Côte de Liesse Road
100 Laurentian landscape $500
1947 91 Panorama of Bic, Quebec
92 Late afternoon
1949 33 The wharf, Bic, Quebec $750

GARWOOD, AUDREY ELAINE (m Herb R. Hosie)
7 Jul 1927, Toronto CWW84 M WWA84
addr: Toronto, 72 Avenue Rd
1955 32 Pineapple $100

GASS, MABEL see MCCULLOCH, MABEL

GASS, MARJORIE EARLE
9 Jan 1889, Saint John 1928, Montreal M NGC
addr: Westmount: 4339 Westmount Ave, 1915-17; Westmount, 1918. Montreal, 5039 Sherbrooke St W, 1919. Westmount, 50 Chesterfield Ave, 1920-2; Montreal, 414 Mackay St, 1923-7
1915 141-2 Winter scene pastel $15 each
143 The boats pastel $15
1916 114 Sketch pastel
115 Peacock pastel
116 Winter day
117 Winter sketch
1917 152 The children $75
153 Sketch pen & ink $10
154 Winter day $15
1918 141 Sand pile
142 Sketch
143 Bonsecours, interior
144 The market
1919 135 Old Château de Ramezay $35
136 Arabian nights, composition $25
137 A summer afternoon $30
138 Sketch $10
1920 105 September day $20
106 The stream $30
107-8 Old house, Vaudreuil $30 each
1921 95 Spenser's Faerie Queen
96 Child feeding geese
97 Curios
1922 119 Winter $75
120 A street in Vaudreuil $75
121 Tête-à-tête $75
122 The green vase $30
1923 96 On Lake Memphremagog $225
97 Old courtyard $200
98 Bonsecours $200
1924 87 Landscape, Knowlton $300
88 Autumn $275
1025 119 A late autumn day $250
120 Scene at night $225
121 River scene $35
1927 69 A winter scene $150
70 Dominion Square on a wintry day $200

GAUCHER, YVES
3 Jan 1934, Montreal AGO B CC2 CE M WWA84 Juror
addr: Westmount, 424 Roslyn Ave, 1960-2. Montreal: 2625 Albert St, Apt 1, 1963; Montreal, 1968

1960 157 143° nm $50
1962 44 Nako nm $50
1963 77 SA nm $125
78 AJI nm $125
1968 100-01 Alap acry 108 x 80
(one MBAM)
102 Alap acry 80 x 120

GAUDET, ALICE
addr: Montreal: 3406 St Denis St, 1936;
4564 Boyer St, Apt 3, 1937
1936 164 The painted doll pastel $35
1937 121 A study pastel $90

GAUGUET-LAROUCHE, JEAN
6 Oct 1935, La Malbaie, Que
addr: Montreal, 2078A Panet St, 1963.
Cartierville, Que, 12270 Jasmin, 1965
1963 102 Cybèle en escarpin d'hiver
iron $750
1965 36 Cosmogonie 7 metal & stone $650

GAULT, GEORGIA M.
addr: Montreal: 763 University
1917; 75 Mount Royal Ave, 1921-3
1917 148 Moonrise $40
149 At the end of the lake $40
150 The road to the village $40
1921 98 My hour $100
99 Franklyn Canyon, California
$50
1922 Georgina M.
123 In the silence of the mountain
1923 99 A gray day $25
100 The last load $25

GAULT, MARGUERITE
addr: Montreal, c/o Charles Edlington,
146 Mansfield St
1917 151 Noirot

GAUTHIER, JEANNETTE
addr: Montreal, 5476 Côte St Antoiné Rd
1943 78 Vue du 6è étage $150

GAUTHIER, O.
addr: Montreal, 1442 Fullum St
1937 122 The shack wc $40

GAUTHIER-CHARLEBOIS, ALYNE (m R.H.
Charlebois)
addr: Montreal, 75 Sherbrooke St W,
1932-3; 2273 Wilson Ave, 1942
1932 103 Dimanche matin wc $40
104 Blanchisseuses wc $30
105 Sambo wc $20
106 Vieux Tchèque wc
1933 105 Eglise de Sillery, Quebec
1942 60 Sieste $100
61 Première neige $100

GAUVREAU, GILLES
29 Jul 1924, Quebec M
addr: Montreal, 4399 St Dominique St,
1955. Pointe des Cascades, Que, 1958-
62
1955 33 Pochade 112
1958 18 Le fleuve en hiver $40
1962 9 Paysage cascadian $45
10 Pointe des Cascades $45

GAUVREAU, PIERRE
23 Aug 1922, Montreal CE M
addr: Montreal: 75 Sherbrooke St W,
1947-9 ; 358 St Joseph Blvd E, Apt 4,
1953; 1905 Tupper St, No 72, 1961
1947 93 L'oblongue étalène $150
1949 34 L'ascension d'Ubu $100
1953 76 Merci pour demain $150
1961 76 Ascension nm $225

GEARY, JOHN
addr: Montreal, 2070 Mance St, 1927-9
1927 Gearey, 1927-8, mispr
308 The old woman plaster
1928 341 Eleanor plaster
342 Girl of Caughnawago plaster
$75
1929 370 Log harvest plaster

GECIN see SINDON, GERARD

GEDDES, FRANCES MILDRED (Mrs)
1888, Tring, Eng
addr: Toronto, 101 1/2 King St W,
1919 139 The letter $75
140 A gipsy $150
141 The peace pipe $100

GEDEON, F.
addr: Montreal, 244 Sherbrooke St E,
1945-6
1945 100 The fountain, Montreal
Botanical Garden pastel $50
1946 101 The church at Sault-au-
Recollet, Que $50

GEES, FRANZ BERNHARD (BRUNO)

30 Nov 1922, Bielefeld, Germ
addr: Montreal, 2685 Darling St, 1957-60
1957 34 Landscape $300
1958 19 Standing figure $500
1960 158 Fossilized form nm
159 Indian nm

GENDRON, PIERRE
3 Jul 1934, Montreal CC1 M TB3
addr: Montreal, 6979 d'Iberville Ave, Apt 6, 1956-60
1956 24 Paysage $40
1957 35 Nature morte No 1 $75
1960 37 Fugue en jaune $200
160 Hommage à Schoenberg nm $75

GENEREAUX, MARIE ARLINE
6 Feb 1897, Quebec
addr: Quebec: 16 Saunders St, 1930-2
130 Aberdeen St, 1935-9
1930 269 Vue arrière ancien Manoir Gourdeau, Ile d'Orléans etch $12
270 Entrance to Cathedral of the Holy Trinity, Quebec etch $5
1932 385 Diane wash drwg
1935 126 Old roofs on Conroy Street, Quebec wc $20
1938 51 Strange roofs wc $25
52 In an old quarter of Quebec City wc $25
1939 145 Sunday quiet, Lower Town, Quebec wc $20

GENSONNET, CATHERINE LYBIA EXARCHOU (m A. Gensonnet)
17 Sep 1921, Athens, Greece
addr: Montreal: 2173 Marcil Ave, 1957; 2259 Grand Blvd, 1963
1957 36 Impression $100
1963 79 Cosmique nm $150

GENUSH, LUBA (m Peter Gloor)
9 Sep 1924, Odessa, Russia M TB3
addr: Montreal: 7777 Stuart Ave, 1956-8; 5260 Cumberland Ave, 1960-1
1956 100 Integration nm $75
1957 116 Three figures nm $80
1958 62 Industrial landscape nm $120
1960 161 Mother and child nm $90
162 Two figures nm $90
1961 77 Standing figure nm $180

GEORGE, R. G. N.
addr: Galt, Ont
1934 444 An old farm bridge etch $15
445 Ghost trees etch $7.50

GERIN-LAJOIE, CLAUDE
addr: Outremont, 275 ave Outremont
1951 99 Nature morte avec nappe quadrilée $45

GERIN-LAJOIE, MARCEL
addr: Outremont, 275 ave Outremont
1946 102 La forêt tourmentée wc $35

GERMAIN see PERRON, GERMAIN

GERSOVITZ, SARAH VALERIE GAMER (m Ben Gersovitz)
5 Sep 1920, Montreal CWW84 M WWA84
addr: Montreal, 5173 Mayfair Ave, 1957-64
1957 117 The sisters nm $25
1958 63 The unloved nm $25
1960 163 Triceratop and friends nm $75
1961 78 Of all he surveys nm $60
1963 80 Fossils nm $50
1964 90 Entr'acte nm $55

GERSTENBERGER, LUJZA
1 Dec 1912, Budapest
addr: Montreal: 3490 Hutchison St, 1953; 451 Sherbrooke St W, 1955
1953 Lujra mispr
58 Homeless sepia $50
59 Refugees sepia $50
1955 108 Refugees nm $30

GERVAIS, J. ETIENNE LEO
22 Mar 1917, Montreal M
addr: St Vincent de Paul, Que, 1131 Belleville Ave, 1960-4
1960 232 Boeuf-musqué wd $75
233 Boeuf wd $75
1964 120 Plentitude polyestre $150

GERVAIS, LISE
2 Sep 1933, St Césaire, Rouville, Que CC1 M
addr: Montréal: 17 ch Côte Ste Catherine, Apt 9, 1961; 3419 rue Peel, 1962-4; Montréal, 1967
1961 18 La joie d'aimer illus $250. Mention hon. 1967-23, 75 x 42 1/2 (Galerie du Siècle, Montreal)

1962 11 Jaune eclat du rire $800
12 Rose des vents $800
1963 32 Invention à IV voix op 1 $675

GERVAIS, SUZANNE
addr: Montreal, 742 Wiseman Ave
1960 38 Joie $250

GESNER, GLADYS MARY
14 Jul 1906, Halifax M
addr: Halifax, 31 Cogswell St
1956 101 Bouquet nm

GEYMONAT, A. M. (Miss)
Addr: Montreal, 3285 Barclay Ave, Apt 14
1955 34 Flowers $15

GIBB, AMY
addr: Montreal, 5890 Côte St Antoine Rd
1950 117 Country scene

GIBB, DAVID ALEXANDER
21 Apr 1884 - 24 Mar 1971, Galt, Ont
M PMC W78
addr: Galt, Ont
1915 144 The hillside copse $35
145 The stoney lane $25
146 The homestead $25
147 Fields in dry weather

GIBBONS, DOROTHY
addr: Montreal, 3488 Côte des Neiges Rd
1938 194 Laughter plaster

GIBSON, BESSIE
b Australia fl 1905-26 B DBA
addr: Paris, 8 bis rue Campagne Première
1912 155 Lady Drummond min

GIBSON, THOMAS KENT HAMILTON
11 Dec 1930, Edinburgh CE
addr: Toronto, 404 Jarvis St, 1962-3
1962 13 Zero $400
14 Krishna's flowers $400
1963 27 Beach $500
28 Crescent Grill $450

GIDDINGS, M. BEATRICE
addr: Montreal, 199 Vinet St, 1906-10
1906 69 Still life $40
232 The Pearl House, Ores Island wc $35
1909 148 The bridge, Dixie wc $40
1910 147 Pasture, Granby $50

GIGUERE, E. LOUISE DE MONTIGNY see MONTIGNY, E. LOUISE DE

GIGUERE, ROLAND
4 May 1929, Montreal CC2 CE M
addr: Paris, 5 rue Manuel, 1961. Montreal, Galerie Libre, 2100 Crescent St 1962
1961 79 Voilier de nuit nm illus
Purchase award (MBAM)
1962 45 La fenêtre du tempestiaire nm $160

GIHON, CLARENCE MONTFORT Amer
25 Oct 1871, Philadelphia 1 Jan 1929, Dax, France B DBA TB1/1 WWW
addr: Montreal, c/o A.R. Doble, 804 Sherbrooke St W
1914 147 Old street, Montreuil-sur-Mer $175
148 After the thunderstorm $300

GILBERT, HELEN MAR
1888 18 Country road $125

GILHOOLY, DAVID JAMES
15 Apr 1943, Auburn, Cal CWW84 IO WWA84
addr: Regina
1970 white earthenware
27 Froghell 14 x 10 1/2
28 English frog explorers arrive at frog Tut's burial chamber 10 1/2 x 13 1/2 x 13
29 Frog baccanal
30 The anatomy lesson of Dr Tulip 11 x 9 illus

GILL, CHARLES IGNACE ADELARD
21 Oct 1871, Sorel, Que 16 Oct 1918, Montreal CC1 CE EC M W78
addr: Montreal: Jacques Cartier Normal School, 1901; Montreal, 1903; 502 Parc Lafontaine, 1905-6; Montreal, 1908; 42 Chambord St, 1910-12
1901 43 Portrait
1903 58 Remorse $100
1905 55 Les neiges de l'été $80
1906 70 Un vieux berceau $150
71 La problème $200
72 La gardien du jardin $75

73 Matinée de juillet $15
74 Devant la cuisine $20
75 Avoine verte $15
307 Octogenaire b&w $8
1908 66 L'effort $75
57 Le Cap Trinité $20
1910 148 After the game $75
1912 156 Le rêve et la raison $300
157 Portrait
port: by Edmond Dyonnet, 1901-30; bust, Alice Nolin, 1931-437

GILL, MARY C. (MINNIE)
Pierreville, Que AAA1900 H
addr: Lennoxville, Que, 1897-1920
1897 Minnie, 1897-1901
48 Passing shower $25
49 The Murray River $30
1898 147 Farm at Murray Bay wc $17.50
148 Pont au Saumon wc $12.50
149 Tarn among the Laurentians wc $12.50
1900 41 Laurentians bowlders $40
1901 44 La Loutre Beach, Cap à l'Aigle $20
130 Early December, Lennoxville wc $10
1903 172 Eventide, Murray River wc $25
173 Misty morning, Murray Bay wc $15
1905 56 Dawn at Cap à l'Aigle $23
1906 76 Harvest at Cap à l'Aigle $25
233 Sunset, Drummondville pastel $25
234 The beginning of a breeze pastel $25
235 Wayside Cross, St Irene wc $10
1908 203 Le Heugh, Cap à l'Aigle pastel $30
1909 149 A vetch field, Cap à l'Aigle pastel
1914 149 Shades of evening pastel $40
150 Autumn leaves wc $10
1915 148 By Lake Nairn, Murray Bay pastel $30
1917 156 The valley of Le Gouffre pastel $35
157 A July field, Cap à l'Aigle pastel $30
158 An old smoker pastel $25
1918 146 Mustard field after rain, Cap à l'Aigle $50
1919 143 Early winter, Lennoxville $60
1920 110 Meadow land

GILLIES, JOAN
addr: Montreal, 1675 Lincoln Ave
1946 259 Bill charcl

GILMOUR, MARY
addr: Montreal, 3480 Côte des Neiges Rd
1933 106 Breton girl $300
107 Neapolitan $200

GILSON, ENID A.
addr: Montreal, 5779 5th Ave, Rosemount
1942 62 Bleury Street wc $25
63 Autumn afternoon wc $25

GIOVANELLI, V.
addr: Montreal, 936 St Lawrence St
1909 388 Princess d'Orleans marble $200
389 Pansies sculp $25

GIRUARD, CLAUDE
30 Nov 1938, Chicoutimi, Que CWW84 M
addr: Québec, 2 ave St Denis
1961 19 Ces soleils mouillés $225

GIROUX, BRUNO
addr: Montreal, 7659 St Hubert St
1942 236 Fleurette Beauchamp plâtre patine

GIRVIN, GEORGE
addr: Toronto 293 Mossom Rd
1926 61 August $50
62 October $50

GISSING, ROLAND
14 May 1895, Broadway, Eng 29 Sep 1967, Okotoks, Alta M W78
addr: Cochrane, Alta, 1931-3. Ghost River, Cochrane, Alta, 1934-6
1931 103 The Chinook Arch $75
1932 107 Storm on Cascade Mountain $55
1933 108 Wind clouds $125
1934 118 Morning, Moraine Lake $100
1936 Ronald, mispr
165 Blue shadow, Bow Valley $75

GIUNTA, JOSEPH
2 Oct 1911, Montreal
addr: Montreal: 6691 Papineau Ave, 1934; 7112 Drolet St, 1940-5; 6960 Sherbrooke St W, 1946-7; 5543 Queen Mary Rd, 1957-63
1934 Guinta, mispr

130 Still life $30
1940 125 Gloucester harbour $150
1945 101 Autumn, Montreal North, Boulevard Gouin $200
1946 103 Winter in Gloucester, Mass $400
1947 94 A bit of old Montreal $250
1957 37 Afternoon shadows, Bonsecours Market $300
1963 29 Composition No 2 $500

GLADSTONE, GERALD
7 Jan 1929, Toronto AGO B CC2 IO M TB3
addr: Toronto: 1263 Gerrard St E, 1957; 736 Bay St, c/o Isaacs Gallery, 1958-1961; Dorothy Cameron Gallery, 1963; 47 Colborne St, 1964; Toronto 1968
1957 38 The coming struggle $125
1958 20 Female $300
1960 234 Automatic bird metal $600
235 Earth's elbow metal $250
1961 111 New sun steel $350
1963 103 Optical-orbital No III wld steel $900
1964 121 Moon 2 wld wire & plak $2,500
1968 103 Glass cubed sculpture No 10 clear acry & steel 15 x 10 x 10 $1,200

GLADU, JEANNETTE (m Gerard Guerin)
c 1939
addr: Montreal, 3509 Cartier St, 1960-2
1960 Guerin
169 Atomes nm $75
1961 Gladu-Guerin
80 Embryon nm $175
1962 Guerin
59 Centenelle de rêve nm $75

GLEASON, HELEN H (m Arthur Gleason)
addr: Montreal: Herald Bldg, 1910; 45 Overdale Ave, 1911
1910 436 Bowl, landscape
437 Plate
438 Vase
439 Candlestick
1911 Mrs Arthur Gleason
321 Bowl, landscape
322 Blue vase
323 Candlestick
324 Cup & saucer, poppy

GLEN, EDITH M.
addr; Westmount, 586 Lansdowne Ave
1936 166 Cyclamen pastel $35

GLEN, EDWARD RANDOLPH
1887 - 4 Feb 1963, London, Ont AGO
addr: Paris, 84 rue Notre Dame des Champs
1921 103 Flower girl, Etaples, France $200
104 Picardy poplars, Etaples, France $200

GLYDE, HENRY GEORGE
18 Jun 1906, Luton, Eng AGO CC2 CE CWW84 M NGC TB3 WWA84
addr: Calgary, 1933 24th St W, 1942. Edmonton, 11019 80th Ave, 1946
1942 64 Ice fields $150
1947 95 Manoeuvres $200
96 Yukon, Alaska Highway $100

GLYDE, HILDA
addr: Victoria, RR1, Box 3391
1949 35 Evening, gravel pit $150

GNAEDINGER, ELAINE
addr: Montreal: 1484 Sherbrooke St W, 1939; 1548 St Matthew St, 1941
1939 146 Italian window wc $35
147 L'aubergine wc $35
1941 79 Lower St Lawrence frieze wc $30

GODFREY, MARY S.
addr: Montreal: 293 Peel St, 1891; 770 Sherbrooke St, 1892
1891 160 Autumn tints wc
161 Below the pines, Mount Royal wc
1892 172 Emerald pool, White Mountains wc

GODFREY, WILLIAM FREDERICK GEORGE
12 Jun 1884, London, Eng 2 Mar 1971, Toronto AGO CWW70 M
addr: Toronto: 40 Wood St, 1924-5; 186 Fern Ave, 1927-9; 1099 Dundas St W, 1930; 2 Manor Rd, 1931; 131 Lawrence Ave W, 1936
1924 89 Scarboro Bluffs, evening wc $25
90 Lake Vernon, late fall wc $35
91 The Capilano valley pastel

1925 122 Coast near Victoria B.C. wc
347 Still life drwg $20
1927 274 The hilly road etch $12.50
1929 324 Shadows on a hilltop block pr $10
1930 81 Downtown, Montreal wc $200
1931 104 Old Montreal $200
105 The Market House, Montreal wc $100
106 In Chinatown, Toronto wc $200
379 Winter, St Maurice St, Montreal lino cut $15
380 Site of the Sun Life Building, Dominion Sq, Montreal lino cut $20
1936 539 Night in Muskoka wd cut $8.50
540 The crossroads farm wc cut $8.50

GODWIN, EDWARD WILLIAM (TED)
13 Aug 1933, Calgary AGO CC1 CWW84 M
addr: Regina
1968 104 A tartan for Apollo rising elvacite 74 x 84 $1,090
105 A tartan for me running elvacite 75 x 99 $1.285
106 Bwana white hunter No 1 mm 20 x 26 $115
107 Bwana white hunter No 2 mm 20 x 26 $115

GOETZ, PETER HENRY
8 Sep 1917, Slavgorod, Siberia CWW84 IO M WWA84
addr: Waterloo, Ont, 59 Allen St W, 1955-60
1955 109 Church on the hill nm
1956 102 The roller coaster nm
103 Village church nm $50
1957 118 Serenity nm $100
119 Theme in blue nm $85
1960 164 Halifax harbour nm
165 Liberty, N.Y. nm $150

GOGUEN, JEAN
15 Mar 1927, Montreal
addr: Montréal: Galerie du Siècle, 1494 rue Sherbrooke O, 1964; 1052 rue Sauvè est, 1965
1964 33 S'yl-vie $500
1965 7 Dynamique No 7 $425

GOLD, ALAN
13 Aug 1930, Ottawa
addr: Montreal: Dominion Galleries, 1438 Sherbrooke St W, 1952-3; 4839 Lacombe Ave, 1954; 1433 Crescent St, Apt 4, 1958-61
1952 Allan, mispr
13 Still life with Chinese lily $100
1953 16 The red jacket $165
1954 38 Play ground $145
1958 21 Green shirt
1959 8 The top
1960 39 Abalone shell $150
40 Locks $150
1961 20 Hawk $300

GOLDBERG, ABE
addr: Montreal, Clarke St (no number), 1942; 69 Marie Anne St W, 1946-50
1942 65 The drunkards $45
66 Contrasts $40
1946 104 Portrait of a boy
105 Portrait of a girl
1947 97 Italian girl $75
1950 11 The alley $250

GOLDBERG, E. ERIC
28 Oct 1890, Berlin, Germ 17 Feb 1969, Montreal M NGC WWA62 Juror
addr: Montreal, 2151 Lincoln Ave, 1935. Westmount, 335 Clarke Ave, 1939; 331 Clarke Ave, 1942-56
1935 127 Jardin du Luxembourg $400
1939 148 Village, south of France $375
1942 67 Landscape wc $125
1945 102 Arlequin $225
102A Backstage $250
1947 98 Railway bridge, Port Daniel $275
99 Percé Rock $250
1948 12 Women cleaning fish $350
1949 36 Basket weavers $300
37 Oriental women $275
1954 39 Ballet dancers $350
1956 25 Gaspé couple $475

GOLDBERG, REGINA see SEIDEN, REGINA

GOLDHAMER, CHARLES
21 Aug 1903, Philadelphia AGO CE CNS40 CWW84 IO M NGC TB2 WWA82
addr: Cooksville, Ont, 2064 Centre Rd S
1955 110 Spirits of the forest king nm $90

GOLDIE, CHARLES A. Eng
fl 1858-13 B DBA DVP G RA TB
addr: St Servan, France, la Scellerie
1913 154 An episode of the French Revolution 1793, Breton Royalists on their way to be shot $2,000

GOLDMAN, HARRIET
addr: Montreal, 4810 Roslyn Ave
1956 26 Broken vase $50
27 Still life $50

GOLDSMITH, MARION
addr: Westmount 4123 Western Ave
1949 128 Lilies gouache $100

GOLDSMITH, SIDNEY CHARLES JOSEPH
29 Jan 1922, Toronto M NGC TB3
addr: Ottawa, 154 Montfort St, Eastview, 1951-5. Ste Genevieve de Pierrefonds, Que, 1959-60
1951 129 Chestnuts unfolding wc $60
1954 40 The elevation $125
1955 35 On stilts $80
1957 39 Street scene $140
1960 166 Chalice nm $40

GOMEZ, RICARDO VINCENTE JOSE
20 Feb 1942, San Francisco
addr: Regina
1968 108 Untitled lacquered cast lead 5 x 27 x 8 $600

GONTARD, LUDWIG VON
b 1922
addr: Westmount, 441 Victoria Ave
1955 81 Saint Martin $240

GOODALL, JOHN E.
addr: Montreal, 2046 University Ave
1947 100 Stormy night, Montreal wc $60

GOODFELLOW, MEDORA
addr: Cartierville, Que, 4317 Gouin Blvd W
1932 467 An old habitant plaster $50 bronze $100

GOODFELLOW, S.
addr: Woodlands, Que
1914 503 Toilet set, 3 pieces

GOODIN, F. GLANVILLE
addr: Montreal, 1456 St Mark St
1931 279 Studies for a cathedral, Guildford, Eng competition des

GOODSTONE, ALBERT J.
addr: Montreal: 2055 Mansfield St, 1937-9; 76 Drummond Apts, 1943
1937 123 On Lachine Canal
124 Vacant lot, winter
125 Vacant lot, summer
1938 53 Still life
1939 149 Pani Mama
150 From my window $200
1943 79 Dead chrysanthemum $120
80 Mother

GOODSTONE, ALLIERE
addr: Montreal, Drummond Apts
1941 78 Papillon
79 Havana Cathedral wc

GOODWIN, BETTY ROODISH (m Martin Goodwin)
19 Mar 1923, Montreal CE M
addr: Montreal, 3515 Durocher St, Apt 72, 1947. Ottawa, 98 Research Rd, RR1, 1949. Montreal, 860 Rockland Ave, 1955. Westmount, 517 Lansdowne Ave, 1957-61
1947 304-5 Contour drawing pen
1949 129 Snowball fight casein $20
1955 36 Still life $100
1957 40 Summer still life $200
1958 22 The windmill $200
1959 9 Flowers $200
1960 41 The bouquet $500
42 Still life $350
1961 21 Winter still life $385

GOODWIN, E. A.
addr: Cartierville, Que, 28 De Venise Ave
1944 Lieut RCNVR
50 Towards the river, Cartierville wc

GOODWIN, HAROLD
addr: Montreal, 1442 Stanley St
1942 68 Allegory $100

GORDANEER, JAMES EDWARD
14 Apr 1933, Toronto M
addr: Toronto: 21 Sussex Ave, Apt 6A, 1961; 314 Lonsdale Rd, 1962
1961 22 Requiem for a bird $275

1962 15 Kataga $400

GORDANIER, ADDIE
addr: Laprairie, Que, c/o W.H. Montgomery, Box 47
1916 118 Lilacs and snowballs wc $150

GORDON, ARTHUR WILLIAM
21 Feb 1903, London, Eng
addr: Montreal, 4110 Harvard Ave
1957 41 Studio $100

GORDON, DONALD MACPHERSON
b 1875 24 Feb 1955, Montreal
addr: Montreal, 2049 McGill College Ave, 1931-3
1931 Gordon & Thompson
280 Barclay School, Wiseman Ave
281 Automobile showroom, Ottawa
282 Film Exchange Building, Monkland Ave
283 Garage building, Bleury St
1933 377 Proposed church, Montreal
378 House, Sutton, Que
Gordon & Thompson
379 Barclay School
380-2 Community building, Notre Dame de Grace, Montreal

GORDON, GEOFFREY DAVID
15 Jun 1944, London, Ont
addr: London, Ont
1969 3 Too much acry, 3 parts 117 x 80, 120 x 75, 98 x 62

GORDON, HORTENSE CROMPTON MATTICE
(m John Sloan Gordon)
24 Nov 1887 - 6 Nov 1961, Hamilton, Ont
AGO CC2 CWW58 M W78
addr: Hamilton, 101 Spadina Ave, 1929-50
1929 84 Market place, Etaples, France $200
1930 82 Church at Hesdin, France $175
1931 107 Waterdown Valley, Ont $75
382 Printed textile des wc $50
1932 108 Garden flowers $150
1933 109 L'Tacq, Jersey, C.I. $40
110 Study of flowers $75
111 Corbier Lighthouse, Jersey, C.I. $100
1934 119 In port, Gloucester $100
1935 128 At Friendship, Maine $200
129 Old street, Rouen, France wc $40
1936 167 Flower rhythm $150
168 Le Havre, France wc $40
1937 126 St Margaret's Bay, Kent, Eng $75
127 Old inn, Folkstone, Eng $50
1947 101 Rope, cork and seaweed $200 (RM)
102 Radar abstraction $100
1950 12 Interior, in space oil on gesso $125

GORDON, J. K.
addr: Montreal, 3628 Lorne Crescent
1934 120 Ellie's Cove

GORDON, JOHN SLOAN
6 Jul 1868, Brantford, Ont 1940, Hamilton, Ont CWW36 M NGC TB3
addr: Hamilton: 1908; 28 1/2 King St W, 1909; 101 Spadina Ave, 1933-7
1908 68 The Japanese gown $200
69 The clock tower $150
1909 150 Old Kirby mill, Brantford $150 (NGC)
151 The naiad
152 Wisteria
1933 112 Ya Honk (geese) wc $50
113 Wintry weather, Normandy coast wc $50
114 Gale on Channel Islands wc $50
1934 121 Fish wharf, Friendship, Maine pastel $75
122 Study of rocks, Maine pastel $25
1935 130 The gate, Longpont, France $150
1936 169 Barbadoes, B.W.I. wc $50
1937 128 Green light wc $25
port: by Ottilie Palm, 1909-275

GORDON, MARGARET
addr: Montreal, 22 Côte des Neiges Rd
1919 144 The charlady pastel $10

GORE, MILLICENT see ANDERSON, MILLICENT

GORESKO, J, or W. J.
addr: Montreal, 126 Laurier Ave W, 1945-6
1945 J.
103 Still life, in memoriam $150
1946 W.J.
106 Pleasures of youth $200
107 The Lord and Susan $200

GORMAN, RICHARD BORTHWICK
20 Dec 1935, Ottawa AGO M
addr: Toronto: 3 Bedford Rd, 1961; 11 Yorkville Ave, Apt 1005, 1962. London, Eng, 1967
1961 23 Form number two, in flight illus $300. Jessie Dow prize. 1967-24, oil & lucite 66 x 66 (Agnes Etherington Art Centre, Queen's University, Kingston, Ont. gift of Mr & Mrs S.J. Zacks, 1962)
1962 16 Familiar and internal $300

GORMLEY, ANNA
fl 1894-1907 H
addr: Toronto, 89 Canada Life Bldg
1894 189 Island sketch, Toronto wc $20

GORUP, GUY
addr: Montreal North, 10850 Wilfrid St-Louis St
1960 167 Amour visuel, canadien nm $300

GOSLING, WILFRED GILBERT
1863, Bermuda H
addr: St John's, Nfld
1914 151 St John's harbour, Nfld $80

GOSSAGE, EDITH see CHATFIELD, EDITH

GOTCH, THOMAS COOPER Eng
10 Dec 1854, Kettering, Eng 1 May 1931 Newlyn, Eng B DBA G TB1/2 WBA WWB29
1883 149 Forgotten

GOUIN, LOMER
addr: Montreal, 265 Craig St W
1952 71 Marchandage ink $100

GOULD, JOHN HOWARD
14 Aug 1919, Toronto IO M WWA84
addr: Toronto, 20 Rathnally St
1960 168 Girl with flowers nm $160

GOULD, STELLA see GRIER, STELLA

GRAHAM, JAMES LILLIE
2 Aug 1873, Belleville, Ont AGO H M NGC TB3
addr: Montreal: 129 Bleury St, 1891-2; 128 Marie Anne St, 1894; 709 Dorchester St, 1895. England, 1898. London, Eng, 1900. Montreal: c/o Art Assoc, 1905; no addr, 1908; Montreal, 1910; 66 Jacques Cartier Sq, 1911. Toronto, 195 Dunn Ave, 1920. Montreal: 372 Dorchester St W, 1921; 255 Bleury St, 1922-4; 305 Beaver Hall Hill, 1925; 676 Sherbrooke St W, 1929; 84 Monkland Ave, 1930; 5430 Monkland Ave, 1931; 1096 Beaver Hall Hill, 1933-40; 542 Sherbrooke St W, 1945; Montreal, 1967
1891 55 Horse's head $25
56 Portrait of a horse $25
1892 62 Toiling homewards $125
63 Oxen under yolk $125
64 Cow and calf
1894 66 Across the lea (NGC)
67 Interior of stable, Logan's Farm $50
68 Study of a lion $50
1895 46 By the birch grove
47 At the close of day $100 (MBAM)
1898 35 The rector's garden $75
1900 42 A roadside pasture $60
43 At milking time $50
1905 57 Ploughing $125
58 Return from work $150
59 Mid-day rest $80
60 The harvest field $125
John L, mispr. addr, England
207-8 Greyhound pastel $25 each
1908 70 The pasture $40
1909 153 The drinking place $95
1910 149 The prodigal son $900 (AGO)
150 Toward evening in the pasture
151 Stable interior $250
152 Evening on the pasture $250
153 A corner of the pasture $125 (NGC)
1911 114 Autumn morning by brookside and pasture $300
115 On an upland pasture $225
116 Portrait study pastel
117 Tiller of the soil $225
1920 111 Morning in a pasture near Antwerp $450
112 At nightfall in a barnyard $400
113 On the road near Antwerp $110
114 Scene at mounted sports, Witley camp wc $100
1921 105 Deer in the forest $360
106 In Rouen $200
107 Study of a tiger pastel $95
108 Moonrise, Green Park, London wc $95
1922 125 Normandy pasture $135

126 Pasture at moonlight $145
127 Interior of Church of St Ouen, Rouen $135
128 Autumn in the glen pastel $110
1924 92 Place d'Armes $600. 1967-25, 35 x 31 Jessie Dow prize (Musée du Québec)
93 Au Marché de Bonsecours $450
1925 123 Autumn at sundown, Flemish pastoral $325
124 Close of September day, Flemith pastoral $200
125 After snowfall, Christ Church Cathedral, Montreal $300
126 Grey morning on coast at Laguna, California wc $110
1929 85 Summertime pastoral $700
86 Workers at sundown by the docks at Antwerp $650
87 Inside the stable door $375
88 A cabstand on a winter evening at Montreal $180
1930 83 Early morning sunlight, a milking scene $150
84 Return herd at the ford $100
85 Returning from pasture $90
86 Along a quiet road at close of day $80
1931 108 A scene in peasant life $150
109 In pasture after a day of showers $95
110 Autumn scene at Murray Bay $140
1933 115 Ploughing in the Low Country $100
116 Market day, back of Château Ramezay $130
117 At sundown $190
1934 123 Along a river's edge, near Bic $120
124 Summer evening, at La Malbaie, Murray Bay, Que $125
1937 129 Winter, Bonsecours Market $550
130 Evening at La Malbaie $75
1939 151 January thaw $300
1940 126 Autumn sunlight by a woodland brook $160
1945 105 At the close of an autumn day $500
1894-5 Assoc. Student's 1st prize 1892

GRAHAM, JOHN G.
addr: Toronto, Balmy Beach
1910 154 Aysgarth Falls $20
155 On the Tyne $30

GRAHAM, MONICA (Mrs)
addr: Montreal, 532 Grosvenor Ave, 1940-1
1940 127 Miss Nancy Bignell min
128 Master David Casgrain min
1941 80 Josette Lacaille min

GRANSOW, HELMUT
10 Jan 1921, Chemnitz, Germ IO M
addr: Morin Heights, Que, Box 112
1952 72 Riverside pr $45

GRANT, DUNCAN EDMUND
16 Mar 1846, Roseneath, Scot flg 1924 H
addr: Montreal: 1880. Quebec: 33 d'Artigny St, 1892; Quebec, 1895-8. Como, Que, 1903
1880 17 On the lower St Lawrence
104 View on the St Maurice wc
107, 120 Landscape wc
182 Hazy day wc
1881 72 An old favourite wc
1885 101 On the Jacques Cartier River wc
131 On Beaupré flats wc
139 Mount St Anne, Que wc
141 A bit of nature wc
146 Falls of Feréol wc
1892 173 Château Bigot, ruine wc $75 (NGC)
1895 162 October wc
163 Lake of Two Mountains wc
1898 150 A royal oak
151 Magdalen River wc $40
152 Stranded wc $40
153 Lost on Anticosti wc $45
1903 174 Oka wc $30
175 Ouatchewan River wc $25

GRANT, LEWIS JOHN MASON
1881, Bhagulpur, Bengal, India d 1909
DBA DVP
addr: Toronto, 20 McKenzie Ave, 1910-13
1910 156 Woodland stream wc $100
157 After a shower wc $50
1913 155 Daffodils $40
156 Azalea wc $40
157 Narcissi wc $30

GRANT, MARY
1872, Huntington, Que d 1957 NGC
addr: Montreal: 3 Stanley Court Apts, 1922-5; 205 Mansfield St, 1927; 2055 Mansfield St, 1928; 5530 Queen Mary Rd, 1931-5
1922 129 Market slip, Saint John, N.B. $50
130 Low tide, West Saint John $50
1923 101 Blue Rock harbour, N.S. $125 (NGC)
102 North Head, Grand Manan $35
103 Off the coast of Nova Scotia $40
1924 94 Norton's Reef, Monhegan, Maine $175
95 Monhegan harbour $125
96 Castalia, Grand Manan $75
1925 127 Incoming tide $175
128 The close of the day $60
1927 71 Surf and seaweed at Peggy's Cove $250
72 Herring Cove $200
73 Drying the sails $200
74 March at the canal $75
1928 75 The beach $90
1931 111 A harbour of bygone days $200
1933 118 The restless sea $300
119 New Brunswick fishing boats $300
120 Nova Scotia schooners $160
1934 125 Windswept surf on Cape Breton coast $300
1935 131 Home from the Grand Banks $300

GRANT, WILLIAM J.
addr: Montreal, 8665 St Denis St, 1945-7
1945 106 Home pastel $50
1946 108 Eastern Townships pastel $35
1947 103 Haven $50

GRAVEL, RAYMONDE
18 Jun 1913, Montreal M
addr: Orono, Ont, 1942. Ottawa, 11 Ross Ave, 1945-6. Montreal, 7565 de l'Epée Ave, 1948-9
1942 69 My Mother reading
1945 107 Still life $100
1946 109 The curtain falls $200
110 Noel chez l'artiste $250
1948 13 Spring flood $175
1949 38 Le bon pain $175

GRAVES, FRANK W.
16 Oct 1887
addr: Pointe Claire, Que, 25 Condover Rd, 1925. Montreal, 326 Beaver Hall Hill, 1927
1925 298 Barn at Exceat, Sussex
1927 207 Sketch for house near Montreal

GRAY, FRANCIS WILLIAM
15 Apr 1877, Yorkshire, Eng CWW38
addr: Ste Anne de Bellevue, Que
1921 294 Head of a child, portrait study sculp

GRAY, JACK LORIMER
1927, Halifax 28 Aug 1981, West Palm Beach, Fla M
addr: Halifax, 4 Waterloo St, 1945-7. Montreal, 3650 Ste Famille St, 1952
1945 108 Evening departure $40
109 Abandoned mine wc $15
1947 104 Dawn, Quero Banks wc
1952 14 East wind, Halifax

GRAY, JOHN WARREN
1824, England 26 Feb 1912, Maisonneuve, Que H
addr: Montreal: 1880; 7 Thistle Terrace, 1900; c/o Johnson & Copping, Craig St, 1901-3; 868 St Catherine St W, 1909
1880 69 A summer's afternoon, Essex
1881 12 Cape Blomidon, low tide
17 Under the pines, Mount Royal Park
19 Autumn, passing showers
48 Looking towards Nun's Island, moonlight
1883 4 A tranquil moment wc
10 Old mill on the Cobiquid Mountains, N.S. wc
98 Sunset hour, Mount Orford, from Magog
1885 1 Landscape
24 Evening hour
83 Autumn
1900 44 A bend of the brook $18
1901 45 Evening hour $15
131 An old mill, Surrey, England wc $30
1903 59 Interior
176 The Bluffs, Dutch Valley, N.B. wc $35
1909 154 Longleat Park, Westminster $75

GRAY, KATHARINE E.
addr: Montreal: 621 Sherbrooke St W, 1928; 3449 Peel St, 1929-34
1928 76 Portrait study $75
77 The farm wc $25
299 The cobbler wd engr $10
300 Murray Bay wd engr $10
1929 325 Dancers at the London Coliseum wd engr $10
1930 Katherine E, 1930-1
271 Firelight wd engr $15
272 The organgrinder wd engr $15
273 Railway waiting room wd engr $12.50
274 Old houses, St Amable Street, Montreal wd engr $12.50
1931 382 French Canadian dancers wd engr $15
383 Campus, McGill University, Montreal wd engr $15
1934 126 Côte de Liesse Road, November wc $25

GRAYSON, JOSEPH see LEE-GRAYSON, JOSEPH

GRAYSON, WALTER C.
addr: Montreal, 5878 McLynn Ave, 1945-6. Valois, Que, 2 Summerhill Ave, 1957-8
1945 110 Winter's end wc $50
111 Sugaring time wc $35
112 Spring wc $50
1946 111 Bate's farm wc $75
1947 105 Sugar camp wc $75
1948 79 Farm in Drummondville wc $100

GREENAWAY, ROY
15 Aug 1891 - 18 Nov 1972, Toronto M
addr: Toronto, 76 Alexandra Blvd, 1940-6
1940 129 Winter fishing, Toronto $35
1946 112 The other side of the tracks $125

GREENE, LORNA G.
addr: Westmount, 368 Wood Ave, 1940-1
1940 325 Interior design, dining room
357 Victorian group, New York City wc
1941 263 Wallpaper showroom, interior design, modern

GREENE, MARIE ZOE (m Wesley H. Greene)
31 Mar 1911, Madison, Wis M WWA62
addr: Ottawa, 130 Sunnyside Ave, 1946. Chicago, 5649 Blackstone Ave, 1947
1946 285 Mother and two sons plaster $64
286 Figure in rotation plaster $35
1947 334 Agnes bronze $150

GREENE, THOMAS GARLAND
12 Sep 1875, Toronto 22 Nov 1955, Orillia, Ont AGO CNS36 M NGC
addr: Willowdale, Ont
1924 222 Grand Council at Sault Ste Marie, 1671. Shown at RCA 1923, mural decorative painting competition

GREENHAM, ELVINA see CRABTREE, ELVINA

GREENLEES, H. NANCY see RHIND, H. NANCY

GREENSTEIN, ANNE (m Sam Greenstein)
11 Oct 1914, Warsaw M
addr: Montreal: 7221 de l'Epée Ave, 1944-7; 7429 Bloomfield Ave, 1952-7
1944 51 The foals $50
1946 113 Country kitchen
1947 106 Country stove on week-end
1952 15 Portrait of artist
1957 42 Elaine

GREENSTONE, MARION (m Myron Greenstone)
30 Mar 1925, New York M TB3 WWA84
addr: London, Ont: c/o 508 Wellington St, Apt 3, 1960; 246 Ridout St S, 1961. Brooklyn, N.Y, 1967
1960 43 Composition No 90 $600
44 Composition No 91 illus, $650 Jessie Dow prize. 1967-26, 50 x 56 (Ayala and Sam Zacks, Toronto)
1961 24 Composition No 138 $800

GREENWOOD, DOROTHY (Mrs) and GREENWOOD, G. F. (Mrs) may be the same artist, see also Greenwood, M.F.
addr: Montreal: (Dorothy) 381 Mountain St, 1911: (Mrs D.) 180 Mansfield St, 1914; (Mrs, no initial) 381 Mountain St, 1912; (Mrs G.F.) 381 Mountain St, 1913. (Mrs G.F.) Woodstock, N.Y, 1915
1911 Dorothy
118 Landscape pastel
119 The hay field pastel
120 Portrait sketch pastel

121 Study in yellow pastel
1912 Mrs (no initials)
158 Pussy willows $100
159 Autumn afternoon $50
160-1 Landscape $50 each
1913 Mrs G. F.
158 Summer pastel $75
159 Owl's Head Mountain pastel $65
160 A study pastel $85
161 Still life pastel $50
1914 Mrs D.
152 The Russian ikon $85
153 Still life $40
154 Approaching storm pastel $100
1915 Mrs G. F.
149 Winter in the Catskill $100

GREENWOOD, M. F.
addr: Montreal, 381 Mountain St
1909 390 Head of a child plaster

GREGER, HANS JURGEN
c 1935, Hamburg, Germ
addr: Pointe Claire, Que, 179 Cartier Ave
1963 104 Composition No 28 metal

GREGOR, THOMAS A.
addr: Quebec, 22 Mount Carmel St
1895 164 Nearing port wc $40

GREGORY, MARY see PATTULLO, MARY

GREIG, WILLIAM
fl 1887-1916 H
addr: Westmount, 1908. Montreal, 141 St Peter St, 1909. Westmount, 86 York Ave, 1913. Montreal, 141 St Peter St, 1915-16
1908 Grieg, mispr
204 Sand Point, Lac Tremblant wc
1909 417-18 Heraldis emblazoning
1913 162 Frame of etchings dry point and mezzotints
1915 150 A misty morning
1916 119 In the English Channel $30
120 Morning

GREMINGER, JUAN
26 Aug 1923, Buenos Aires
addr: St Eustache-sur-le-Lac, 1608 Oka Rd, 1955-7
1955 37 In a blue sweater $200
1956 28 Serenade for Silvia $300
1957 43 The ship Belinda $300

GRENIER, MARY
addr: Westmount, 4330 Sherbrooke St W
1934 127 Back yard wc $15

GRENON, CAROL
addr: Laval des Rapides, Que, 364 Blvd des Prairies
1965 37 Mutation ciment, céramique $300

GRESHAM, ARTHUR
1891, Sheffield, Eng
addr: Toronto: 49 1/2 Helena Ave, 1928; 46 Joicey Blvd, 1931
1928 78 Vera wc $75
79 Vanity wc $100
1931 112 Porcelain and pewter wc $50

GREY, J. O.
1871, Wales 1954, Terrebonne Heights
addr: Pointe Claire, Que, 44 Waverley Rd, Bowling Greene, 1944-5. Dorval, Que, 7 Decarie Blvd, 1946
1944 52 Falling barometer, south of the Cape $250
1945 Captain
113 Sabbath quietude, port of Montreal $450
1946 114 Out of the fog $200

GRIER, EDMUND GEOFFREY
22 Nov 1899, Toronto 9 Sep 1965, Ottawa M
addr: Westmount, 561 Côte St Antoint Rd
1945 114 On the bridge $750

GRIER, EDMUND WYLY, Sir
26 Nov 1862, Melbourne, Australia 7 Dec 1957, Toronto AGO B CC2 CNS36 CWW55 EC H M Mo98/12 NGC TB1/2/3 W78 WWA53
addr: Toronto: 37 Canada Life Bldg, 1892-4; Imperial Bank Chambers, 1900-17; 771 Yonge St, 1922; 6 Crescent Rd, 1940. Lennoxville, Que, Fairview Inn, 1942
1892 65 The golden lion $100
66 The rising moon $50
67 Portrait of a physician
68 The fates, a rehearsal $500
1894 69 Bereft $2,000

1900 45 E.F.B. Johnson, QC
1906 78 Daughter of the Empire
1908 71 Sutherland Maclem, Esq
1909 156 The dreamer $750
1917 159 Principal Ross, DD
1922 131 The cameo $500
1940 130 H.W. Eddie, Esq
131 Arthur B. Wood, Esq, FIA, FAS
1942 202 Mrs Stewart-Smith drwg

GRIER, ELDON BROCKWELL
13 Apr 1917, London, Eng CC2 M
addr: Westmount, 4077 Tupper St, 1941. Montreal: 1630 Lincoln Ave, Apt 1, 1942-9; 5520 Victoria Ave, Apt 15, 1950-1. Town of Mount Royal, 221 Dresden Ave, 1957
1941 227 Pen & ink drawing $20
228 Brush drawing $15
1942 70 The bathers $60
71 Red building $30
1947 107 The ovation, Mexico $200
1949 39 Still life $125
156 Sunday etch
1950 148 Figure lift ground etch $10
149 Portrait of a woman charcl $25
1951 127 Reclining figure No 2 pencil $15
1957 120 View from Quebec nm $15
121 Landscape nm $20

GRIER, STELLA EVELYN (m A.E. Gould)
6 Jan 1898, Toronto M TB2
addr: Toronto: 891 Bay St, 1929; 6 Crescent Rd, 1934-5. Compton, Que, King's Hall, 1937
1929 89 In the window $100
90 The engineer
1934 128 Dr J. Fleming Goodchild
129 Mother and child $200
1935 132 Helena $100
1937 131 Harvesting, Eastern Townships

GRIFFIN, CONSTANCE M.
addr: Montreal: 20 Bayle St, 1924; 1028 Côte des Neiges Rd, 1929; 4932 Côte des Neiges Rd, 1932; 1501 St Catherine St W, 1936-7; 1260 Mackay St, 1938-9. Town of Mount Royal, 141 Dunrae Ave, 1940
1924 97 Study of a Chinese girl pastel $35
1929 91 A Chinese girl pastel $35
326 Portrait sketch crayon
1932 109 A new Canadian $250
110 Derek pastel
1936 170 Mrs Gordon Russell pastel
171 Miss Cecile Lefort pastel
172 My sister pastel
541 The habitant drwg $20
1937 132 The green hat pastel
400 Portrait charcl
1938 161 Portrait charcl
1939 404 Portrait sketch charcl
1940 358 Portrait drwg

GRIFFITHS, JAMES
1814/25/ or 27, Newcastle, Eng 10 Aug 1896, London, Ont EC H M NGC W78
addr: London, Ont
1880 48 Peonies (NGC)
106 Hollyhocks wc
110 Flowers and fruit wc
112 English roses wc

GRIGGS, ALICE JEPHSON
addr: Sherbrooke, Que, 21 Walton St
1923 104 The old bridge wc

GRIGNON, V. J, or de V. L. (Mme)
addr: Ste Scholastique, Que, 1900-6
1900 V. J.
46 Fruit $25
1901 de V. L, 1901-6
46 Outremont in winter $15
1906 79-80 Still life $30 each

GROSS, HELEN see OMANSKY, HELEN

GROSS, MARIO
c 1927, Berlin, Germ
addr: Montreal, 38 Rosemount Ave
1951 14 Backyard in St Henry $80

GROSSMAN, IGNACE
addr: Montreal, 1255 St Mark St, 1946-7
1946 115 Backyard
1947 108 Spring in Montreal
109 New York

GROVES, NAOMI see JACKSON, NAOMI

GRUPPE, CHARLES PAUL Amer
3 Sep 1860, Picton, Ont 30 Sep 1940, Rockport, Mass

B CWW36 DBA F H NGC TB1/2 WWA40/47
addr: Rochester, N.Y, 609 Powers Block, 1892. New York, 106 W 55th St, 1913
1892 69 The herring fishers coming on the beach $500
174 A misty morning, Rotterdam wc $175
1913 163 The ploughman $400
164 A bit of Holland $300
165 The woodcutter wc $200

GUAY, MIMI
addr: Montreal: 3449 Shuter St, 1936; 120 Sherbrooke St W, 1937-9
1936 542-3 Nude drwg $50 each
1937 401 Marcel Guay, CA drwg
1939 405 Portrait drwg

GUERIN, CARROLL
addr: Montreal, 1321 Sherbrooke St W
1958 23 Impression No 7 $150

GUERIN, JEANNETTE see GLADU, JEANNETTE

GUERY, ARMAND French
1850, Reims, France July 1917, Gueux, France B DBA TB
addr: Paris
1898 36 The falling of the leaves $1,100
37 A summer evening in Champagne, France $1,100

GUEST, MARIE see HEWSON, MARIE

GUIGNON, EUGENE
addr: Montreal, 832 St André St
1910 158 Old church $30
159 River scene $30

GUILLAUME, JANINE LEROUX
17 Aug 1927, St Hermas, Que
addr: Montreal, 1554 St Denis St
1960 170 Infiltration lapidaire nm $55
171 Tournoiment incandescent nm $50

GUILLET, MICHEL
addr: Montréal, 3943 rue Berri
1961 81 Ville de sang nm $50

GUISE-HITE, C. DE
addr: Montreal, 1650 Sherbrooke St W
1934 80 Portrait study of artist
438 Mary Joly de Lotbinière chalk
439 John Stikeman nm

GUITE, SUZANNE (m Alberto Tommi)
10 Dec 1927, New Richmond, Gaspé, Que
M WWA82
addr: Percé, Que
1961 112 La mère debut bronze $2,000

GULNICK, MARION
20 Aug 1924, Montreal
addr: Montreal, 5649 Jeanne Mance St, 1953-7
1953 77 Still life $75
1957 44 Pastorale

GUNN, PATRICIA see O'BRIEN, PATRICIA

GURD, FRASER BAILLIE
7 Jan 1883, Montreal Mo12 CWW48
addr: Montreal: 124 Bishop St, 1906; Montreal, 1908; 406 Mackay St, 1916; 731 Sherbrooke St W, 1919-21
1906 81 Montreal harbour $15
82 A grey afternoon $15
1908 72 Evening, Montreal harbour
1916 121 Biplanes over French Flanders wc $35
122 Canadian dug-outs in Belgium, German flares in distance wc
1919 Major, M.D, A.M.C.
145 Canal de la Lys
146 Archies in action wc
147 A farm yard in Flanders wc
148 Biplane landing in the snow wc
1920 115 After the storm wc
116 Auchel wc
1921 109 The chalk pits, Notre Dame de Lorette wc $80
110 Harvest evening wc $50

GUTTMAN, FREDA
addr: Westmount, 651 Lansdowne Ave
1957 122 Providence, R.I. nm

H

HABICH, WILFRIED FRANZ JOSEPH KAY
23 Feb 1926, Buhlertal, Germ
addr: Montreal, 6421 St Denis St, 1953. Ville St Laurent, Que, 1440 Decarie Blvd, 1955

1953 78 Still life, flowers $60
1955 111 Near the borders of night nm $50

HADDOCK, WILLIAM RICHARD
2 Mar 1909, Birmingham, Eng M
addr: Montreal, 648 Sherbrooke St W
1936 173 About the waterfront $125
174-5 Morning in the city wc $30 each
176 In McGill grounds wc

HAGAN, ROBERT FREDERICK
21 May 1918, Toronto IO M WWA84
addr: Toronto, 305 Ontario St
1941 81 Still life $60

HAGAR, FLORENCE L.
addr: Montreal: 111 Metcalfe St, 1901-3; 148 Hutchison St, 1905-11; 313 Peel St, 1913
1901 230 Salad bowl and tray
231 Bouillon cup & saucer
232 Violet vase $5
233 Dessert plate $6
234 Nut bowl $3
1903 285 Jardiniere and stand
286 Vase $13
287 Cup & Saucer $10
288 Vase, roses $8
289 Cologne bottle $4
290 Spoon tray $4.50
291-2 Cup & saucer
1905 304 Cologne bottle
305 Plate $9
306 Stein $6
307 Vase $6
308 Compote $5
309 Cream bowl $4
310 Heart shaped box $3
1906 402 Blue and silver pitcher $20
403 Vase, dragon fly $12
404 Vasë, nastúrtiums $8
405 Bowl, poppies $10
406 Fern dish $7
407 Small vase $4.50
408 Bonbon dish $5
409 Plate
1908 381 Vase, cactus $10
382 Vase, peacock's feathers $9
383 Compote $8.50
384 Small compote $4.50
385 Small vase $4
1910 440 Bowl $6
1911 325 Satsuma bowl $10
326 Fruit dish $8
327 Plate $6
328 Satsuma vase $4
1913 469 Vase $20
470 Bowl $15
471 Vase, Satsuma $10

HAGARTY, BEATRICE see ROBERTSON, BEATRICE

HAGARTY, CLARA SOPHIA
28 Jun 1871 - 18 Jan 1958, Toronto AGO CNS36 CWW55 M Mo12 PMC
addr: Toronto: York Chambers, 1898; 36 Toronto St, 1906; 13 Spadina Rd, 1909
1898 38 Spinning, Dutch interior $50
39 Waiting, Dutch interior $40
1906 83 The lady in black $75
84 The old housewife $50
1909 157 Col Biscoe
158 In the window $200

HAGARTY, MARY S. Eng
fl 1882-1938 B DBA DBW DVP G RA TB
addr: London, Eng, 26 Christchurch Rd, Streatham Hill, 1913-14
1913 166 Houses of Parliament, from the Embankment wc $25
167 St Paul's, from the Embankment wc $25
1914 155 The Whife Cliffs of England wc $26
156 The Towers of Westminster Abbey wc $26
157 St Paul's from Blackfriars wc $26
158 Waterloo Bridge and St Paul's wc $20

HAHN, EMANUEL
30 May 1881, Reutlingen, Germ 14 Feb 1957, Toronto AGO CC1 CWW55 EC M NGC W78 WWA56
addr: Toronto, 32 Adelaide St E
1940 408-9 Julian C. Smith, memorial medal, for Engineering Institute of Canada plaster models, obverse reverse

HAINES, FREDERICK STANLEY
29 Mar 1879, Meaford, Ont 21 Nov 1960, Thornhill, Ont AGO CC2 CWW58 EC M NGC PMC TB2 W78 WWA62

addr: Meadowvale, Ont, 1908. Thornhill, Ont, 1927. Toronto, Ontario College of Art, 1940
1908 73 Holstein calves $25
74 Barn, interior $75
1927 76 The beech tree $450
1940 132 Grace Lake $400

HALDORSEN, PATRICK ROY
17 Mar 1919, Dryden, Ont
addr: Ottawa, 65 rue Robert
1950 13 Rue St Redempteur, Hull $50

HALFHIDE, EWALT W
b Trinidad
addr: Montreal, 6185 Hudson Rd, Apt 3
1952 120 Still life wc $50

HALHEAD, HARRIET Eng
b Australia fl 1890-1911 B DVP G TB
addr: London, Eng, 8 Trebovir Rd
1912 162 Mr Louis Deschamps $500
163 Mrs Harrod

HALL, JOHN ALEXANDER
10 Oct 1914, Toronto AGO CWW84 IO M WWA84
addr: Toronto, 10 Kilbarry Rd
1940 133 Woman reading $250

HALL, ROBERT
28 Jun 1925, Winnipeg
addr: Toronto, 148 Glenrose Ave
1949 40 Early morning, Quebec City $150

HALL, THOMAS HERBERT
6 Mar 1885, Ackworth, Yorks, Eng 17 Apr 1972, Pointe Claire, Que M
addr: Montreal: 303 St James St, 1914; 747 de L'Epée Ave, 1915; 2002 Victoria St, 1935-48
1914 159 A nameless lake wc
160 A winter afternoon wc
161 On the Rivière des Milles Isles wc
162 Birches in springtime wc
1915 151-2 Winter sketch wc $25 each
153 Mending the birch bark canoe wc $25
154 Moose hunters returning $50
1935 133 Old farmhouse, Staten Island $35
134 Tree tops, Staten Island, N.Y. $35
135 The camp, Lac Tremblant $35
1936 177 Summer cottage in winter $25
178 Early snow $25
1946 116 Mellowed sunlight $200
1947 110 Birches on Mount Royal wc $75
1948 80 Newago, Quebec wc $75

HALLAM, JOSEPH SYDNEY
19 Jul 1899, Manchester, Eng 26 Nov 1953, Toronto AGO CWW49 M NGC WWA56
addr: Toronto, 184 Dinnick Cr
1949 41 Street market $150
42 Track $200

HALLIDAY, FRANCIS ROBERT
11 Jun 1884, Toronto
addr: Toronto, 148 Shuter St
1909 159 A country cousin $25

HALPIN, JOHN J.
addr: Ottawa, 676 Cooper St
1918 147 Summer evening $50
148 Clouds at Ridgemont $50

HAMANN, ANDRIES
1936, Netherlands
addr: Aylmer, Que, 22 Bancroft, 1959. Kirk's Ferry, Que, 1964
1959 10 Growth $130
1964 34 Untitled $500

HAMEL, GUY
addr: Montréal, 3623 rue St Denis, ap 11
1964 91 L'enlèvements des Sabines nm $50

HAMEL, JOSEPH ARTHUR EUGENE
14 Oct 1845 - 20 Jul 1932, Quebec
EC H M NGC TB3
addr: Quebec
1880 5 Portrait of a Belgian military gentleman (NGC)
51 Fruit
70 Roman peasant girl
181 Ruins of the tomb of St Gobert wc

HAMER, GLADYS
addr: Halifax, 117 Oxford St, 1940-1
1940 359 Spar yard etch $10
1941 229 The fisher girl etch $10

HAMER, JACK
20 Aug 1914, Brighouse, Eng IO M
addr: Peterborough, Ont 109 James St
1949 130 Snow water wc $60

HAMILTON, ARTHUR, Lt Col
addr: Montreal, Bell Telephone Bldg
1909 160 Shoal waters wc
391 Brass box $50
392 Blotter $10

HAMILTON, IDA GERTRUDE
26 Jun 1887, St Mary's, Ont
addr: Toronto, 21 Avenue Rd, 1930. Hamilton: 27 Bold St, 1931; 99 East Ave S, 1932; 94 Longwood Rd S, 1933-6; 88 Flatt Ave, 1937-9
1930 87 Morning sunshine $100
88 The float, Rocky Neck, Mass $150
1931 113 A snowstorm, Toronto, 1929 $250
114 A byway, Gloucester, Mass $100
115 A summer sketch $50
1932 111 Wharves and small boats $175
1933 121 Still life, apples and bowl $150
1934 131 The downs $150
132 The fishing fleet $125
1936 544 Erin, Ontario lino cut $7.50
545 Houses lino cut $7.50
1937 133 Willow branches wc $25
402 Old willow lino cut $7.50
1939 152 Winter, West Hamilton wc $35

HAMILTON, JAMES H.
addr: Montreal, 1330 Sherbrooke St W
1965 8 Etruscan game for two $280

HAMILTON, KATHLEEN ANITA
18 Aug 1931, Vancouver M
addr: New Westminster, B.C, 835 12th St
1960 45 City I, the alley $175

HAMILTON, MARY RITER (m Alexander H. Hamilton)
1873, Teeswater, Ont Apr 1954, Vancouver M Mo12
addr: Winnipeg, Canadian Bank of Commerce
1912 164 Notre Dame, twilight
165 Notre Dame, interior
166 The Pantheon, interior
167 Abazia di San Gregorio, Venise (Salon 1905)
168 Les sacrifiéer $500
169 La toilette wc $200
170 Memories wc
171 Notre Dame wc
172 Old Kay pastel

HAMMOND, JOHN A.
11 Apr 1843, Montreal 10 Aug 1939, Sackville, N.B. B CWW36 DBA G H M Mo98/12 NGC TB3
addr: Saint John, N.B, c/o Owens Art Gallery, 1891-2. Sackville: 1894-5; Mount Allison College, 1897-1928. Montreal: 1405 Bishop St, 1930; 270 Côte des Neiges Rd, 1931. Sackville, Salem St, 1932-3
1883 128 Carlton Flats, Saint John
135 Gasperaux fishing
141 Bay shore, Saint John, N.B.
145 Little River, Courtney Bay,
146 Low tide, Courtney Bay, N.B.
1888 15 Runswick, Yorkshire $50
36 Old Antwerp $100
77 Evening, Holland wc $90
90 Lac d'Amour, Bruges, Belgium wc $90
1889 130 At close of day wc $110
1891 57 Saint John harbour $75
58 A Belgian farm $75
59 A frost effect
60 Children's flock
61 Hay barge on the Seine
1892 70 Sunset, Saint John Harbour $100
71 Kimberdyke $40
72 Salmon fishing $40
73 Evening $150
74 Sunlight and fog $150
75 Harbour of Saint John $500
76 Homeward
1894 70 Herring fishing
71 On the Oise
72 Windmill, Holland
73 Fishing, Bay of Fundy
74 Dulce gatherers $250
1895 48 Fishing boats, Bay of Fundy $400
49 Windmill, Holland $350
50 Sunrise, Bay of Fundy $300
51 The old barn $300
1897 50 Herring fishing $300
51 The Tantramar $300

52 Sunrise $250
53 Grand Pré $200
1898 40 Gaspereaux Valley $300
41 Sunset, Holland $250
42 Morning $200
43 Evening $200
1901 47 Sunrise, Bay of Fundy $300
48 Blackfeet encampment $200
49 On the river at Canton $250
50 Honk Kong $45
51 Sunset, Japan $45
52 Fugi, Japan $25
53 Mount McKay $25
1903 60 Evening, Holland $300
61 Gaspereaux fishing $250
62 Tantramar Marsh $200
63 Sunset, Bay of Fundy $60
64 Mount Baker, Oak Bay, B.C. $30
65-6 Montmorency Falls $30 each
1905 61 Outward bound $250
62 Inward bound $200
63 Gaspereaux fishing $65
64 Sand Cove, Bay of Fundy $65
65 Sunrise $150
1906 85 Low tide at Saint John $250
86 Belfry of Bruges $200
87 Bruges $200
88 Sheep ranch $65
1907 75 Willow Marsh $250
76 Marsh lands $225
77 Fishing boats $200
1908 78 Buttermilk Channel $85
79 Evening $85
80 Solitude $85
1909 161 Landscape, France $250
162 Willow Creek, Sackville $225
163 Market slip, Saint John $200
164 Summer $75
1910 160 Knocke, Belgium $200
1911 122 Marsh lands $300
123 Evening $250
124 Sand dunes $200
1912 173 Konderdyke $250
174 Dutch scene $200
175 Summer $75
176 Inward bound $75
1913 168 Sackville, N.B. $300 (NGC)
169 Barbizon $300
170 Courtney Bay $250
171 The weirs, Saint John $200
1914 163 Market slip, Saint John $300
164 Entrance to the forest $250
165 Fort Cumberland, N.B. $200
166 Evening, Bay of Fundy $75
1915 155 Windmill, Holland $250
156 Canal at Amsterdam $75
157 Bruges, Belgium $200
1916 123 Sunset, Barbizon $300
124 Bruges, Belgium $200
125 Dinant, Belgium $200
126 Morning mist $75
127 Knocke, Belgium $75
128 Canal, Vanice $75
1927 77 The market slip, Saint John $400
78 The old barn, Sackville, N.B.
79 Sunshine and fog, Bay of Fundy $100
80 French landscape $600
1930 89 Market slip, Saint John $500
90 Harvest scene, Sackville $250
1931 116 Rouen $1,000
117 On the Meuse $300
1932 112 Saint John harbour $300
113 Landscape, Sackville $250
1933 122 Allen's Creeke, N.B. $150
1894-7 Assoc Hon mention, seascape 1892
port: by Robert Harris, 1898-48; Edmond Dyonnet, 1913-122

HAMMOND, RODY see COURTNEY, RODY

HAMON, HECTOR T.
addr: St Lambert, Que, 311 Mercille Ave
1948 14 Mrs Phillip S. Hamon

HAMPSON, A. E.
addr: Montreal, 7 Ontario Ave
1922 132 Margareta $200

HAMPSON, BEATRICE MARY STEPHEN CANTLIE (m Robert Hampson)
7 Sep 1897, Montreal
addr: Westmount, 31 Forden Ave, 1949-55
1949 43 Calendulas $75
1951 100 Memories
1955 38 Star fish and shells $125

HANCE, JAMES BUSICK
19 Jan 1847, England d 1915 AAA1900 CWW10 H
addr: London, Eng, and Montreal, 72 McGill College Ave, 1897-8. Quebec, 1903
1897 54 A Surrey road, near Esher $40
157 The Three Sisters, Rocky Mountains wc $40

158 The Capilano Canyon, Vancouver, B.C. wc $35
1898 44 On the Alyn, north Wales $60
45 Near Cap Rouge, Quebec $45
154 Sketch, Murray Bay wc $30
1903 67 Winter sunset, from the glacis $500
68 Wolfe's Cove, Quebec $250
177 Quebec from the river wc $50

HANCOCK, HENRIETTA see BRITTON, HENRIETTA

HANDY, ARTHUR
6 Feb 1933, New York AGO IO M
addr: Toronto
1968 109 Aphrodite yawns fibreglass & polyester resin 12h $300

HANKEY, ROLAND ALERS
addr: Montreal, 3459 Mc Tavish St
1935 404 Bowl of wild flowers drwg $20

HANKIN, MOLLIE E.
addr: Westmount, 648 Murray Hill Ave, 1935-7
1935 136 Portrait study $75
1937 134 Miss Nora Hankin

HANNAFORD, MICHAEL
1832, Stoke Gabriel, Devon, Eng 7 May 1891, Toronto H W78
1881 35 In the Waimakariri Range
40 The natural steps, Montmorency
45 On the Dart, Horse Shoe Fall
79 Banshee Tor, New Zealand wc
1883 84 The home of the sea gull, coast of Devon
122 The Don Valley
156 On Lake Muskoka

HANNIBAL, ERIC
addr: Montreal, 1229 Mountain St
1934 500 Mr E.H. bust plaster

HANNING, JOSEPH D.
addr: Montreal: 1196 Bishop St, 1935; 1830 Bayle St, Apt 7, 1939
1935 405 Adirondack pines pendrwg $10
406 Old friends pendrwg $10
1939 353 Architectural rendering, club
354 Architectural rendering, Lakeside hotel

HANSON, GERTRUDE JEAN (m John A. Elphick)
27 Sep 1933, Toronto CWW84 M WWA84
addr: Toronto, 74 Runnymede Rd, 1956; Oakville, Ont, 1193 Sarta Rd, 1962-3
1956 29 Midnight suns and snow $180
1962 46 Nature's cradle nm $110
1963 30 Fragments of an ancient world $450
31 Dream voyage $290

HARBISON, CATHY see SENITT, CATHY

HARDENBERGH, ELIZABETH RUTGERS Amer
b New Brunswick, N.J. WWA40
addr: New York, Van Dyke Studios, 939 8th Ave
1912 177 Devonshire, wild flowers wc $25
178 Pansies wc $20

HARDIE, A. ISOBEL HART (m William Hardie)
b Perth, Ont d 4 Mar 1943, Ottawa
addr: Ottawa, 71 Russell Ave
1932 386 Old Bank of Montreal, Ottawa etch $8

HARDING, EDITH NEILSON (EDYTHA)
addr: Montreal, 3783 Hampton Ave, 1932-37
1932 Edith A.
114 The barn yard $75
1933 123 From the mountain $75
1934 133 Grey day, in Laurentians $60
134 Mount Rolland $60
1935 137 March thaw $75
138 Pointe Gatineau, Ottawa $75
1936 Edytha, 1936-7
179 Northern landscape $200
1935 135 The market place, Kingston, Jamaica $100

HARDMAN, JACK NELSON
2 Oct 1923, New Westminster, B.C. M
addr: New Westminster, 570 Goodlad St, 1956. North Burnaby, B.C, 390 N Hythe, 1957
1956 104 Stellar myth nm $15
1957 160 La belle et la bête ter cot $45

HARMAN, JACK KENNETH
31 Jul 1927, Vancouver M WWA80
addr: South Burnaby, B.C, 4265 Bond St
1961 113 Figure bronze $425

HARNEY, KATE
addr: Montreal: 570 Cadieux St, 1909; 194 Ontario St E, 1910-11
1909 46 Plates, six $2.50 each
47 Plate, rose $7
48 Framed tile $20
49 Coffee pot $7
1910 441 Dutch tile $10
442 Plate $8
1911 329 Vase $45

HARNEY, PHOEBE SPROULE
addr: Montreal: 194 Ontario St, 1910; 107 St Famille St, 1912-14
1910 356 Bust
357 Bas-relief
1912 405 May sculp
406 Billy sculp
1913 402 Cushla ma chree, pulse of my heart sculp $150
1914 432 The voice sculp $100

HAROLD, ALEXANDER
b Scotland H NGC TB3
addr: Montreal, 75 Aylmer St, 1891-2
1891 62 Mountain stream $100
63 A summer morning $15
1892 77 Horse and haycart $30

HAROLD, ALICE
addr: Montreal, 8 Desrivières St (Desrioreres, mispr)
1918 149 A bit of old Montreal $200

HAROLD, ELIZABETH M.
addr: Westmount, 236 Wood Ave, 1912-17. Montreal, 335 Northcliffe Ave, 1921-2. Westmount: 360 Claremont Ave, 1927; 339 Victoria Ave, 1931-6
1912 451 Vase $8
452 Bowl $4
453 Stein
454 Cup & saucer $2.50
1913 472 Jardinere $20
473 Vase $7
474 Dessert plate $5
1914 504 Dessert plates (8) $40
505 Box $5
506 Coffee cups (8) $35
1915 442 Satsuma vase $12
443-4 Pitcher $5, $3.
1916 370 Salad dish $6
371 Chocolate pot $7
1917 424 Biscuit jar $10
1921 111-12 Décarie Boulevard, sketch $20, $15
1922 133 St Paul Street $75
134 Mountain and St James Street $50
135 The canal $50
1927 80 Old house, St Paul Street $60
1931 118 Young Negro girl pastel $30
119 Miss Cynthia Percey pastel
1932 115 Mrs George Wheeler pastel
1936 180 Old houses, St Martin, Que $50

HARPER, J. (Miss)
addr: Montreal, 1131 Dorchester St
1900 227 Bonbon box, rococo des
228 Cup & saucer, Queen's Jubilee
229 Service plates, Persian des

HARRINGTON, ANNA LOIS DAWSON (m Bernard James Harrington)
addr: Montreal: 295 University St, 1912; 851 University St, 1915
1912 179 A summer day wc
180 Sketch wc
1915 158-160 Cap à l'Aigle wc

HARRINGTON, LOUIS S.
addr: Montreal, 295 University St
1912 181 When day is over

HARRINGTON, REBECCA CHRISTINA (m E.A. Harrington)
21 Apr 1869, Toronto d 1930 M
addr: Toronto: 34 Dunbar Rd, 1925; 55 Elm Ave, 1928-30 (1928, Westmount, 55 Elm Ave, mispr)
1925 129 Juniper trees, petunias wc $500
1928 81 Arrowhead-bed wc $400
1929 94 Garden flowers wc $400
95 The Royal Richmond wc $400
96 An autumn rhapsody wc $300
97 Noon-day wc $500
1930 91 Christmas flowers wc $350
92 Streposelon, or golden shower wc $350
93 Summer flowers wc $500
94 Early spring wc $400

HARRINGTON, RUTH M.
addr: Montreal
1908 81 Autumn $20
82 Kennst du das land
205 The dying day pastel $20
206 At evening wc

HARRIS, ALFRED PETER
4 Apr 1932, Toronto IO M WWA84
addr: Toronto, 26 Duncannon Dr, 1960. St Catharines, Ont, 1968
1960 46 Self portrait $200
1968 110 Resting figure mm 16 x 20 $400
111 Paint tray paint on metal 8 3/4 x 9 1/4 $200

HARRIS, BESS LARKIN (m Frederick Broughton Housser. m Lawren Stewart Harris)
18 Nov 1890, Brandon, Man 28 Sep 1969, Vancouver M
addr: Vancouver, 4760 Belmont Ave
1947 110A In southern sunlight $75

HARRIS, LAWREN PHILLIPS
10 Oct 1910, Toronto AGO B CC1 CWW73 M NGC TB3 WWA84
addr: Toronto, 25 Severn St, 1939. Sackville, N.B, 1968
1939 155 Amos $250
1968 112 Yellow suite 36 x 46 $850
113 Perpendicular plan 48 x 30 $800
114 Interchangeable form latex 58 x 36 $950
115 Sextet flex-tex & gesso 42 x 54 $800

HARRIS, LAWREN STEWART
23 Oct 1885, Brantford, Ont 29 Jan 1970, Vancouver AGO CC2 CE CWW67 EC M NGC TB2 W78 WWA70
addr: Toronto, Studio Bldg, 25 Severn St, 1939. Vancouver, 4760 Belmont Ave, Vancouver
1939 153 Lake Superior nm (MBAM)
154 A lake in Labrador
1947 111 Subjective painting, mountain experience

HARRIS, MARGUERITE V.
addr: Montreal, 290 Peel St
1909 165 Finhauts, Switzerland wc
166 Near Lausanne wc

HARRIS, PETER see HARRIS, ALFRED PETER

HARRIS, ROBERT
18 Sep 1849, Tyn-y-Groes, Wales 27 Feb 1919, Montreal AGO B CC1 CE CWW10 EC H L M Mo98/12 NGC R1 TB1/3 W78
addr: Toronto, 1880. Montreal: Fraser Institute Bldg, 1891; YMCA Bldg, 1892; c/o Art Association, 1894-1911; 11 Durocher St, 1912-18
1880 1 The news boy (AGO)
13 A chorister (NGC)
37 The rejected suitor
47 Boy's head, study
50 The exile, study
55 The curate's daughter
1881 2 Lobster fishers landing the catch
8 The young genius
9 A man of no account (MBAM)
1883 138 Chaff
151 Cut-out
152 'And whatsoever the fight's event, he keeps his honest soldier's name' R. Browning
153 Finishing touches
154 From the Quartier Montmarte, Paris
155 Charcoal dealer's yard, French village
157 Model, from the Via Sistine, Rome
165 The knitter
166 An introduction
1885 10, 74 Portrait
15 Comrades
30 Sympathy
40 On the shore of Gaspé Bay
119 In the dumps wc
1886 52 Watching the boats run in before the squall
53 Portrait
54 Abou-ben-Adhen and the Angel
55 Taking it easy
56 Talitha cumi
58 A religious procession in a French Canadian town
62 Le June, first Jesuit Superior in Canada, meditating in solitude when living with Indians (MBAM)
65 Maisonneuve killing the Indian chief while covering the retreat of his men in the sortie

from the Montreal Fort, March 30th 1641
70 John McLennan, Esq
72 Contrasts
83 Adversity
100 The studio boy's private view
1888 5 Miss T....n
16 An exile $60
20 Rev Canon Norman
24 Composing his serenade $250
38 Children of J. Burnett, Esq
46 Little gossips $100
47 Harmony $100 (NGC)
63 Autumn $60
64 A Chelsea pensioner $60
1889 26 D. Lorn MacDougall, 1st Pres Montreal Stock Exchange
27 Principal Grant
28 The Pilot of the Galilean Lake $125
29 The local stars, Pine Creek School District $800
30 Bad dog $60
31 Near Sturgeon Point $50
32 In a studio $50
33 A nut brown maid $80
131 Little gossips wc $50
132 Two of a kind wc $50
1891 64 Rt Hon Sir John A. Macdonald
65 Portrait of a lady
66 Prof H.T. Bovey
67 The prelude $250
68 A monk $80
69 The cottage steps $135
70 The cow pen, P.E.I. $40
71 On Sturgeon Lake $40
72 In the woods, P.E.I. $25
73 Going wrong $450
1892 78 Master Guy Drummond
79 Portrait of a lady
80 Mr H.L. Putnam
81 The sands of Dee $550
82 Pastoral, lower St Lawrence $250
83 Harvested, P.E.I. $40
84 A meditative pipe $150
1894 75 Mr A.F. Gault
76 Mrs P.A. Peterson
77 Canadian backwoodsman $400
78-9 Study of a head $75 each
80 On the sands, Kennebunkport $60
241 The maple wreath pastel $50
1895 52 His Excellency the Earl of Aberdeen, Governor General of Canada
53 Mr E.B. Eddy
54 Portrait
55 The wharf by moonlight $200
56 Head $175
57 Landscape $100
1897 55 Mrs H. Montague Allan
56 Samuel Finley, Esq
57 Mrs Finley
58 F. Fairman, Esq
59 Mrs Edward Parker
60 Master Harold Stanley Bagg, son of R. Stanley Bagg, Esq
61 Come if you dare $350
62 The summer moon, fishing village $200
1898 46 Rev Canon Ellegood, painted to commerate 50th anniversary of his ordination
47 Robert Lindsay
48 John Hammond, RCA
49 T.B. Brown, Esq
50 Miss Stevenson Brown
51 The miniature
52 Young Canada $450 (NGC)
53 The nihilist $100
155 Mrs A.T. Taylor pastel
156-7 Head pastel $50 each
1900 47 Hon W.H. Tuck, Chief Justice of New Brunswick
48 Frances, daughter of George Smithers, Esq
49 Canadian adventurer, time of Maisonneuve $500
50 Portrait $450
51 Study of a head $250
1901 54 Mrs James Ross
55 Mrs Louis Sutherland, and son
56 Prof Dupuis, Queen's University, Kingston
57 George Rutherford, son of George Caverhill, Esq
58 Mrs Hayter Reed
59 Georgina, daughter of George Smithers, Esq
60 Mrs A.F. Riddell
61 The banjo boy
62 The coming storm, Gaspé coast
1903 69 H E, Countess of Minto commissioned by Art Association of Montreal Council (MBAM)
70 Portrait
71 The late Principal MacVicar
72 Mrs R. H.
73 Still life, emtremes meet $100

1905 66 Miss Lindsay
67 C.R. Hosmer, Esq
68 Before the song
69 Panel for chancel, The Good Shepherd
70 'A thought ungentle canna be The thought o' Mary Morrison' Burns
1906 89 Hugh Graham, Esq
90 Mrs Leonowens
91 Mrs W. Stanway
92 Mrs F. Cleveland Morgan
93 Mrs Robert Lindsay
94 Mrs Henry Joseph, and Master Joseph
1908 83 Mrs J.K.L. Ross, and children
84 Dr T.G. Roddick
85 W. Markland Molson, Esq
86 Thomas Fyshe Esq (Bank of Nova Scotia commission)
278 Mrs R. H. bust, plaster
279 T. J. H. bust, plaster
1909 167 Lord Strathcona and Mount Royal
168 Dr Robert Craik, MD LLD
169 Eugene Lafleur, KC
170 Portrait
171 The skipper's daughter $450
172 Posing $450
173 At anchor, afternoon $300
174 H.N. Bate, Esq, Ottata
1910 161 Daughter of Rev Principal Hill, DD
162 Miss Brenda Hebden
163 The late Andrew Allan
164 Summer time $500
165 Man's head, study $275
1911 125 W. de M Marler, Esq
126 Roswell Fisher, Esq
127 Gumming the canoe
128 Still life $150
129 Bavarian mountaineer $250
130 Study, man's head $250
131 Study, old man's head
1912 182 David Morrice, Esq
183 Derelict $900
184 Marie $500
185 The post office, Etaples $25
186 On the Canache $25
1913 172 Crochet $900
173 Self portrait (NGC)
174 Evening $250
175 Coming from berrying $200
1914 167 Prof John Clarke Murray, LLD
168-9 Nude study
170 Girl's head pastel
1915 161 J.E. Martin, KC
162 The late C.M. Hayes, Esq (NGC)
163 Composing his serenade $600
1916 129 Old fisherman Pas de Calais
1917 160 Late Lieut Murdoch Laing, 24th Battalion
161 In summertime
162 My old Montreal model (NGC)
163 Yale, B.C.
1918 150 Lady Roddick
151 Late Peter Whiteford Redpath, B Sc
152 David Morrice, Esq, Jr
153 R. Ward S. Robertson, Lieut
154 Frame of four sketches
1894-7 Assoc prize, 1892, portrait medal Chicago 1893

HARRIS, SALMON see PRODNUK, FRANK G.

HARRIS, WILLIAM CRITCHLOW
30 Apr 1854, Bootle, Eng 16 Jul 1913, Halifax
addr: Charlottetown, P.E.I.
1895 223-4 St Dunstan's Cathedral, Charlottetown, exterior, interior perspectives
225 St Paul's Church, Charlottetown, exterior perspective

HARRIS, ZAIDEE (Mrs)
addr: Montreal, 2 MacGregor St
1903 178 Split Rock, Murray Bay wc

HARRISON, ALLAN see HARRISON, WILLIAM ALLAN

HARRISON, EDITH ELIZABETH (m W.E.C. Harrison)
6 Apr 1907, London, Eng M
addr: Kingston, Ont: 77 Queen's Cr, 1940; Queen's University, 1943
1940 134 Cold morning $45
1943 81 Taking in stores, HMCS Ironbound wc $45

HARRISON, WILLIAM ALLAN
27 Dec 1911, Montreal CWW84 M WWA84
addr: Montreal: 2 Oldfield Ave, 1939; 1185 St Mark St, 1941; 1843 Dorchester St W, 1942
1939 156 Toulon $75

157 Panorama, Montreal $75
158 The campus, McGill University $40
1941 Allan, 1941-2
230 Yvonne pen drwg $15
231 Street in Arles pen drwg $15
1942 72 Portrait study $75

HARTLEY, MURIEL see COTTINGHAM, MURIEL

HARVEY, DESMOND VACHELL (signs Desmond Vachell)
addr: Montreal: 15 Hope Ave, 1925; 1564 Summerhill Ave, 1931-4
1925 348 Billet-doux drwg $75
349 Italian peasant charcl $35
1931 Desmond Vachell, 1931-4
236 W.E. Ford, Esq
1932 315 Portrait, young lady pastel
1934 349 G. Serge Lecours, Esq pastel

HARVEY, DONALD
14 Jun 1930, Walthamstow, Eng CWW84 M WWA84
addr: Victoria: 1025 Joan Cr, 1963; Victoria, 1968
1963 32 Guardian $300 (MBAM)
1968 silkscreen, 116-18
116 Voices of authority 26 x 32 $85
117 Overtake 26 x 32 $85
118 4 squares on the move 26 x 32 $85
119 Yes, yes acry 57 1/2 x 80 1/2 $1,000

HARVEY, ERIC
addr: Toronto, 54 Shuddell Ave, 1928-9. Montreal, 1126 Stanley St, 1940
1928 301 The cat lino cut $75
1939 327 Irish terrier $75
1940 135 Head of a man scraperbrd $15

HARVEY, MARGARET M.
addr: Westmount, 4007 Dorchester St W, 1935-6
1935 139 Polish peasant $100
1936 181 Portrait study crayons $15

HARVEY, NELLIE Eng
b London, Eng fl 1890-1938 DBA TB1/2 WWB 34
addr: Gowanbrae, Stirling, Scot
1914 171 Blairdrummond Moss and Ben Ledi wc $20
172 A croft, Sutherland wc $20

HARVEY, PHYLLIS NELSON (m Cecil Richards)
17 Nov 1906, Montreal M
addr: Toronto, 25 Severn St
1933 124 Gladoli $35

HARVEY, REGINALD LLEWELLYN
8 Jan 1888, Southampton Eng Dec 1973, Victoria M
addr: Calgary, 1740 13th Ave W
1929 98 In Sarcee Reserve, Calgary pastel $50
99 On Moraine Lake Road, Canadian Rockies pastel $50

HARVEY, SYDENHAM PARKER
2 Jan 1914, Cobden, Ont M
addr: Toronto, 57 Palmer Ave, 1936-40
1936 595 Duck bronze $75
596 Grouse bronze $75
1937 460 Flight plaster $40
461 Form wd $50
462 Twelve wd $50
1940 410 Partridge plaster $47.50

HARVIE, MABEL E.
addr: Westmount, 355 Metcalfe Ave, 1910-12
1910 166 Sketch b&w
167 Springtime
1911 132 The lake in the hills wc
133 The mouth of the river wc
1912 187 Beach, Little Metis $10
188 Lowtide, Little Metis $10
189 The wharf, sketch $10
190 Sketch $10

HASKELL, LOUISA
addr: Montreal
1908 386 Cider jug $5.50
387 Rose jar $6
388 Small bowl $2

HASLEY, ARTHUR
addr: Montreal, 57A St Luke St
1914 433 My daughter sculp

HASPEL, TUTZI (BERTHA Mrs Seguin)
14 Oct 1911, Bucharest IO WWA70
addr: Toronto, 43 Camberwell Rd, 1954-60
1954 Haspel-Seguin, 1954-5
103 Wellfleet, Cape Cod wc $150

1955 112 Saguaros nm $50
1960 Seguin
215 Why? nm $40

HASS, JOHN
25 Mar 1925, Renfrew, Ont M
addr: Montreal, 1940 Lincoln Ave, Apt 12
1955 113 Evening from inside the barn nm $100

HASSELL, HILTON MACDONALD
14 Mar 1910, Lachine, Que 2 May 1980. CWW81 IO M
addr: Port Credit, Ont, 1761 Minaki Rd, 1960-1
1960 47 Quarry facets $350
48 Beach kaleidoscope $750
1961 25 Sands of Wingaersheek $750

HATCHER, JOHN JOSLYN
17 Mar 1931, Winnipeg M
addr: Winnipeg, 955 Garfield St, 1953; 810 Sargent Ave, Apt 5, 1957
1953 104 Canmore etch $25
1957 45 Manhattan street $150

HATFIELD, ANNA see ADAMSON, ANN

HAUSER, CONRAD J.
1900-1970
addr: Toronto, 390A Huron St
1939 159 Sketches of 1938 $10

HAWKSLEY, FREDERICK (or J. Frederick)
H
1885 79 The Pond-Locks Mills

HAWORTH, COLIN REID
11 Mar 1916, Ottawa M
addr: Montreal West, 126 Brock Ave N
1958 64 October prospect nm $35

HAWORTH, PETER
28 Feb 1889, Oswald Twistle, Eng 7 May 1986, Toronto AGO CC2 CNS40 CWW82 IO M NGC TB2/3 WWA84
addr: Toronto, 111 Cluny Dr, 1939-61; Toronto 1967
1939 161 Barn and plough wc $50
1952 64 Orchard wc $125
1954 105 Driftwood wc $150 (NGC)
106 Golden acre, abstraction wc $150
1955 114 Northern lake nm $150 (AGO)
115 Boats at anchor, Percé nm $125
1956 106 Mist on the lake wc $175 (listed 1967, Jessie Dow prize)
107 Mountain forms nm $125
1957 124 Autumn mood nm $175 (UG)
1960 172 Tree forms in winter nm $250
1961 83 Dusk, Mal Baie harbour nm $250
1967 28 Still water. 1960 wc 20 x 25

HAWORTH, ZEMA BARBARA COGILL (BOBS)
(m Peter Haworth)
20 Jan 1904, Queenstown, S Africa AGO CC1 CNS40 CWW84 IO M NGC TB3 WWA84
addr: Toronto, 111 Cluny Dr, 1939-67
1939 160 King Ridge, autumn temp $75
1952 63 Estuary wc & gouache $125
1967-27, 20 x 25 Jessie Dow prize
1953 55 Quarry gouache $125
1954 104 Drying nets, Gaspé gouache $100
1956 105 Of harbour boats, and fish, and things nm $150
1957 123 Autumn tapestry nm $175 Hon mention
1961 82 Shoreline shapes nm $300

HAWTHORNE, MARION MCCLURE
14 Mar 1897, Montreal CNS36
addr: Montreal, 4505 Cumberland Ave, 1934-44
1934 135 Sunflowers $50
1936 182 Cyclamen
183 Azalea blossoms $50
1937 136 Asters $45
137 Spring shower $35
1938 54 J.T. portrait
55 White azalea $35
1939 162 Mrs David Hawthorne
163 Still life $45
1940 136 Portrait in a striped dress $150
1941 82 Portrait in grey and yellow
1944 53 Flying Officer M.F. Doyle

HAY, NORMAN KYLE
1883, Ottawa
addr: Halifax, 31 South St, 1933-5
1933 125 Rocks at Peggy's Cove, N.S. wc
1935 140 Rock formation, Prospect, N.S. $50

HAYES, NORMAN

addr: La Tuque, Que, 51 St Louis St
1946 117 Momocciam Street wc $15
118 Suk wc $20

HAYMAN, STANLEY
30 Nov 1910, Toronto M
addr: Peterborough, Ont, 397 George St
1954 134 Medals: Rt Hon Viscount Montgomery. Robertson Davies, playwright. Victory. Pandora. St James United, Montreal

HAZELL, FRANK
7 June 1883, Hamilton, Ont d c 1957
AAA33 F TB2 WWA56/obit 59
addr: Montreal, 652 Sherbrooke St
1906 236 Autumn sketch wc $10
237 Reflections wc $15
238 Old shack, Rideau River wc $15

HEAD, GEORGE BRUCE
14 Feb 1931, St Boniface, Man CC1
CWW84 M WWA84
addr: Winnipeg: 264 Wellington Cr 1957; 770 Minto St, 1960. Transcona, Man, 50 Brewster Bay, 1961
1957 46 On the north-east shore $80
1960 49 Aquatic garden $125
173 The stockade nm $75
1961 84 Untitled exterior nm $100

HEALY, SINCLAIR DAVIS
3 Oct 1925, Moncton, N.B. M
addr: Fredericton, N.B, 426 Needham St
1960 50 Greenhouse $175

HEASLEY, DONALD JAMES
28 Aug 1897, Montreal
addr: Montreal, 116 Jeanne Mance St
1924 308 Ski runner sculp

HEATER, C. B. (Mrs)
addr: Outremont, Que
1918 429 Satsuma bowl gold & enamels

HEAVEN, ETHEL R.
fl 1897-1906 H
addr: Toronto: York Chambers, 1900; c/o McKenzie & Co, 1903; 131 Bloor St, 1906
1900 135 Study of an Indian pastel $50
136 Portrait study pastel $75
1903 179 Vrouw knitting wc $50
180 Moonrise in Holland wc $35
181 Sunset, view of Lion, and St Marks wc $25
1906 239 The Ponte Vecchio, Florence wc $50
240 Houses on the Arno wc $30
241 Vici dei Neri, Florence, night wc $30
242 Serenata, Grand Canal, Venice pastel $30

HEBBLETHWAITE, WALTER BENSON
11 Apr 1929, Ridgetown, Ont M
addr: Ridgetown, Ont RR 1
1956 30 Eulogy to a poet $150

HEBERT, ADRIEN
12 Apr 1890, Paris 7 Jun 1967, Montreal B CC2 CE CNS36 CWW61 M NGC TB2 W78 WWA53 Juror
addr: Montréal: 217 rue Berri, 1909-11; 34 rue Labelle, 1913-18; 1923; 7 rue Ste Julie, 1919-21, 1924-6; 341 Place Christin, 1934-46; 1227 rue Berri, 1947-50; 1238 rue Labelle, 1951-67
1909 175 Le jardin potager $30
1910 168 L'automne $25
169 Paysage - sunset $10
1911 134 Danse matinale
1913 176 Une voile $50
177 Vielle diligence $70
1915 164 Soleil couchant dec panel $150
1916 130 Crépuscule
131 Autumne esquisse panneau déc $50
1917 164 L'appel, hunting scene $75
1918 155 La terre
1919 149 Une nuit un faune appleait $350
150 Marine $200
151 Le laboureur b&w
366-7, sculpture, Adrian is name error for Henri Hébert q.v.
1920 117 La littérature $250
118 La peinture $250
1921 113 Retour du bois $150
114 Marine $75
1923 105, 107 Antraigues-sur-Volane, France $100, $75
106 Vogué, Ardèche, France $100
108 Vals-les-Bains, France $75
1924 98 Le ruine babines
99 Le château $200
100 La Truyère

101-2 Portrait
279 Three wood cuts for 'Les conteurs canadiens'. Edition du Monde Nouveau, Paris
1925 130 La Place, St Henri $250
131 S.S. Montclare $350
132 Dechargement de plâtre $550
133 Un cargo $250
1926 195 L'élévateur charcl $75
196 Un cargo charcl $75
1934 136 Parc Lafontaine $350
1935 141 Place Jacques Cartier $175
407 Montréal, la nuit drwg $75
408 Clair de lune drwg $50
1936 184 Outward bound $350
185 Matin d'hiver $200 (listed 1967 Jessie Dow prize)
1937 138 Christmas spirit $300
139 La vitrine des jouets $450
1938 56 La rue, soir $400
57 Le marché
1940 137 Parc Montmorency, Qyébec $250 1967-29, 33 3/16 x 27 5/16 Jessie Dow prize (Musée du Québec)
138 Vue de Québec $300
139 La pluie, Montréal $400
1941 83 Les patineurs $1,000
84 Les toits sous la pluie $225
85 La neige $200
1942 73 Le port $500
74 Paysage, Québec $300
75 Paysage, Isle Belair $150
1943 82 L'amateur $150
83 Rue Notre Dame de Lourdes $150
84 Le port $300
1944 54 Le port $300
1945 115 L'hiver $375
1946 119 L'église du Bic $250
120 Place Jacques Cartier $250 (MBAM)
1947 112 Le port $500
1949 44 La pluie $600
1950 14 La forge $250
1951 15 Rue Dorchester $300
16 Coin d'atelier $300
1952 16 Le port $400
1953 17 S.S. Empress of Canada $500 (listed 1967, Jessie Dow prize)
1954 42 Remorqueur $350

HEBERT, HENRI
3 Apr 1884 - 11 May 1950, Montreal
AGO B CC2 CE CNS48 CWW48 M NGC TB2
WWA53 Juror
addr: Montreal, 34 Labelle St, 1910-26; 1238 Labelle St, 1928-47
1910 358 The old notary bust $100
359 Mons Devries, de l'Opera Comique bust
360 Monsieur bust
361 La vie est parsemée de ronces et d'epines statue $150
362 Antique dance statuette $20
1911 288 My father bust
289 Study sculp $10
1912 407 My sister Pauline bust
408 Adam and Eve mantlepiece
1913 403 Jean Donner plaster $10
404 L'Abbé Mélancon bust, plaster $10
1914 434 Mr E. Monpetite bust, plaster
1915 367 Kultur sculp $100
368 Life is full of thorn sculp $100
1916 315 Variation sur un thème ancien sculp $15
316 Apollo sculp $10
317 Arthur D sculp
1918 371 Fatum sculp $25
1919 Adrien, name error for Hénri
366 Mr G. Desaulniers sculp
367 1914 sculp (NGC)
1920 299 Evangeline plaster
300 To the trenches plaster
1921 295 Apollo bronze $35
296 Les sucres plaster $25
1922 336 Evangeline bronze $175 (NGC)
337 The wind plaster (Mr Ernest Rolland)
338 Sir Alexander Lacoste sculp
339 Mr A.F. Gault sculp
1923 109 Clo pastel
110 Cé pastel
252 Monument sculp des
1924 103 A la barre pastel $75
104 Danseuse pastel $40
105 Mme P. Rolland pastel
309 Bacchante sculp
310 Outremont War Memorial sculp
311 Termae sculp $150
312 Françoise sculp
1925 389 Marcel Dupré sculp, copy $25
390 Eternelle chanson, Eros sculp $100
391 Eternell chanson, La femme sculp $100
1926 241 Alphonse Jongers plaster $50 (bronze AGO MBAM NGC)

1928 343 M J.A.E. Dubuc, Chicoutimi plaster
344 M J.P. Vaillancourt plaster
345 Monument plaster
346 The charleston plaster $20
1929 371 Miss A.C, dancer of Oslo plaster $50
372 Dr A. LeSage plaster
373 M Guy P. Couture, KC plaster
374 Hon Alphonse Racine plaster
1931 421 La brise plaster
422 Pamphile Lemay, poete plaster
423 Mr L.H.P. medln plaster
1939 455 Linne, 1707-78, Jardin Botanique, Montreal medln plaster
1945 267 Monument à l'Hon Sénateur L.O. David, Montréal
268 Monument à l'Hon Sénateur L.O. L'Esperance, Montmagny, Qué
269 Monument commémoratif à J. de Lesseps, Gaspé, Que
1947 335 Etude de tête plaster
port: by Joseph St Charles, 1903-257; Henriette Fauteux, 1949-28

HEBERT, LOUIS PHILIPPE
27 Jan 1850, Ste Sophie d'Halifax, Megantic Co, Que 13 Jun 1917, Montreal
B CCI CE CWW10 EC M Mo98/12 NGC RI TB1/3 W78
addr: Montreal, 34 Labelle St, 1895-1915
1886 112 Monument to Capt Jos Brant, Thayendanegea des
113 Lucien bust
114 Blanche bust
1895 226 Un duel bronze
227 Buste d'enfants bronze
1897 237 Madame H bust bronze
238 Hon L.J. Forget bust bronze
239 Convoitises plaster group $40
1903 261 Sans merci plaster
1906 354 L'évasion sculp
355 Soupir du lac bronze $75
1908 280 Coureur de bois plaster
281 Mdlle De Vercheres bronze $60
1909 393 Coureur de bois bronze $100
394 Acadiens plaster
1910 363 Hon Honore Mercier bronze
364 Les Acadiens, groupe bronze
365 L'évasion, groupe bronze $130
366 Le printemps, groupe plaster $25
1911 290 Le Moyne de Ste Hélene sculp $20
1913 405 Martine Messier bronze $200
1915 369 Sir Thomas Shaughnessy buste plâtre
port: by Joseph St Charles, 1903-107; bust, Henri Hébert, 1911-288

HEBERT, MAURICE
addr: Quebec, 1 Couillard St
1930 275 Paysage etch $10

HECHT, ESTELLE
b Montreal d 1971 M
addr: Montreal, 1120 Bernard Ave W, Apt 10, 1958-63
1958 65 Windows nm $25
1960 174 Enchanted city nm $30
175 The shadows deepen nm $20
1961 85 Unknown landscape nm $25
1963 81 Sentinels nm $30
82 Winter trees nm $30

HECHT, ETHEL
addr: Montreal: 401 Marcil Ave, 1928-30; 3797 Marcil Ave, 1931-2
1928 82 Summer temp
1929 100 Gladioli temp $25
101 Spring flowers temp $20
102 A bowl of flowers temp $12.50
1930 95 Spring flowers temp $15
96 Tulips and narcissi temp $15
97 Flower study temp $12.50
1931 120 Nasturtiums temp $15
121 Marigolds temp $15
1932 116 Tulips temp $15
117 Spring flowers temp $20

HEDRICK, ROBERT
1 May 1930, Windsor, Ont AGO IO M
addr: Toronto: 605 Yonge St, 1960-1; Isaacs Gallery, 832 Yonge St, 1962; Toronto, 1968
1960 51 Sea wall $500
1961 26 Shifting fields $450
1962 17 Anatomy for figure $800
1968 120 TS/1 acry 78 x 48 $1,750

HEFFLON, RUTH E.
addr: Montreal, 10 Torrance St, 1918. St Albans, Vt, 235 N Main, 1921
1918 156 Sketch b&w
157 Sketch
1921 115 Sketch

HEIMLICK, HERMAN

18 Jun 1904, Satoraljaujhely, Hungary
addr: Westmount, 1215 Greene Ave, 1937-41. Montreal, 1501 St Catherine St W, No 11, 1942-55
1937 403 Mr L. Sperber drwg
1938 162 Miss E. R. charcl
1940 140 Peonies $75
1941 86 Boy from Orient pastel $60
87 Reclining nude $100
1942 76 Sitting girl, study $120
1944 55 Nude pastel $50
1945 116 Nude, study $250
1947 113 Boat house $110
1954 43 Flower, still life $125
1955 39 Girl of Brittany $175
port: by Ernest Neumann, 1938-174

HELME, JAMES BURN
29 May 1897, Smith Falls, Ont 12 Nov 1945, Pennsylvania CWW36
addr: Smith Falls, Ont, 1932: John St W, 1933
1932 387 Waddell, Pennsylvania wd engr
388 Burgos, Spain wd engr $15
1933 126 Valley farm wc $60

HEMMING, EDITH Eng
fl 1896-1911 DBA G H RA
addr: Montreal, 525 Sherbrooke St
1903 182 The late Henry Hemming wc

HEMPSTEAD, J. H. (Mrs)
1886 122 Portrait

HENDERSON, BEATRICE M.
addr: Montreal, Birks Bldg (address, listed as M. Beatrice)
1903 74 Rev Jas Barclay, DD
183 A young artist wc $25
235 Portrait of a child nm
236 Portrait study nm

HENDERSON, JAMES
21 Aug 1871, Glasgow 5 Jul 1951, Fort Qu'Appelle, Sask EC M NGC W78
addr: Fort Qu'Appelle, Sask, 1931-6
1931 122 Near Fort Qu'Appelle, Sask
1932 118 Near Fort Qu'Appelle $350
119 Winter, Qu'Appelle Valley, $250
1936 186 Winter glory, Qu' Appelle Valley $350

HENDERSON, PETER
24 Jun 1884, Dundee, Scot 23 Nov 1944, Montreal
addr: Montreal, Windsor Street Station, Room 401
1928 238-9 Banff Springs Hotel, upper and lower lounge

HENDRY, WILLIAM A.
addr: Montreal West, 63 Ballantyne Ave N, 1933. Ste Anne de Bellevue, Que, Ste Marie Rd, RR 1, 1940-2
1933 127 Burnt land, district of Cochrane, Ont wc $25
1940 360 Peddlar drwg
1941 233 Hill top wd engr $5
1942 203 Stoker wd engr $5

HENEKER, EVELYN ELIZABETH (EVE)
addr: Montreal: 453 Mackay St, 1916-27; 1533 Mackay St, 1928. Morin Heights, Que, c/o Mrs Archie Hamilton, 1932. Montreal: 1445 Bishop St, Apt 4, 1944
1916 132 The High Rocks, Prout's Neck wc
1917 165 Mists rising from the water at sunset wc
166 From the pasture at Ardintoul wc
1927 81 The carpenter's shop
1928 83 Still life
84 View from my Gloucester studio
1932 389 In summer drwg $25
1944 56 Listening house $50

HENEY (Miss)
1886 126 A life study
131 A study

HENEY, IRENE S.
addr: Westmount: 411 Metcalfe Ave, 1912-14; 476 Roslyn Ave, 1924
1912 455 Vase $12.50
456 Satsuma urn $4.50
457 Cream jug $2
458 Bowl $4
1913 Henry, Irene mispr
475 Belleek bowl $20
476 Satsuma vase, flat enamels $18
477 Satsuma pot $3.50
478 Plate, wild cucumber $3.50
479 Coffee set, green and silver
480 Bowl, flat enamels $5
1914 507 Plate, flat enamels $5
508 Plate, lustre $4.50

509 Bowl, enamel $10
510 Chocolate pot $10
1924 355 Belleek jar, enamel
356 Bowl, enamels
357 Box
358-9 Jug

HENNESSEY, FRANK CHARLES
12 Jan 1893 - 7 Nov 1941, Ottawa AGO CC1 EC M NGC W78 WHC
addr: Ottawa: 3 Buckingham Apts, 400 Cumberland St, 1922; 91 Rideau St, 1924-32; 176 1/2 Nepean St, 1939-40
1922 136 Crows $75
137 Ravens $100
1924 106 Trapper's cabin $150
107 Little girl pastel $150
1925 134 Gulls, Gaspé $150
135 Canada geese $100
1930 98 Sunday morning $150
99 Late afternoon $150
1931 123 In the hills pastel $50
124 Near Luskville, Que pastel $50
125 At Muskoka Lake pastel $50
126 Near Masham, Que pastel $50
1932 120 Sketch for picture pastel $75
121 Gatineau in March pastel $75
122 Village of Lac Ste Marie pastel $75
123 March thaw pastel $75
1939 164 The setting sun $700
1940 141 The woods in spring $700

HENRY, LEO
addr: Montreal, 2336 Hingston Ave
1950 150 Car barns, St Henri pastel

HENRY, VERA L.
addr: Vaudreuil Station, Que
1924 batik
108 Combat of Menelaos and Hector $35
109 The sun worshipper $20
110 The death of Sir Lancelot $50
111 Rennaisance design $15

HENSHAW, A. N.
1885 37 Hot house grapes
444 Flowers

HENSHAW, ARTHUR S.
AAA28 H
addr: Montreal: 144A Durocher St, 1897-8; 739 Sherbrooke St, 1901
1897 63 Autumn, bit of Como Road
64 Hudson Heights
1898 54 A corner of Greenwood farm, Como
1901 63 White Head, Cushing's Island

HENSHAW, RUTH BEATRICE
1895, Montreal
addr: Montreal: 149 Drummond St, 1922-3; 747 St Catherine St W, 1925; 581 Sherbrooke St W, 1928; 1227 Sherbrooke St W, 1929; Ritz Carlton Hotel, 1930-1; 1509 Sherbrooke St W, 1932-4; Ritz Carlton Hotel, 1936
1922 138 The lady in blue
1923 111 Mrs Ross Robertson
1925 136 Mrs Hobart Molson and Andy
1928 85 Drying clothes by the Jumna River $45
86 Near Quetta, Baluchistan temp $30
1929 103 The mandarin's coat $60
1930 100 Aviles Street, St Augustine wc $30
101 Old boats, St Petersburg, Florida wc $30
1931 127 Old house, St Augustine, Florida wc $35
1932 124 Head of a child
125 Old house near Rigaud wc $25
126 A habitant cottage wc $25
1933 128 Farm house, Ste Marguerite $25
129 Old house at Como, Que $10
1934 137 Helen wc $10
1936 187 Old house near Rigaud wc $30
188 November day wc $15

HERBERT (Mrs)
1886 115 The monastery

HEREFORD, SALLY (Mrs)
addr: Ottawa, 270 Fairmont Ave, 1933-40
1933 pastel, 1933-40
130 Zinnias $75
131 Autumn flowers $100
132 Pewter and iris $110
133 Daffodils $125
1935 142 Gladoli $50
143 Geranium $50
1936 189 Peonies $75
190 Spring flowers $50
1939 165 Gladioli $100
1940 142 Gladioli $100

HERIOT, JOHN CHARLES ALLISON
1861, Georgeville, Que 24 July 1921, Montreal
addr: Montreal: 2A Berri St, 1892; 104 Union Ave, 1916; 628 Union Ave, 1917-19
1892 223 Country house des
1916 331 Heraldic painting, Sir Edward Gordon Johnson, Bart ensigns amorial
332 Suggested changes in British Infantry colours
1917 373 Colours of 193rd Overseas Battalion, Nova Scotia Highland Brigade heraldic drwg
1918 392 Heraldic drawing
393 Proposed new Coat of Arms, Dominion of Canada. Suggested method of differencing the British national flag and ensigns, for use in Canada, as approved by Historical Societies of Montreal and Toronto
1919 387 Maj Gen James Wolfe, amorial bearings

HERMAN, JOY
24 Mar 1943, Montreal
addr: Town of Mount Royal, Que, 70 Devon Ave
1962 60 Country quiet nm $100

HERMES, GERTRUDE ANNA BERTHA Eng
(m Blair Hughes-Stanton)
18 Aug 1901, Bromley, Kent, Eng DBA RA TB2 WBA WWB82
addr: Westmount: 4187 Sherbrooke St W, 1943; 369 Clarke Ave, 1944-5
1943 229 The warrior's tomb wd eng $60
257 Katherine Paterson plaster
1944 161 P.K. Page plaster $250
1945 258 Adam and Eve wd eng $35
259 Two people wd eng $35
278 Prof Frank Scott plaster $250

HERTZBERG, PHYLLIS see ARMOUR, PHYLLIS

HESS, WILLIAM HUNTINGTON
31 Mar 1882, St Thomas, Ont
addr: Montreal, 188 no 2, St Urbain St, 1910-14
1910 170 Still life $75
1911 135 An afternoon cup $100
1912 191 Grandad at the game pastel $15
1913 178 A harbor view $20
179 The lumber mill wc $20
180 Howard S. Ross, Esq, KC b&w
1914 173 Mansfield House, Esq
174 Rev O.C.S Wallace, DD, LLD

HESSON, FRANCES G.
addr: Montreal, 213 Peel St
1901 235 Vase, poppies $40
236 Jardiniere, roses $25
237 Jardiniere $12
238 Tankard $12
239 Vase $12
240 Plaque, grapes $10
241 Plaque $10
242 Fruit dish $8
243 Tray $6
244 Cup & saucer $6
245 Olive dish $4.75
246 Stud box $2.50
247 Plates, set of 6 $10.50

HEWARD, BARBARA HAMILTON
26 Jul 1928
addr: Westmount, 18 Rosemount Ave, 1946-7
1946 121 Still life $50
1947 114 Adventure in colour $35

HEWARD, DOROTHY BURTON
30 Sep 1888, Montreal d 22 May 1912
addr: Montreal: 39 Lorne Ave, 1906; Montreal, 1908; 258 University St, 1910-11
1906 309 Study of a head chalk
1908 207 The white hat chalk
1910 171 Illustration
172 Prue, portrait sketch
173 Study in brown
174 The straw bonnet $50
1911 136 Prudence
137 Landscape
138 Mordkine, the Russian b&w $10
139 Pavlov, the Russian b&w $10

HEWARD, EFA PRUDENCE
2 Jul 1896, Montreal 19 Mar 1947, Los Angeles AGO CC1 CE EC M NDG W78 WWA53 Juror
addr: Montreal: 802 University St, 1914-15; 302 Prince Arthur St, 1920; 390 Sherbrooke St W, 1922-4; 3467 Peel St, 1939-45
1914 175 Sketch b&w $5

1915 165 Nonnie $5
1920 119 Sketch
1922 139 Mrs Hope Scott
1923 112 Portrait study
113 McGill campus on a rainy day
1924 112 Eleanor $200
113 Portrait of a man $200
1939 166 Rosaire $600 (MBAM)
167 Clytie $450
168 Bermuda house $150
1941 88 Skier $200
89 Winnie $150
1945 117 Young girls $700

HEWITT, VIOLA F.
addr: Montreal, 385 Melrose Ave
1923 114 A study

HEWLETT, JAMES MONROE Amer
1 Aug 1868 - 18 Oct 1941, Lawrence, N.Y. B F TB1/2 WWA40
addr: New York, 345 Fifth Ave
1909 mural proofs for decoration
419 Magdalen College, Oxford $65
420 The Tiber, Rome $65

HEWSON, MARIE OLIVIA (m Benson Guest)
21 Aug 1880, Oxford, N.S. d c 1965 M
addr: Amherst, N.S, 1915. Winnipeg, 109 Lenore St, 1929
1915 166 The Quai Verte, Bruges wc $25
1929 Guest
92 Prelude $65
93 Ukrainian girl $300

HEWTON, BENEDICTA ISABEL ROBERTSON (Mrs Monk. m Randolph Stanley Hewton)
addr: Westmount, 4136 Dorchester St, 1933; 1850 Lincoln Ave, 1930
1922 Monk
201 Mrs Angus MacKay
1930 102 Gloucester wc $50
276 Still life wd block $15
277 Circus wd block $15

HEWTON, RANDOLPH STANLEY
12 Jun 1888, Maple Grove, Megantic, Que 17 Mar 1960, Trenton Ont AGO CC1 CE CWW58 M NGC PMC TB2 WWA59
addr: Lachine, Que, 1908. Paris, 21 rue Lauriston, 1909. Lachine, 1910; Paris, 26 rue de Fleurus, 1911-12; Lachine, 76 44th Ave, 1913-15. Montreal: 258 Bishop St, 1921-4; 1850 Lincoln Ave, 1930-3

1908 87 The sea shore $40
88 The barn $15
1909 176 Moonlight
177 The beginning of the storm, Portrush
178 The end of the storm
1910 175 Pont St Michel $20
176 A grey day $20
177 In the harvest time, France $20
178 Apres la pluie $20
179 Moret sur Loing $30
1911 140 En automne, Jardin du Luxembourg $225
141 Pentreath in a mist, Cornwall $300
142 Fishing quarter, Venice $150
143 A wintering evening, Paris $90
144 Rue de Fleurus, Paris $90
145 Au prentemps, Jardin du Luxembourg $40
1912 192 Jardin du Luxembourg, winter $225
193 A Venetian canal $225
194 Un paysage français $200
195 Camaret sur Mer, France $200
196 Grand Canal, Venice $30
197 Corner of Doge's Palace, Venice $30
1913 181 Queen Aholibad dec
182 The bath
183 Picnic under the trees
184 Street scene, Jerusalem
185 Venice wc
186 Cliffs, Camaret wc
187 Lake in Italy wc
188 Painted houses of Venice wc
1914 176 Fons solis dec
177 Portrait
178 Landscape $200
179 Sketch, Jerusalen $30
180 Sketch, Lachine wc $25
181-3 Sketch wc $25 each
1915 167 A Venetian canal $200
168 The barn yard $200
169 A spring day $200
170 The white cottage $200
171 Old gate and gondola, Venice wc $75 (listed 1967, Jessie Dow prize. Old gateway and gondola, Venice)
172 Canal and gondola wc $60
173 Venetian canal wc $50

1921 116 Miss Audrey Buller (NGC)
1922 140 Mrs Walter Stewart
141 Mrs Angus McKay
142 Landscape $200
143 Interior wc
1923 115 The red shawl
116 The bathers $75
117 Tadousac wc $30
118 Cap à l'Aigle wc $30
1924 114 Portrait
1930 103 Miss Freida Wonham
104 Miss Ethel Williams
105 Landscape $200
1933 134 Winter landscape $400
135 Miss H. Craig
136 Autumn landscape $400
137 Village of Bic $200

HEYMANN, GUNTER
1 Jan 1908, Berlin, Germ d 1960 M
addr: Montreal: 1527 Crescent St, 1944-5; 1556 Guy St, 1947
1944 57 Mr Bimson
1945 118 The back stairs $150
119 Still life $250
1947 115 Mrs Paine
116 Anna
117 Fairy tales wc

HEYVAERT, PIERRE
12 Nov 1934, Flanders, Belg M
addr: Montréal, 2158 rue du Havre
1964 122 Petaloide métal et bois $275

HIBBERT, MARGARET
addr: Halifax, 9 Vernon St
1939 169 Pattern wc $20
170 ...and points west wc $20

HICKLING, WALTER ROBERT
1 Mar 1924, Delhi, Ont M WWA62
addr: Burlington, Ont
1968 121 Boatman II acry 53 x 45 $450
122 Boatman III acry 48 x 54 $500
123 Over acry 37 1/2 x 48 $300
124 Over Icaria acry 48 x 56 $500

HILDER, CHARLES SNOWAD
30 May 1915, Carmen, Man
addr: Montreal: 5475 Victoria Ave, Apt 3, 1945-7; 1452 Bishop St, Apt 23, 1949; 754 Sherbrooke St W, 1951
1945 120 Haunted house $75
1946 122 The rock $200
123 M. Heath $50
1947 118 Fishing stages, Pouch Cove, Newfoundland $150
1949 45 Stephanie
157 Jan Veen chalk
1951 66 Lethe pastel $35

HILL, CLAUDE
addr: Montreal, c/o 1108 Elgin Terrace
1940 361 J.A.K. drwg

HILL, DONALD RICHINGS
12 Jun 1900, Buffalo, N.Y. 1939 Toronto M
addr: Westmount: 361 Kensington Ave, 1919-28; 234 Kensington Ave, 1929; 16 Willow Ave, 1935
1919 152 Betty
153 Dusk
1920 120 St Lawrence River, sketch $10
1921 117 Miss Laura Price
1922 144 Miss Elizabeth Rudel
1923 119 Mrs W.D. Lighthall min
120 Rita S. min
1924 115 Peggy
116 Case of miniatures wc
1925 137 Marjorie Bremner
138 Harry Morgan, 3rd, John MacKenzie min (2)
1926 63 My confrère $100
1927 82 Case of miniatures A-Girl in blue. B-Lorraine Morgan. C-late Sir Alexander Bertram. D-Mrs S.W. Ewing
275 Miss Elsie Forsythe charcl
1928 87 Mrs Wm. Boyle
302 Mrs Leslie Speer crayon
1929 104 Miss Sheila MacFarlane
1935 144 Evelyn

HILL, GEORGE WILLIAM
6 May 1862, Shipton, Que 17 Jul 1934, Montreal CC2 M Mo12 NGC PMC TB2 W78
addr: Montreal: 209 Board of Trade Bldg, 1895-7; YMCA Bldg, 1898-1901; Montreal, 1908: 255 Bleury St, 1909-19
1895 228 Sir John A. Macdonald bas rel $3
229 Portraits bas rel
1897 240 Mr and Mrs M. bas rel
241 Miss T. bust
1898 230 Sir Wilfrid Laurier, KCMG bas rel $50
231 Portrait bust $15

1901 209 Master Bruce Reford bust
1908 282 Master Fred Ulley bust bronze
283 Rt Hon Lord Strathcona and Mount Royal bust bronze replica $250
1909 395 John Hamilton Graham, LLD bust bronze
1910 367 The age of electricity plaster $100
368 Fred Ulley bust marble
1915 370 Equestrian statue of Edward VII sketch model
371 Monument for Edward VII sketch model
372 Joy of freedom sculp $25
1916 318 Panel, four portraits bas rel
1917 361 South African mounted scout sketch
1919 368 Dr Wm Henry Drummond bust plaster, bronze replica $375 (bronze NGC)

HILL, HULDA (Mrs)
addr: Kingston, Ont, 220 Frontenac St, 1945-6
1945 121 Summer flowers egg temp $40
1946 124 The trail egg temp $25

HILLENBRAND, JOSEPH F.
addr: Westmount, 4643 Sherbrooke St W, 1934-6
1934 446 Study in sanguine drwg $25
447 Moonlight on the river wd engr $8.50
448 Trees lino cut $5
1935 409 Tree shadows wd engr $12.50
1936 546 Mountain stream, Gratten Lake, Que lino cut $10

HINCHCLIFFE, E. IRENE (Mrs)
addr: Toronto, 62A Edgewood Ave, 1945-7
1945 122 Geranium $45
1947 119 Mark

HINGSTON, LILLIAN ISABEL PETERSON (m Donald Alexander Hingston)
Aug 1881 - 29 May 1967, Montreal M
addr: Montreal, 1000 Sherbrooke St W, 1929-39; Westmount: 424 Metcalfe Ave, 1940-44; 310 Roslyn Ave, 1945-8
1929 105 Red tulips $150
106 Pink tulips $150
1930 106 Apple blossoms $150
107 Roses $60
1931 128 Spring flowers $60
1932 127 Peonies $150
1933 138 Chrysanthemums $100
139 Sweet peas $75
140 Spring flowers $45
1934 138 Spring flowers $150
1935 145 Spring flowers $175
1936 191 Salpiglossis $100
1937 140 Petunias $100
1939 171 Melting snow $25
1940 143 McGill grounds $125
1941 90 Petunias $100
1942 77 Frozen mist $200
1943 85 L'Hôtel Dieu $200
1944 58 Sherbrooke Street $80
1945 123 Winter's end $150
124 After the storm $125
1947 120 Winter street scene $125
1948 15 Snow clad $200

HIRSCHBERG, MARTIN
9 Nov 1937, Toronto IO M
addr: Toronto, 14 Gulliver Rd
1964 35 The lady must go $250

HOBSON, ARTHUR
addr: Montreal, 200 Mazarin St
1925 139 Chez l'habitant $50

HODGES, J. SIDNEY WILLIS Eng
4 Apr 1829, Worthing, Eng Jul 1900.
B DBA G H TB
1886 50 Peter Redpath, Esq

HODGINS, AIMEE GERTRUDE BURGESS (m C.R. Hodgins) (signs le/de Moncy, Ai)
1866, India CWW38 H
addr: Victoria, RR1, Colwood, 1935-6
1935 146 Queen Victoria min $50
147 Lady Fisher, portrait from life min
148 Mrs Piggott, portrait from life min
149 Baby Barbara Sellars, aged 4 years, Edmonton, Alta min
1936 192 Sir Henry Norman, KCB, KCSI wc
193 2d Lt Charles Francis Burgoyne Hodgins, Wiltshire Regiment min
194 Portrait of a lady min
195 195 George Washington, after Cosway min

HODGSON, THOMAS SHERLOCK

5 Jun 1924, Toronto AGO CC2 M NGC
addr: Toronto: 304 Lakeshore Ave, Centre Island, 1954-55; 38 Ellis Park Rd, 1958; 43 St Olaves Rd, 1963
1954 107 Brown beach wc $100
1955 40 Rusty go-cart $90
1958 24 The very end $600 Hon mention
1963 33 Pink negligee $1,000

HOFMANN, GRETA
addr: Montreal, 4268 Madison Ave
1956 108 Eva nm $50

HOFMANN, ROBERT
addr: Montreal, 4268 Madison Ave
1949 158 Ivan Mestrovics, sculptor pastel

HOGENKAMP, CLAIRE FLORENCE (m Alfred Pinsky)
15 Mar 1940, The Hague M
addr: Montreal
1970 polyester resin
31 Discotheque couple 69 1/2h
32 Waltzing couple 69h

HOGG, GRACE MARY ISABEL MACKENZIE (m James D. Hogg)
Oxbow, Sask M
addr: Saskatoon, 1014 7th St E
1957 125 Prairie pattern nm $25

HOLBROOK, ELIZABETH MARY BRADFORD (m John C. Holbrook)
7 Nov 1913, Hamilton, Ont CWW84 M WWA84
addr: Hamilton, 137 Sherman Ave S, 1948-50. Ancaster, Ont, Sunny Hill Farm, Mohawk Rd, RR 1, 1956
1948 116 Geo. M. Nelson bust cast stone
1949 172 Perce Tacon, MA B Paed plaster
1950 89 Figure for fountain in children's park plaster $300
1956 143 Harry Somers, Canadian composer plaster for bronze

HOLDEN, SARAH B. (SARA) (Mrs Hunter)
Belleville, Ont H
addr: Paris, 226 blvd Raspail, 1892. Montreal: 49 Belmont Park, 1894; 377 Mountain St, 1897
1886 88 Tired of study
1889 Sara B.
34 Reading to sister $75
35 Hark! What do I hear? $125
1892 85 Serious thought $60
86 The dunce's stool $25
1894 81 Widowed, but not forsaken $400
82 A grey day at Lachine $150
83 An Italian Grannie $75
1897 65 Portrait, 'Paint me, Auntie'
66 J.C. Holden, Esq
67 The dunes in flower, Holland
1894-97 Assoc 2nd price, 1892, student under 30. Medal, Chicago 1893

HOLESCH, DENES DE
1910, Czechoslovakia
addr: Montreal, 5385 Coolbrook Ave
1947 121 Gypsy boy $125
336 R.T. Downing head plaster

HOLGATE, EDWIN HEADLEY
19 Aug 1892, Allandale, Ont 21 May 1977, Montreal AGO CC1 CE CNS36 CWW36 EC M NGC TB2 WWA76 Juror
addr: Westmount, 44 Rosemount Ave, 1912-20. Montreal: 67 Ste Famille St, 1923; 3535 Lorne Ave, 1934-43. Morin Heights, 1967
1912 198 Oaks in autumn $10
199 Sketch $10
200 Phillips Square $10
201 La cigale et la fourmi wc $25
202 The market wc $25
1913 189 Sous le Cap, Quebec pastel $15
190 Little Champlain Street, Quebec pastel $15
191 Rue Ancien Chantier, Quebec pastel $15
192 Canal smoke, Montreal $15
1914 184 An alley, Florence b&w $25
185-6 A street in Siena b&w $25 each
187 Fantasy b&w $25
1915 174 Night, Little Russia $30
1916 133 The bridge, night $75
134 Old convent $75
135 Study pastel
136 Three sleighs pastel $15
137 The lantern $50
138 At the market pastel $15
1918 158 York Cliffs
159 Mount Royal

160-1 Venice b & w
1919 153 The Rolland house, Côte des Neiges hill
1920 121 Amiens Station, March 29th 1918 $150
122 Dug-out in the chalk, before Arras $100
123 Houdain wc
124 The church, Ablain, St Nazaire $25
1923 121 The 'cellist
122 Market, Brittany $125
123 An old woman, Brittany b&w $50
1934 139 By the lake $400
140 A.E.S, portrait
1938 58 Lazy snow $300 (listed 1967, Jessie Dow prize)
59 Little nude $120
60 A study
1943 86 Stephen Leacock (NGC)
1967 30 The bathers 32 x 32 (MBAM)

HOLLAND, ETHELWYN HAMMOND (m G.A. Holland)
12 Nov 1877, Montreal
addr: Montreal West, 134 Ballantyne Ave N, 1946-7
1946 125 Sweet Williams $25
126 Hydrangeas
1947 122 Flower study

HOLLAND, J. JEFFERY
addr: East Riverside, N.B, P O Box 80
1964 36 Snowbound harbour $40

HOLLAND, LUCY M. (Mrs)
addr: Sherbrooke, Que, 2 Moore St
1910 180 St Francis River $150
181 In the woods wc $50

HOLLAND, MIRIAM RAMSAY
19 Aug 1904 - 13 Apr 1953, Montreal M
addr: Montreal: 1477 Fort St, 1930-4; 1447 Chomedy St, 1935-6; 1471 Closse St, 1937-52
1930 108 Fish shacks $125
1931 129 Boats at low tide, Concarneau, Brittany $120
1932 128 The farmhouse on the hill $100
390 Head of W.G. chrcl & pastel
1933 141 Gollage of St Hippolyte $125
451 A. Laliberte, RCA charcl & pastel
452 L.G. charcl & pastel
1934 141 Houses by the road, Gaspé Peninsula $200
449 Arthur charcl & pastel
1935 150 Lake shore $100
151 Mrs A.D. Skelton, Ottawa pastel
1936 196 Fishing boats, Grand River, Gaspé $150
197 M. Lockheart pastel
1937 141 Late afternoon, St Martin, N.B. $150
142 My mother, sketch
405 Miss Winsome Holland pastel
1939 172 Dappled sunlight $75
1940 144 Farm houses $150
145 Village street $50
1941 91 The highway in spring $50
1942 78 Rockcliffe Park, Ottawa $50
1943 87 Side street $125
1944 59 The Bedard house $150
1945 125 Valerie pastel
1952 17 Geranium on a windowsill

HOLLAND, NORMAN (Mrs)
addr: Westmount: 1915; 606 Grosvenor Ave, 1916-19
1915 175 The elm tree $20
176 Street in Carillon $20
1916 139 The top of the hill $10
140 The distant hills $10
1917 167 Portrait
1918 162 Lake Champlain, sketch $15
1919 155 Early spring, sketch $15
156 Little birches $15
157 Portrait study

HOLLAND, R. I.
addr: Montreal
1918 163 A V.A.D. b&w

HOLLENBACK, WILLIAM GRANT
4 Jan 1919, Canada IO
addr: Niagara Falls
1968 125 Banner acry 48 x 50 $400
126 Manifesto acry 48 x 50 $400
127 Souvenir acry 48 x 48 $400

HOLLISTER, FRANK S. J.
addr: Montreal, 92 Union Ave
1909 421 The Angel of the Resurrection nm
422 The Good Samaritan nm

423 Classic design nm
424 Figure of St Barnabas nm
425 Mary and Martha nm

HOLMBERG, K.
addr: St Laurent, Que, 1585 Ouimet St
1961 114 North wire $150

HOLMDEN, KENNETH HENSLEY
23 Feb 1893 - 8 May 1963, Montreal
addr: Montreal: 1483 Closee St, 1933; 1830 Bayle St, 1935. Westmount, 388 Olivier Ave, 1936. Montreal, 1490 Sherbrooke St W, 1940-50
1933 142 The phoenix $200
143 Romantic landscape $90
144 The call to arms, an incident in the life of a medieval town $70
1935 152 Iris and columbines dec panel $75
1936 547 Decorative panel oils & metal colours $60
1940 146 Boys fighting, an incident, 18th century Montreal $100
1941 92 Kathleen in black and red, portrait $150
93 Zinnias and African marigolds oil & metal colours $50
1944 60 The back pack $250
1946 127 March snowstorm metal colours $125
128 Winter, Mount Royal $125
1947 123 Corner in Montreal, winter $150
124 Bit of roof garden $100
1950 15 Apple blossom $150
16 January $400

HOLMES, EYRE
addr: Ottawa, 18 Rideau St
1933 145 Intermission pastel $50
146 A Gatineau lake $50

HOLMES, ROBERT H.
25 Jun 1861, Cannington, Ont 14 May 1930, Toronto AGO CC2 H M NGC R1 TB2 W78
addr: Toronto: 1908; Graphic Arts Club, 1909; 140 Bond St, 1912
1908 207A Autumn glory wc $125
1909 179 Trilliums wc $75 (AGO)
180 Lobelias wc $75
1912 203 Hepaticas $100
204 Cardinal flowers wc $100
205 Pyrolas wc $100
206 Ragged orchis wc $100

HOLMFELD, HELMUTH EMANUEL BERNHARD EDWIN (Baron de Holmfeld, baron Holy Roman Empire, Baron Dirckinck-Holmfeld, Danish baron)
7 Jul 1835, Schwarzenbeck, Holstein, Denmark 11 Sep 1912, Seattle B TB
addr: Montreal, 98 Stanley St
1895 Holmfeld, Baron
58 Mr James N. Patton
59 Sunset on the Elbe
60 Morning in autumn, Brome Lake $80

HOLMSTED, MARIE H. (Mrs)
4 Mar 1857, Toronto 26 Dec 1911, Moose Jaw, Sask H
addr: Dundas, Ont, Bank of Commerce, 1897-8. Simcoe, Ont, The Terrace, 1903
1897 159 Marsh hawk wc $50
1898 158 Owl and blackbird wc $40
1903 184 On the road to Ste Anne's wc $50
185 Coming storm at the Rocks wc $35

HOME, MARY W.
addr: Quebec, 38 St Louis Rd, 1915-16
1915 445 Parrot plates six $45
1916 372 Cup & saucer six $40

HOO, SING (HOO SING YUEN)
c May 1909, Canton CWW84 M WWA84
addr: Toronto: 473 Western Rd, 1943; 139 Livingstone Ave, 1949
1943 259 Prayer sculp
1949 173 The thought plaster $500

HOOD, HARRY
7 Feb 1876, Cupar, Scot 10 Jul 1956 Vancouver
addr: Vancouver, 1103 Robson St, 1935-40
1935 153 The stove wc $30
154 The stone floor wc $35
1936 198 Ships that pass in the day wc $40
199 The north window wc $50
1938 61 The red fence $200
62 Joan
1939 173 Reflections $40

174 Shingle mill, Vancouver, B.C. $50
175 Old mill, Vancouver, B.C, $50
1940 147 Shingle mill, Vancouver $40

HOOKER, MARION see NELSON, MARION

HOOPER, JOHN
1926, Southampton, Eng M
addr: Hampton, N.B.
1968 128 Man cedar 42h $1,500
129 City of wood wd shingles 48 x 96 $1,050

HOPE, CLARK MIDDLETON
addr: Westmount, 4328 Montrose Ave, 1933-5
1933 147 Thelma
1934 142 The fresh green of mid-summer $300
143 Distant mountains after rain $350
144 September sunshine, Black Lake $350
1935 155 Chinese head $60

HOPE, WILLIAM R.
May 1863 - 5 Feb 1931, Montreal H M Mo12 NGC W78
addr: Montreal: 1226 Dorchester St, 1895-7; 291 Mountain St, 1898-1903; Montreal, 1908-10; c/o Scott & Sons, 1912; 994 Dorchester St W, 1920-5
1889 36 Tarbert, Loch Fyne $500
1895 61 Moonlight on the Loing, France $300
62 In the forest of Fontainebleau $300
1897 68 Departing day $150
69 Moonlight $60
70 On the Loing, France $50
1898 55 Salmon fishing in Gaspé $200
1900 52 Hay making, St Andrews, N.B. $100
53 Summer day, St Andrews $100
54 Evening $50
1901 64 York Beach, Maine $250
65 Evening, Back River
1903 75 June twilight $1,000
76 Moonlight
77 St Andrews, N.B. (NGC)
1908 89 Dante and Virgil at the Gate of Dis. Inferno, canto VIII $1,000
1910 182 The souls of the lost
1912 207 A squall $750
1920 125 The track of the column $300
126 Prisoners $200
127 Side street, Valenciennes $150
1924 117 The kirk, St Andrews, N.B.
1925 140 Mons $750
port: by Alphonse Jongers, 1927-90

HOPPER, ENID
addr: Sherbrooke, Que, 472 Quebec St
1955 116 Peter nm

HORLOR, GEORGE W. Eng
fl 1849-90 B DBA G TB
1885 6 Mountain sheep

HORNER, STAN
addr: Pointe Claire, Que, 15 Cartier Ave
1961 27 Secret night $300

HORNYANSKY, NICHOLAS (NICHOLAUS)
11 Aug 1896, Budapest 25 May 1965, Toronto AGO CWW61 M TB3 W78 WWA66/70
addr: Toronto: 83 Madison Ave, 1931; 22 Rathnelly Ave, 1932; 16 McMaster Ave, 1933-5; 228 Cottingham St, 1936; 24 Harbord St, 1937; 83 1/2 Yonge St, 1939; 16 Vermont Ave, 1940-2; 44 Westmorland Ave, 1949-60
1931 130 Brass and pewter $200
384 The Kloveniersburgwall in winter, Amsterdam etch $60
1932 391 Barbara stone point etch
392 Early days, from 'A life' col etch $20
393 Montelbaanstoren, Amsterdam etch $20
1933 453 Fishermen's homecomming, Holland col etch $25
454 The frozen waterfall etch $25
1934 450 St Stephens' on Bellevue col etch $5.50
451 Weavers' Quay, Nurnberg col etch $20
452 Dome des Invalides, Paris col etch $20
1935 410 Fishing village, Lake Ontario etch $10
411 Quebec City from the east col aqua $6

412 Ontario ravine etch $10
1936 548 Rijndijk village, Holland col etch $25
1937 406 Sagittaria col etch $18
407 Detroit from the river col etch $15
1939 176 March weather, Lierre $200
1940 362 Sunset on Rice Lake aqua $15
1941 233 Winter's white sun col aqua $12
1942 79 Sunset on Rice Lake col aqua $12
80 October sun col aqua $15
1949 46 Lifelong neighbours $500
159 St Jean, Quebec col aqua $15 (SPL)
1950 83 Old French brigs soft ground etch
84 Rideau mill col aqua $35
1951 17 The cub $110
1952 18 Turtle Cove $120
1954 123 Predawn aqua $27
1960 176 Boreas nm $45

HOUGHTON, C. G.
addr: Outremont, 637 Côte Ste Catherine Rd
1940 148 Spring, Fresnière, Que wc

HOUGHTON, FRANK
fl 1887-1925 H
addr: Montreal: 118 Tupper St, 1891; 371 Mance St, 1917; 224 Sherbrooke St E, 1919-20; 58 Park Ave, 1924; 3154 Park Ave, 1925
1891 162 Mr Bogg's first bear wc $30
168 River Guardian's camp, Metis wc $20
169 Old house, Grand Metis wc $10
170 Deserted mining camp, Cobalt country wc $10
1919 158 The outskirts of the village wc $10
159 Lumber camp, Lake Wahnapitae wc $10
1920 128 Fort Senneville $20
1924 118 Winter among the birches $80
1925 141 A bit of Mount Royal $50
port: by Dorothy Rhynas Coles, 1919-80

HOUGHTON, MARGARET (MAY) (m Jules Brunn)
23 Sep 1865, Montreal B H Mo12 TB
addr: Paris, 9 rue Campagne Première, 1891. Montreal: 44 Lorne Ave, 1892; YMCA Bldg, 1894; Bleury St, 1895; 35 Tupper St, 1897. Concarneau, France, 1903. Paris: 1909-10; 278 rue St Jacques, 1911. Montreal, 58 Park Ave, 1922
1891 74 Autumn on the Loing $55
1892 87 Rest $200
88 Feeding chickens
1894 84 The evening of life $200
85 A foggy evening over the bar $40
86 A group of old fishing stages $50
1895 63 A bleak pasture $100
64 Giving salt to the sheep $80
65 Morning $60
1897 71 A game of cards $150
72 Torsile $40
73 Summer fields $20
74 The family shoemaker $40
1903 78 Rest $200
237 In the orchard pastel $75
238 The golden moon pastel $75
1909 181 Old Breton farm house wc $10
182 Waiting wc $15
183 Grand'mère wc $25
184 Fisherman's daughter wc $15
1910 183 Prière $150
184 Goose girls wc $25
185 The little mother wc $25
186 The fountain wc $25
187 Evening light wc $25
1911 146 A coming storm, La Cotinière wc $25
147 Old houses, La Cotinière wc $25
148 Peeling corn cobs wc $25
149 Grandpère est faché wc $20
1922 145 Breton peasant wc $30

HOUGHTON, P.
1886 133 On the north shore of Lake Superior

HOULE, MAURICE
addr: Ville d'Anjou, Que, 7651 ave de la Seine
1960 237 Boeuf métal $250

HOULE, ROMEO

addr: Ville d'Anjou, Que, 7621 ave de la Seine
1961 28 Estuaires $150

HOUSTON, GEORGE Scot
20 Feb 1869 - 5 Oct 1947, Dalry, Ayrshire, Scot B DBA DVP TB1/2/3 WBA WWB34
addr: Glasgow
1908 208 An Ayrshire farm wc
209 The mill in the glen wc

HOUSTOUN, DONALD MACKAY
27 Nov 1916, Stevensville, Ont AGO IO M
addr: Toronto, 377 Brookdale Ave, 1955-60
1955 41 Beach stones $250
1960 52 Landscape $700

HOVEN, C.
addr: Halifax, 1891-2
1891 75 Landscape $200
1892 89 Landscape $300

HOVERMANN, WILLY
addr: Montreal: 3531 Shuter St, 1940; 461 Mayor St, 1946-7
1940 363 Chapel in the woods etch $12.50
1946 129 Trees pastel $100
1947 125 The red house $150

HOWARD, NORMAN DOUGLAS
13 Apr 1899, Nottingham, Eng d 1955 DBA
addr: Montreal, 1410 Stanley St
1933 148 The Ramesseum, Thebes $175
149 Ladies of the lake $95

HOWARD, STEWART (Major)
addr: Montreal, 225 Sherbrooke St W
1916 141 North River wc $10
142 North River rapids at Belisle Mills wc $10

HOWARD, WILLIAM ALFRED
13 Dec 1902, London, Eng
addr: Toronto, 47 Bellefair Ave
1932 394 Scarboro Bluff pen & ink $10
395 Birch trees pen & ink $10
396 The old halfway house, Kingston Road col wdcut $10

HOWE, GEORGE see BLACKADER, GORDON HOME, 1912

HOWELL, J. CONSTANCE
addr: Montreal, 2673 St Catherine St, 1892-5
1892 90 Triliums $25
175 Floats and snells wc $20
176 View on the coast near Gloucester, Mass wc $10
1895 66 Wharf at Gloucester $25

HOYT, EDITH Amer
10 Apr 1894, West Point, N.Y. F TB2 WHC WWA47
addr: Washington, D.C, 1301 21st St, 1929-40
1929 107 A summer day $75
108 The Garden of the Gods $50
1940 149 Mount Robson, B.C. $250

HRUBY, MALENKA ELEANORA
23 Jan 1930, Prague, Czecho M
addr: Montreal, 2118 Maplewood Ave, 1956. Ottawa, 57 Rosebery Ave, 1963-4
1956 31 Nude $60
1963 34 Looking through $200
1964 37 A breath of fresh air $300

HUANG, JUDITH (m Ting Young Huang)
addr: Ottawa, 679 Chapman Blvd
1964 92 Recollection nm $80

HUDDELL, IDA M.
b Montreal
addr: Ville St Pierre, Que: 445 St James St, 1913-24; 471 St James St, 1925-46
1913 481 Large vase $25
482 Tray enamels $4
483 Box enamels $8
484 Lemonade jug $8
1914 511 Large vase $25
512 Tray $9
513 Salt, pepper shakers $5
514 Nut bowl (sold)
515 Marmalade jar $6
1915 446 Syrup jug enamels $7
447 Tray enamels $8
448 Satsuma box $9
449 Lemonade jug $15
450 Lemonade cups $3 each
451-2 Fruit bowl $10 each

1916 373 Satsuma tea caddy $7
374 Satsuma box $5
375 Satsuma vase $12
376 Hot milk jug
377 Tray $10
1917 425 Jug, morning glory $13
426 Jug, conventional des $12
427 Jug, bittersweet $10
428 Vase, conventional poppy $16
1918 430 Satsuma rose jar $10
431 Satsuma vase, morning glory $16
432 Vase, holyhock matt cols & lustre $30
433 Belleek biscuit jar $12
434 Bowl, conventional grape des $15
435 Green china jug, water lily des $7
1919 421 Vase matt colours $15
422 Jardiniere, conventional $20
423 Belleek stamp box enamels $4
424 Satsuma tea caddy $9
425 Muffin dish $10
426 Fruit bowl $10
1920 332 Vase, semi-conventional nasturtium des $9
333 Pair candlesticks $15
334 Vase with lamp shade, and electrical attachment $40
1921 336 Cheese dish $7
337 Coffee set $50
1922 380 Satsuma jar in enamels
1923 279 Satsuma lamp, semi-conventional poppy des, enamels $45
1924 360 Vase, semi-conventional grape des $16
361 Satsuma candlestick $12
362 Candlestick, semi-conventional iris des
1925 316 Vase, matt colours semi-conventional des
317 Bowl, conventional des
318 Candlestick
1926 162 Vase, semi-conventional des
163 Muffin dish, conventional des
164 Box, matt colour
1928 88-9 Study of roses $40 each
1929 109 Study of flowers $30
110 Zinnias and phlox $30
1930 109-10 Study of Chinese woman $30 each
111 Still life $40
1932 129-30 Study $25 (1) n.p.(1)
1933 150 Late autumn day $20
151 Mrs A.S. Noad
1934 145 A descendant of the Cree tribe $25
146 Miss Jessie Baillie
1936 200 Portrait study
1937 143 Petunias $20
1940 150 Portrait of a school girl $25
1941 94 Hollyhocks $20
1944 61 One who guards our coasts
1946 130 A native of Trinidad

HUDON, NORMAND
5 Jun 1929, Montreal M
addr: Montreal: 6832 Des Erables St, 1949-51; 1668 St Luc St, 1954
1949 47 Pointe au Pic $100
1951 18 Maisons de faubourgs $100
1954 44 L'atelier $200

HUDON, SIMONE MARIE YVETTE (m Henri Beaulac)
9 Sep 1905, Quebec M WWA53
addr: Quebec, 42 Laurier Ave, 1930-40
1930 278 Porte de convent, Québec etch $5
279 La Place Royale, Québec etch $10
280 Coté à Coton, Québec etch $8
281 La Halle Montcalm, Québec etch $12
1933 455 Maison bicentenaire à Québec etch $12
456 Monastière des Ursulines à Québec etch $10
457 Vieille maison, rue Ste Monique, à Québec etch $9
1937 408 Crèpuscule, Québec col etch $12
409 Côte du Palais à Québec col etch $10
410 Sur le Cap à Québec col etch $8
411 Goelette col etch $4
1938 163 Rue Sous le Cap, Québec etch $7
164 Escalier à la Basse Ville, Québec soft ground etch $8
1940 364 Québec, 1938 etch $3
365 Québec etch $3
366 Parvis de la Cathédrale

Anglicane aqua $6
367 L'ancienne Place d'Orleans à Québec etch $4

HUDSON, ANDREW
9 Jul 1935, Birmingham, Eng M
addr: Saskatoon, 906 Saskatchewan Cr E
1964 38 Out of the lake $400

HUESTIS, FLORENCE
addr: Sackville, N.B, Ladies' College
1924 363 China bowl, Moorish $50

HUET, JACQUES
6 Aug 1932, Montreal M
addr: Montreal, 4582 rue Parthenais
1963 105 Mygale bois $450

HUFFMAN, ISOBEL MARY KNOX (m Percival Huffman)
18 Jan 1895, Toronto DBA WWB34
addr: Toronto, 27 Rosedale Rd
1934 147 Desmond wc $25
148 Leslie Reid, author of 'The rector of Maliseet' $25
149 A little girl min $100
150 The empty teacup $150

HUGGINS, ROSS
1916, Toronto M
addr: Montreal, 7410 de Berniers St, 1960-4
1960 53 The quiet season $400
1964 39 Two black horses $250

HUGGINS, WILLIAM H.
addr: Ottawa, 447 Somerset St
1917 191 Little Metis Beach, Que wc $20
172 Near Field, B.C. wc $15

HUGHES, EDWARD JOHN
17 Feb 1913, North Vancouver, B.C. AGO CC1 CE CWW84 M NGC WWA84
addr: Montreal, c/o Dominion Galleries, 1438 Sherbrooke St W, 1953-64
1953 18 Pilot Bay, Gabriola Island, B.C. $450
19 Hopkins Landing, Howe Sound, B.C. $375
1954 45 Low tide, Saseenos, B.C. $385
1955 42 The cannery at Namu, B.C. $385
1957 47 The store at Allison Harbour, B.C. $575
1964 40 The Thompson Valley $1,950

HUGHES, HAROLD
addr: Verdun, Que, 793 6th Ave, 1936-7
1936 201 Winter solitude wc $40
1937 144 Open water wc $60

HUGHES, MARY
addr: Montreal West: 249 Westminster Ave, 1924; 49 Brock Ave N, 1926. Montreal, 5004 Clanranald Ave, 1931-2
1924 119 A favourite model min $50
120 At the well, Verre, Holland wc $15
1926 64 Miss Zabelle Boyajian, Armenian poet and painter min $150
1931 131 A south sea belle min $20
1932 131 Head of a monk $500

HUGH-STANTON, GERTRUDE see HERMES, GERTRUDE

HUI, MOLLY LAI MUI (m W.K. Lore)
24 Nov 1916, Victoria, Hong Kong
addr: Ville St Laurent, Que, 650 Laurentian Blvd
1954 108 Spring herder wc $375

HULL, LINA A.
addr: Hamilton, 295 Charlton Ave,
1927 83 Still life $50
84 Peonies $200

HUMPHREY, JACK WELDON
12 Jan 1901 - 23 Mar 1967, Saint John, N.B. AGO CC2 CE CWW 64 M NGC TB3 W78 WWA66/70
addr: Saint John: 54 Orange St, 1931; 108 Prince William St, 1942-8
1931 132 Still life of brass $120
133 Still life with bottle $120
1942 81 People waiting $200
82 Portrait $160
1943 88 Winnifred $175
1948 81 The Fairhaven Queen at South Wharf wc $50

HUMPHRIES, JOHN
6 May 1882, Blockley, Glos, Eng 15 Dec 1958, Lachine, Que CNS36 M
addr: Montreal: 616 Marquette St, 1922; 4849 Esplanade Ave, 1930; 2244 Harvard Ave, 1934; 2230 Harvard Ave, 1935-7; 4324 Harvard Ave, 1945-7
1922 146 A memory of dawn wc
1930 112 A Laurentian mountain slope wc $25

1934 151 Old farm and barn, Kamouraska, Que wc $25
152 Karmouraska, Que wc $10
1935 156 A lower St Lawrence shore wc $50
157 A Laurentian mountain velley wc $30
1936 202 Ancient and modern, corner of Craig and Main Streets, Montreal wc $350
203 Where the North River slumbers wc $150
204 The road to the shore wc $150
205 Down from the lakes $100
1937 145 Ramparts of a mountain stream, the North River wc $100
146 A bend in the North River wc $100
147 The old homestead wc $75
148 A lower St Lawrence port wc $50
1945 126 A village of the lower St Lawrence wc $150 (listed 1967, Jessie Dow prize) (MBAM)
1946 131 Quebec from the Levis shore wc $200
1947 126 Shore road, the lower St Lawrence wc $200

HUNSICKER (Miss)
addr: Montreal, 139 Mackay St
1900 230 Service plates, marine views

HUNT, DORA A. (m H.L. Hunt)
addr: Vancouver, 1637 Harwood St, 1960-1
1960 54 Still life, green and white $100
1961 29 Borodin $175

HUNT, JOHN POWELL
14 Dec 1854, St Mary's, Ont 1932, London, Ont H
addr: London, 423 Dundas St, 1911-14
1911 150 Winter, London, Ont $50
151 On the Medway wc $15
152 Near Meadow Lily Mills wc $15
1912 208 On the Thames, London, Ont $50
209 The rustic fane $50
210 At Broughdale, Ont $75
1913 193 Autumn pastoral $300
194 Landscape, near London, Ont $75
195 Corn harvest $75
196 Morning on Lake Nipissing $75
1914 188 Storm beaten $500
189 Thames Valley, Ontario $60
190 On the Thames, Ontario $75
191 West London, Ontario $75

HUNT, THOMAS L. Amer
AAA25 F Y
addr: Cleveland, Ohio, 127 Bender Ave
1914 192-3 Winter evening, Euclid village

HUNT, WILLIAM EDWARD
addr: Montreal: Witness Office, 1905; 927 St Urbain St, 1906; 1293 St Urbain St, 1909
1905 209 Autumn solitude pastel $35
210 Evening light pastel $25
211 Willows pastel $35
1906 95 Golden light $25
96 Indeterminate afternoon $25
97 Poor people's palaces $50
243 Point-aux-Trembles, September pastel $35
244 Among the Chenails wc $15
1909 185 Golden, glorious summer wc $100
186 Nature in many moods wc $100
187 The spirit of autumn wc $35

HUNTER, ALBERT P.
1901, Ottawa 1970, Winnipeg
addr: Winnipeg, 195 Queenston St
1947 127 Public wharf, Woodlands, B.C. wc $80

HUNTER, I. (Mrs)
addr: Pointe Clair, Que, 91 Cedar Ave
1926 165 Jar, grape des
166 Jar, green-blue majolica

HUNTER, RAOUL
19 Jun 1926, St Cyrille, Que M
addr: Québec, 470 rue Lemesurier
1960 238 Torse wd

HUNTER, SARAH see HOLDEN, SARAH

HUNTLEY, WALTER EDWIN
1887, Newark, N.J. 1 Feb 1931, Toronto M

addr: Toronto, 66 Bond St
1927 85 North lake country $375

HUOT, CHARLES EDOUARD MASSON
26 Mar 1855, Quebec 27 Jan 1930, Sillery, Que CC1 H M NGC PMC W78
addr: Quebec: 1894-1908; 24 St Stanislaus St, 1909
1894 87 Moonlight scene, lower St Lawrence $100
1908 90 Through grief and sorrow
1909 188 Tête d'étude
189 Interieur d'atelier

HURTUBISE, JACQUES
28 Feb 1939, Montreal AGO CC2 CE M WWA84
addr: Montréal: 8558 rue Waverley, 1958; 673 rue Vitré, ap 2, 1960; 3665 rue St Christophe, 1962. Rivière des Prairies, Que, 10221 52 ème ave, 1963-4. Montréal, Galerie du Siècle, 1494 rue Sherbrooke O, 1965.
1958 25 Le sentier $50
1960 55 Sous les ponts rouges $200
239 Nue couchée limestone $250
1962 18 Radio activité nu 17 $225
1963 35 Peinture nu 44 $525
1964 41 Terrible douceur $400
1965 9 Bérénice $600

HUTCHINGS, GEORGE H.
addr: Montreal, 6 Beaver Hall Sq
1909 426 Reception hall

HUTCHINSON, GRACE see FULGER, GRACE

HUTCHINSON, LEONARD
9 Apr 1896, Manchester, Eng May 1980, Thornhill, Ont CE IO M
addr: Mount Hamilton, Ont, 109E 19th St, 1932-9
1932 397 The city col pr $15
398 Evening, Desjardins Canal col pr $15
399 The red dome col pr $15
400 The park col pr $15
1935 413 Above Twelve Mile Creek col pr $15
414 Windy morning col pr $15
415 Mount Albion col pr $15
1936 206 After rain col wd cut $15
207 Cayuga col wd cut $15
1937 412 The grist mill engr $12.50
413 Ontario landscape col wd cut $15
1938 165 Plenty o' nothin' engr $7.50
166 Communist? engr $7.50
1939 177 Drought engr $10
178 Recessional engr $10
179 Tobacco engr $10

HUTCHISON, ALEXANDER COWPER
2 Apr 1838 - 1 Jan 1922, Montreal CWW10 EC H Mo98/12 NGC W78
addr: Montreal: 181 St James St, 1894-1900; Montreal, 1908; 2 Place d'Armes, 1909; 50 Royal Insurance Bldg, 1911-16; 204 Notre Dame St W, 1933
1894 264 YWCA building, Drummond St, perspective
265 Mr W.W. Ogilvie's summer residence, The Rapids Farm perspective
1900 Hutchison & Wood, 1900-08
180-1 Merchants' Bank, section, alterations des
182 McIntyre Block, Victoria Sq and Craig Street des
1908 319 Proposed St Andrew's Church, Westmount
1909 Hutchison, Wood & Miller 1909-16
427 Protestant Infants' Home
428 Residence
1911 296 First Presbyterian Church
297 House in Westmount
1912 413 Commercial building
414 Residence, Westmount
1914 450 Stanley Presbyterian Church
451 Westmount residence
452 Study for church building
453 Transportation station
1916 333 CPR freight terminal bldg, Toronto
334 Proposed Whitlock Golf Club House, Hudson Heights
1933 383-4 St Matthew's Church, exterior, interior
385 Store, St Catherine Street

HUTCHISON, FREDERICK WILLIAM
13 Mar 1871, Montreal 1 May 1953, Hudson Heights, Que AGO CWW49 M NGC WWA53
addr: Montreal: Fraser Institute, 1903; 51 St Catherine St W, 1911. New York,

43 E 59th St, 1912, 1914. Westmount, 4404 St Catherine St W, 1913. Montreal, 99 Notre Dame St W, 1928. New York, 36 W 12th St, 1931. Montreal, 1450 Drummond St, 1933. Hudson Heights, Que, 1951
1903 79 Promenade, Roscoff, Brittany $75
80 Landscape $20
81 Barnyard $20
1911 153 September morning $400
1912 211 A fisherman $300
1913 197 Oka village
198 The shore $300
1914 194 An old section $800
1928 90 Oxen resting
1931 134 St Simeon
1933 152 Sheltered harbour, Petite Revière, Que $500
153 Over the hills, Percil Bay, Que $700
154 Fortin's mill $500
155 Barachois Bay $400
1951 19 Street in St Urbain $1,000

HUTCHISON, JOHN CAMERON
addr: Montreal: 698 St Antoine St, 1900; 234 Guy St, 1901-3
1900 173 Eventide b&w $5
183 Heraldic emblazoning
1901 190 A glimpse of Wells Cathedral b&w $15
199 Achievement of arms
200 Ornamental heraldry
1903 186 Maple leaves wc $20
187 A Muskoka pathway wc $10
188 September in Muskoka wc $15
239 Study in black and white $10

HUTCHISON, LILLIE J. (Mrs)
addr: Montreal
1908 210 High Street, Edinburgh
211 Craig Millar Castle pen & ink

HUTTON, GWENDOLEN see LAMONT, GWENDOLEN

HUYCK, LAURA G. TALMADGE (Mrs) Amer WWA40
addr: Albany, N.Y, 40 Marion Ave
1935 158 Opus 27, twilight pastel $250

HYDE, GEORGE TAYLOR
23 Aug 1879 - 23 Jun 1944, Montreal CNS27 CWW38
see Nobbs, Percy Erskine, 1915-44

HYDE, LORA
addr: Montreal, c/o A.R. Doble, 804 Sherbrooke St W
1914 195 Girl with letter
196 Le Cour de Blanchisseuse, Marlotte $75

HYNDMAN, ROBERT STEWART
28 Jun 1915, Edmonton M WWA62
addr: Ottawa, 74 Acacia Ave
1952 19 The soldier $250

I

IACURTO, FRANCESCO (FRANK)
1 Sep 1908, Montreal CWW84 M WWA84
addr: Montreal: 6 Jean Talon St W, 1933; 7181 St Denis St, 1935; 7459A St Denis St, 1937. Quebec, 10 McMahon St, 1946. Montreal, 1472 Sherbrooke St W, 1947-9. Quebec, 20 St Anne St, 1950. Montreal, 8950 St Lawrence Blvd, 1952-3
1933 156 Young Indian, from Caugnawaga $150
1935 159 Chief Judge G. Perrault
1937 149 Nude, study pastel $75
1946 132 Edith Wills Henderson
1947 128 Afternoon of life $2,500
1948 16 Kitty
1949 48 Ed Dyonnet, RCA
1950 17 Farmer, Ils d'Orléans
1952 20 Reminiscing
1953 20 Calèche driver $1,500

IDE, KATHARINE
addr: Ottawa, 447 Riverdale Ave, 1940-2
1940 151 Gaspé fishing boats $35
1942 83 Study of a child pastel $35

ILLSLEY, HUGH PERCIVAL
15 Feb 1896, Montreal
addr: Westmount, 134 Clandeboye Ave, 1923-5, 1927. Montreal, 326 Beaver Hall Hill, 1926
1923 268 Bank des
269 Sketch
1924 330 War memorial
1925 299 Sketch
1926 147 Residence
1927 208 Sketch $20
see also Archibald, Ian T, 1940

INGALLS, HELEN A.

addr: Laprairie, Que, 1914-15
1914 197 Minette b&w $10
1915 177 Stone for King Edward Road, Laprairie $10

INGALLS, LORNA WENTWORTH
addr: Montreal: 242 Mountain St, 1913; 3457 Shuter St, 1937
1913 406 Cows and a duck sculp $25
407 Enough for one sculp $15
1937 L.W. Ingalls
150 The green balloon wc $25
151 The ginger jar wc $15

INGLE, BERTHA MAYLAW
1878, Nassagaweya, Ont 20 Oct 1962, n Guelph, Ont
addr: Toronto, 310 Bloor St
1910 188 The goose girl $75

INNES, ALICE AMELIA
1890 Brooksdale, Ont 30 Dec 1970, St Thomas, Ont M
addr: Toronto, 25 Severn St, 1943-5
1943 89 The Narrows $300
1945 127 December $350 (listed 1967-30A, Jessie Dow prize)

INWOOD, ELIZABETH
addr: Westmount, 229 Melville Ave
1948 17 Still life $75
99 Figure composition aqua $10

IRVING, THOMAS
addr: Montreal, 64 Aylmer St
1895 165 Old Leuchars Church, Fife-shire, Scotland wc $50
166 Interior pen & ink $6

IRVING, VERA ISABEL MATTHEWS (m Lawrence Irving)
1 Sep 1913, Toronto
addr: Toronto, The Palisades, 1947-55
1947 129 Topic, famine egg temp $150
1949 49 Life is tedious $100
1950 18 Swimming lesson
67 Pen ball gouache $100
1955 43 Flight cancelled $125

IRWIN, M. ELEANOR
H
addr: Montreal: 43 Belmont Park, 1898-1901; Place Viger Hotel, 1909-10
1898 56 Still life $20
1901 132 5th February 1901 wc $10
1909 190 The Eure at Les Damps wc $40
191 Laroche in the Ardennes wc $20
192 Rio Della Toresela, Venice wc $15
1910 189 A street in Bruges wc $25
190 Dinant wc $20

ISKOWITZ, GERSHON
24 Nov 1921, Kielce, Poland AGO B CE IO M WWA84
addr: Toronto, 435A Spadina Ave
1964 42 Spring $550

IVES, ANTOINETTE
fl 1882-9 H
1889 37 An old New Englander $60
133 Noon-day rest wc $50
134 Portrait wc

J

JACK, LEIGH
addr: Montreal, 3683 Hutchison St
1933 515 Leona plaster
516 Jobless plaster

JACK, MARION ELIZABETH
Saint John, N.B. fl 1898-16 DBA Mo12
addr: Saint John: 1908; 162 Union St, 1913-14. Montreal: 14 Tower Ave, 1915; c/o Copping Art Store, 1916
1908 91 French woodland scene $75
1913 199 Old cottages at Benfleet, near the mouth of the Thames $45
200 The hillside farm $45
1914 198 Birches and maples $117
199 Church interior, Southwold, Sussex $117
200 Coming storm $135
201 Spring in England $135
202 Bunyan's house, Elstow b & w $50
203 Abdul Baha pastel $50
204 Valley of the Stour wc $50
205 A bit of English country wc $50
1915 178 An autumn day, Eliot, Me $125
179 Green Acre, Me $150
180 The harbour, St Andrews-by-the-sea pastel $35

1916 143 The old road, Green Acre $250
144 Turkish fortress, Acca, Syria $25
145 Etude, Mount Carmel from the Mediterranean wc $15

JACK, MARTHA SHARPE FORRESTER (PATTI)
1850's, Gatehouse of Fleet, Kirkcudbrightshire, Scot 1908, St Andrews, Scot DBA G H
addr: Ottawa, 206 O'Connor St
1900 Patti
55 Highland interior, Trossacks, Scotland $50
56 Tinkers tents on Fife moor, Scotland $50

JACK, RICHARD
15 Feb 1866, Sunderland, Eng 30 Jun 1952, Montreal B DBA DVP G H M RA TB1/2/3 WBA WWB29 Juror
addr: Westmount, 563 Victoria Ave, 1936. Montreal, The Cottage, 3484 Peel St, 1942-8
1936 208 W.A. Black, Esq
209 Mrs G. Victor Whitehead
210 Winter in the Laurentians $500
1942 84 Still life, Tang horse
85 Still life, Buddha
86 Storm mountain
1943 90 Flower piece $500
91, 93 Still life $500 each
92 Mount Stephen $500
1944 62, 64 Still life $850, $650
63 Lake O'Hara $750
1945 128-9 Still life $400, $650
130 Market place, Cahors $350
1946 133 The vision
134 Interior $700
135 Mrs G.V. Whitehead
1947 130 Spring day in the Laurentians $500
131 Still life $650
1948 18 Spring flowers $500

JACKS, ROBERT
8 Mar 1943, Melbourne, Australia CWW70 IO
addr: Toronto
1969 4 Big mauve acry 78 x 114

JACKSON, ALEXANDER YOUNG
3 Oct 1882, Montreal 5 Apr 1974, Kleinberg, Ont AGO B CC2 CE CWW70 EC M NGC TB1/2 W78 WWA73
addr: Montreal, 76 Park Ave, St Henri, 1903. Westmount, 69 Hallowell Ave, 1906-13, 1915, 1923. Toronto, Studio Bldg, Severn St, 1914, 1922, 1929-46
1903 189 November wc $15
1906 98 Cloud and sunshine $18
99 Meadow land $20
245 After the winter wc $18
1909 193 Moonlight, Etaples $20
194 Salt marsh, Etaples $25
1910 191 Early spring $100
192 Misty morning $80
193 November morning, Episy $135
194 The River Loing $100
1911 154 Grey day in March $100
155 Summer clouds $25
156 Evening, Georgian Bay $25
157 The old sugar shanty $25
1912 212 Canal de Loing, France $100
213 The Ramparts, St Malo, by moonlight $40
214 Old courtyard, St Malo $25
215 Return of St Pierre Miquelon fleet, St Malo $100
1913 201 The fountain $250
202 Assisi, from the plain $250 (AGO)
203 A village in Picardy $150
204 Morning, St Malo $150
1914 206 A squall on Georgian Bay $250
207 The land of the leaning pine $200
208 Evening $50
1915 181 A frozen lake $500 (NGC)
182 Autumn $500
183 Northern lights $300
1922 147 A Nova Scotia village $350
148 A lake in the hills $350
149 Morning after sleet 1967-31, 25 1/4 x 31 1/4 (National Gallery of Canada)
1923 124 Pic Island
1929 111 The north shore of Baffin Island
112 Baffin Bay $500
113 Early spring in Quebec $400
1932 132 Night, Pine Island $400
133 Winter, St Fidele $275
134 Winter, Ruisseau Jureux $275
1933 157 Grey day, les Eboulements $225
158 The St Lawrence at les

Eboulements $275
159 Hills, Killarney, Ont $300
1934 154 The valley of the Gouffre $300
155 Labrador $400
156 St Hilarion $225
1939 180 Great Bear Lake, autumn $300
181 Spring in Algoma $350
1946 136 Wild woods $200
port: by Lilias Torrance Newton, 1939-249

JACKSON, CECILIA
addr: Montreal, 110 Union Ave
1895 249 Plate
250 Bonbon box

JACKSON, ERNA NOOK
30 Nov 1886, Petrolia, Ont
addr: Toronto, 19 Oaklands Ave, 1928-36
1928 91 The market, St Thomas $45
1931 135 Still life $30
136 Full blown $50
1935 162 On Vancouver Island $40
1936 213 Murray River, Quebec $100

JACKSON, HENRY ALEXANDER CAMERON
25 Aug 1877, Montreal d 1961
addr: Montreal, 76 Park Ave, St Henry 1901-3
1901 133 A collier in the harbour wc $15
134 Through sweet clover wc $15
1903 190 In old Montreal wc $20

JACKSON, NAOMI CATHERINE ADAIR (m J. Walton Groves)
1910, Montreal M WWA84
addr: Montreal West, 35 Campbell Ave, 1934-43
1934 157 North Beach, Percé, Gaspé $75
1935 160 October day, St Sauveur, Que $25
161 Georgian Bay, Ont $20
1936 211 Hedemowa Church, Sweden $25
212 Aarhus harbour, Denmark
1943 94 Arctic baroque

JACKSON, SARAH JEANETTE
13 Nov 1924, Detroit IO M TB3 WWA84
addr: Montreal, Galerie Libre, 2100 Crescent St, 1964-5
1964 123 Danseur bronze $1,350
1965 38 Tête brune bronze $950

JACKSON, WILLIAM HENRY Amer
1843, Keesville, N.Y. 30 Jun 1942, New York WWA40/47
addr: Tompkinsville, Staten Island, N.Y, 144 Cebra Ave, 1926. Montreal, c/o Miss Marguerite Jackson, Montreal General Hospital
1926 etchings, 1926-30
197 Quebec
198 Champlain Street, Quebec
199 Cottage, Longforgan, Scotland
200 Ships
1930 282 Bermuda
283 Old work shops
284 City Hall, New York, 1654
285 Sailing yacht

JACOBI, OTTO REINHOLD
27 Feb 1812, Konisberg, Prussia 20 Feb 1901, Ardoch, N.D. AGO B EC H M Mo98 NGC R2 TB W78
addr: Toronto: 1880; 80 Summer Hill Ave, 1892-8
1880 2 Landscape
6 Falls of St Anne, near Quebec
16 The Splungen Torrent
25 The Splugen Pass (MBAM)
26 A solitude
33 Shawenegan Falls (Shewanegan, mispr)
34 View on the Mississipi, valley of the Ottawa, animals by A. Vogt
129 Landscape wc
148 Thousand Islands wc
1888 10 Scene on the Georgian Bay $84
37 Scene in the backwoods $84
93 Rock elms wc $90
120 In the bush wc $30
123 On Georgian Bay wc $40
129 Sunset wc $40
132 Burning brush wc $30
1889 135 Sunset in the woods wc $40
136 Evening in the north west wc $40
1892 91 Scene in the backwoods $84
92 Scene on Georgian Bay $84
1894 88 Sunset $30
89 Madoc Falls, St Maurice River $30
90 Near Fort William $40
1898 57 Boating on the Humber $50
58 Afternoon on the Humber $50

port: by M. Cary McConnell, 1895-82

JACOBS, MICHEL
10 Sep 1877, Montreal 4 Feb 1958, Rumson, N.J. B CWW61 F TB2 WWA56/obit 59, WWB34
addr: Montreal, 6 Beaver Hall Sq
1914 209 Portrait head
210 Samuel Cohn
211 Viola
435 The rock of all ages brass replica $40

JAENICKE, BEULAH IRENE (m Edward J. Rosen)
16 Jun 1918, Leader, Sask M
addr: Vancouver, 1103 Robson St
1938 63 Daffodils $32

JAMIESON, MARTHA GREENING
22 Jan 1918, Calgary M
addr: Kingston, Ont, 33 George St, 1944-55
1944 65 Freda Leibov $40
66 The new hat $25
1955 44 Comedy team $75

JANES, PHYLLIS HIPWELL (m Henry F. Janes)
15 Feb 1905, Alliston, Ont M WWA62
addr: Toronto, 320 Keewatin Ave
1960 56 Resignation $350

JANITSCH, MARGUERITE D.
b Québec M
addr: Québec, 1115 ave des Laurentides
1958 26 Nature morte à l'horloge $100

JAQUE, LOUIS (b Louis Jacques Beaulieu)
1 May 1919, Montréal M WWA84
addr: St Vincent de Paul, Qué, 3500 blvd Levesque, 1955-6. Montréal, 10520 rue Meilleur, 1958-61; Montréal, 1967-8
1955 117 En tant que dueront les fruits amers nm $85
1956 109 Le pêcher d'ombus-nourrices nm $85
1958 66 A Giorno nm $90
67 Port Bourgade nm $90
1960 177 Après le deluge gouache $185 (listed 1967, Jessie Dow prize)
178 Le monument perpétuel nm $65
1961 86 Tanagra illus nm purchase award (MBAM)
1967 32 Grégorienne. 1967 51 x 38
1968 130 Rythmopée No 5 39 1/2 x 32 $400
131 Module paramétrique No 3 38 x 51 $600
132 Diatons No 1 39 1/2 x 39 1/2 $500
133 Altimètre 32 x 39 1/2 $400

JAQUES, BETTY
addr: Montreal, 1639 Lincoln Ave, 1943. Westmount, 5 Park Place, Apt 7, 1947
1943 95 Death dance of an iris $25
1947 132 White cyclamen wc $25
133 African carving wc $25

JARVIS, LUCY MARY HOPE
27 Jul 1896, Toronto M
addr: Fredericton, N.B.
1932 135 Tangled bank by the sea wc $35

JASMIN, ANDRE
7 Dec 1922, Montreal CC2 M
addr: Montreal: 8479 Berri St, 1945; 8300 Lajeunesse, Apt 1A, 1950
1945 131 Les trois danseurs $150
1950 118 Petite fille à la fleur $90

JEAN, MARCEL
1 Feb 1937, Québec M
addr: Québec
1968 134 No 2150 dessin 24 x 30 $500
135 No 2160 dessin 22 x 22 $400

JEAN-LOUIS, DONALD CHARLES
17 May 1937, Ottawa AGO IO M
addr: Toronto, 67 Lowther Ave
1963 83 3 organic forms nm $80

JECKLEY, D. (Jectkey, D, same addr in Royal Canadian Academy 1920 exhibit)
addr: Montreal, 3167 St Denis St
1920 129 October evening
130 Sketch

JEEVES, BARRY RICHARD
addr: Montreal, 4600 Cumberland Ave
1955 118 Neglected nm $15

JEFFERIES, GERALD F.
1914, Halifax M

addr: Halifax, 31 Cornwallis St
1946 137 Unloading hay wc $40

JEFFERYS, CHARLES WILLIAM
25 Aug 1869, Rochester, Kent, Eng 8 Oct 1951, York Mills, Ont AGO CC2 CE CWW49 EC M Mo12 NGC PMC TB2 W78 WWA47
addr: Toronto: 402 Wellesley St, 1894-5, 1900; c/o H & J Mathews, 1898. New York, 53 W 24th St, 1901. Toronto: Medical Council Bldg, 1905; Toronto, 1908; 216 Garden Ave, 1909. York Mills, Ont, 1942
Jeffreys, 1894, 1895, 1901, 1908. Jeffries, 1905
1894 190 A day in June wc
1895 67 Afternoon at Quebec $30
167 Côte Beaupré, Québec wc $25
1898 159 Evening, Toronto Bay wc $35
160 November morning wc $35
1900 57 St Denis, Richelieu River $35
137 Pines at Sorel wc $25
1901 66 On the Richelieu $40
1905 71 Sundown in the pine wood $40
1908 212 Sundown at Keewatin wc $35
213 The Boulder, Lake of the Woods wc $35
1909 195 Church at St Joachim, Chateauguay wc $35
1942 87 Racketty Creek, Haliburton wc $150

JEFFERYS, JEAN ADAMS
addr: Toronto, c/o H & J Mathews
1898 161 A nocturne wc $25

JEMMETT, MARY ELLA MAUD MARTINEAU (m Douglas M. Jemmett)
20 Oct 1892, Cermisco, Italy
addr: Kingston, Ont, Elmhurst, 1946-7
1946 138 Mexican jug m tech $10
1947 134 Ships, Kingston Regatta temp $100

JEROME, JEAN-PAUL
19 Feb 1928, Montreal M TB3
addr: Montreal, 1879 Casgrain Ave, 1950-1
1950 151 Tête charcl $40
1951 101 Nature morte $200

JOBIN, IVAN
25 Jan 1885, Montreal M
addr: Montreal: 126A Mentana St, 1914-16; 1260 Mentana St, 1917; 757 Berri St, 1918-19; 173 St Joseph Blvd W, 1920; 732 Berri St, 1921; 278 Berri St, 1924-6
1914 212 Early morning, Ste Adèle wc $10
213 The eclipse, March 1914 pastel $25
1915 184 Le matin, Keeseville, N.Y. wc $50
185 Partie interiéure du Fort Chambly wc $50
186 La tempête wc $45
187 Ce qui reste de l'hiver, sur Mont Royal wc $10
188 L'orage pastel $75
1916 146 Paysage, Rivière des Prairies pastel $30
1917 173 L'été pastel $75
174 Lever de lune pastel $30
175 Le champ de blé pastel $25
1918 164 Grand moulin, St Eustache pastel $20
165 Lever de lune St Eustache $20
372 Le bain sculp $4
1919 369 La poseuse sculp $5
1920 131 Nudités pastel $75
1921 118 Le chemin de campagne $35
1924 280 La brise wd cut $5
281 Qui cherchez-vous? wd cut $5
1925 350 Un canadien français drwg
351 M. Edouard Montpetit wc cut
1926 201 La fuite en Egypte wd cut
202 M. Jean Flahault wd cut

JOHANSSON, LINNEA
addr: Montreal: 2050 McGill College Ave, 1934; 3449 Ontario Ave, 1937; 1245 Mackay St, 1938
1934 502 Portrait plaster
1937 463 Self portrait plaster $150
1938 195 Portrait study plaster

JOHNSON, BRUCE HENDERSON
18 Mar 1926, Toronto M
addr: Montreal, 4836 Grosvenor Ave
1960 179 Pretty girl bathing in the nude nm $400

JOHNSON, DOROTHY
addr: Toronto, 146 Dunn Ave
1932 136 Fall weather, Muskoka $125

JOHNSON, ELAINE

addr: Montreal: 4554 Old Orchard Ave, 1937; 2047 Victoria St, 1938-9. Westmount, 1375 Greene Ave, 1940-2
1937 152 Jean pastel
153 Mrs Dent Harrison, Jr wc min
1938 64 Isobel
1939 182 Beverley - Anne Harrison wc
183 Doris
184 The tired model $100
1940 152 Portrait of Betty
1941 95 Miss Meyer wc min $35
96 The teacher wc min $35
1942 88 Mrs Henry Fetherstonhaugh wc min
89 Mr Henry Fetherstonhaugh wc min

JOHNSON, HELEN G.
fl 1893-4 H
addr: Burlington, Vt, 204 Pearl St
1894 91 Chrysanthemums $50
92 Pigeons $25
93 Corn $20
94 Still life $20

JOHNSON, JEANNE see PAYNE-JOHNSON, JEANNE

JOHNSON, LUCY G.
addr: Montreal, 117 Metcalfe St
1894 191 A bit of beach, Murray Bay wc $20

JOHNSON, PAULINE F. (Mrs)
Juror
addr: Montreal, 4 Chelsea Pl, 1934-5
1934 502 Chang plaster
503 Mr Horio plaster
1935 465 Raymonde plaster
port: by Orson Wheeler, 1948-119

JOHNSTON, FRANCES ANNE (m George Franklin Arbuckle)
9 Oct 1910, Toronto CWW84 IO M
addr: Montreal, 4100 Côte des Neiges Rd, 1946-57. Toronto, 52 Lascelles Ave, 1960
1946 139 The jug and feather $200
140 Supper $300
141 Midsummer flowers $100
1947 135 South window $600
1949 50 Interior $400
51 Victorian sitting-room
1950 19 Great-grandmother's chair $325
1951 20 The saint, the lady and the knight $450
1952 21 Green and gold $350
1953 21 Still life and flowers $150
1954 46 Concerto grosse $100
1955 45 Bottles and gourds $350
1957 48 Pochette $300
1960 57 Still life $500
58 September $400

JOHNSTON, FRANCIS HANS (FRANZ)
19 Jun 1888 - 9 Jul 1949, Toronto AGO CC1 CE CWW48 EC M NGC PMC TB2/3
addr: Toronto, 2474 Yonge St
1927 86 Silver heights $300

JOHNSTON, FREDA see DREANY, FREDA

JOHNSTON, GRAHAM Eng
DBA
addr: Montreal, c/o J.C.A. Heriot, Esq, 104 Union Ave
1916 Official herald painter
335 Heraldic painting, achievement of arms

JOHNSTON, MARY
1889 38 A study table $100

JOHNSTONE, JOHN YOUNG
12 Nov 1887, Montreal 13 Feb 1930, Havanna M NGC TB3 W78
addr: Montreal: Art Association, 1911-13; 223 Ontario St W, 1915-21; 781 University St, 1922-5
1911 158 Indian maid b&w
159 Sketch b&w
1913 205 Sketch, Volendam $15
1915 189 Le Quai des Menétriers, Bruges $100 (NGC)
190 The lace makers of Bruges $100
191 Quai des Augustine, Bruges $100
192 Sketch of belfry b&w $12
193 Sketch of Chat-noir b&w $12
1916 147 Bonsecours Market $100 (NGC)
148 Early morning $100
149 La ville Close, Concarneau wc $15
150 Pont Aven, Bretagne wc $15
151 Going home $60
1917 176 Squaw, Bonsecours Market $150
177 Craig Street, Montreal $100

178 Two squaws, Montreal $100
179 Panet Street, Montreal, sketch $20
180 In the Bonsecours Market, sketch $20
181 On the rue des Carrières, sketch $20
1918 166 Bonsecours Market $200
167 Café d'Or, Paris $150
168 Cote de Beaupré $20
169 On rue des Carrières $20
170 Laiterie, Paris $20
1919 160 A sail boat, Beaupré, Que $125
161 The farm house, Weggie, Switzerland $40
162 Beupré, Quebec, sketch $25
163 View from the Rigi, Switzerland
164 Bruges, Belgium, sketch pastel $25
1920 132 Old courtyard, St Vincent Street $150
133, 135 St Joachim Road, sketch $50 each
134 Ste Anne de Beaupré, sketch $50
1921 119 The road, St Joachim wc $75
120 Old chateau, Chateau Richer $75
121 Pont Aven, Bretagne, sketch $60
122 Paris, France, sketch $60
1922 150 Le Bassin Louise à Québec $500 (NGC)
1923 125 Tell's Chapel, Switzerland, $60
126 Beaupré, Switzerland, sketch $60
1924 121 The road, St Joachim $500 (NGC)
122 Beaupré, Quebec, sketch $50
123 Murray Bay, sketch $75
1925 142 Côte de Beaupré $100
143 Below Quebec $75
144 Switzerland, sketch $75
145 Place Mouffetard, Paris $70

JONES, DENNIS GORDON
1932, London, Eng M
addr: Montreal, 2170 Bishop St
1965 10 Limpopo $225

JONES, EVAN
c 1896, Wallasey, Eng 5 Nov 1949
DBA
addr: Montreal: 34 Harvard Ave, 1928; 6321 Iberville St, 1934
1928 92 Renaissance well, Arquata Scrivia, Italy wc $25
303 Based on the purple orpine drwg
1934 158 On the Giudecca, Venice wc $30
159 On the Ponte Vecchio, Florence wc $15
453 Porta Santa Susanna, Perugia etch $7.50

JONES, FRANCES MARTHA (m Robert Victor Rosewarne)
15 Sep 1916, Smith Falls, Ont IO M
addr: Ottawa: 63 Lees Ave, 1956-7; 233 Argyle Ave, 1960
1956 110 The autumn land nm $25
111 The heart in the forest nm $15
1957 126 The cedar wood nm $25
1960 180 October nm $40
181 Forest visitation nm $40

JONES, HELEN
addr: Montreal: 312 Peel St, 1911; 289 Stanley St, 1913
1911 160 Montreal from the mountain wc $35
161 Hadrian's Villa, Rome wc $30
162 Petersfield, Cape Breton wc $15
163 Bordighera wc $15
1913 206,207 Sketch, Florence wc
208 Near Rome wc
209 On the mountain wc

JONES, HENRY WANTON
11 May 1925, Waterloo, Que M
addr: Westmount, 4166 Sherbrooke St W, 1951. Montreal: 1548 Stanley St, 1954-57; 2048 Stanley St, 1958-61. Montreal, 1967
1951 102 North light $85
103 Repas sur la table bleu $110
1954 47 The exile $125
48 Two musicians $150
1956 32 Painting in yellow $110
144 Figure sculp metal $100
1957 49 Red figure $155
50 Painting $185

1958 27 Boat $185
79 Reclining figure metal $110
1960 59 Still life $185
60 Interior with still life $300
1961 30 Interior with two figures illus $450 Hon mention 1967-33, 60 1/2 x 36 1/2 (Mr Sam Tata, Montreal)

JONES, HUGH GRIFFITH
3 Dec 1872, Randolph, Wis 16 Sep 1947, Montreal CE CWW36 M NGC PMC
addr: Montreal: King Edward Apts, 10 Oldfield Ave, 1909-22; 410 Drummond St, 1922; 276 Pine Ave W, 1924-9; 456 Pine Ave W, 1930; Château Apts, 1227 Sherbrooke St W, 1932-47
1909 196 North Dakota Bad Lands wc
197 Sand dunes, Oak Island wc
198 Evening, Hudson River wc
199 Breezy day, Fire Island wc
1910 195 Cloudy afternoon wc
196 Beach, Fire Island wc
197-8 Study for decoration
389 Porto Rico capitol, elevation competition
1911 164 After the storm, Gloucester wc $100
165 Morning on the plains wc $100
166 Fishing boats, Gloucester wc $100
167 Summer afternoon, New Jersey wc $100
168 Decorative study wc $100
1913 210 Lake Louise wc
211 Along the Columbia River wc
212 Late afternoon, Oak Beach, L.I. wc
213 Morning, Hudson River wc
1914 214 Passamaquoddy Bay, St Andrews
215 Evening wc
216 New London, Conn wc
1915 194-5 Sketch, Lachine Canal
196 Sketches, Canadian Rockies
197 Night, Hudson River
1916 152 Evening, Hudson River valley wc
153 Spring wc
1917 374-5 Fulford Memorial Home, Brockville, living hall, entrance
376 St John's Church, Moncton, N.B. photo
1918 171 St Joachim Road, Beaupré, Quebec
172 Late afternoon
173 The river
174 Evening shadows
394 Fulford Memorial Home, Brockville, Ont
1919 165 Late afternoon, Quebec
166 Autumn landscape, British Columbia
1920 136 Winter afternoon, Lake Superior
137 Evening, Lake Superior
138 Staten Island, New York
139 Milwaukee River, sketch
1921 123 Late afternoon, Charlemagne, Quebec
124 Orlean's shore, Quebec
125 Winter, Rainy Lake
1922 151 Cottage, Castle Coombe, England
152 Canterbury, England
367 Farm house, W.B. Somerset, Esq, Burlington, Ont
368 CPR station and office building, Moose Jaw, Sask
1924 124 Afternoon, lower St Lawrence wc
125 Interior, St Bartholomews, London wc
126 Evening, Iffley Church wc
127 Evening on the River Thames wc
1925 147 St Martin's Church Yard, Canterbury, England
1926 65 Rocks and surf, Gloucester wc
66 Gray day, Gloucester wc
67 Bushy Parks, evening wc
68 Chalk cliffs, Dover wc
1927 87 Winter haze, Lake Superior
88 Afternoon near Sudbury
89 Street in Rouen, France wc
209 Section of façade of a Canadian railway station, study
210 Montreal South Shore Bridge, St Catherine Street piers
211 Pazzi Chapel, Florence, sketch
212 San Marco, Venice, sketch
1928 93-6 Saguenay wc
1929 114 Valley, afternoon, near Georgeville

1930 113 Ramparts, Algiers wc
114 Winter day, Sicily wc
115 At Kasbah Gate, Algiers wc
116 Lost River Pass, White Mountains wc
1932 137 Distant chalk hills, Normandy
138 Capucini Monastery, Syracusa wc
139 Château Gaillard, Normandy wc
1935 163 Venice, lagoon, boats wc
164 A Venetian campo wc
165 A church in Siena wc
1936 214 The Diocletian Cloister, Rome wc
215 Ruins, Roman Theatre, Taormina wc
216 Evening, Cotswolds
217 Afternoon, the Clyde
1943 96 Dalmatian coast at Ragusa, Dubrovnik
1944 67 On the Ombla, Dalmatia
67A Cloister, Ragusa, Dubrovnik
1945 132 Dalmatian garden
133 Winter shadows
1946 142 An English church yard
1947 136 A road in Ragusa, Dalmatia
see also Ross, George Allen, 1916

JONES, MAXWELL W.
addr: Montreal, 8 Amesbury Ave
1937 154 Gertrude wc

JONES, RUPERT
18 Dec 1924, Sandys Parish, Bermuda M
addr: Westmount, 476 Roslyn Ave
1960 240 Diane illus plaster 1967-34 21"h Ladies Comm prize

JONGERS, ALPHONSE
17 Nov 1872, Mézières, France 2 Oct 1945, Montreal B CC1 M NGC TB Juror
addr: Montreal: Fraser Institute, 1897; 9 University Ave. 1898. Paris, 1900. New York, 1905-24. Montreal, Ritz Carlton Hotel, 1925-45 Juror
1897 75 Portrait of a lady
76 Maxime Ingres, Esq
77 Andrew Macphail, Esq, MD
78 Lt Col Jeffrey Burland
79 Portrait, study
160 Sketch, F.R. Heaton pen & ink
1898 59 Robert Craik, MD LLD, Dean of Faculty of Medicine, McGill University
60 Mrs A.A. Browne
61 Mrs Yates
62 Mrs Masson
63 Mrs Fayette Brown
64, 68 Portrait
65 W. Scott, Esq (MBAM)
66 J.G. Adami, MD
67 Miss Adami
69 Study
1900 58 Mrs F..L. Wanklyn and child
59 Mrs J.G. Adami
60 Mrs Jeffrey Burland
61 Mrs C.W. Colby
62 Dr C.W. Colby, MA
63 Mrs William Hope
64 Mrs A. Macphail
65 Mrs E.J. Major
66 Portrait
67 A child, sketch
1905 72 Portrait of a child
1924 128 Sir Andrew Macphail
1925 146 Mrs Angus
1926 69 Lord Atholstan
70 Madame Henri Rainville
71 Panny
1927 90 William Hope, Esq, RCA
1929 115 Sir Herbert S. Holt
116 Mrs E.G. M. Cape
117 George E. Armstrong, CMG MD
1930 117 Mrs MurrayVaughan
118 Elwood B. Hosmer, Esq
119 Portrait of a boy
1931 137 W.W. Chipman, Esq MD LLD
138 John L. Gilmour, Esq
1932 140 Sir Charles Gordon
141 Madame Paul Rodier
1933 160 Dr E.W. Archibald
161 Norman Dawes, Esq
162 Miss Mimi Labrecque
1934 160 Col George Cantlie
161 J.E. Aldred
162 Dr Lionel Lindsay
163 Miss Jennie Webster
1935 166 Ward C. Pittfield, Esq
1936 218 Lord Duncannon
1937 155 D. Forbes Angus, Esq
156 Mr René Turch, Consul General of France
1938 65 Dr Chas. F. Martin
66 Air Vice Marshall Bishop
67 Mrs Howard Pillow
68 Vicomte Roger de Roumefort
1939 185 Hon Chief Justice Greenshields

186 F. Ronald Graham, Esq
187 Master Hugh Hallward
1940 153 J.D. Johnson, Esq
154 Dr Norman Brown
155 Miss Thériault
1941 97 Mrs R.F. Graham
98 Salome
1942 90 Madame Thériault
1943 97 Leontine
98 My friend Jerry
99 Sub Lieut Edmond Joly de Lotbinière
100 Trallero
1944 68 Mrs Leo Timmins
69 Earl Spafford, Esq
70 Himself
1945 134 The blue sweater
135 George B. Foster, Esq
136 Louise Thiesen, Esq
port: by Henri Hébert, 1926-241

JORDAN, MARION CURTIS
addr: Montreal, 2278 St Catherine St
1901 248 Bacchus
249 Vase, blue underglaze
250 Modeled tile
251 Beer stein
252 Vase, blue underglaze $10
253 Brown vase $5
254 Cup & saucer $2
255 Vinegar cruet

JORGENSEN, FLEMMING
29 May 1936, Aalborg, Denmark M WWA84
addr: Victoria: 60 Boyd St, 1960; 1268 Reynolds Rd, 1961; 3904 Cadboro Bay Rd, 1964
1960 182 Harbour at night nm $75
1961 31 Resting figure $125
1964 43 Spring morning $300

JORON, M. F. (Mrs)
addr: Westmount, 464 Elm Ave
1940 156 Peonies $100

JOST, OTTILLE see PALM, OTTILLE

JOUBERT, LEON
b Quimper, France fl 1876-1920 B TB
1883 107 La lande de Kerongosquer

JOUDRY, B. KENNATHA (Mrs)
addr: Montreal, 4251 Marcil Ave, Apt 2
1936 219 Winter $75

JOURDAIN, JACQUES
6 Jan 1931, Trois Rivières M
addr: Cap-de-la-Madeleine, Qué, 433B rue Notre Dame
1960 61 Petit Champlain, Québec $200

JUDAH, DORIS MINETTE TROTTER (m E. Lionel Judah)
7 Mar 1887, Montreal d 1965 CNS36 M
addr: Montreal: 99 Durocher St, 1919-20; 744 Shuter St, 1925; 3638 Durocher St, 1933-40
1919 sculpture 1919-40
370 Miss Margaret James at study
371 J. Dawson Morphet, Esq
1920 301 Lt Col W. Watt Burland, DSO
302 Ellen, daughter of Dr Alfred Stanfield, FRSC
1925 392 Mrs Thomas Caverhill
1933 517 Juliette plaster
1934 504 A portrait bust plaster
505 Healing hands plaster $100
1935 466 Etudiante plaster $100
467 Masque orientale plaster $25
1936 597 Pipe dreams plaster $50
1937 464 George M. Brewer, FAGO, as Dr Raymon Lull in 'The Spanish miracle' plaster
1940 411 Molly Harrow-Erickson, PhD plaster $100

JUDGE, ALICE ELIZABETH PHILLIPS
20 Jan 1930, Montreal
addr: Westmount, 302 Grosvenor Ave
1953 98 The pear tree wc $25

JUDSON, WILLIAM LEE Amer
1 Apr 1842, Manchester, Eng 1928, Los Angeles AAA28/obit 29 B F H
1883 5 Indian Beach, Grand Manan wc
11 An arrangement in primaries and gray wc
123 Rolling in wealth
140 Summer morning on the Thames, Ont
1885 2 Cabbage
32 Going to market
1889 175 Roses pastel $40
176 Portrait pastel $100

JULIEN, GRATIA
addr: Ottawa, 51 Sweetland Ave, 1936-44
1936 220 Lys et lupins pastel
221 Des antiques pastel

1937 157 Une rose crayon & wc $7.50
414 Etude drwg
1944 71 La cour pastel

JULIEN, OCTAVE HENRI
14 May 1852, St Roch, Que 17 Sep 1908, Montreal CC2 CE H M R2 W78
addr: Montreal, 1908
1908 92 Old French Canadian auction sale
1916 deceased
154 Josette, Ste Rose wc
155 Le paysan wc
156 La messe de minuit wc
157 Allant au marché wc

JULIEN, RACHEL
addr: Montreal, 264 de l'Epee Ave
1932 142 Tête décorative gouache $10

JUNEAU, DENIS
30 Sep 1925, Verdun, Que B CWW84 M TB3
addr: Verdun, 5547 Bannantyne Ave
1952 134 Femme lisant charcl $20

JUTRAS, JOSEPH
18 Feb 1894, Montreal M
addr: Montreal: 1421 Papineau Ave, 1922; 1739 Papineau Ave, 1923; 5270 Papineau Ave, 1926; 2633 Masson St, 1936
1922 153 Scène d'hiver $125
1923 128 Coin de la Seigneury Lussier $35
129 Residence de la ferme St Gabriel $250
1926 72 On Sherbrooke Street West $75
1936 222 Ferme McAvoy pastel $10

K

KACERE, JOAN BRIERLY
addr: Winnipeg, 502 River Ave
1953 105 Gamut drwg $50

KACERE, JOHN
addr: Winnipeg, School of Art, University of Manitoba, 1951-2
1951 104 Image No 5 $150
1952 135 Oratorio col intaglio $40

KAHANE, ANNE (m Robert Langstadt)
1 Mar 1924, Vienna AGO CC1 CE M NGC TB3 WWA80 WWB54 Juror
addr: Montreal: 3940 Côte des Neiges Rd, 1947; 2425 Maplewood Ave, 1948; 4046 Maplewood Ave, 1949-55; 3125 Maplewood Ave, 1956-9; 3281 Forest Hill Ave, 1960; 3794 Hampton Ave, 1963-5; Montreal, 1967
1947 337 Father and son sculp
338 Starving youth sculp
1948 19 Still life $100
1949 52 The evening paper $150
174 The pigeon copper $75
1950 158 Bird wire $40
159 Three figures mortar $60
1951 145 Cellist mortar $90
1952 146 Seated man wc $150
147 Man with child wc $150
1954 135 Three figures sculp $225
1955 146 The rider wc $250
147 Queue wd $250 (NGC)
1956 145 Passerby wc $500 (AE)
146 Ball game 1955 wd $350
1957 161 Park bench wd $450
1959 51 Follow the leader wd $750
1967-35, 38h. Ladies Comm prize (Winnipeg Art Gallery)
1960 183 Head $50
1963 106 Distant figures wd $1,600
1964 124 Falling man wd $500
1965 39 Lonnie Lohn wd & metal

KAISER, RITA ELIZABETH
8 Nov 1923, Montreal
addr: St Eustache-sur-le-Lac, Que 45 11th St
1962 61 The happy time nm $60

KAKINUMA, THOMAS
4 Oct 1908, Tochigi-Ken, Japan M
addr: South Burnaby, B.C, 4607 Irmin St, 1959-60
1959 52 Children at play ter cot $50
1960 241 Madonna and child ter cot $100
242 Cityscape cer $100

KALENDA, JOSEPH
addr: Montreal, 3850 Côte St Catherine Rd
1949 131 Grain elevator wc $100

KALMAN, MAXWELL MYRON
31 May 1906, Montreal
addr: Montreal: 630 Dorchester St W,

1938: 4914 Victoria Ave, 1941
1938 139-40 Residence drwg
1941 Kalman & Fisher
264 School, Waverley and Fairmount Streets, Montreal

KAPLAN, JULIUS
addr: Montreal, 5164 Jeanne Mance St, 1934-6
1934 164 The tea service $45
1936 223 Our back lane wc $50
549 Male head, study drwg $40

KARMAN, ROBERT
17 Feb 1933, Montreal M
addr: Scarborough, Ont 51 Gaiety Dr, 1958-60
1958 28 Forlorn $80
1960 62 Quatre bateaux $225
63 The snow fence $125

KAUNOT, HANS
addr: Montreal, 3429 Famille St
1960 243 Horse composition ter cot $100

KEEFER, EMAIME (m T.C. Keefer)
addr: Westmount, 4323 Western Ave, 1935-40
1935 167 Still life $60
1940 157 Candlelight $50

KEENE, CALEB
1862, Stourbridge, Eng Aug 1954, Oakville, Ont M
addr: Westmount: 1215 Greene Ave, 1914; 14 Oldfield Ave, 1915-16
1914 217 Groot Drakenstein Mountain, South Africa
218 Hex River Valley, South Africa
219 Still life
1915 198 Lac Gauthier, Laurentians $195
199 Red lacquer cabinet $450
200 Black lacquer screen $300
1916 158 The falls, Cache River, Laurentians $200
159 On the Boule River, Laurentians $35
160 In the Laurentians $20

KEENE, LOUIS
21 Sep 1888, London, Eng M
addr: Westmount, 1215 Greene Ave
1914 220 The King George V giving a broadside
221 The Battle of the Whip and the Broom wc $250
222 The Battle of Camperdown wc $250
223 The lights of the Halfway House, Cape Town wc $250

KEENE, VIOLET (m Harold E. Perinchief)
1893, Rosehill, Bath, Eng
addr: Montreal, 14 Oldfield Ave
1915 201 Lefroy Glacier, Canadian Rockies wc

KEILLOR, NELLIE
addr: Sudbury, Ont, 188 College St
1950 68 Blind River wc $25

KELEMEN, NICHOLAS J.
addr: Toronto, 190 Heward Ave
1947 137 Island scene $200

KELLY, ELIZABETH MAY
b 1888, Clarkson, Ont
addr: Clarkson, Ont, 1933-40
1933 458 Across the bay, Allendale, Ont col pr $5
459 February col pr $5
1934 454 Birches and maple col pr $10
455 The old pine lino cut $7
1935 416 The afterglow col pr $8
1937 415 Sunset col pr $7
416 August afternoon lino cut $5
1940 368 The barren mountains of Haiti col pr $7
369 Old boat house, Cobourg, Ont nm $7

KELLY, HANNAH RUSK (m Samuel L.P. Kelly)
1860, Elderslie, Ont H
addr: Hamilton, Ont, 18 East Ave
1924 Kelley, mispr
129 June min $100

KELLY, JOHN DAVID
15 Oct 1862, Gore's Landing, Ont 27 Dec 1958, Toronto AGO H M W78
addr: Toronto, 461 King St W
1913 214 Storm on Lake Nipissing b&w $75
215 The woodsman b&w $50

KELSEY, CHARLES WILLIAM
19 Apr 1877, London, Eng 27 Jan 1975, Montreal M PMC
addr: Montreal, 155 Mance St, 1923. Westmount, 19 Staynor Ave, 1924-5. Montreal, 278 West Hill Ave, 1926-8. Westmount: 4148 Dorchester St W, 1929-34; 4475 Western Ave, 1935-8; 136 Clandeboye Ave, 1939-45
1923 228 The first missionary from the east, forming the community of Glastonbury, Eng des $500
229 The angel of life des $200
230 The first four incidents in the life of our Lord $100
1924 130 The Crucifixion of our Lord $200
131 Glace Bay, Cape Breton $60
282 Christ in glory as King of of Life st gl window wc
1925 352 Chaucer's portrait, title page, and 'Story of the Chanticleer' pen & ink
353 The Nativity st gl cart
1926 203 Joshua st gl
204 Proposed east window, Trinity Memorial Church
1927 91 The two gentlemen of Verona, Shakespeare wc $250
276 The Virgin and Child, with adoring angels st gl des
277 The story of the Rosary st gl des
1928 97 Sylvia, daughter of artist
98 John and Sebastian Cabot sight land off north coast of America, 1497 wc $200
1929 118 'My heart is singing like a bird', Christina Rossetti's poem wc $200
245 Worthington Memorial, Christ raising Jairus' daughter nm
246 Reredos and panelling, St Mathias Church, Westmount photo
1930 120 King Arthur and his Knights wc $200
286 Raising of Jairus' daughter, St Barnabas Church st gl sketch
1931 139 St Jeanne d'Arc at age of twelve, listening to the voices of St Michael, St Catherine and St Margaret to save France $1,000
284 Verdun United Church 3 cart
285 The Resurrection st gl window
1932 143 The sleeping beauty wc $50
144 Early spring $50
401 St Luke's United Church, st gl window
1933 386 St Barnabas Church, window, The Nativity, Crucifixion Resurrection st gl cart
1934 165 David, prepared to meet Goliath $40
166 Miss Murray
1935 168 The cigarette girl wc $125
1936 224 A worker of Sir Wilfred Grenfell Mission, Canadian Labrador $200
225 The letter $125
550 The magi and shepherds st gl drwg
1937 158 The dancer wc $75
1938 167 Fraser window, sketch des & drwg
1939 355 Windows, Diocesan College Chapel photo
1940 158 Château de Ramezay wc $50
370 Stained glass window des pen & wc
1941 234 Medallion window des
1943 101 Decoration of sanctuary des
1944 140 Pat Christie window, Erskine Church des drwg
1945 260 St Paul's Church, Knowlton, Que, Nativity st gl des 3drwg
see also, Nobbs, Percy E, 1925

KELSEY, DORA see WOODHEAD, DORA

KELSEY, LEONARD EDGAR
12 Dec 1883, London, Eng 3 Jul 1975, Vancouver M
addr: Montreal, 2155 Esplanade Ave, 1914. Montreal West, 328 Ballantyne Ave, 1934-47
1914 224 Bookplate des b&w $20
1934 167 Thatched cottages, Bury St Edmonds wc $45
1935 169 Log boom, Lac Tremblant wc $35
1936 226 Sunset, Cache River wc $25
1943 102 Mont Rolland, St Adèle wc $35
1945 137 On Gouin Boulevard wc $55
1947 138 Musical romance, Molson Stadium wc $100

KEMP, FLORENCE see PROCTOR, FLORENCE

KEMP, JAMES ALEXANDER

6 Oct 1914, Toronto CWW70 IO M
addr: London, Ont, 519 Canterbury Rd, RR3
1955 46 Figure with mandolin $160

KEMP, V. ELIZABETH
addr: Montreal, 900 Sherbrooke St W, 1937-40
1937 417 Kentucky sisters copper plate etch $10
418 The mouth organ copper plate etch $10
419 Spring exhibition dry pt $5
420 Armenian dry pt $5
1938 69 Hay cart
70 West wind, Cacouna, Que
168 Taxi fare etch $10
169 Mount Rolland Station, Que etch $7
1939 188 Mud flats, Cacouna $50
407 Express dry pt $10
1940 371 Skiers' snack bar etch $10

KENNEDY, GARRY NEILL
6 Nov 1935, St Catharines, Ont CE M
addr: Halifax
1968 136 Untitled laminated plastic 48 x 96 $700

KENNEDY, JAMES
b 1884
addr: Montreal, 792 Shuter St, 1914-16. Westmount, 432 Grosvenor Ave, 1932-3
1914 225 Winter evening wc
226 Place d'Armes Square wc
1916 161 Dominion Square, Montreal wc
1932 402 Lachine Canal lino cut unfr $4
1933 387 Watson Art Galleries
460 Greeting card lino cut

KENNEDY, JEAN M.
addr: Montreal, 112 Crescent St
1922 154 Sketch near Ste Agathe pastel $15

KENNEDY, SYBIL
13 Aug 1899, Quebec CWW73 M NGC TB3
addr: Montreal: 3600 Atwater Ave, 1929; 1321 Sherbrooke St W, 1931. Westmount, 1215 Greene Ave, 1945-6. Montreal, 3940 Côte des Neiges Rd, 1947; Dominion Galleries, 1438 Sherbrooke St W, 1956. New York, 64 E 94th St, 1961
1929 375 Statuette plaster $100
1931 424 Coloured boy plaster $100
1945 279 Sailor plaster, bronze $225
1946 287 Mother and child bronze $300
1947 339 'Cellist bronze $450
1956 147 Patient woman bronze $675
148 Young mother bronze $250
1961 115 Girl reading bronze $1,500

KENNEY, GAIL
addr: Montreal, 3558 Clark St
1964 125 Birth of a bird soapstone $150

KENNY, GWENN
addr: Ottawa, 372 McKay St
1955 119 Still life, fruit nm $50

KERGOMMEAUX, DUNCAN ROBERT CHASSIN DE
15 Jul 1927, Premier, B.C. CC1 CWW84 IO M NGC TB3 WWA84
addr: Ottawa: 15 Chestnut St, 1956; 49 Cherrywood Dr, 1962-64
1956 15 Structure of a night forest $200
1962 6 Landscape $350
1963 17 No 18/62 $350
1964 22 No14/63 $750

KERR, ESTELLE MURIEL
16 Apr 1879, Toronto Nov 1971, Toronto H Mo12
addr: Toronto, 80 Spadina Rd
1923 130 The costume ball $200

KERR, GERTRUDE
addr: Toronto, 69 Madison Ave
1912 216 Study, girl's head $30
217 Newlyn harbour slip $25
218 Sketch, Polperro harbour wc $25

KERR, ILLINGWORTH HOLEY
20 Aug 1905, Lumsden, Sask CC1 CE CWW84 M NGC TB2/3
addr: Montreal, 2031 Jeanne Mance St, 1939. Calgary, Coste House, 1948
1939 189 Soho, London wc $40
190 Storm over the Cotswolds wc $40
191 Bitter aloes, La Plage, France wc $35
408 Beech woods, Hampshire reed pen $35
1948 82 Prairie road wc $60

KERR, RONALD
addr: St Lambert, Que: 24 Mercille Ave, 1923; 104 Birch Ave, 1924-5. Outremont, Que, 1056 Durocher St, 1926. Montreal: 820 Troie Ave, 1927-31; 6554 Durocher St, 1933-46; 5591 Côte des Neiges Rd, 1947
1923 pastel, 1923-47
131 Winter, Longueuil $15
132 February morning $15
1924 132 The yard in winter $25
1925 148 Fifth Avenue $20
149 Street, Quebec $20
1926 73 A beach on the Ottawa $15
1927 92 The backyard
1930 121 Suburban park $15
1931 140 The river in June $15
1933 163 The veil of evening $15
164 Winter's gold and blue $15
1934 168 Deep winter $25
169 March sunshine $30
1935 170 March shadows $20
171 Houses, St François de Sales $20
1936 227 Noon in January $10
1937 159 February afternoon $20
160 Sunlight on the flats $20
1938 71 Suburban winter scene $25
1939 192 Village church $25
1940 159 Thaw after the first snow $25
160 Roofs $25
1941 99 Below Cartierville $25
1943 103 Early morning car $25
104 The barn in January $25
1944 72 The last snow $25
1946 143 Winter silhouette $25
144 Suburban vista $25
1947 139 Corridor $30
140 The cliff edge $30

KERR-LAWSON, JAMES see LAWSON, JAMES KERR

KETS, A
addr: Westmount, 1240 Greene Ave
1925 150 Manchu antiquary $800
354 Manchu old man drwg $350

KETTLE, HORACE GARNARD
14 Dec 1906, London, Eng M WWA53
addr: Toronto, Upper Canada College
1940 161 January thaw wc $40
162 Ontario landscape, near Huntsville wc $40

KEYSER, NICOLE DE
2 Nov 1936, Ostende, Belgium
addr: Montreal, 240 Milton St
1963 18 Composition I $300

KIDD, JOSEPH M.
Athlone, Ont fl 1892-1905 H
addr: New York, 215 W 57th St
1894 95 Shady trees in a harvest field $50
96 Wheat sheaves near Athlone $35

KIERAN, ALBERT L.
addr: Beaurepaire, Que, 72 St Louis Ave
1940 163 Animal decoration, deer wc $20

KIERAN, PHILIP PETER
30 Apr 1888, Dublin
addr: Beaurepaire, Que, 72 St Louis Ave, 1933-43
1933 461 Group of book plates engr
1934 456 Australian birds dry pt etch $10
1935 172 Beta splendins dec wc $25
1936 228 The spinnaker pastel $25
229 Gaspé fishermen, Percé $40
1937 161 Laurentian valley, Huberdeau pastel $25
1938 170 Nude etch $10
1940 164 Little Magog Lake $25
1942 91 Wind and rain pastel $40
1943 105 Torpedoed dry pt
106 HMCS Assiniboine attacking sub in fog nm

KILGOUR, ANDREW WILKIE
1868, Kirkcaldy, Scot 28 May 1930, Strathmore, Que M NGC TB3
addr: Montreal: 176 Fairmont Ave, 1911-21, 1924; 84 St François Xavier St, 1922-3. Outremont, 1445 Van Horne Ave, 1925-6. Montreal, 275 Craig St, 1927. Outremont, 963 Hartland Ave, 1928-9. Montreal, 1070 Bleury St, 1930
1911 169 Daffodils $150
170 Unloading bricks, on the Thames $80
330 Blue plaque, teasel des $60
1912 219 A mild spell in December $50
220 A fresh morning $30

221 Dawn, a summer idyll $70
222 This winter's weather it waxeth cold, and it freezeth on every hill $60
1913 216 George Booth, Esq
217 In the Laurentians $150
218 The mill at Sixteen Island Lake $25
219 Morning, the mill at Sixteen Island $25
1914 227 Portrait of a curler
228 Old canal, Lachine $80
229 Evening, Fraser's Point $35
1915 202 Evening reflections, Carillon $75
203 Snow flurry, Laurentians $30
204 Winter's ragged hand relaxes $30
205 October afternoon, Lachine $30
1916 162 Over the house-tops $30
163 Close of a winter's day $50
164 Choir girl
165 By the margin of the pond wc $20
1917 182 Study of a head $30
183 Pearl $50
1918 175 Lemay's Island, Lake St Francis $100
176 An old Contemptible $50
177 Portrait study
178 The fishers shack, evening $20
179 Dorothy
180 Pauline
1919 167 L'été $150
168 The bather $150
169-70 Portrait study
171 Cover design, red & black (Veteran Ltd) wc
1920 140 Spring's carpet $350
141 Gray morning, River Rouge $35
142 Autumn afternoon, River Rouge $35
143 On the North River, St Andrews $35
1921 126 The lopped cedars $200
127 September, Fraser's Point $80
128 The bridge at Ste Anne's $40
129 Summer skies $40
1922 155 The graduation play princess $350
156 The last of the snow, Laurentians $80
157 E.I. Parry, Esq
158 March, Sixteen Island Lake $40
1923 133 Frosty morning wc $35
134 November in the Laurentians wc $35
135 Thanksgiving wc $35
136 Autumn in the Laurentians wc $35
1924 133 October's misty veil $300
134 The mountain road $300
283 Music cabinet, dec panels temp $175
1925 151 December, Morin Heights $150
152 On the North River $150
1926 74 The icy fringe $150
75 December afternoon $50
1927 93 The road to Father's Rest
1928 99 Forecast, rain or snow $125
100 March evening, the break-up $125
101 Winter's thraldom broken $125
102 Early snow $50
1929 119 March morning, Black Creek $125
120 Evening shadows, North River $125
121 October morning, Little Chub $150
122 Winter's reign is waning $150
1930 122 January morning in Laurentians $250
123 Follow the leader $200
124 Winter sunlight $100

KILLAM, MABEL see DAY, MABEL

KILPIN, LEGH MULHALL
5 Nov 1853, Ryde, Isle of Wight 3 Nov 1919, Montreal DBA H M RA
addr: Westmount, 1908. Montreal: 147A Stanley St, 1909-11; 3 Beaver Hall Sq, 1912-13; 203 Esplanade Ave, 1914. Westmount: 4125 Sherbrooke St W, 1915-17; 4472 Sherbrooke St W, 1918-19
1908 214 John Ogilvie, Esq qc $200
215 Normandy peasant wc $75
291 Set of 5 miniatures
292 Miss Norah Bailey min
293 Miss Adelaide Neilson min
294 Miss Ivy Moss min
295 Mr W. Smith min
296 Master J. Gordon min
297 Miss Reid min
298 Child head gold frame with pearls
1909 200 Lady Van Horne wc

201 Mrs Kilpin wc
202 Twixt winter and spring wc
203 Ste Agathe des Monts wc $65
204 Frost and fog on the Thames $135
1910 199 Miss Kilpin wc $250
200 Miss Adami wc
201 Pearl of the maelstrom wc $150
202 The mower $160
203 October morning, Normandy $140
1911 171 Muriel
172 On St Maurice River $50
173 Artist's mother at 93 wc
174 Snipe wc $80
1912 223 Tadousac Bay
224 On the Saguenay
225 Agnes
226 Hetty Sorel wc $200
227 On the St Lawrence $120
228 Fog lifting, Saguenay wc $50
1913 220 The coming storm wc $300
221 Rising moon wc $200
222 Shade and sunshine wc $250
223 Snow in the Laurentians wc $80
224 The bride $250
225 Miniature wax relief $100
1914 230 Seeding potatoes $120
231 Peace $100
232 Homeward $75
233 Chums $65
234 Candies wc $160
235 A London fog pastel $80
1915 206 Late J.B. Learmont, Esq
207 Inspiration $200
208 The temple of fame wc $250
209 The hill farm wc $200
1916 166 A good one wc $200 (NGC)
167 Memphremagog Lake wc
1917 184 Owl's Head, Memphremagog wc $200
185 Piedmont Bridge wc $125
186 Bridge, Cartierville etch $20
187 Log mill, Cartierville etch $20
188 Coming storm etch $20 (or $60 for set 186-188)
1918 181 The back gate $200
182 Farm at Lesage pastel $175
183 Moonrise $200
184 Devil's Bridge, St Gothard etch $30
185 St Anne de Beaupré etch $25
186 St Joachim etch $25
187 Italian fishing village etch $30
188 The garden wall $30
189 At Lands End $30
190 On the Thames $30
1919 172 In Flanders fields where poppies grow $350
173 Dreamland $200
174 The fringe of the wood mono $30
175 Near Dorval mono $30
176 In Cambridge Marshes etch $20
177 Richmansworth etch $20
178 Off St Ives, Cornwall etch $15
1921 late (Mrs L.M. Kilpin, 174 Hampton Ave, Montreal)
130 Laurentian farm $80 (NGC)
131 Spring morning wc $50

KIMBER, HETTY DONNE
c 1854, Oxford, Eng 6 Jun 1946, Sydney, N.S. AAA1900 H
addr: Sydney, N.S. 1891-98. Montreal, 50 Ontario St, 1900. Sydney, 1905-14. Montreal, 50 Ontario St, 1918. Sydney, 88 Park St, 1920-22
1891 163 Montreal wc
164 In Cape Breton wc
1895 168 Near Sydney, Cape Breton wc $20
169 On the River Charles, Dedham, Mass wc $18
170 A field of golden rod wc $15
1897 161 October day in the woods wc $25
162 Willows on the River Charles wc $17.50
163 Sydney harbour in the winter wc
1898 162 A Louisburg moor wc $30
163 Squall, East River, New York wc $15
164, 167 Evening on the East River, New York wc $15, np
165 Wind and city dust, East River, New York wc $15
166 A breezy day in summer, Cape Breton wc
1900 138 The old orchard wc $18
1905 161 Evening stillness, Adirondacks wc $35
1908 216 Mist rising, River Charles wc $16

217 Mother Brook wc $12
218 Bridge on the Charles wc $10
1909 205 A breezy point wc $15
206 Storm, valley of the Margaree, Cape Breton wc $15
207 A Cape Breton homestead wc $15
208 Evening wc $15
1910 204 The McLean farm, Sydney wc $15
205 The home field wc $15
206 The winding Margaree wc $10
1911 175-79 Winter in the Adirondacks wc $35, $15, $12, $12, $10
1913 226 The woods, Lake Palcid wc $25
227 From the I.C.R. wc $25
228 Grand Narrows wc $15
229 Whycocomagh, C.B. wc $15
1914 236 Cape Breton woods wc $30
237 Dawn in the mountains wc $30
1918 191 The brook wc
192 Sidney River, C.B. wc $15
193-96 Sketch wc $10 each
1920 144 Cape Breton woods wc $30
145 Near Woodstock, Vermont wc $18
1922 159 Winter in the Adirondacks wc $30

KING, ADDISON H. (Mrs)
addr: Montreal, 249 Mountain St
1916 379 Vase, matt blue with white birds $15

KING, ETHEL M.
1878, Prescott, Ont
addr: Westmount: 17 Melbourne Ave, 1901-9; 2 Belvedere Rd, 1910-15
1901 135 Rocks, Kennebunk Port wc $10
136 Old windmill, Lachine wc $10
1903 191 Pine woods, Kennebunk Port wc $25
293 Ornamental plate
294 Miniature on china
295 Minatures, fancy heads
296 Tall vase
1905 311 Cup & saucer
312 Vase, pansies
313 Sugar bowl
1906 410 Wall plate, fancy head
411 Vase, figure subject
412 Three dessert plates
413 Vase, nasturtiums
1908 218A A shady pool wc $20
389 Vase, figure subject $15
390 Bureau set, 5 pieces
391 Bonbon dish $3
392 Fancy buttons, set of 5 $3
393-4 Fancy buttons, set of 4 $2.50 each
1909 209 Surf, Biddeford nm $25
210 Westmount Public Library nm $12
50 Vase, figure $45
51 Spring scene, framed $40
52 Vase $8
53 Vase, yellow roses $4
54 Bonbon dish $3
55-6 Cup & saucer $5.50, $4
57 Fancy buttons, pink roses, 4 $3
58 Fancy buttons, violets, 3 $2.25
59 Fancy buttons, yellow roses, 3 $2
60 Fancy buttons, small roses, 4 $2
1910 207 A shady corner, Westmount Park wc $25
208 Ruins, old Ville Marie Convent wc $10
1911 180 November afternoon wc $20
181 The house in the snow wc $20
182 A grey day in the woods wc $25
331 Tea caddie $5.50
332 Cup & saucer $4.50
1912 229 A hillside $25
230 A summer day, Beaupré $25
1913 230 Grey day, St Andrews $50
231 Autumn morning, St Andrews wc $25
232 First touch of frost wc $8
1914 238 A snowy evening $30
239 The two poplars $18
240 Evening wc $20
1915 210 Winter twilight $75
211 A snowy evening $50

KINGSLEY, ALBERT
addr: Ottawa, 68 Cedars, Eastview 1940-3
1940 165 Village sur le Richelieu $125
166 L'enterrement $125
1941 100 Festival
1943 107 Le déjeuner

KINNAIRD, F. GERALD Eng
fl 1864-85 DBA G TB1
1885 Kinnair, mispr
21 Not for you

KINNEY, ALICE R.

addr: New York, 25 Madison Ave
1892 178 La France roses wc $35
179 Mermet roses wc $40

KINNIS, WILLIAM GILBERT
1921, Trail, B.C. M
addr: Montreal, 1158 Beaver Hall Sq, 1950. St Hilaire, Que, 12 Desrochers Ave, 1960
1950 119 Landscape at Bair St Paul $80
152 Seated figure drwg $25
1960 64 River at Baie St Paul $100

KINSMAN, KATHARINE NIXON BELL (m Ronald Desmond Lewis Kinsman)
1909, Los Angeles M
addr: Town of Mount Royal, Que, 1270 Regent Rd, 1949. Montreal, 4870 Côte des Neiges Rd, 1964
1949 132 Landscape gouache
1964 93 Vieille maison, Montréal nm $100

KINTON, E. JERRINE WELLS (Mrs)
1892, Waterloo, Ont M
addr: Toronto, 433 Durie St, 1932-3
1932 145 Hungry Bay, Bermuda $175
342 Kitchener Public Library st gl window
403 Borgarfjorthur, Iceland wd cut $6
1933 388 Stained glass drwg

KIRBY, EMMA
addr: Ottawa, 194 Maria St
1894 97 Still life

KIRSHNER, SAMUEL S.
addr: Montreal: 628 St Catherine St W, 1925-6; 69 Drummond St, 1927; 1475 St Catherine St W, 1929
1929 153 Street scene in Montreal pastel
154 Montreal harbour pastel $25
1926 242 Adolphe sculp
243 Study sculp
244 Thos Bach K.M. McAnespie bust
1927 309 Max Panteleieff, baritone, as Boris Godunoff sculp
1929 376 Mr D. Sylvers plaster
377 Ancienne femme plaster $200
378 Young man plaster $200

KITCHENER, MADGE
addr: Westmount, 7 Holton Ave
1913 233 Jeanette $50

KIYOOKA, HARRY MITSUO
18 Feb 1928, Calgary CC2 M
addr: Winnipeg, 289 Assiniboine Ave, 1953. Calgary, 1968
1953 79 Ascension $150
1968 acry polymer
137 The horizontal centre 46 x 70 $1,000
138 Horizontal interchange 46 x 70 $1,000
139 Dechevron 46 x 66 $1,000
140 Green tangents 46 x 66 $1,000

KIYOOKA, ROY KENZIE
18 Jan 1926. Moose Jaw, Sask AGO CC1 M NGC TB3
addr: Regina, 1510 College Ave, 1960. Vancouver, 2426 W 5th Ave, 1964. Montreal, 1968
1960 184 Non-still life '57 nm $450
1964 44 Duo-deme $500 (MBAM)
1968 141 Blue bridge acry 109 x 109 two parts $2,750
142 Noctua acry 109 x 109 2 parts $2,750 (MBAM)

KLINCK, RONALD W. (Mrs)
addr: Montreal, 1532 Mackay St, Apt 5
1947 306 The Creation, Genesis, chap 1 illum on vellum
307 Benediction, from St Jude dec panel, Norwegian pine
308 15th century carol Gothic lettering, pen

KNOPF, ERNESTINE
b Toronto d 1976 M
addr: Montreal: 1041 Decarie Blvd, 1929; 5389 Decarie Blvd, 1930; 1102 University St, 1931; 11 Norwood Ave, 1932; 1379 Sherbrooke St W, 1935
1929 123 Pensive
124 A study
1930 125 Mrs M.M. Knopf
1931 141 Roses $20
1932 146 A study $35
1935 173 Fanya
174 Constance, a study

KNOWLES, DOROTHY ELSIE (m William Perehudoff)

7 Apr 1927, Unity, Sask AGO CE M
WWA82
addr: Saskatoon
1968 143 The Northern Saskatchewan River 72 x 58 $800
144 The pool 33 1/4 x 50 1/4 $500
145 Young willows 76 x 56 $800
146 The fall trees 48 x 42 $500

KNOWLES, ELIZABETH ANNIE BEACH (m Farquhar McGillivray Strachan Stewart Knowles)
8 Jan 1866, Ottawa 4 Oct 1928, Riverton, N.H. AGO CWW10 H M Mo12 NGC R2 W78
addr: Toronto: 340 Bloor St W, 1906-12; 278 Bloor St W, 1913-15. Peekskill, N.Y, 100 Smith St, 1921. Toronto, Robert Simpson Co, 1927. Montreal, 679 St Catherine St W, 1928
1906 100 Moonrise $75
1909 211 Evening $50
212 A winter twilight $35
213 A chicken yard $30
214 In durance vile $40
1910 209 Early morning $60
210 The lord of the barnyard $30
1912 231 Case of miniatures
1913 235 Case of miniatures wc $175
1915 212 Case of miniatures $150
213 Spring $150
1921 132 Interned $125
133 A ray of light $125
1927 94 Return of the truants $150
1928 103 The call to dinner $200

KNOWLES, ETHEL M.
addr: Montreal, 362 Melrose Ave
1926 76 A bit of old Scarboro' wc $35

KNOWLES, FARQUHAR MCGILLIVRAY STRACHAN STEWART
22 May 1859, Syracuse, N.Y. 9 Apr 1931, Toronto AGO B CWW10 H M Mo12 NGC R2 TB1/2 W78 WWW
addr: Toronto: 162 Jarvis St, 1891; Toronto, 1892. Bushey, Eng, 1894. Paris, 1 rue Cervantes, 1895. Toronto: 144 Yonge St, 1897-8; 5 Confederation Life Bldg, 1901; 340 Bloor St W, 1909-12; 278 Bloor St W, 1913-15. Peekskill, N.Y, 100 Smith St, 1921-2. Toronto, Robert Simpson Co, 1927. Montreal, 679 St Catherine St W, 1928. Toronto: 214 Jarvis St, 1930; Robert Simpson Art Gallery, Yonge St, 1931; 262 Jarvis St, 1932
1891 165 Percé wc $300
166 Noon wc $100
167 Coming storm wc $75
168 Twilight wc $30
1892 177 Wolfe's Cove, Quebec wc $300
1894 98 A Yorkshire lane $100
99 Tower of London $100
100 Logan's Rock Point, Cornwall $80
192 A farm lane wc $75
1895 68 Cancalase fisher wives $100
69 The critics $75
70 In port $60
71 Return of the fisher girls $30
1897 80 A Brittany spinner $100
81 Fishing boats, Cancale Bay $40
82 Surf, coast of France $40
83 Orchard in Tregony, Cornwall $20
84 Study of a girl's head
1898 70 Limehouse Reach, Thames River $225
71 Inspiration $100
72 Falmouth Bay $75
1901 67 The Thames near Gravesend $75
1909 215 Queen of night $250
216 Heavy weather $75
217 Moonrise $200
218 Fisher folk of Cancale $75
1910 211 A dancing girl $150
212 At Cancale, Brittany $150
213 La Grande River, Beaupré $800
1912 232 August afternoon $150
1913 234 In the gloaming $350
1915 214 A breeze day on the coast $250
215 Wood gatherers, Quebec $150
1921 134 The shades of evening $700
1922 160 Mount Anne, Beaupré, Quebec $300
1927 95 London Pool $200
96 Misty moonlight $250
97 Heavy westher $1,000
1928 104 A rocky shore $500
1930 126 Percé Rock $1,000
127 Bay of Fundy $500
128 Moonlight on the coast $250
1931 142 Old homestead, Lake Magog (listed 1967, Jessie Dow prize)

143 Autumn splendour $800
1932 147 Between sunset and the moon $1,200
148 Coming storm $400

KNOWLES, LILA CAROLINE TAYLOR (m Farquhar McGillivray S. S. Knowles)
10 Sep 1886, Granton, Ont M
addr: Toronto: 214 Jarvis St, 1931; 262 Jarvis St, 1932
1931 Taylor
229 On Grand Manan $100
1932 149 Rugged coast $100
150 Edge of the wood $75

KNOWLTON, JONATHAN
23 Feb 1937 New York WWA84
addr: Edmonton
1968 147 Black & blue over U stained acry 129 x 174 S2,000 (MBAM)

KNOX, AGNES see EARLE, AGNES

KNOX, ISOBEL see HUFFMAN, ISOBEL

KNOX-LEET, E. H.
addr: Montreal, 310 Mansfield St
1921 135 Vlamertinghe, Ypres salient wc $25
135 The square, Bethune, 1918 wc $25

KOCHANSKI, VERA (Mrs Worling)
22 Jul 1928, Oshawa, Ont M
addr: Ottawa, 21 Arundel Ave, 1951. Toronto: 40 Earl St, 1960: Toronto, 1967
1951 60 Out to play wc $50 Jessie Dow prize. 1967-75, 18 1/2 x 14 1/2, Worling
1960 185 Twilight nm $75

KOLISNYK, PETER HENRY
30 Nov 1934, Toronto CWW84 IO M
addr: Toronto: 22 St Mary St, 1960; 215 Cottingham St, 1962. Cobourg, Ont, 1969
1960 65 Still life in green $185
1962 47 Moment nm $110
1969 5 Refraction III bronze, plexiglass 144 x 72 x 16

KOOCHIN, WILLIAM
15 Dec 1927, Brilliant, B.C. M WWA84
addr: Vancouver, 730 Nicola St, 1960. Santa Monica, Ca, 1524 Grant St, 1961
1960 244 Cock wld metal $300
245 Running horse wld metal $160
1961 116 Nude sitting wld copper $700

KOPMANIS, AUGUST ARNOLD
17 Mar 1910, Riga 27 May 1976, Genoa
CWW73 M WWA78
addr: Toronto: 372 Brunswick Ave, 1954; 19 Millbrook Cr, 1955-60
1954 136 Mother and child sculp $30
1955 148 Relaxing boy ter cot $50
1956 149 Mother snd child copper
1957 162 Fisherman sandstone $200
1959 53 Descent marble $400
1960 246 Player stone $175

KORNER, JOHN MICHAEL ANTHONY
29 Sep 1913, Novy Jicin, Czecho AGO CC2 M NGC TB3 WWA82
addr: Vancouver, 6626 Adera St, 1957-64
1957 51 Foreign craft $250
52 Nocturnal $300
1960 66 Coast glitter (26) $600
1964 45 HMS Plumper exploring Johnstone Strait, 1862 $600

KOZLOWSKI, Z.
addr: Montreal, 5475 Queen Mary Rd
1947 141 Clouds over Lake Archambault wc $60

KREBSER, LUDWIG
addr: Montreal, 691 Shuter St
1914 241 Interior $90

KRIEGHOFF, CORNELIUS
19 Jun 1815, Amsterdam 8 Mar 1872, Chicago AGO B CE DCB EC H M NGC TB W78 WHC
1880 deceased
57 On the way to market
58 Indian camp
76 Canadian scene
1883 164 Returning from market
168 Indian camp
1886 103 Lake St Charles, Quebec

KUCHMIJ, NICHOLAS
1936, Montreal M
addr: Town of Mount Royal, 899 Graham Blvd
1957 127 Portrait nm $35

KULBACH, RENE L.

c 1909, Estonia d 1960 M
addr: Montreal, 1431 Pierce St
1935 417 Bear lino cut $15
418 Deer lino cut $15
419 Swans des $50

KURELEK, WILLIAM (WASYL)
3 Mar 1927, n Whitford, Alta 3 Nov 1977 Toronto AGO CC1 CE M WWA78
addr: Toronto, Isaacs Gallery, 832 Yonge St
1964 46 The Agony in the garden $650

KURRLE, W.
addr: Montreal, c/o Scott & Sons
1894 277 Decorative panel wd carv $350
Medal, Chicago 1893

KYLE, GWENDOLEN (GWENDOLYN)
20 Dec 1880, Brockville, Ont
addr: Westmount, 421 Mount Stephen Ave, 1915-26. Montreal: 811 Drummond Court Apts, 1927; 1201 Dorchester St W, 1933-4; Westmount: 4656 Sherbrooke St W, 1935; 4129 Western Ave, 1936
1915 216 The mill, St Andrews, Que $15
217 A path through the woods, Cap à l'Aigle $15
1916 168 The potato patch $15
169 Wheat field, Cap à l'Aigle $15
1917 189 Paysages, minisculus etch $5
190 Sketch $10
1918 197 Sketches min $5 each
1919 179 Roslyn, sketch $25
180 Miniature sketches $5 each
1920 146 On the beach $50
147 The coming storm $60
1921 137 Sunshine and shadow $75
138 The green umbrella $75
1922 161 The passing storm $60
1923 137 Case of thumb-nail sketches $10 each
1924 135-8 Sketches $10 each
1925 155 Case of thumb-nail sketches A. One summer day B. Mid-day C. Rough sea D. Serenity $15 each
1926 77 Case of miniatures A. Early thaw B. Winter light and shadow C. Snow flurries D. Golden glow $10 each
1927 98 Case of miniatures A. Silver strand B. Notre Dame de Victoire, Quebec C. Snow bound D. The Mance, Quebec $10 each
1933 165 Market square $10
166 Verdugo Mt, California $15
167 Strait of Juan de Fuca, Victoria, B.C. $15
168 Snow bound $10
1934 170 Ontio Beach, Ogunquit, Maine $10
171 One summer day $15
172 Blossoms $10
173 Reflections $10
1935 175 Spring $10
176 Summer $10
177 Autumn $10
178 Winter $10
1936 233 (1) Fog bank $15 (2) Fall colouring $10 (3) The brook $15 (4) Jewel coast of Ogunquit, Maine $20

KYLE, JEAN DOUGLAS
addr: Westmount, 467 Côte St Antoine Rd
1932 151 Ice breakers, Montreal harbour $45

L

LABELLE, HENRI SICOTTE
15 Jan 1896, Montreal CNS44 CWW70
addr: Montreal: 5300 Park Ave, 1927; 719 New Birks Bldg, 620 Cathcart St, 1928-32. Outremont, 3 Kelvin Ave, 1937-9
1927 213 J.B. Baillargeon Express Bldg, Queen St
214 Banque Provinciale, Ste Hyacinthe
215 Apartment house, Fort St
1928 240-1 Club, Chapleau-la-Minerve, Que, interior, exterior views
242-3 House, Pierre Charton, Esq, Ville Lasalle, Que, house, view of garden
1931 286 Laundry building, New Method Washing Ltd
287 Town hall, fire station, St Eustache-sur-le-Lac
288 Residence, Donat Langeliere, Esq
1932 343 Loyola College, chapel
344 Residence, Sunset Ave, Outremont

345 Residence, Dr R Vance Ward
1937 342 Eglise St Antoine de Padoue, Timmins, Ont
343 Residence, Ville La Salle
344 Residence, Warwick, Que
345 Residence, Outremont
1939 356 Magasin Dupuis Frêred Lte
see also Parent, Ovide L.A, 1929; Lofvengren, Thomas A, 1935-356, 1936-482

LABELLE, JOSEPH
c 1882 - 18 May 1939, Montreal
addr: Montreal: 136 Parc Lafontaine, 1905-21; 243 Blvd Decarie, 1927
1905 237 Study of a head drwg $10
1921 139 Winter scene pastel $25
1927 99 Head of an old man $50

LABELLE, LOUIS see VENNE, JOSEPH, 1905

LABRECQUE, PIERRE
addr: Beloeil Station, Que
1951 146 Figure antédiluvienne bronze $225

LACROIX, JOSEPH SAMUEL RICHARD
14 Jul 1939, Montreal AGO B CC1 CWW84 M WWA84
addr: Rosemount, 5047 4th Ave, 1960. Montréal, Galerie Agnes Lefort, 1504 rue Sherbrooke O, 1962-3. Outremont, 649 ave Querbes, 1964
1960 67 Eveils maritimes $40
1962 48 Hélianthée nm illus Purchase award (MBAM)
1963 84 Alfatière nm $60
1964 94 La feuillée nm illus $80 Hon mention

LACROIX, MARIE
addr: Montreal, 351 Mount Royal Ave E
1924 139 Prunes bleues $20

LAFANE, ROY (Mrs)
addr: Westmount, 21 Holton Ave
1918 198 Corner of park in Detroit, Mich $40
199 Mid-day $50

LAFONTAINE, MARGUERITE DE MONTIGNY
(m Georges Lafontaine)
21 Aug 1890, Montreal CNS36
addr: Rosemount: 5739 11th Ave, 1929-36; 5673 11th Ave, 1938; 5691 11th Ave, 1939; 5856 11th Ave, 1942
1929 379 Mlle Helene Charbonneau plaster $150
1930 307 Prière, tête de jeune fille plaster $150
308 Tête de jeune homme plaster $150
1931 425 Rodolphe Plamondon marble $500
1934 de Montigny-Lafontaine, 1934-9
498 Marielle, enfant du Dr et Mde Henri Lemieux plaster $250 marble $2,000
499 Georges André, fils M et Mde O.P. de Montigny plaster $150 marble $2,000
1935 464 Dr Georges Dupont $250 plaster $50
1936 594 Régor plaster $150
1938 181 Rene Sarrasim plaster $250 copy $50
1939 450 Mr José de Laquerrière, musician plaster $50 bronze $250
1942 Montigny-Lafontaine
240 Etude, rèreries plaster $50

LAFONTAINE, YVAN
b 1943
addr: Montreal, 3623 rue St Denis
1964 47 Paysage Gaspésien $150

LAFOREST, FRANZ JEAN MIGUEL
8 Dec 1921, Valparaiso, Chile
addr: Montreal, 3768 Parc Lafontaine, 1940-1. Hull, Que, 227 Laurier St, 1942
1940 167 Etude de tête pastel
1941 101 Bure pastel $175
Miguel 102-3
102 Cocktail de fleurs
103 Composition, village canadien
235 Etude d'arbre charch
1942 92 Nuque blonde $50

LAGACE, JEAN BAPTISTE
fl 1894-1918 H
addr: Montreal: 1895; 836 St Hubert St, 1917-18
1895 Legacé, mispr
172 In the park pen & ink $25
1917 191 Saules et peupliers, Lac St François wc $15

192 Le couchant dans les saules wc $15
193 Les nuages dorés wc $15
194 Soir d'automne wc $15
195 Le maison rouge, St Zotique wc $15
1918 200 Matin wc $15

LAING, AGNES
d 1936
addr: Winnipeg, 139 Machray Ave, 1930-1
1930 129 Old bridge on Brokenhead River, Man wc $15
130 Between the lights, Victoria Beach, Man wc $15
1931 144 The old lilac bush wc $25

LAING, MARION
1849, Quebec Mar 1932, Montreal H
addr: Montreal, 123 Mackay St, 1892-1900
1888 79, 85, 102, 105 Colorado wild flowers wc
112 Collection of Colorado wild flowers wc
1892 180 May flowers wc
181 Pansies wc $15
182 Wild roses wc $10
1894 101 Yellow roses $35
1897 85 Violets $60
86 Roses $100
1898 73 Phlox $40
1900 68 Clover $15

LALANDE, EDITH see PATTERSON, EDITH

LALIBERTE, ALFRED
18 May 1878, Ste Elizabeth, Que 13 Jan 1953, Montreal B CC2 CE CNS36 CWW49 EC M NGC PMC TB1/2/3 WWA53
addr: Montreal: 1908; Monument Nationale, 296 blvd St Laurent, 1909-17; 67 Ste Famille St, 1919-27; 3531 Ste Famille St, 1928-52
1908 284 Louis Payette, Mayor of Montreal bust plaster
285 Mr Thomas Gauthier, Pres Council of Arts & Manufacturers bust plaster
286 Head study plaster
287 Notre chimère plaster
1909 396 Desepoir, group plaster (MBAM)
397 Rt Hon Sir Wilfrid Laurier plaster
398 Head study bronze
399 M Archambault, founder Artisans Canadiens-Français sculp
400 Country musician sculp
1910 369 Mendiant statuette $750
370 O Canada, mon pays et mes amours, groupe plaster
371 L'échec, figure plaster
1913 408 Le semeur plaster (MBAM)
409 L'amour triomphe du temps sculp
410 Tête, Nelligan sculp
411 L'Acadie sculp
1914 436 Gov Pothier buste plâtre
437 Mr Sexton buste plâtre
438 Tête de jeune fille buste plâtre
1915 373 Col Gaudet bust
374 Dollard bust
375 L'abime, groupe sculp
376 Vers l'idéal sculp
1916 319 La pioche sculp
320 La muse sculp $150 (NGC)
321 Tête d'enfant sculp $100
322 Ma pauvre Mère sculp
1917 362 Mon frère bust plaster
363 Napoléon Bourassa bust plaster
364 Etude de tête plaster équisse terre cuite 165-67
365 Les larmes $25
366 La faim $25
367 Midi $25
1919 372 Tête de jeune fille plâtre
373 Une jeune héro bas rel plâtre
1920 303 Vanité des vanités, figure plâtre
304 Dollard des Ormeaux, groupe plâtre, demi-exécution
305 Alphonse Venne buste plâtre
306 Tête de Dollard bas rel plâtre
1921 297 Henry Norton bust plaster
298 Miss J.C. McCaw medln plaster
299 Laurier Monument, Arthabaska buste plâtre
300 Monument Laurier, sur sa tombe à Ottawa maquette plaster
1922 340 Pierre Boucher statue plâtre
1923 253 Le réveil sculp

254 Déese sculp
1924 313 Les ailes brisées sculp
314 L'emprise de la pensée sculp
315 Dollard bust bronze
316 A.L. Caron sculp
1925 393 Canada plaster
394 Nos mères canadiennes plâtre
395 La barque de la vie bronze $200
396 Feuille d'érable bronze $200
1926 245 Le fils de ses oeuvres sculp
246 Ame et sentiment sculp
247 La terre qui meurt sculp
248 Ame et matière sculp
1927 310 Muses plaster (MQ)
311 M Cullen, Esq bust (AGH)
312 Terre mourante marbre $350
313 Tête de femme marbre $250
1928 347 L'aquarrissage plaster
348 Surtout de table, l'orgie bronze $450
349 Tête de femme marbre $200
350 Le menuet plaster
1929 380 Triomphe mécanique plaster
381 La chaudronné de sucre plaster
382 Etude de tête écheur plaster
383 L'ouvrier, tête plaster
1930 309 Mlle Helene Charbonneau, OA plaster
310 Le charron bronze $250
311 Le vanneur bronze $200
312 Le battoir bronze $200
1931 426 Les boeufs à la furse bronze $350 (MBAM)
427 Le tonnellier bronze $250
428 Le notaire bronze $300
429 Le cultivateur bronze $300
1932 468 Le fondeur bronze $250 (MBAM)
469 Le chargeur de fusil bronze $250
470 Le laveur d'or bronze $250 (MBAM)
471 Le jongue bronze $200
1933 518 Les pêcheurs aux flambeau bronze $350
519 Le diable aux forges St Maurice bronze $300
520 Le faiseur de rouet bronze $300
521 Le paiement des barrières bronze $400
1934 506 L'ère de la mécanique plâtre
507 L'Hon J.A. Perrault plâtre
508 Jos St Charles plaster
1935 468 Jean Rivard, le défricheur plaster
1938 196 Suzor-Coté plaster
1942 237 Chargeur de fusil à pierre bronze $300
1952 81 Thibaudeau Rinfret bronze $2,000
port: by Joseph Charles Franchère, 1920-93; Alice Nolan, sculp, 1922-344; Miriam R. Holland, 1933-451; Thérèse Dionne, sculp, 1946-278

LALONDE, A. GODFROY
addr: Montreal, 4330 Berri St, 1946. Westmount, 179 Selby St, 1962
1946 145 Cathedral of Montreal $250
1962 62 Cirque nm $100

LALONDE, J. A.
addr: Montreal, 4355 Walkley Ave
1953 80 Victoria Pier $200

LAMARCHE, E. ULRIC
15 Dec 1867, Oakland, Ca 1921 Montreal H M
addr: Montreal: 406 Sherbrooke St, 1897; 1488 St Hubert St, 1909; 618 Mentana St, 1910
1897 87 Nature morte $50
1909 Ulric, 1909-10
219 Soir d'été $75
220 Vielle cabane à sucre $75
221 Etude $25
1910 214 Les moyettes $100
215 Paysage $40

LAMARCHE, GAIL L.
M
addr: Beaconsfield, Que, 111 Florida Dr
1957 128 Still life nm $35

LA MARCHE, JEAN LOUIS
addr: Québec, 1036 rue Scott
1960 68 Espoir pour un monde meilleur $200

LAMARTINE, GERT LOUIS
20 Jul 1898, Uiffingen, Germ d 1965 CNS59 M
addr: Montreal: 4595 Harvard Ave, 1932; 10 Trafalgar Pl, 1933

1932 152 Mr T. Horio, portrait sketch gesso $200
153 Crucification, Stations of the Cross, College St Laurent enamel, gesso $185
154 Flowers $135
346 Interiors
1933 169 Portrait study gesso
170 H. Schafhausen, Esq gesso

LAMB, HAROLD MORTIMER
21 May 1872, Leatherhead, Eng 25 Oct 1970, Vancouver M Mo12
addr: Westmount, 68 Westmount Ave, 1912-13
1912 233 Poplars $50
234 Sunset $50
1913 236 Foul Bay, Victoria, twilight $35
237 The lovers $25

LAMB, MOLLY see BOBAK, MOLLY

LAMBE, AGNES M.
addr: Montreal, 2 Macgregor St, 1897-1903
1897 164 Scotch thistles wc
1901 138 Under the pines, Mount Royal wc $25
139 Over the riding park Mount Royal wc $25
1903 192 Up the Murray River wc

LAMBE, ANNIE M.
H
addr: Montreal, 2 Macgregor St, 1897-1903
1897 165 La Coupe, Tadousac wc
166 Michaelmas daisies wc
1901 140 Under the pines, Mount Royal wc $25
1903 193 A view in Rossland wc

LAMBE, ELIZABETH HAINES (LIBBIE)
addr: Montreal, 2 Macgregor St, 1901-3
1888 107 A blizzard wc
1901 137 Spruce trees, study wc $10
1903 194 View of Murray Bay wc $10

LAMBE, LAWRENCE MORRIS
27 Aug 1863, Montreal CWW10 H Mo12
addr: Ottawa, Geological Survey, 1891
1885 109 Mount Stephen wc
115 Kicking Horse Pass wc
1888 92 Cap Blanc, Murray Bay wc
104 Cliffs at Murray Bay, Point à Pic wc
109 Sea shore, Cap Rosiers, Gaspé, Que wc
1891 76 Kicking Horse Pass, Rockies $50
77-8 Sketch, near Aylmer $40, $20
169 Sketch, near Aylmer wc $20

LAMBE, SARAH M. (ZAIDEE)
1888 Zaidee
127 Study of lilacs wc

LAMBE, WILLIAM BUSBY
9 Jan 1826, Montreal H Mo98
addr: Montreal, 2 Macgregor St, 1891-5
1888 75 Lac Lorne, Point à Pic, Murray Bay wc
101 Study of maple leaves, autumn tints wc
1891 170 Micmac camping grounds, Métis wc
1895 171 Percé Rock wc

LAMBERT, C. A.
addr: Montreal, 607 University St
1919 181 Upper Melbourne wc $15
182 Covenhaven woods, N.B. wc $20
183 On Minsters Island, N.B. wc $15

LAMBERT, PHYLLIS see BRONFMAN, PHYLLIS

LAMBERT, RONALD M
26 Aug 1927, Oshawa, Ont AGO M
addr: Oshawa, Ont, 481 Masson St, 1951-2
1951 105 Moonlight $100
1952 136 Illustration, Shakespeare's Macbeth pencil $100

LAMONT, GWEN KORTRIGHT HUTTON (m John M. Lamont)
17 Apr 1909, Fort Macleod, Alta 30 Dec 1978, Kelowna, B.C. M
addr: Sudbury, Ont, 48 Roxborough Dr, 1934. Victoria: 1758 Armstrong Pl, Oak Bay, 1936; 1133 Monterey Ave, 1937
1934 Hutton
153 Celery field, B.C. $35
1936 234 Peace River pioneer
1937 162 Chris $25

LAMPRECHT, GISELA HELEN LOUISE VON EICKEN (Mrs)

26 Feb 1899, Munich M
addr: Montreal, 1452 Sherbrooke St W, Apt 2. 1954-5
1954 137 Portrait of my daughter plaster
138 Nichel fired clay
1955 149 Jerry T. fired clay

LANDORI, EVA (m Rudolf Hoffman)
3 Mar 1912, Budapest M
addr: Westmount, 418 Claremont Ave, Apt 47, 1953. Montreal, 3531 Vendome Ave, 1956-63
1953 81 Between walls $165
1956 33 Annonciation $150
1957 53 Pieta Hungarica $600
1958 29 Eruption $400
1959 11 Epanouissement
1961 87 Floating movement nm $180
1963 85 Drawing No 8/63 nm $150

LANDSLEY, PATRICK ALFRED
13 Aug 1926, Winnipeg CC2 M
addr: St Boniface, Man, 398 Taché Ave, Apt 2, 1954. Montreal: 3560 Mountain St, 1955-6; 3614 Ontario Ave, 1958-61
1954 49 Interior with two women $200
1955 47 Winter $90
1956 34 Laurentian landscape $115
1958 30 Dark trees $275
1960 69 Dark forms in winter $300
1961 32 Charred tree $200

LANG, BYLLEE FAY
4 Dec 1908, Didsbury, Alta 10 Dec 1966, Bermuda M W78
addr: Montreal, 4131 Côte des Neiges, 4, 1945. Hamilton, Bermuda, Bank of Bermuda, 1946
1945 280 Senator T.D. Bouchard col plaster
1946 288 Babouchka col plaster $250
289 Joan Mercer oiled plaster $250

LANGELIER, PAULINE
addr: Montreal, 437 St Hubert St
1923 255 Etude sculp

LANGHAM, E. (Hon Mrs) Eng
fl 1879-82 DBA DVP H
1880 72 Sketches

LANGLOIS, FERNAND
addr: Montreal, 10589 rue Parthenais
1963 36 Chambre funéraire $300

LANGLOIS, JEAN
17 Jan 1916, Montreal M
addr: Montréal, 7432 blvd St Laurent, 1938-49
1938 72 Dimanche matin, Rigaud $125
73 L'arrivé au marché $85
1939 193 Matin d'hiver $85
194 La débacle $70
1940 168 Jour gris $75
169 Vallée de l'Outaouais $125
1941 106 Solitude $50
107 La ferme $100
1942 93 The thaw $125
94 July $75
1943 108 A summer day $125
109 Quiet day, Rigaud, Que $175
110 Irish girl $100
1944 73 August $200
74 Early spring $150
1945 138 Poultry market $100
139 Béloeil, Que $75
1946 147 Market in March $100
148 The sowers $60
149 Ste Eustache $60
1947 145 Circus $150
146 Oka road $100
1949 54 Portrait $150

LANGLOIS, MARIE
30 Apr 1929, Montreal
addr: Montreal, 5539 Woodbury Ave, Apt 20, 1957-60
1957 54 Paysage $100
1960 70 Madère $150

LANGSTON, HENRY THOMAS
1 Oct 1913, Sidney, Australia
addr: Montreal, 5015 Clanranald Ave, 1946. Westmount, 522 Clarke Ave, 1947
1946 150 Autumn, St Sauveur $100
1947 147 Spring thaw near Ste Adèle
148 Indian summer
149 Through the trees $350

LANSLOOT, ROBERT
addr: Montreal, 994 Des Erables St
1916 170 La rue de Lille, Ypres $60
171 A mountain view, Eastern Townships, Que $25

172 Le Ruitchmolers, Bruxelles $40
173 La Senne, á la Petite Ile, Bruxelles $35

LA PALME, PIERRE GABORIAU (GABO)
2 May 1935, New York M
addr: Montreal, c/o Dominion Gallery, 1438 Sherbrooke St W
1964 48 South Utopia $700

LA PIERRE, THOMAS
28 Dec 1930, Toronto CWW84 IO M WWA84
addr: Toronto, 12 Glenaden Ave E
1960 186 Seed nm $150

LAPIERRE, VIATEUR
17 Sep 1917, Montreal
addr: Montreal, 6326 Christophe Colomb St
1946 151 Shawbridge wc $50

LAPINE, ANDREAS CHRISTIAN GOTTFRIED (b Andrejs Lapins)
27 Oct 1866, Shujen, Riga, Russia 27 Feb 1952, Minden, Ont AGO CC1 CWW49 H M NGC TB3
addr: Toronto: 1908; Yonge Street Arcade, 1909; 160 Richmond St W, 1916-24; 86 King St W, 1927; Mosson Road, Old Mill, 1929; 101 King St W, 1931; 222 Pacific Ave, 1935; 15 Alcorn Ave, 1940
1908 93 Horses in stall $100
219 A farmer's Sunday morning wc $80
1909 222 When the leaves are fallen pastel $35
223 The lumber mill wc $60
1916 174 Victims of war b&w $100
175 Hay ricks, Manitoba $250
176 End of the day's toil $150
177 Wagon shed $150
1920 148 Early morning wc $250 (listed 1967, Jessie Dow prize)
149 Late afternoon wc $250
150 Le rire drwg
1924 140 Bergere, Latvia $80
141 Le canal, Hollande $100
1927 100 At the river bank $100
101 Spring wc $100
278 The book drwg
1929 126 La Noni wc $200
1931 145 Going home $600
1935 179 Noon hour wc $80
180 At the warehouse wc $60
181 From Ward's Island wc $80
182 The lane wc $80 (listed 1967, Jessie Dow Prize)
1940 170 The pioneers $250

LA ROCQUE, PIERRETTE
addr: Montreal, 6583 Boyer St, 1950-1
1950 120 Nostalgie $100
1951 106 Nature morte $60

LAROSE, LUDGER
1 May 1868, Montreal 1915, Montreal CC2 CE M
addr: Montreal: 530A Lagauchetière St, 1895; 105 St Lambert Hill, 1898; 813 Mount Royal Ave, 1900; 983 Mount Royal Ave, 1905; Montreal, 1908: 212 Prud'homme Ave, 1912-13
1895 72 La leçon maternelle $150
73 A Tunisian $100
1898 74 Nature morte $50
75 Canadian loom $80
1900 59 Plants in a city green house $100
70 In the conservatory $150
1905 93 Portrait of a child
1908 93A Laval Avenue, winter $120
1912 235 My three jewels
1913 238 Westmount heights $30

LARSEN, HENRI V.
addr: Montreal: 123 Ontario St W, 1927; 181 Hutchison St, 1928; 3609 Hutchison St, 1929
1927 279 The Point litho $5
280 The fountain, Place Viger litho $5
281 The lake litho $5
282 Bonsecours Market, Montreal litho $5
1928 304 Dancing in the street litho
305 The jackpine litho
306 The kitchen window litho
307 Hotel Dieu, Montreal litho
1929 127 Autumn wc $25
328 The old ship litho $6

LA RUE, J. A.
addr: Outremont, 5711 Durocher Ave
1931 289 Groupe monastique á Québec

LASNIER, RAYMOND
28 Feb 1924, Quebec 10 Feb 1968
Trois Rivières, Que M
addr: Trois Rivières: 42 rue Des Casernes, 1955-7; 66 rue René, 1961
1955 48 Composition $90
1957 55 Poisson
56 Etude
1961 33 Nocturne No 2 $200

LASSING, ANTON
1928, Amsterdam
addr: Toronto, 56 Division St
1957 57 Brief encounter $150
129 Spring nm $50

LATTER, HENRY HAVELOCK
addr: Montreal, 3548 Vendome Ave
1933 171 La place du vieux cimetière, Vence, France $20
172 Baou Blanc, Alpes Maritime, France $20

LAUDA, GEORGES JIRI
17 Jan 1925, Prague M
addr: Montreal, 3421 Ste Famille St, 1953-7
1953 106 Le corsage noir litho $20
1954 124 Danseuse litho $20
1955 49 Quartet rehearsal $150
1956 112 Italian septet nm $20
113 Girls' quintet nm $20
1957 58 Rehearsal $180

LAUGHTON, MINNIE M.
addr: Montreal: 334 Mackay St, 1924; 1662 St Luke St, 1929
1924 364 Fruit plate $15
365 Vase, orange lustre
1929 128 L'italienne $75

LAURIE, ISABELLA see OGILVY, ISABELLA

LAUTERMAN, DINAH
6 Aug 1889 - 14 Jun 1945, Montreal M
addr: Montreal, 196 Peel St, 1922-9. Westmount, 33 Cote St Antoine Rd, 1935-9
1922 341 Sandy sculp
1923 256 The suppliant sculp
1927 314 The organ grinder plaster
1929 384 Late Chief American Horse, of Caughnawaga
385 Portrait bust
1935 469 Late Dr Maxwell Lauterman bust
1939 456 Study of a head, from composition 'Progress' plasticene

LAUZE, BERNARD M.
addr: Montreal, 4422 St Denis St
1945 140 Back River $40

LAUZON, GILBERT
addr: Montreal, 6862 St Dominique St
1951 107 Woman at the piano $135

LAUZON, NORMAND
17 Apr 1925, Montreal M
addr: Montreal, 6362 Casgrain St
1954 50 St Henri Street $100

LAVALLEE, ANDRE
c 1935
addr: St Lambert, 651A Victoria St
1960 71 Ombre violacée $60

LAVALLEE, DENYSE
addr: Montreal, 2062 Jeanne Mance St, Apt 1, 1946-7
1946 152 La lecture $50
260 Les deux soeurs drwg $25
1947 309 Rose souris drwg $40

LAVERY, JOHN, Sir Eng
Mar 1856, Belfast 10 Jan 1941, Kilmaganny, Ire B DBA DVP RA TB1/2 WWB34
addr: London, Eng
1913 239 The wreck of the Delphi $150
240 A moonrise landscape $150
241 The beach, evening, Tangier $750
242 The Pompadour gown $750

LAVOYE, MARIE ANN JULIETTE (b Lavoie)
25 Jun 1903, Montreal M
addr: Montreal, 1820 McGregor St, Apt 408, 1943-5. Detroit, Mich, 212 David Whitney Bldg, 1946. Montreal, 3534 Mountain St, 1949
1943 111 Mrs Lucy Ann Farrar Hutton min wc
112 Grandmother at twenty wc
113 Miss Pauline Timmins wc
1944 75 Mrs John J. Heney min wc
76 Miss Joan Timmins min wc
77 Barbara min wc

78 My brother min wc
1945 141 Miss Julia Timmins min wc
142 My father min wc
1946 153 Miss Gloria Timmins min
1949 133 Mrs Harold T. Pepin wc

LAW, CHARLES ANTHONY FRANCIS
15 Oct 1916, London, Eng CWW70 M WWA84
addr: Quebec, 89 Claridge, 220 Grande Allee, 1938-40. Ottawa, 287 Metcalfe St, 1951. Armdale, N.S. 1967
1938 74 Windy day, St André, Que $75
75 Rivière à Claude, Gaspé $75
1939 195 Cold winter day, Que $50
1967-36 40 x 36 (Mr J.D. McKeown, Montreal) Jessie Dow prize
1940 171 Weathered, Ontario $50
1951 22 After the shower, Paris $300 (listed 1967, Jessie Dow prize)

LAWLEY, JOHN DOUGLAS
1905, Glace Bay, N.S. CWW67 M
addr: Montreal, 2025 Grey Ave, 1943-51
1943 114 Strike at the coal mine
1944 79 Two miners go to heaven $60
80 Cape Breton farm in spring $55
1945 143 Breezy day on the Bras d'Or
1946 154 East Bay, Cape Breton $50
1947 150 Death under the Atlantic $150
1951 23 At the chalet $125

LAWSON, ARTHUR WENDELL PHILLIPS
25 Sep 1898, Toronto 10 Jun 1952, Columbus, Ohio M
addr: Leaside Ont: 1929-31; Eglinton & Bayview, 1934: Eglinton Ave E, 1936
1929 129 The Spanish bridge, Ronda, Spain wc $75
1930 131 Rome wc $50
132 Ronda, Spain wc $75
1931 385 Eglise St Jacques, Dieppe litho $10
386 Dieppe litho $10
387 Albi litho $10
1934 174 St Gabriel, Bouchetts $175
1936 235 Honfleur, Normandy wc $50
236 Full moon, high tide and fog wc
237 Louisbourg, Nova Scotia wc

LAWSON, CECIL C. P. Eng
b London, Eng fl 1907-23 DBA TB
addr: Paris, 2 rue Cassini
1914 242 The 'Fencibles' at Battle of Chateauguay $150

LAWSON, EDITH see COOMBS, LAWSON

LAWSON, HAROLD
15 Jun 1885, New York 23 Jun 1969, Montreal CNS51
addr: Montreal: 5864 Sherbrooke St W, 1919; 127 Stanley St, 1920-4; 374 Beaver Hall Sq, 1925-7; 1164 Beaver Hall Sq, 1928-31; 810 Architects Bldg, 1932-5; 1227 University Tower Bldg, 1936-9
1919 388 Semi-detached house
1920 316 House, Summit Cr, Westmount wc
317 Architectural rendering pen & ink
1924 Lawson and Little, 1924-39
331 Bank of Montreal, Kingston branch
332 Residence, H.R. Little
333 Proposed residence, Westmount
334 Residence, W.E.C. Irwin
1925 300 Proposed school, Hampstead
301 Proposed memorial hall and civic centre
302 Suggested union plaza for two transcontinental rental systems
303 Branch bank building, Fredericton, N.B.
1927 216 Bank of Montreal, Quebec, prelim study
217 Bank of Montreal, Kingston
218 Bank of Montreal, Fredericton, N.B.
1928 244 Bank of Montreal building, Quebec, corner and entrance scale model
245 The Hermitage, office study
246 Westmount Realties Co, office building
1929 247 The Hermitage
248 Singer Building
249 Architectural composition
1930 222 Residence, A.C. Price, Esq Quebec
223 Residence, V.E. Price, Esq,

Knowlton, Que
224 Bank building des
1931 290 Cabin at Lucerne, Que
291 Industrial Life Building, Quebec
292 Royal Victoria Hospital, addition
1932 347-50 Lucern, Quebec, fireplace, log chateau, swimming pool sports clubhouse
1933 389 Royal Victoria Hospital, Nurses' Home, extension
390 Residence, Knowlton
391-2 Seigniory Club, member's cabin, and interior
1934 393 Entrance gates, proposed cemetry
394 Proposed residence, Cedar Ave
1935 352 Entrance gates and adjoining buildings, Montreal Memorial Park
478-80 Views of guest house from porch of main cabin; guest house, moonlight view from road; main cabin from garden; A.A. Martin, Seigniory Club, Que
482 High school, Grand Falls, Nfld
1937 346 Proposed mausoleum, Montreal Memorial Park
1938 141 Proposed office building
142 Country house, sketch
143 Residence, Stanley Stranger, Esq, Hampstead, Que
1939 357 Guardian Trust Building
358 House, Seigniory Club

LAWSON, JAMES KERR
28 Oct 1862, Anstruther, Scot 1 May 1939, London, Eng B CC1 DBA DVP H TB1/2 WBA
1883 80 Winnowing
109 The cactus bower, Capri
130 A Capri landscape, twilight
1885 3 After the carnival
14 An old fisherman
60 Twilight
69 Village green, Runswick, Eng
75 Piping Pan
1888 9 Jacques Bonhomme (written in ink, printed title obliterated)

LAWSON, WENDELL see LAWSON, ARTHUR WENDALL PHILLIPS

LAWTON, E. STRAKER
addr: Montreal, 1758 Hutchison St, 1914-16
1914 243 Still life wc
1915 218 A sketch pastel
1916 178 Old china: still life wc
179 Cottage, old Hornsey wc $10
180 Lake Ontario, Toronto Island wc $15
181 Old house, Fletcher's Field wc $12

LAWTON, PIERRE
c 1933, Chicoutimi, Que M
addr: Westmount, 476 Roslyn Ave
1960 72 Rooftops $150

LEAHY, HENRY BERNARD
20 Nov 1881, Stellarton, N.S.
addr: Sydney, N.S.
1911 183 Pierrette $25
184 Florence Thompson $50

LEATHERS, WINSTON LYLE
29 Dec 1932, Miami, Man CWW84 M WWA84
addr: Winnipeg
1968 148 Nebular reorder No 9 airbrush 22 x 28 $300
149 Nebular readjustment airbrush 22 x 28 $200
150 Cosmic order No 2 airbrush 22 x 28 $200
151 Cosmic order No 3 airbrush 22 x 28 $200

LE BEL, MAURICE
28 Aug 1898 - 26 Jun 1963, Montreal CNS36 M
addr: Montreal: 6513A de Normanville St, 1930-2; 5992 Christophe Colomb St, 1936-7; 6605 Christophe Colomb St. 1942-52
1930 287 Les outardes lino $15
288 Paysage au Lac Tremblant lino $10
1932 404 Leda au cygne wd cut $8
405 Stephen, sketch drwg
1936 238 Cargo boat $25
551 La charge de bois wd cut $8
1937 Le Bell, mispr
163 Laurentian sketch $25
164 Still life $20
1942 95 Composition $75
96 The poplars $100

1943 115 Wartime traffic $50
1944 81 Still life $75
1946 155 Marine, Gaspesia, Que $50
261 Esmeralda col lino $15
1947 151 Marine wc $40
152 The tavern wc $40
1949 55 The terminal, Canada Steamship Line, Bagotville, Que
1952 23 Grey day, November, Shawbridge

LE BEUF, C. (Mrs)
addr: Westmount, 21 Holton Ave
1918 202 Capt G.H. Trudeau, RFC min
203 Cadet C. Le Beuf, RFC min
204 Mrs C. Le Beuf min
205 Baby, J. Le Beuf min

LE BEUF, JEAN GUY
6 Jan 1932, Quebec M
addr: Sillery, Que, 1321 Lemoine Ave, 1958-9
1958 68 Paysage nm $60
1959 12 Construction No 6 $250

LE BLANC, G. V.
addr: Montreal, c/o Edlington's
1924 142 Le fin d'hiver wc

LEBLANC, JEANNE (m Gerald Rhéaume)
15 Apr 1915, Montreal B NGC
addr: Westmount, 457 Mount Stephen Ave, 1937-41, 1947-50. Montreal, 4870 Queen Mary Rd, 1942-6; Dominion Gallery, 1438 Sherbrooke St W, 1953-4. Florence, Italy: Erta Canina, 22, 1957; Via Giovanni Prati, 9, 1958-9. Montreal, 3003 Cedar Ave, 1960. Florence, 1967
1939 196 Les Eboulements $75
197 Ferme des Eboulements $75
1940 172 Deception $100
1941 108 Février $40
109 Saint Adèle $60
1942 Rhéaume, 1942-67
139 Dominicain
140 Andrée $60
1943 170 Paysage $35
1945 186 Etude $100
187 Nature morte $60
1946 201 Nature morte aux fleurs $150
1947 228A Nature morte $150
1948 50 La chaise longue $350
1949 85 Nature morte $200
1950 134 Nature morte $175 Jury II prize (listed 1967)
1953 33 Cyprès noirs $200
34 Narcisses et tulipes $250
1954 72 Antella $225
1957 79 Paysage Florentin $350 Jessie Dow prize (listed 1967)
80 San Casciano $350
1958 73 Romola wc $250 1967-56 25 x 26
74 Ospedaletto nm $250
1959 35 Certosa nm $250
1960 208 Choux fleurs violets nm $275
209 Paysage, Grassina nm $275

LEBLANC, LUCIEN
4 Sep 1893, Montreal 17 Jun 1966, Cornwall, Ont
addr: Montreal, 8069 St Denis St
1929 250 L. Prefontaine Apartments

LE BOUTILLIER, RUBY VIVIAN
b Montreal
addr: Westmount, 486 Argyle Ave, 1931-45
1931 293 A Spanish living room
294 A modiste shop, Louis XVI period
295 A basement tea room
1932 155 Daffodils wc $25
156 Louis XVI period bedroom, Metropolitan Museum, N.Y. wc $25
351 Panelling, Georgian dining room $20
1933 173 Nasturtiums $40
174 Les Boules, lower St Lawrence wc $40
462 Chinese lacquer cabinet, in Metropolitan Museum, N.Y. des
1934 175 Spring flowers wc $75
176 Sous le Cap, Quebec wc $20
1935 420 Campanula wc des $20
1936 239 Anemones $25
240 Plantain lily wc $25
241 Bow River, Banff, Alta wc $35
1937 165 Rosy morn petunias $50
166 Trillium wc $35
1939 198 Peonies wc $40
1940 173 Spring companions $40
1945 144 Trilliums $40

LE CLAIRE, ALPHONSE
20 Jul 1843, Montreal
addr: Westmount, 441 Strathcona Ave
1924 penknife carving
145 Mahogany frame
146 Book cover

147 Chain
148 Pillars

LECLAIRE, IRENE
addr: Viauville, Que, 131 Second Ave
1915 453 Vase, roses
454 Jewel box

LE COCQ, DORIS (m Fred T. Tabuteau)
London, Eng M
addr: Montreal, c/o W. Scott & Sons, 1490 Drummond St
1936 598 Sea phantasy plaster $35

LE DAIN, BRUCE
1928, Montreal M
addr: Montreal, 4586 Decarie Blvd, 1949-53
1949 56 The Quebec scene, Chesterville $150
1952 24 The old carriage house, Masonville, Que $200
1953 22 The pond in October $300

LEDUC, FERNAND
4 Jul 1916, Montreal CC2 CE M NGC
addr: Montreal, 1149 St Joseph Blvd E
1953 82 Les bons augures $175

LEDUC, OZIAS
8 Oct 1864, St Hilaire, Que 16 Jun 1955, St Hyacinthe, Que B CC1 CE CWW48 H M NGC PMC TB3 WWA53
addr: Montreal, 202 St Martin St, 1891-2. St Hilaire, Que, 1894-1921
1891 79 Nature morte, violin $40
80 Mater Dolorosa
1892 93 Nature morte, livres $40
1894 102 Liseuse (MQ)
1895 74 Still life $50
1897 88 The young student $75
1898 76 Still life $40
1900 71 Pigeons $40
1912 236 Guy Delahaye, poet (MQ)
1913 243 Cumulus bleu $25
1914 244 Effet gris, neige $125
1915 219 Pommes vertes $225 (NGC)
1916 182 Lueurs du soir $80
1917 200 The good shepherd $75
201 L'orage b&w $15
202 Pommiers en fleurs b&w $15
368 Mme Louise Lecours medln
1921 140 L'heure mauve $350 (MBAM)
1894-5 Assoc 1st prize, artist under 30

LEE, AMICE
addr: Westmount, 4319 Montrose Ave
1920 151 Roll of honour, Faculty of Law des wc
152 Decorative panel wc

LEE, ETHEL W.
addr: Westmount, 318 Grosvenor Ave 1912-14
1912 459 Teapot $7
460 Chocolate pot, Satsuma $2
1913 485 Jardinière $12
486 Berry set, bowl $20
487 Celery dish
1914 516 Cylinder vase $12
517 Salad bowl $8
518 Plate $5

LEE-GRAYSON, JOSEPH HENRY
10 Dec 1875, Harrogate, Eng 1954, Summerland, B.C. M
addr: Regina, P O Box 93, 1927-33
1927 75 Abandoned $165
1932 157 More snow coming wc $50
158 The Battle Hills, Saskatchewan wc $50
1933 175 The Wascana, Regina wc $50
176 A northern post, RCMP wc $50
177 After rain, the south-west wind wc $50

LEE-SMITH, MARIANNE
1872, Sutton-on-Hull, Eng
addr: Toronto: 41 Dunloe Rd, 1929; Hotel Marlboro, Jarvis St, 1930; 760 Yonge St, 1932; c/o Mr F. Currie, 460 Yonge St, 1933; 174 Cottingham St, 1935-6
1929 Smith, Marianne Lee
200 Bridge over canal, Ottawa $100
1930 133 Still life $50
1932 159 A posey $40
160 Still life $70
1933 178 The copper kettle $100
179 Still life $25
1935 183 The copper kettle $90
1936 242 Still life $100
243 Autumn bouquet $50
244 Silver and blue $50

LEES, CHARLES Scot
1800, Cupar, Fifeshire, Scot 28 Feb 1880, Edinburgh B DBA DVP G TB

1883 102 A summer evening on Musselburgh Links

LEFKOVITZ, SYLVIA
29 Aug 1924, Montreal M
addr: Montreal, 3631 City Hall Ave, 1944-6
1944 82 A Canadian school girl
1946 262 Etude charcl

LEFORT, MARIE AGNES
5 Jan 1891, Nappierville, Que 9 Feb 1973, Montreal M WWA62 Juror
addr: Montreal: 712 St Hubert St, 1924; 2058 Maplewood Ave, 1932-3; 1414 Drummond St, 1936-40; 2 Amesbury Ave, 1941-8
1924 143 Head of an old man $60
144 Louise pastel
1932 161 Still life
162 July $75
163 Portrait pastel
1933 180 Zinnias
1936 245 Shawinigan Bey $100
246 Before the storm, Chambly $75
247 Golden youth, nude
248 Winter in Como $75
1937 167 Skier, portrait of Miss M.S.
1938 76 La femme au divan bleu, portrait
1939 199 La madone des iles $400
1940 174 Relaxation $100
175 On Batiscan River $60
1941 110 Les masques en fête $100
111 Mireille sous les pommiers
1942 97 Les doulers, composition $150
98 Nature morte $50
99 Quartier du chemin de fer $35
1943 116 Les abords du chemin de fer
1944 83 Les poires $60
1946 156 Portrait
157 Marine
1948 21 Monique $350

LEFORT, ANDRE
addr: Ottawa, 138 Percy St
1964 95 Chronique V nm

LEGACE, JEAN see LAGACE, JEAN

LEGENDRE, IRENE
19 Nov 1904, Fall River, Mass M
addr: Montreal, 430 St Joseph Blvd, W
1946 158 Mère et enfant $300
159 Notre Dame du Portage $175

LEGENDRE, SOLANGE
addr: Montreal, 967 St Joseph Blvd E
1952 25 Nature morte $60
73 Cour aqua $15

LEGER, J. A.
(C.A, mispr 1908, 1912-13, 1919)
addr: Maisonneuve, Que. 1908. Montreal: 83 Desjardins Ave, 1909; 17 Bleury St, 1910; 373 Lartigue St, 1912; 37 Notre Dame St, 1913; 681 Ontario St E, 1916; 250 Saguinet St, 1917; 567 St Catherine St E, 1918-19
1908 220 Printemps pastel $15
1909 224 Tête d'enfant $15
225 Paysage $25
1910 216 Gardeuse d'oies $125
1912 409 M.Z. Juteau bust
1913 412 Evangeline sculp
413 Pauvre cigale sculp $25
414 Lt Col Burland sculp
1915 see Léger, Onésime André, listed as O.A, may be error for J.A.
1916 183 Le matin et le soir de la vie b&w $15
184 La mendiante pastel $15
185 La lettre pastel $25
1917 203 La mort d'Etienne Dolet pastel
204 La dernier étincelle pastel
205 L'automne pastel
1918 206 Sans asile pastel
207 Mme V.L. b&w
1919 184 Le repose $200
185 Le fagot $150

LEGER, ONESIME ANDRE
b 1881 24 Mar 1924, Quebec
addr: Montreal, 70 St James St, 1915. Maisonneuve, 569 St Catherine St, 1920. Montreal, c/o Art Assoc, 1925
1915 listed O.A, may be error for J.A.
377 L'adieu sculp $25
378 La pensée sculp $25
1920 153 Le crépuscule $200
154 Portrait de ma mère pen & ink
1925 late
156 Les ronces $650
157 La transition wc $1,000
158 La defense du foyer wc $800
159 Ximenes wc $1,000

LEIBOVITCH, NORMAN
20 Nov 1913, Montreal M
addr: Montreal: 5551 Waverly St, 1940-1; 3669 St Urbain St, 1942
1940 176 Feline design wc
1941 112 Deer $100
1942 238 Horse glazed plaster $200

LEIGHTON, ALAN
addr: Montreal, 1239 Sussex Ave
1949 57 Wharf houses, Kennebunk Port $250 (Kenneburk, mispr)

LEMASNIE, GAMBLE SHERIDAN
fl 1905-33
addr: Montreal: 20 University St, 1905; Montreal, 1908
1905 162 Nightfall in June wc
163 A light wind wc
1908 221 The carpenter's shop wc
222 Arundel Lake, England wc
223 Tiger's head wc

LEMIEUX, EMILE
30 Apr 1889, Montreal M
addr: Montreal: 1105 St Denis St, 1913-14; Goodwin's Ltd, 1920; 1816 St Urbain St, 1922; 5403 Durocher St, 1935-49; 3675 Côte des Neiges Rd, 1950-1
1913 244 Strathcona Horse b&w $10
245 St Catherine Street, east of Peel wc $10
246 Mr E.L. b&w $10
1914 245 Forêt de Mendon $45
246 Royal George b&w $15
247 On the canal b&w $20
248 Barges b&w $20
249 La phare b&w $15
1920 155 Bouleaux, sketch $80
156 La route neuve, sketch $80
157 Vieille maison, sketch $80
158 Beaupré, sketch $80
1922 162 Eveil $100
163 Helios wc $75
1935 184 Les sucres $175
185 Early spring $175
1936 249 Enneigée $150
250 L'heure mauve $150
251 Fin d'après-midi $150
1941 113 Hiver, Val David $350
1943 117 October in the Laurentians $250
118 Start of Rapids, Lac Raymond $250
119 Hiver Laurentien $250
120 Récolte, St Augustin $250
1944 84 Vieille grange $250
85 Still life $250
1945 145 Le vase blanc $250
146 Maison canadienne $250
1946 160 Québec matinal $300
1949 58 Au vieux moulin, Baie St Paul $350
1950 21 Blue flowered plate $200
22 French horns $350
1951 24 Les sucres $250
port: by Marjorie S. Winslow, bust 1946-296

LEMIEUX, JEAN-PAUL (MARIE JOSEPH JEAN PAUL)
18 Nov 1904, Quebec AGO B CC1 CE CWW84 M NGC TB2/3 WWA84 Juror
addr: Montreal: 406 Pine Ave W, 1931; 3610 Durocher St, 1933-5; Quebec: 46 Marquette St, 1938; 37 St Joachim St, 1940. St Louis de Courville, Que, 1942
1931 146 Nature morte temp $50
147 Sept de trêfle temp $50
1933 181 Interior $75
182 Temps calme wc $20
1935 186 Nuages sur la côte nord $125
1938 77 Les beaux jours $50
1940 177 Eglise, Baie St Paul gouache $35
178 Patineurs à Montmorenci gouache $35
1942 100 Notre Dame Protégeant, Québec oil on panel

LEMIEUX, LUDGER
9 Feb 1872, West Farnham, Que 27 Oct 1953, Montreal
addr: Montreal, 1260 University St
1931 296 Chapelle Bourget, Cathedral, Montréal
297 Chapelle Ste Therèse, Eglise St Charles, Montréal photo
298 Eglise St Vincent Ferrier, Montréal
Lemieux & Lemieux
299 Marché municipal

LEMIEUX, MARGUERITE
11 Mar 1899, Montreal CNS36 M
addr: Montreal: 1260 University St, 1930-2; 5201 Brillon St, 1933
1930 134 Ste Agathe, residence, Hon Alphonse David wc $150

135 Intérieur, Saint Julien le Pauvre, Paris wc $150
1931 148 Nature morte pastel $60
149 Vase, persan et tanagra $60
1932 164 Le Pont Neuf wc $30
1933 183 Le Pont Neuf wc $40
184 Le Parc de Westmount wc $25

LEMIEUX, PAUL M.
25 Jan 1902 - 26 Dec 1968, Montreal
addr: Montreal, 1260 University St, 1931-7
1931 150 Oratoire à Carolles, Normandie, France wc $40
151 Villefranche, Alpes Maritimes, France wc $50
1934 395 Autel privé en verre sculpté, et chandeliers en aluminium
1935 353 Musée Catholique Canadien, perspective
354 Residence, Mr C.A.
355 Eglise, perspective
1937 347 Une gentilhommière bretonne
see also Lemieux, Ludger, 1931-299

LE MOINE, BERTHA see LE MOYNE, BERTHE

LEMOINE, EDMOND
1877, Quebec d 1922 M
addr: Quebec: 1908; 21 rue des Ramparts, 1909-13; 139 St Jean St, 1915-17
1908 Edward, 1908-9
94 Rivière Malbaie $25
95 Marine $25
1909 226 Moutons au paturage $30
227 Etude
1913 247 Toits enniegés $60
248 Quai au Cap à l'Aigle $50
249 Type italien $40
1915 220 Québec, vu de Maiserets $40
221 Etude $35
222 Goélette au bassin $25
1916 186 Intérieur canadien $75
187 Nature morte $40
1917 206 Paysage et moutons, Rivière Malbaie $50
207 Goélette en déchargement, La Malbaie $25

LE MOYNE, BERTHE
addr: Montreal: 1915; 262 Lafontaine Park, 1916-18
1915 Le Moine, Bertha, mispr
223 Château de Carillon
1916 188 A study $60
1917 208 Composition
209 Illustration, La sorcière b&w $5
1918 208 Un sentier dans la montagne $40

LENDVAY, ISTVAN (STEPHEN)
8 May 1929, Csorna, Hungary M
addr: Don Mills, Ont, 4 Vendome Pl
1965 24 Wild flowers at Lake Nipigon nm $125

LENNIE, EDITH BEATRICE CATHARINE
16 Jun 1904, Nelson, B.C. 1 Jun 1987, West Vancouver M WWA84
addr: Vancouver, 1737 Matthews Ave
1935 421 Orphan boy chalk drwg $50

LENNOX, MAY
addr: Montreal, 2161 Prud'homme Ave
1936 252 Old mill pastel $12

LEO, ANSEL
fl 1884-97 DBA G
addr: Montreal, 20 Park Ave
1897 242 Portrait bust $150

LEONARD, JEAN
addr: Outremont, 771A Querbes Ave, 1945-7
1945 147 Paysage $40
1947 153 Femme et enfant $50
310 Femmes au masque drwg $35

LEONARD, JOHN CHARLES
5 May 1944. Oxted, Eng CWW84 M
addr: Toronto
1970 33 Smith & Wesson K22 acry 44 x 58
34 Ruger single six acry 48 x 100

LEONARD, O. DE L. (Mrs)
addr: Windsor Mills, Que
1910 372 Portrait medln bronze

LE PAGE, TERRANCE D.
addr: Vancouver, 1164 Pacific St
1960 73 Theme SFB variation VI $200

LEPROHON, ROBERT R.
addr: Montreal, 5255 Rosemount Blvd

1951 25 Nature morte à la nappe rose
$125

LE QUESNE, DONALD CORBEL
20 May 1932, Montreal M
addr: Montreal, 7538 Wiseman Ave, 1954-5
1954 51 Girl in repose $125
1955 50 Abstract $125

LE ROY, HUGH ALEXANDER COTE
9 Oct 1939, Montreal B M CWW84
addr: Westmount, 220 Redfern Ave, 1965. Montreal, 1968
1965 40 Panel compression wd $500
1968 152 Sand box fibreglass
84 x 84 x24 $3,500

LESSEL, MARIAN I.
addr: Bridgetown, N.S.
1937 168 Isabel

LE TARTE, JEAN-PAUL
28 Apr 1933, Montreal M
addr: Montreal, 2141 Maplewood Ave, Apt 6, 1954-6
1954 52 Nature morte $60
1955 51 Vie du port $175
1956 35 Composition $75

LETENDRE, RITA (m Kosso Eloul)
1 Nov 1928, Drummondville, Que AGO B CC2 CE CWW84 IO M TB3 WWA84
addr: Montreal, 4371 Harvard Ave, 1961-2
1961 34 L'èclat de midi
1962 19 Structure du silence $900

LEVEILLE, FRANCOISE
addr: Montreal, 3791 Old Orchard Ave
1933 185 St Jean de Matha

LEVINE, ANNE
15 Nov 1915, Montreal
addr: Montreal: 4327 Coolbrook Ave, 1949; 4372 King Edward Ave, 1956
1949 160 Still life pastel $50
1956 114 Mother and children nm $50

LEVINE, MARILYN
22 Dec 1935, Medicine Hat, Alta M
addr: Richmond, Cal
1970 stoneware clay
35 Jacket, lying, dark brown 22 x 12
36 Jacket, lying, buff colour
24 x 13
37 Jacket, hanging, black-brown
30 x 20

LEVIS, RAQUEL
7 May 1907, Shanghai
addr: Toronto, 602 Lonsdale Rd, Apt 1
1953 83 Fish vendor $250

LEWIS, GLENN ALUN (signs Flakey Rose Hip)
26 Oct 1935, Chemainus, B.C. M WWA84
addr: Vancouver
1970 Glenn Lewis & Michael Morris
38 Did you ever milk a cow? cow, gallery, paintings, straw, feed, water plus cow's requirements

LEWIS, STANLEY
28 Mar 1930, Montreal M WWA84
addr: Outremont, 982 Pratt Ave, 1951. Montreal: 3020 Van Horne Ave, Apt 11. 1952-6; 4145 Blueridge Cr, 1960
1951 138 Fish etch $20
1952 148 Torso limestone
1953 107 At the circus pen & ink $20
1956 150 Profile soapstone $100
1960 247 Fallen bird limestone $650

LEWIS, WINIFRED D.
addr: Galt, Ont, 1918. Westmount, 4277 Western Ave, 1932-6
1918 209 Little Joe Lake, Algonquin Park wc
1932 165 Dawn at Minnesing, Algonquin Park pastel $35
1933 186 Hard times pastel $60
187 March woods, Hudson Heights, pastel $75
188 A bit of French Canada pastel $60
1934 177 The potato crop pastel $60
178 Road to the sugar bush pastel $100
1936 253 Le Bouvelard, Pointe aux Pêres pastel $100

LEY, CECILE SENECAL (Mrs)
addr: Montreal: 3500 Durocher St, 1937; 5798 Darlington Ave, 1941
1937 169 Gertrude
1941 114 Miss Joan Cameron
115 Study $40

LICUSHINE, DIMITRY SEMENOFF
24 Oct 1896, Rostoffen, Russia M
addr: Montreal, 3427 St Lawrence Blvd, 1936-52
1936 254 Interior $100
255 Still life $100
1937 170 Still life, after rehearsal $200
171 Still life, red onions $100
1952 26 Chef $200

LIEBICH, KATHLEEN CHIPMAN SWEENY (Mrs)
21 Jan 1892, Toronto M
addr: Westmount, 236 Redfern Ave, 1937-47
1937 172 Still life $20
1939 200 Garden, Montreal West wc $25
1941 116 Zinnias temp $25
117 Flower study wc $20
1943 121 Roses wc $25
1944 86 Roses wc $30
1947 154-5 Pansies wc $35 each

LIGHTBODY, MAYA (b Maria Antoinette Smodlibowski. m Russell N. Lightbody)
22 Aug 1933, Lwow, Poland M
addr: Regina, 3219 Westgate Ave, 1958. Montreal, 692 Canora Rd, 1960. Knowlton, Que, 1964
1958 69 Cats at night nm $15
1960 187 Pods nm $30
1964 97 Toad nm $35

LIGHTSTONE, HATTIE (Mrs)
addr: Westmount, 471 Strathcona Ave, 1946-7
1946 161 Elaine $200
1947 156 Little Joe $500

LILLEPOLD, EDWARD
1919, Estonia
addr: Montreal, 3495 Girouard Ave
1951 108 City at night $175

LILLEY, ALBERT E. V. Eng
fl 1892-1940 DBA DVP G RA WBA
addr: Wolverhampton, Eng
1909 228 The Quai Vert, Bruges $100
229 Fishing village, Devon wc $50
230 The captain's garden wc $50
231 A summer morning wc $40

LINDNER, ERNEST
1 May 1897, Vienna AGO CC1 CE CWW84
M WWA84
addr: Saskatoon: 104 London Block, 1933; 414 9th St E, 1962-4; Saskatoon, 1970
1933 189 Early thaw wc $60
1962 49 Wood forms nm $60
1964 97 A secluded wood nm $350
1970 39 Regeneration acry 40 x 30
40 Core of a tree acry 40 x 30 illus
41 Uprooted acry 40 x 30
42 The vine acry 40 x 30

LINDOE, LUKE ORTON
8 Mar 1913, Bashaw, Alta M
addr: Calgary: Coste House, 1948; Institute of Technology and Art, 1949
1948 83 Promised land wc $60
1949 134 Geranium wc $40

LINDSAY, ELLEN TRIDER
16 Dec 1900, Saint John, N.B. CWW61 M
addr: Halifax, 83 Morris St, 1942-3
1942 101 Kitchawan woods wc $35
1943 122 Bound for Britain, toys made for the children of Britain wc $20

LINDSAY, IAN GRAHAM
addr: Montreal, 456 Pine Ave, 1935-8. Westmount, 4275 Western Ave, 1939-40. Montreal, 1243 Bishop St, 1942. Ottawa, 65 St James St, 1947
1935 422 Trees in winter wash drwg $15
1936 256 Mountain swamp, Mount Royal wc $15
257 Rainy day, Laurentian Mountains wc $15
552 Decorative initial letters for books temp des
1937 421 The derelict, Quebec City charcl $20
422 Ex libris des pen & wash
1938 171 Illustrations 'Book of Genesis'. Creation, the fish of the sea, the seeds of the earth drwg (2)
1939 409 The yellow boat, St James' Cathedral reed pen & wc $20
410 Japanese legend, illustrations des $60
1940 372 The marionette dance des $25
373 The dragon of the mushroom

forest, Chinese legend des $30
374 The fairy monkey of Flower and Fruit Mountain, Chinese legend des $30
1942 204 Indian moons (calendar) drwg $70
1947 157 Pulp logs wc $45
158 Oil depot, Hull, Que wc $40

LINDSAY, MARGUERITE
addr: Montreal, 455 Sherbrooke St W
1915 477 Waste paper basket leather
478 Suede blotter

LINDSAY, ROBERT HENRY
23 Apr 1868, Prescott, Ont Mar 1938, Brockville, Ont H M
addr: Brockville: 1910-24; 38 King St W, 1925-34
1910 217 Gold and brown $25
218 Coal docks, Brockville $35
219 Winter evening $15
1911 185 An old street, moonlight $50
186 Hillside farm, winter $35
187 Winter $35
1912 237 Scarlet and gold $40
238 The green porch $60
239 Winter morning $40
240 Sunlit woods $15
1913 250 Twilight $200
251 The pool $60
252 Sunlit woods $40
1914 250 Winter
251 Sunset in the hills $25
252 The frozen stream $20
253 Winter sunset $20
1915 224 The coast of Antrim $25
225 Belfast Lough $50
1917 210 The new moon $75
211 The lake
212 The pool in the meadow
213 Grey weather
1918 210 Marauders $75
211 October $50
212 Evergreens
213 Winter morning on the St Lawrence $15
214 The lock keeper's home $15
215 Birch and pine $12
1919 186 Rockcliffe Park, Ottawa $50
187 The silent woods $50
188 A shady road $50
189 Belfast Lough $10
1920 159 The pines pastel $50
160 A French river $25
1921 141 Palmettos, Florida $15
142 Toll house on bridge, Halifax River $15
143 Florida sunshine $15
144 Florida landscape $15
1922 164 The little gray house
165 Snow storm $20
166 The garden gate, sketch $20
1923 138 Corn under snow $50
1924 149 Old fences $50
150 A summer day $15
151 After the storm $30
1925 160 The ravine $40
161 Ice going out pastel $50
1926 78 Ice going out $25
1927 102 A woodland $40
103 The Chinese grocery, Toronto pastel $40
1929 130 Ice moving out $30
1932 166 Spring, Buller's Creek, Brockville $40
1933 190 Fernbank, Brockville $50
191 The ogre and the lady $25
192 The veteran pine wc $20
1934 179 End of winter wc $20
180 The old farm $150

LING, JOYCE REJEANNE
addr: Montreal, 7011A Pie IX Blvd
1962 63 The new paradise nm
64 Joseph and Mary also went to register nm
65 Flowers for mother nm $25

LIPARI, FRANCOIS AMEDEO ANGELI (FRANK)
21 May 1927, Montreal M
addr: Montreal West, 434 Wolesley Ave N, 1958-60
1958 31 Winter harvest $300
1960 74 City under rain $200
188 Welcome and reluctance nm $120

LISKIND, SABINE (Mrs)
addr: Montreal, 20 Pine Ave W
1929 386 A bust of the family plaster

LISMER, ARTHUR
27 Jun 1885, Sheffield, Eng 23 Mar 1969, Montreal AGO B CC2 CE CWW64 EC M NGC PMC TB2 WWA62 Juror
addr: Montreal: 1485 Fort St, Apt 4, 1941-59; 2055 Fort St, Apt 4, 1960;

Montreal, 1968
1941 118 Rock and pine wc $150
236 Fishing gear, Nova Scotia reed pen $60
237 Incoming tide, Cape Breton Island reed pen $60
238 Driftwood reed pen $60
1942 103 Shoreline litter $350
104 Spring in the garden $150
1943 123 Beach on Fundy $200
124 Killicke $150
230 Fishing gear drwg $75
231 Laurentian waterfall drwg $75
1944 87 Northern river $200
141 Pine tree drwg $60
142 Nets and gear drwg $60
1945 148 Dark pool, Georgian Bay $325
149 Twisted Island $225
1947 159 Reflections, Georgian Bay $300
311 Fishing gear drwg $60
312 Georgian Bay islands drwg $75
1948 22 Fisherman's gear with pail $350
23 Dead pine, Georgian Bay $200
100 Pine roots, Georgian Bay ink drwg $75
1949 59 Backwater, Georgian Bay $250 (MBAM)
161 Fishing gear, Nova Scotia b&w $60
1952 27 Morning in the forest, B.C. $225
28 Forest and shore, Vancouver Island, B.C. $350
1953 23 Beach texture II $250
1954 53 Ghost tree, Vancouver Island $350
1955 52 Rock and sumac $200
1956 36 September in Georgian Bay $400
1957 59 Shells & cones $250
1959 31 Shore line, Vancouver Island, B.C. nm $100
1960 75 Forest tree, B.C. $450
1968 153 Landscape 16 x 20 $250
154 Landscape 18 x 14 $250
155-6 Forest trees 15 x 20 ink drwg $15 each

LITKE, LUCILLE THELMA
26 Mar 1932, Beausejour, Man
addr: Winnipeg, 165 Parkview St
1955 120 Flower study nm $8

LITTLE, HAROLD ROBERT
1866, London, Ont 14 Sep 1948 Montreal
see: Lawson, Harold, 1924-1939
Perry, Alfred Leslie, 1939

LITTLE, JOHN GEOFFREY CARUTHERS
28 Feb 1928, Montreal M NGC TB3
addr: Town of Mount Royal, Que, 470 Stanstead Ave, 1946-50. Montreal: 2077 Tupper St, Apt 14, 1953; 2066 Lincoln Ave, 1954. Town of Mount Royal, 1140 Dunraven Rd, 1961
1946 162 Looking at Jersey fron Ninth Avenue temp pastel $40
1947 160 Saturday afternoon $50
161 Frustrated Gershwin $50
1949 135 Rivington Street, New York City ink & wc
136 Stern-wheeler on the Yazoo ink & wc $100
1950 23 November afternoon $50
69 Mulberry Street, Little Italy ink & wc $80
1951 26 Back of the yards $75
27 Crescent City jazz $65
1952 29 Jeanne Mance Street $80
1953 24 Harlem jug band $100
1954 54 Rue Sous le Cap, Québec $150
1961 35 Sunday, Lagauchetière Street $500

LITTLE, NEIL
addr: Montreal, 1509 Sherbrooke St W
1946 163 Manhattan

LIVING, A. MARION
H
addr: Ottawa, 160 Lyon St, 1894-7
1894 193 Daffodils wc $25
194 Roses wc $25
1895 75 A working woman
1897 167 Roses wc $18
168 Little gipsy wc $25

LIVINGSTON, ALICE
fl 1891-7 H
addr: Paris, 1891. Montreal: 164 Mansfield St, 1892; Turkish Bath Hotel, 1894-5; 1018 Sherbrooke St, 1897
1891 171 Study, still life wc $15
172 Roses wc $20
1892 94 Tisane pot with buttercups $60
95 Fragment, after Fragonard
1894 Roses wc $20

196 Miss Dorothy Shepherd min on china
249 Vase, azaleas $25
250 Plate, decorative head $15
251 Fruit dish, Royal Berlin china $15
252 Wild rose plate $10
253 Cup & saucer, Sèvres blue $5
254 Plate, with monogram
255 Decorative glass, 2 pieces
1895 76 Old favorites $50
173 Sweet peas wc $25
174 In early spring wc $10
251 Dresden bowl, 6 plates $20
252 Clock, Sèvres blue $15
253 Plate, Sèvres blue $15
254 Vase $10
255 Bonbon dish $7
256 Tea cup $6
257 Cup, Coalport $5
258 Cup $3
259 Plate $5
260 Head, after picture in Louvre
1897 169 Old houses off St Louis St, Quebec wc $25
170 Sous le Cap, Quebec wc $20
171 Along the shore, Ile d'Orleans wc $15
172 A gray day wc $20

LIVINGSTON, GRACE M.
addr: Montreal, Turkish Bath Hotel
1895 261 Toilet tray and boxes
262 Tea cup $5
263 Tea cup, Dresden $1.50

LOCHHEAD, KENNETH CAMPBELL
22 May 1926, Ottawa AGO CC1 CE CWW84 M NGC TB3 WWA73
addr: Regina, School of Art, University of Saskatchewan, 1962-4. Winnipeg, 1967
1962 20 Perpetual illus Purchase award (MBAM)
1963 37 Blue extension illus $800 Jessie Dow prize 1967-37 80 x 97 3/4 acry
1964 49 Yellow rise illus $1,000 Grand award listed 1967, acry

LOCKERBY, ISABEL
addr: Montreal, 408 Mackay St
1913 253 The outcast wc $10
254 The Pied Piper wc $10
255 The fair wc $10
256 The boat wc $10

LOCKERBY, MABEL IRENE
13 Mar 1887 - 1 May 1976, Montreal
AGO M NGC TB2
addr: Montreal: 408 Mackay St, 1913-26; 1444 Mackay St, 1928-56; Montreal, 1967
1914 254 Sketch, Phillipsburg $10
255 Sketch, St Eustache $10
256 The swineherd $15
257 Summer $15
1915 226 Little Miss Muffet $15
227 The shepherdess $15
228 The pink lantern $15
229 A sunny day $15
1916 189 The pink cockatoo $60
190 The little goose girl $15
1917 214 The grey gander $75
215 The orange scarf $75
216 Spring $15
217 On the quay $15
218 Sketch on Mount Royal $10
219 The market pastel $15
1918 216 The kitten $75
217 The blue barges $25
218 Boys and birds $15
219 A summer day $15
220 Playmates $15
1919 190 The mermaid $50
191 Boy and squirrel $15
192 The red umbrella $15
193 The goose girl $15
194 Sketch of a soldier $15
195 Winter pastel $15
1920 161 Music $20
162 The boat $20
163 Homeward $20
164 Happy hours $20
1922 167 In the orchard $200
168 Boy and birds $50
169 The market wc $30
1923 139 Decoration $150
140 Joy pastel $40
1924 152 The turkey $75
153 Evening $20
154 Ploughing $20
155 Decoration $20
1925 162 The heron $15
163 The pond $15
164 In the garden wc $15
165 The fawn wc $15
166 A summer day wc $15
1926 79 On the canal $20

80 The jade necklace wc $15
1928 105 After the snowstorm, Caughnawaga $75
106 Waiting $15
107 Feeding the pigeons $15
1929 131 Late snow $150
132 Trout stream, Hudson $15
133 Melting snow $15
1932 167 On Dorchester Street $75
168 A starry night $75
169 The picnic $15
170 In Montreal $15
1933 193 The fountain $150
194 The china pigeon $50
195 A cat wc $10
196 A rooster wc $10
1935 187 After a snowstorm $20 (MBAM)
188 The pond $30
189 The old pink house $150
1936 258 Farm in Ste Marthe, Que $150
1938 78 Red apples $75
1939 201 Lucile et Fifi $200
202 Scarlet tulips $60
1942 105 The lily $50
1946 164 Old towers $100 1967-38 24 x 20 Jury II prize (Art Gallery of Hamilton)
1947 162 A waterfall $100
1948 24 The gold brooch $100
1951 109 Trees $50
1954 55 Bird bath $150
1956 115 Cat and stars nm $50

LOEMANS, ALEXANDER FRANCIS
fl 1882-94 H
1883 117 View on the Catskill Mountains

LOFVENGREN, THOMAS A.
addr: Montreal: 3630 Durocher St, 1929; 3717 Jeanne Mance St, 1931; 757 Vitre St W, 1934-5; 3180 St Antoine St, 1936
1929 251 Suffer little children to come unto me
252 Faith, hope, charity
253 Domestic windows
254 Charity
1931 300 Figure, hope st gl window
301 Life everlasting cart
302 Windows, Fairmount St Giles Church photo
303 Fortitude, devotion, loyalty
1934 396 St Matthew and St Mark st gl cart
397 St Luke and St John st gl cart
398 Medallion window st gl cart
1935 356 Project for Valleyfield Cathedral, H.S. Labelle, archi
357 Stained glass sketches
358 Romanesque, Gothic, Renaissance
369 Four Evangelists
1936 482 Jesse tree window, Valleyfield Cathedral, H.S. Labelle, archi
483 Ascension, east window, St Judes Church, sketch
484 Window, St Peter and St Paul sketch

LOGAN, MARTHA ALEXANDER
27 Jul 1863, Hartford, Conn c 13 Aug 1937, Toronto H M
addr: Toronto, 618 Ontario St, 1905-6; Toronto, 1908
1905 164 In the Don Valley wc $35
165 A country road wc $30
166 Sand dunes, Lake Erie wc $20
1906 246 October wc $35
247 August foliage wc $20
248 Cottage at Lambton wc $20
249 A German home wc $20
250 A country road wc $15
1908 Mary, mispr
96 Hollyhocks $20
224 Beaupré wc $50

LOGGIE, JOHN MILLAR
7 Jun 1896, Langside, Scot CNS36
addr: Montreal, 1321 Sherbrooke St W
1934 181 Morning on Medicine Lake $425

LOHSE, WALTER C.
addr: Montreal: 6014 Park Avem 1932-3; 758 Victoria Sq, 1946
1932 171 Menace $200
1933 197 Mural, Diana temp $60
1946 165 Family coat of arms temp

LOMER, LORNA GERTRUDE (m Robert E. Macaulay)
18 Jul 1881, Montreal M
addr: Montreal: 206 Peel St, 1905; 9 University Ave, 1906; Montreal, 1908. St Anne de Bellevue, Que, 1924. Gardenvale, Senneville, Que: 1929-31; 1 Elm-

wood Ave, 1932-47; 2 Elmwood Ave, 1949
1905 74 French Canadian milk house $20
75 Sweet sixteen $40
76 Claire
77 Miss Kathleen Draper
78 Miss Dorothy Holland
79 Chrysanthemums $15
1906 101 The spinning wheel $25
102 October evening $25
103 Little Dutch girl $20
104 A Dutch bride $25
105-6 Portrait
231 Baby boy pastel $10
310 Good night b&w $10
1908 97 In Bois de Boulogne $25
98 The morning $25
99 Out to sea $25
225 Asleep pastel $15
1924 Macaulay, 1924-49
1924 160 Janet pastel
1929 136 Kathleen Woodcock pastel
137 Janet pastel
1930 138 Hester Spriggs pastel
1931 156 Petunias pastel $60
157 Bittersweet pastel $50
1932 176 The turn of the road, Ste Geneviève pastel $50
177 Hawthorns after the storm pastel
178 Mrs Donald Macaulay pastel
1933 464 Self charcl
465 Helen charcl
1934 186 On the St Charles Road, Beaconsfield pastel
457 Helena Jocelyn drwg
1935 194 In Ste Geneviève pastel $100
470 Young boy plaster
1936 261 On the Baie de Chaleur wc $75
1937 175 Miss Gertrude Morrison $250
1939 205 On the North Shore road $80
1940 182 Afternoon, Isle of Orleans wc $100
1941 121 Bass woods, September $200
1943 126 Old church and presbytère, Ste Anne $125
1944 90 Basil Brooke Carter, Esq
91 Toronto roof tops wc $75
1945 151 Late winter afternoon, Toronto $200
152 Here, where the world is quiet pastel $150
1946 248A Sheila Grace
1947 165 Miss Truda Morrison $500
1949 60 Senneville, lindens and elms $500

LONDIGNY see BAILLARGEON, GERARD

LONG, BEATRICE MARY CARTER (Mrs)
5 Nov 1877, Kirton, Eng M
addr: Mount Royal, Que, 107 Wickstead ave
1932 172 A reverie

LONG, MARION
19 Sep 1992 - 19 Aug 1970, Toronto
AGO CWW67 M NGC TB2/3 W78 WWA66
addr: Toronto, Studio Bldg, Severn St
1919 196 God pity them, the womenfolk who mourn $300

LONGLEY (Miss)
1886 95 A Montreal news boy

LORANGER, GEORGES
1931, Sherbrooke, Que M
addr: Ottawa: 218 MacLaren St, 1960; 422 Queen St, 1961
1960 189 Kammermusik nm $60
1961 88 Medieval town nm $125

LORCINI, GINO
7 Jul 1923, Plymouth, Eng B CWW84 IO M WWA84
addr: Pointe Claire, Que, 1 Canterbury Park, 1960-5; Pointe Claire, 1967-8
1960 190 October etude nm $35
191 Hibernal nm $35
1962 74 Structural relief No 7 wd $225
1965 25 Alpha IX illus $475 1967-39 structural rel alum on perspex 24 x 36 Jessie Dow prize (Miss Frances Plaunt, Peterborough, Ont)
1968 157 Triple fugue alum on board 44 x 65 $1,000
158 Prélude and fugue alum on board 37 x 17 $1,600
159 Prismus F S major alum 23 h $1,200
160 Prismus B A B major alum 23 h $1,200

LORD, WALTER H.
b 1913
addr: Toronto, 338 George St, 1939-40
1939 wood engraving, 1939-40
411 Popcorn vendor $10
412 Old Dad's book shop $15
413 Night watchman $10

414 Woman in the window $10
1940 375 Passive resistance $10
376 Solace $10
377 Call of the soil $10

LORENZ, CHARLOTTE EMILY
5 May 1871 - 4 Oct 1950, Montreal
addr: Montreal: 477 Berri St, 1905; 1475 St Hubert St, 1910-11. no addr 1912
1905 80 The brook in the glen $10
1910 220 In the glen $18
1911 182A Still life $25
1912 241 Village home, Bristol Corners $20

LORIMIER, GUILLEMETTE DE
addr: Montreal, 1501 Closse St, 1940-1. Westmount: 2 Grove Park, 1944-6; 425 Wood Ave, 1948-51
1940 179 Snow storm, Ste Marguerite $30
180 Kate Vale $30
1941 119 Troisème Rang, Knowlton $25
1944 29 Côtes 40 and 80 $40
1945 66 Madame Rolland
1946 63 Sur le chemin de Ste Agnès
1948 26 Un coin de Paris
1951 28 Automne $100

LORIMER, PETER B.
addr: Montreal, 1445 Plessis St
1948 117 Pregnant woman plaster & sand $100

LORING, FRANCES NORMA
14 Oct 1887, Wardner, Idaho 5 Feb 1968, Newmarket, Ont AGO CC2 CE CWW64 EC M NGC W78 WWA62
addr: Toronto, 110 Glen Rose Ave
1922 341A The rod turner bronze $350
341B The oiler bronze $350 (NGC)

LORRAIN, ROBERT
c 1941, St Jean, Que
addr: St Jean, 182 rue Champlain
1964 126 Petite dame bois $400

LOUDIGNY see BAILLARGEON, GERARD

LOUDON, ISABEL MARY
8 Nov 1884, Toronto M
addr: Ottawa, 230 Chapel St, 1924-6
1924 284 Cretonne des temp $40
285 Foulard dress des temp $15
286 Foulard dress 2 motive des temp $10
1926 205 Book plates 2, $15 each

LOUGHEED, ROBERT ELMER
27 May 1910, Massey, Ont M WWA82
addr: Montreal, 1201 Sherbrooke St W, 1945. New York, 1946. Montreal: c/o Continental Galleries, 1948; 1450 Drummond St, 1952
1945 150 Farm scene, Valleyfield, Que
1946 166 Logging near Lachute $650
1948 25 Haystacks $500
1952 30 Bush scene with horses, near Lachute $450
31 Ploughing team, Baie St Paul $450

LOUVIN see VINEBERG, LOUISE

LOVELAND, LOUISE A. (Mrs Walter F. Loveland)
addr: Victoria, 1311 Point St
1921 145 A July morning, Victoria $25

LOVERING, IDA R. Eng
fl 1881-1915 DBA DBW DVP RA
addr: London, Eng, 24 Yeomans Row
1912 242 Fine feathers make fine birds $500
243 Evening prayer $500

LOVEROFF, FREDERICK NICHOLAS (b Postnikoff)
c 8 Jun 1894, Terpania, Russia 12 Aug 1959, Redwood City, Cal AGO CC2 M NGC PMC TB2
addr: Toronto, 13 Ottawa St
1922 170-72 Sketch $35 (1) $45 (2)

LOW, NESTA
addr: Montreal, 16 Highland Ave
1930 136 Portrait study pastel

LOW, WARWICK J.
addr: Montreal, 4076 Highland Ave, 1933-4
1933 198 Peleated woodpeckers wc $50
1934 182 Rough-legged hawk wc $50
183 Rose breasted grosbeaks wc $50

LOWDEN, CATHERINE V.
addr: Montreal
1908 395 Panel, corn

396 Panel, oranges
397 Vase, blue and white iris
398 Vase, geraniums
399 Vase, roses
400 Jardiniere, trumpet vine
401 Punch bowl, grapes
402 Chop dish, sweet peas

LOWE, NELLIE KEILLOR (m Kenneth Lowe)
c 1917, Baggot, Man 18 May 1967, Sudbury, Ont M
addr: Sudbury, General delivery
1956 116 Oneping Falls nm $60

LOWREY, JOHN D.
d 1945 M
addr: Montreal, 1564 Stanley St
1944 88 Laurentian hills $150

LOYNES, DE (Miss)
addr: Montreal
1909 232 Pavillion de Flore wc
233 Jardins, Grand Trianon wc
234 L'Esplanade des Invalides wc
235 Pont Neuf

LUBICZ, F. R. (or F. H. Lubiez)
addr: Montreal, 990A Sherbrooke St (addr listing, F. H. Lubiez)
1903 82 On the mountain $100

LUCE, CLARENCE
addr: New York, 246 4th Ave
1905 247-8 Country estate, des, courtyard view
249-50 Estate, bird'e eye view, fountain detail
251 Library building des
252-3 New York State Building 2 views

LUCKOCK, CHARLES WARREN
13 Jun 1915, Toronto AGO M
addr: Montreal, 3085 Durocher St, 1937. Toronto, 527 Crawford St, 1938
1937 173-4 Fog No 1, No 2, wc $25 each
423 Ship building reed pen $25
424 November winds reed pen $25
1938 172 Trees, Mount Royal reed pen $25

LUKE, JANE CORBUS (m E.B. Luke)
25 Sep 1881, Chicago M
addr: Montreal West, 41 Brock Ave, 1922-44
1922 173 Lac Mercier at sunset $50
1924 156 Still life $30
1927 104 Still life, peonies $125
1928 108 Main Street $75
109 Calendulas, still life $35
1929 134 Mrs Morley C. Luke
135 French Canadian houses near Montreal $35
1930 137 In Gloucester harbour $85
1931 152 Chrysanthemums and Buddha $100
153 Still life $100
1932 173 Peonies $100
1934 184 The reflection $450
185 Rockport wharf $75
1935 190 Near St Vincent de Paul $50
191 Village street, Ste Dorothée $50
1936 259 In the lagoon $100
260 September afternoon, Abord-à-Plouffe $40
1939 203 Peonies $75
1940 181 The T'ang camel $50
1941 120 Zinnias on the verandah wall $100
1942 106 Pink dogwood and chinese pottery $150
1943 125 T'ang Buddah and chrysanthemums $200
1944 89 Peonies and the Sevres flower sellers $150

LUKE, MARGARET ALEXANDRA (m Marcus Everett Smith. m Clarence Ewart McLaughlin)
14 May 1901, Montreal 2 Jun 1967. Oshawa, Ont CWW64 M TB3 WWA70
addr: Oshawa, 222 Kendall Ave
1950 121 Traveller's palm $100

LUKE, MORLEY CORBUS
12 Apr 1901, Chicago
see Perry, Alfred Leslie, 1928-39

LUND, CARL CHRISTIAN
1874, Newcastle-on-Tyne, Eng M
addr: Ottawa, 20 Hunderson Ave
1920 165 Spring $45
166 October moon $35
167 Winter evening wc $35

LUND, KNUT
c 1909, Norway M

addr: Montreal, 2945 Barclay Ave
1951 71 Torso plaster $75

LYALL, LAURA see MUNTZ, LAURA

LYLE, JOHN MACINTOSH
13 Nov 1872, Belfast 20 Dec 1945, Toronto CO CWW36 NGC TB3
see Ross, George Allen, 1916

LYMAN, IDE
addr: Montreal, 2049 Aylmer Ave
1936 599 Mrs D'hont plaster

LYMAN, JOHN GOODWIN
29 Sep 1886, Biddeford, Me 26 May 1967, Barbados B CC2 CE CWW64 M NGC TB2 WWA66 Juror
addr: Paris, 1910-11. Westmount, 636 Roslyn Ave, 1912. Warwick East, Bermuda, 1914-18. Montreal, c/o Henry Morgan & Co, 1920. Outremont, 21 Peronne Ave, 1928. Montreal: 1490 Drummond St, 1931; 1524 Bishop St, 1935; 3625 Oxenden Ave, 1939. Westmount, 4038 Tupper St, 1947-8. Montreal, 1509 Sherbrooke St W, 1955
1910 221 Tidal river, La Canche $125
222 Paris plage $75
223 Marine $45
1911 188 August afternoon, Normandy $35
189 On the sands, Picardy $35
1912 244-7 Landscape $175, $175, $150 $75
248 Portrait $250
1913 257 Humoresque, the circus $500
258 A brunette $400
259 Wild nature, impromptu $300
260 Bagatelle, a cottage
1914 258 Bermudian essay $40
259 Impromptu $40
1915 230 Bermudian essay 2 $40 (NGC)
231 Portrait, design
232 Portrait, impromptu
1917 220 Portrait $100
221 Sketch $35
1918 221 Portrait
222 Portrait of the artist (MQ)
1920 168 Portrait study
169-70 St Georges, Bermuda
1928 112 In the Pyrenees $275
113 Interior $275
1931 155 On the beach, St-Jean-de-Luz $225
1935 192 Laurentian lake $200
193 Suzanne au bain $300
1939 204 Before the battle $225
1947 163 Hugh MacLennan $350
164 Still life with fruit $225
1948 27 Rose $350 (MBAM)
28 Portrait of the artist $200
1955 53 Blue eyes $500

LYMAN, WALTER KENNETH GORDON
17 Jan 1897 - 10 Sep 1951, Montreal
addr: Montreal: 74 McTavish St, 1921-3; 374 Beaver Hall Hill, 1925; 2058 Victoria St, 1929-34; 3520 McTavish St, 1935; 2058 Victoria St, 1936-7
1921 146 Late afternoon, Pine Avenue wc
147 Selby Abbey b&w
148 Melrose Abbey b&w
149 Durham Cathedral wc
1923 141 Rome b&w
142 Arch of Titus
1925 355 Maples, 1924 etch $20
356 Bridge at Constantine, North Africa litho $20
1929 255 House, P.S. Fisher, Esq
256 House, Lake Memphremagog
257 Proposed house, J.B. Macphail
258 House, 48 St Sulpice Rd
329 Santa Maria Della Salute litho
330 Venice, 1928 litho
331 Villa d'Este, Rome, 1928 litho
1932 174 Naples wc
175 Villa d'Este wc
352 New Rosedale School
353-5 Residence, Montreal, library from hall, stairway, drawing room
406 Venice litho
1933 393 Front door, 56 Belvedere Circle
394 Residence, 3117 Dulac Rd
395 Proposed residence, Lexington Avenue
463 Santa Maria Della Salute litho
1934 399 Interior country residence wc
400, 402 Proposed Montreal residence
401 Residence, 56 Belvedere Circle
1935 360 Park Toboggan Club House, Mount Royal, and interior wc
1936 485-6 Proposed residence, Montreal wc
487 Proposed skiing lodge, Laurentians wc

488 Proposed week-end sports house, Laurentians wc
1937 348-9 Proposed residence, Montreal wc

LYNCH, JAMES O'CONNOR
8 Oct 1908, Sydney, N.S. WWA62
addr: Montreal, 525 Prince Arthur St W
1945 261 J.G. Drouin, Esq drwg

LYNN, VERN
addr: Montreal, 3270 Barclay Ave, 1950. Westmount, 4081 Dorchester St W, 1951-5
1950 122 Mountain village $250
1951 110 Still life $100
1952 97 Musicians $150
98 Town vista $100
1955 54 Musicians $150

M

MCARTHUR, JOHN
fl 1876-86 H
1886 123 Autumn
137 Near St Michaels
138 Autumn, Le Grand Ruisseau

MACAULAY, JOHN PHILIP RANKIN
26 Jan 1926, Montreal M
addr: Montebello, Que, 1952 Arundel, Que, 1954
1952 33 December rain $80
1954 56 Portage, October $145

MACAULEY, LORNA see LOMER, LORNA

MACBEAN, CLARA SOPHIA
1841, Cobourg, Ont H M
addr: Montreal: 390 Mountain St, 1895; 120 Durocher St, 1905; 104 Shuter St, 1909; 17 Shuter St, 1910; 22 Colonial Ave, 1911
1895 77 African oranges
78 Our kitchen friends $30
1905 238 Mustapha inférieure, Algiers drwg $25
1909 236 In Algiers b&w
1910 224 Fresh dates
225 Dr H. McHugh's old barn
1911 190 Mrs Southwick's flour mill, St Hilaire $25

MCBRIDE, DONALD
c 1923, St Catherines, Ont 4 Feb 1971, Niagara Falls, Ont M
addr: Westmount, YMCA Sherbrooke St W
1955 121 Grass forms nm $60

MCBURNEY, ELIZABETH B.
addr: Montreal: 710 St Antoine St, 1925; 125 Prince Arthur St W, 1926
1925 conventional des
319 Yellow cyclamen $5
320 Geranium $4.50
1926 167 Bowl $8
168-9 Plate $3 each

MCCAFFREY, JOHN ALLAN
18 Apr 1904, Liverpool, N.S. M
addr: Halifax: 321 Morris St, 1934; 1 Bedford Row, 1936
1934 215 The appeal $75
216 At dawn $25
1936 291 Rocky shore $25

MACCARTHY, COEUR DE LION
1881, London, Eng 22 Jan 1979, Montreal M
addr: Montreal: 1908; P.O.Box 31, 1911; Studio, 44 Victoria St, 1914; no addr 1915
1908 289 Lt Col A.A. Stevenson bust from life plaster $250
1911 291 A wave sculp $50
292 Seated figure sculp $25
1914 439 A lady statuette plaster
440 Fire place, dec panel plaster
441 Lady min bust plaster
1915 379 Late Miss Jessie Caverhill-Cameron medln $25

MCCARTHY, DORIS JEAN
7 Jul 1910, Calgary AGO CWW84 IO M WWA84
addr: Scarborough Bluffs, Ont, 1955; 1 Meadowcliffe Dr, 1957-61
1955 122 Edge of the ravine nm $85
1957 132 Edge of Loon Lake nm $125
133 La Flamme's lobster house nm $100
1961 91 Woods at Sanctuary Lake nm $150

MCCARTHY, FORREST TIMOTHY
7 Oct 1924, Trenton, N.J.
addr: Montreal, 1445 Plessis St, 1948

Verdun, Que, 434 3rd Ave, 1949. Lac Brulé, Que, 1953. Montreal: 2105 Valois St, 1954; 7460 Champlain Blvd, 1955
1948 102 Reclining figure etch & dry pt $18
1949 163 Montreal street scene dry pt $20
1953 84 Log cabin interior $100
1954 62 Christmas eve at lumber camp $60
63 Les trois chiens $80
1955 62 Woodcutter's lunchtime $80

MACCARTHY, HAMILTON THOMAS CARLETON PLANTAGENET
28 Jul 1846, London, Eng 24 Oct 1939, Ottawa B CWW36 DBA EC G M Mo98/12 NGC PMC TB1/3 W78
addr: Toronto: 12 Lombard St, 1891; Toronto, 1892: 28 Toronto St, 1898. Ottawa: 1908; 377 O'Connor St, 1912
1889 198 Parting of Paul and Virginia sculp $25
1891 218 L.R. O'Brien, Esq, 1st Pres RCA
1892 231 Mr A.T. Todd bust
232 Rev Principal Grant bust
1898 232 The messenger of love sculp $75
1908 288 Sir Sandford Flemming, KCMG, Chancellor of Queen's University bust bronze, from life, replicas $500
1912 410 Rt Hon Earl Grey, PC GCB bust

MCCAUGHEY, BETTY see FRENCH, BETTY

MCCLELLAND, ELIZABETH K.
addr: Westmount, 111 Aberdeen Ave
1940 326 Interior, Adam period des

MCCLUNIN, F. A.
addr: Montreal, 220 Mountain St
1925 182 Through the notch $100
183 The harbour $100

MCCONKEY, GWYNETT
addr: Montreal, 4070 Highland Ave
1940 327 Interior, early colonial des
383 Interior, Metropolitan Museum, N.Y. wc

MCCONNELL, M. CARY
b Blyth, Huron Co, Ont fl 1890-1939 H
addr: Toronto: 86 Dundas St, 1892; 21 Wilton Cr, 1894; 89 Canada Life Bldg, 1895; 1 Pythian Hall, 124 Victoria St, 1898
1892 96 Meadow stream $25
1894 105 Study of a head $30
1895 82 Out-door portrait study of O.R. Jacobi, RCA $50
1898 78 A grey day $30

MCCORKINDALE, JAMES
c 1886, Glasgow 6 Aug 1956, Montreal
addr: Montreal, 2407 Madison Ave, 1937-51
1937 191 Dawn, Gloucester, Mass $250
1940 202 Hazy weather $150
1942 111 Dawn $160
112 Lanesville wc $80
1943 136 Eventide, Nova Scotia $200
1945 161 Lachine Canal wc $100
1946 176 Hauling in the nets $300
1947 189 Pidgeon Cove $200
190 A grey dawn $200
1949 70 Harbour scene, Gloucester $300
1950 28 Gloucester boats $200
1951 31 Old oven, Baie St Paul $200

MCCULLOCH, MABEL (m Donald M. Gass)
b New Glasgow, N.S. d 1977 WWA62
addr: Charlottetown, P.E.I, 80 Longworth Ave
1934 217 Fishing fleet, Grand Etang, Cape Breton $35

MCCULLOUGH, CHARLES R. (Mrs)
addr: Hamilton, 303 John St S
1939 226 Phlox $60

MACDERMOT, AUDREY M.
addr: Montreal, 4200 Côtes des Neiges Rd, 1947-50
1947 168 Eva $40
1950 24 Gwynnie

MCDERMOTT, A. D. S.
addr: Montreal, 2021 St Urbain St
1947 191 Sous-le-Cap, Québec wc

MACDONALD, ALBERT ANGUS
22 Jul 1909, Bristol, Eng CWW84 M
addr: Toronto: 600 Lonsdale Rd, 1934-5; 26 Grenville St, 1937-8. York Mills, Ont, The Mill, RR1, 1949

1934 458 Bluenose, frozen in pr $10
1935 195 The yellow mask $30
1937 176 Chrysanthemums wc $35
177 Zinnia wc $35
1938 79 The press $200
1949 61 Autumn wind $150

MACDONALD, ANNE BELINDA GWENLLIAN
10 Jul 1929, Dibrugarh, India
addr: c/o London Public Library, Ont
1955 55 Portrait $75

MACDONALD, ARCHIBALD ST AUBYN
3 Mar 1931, Verdun, Que M
addr: Montreal: 3920 Rosemount Blvd, Apt 4, 1949-50; 5252 Walkley Ave, Apt 2, 1952
1949 62 Still life with oil lamp $50
1950 123 Still life with potatoes $75
1952 121 Trees by the river wc

MACDONALD, BEVERLEY
addr: Toronto, 4 Rosedale Rd
1941 122 Evening $40

MACDONALD, ELSIE AMY (m N.S. Macdonald)
29 May 1906, Camberwell, London, Eng M
addr: Montreal, 1963 Rockland Ave
1957 60 A backyard scene $75

MACDONALD, EVAN WEEKES
9 Jun 1905 - c 24 Jan 1972, Guelph, Ont CNS36 CWW73 M
addr: Toronto, 68 Grenville St, 1933. Guelph, RR6, 1949-50; 298 Edinburgh Rd S, 1960
1933 199 Algoma panorama $175
1949 63 Figure painting $400
1950 25 Flora Rocks $275
1960 76 Sword fish packers, Lunenburg $450

MACDONALD, GRANT KENNETH
27 Jun 1909, Montreal AGO CC1 CWW84 EC 10 M TB2 WWA84
addr: Toronto, Roberts Gallery, 27 Grenville St, 1941-2. Kingston, Ont, 188 Collingwood St, 1943, 1949-54. Ottawa, HMCS Bytown, 1944. Kingston, 1968
1941 123 Miss Mary Keens
124 Dr Kenneth Macdonald
125 Miss Greer Garson
239 Mr Noel Coward pencil
1942 107 Miss Tamara Toumanova
108 Miss Irina Baronova
1943 127 Eva Lis Wuorio
128 Leading Seaman C. Cattle pastel
232 Tallulah Bankhead drwg
1944 Sub-Lieutenant
92 Old music
1949 64 Standing woman oil & temp $500
1954 57 Two girls $600
1968 161 Generations oil on gesso 48 x 48 $1,000
162 Entourage temp 30 x 24 $550

MACDONALD, JAMES ALEXANDER STERLING
7 Dec 1921, Abbey, Sask CC1 M NGC
addr: Vancouver, 3972 West 36th Ave, 1954-7
1954 109 Priory High Street wc $150
110 Near Covent Garden wc $150
1957 61 Market, Mexico $185

MACDONALD, JAMES EDWARD HERVEY
12 May 1873, Durham Eng 26 Nov 1932, Toronto AGO CC2 CE EC L M NGC R2 TB2 W78
addr: Toronto: 475 Quebec Ave, 1909; 25 Severn St, 1924
1909 244 Quiet morning $30
245 The maple bush $20
1924 223 A friendly meeting, early Canada. Shown RCA 1923 exhibit, mural competition, 1st prize $500

MACDONALD, JAMES WILLIAMSON GALLOWAY (JOCK)
31 May 1897, Thurson, Scot 3 Dec 1960, Toronto AGO CC2 CE CWW58 M NGC TB2 W78 WWA59
addr: Calgary, Provincial Institute of Technology, 1947. Toronto, 4 Maple Ave, 1960
1947 166 Sandpiper wc $85
167 Fish and polliwog wc $78
1960 77 Earth awakening $750

MACDONALD, MANLY EDWARD
15 Aug 1889, Point Anne, Ont 10 Apr 1971, Toronto AGO CC2 CWW67 M NGC TB2 WWA70
addr: Toronto, 56 Grenville St
1938 80 Portrait

MACDONALD, ROBERT HENRY
7 Mar 1875, Melbourne, Australia 18

Dec 1942, Montreal CNS27 CO CWW36 PMC
see Ross, George Allen, 1916-33

MACDONALD, THOMAS REID
28 Jun 1908, Montreal 15 Oct 1978, Paris, France CWW73 M NGC TB3 WWA78
Juror
addr: Montreal: 3506 Durocher St, 1929; 1475 St Catherine St W, 1930-1; 3531 St Famille St, 1932-3, 1937-8; (studio) 1104 Beaver Hall Hill, 1934-6. Sackville, N.B, Mount Allison University, 1946. St Sauveur des Monts, Que, 1947. Hamilton, Ont: 22 Main St W, 1949-51; 24 Sherman Ave S, 1952; 175 Dufferin St, 1954; Hamilton, 1968
1929 138 Still life $75
1930 139 Still life $50
1931 158 Nocturne $100
159 Burlesque $75
160 Self portrait
1932 179 The cast $75
180 Still life $75
1933 200 Winter night $50
201 Stage entrance, winter $35
202 Paul in grey
466 Portrait sketch drwg
1934 187 Two-a-day $100
188 Winter street $40
189 Still life $40 (MBAM)
1935 196 Paul in green $100
197 Deserted farm, autumn $75
198 Tropical plant $50
1936 262 James Crockart, Esq
263 The black bottle $50
264 The hill at night $75
1937 178 The green shed $50
1938 81 Portrait
82 Girl in blue $200
1946 167 Girl and cast $100
1947 169 Man in black overcoat $300
1949 65 Dancer in black $200
1950 26 Brenda $300
27 Two dancers $200
1951 29 Grey gloves
1952 32 Snow on King Street $200
1954 58 Night portrait $200
59 Mr Vincent $300
1968 163 The green shirt 36 x 28 $350
164 Sandra in the mirror 48 x 36 $500
port: by Henry L. Smith, 1933-490

MCDONIC, HENRY REED (HARRY)
24 Oct 1902, West Hartlepool, Eng
27 Nov 1982, Toronto
addr: Toronto, 684 Church St, Apt 1
1939 224 Saint James' Cathedral wc $150
225 Notre Dame de Victoire wc $200

MACDONNELL, HARRIETTE J.
H (p206)
addr: Montreal: 91 Aylmer St, 1891, 1894-1911; Victoria School of Art, 1892; 647 Aylmer St, 1921-2
1888 76 Sketch in Sydney, Cape Breton wc $10
89 When the wave beats wc $20
113 Old houses, Sydney, Cape Breton wc $25
115 The old Bonsecours Church, Montreal wc $20
1889 137 Citadel ruins, Louisbourg, Cape Breton wc $25
138 Louisbourg harbour, C.B. wc $25
139 Old Bonsecours Church wc $10
140 Sketch, Baie St Paul wc $25
141 A landslip, Baie St Paul wc $25
142 An old oven, Baie St Paul wc $25
1891 81 A wayside Cross, Cap à l'Aigle $35
173 Low tide, Murray Bay wc $15
174 On the beach, Cap à l'Aigle wc $25
175 Washing day, Cap à l'Aigle wc $20
176 Still life study wc $20
1892 97 Indian pottery, Mexico $50
183 Stormy weather, Cape Breton coast wc $30
184 English church, Cap à l'Aigle wc $20
1894 197 An emigrant wc $25
198 At a coal pier, Cape Breton wc $15
199 Study wc $15
200 Scotch roses wc $8
256 Toilet tray
257 Powder box
278 Clock case pyro $6
279 Bread plate, knife pyro $3
280 Frame pyro $2
281 Key rack pyro $2
1895 175 At Cap à l'Aigle wc
176 Drying sails wc $25

177 Roses wc $25
178 Chrysanthemums wc $20
264 Tea caddy $8
265 Rose plate $7.50
266 Cream jug, sugar bowl $6
267 Plate, Scotch roses $5
268 Chocolate cup & saucer $2.50
269 Bonbon box $2.50
270 Cup & saucer, Dresden $1.50
271 Pin tray $1.50
272 Match box $1.25
pyrography
291 Mirror $5
292 Bread plate $3
293, 295 Key rack $2.50, $1.75
294 Bonbon box $2
296 Salad fork & spoon $1.25
297 Watch stand $1
298 Match box $1
299 Paper knife $1
1897 173 Château de Grand Maison, 1652, l'Ile d'Orleans wc $25
174 Le maison de René Pelletier, 1689, l'Ile d'Orleans wc $25
175 Lumber bateau, Quebec wc $18
tile, 256-261
256 Citadel, Quebec $2.50
257 Prison in Citadel, Quebec $2.50
258 Quebec $2.50
259 St Joseph $2.50
260 Wolfe and Montcalm Monument, Quebec $2.50
261 Wolfe's Headquarters, Ile d'Orleans $2.50
262 Bonbon box $4
263 Afternoon tea plates, 6 $9
1898 168 Oven at Cap à l'Aigle wc $20
169 Normandy barn, Cap à l'Aigle wc $10
170 Hay boat, Murray Bay wc $12
171 Farm house, Cap à l'Aigle wc $20
172 Un foyer, Ile d'Orleans wc $30
251 Plaque, Chien d'Or, Quebec $5.75
tile, 252-7
252 Old Bonsecours Church, Montreal $2.75
253 Seminary gate $2.75
254 St Gabriel Church $2.75
255 Mountain Hill, Quebec $2.75
256 House where Montgomery's body was carried, 1775, Quebec $2.75
257 Quebec $2.75
258 Châteay Ramezay, Montreal pen tray $2.75
259 Baie St Paul village pen tray $2.75
260 Old mill, Lachine tea pot stand $2.75
261 Towers, Priests' Farm, Montreal tea pot stand $2.75
262 Murray Bay tea caddy $2
263-4 Salve pot $1.25 each
265 Pin tray $1.25
266 Photo stand $1
267-8 Jardiniere $1.75 each
1900 139 The road side, Cap à l'Aigle wc $35
140 Summer wc $18
141 A restful hour, Ile d'Orleans
tile, 231-7
231 Citadel, Quebec $3.50
232 Chien d'Or $3.50
233 Old Breakneck Stairs $3.50
234 Notre Dame Street, 1840 $10
235 Chief Bear Claw Crow $10
236 Chief Pretty Eagle Crow $5
237 Old towers $2.75
1901 141 A vetch meadow, Cap à l'Aigle wc $25
142 The road side, Murray Bay $25
142 Murray Bay $18
1903 195 Farm yard, Cap à l'Aigle wc $20
196 The Seigneur's oven, Cap à l'Aigle wc $15
197 Vetch meadow wc $15
198 The French village, Murray Bay wc $25
199 Before rain, Murray Bay wc $25
1905 167 Under the spruces, Cap à l'Aigle wc $35
168 Post office, Cap à l'Aigle wc $25
169 Pointe à Pic, Murray Bay wc $35
170 Coming rain, Murray Bay wc $18
171 Mushroom growth wc $20
1908 226 In Venice wc $18
227 Near Crickhowell, Wales wc $14
228 Irish coast, Co. Antrim wc $17
1910 226 Le Pont de Lions, Bruges wc $25
227 A side canal, Bruges wc $17
228 In Bruges, la morte $25
1911 191 Monotropa uniflora wc $25
192 In Siena wc $25
193 Quebec wc $15
194 Trout Beck, Cumberland wc $20
1921 150 In Beniguet wood, Cap à l'Aigle wc $45

151 The Points, Murray Bay wc $50
152 A wild garden, Cap à l'Aigle wc $35
153 San Giorgio Maggiore, Venice wc $35
1922 174 In Bruges wc $40

MCDOUGALL, CLARK HOLMES
21 Nov 1921, St Thomas, Ont IO M
addr: St Thomas: 56 Inkerman St, 1950; 51 Redan St, 1953
1950 71 Blossoms in May wc $150
72 The corner store wc $150
1953 85 Buffalo street scene $375

MCDOUGALL, IDA LAWSON (Mrs)
addr: Montreal, 45 McGregor St, 1925. Rosemere, Que, 1940
1925 184 Still life $50
1940 203 Farm yard $125

MCDOUGALL, JAMES CECIL
4 Jul 1886, Three Rivers, Que 20 Apr 1959, Montreal CWW64 PMC
addr: Montreal: 85 Osborne St, 1923-9; 1221 Osborne St, 1931-7
1923 270 Residence, A. Sidney Dawes, Cedar Ave
271 Residence, J.M. Morris
1924 335 Residence, A.S. Dawes, Esq
336 Residence, J.M. Morris, Esq, Montreal
337 Residence, W.A. Morris, Esq, Hampstead
338 St Maurice Power Co, La Gabelle, Que, power house
1927 223 House, Senneville, Que
1929 259 Residence, Westmount, preliminary sketch
260 Residence, Armand Chevalier, Esq, Senneville, Que
261 Residence, F.R. Whittall, Esq, Sunnyside Ave, Westmount
262 Klean-Rite, garage, St Catherine St, Montreal
1931 312 Anglo-American Trust Co, building, Montreal
313 Residence, Armand Chevalier, Esq, Senneville, Que
314 Proposed Jewish hospital, Montreal
315 Montreal General Hospital, Western Division, proposed private pavilion
1933 400 Attic room, residence Geo. C. McDonald
401-3 Protestant Board of School Commissioners, Administration Bldg, board room, secretary's office, entrance hall
1934 403 Proposed residence, Sunnyside Ave, Westmount
404 Proposed residence, Westmount, preliminary sketches
1935 362-4 Montreal General Hospital, Private Patients Pavilion, main entrance hall, south view, main operating room, typical patient's room, main kitchen, typical ward kitchen, metabolism laboratory
1937 356 Proposed residence, Sunnyside Ave, Westmount
see also Fetherstonhaugh, Harold Lee, 1920-2

MACE, S.H. mispr, see MAW, SAMUEL H.

MCELHERON, JAMES THOMAS
21 Feb 1915, Vancouver M
addr: Ottawa, 8 Driveway, 1961. Montreal, 2030 Closse St, 1963
1961 40 Reflections $200
1963 43 Gatineau promenade No 2 $500

MCEVOY, HENRY NESBITT (HARRY)
1828, Birmingham, Eng 21 Apr 1914, Detroit Gr H
addr: London, Ont
1895 83 Dundas Falls, near Hamilton $30

MCEWEN, JEAN ALBERT
14 Dec 1923, Montreal AGO B CC1 CE CWW84 M TB3 WWA84 Juror
addr: Montreal: 4710 Decarie Blvd, 1949-50; 580 Davaar Ave, 1961-5; Montreal, 1967-8
1949 71 Still life with pineapple $100
1950 126 Nature morte avec plante $40
1961 41 Le grande verticals $800
1962 21 Meurtrière traversant le bleu No 3 (MBAM)
1963 44 Mediane travesant le mauve
1964 51 Le drapeau inconnu illus $2,000. Jessie Dow prize. 1967-42 diptyque 78 x 80
1965 11 Blanc et noir comme un livre ouvert $2,500
1968 émulsion polymère

166 Tableau pour Dominique 68 x 78 $2,100
167 Tableau pour Isabelle 70 x 72 $2,100

MACFARLANE, DAVID HURON
1875, Montreal 1 Feb 1950, Mont St Hilaire M PMC
addr: Montreal: Bank of Nova Scotia Bldg, 1905; Beaver Hall Hill, 1909; New Birks Bldg, 1913-16. Westmount, 611 Sydenham Ave, 1921. Mont St Hilaire, Que, 1926-34, 1941. Montreal: Scott & Sons, 1490 Drummond St, 1935, 1937; Johnson Art Galleries, 1340 St Catherine St W, 1939; Edlington's Ltd, 1468 Mansfield St, 1940; Steveens Art Gallery, 1450 Drummond St, 1943
1905 172 The Back River wc
1909 246 Bic Bay wc
1913 261 Isle Massacre, Bic wc $50
430 New Park School, Westmount (arch)
1916 191 Winter morning, Westmount pastel
1921 155 The harbour opposite Bonsecours Market $40
1922 175 Hauling logs, Back River $50
1926 81 A March morning $50
1927 105 On the Beaupré road wc $40
106 View from the Island of Orleans wc $40
1928 114 Skagway harbour, Alaska wc $45
1932 181 Above St Joachim on the Murray Bay road wc $50
1933 203 Rocks and shore, Bic wc $75
1934 190 Cap des Rosiers, Gaspé wc $75
1935 199 Old Quebec wc $35
200 Matane River valley wc $35
1936 265 Evening, Cap des Rosiers wc $75
266 Old lugger, Bic, Que wc $75
267 Grande Vallée, Gaspé wc $75
268 Near Fox River, Gaspé wc $65
1937 179 The meeting wc $35
1939 206 Low tide, Bic wc $40
1940 183 Sun in the woods wc $50
1941 126 A glacier bay, Alaska wc $75
1943 129 Near Bic, Que wc $50
see also Ross, George Allen, 1906-9

MACFARLANE, ELEANOR J.
addr: Montreal: 1918; 670 Sherbrooke St W, 1919-24
1918 436 Lemonade pitcher
1919 197 Still life study $20
198 Old house
427 Stein
1921 154 Homewards
1922 176 Boothbay Harbour, Maine, a bit of the town $55
1924 161 The 'Henry Ford' $50

MCGILL, DAVID
addr: Westmount, 602 Grosvenor Ave, 1932-9
1932 187 L'Abbé farm, Baie St Paul $30
188 Valley of the Gouffre, Baie St Paul $30
1933 213 Autumn, Quebec $40
214 Old mill at Pont Rouge $40
1934 218 Cloud and sunshine, Baie St Paul $80
219 Sous le Cap, approaching Baie St Paul $80
220 Sous le Cap, near St Ferreol $80
221 The silver lining $40
1935 215 Evening glow, Quebec $140
216 Early spring, Vertu Road $35
217 Low tide, Bic $35
218 Autumn evening, St Petronille, Ile d'Orleans $35
1936 292 June evening, St Laurent, Ile d'Orleans $80
293 View from the church at St Petronille, Ile d'Orleans $50
294 Spring, Côte des Neiges $50
295 Self portrait
1937 192 Cap Chat $125
193 Spring, Côte des Neiges $50
194 Baie St Paul $50
195 Autumn near St Pierre, Ile d'Orleans
1939 227 June evening, Chateauguay River $50

MCGILL, MARGARET
addr: Westmount: 127 Arlington Ave, 1923; 602 Grosvenor Ave, 1924-37
1923 145 Old French oven, Cap à l'Aigle wc $15
146 Sketch from model pastel $20
1924 171 Old French Canadian oven wc $15
1932 189 Miss Huddell
1933 215 Portrait study
1934 222 Road to the beach, Longueuil wc $25

223 A Canadian princess $40
1935 219 Sketch from life $45
229 Mr David McGill, Jr
1936 296 Olive $25
297 Miss Doris Butler
1937 196 Miss Ailsa Neilson

MCGILL, WINIFRED see FOX, WINIFRED

MCGILLIVRAY, FLORENCE HELENA
1864 Whitby, Ont 7 May 1938, Ottawa
AAA33 AGO B CWW36 H M NGC TB2
addr: Ottawa, 292 Frank St, 1915-28
1915 245 Contentment $500
246 Tide water $200
1918 234 The factory yard gate, winter $50
235 Still life $30
236 Amidst the shipping, Venice wc $75
237 Venetian fishing boats wc $75
1927 117 Pottery market, Bridgetown, Barbadoes, B.W.I. $300
118 Murphy's Fleet, Ottawa $200
119 San Giorgia, Venice $150
120 Venetian shipping $150
1928 118 Feathery palms $150
119 A Jamaica wharf $75
120 Sun caught, Percé $125

MCGIVERIN, HAROLD MACKINTOSH
28 Jun 1900, Ottawa 4 Mar 1937, Victoria M
addr: Ottawa: Rideau Apt, 1924; 19 Elgin St, 1925; 108 Sparks St, 1930
1924 170 The St Lawrence, among the islands $100
1925 185 Stormy sunset $100
1930 142 Hillside house on a sunny day $100

MACGREGOR, JAMES GAMBLE
1898, Glasgow M
addr: Winnipeg, 822 Banning st, 1934-5
1934 191 Moraine, Canadian Rockies wc $50
192 After the shower wc $45
1935 423 In Van Horne Woods water pr $12

MACGREGOR, JOHN BOYKA
12 Jan 1944, Dorking, Sussex, Eng
CWW84 IO M WWA84
addr: Toronto

1970 43 The only doors in existence wd & metal 93 x 57 x 48 illus (National Gallery of Canada)
44 Six chairs wd 3 pieces 33 x 16 x 16 each

MCIAN
1883 104 Jacobite hiding place

MCINDOE, MARION C. (Mrs Fred C.)
addr: Montreal, 103 Metcalfe St, 1897-1914
1897 Mrs Fred C, 1897-1901, 1905, 1908-9
264 Vase
265 Brush and comb tray
266 Doulton vase $10
267, 270 Cup & saucer $3 each
268 Sugar bowl, cream jug $5
269 Pen wiper $1.50
1900 238 Tankard $40
239, 243 Plaque $18, $9
240 Vase $10
241-2 Plate $5.50 $4.50
244 Framed head $8
245 Desert plates, 12 $36
246 Posteresque plaque $6
1901 256 Tankard $25
257 Vase $20
258 Tea set $13
259 Jewel box $8
260-1 Plate $6 each
262 Cup & saucer $4.50
1903 301 Vase, lustre $15
302, 304, 309 Plaque $10 $6 $10
303 Vase $25
305 Tea set, lustre $15
306 Tankard $25
307 Cologne bottle $7.50
308 Cup & saucer $5
1905 314 Plaque, silver pheasant $20
315 Compote $7
316 Violet holder $3.50
317 Vase, blue and gold $3.50
318-19 Cologne bottle $7.50 $5
320 Loving cup $6
321 Jardiniere $13
322 Rose jar $13
323 Plaque, head $10
324 Cup & saucer $5
325 Game plates
1906 425 Coffee pot $15
426 Tankard $28
427 Stein $10

428 Vase $12
429 Vase, lustre $10
430 Plaque $12
431 Plate $10
432 Fern pot $3.50
433 Cup & saucer $5
434 Candlesticks, pair $5
1908 406 Plaque, cowboy $10
407 Plaque, pair of setters $10
408 Five o'clock tea set $18
409 Panel $10
410 Vase $6
411 Compote $7
1909 61 Vase $18
62 Candlesticks, pair $10
63 Plate $8
64, 66 Cup & saucer $6, $3
65 Tea set, 3 pieces $15
1910 443 Plate $8
444 Bowl $12
445 Vase, etched des $10
446 Vase $16
1911 333-4 Plate $8 each
335 Cup & saucer $4
336-7 Vase $6 $15
338 Plate, peacock des $6
1913 488 Example of dinner set
489 Jardiniere $15
490 Bowl $8
491 Cup & saucer $5
492 Candlesticks, pair
1914 519 Vase $40
520 Candlestick, pair $16
521 Cup & saucer $3

MACINTOSH, MARY
addr: Westmount, 59 Belvedere Rd, 1922-3
1922 177 Portrait sketch
1923 143 Margaret

MACINTYRE, MARJORY SHIVES
1898, Saint John, N.B.
addr: Montreal, 3424 Simpson St
1948 29 Still life $50

MACK, MARY AGNES
12 Jun 1899, Cornwall, Ont M
addr: Cornwall: Goodaal House, 1924-7; Cornwall, 1928-9; 223 Second St E, 1930-43
1924 157-9 Still life wc $15 each
1925 172 The Poiret fan wc $15
173 Still life wc $15
1927 107 Moonlight, Paris $40
1928 115 The Château de Ramezay wc $25
1929 140 The deserted mill, Martintown wc $35
1930 141 La ferme, Fouché, Barbizon wc $15
1931 161 Un ancien Calvaire, Saint Arsene, Que wc $50
162 Village, lower St Lawrence wc $40
1932 184 Village evening wc $50
185 Spring morning, Béguinage St Elizabeth, Bruges wc $50
1933 206 Afternoon shadows, Seminary, Quebec wc $50
207 Road to St Epiphane wc $35
1936 269 Paysage, Temiscouata wc $40
270 Back country, Temiscouata wc $35
1939 209 My neighbour's tree wc $50
1943 130 Cacouna, 1942 wc $40

MCKAY, ARTHUR FORTESCUE
11 Sep 1926, Nipawin, Sask AGO CC2 CE M TB3 WWA84 Juror
addr: Regina: c/o Norman McKenzie Art Gallery, 1962; University of Saskatchewan, School of Art, 1963. Halifax, 1968
1961 22 Mandala illus Purchase award (MBAM)
1963 45 Void 2 $450
1968 168 Ourobouris enamel on board 48 x 48 $1,000

MACKAY, ROBERT
addr: Montreal, 1546 McGregor St
1934 193 Negro boy
194 Chinese woman

MCKEAN, JANET CORDELIA
13 Sep 1887, Pictou, N.S.
addr: Halifax, 32 Kent St
1937 197 Along Market Street, Halifax wc $15

MACKENZIE, ALISON F.
addr: Como, Que, Woodside
1956 151 Miss Marion Hum ter cot

MACKENZIE, ANDREW
addr: Montreal, 236 Mance St
1915 233 Bridge near Rosemere pastel $20

MACKENZIE, JAMES HAMILTON Scot

1875 - 29 Mar 1926, Glasgow DBA DVP WBA TB2
addr: Glasgow, Scot
1915 Hamilton J, mispr
380 Prentice Pillar, Roslyn Chapel etch $25

MACKENZIE, HUGH SEAFORTH
19 Jun 1928, Toronto IO M WWA84
addr: London, Ont, 1051 Colborne St, 1964. Toronto, 1970
1964 99 The bicycle nm
1970 45 The bamboo poles temp 15 x 18
46 The window temp 21 x 25 illus

MACKENZIE, MARGARET
addr: Montreal, 1509 Sherbrooke St W, 1931-2
1931 388 Book illustration wd cut $5.50
1932 407 Torchlight wd cut $8
408 The island lino cut $8

MACKENZIE, MARION A.
addr: Montreal: 16 St Mark St, 1903; 76 St Mark St, 1905-9
1903 297 Biscuit jar, pansy $8
298 Plate $7
299 Cream & sugar, hawthorn $4
300 Cup & saucer, roses $3
1905 326 Jardiniere and stand
327 Vase, fancy head $25
328 Jewel box
329 Chocolate jug $10
330 Vase $10
331 Cup & saucer $6
332 Bonbon dish $3
333 Small punch bowl $20
334 Claret jug $17.50
335 Gold vase $35
336 Miniature belt buckle
1907 414 Vase $12.50
415 Cup & saucer $4.50
416 Sunbonnet $4
417 Shaving mug
418 Vase, spring $22
419 Tray, roses $9
420 Jewel box
421 Stud box $2.25
422 Brown vase $10
423 Tray $3.25
424 Green vase $6.50
1908 403, 405 Plate
404 Fruit bowl, blackberries
1909 67 Vase $12
68 Fruit bowl $10
69 Fern dish $15

MACKENZIE, PERCIVAL M. (Miss)
addr: Montreal: 3425 Redpath St, 1935-41; 8 Redpath Pl, 1943
1935 424 The morning ride lino block
1939 207 Charleston
1940 184 Curtain $30
1941 127 Sketch $75
1943 131 Above St Siméon $100

MACKENZIE, ROBERT TAIT
26 May 1867, Almonte, Ont 28 Apr 1938, Philadelphia AAA33 AGO B CC2 CE CWW36 EC H M Mo98/12 NGC TB2 W78
addr: Montreal: 59 Metcalfe St, 1898-1900; Montreal, 1901; 913 Dorchester St, 1903
1898 173 A study of willows wc
174 A back street at Berthier wc
175 The Windsor corner wc
176 An April day, Phillips Square
1900 142 An old willow, early spring wc
143 Apple blossoms wc
144 Craig Street, November wc
187 The skater bas rel clay
1901 210 The skater sculp
1903 262 Athlete 1/4 life size plaster
263 Medallion, portrait study plaster

MACKENZIE, ROBIN
1938, Pickering Township, Ont IO M
addr: Claremont, Ont
1970 47 Limbwood elm wd 72 x 72 x 81 illus
48 Elm blocks 72 x 48 x 18

MACKIE, STELLA (Mrs)
b England
addr: Montreal: c/o Royal Bank, Stanley St Branch, 1946; 1117 St Catherine St W, No 423, 1947
1946 168 Col H.R. Lynn, RCE pastel
1947 170 Ronald Mackie pastel

MCKIEL, CHRISTIAN (Mrs)
27 Sep 1889, Pictou, N.S. M
addr: Sackville, N.B: 1931-37; Mount Allison University, 1939-44; Sackville, 1946-7
1931 168 Portrait of a man in a blue shirt pastel $25

169 A fair haired girl, sketch pastel $25
170 A dark haired girl, sketch pastel $25
1932 190 Portrait of an old man pastel $20
191 Portrait of a young woman pastel $15
192 The old fisherman pastel $20
411 Mount Allison Library etch $5
1935 221 Delphiniums pastel $75
222 Nasturtiums pastel $20
1936 298 Old mutton $50
299 Portrait study pastel $10
1937 198 Nasturtiums $75
199 Delphiniums $75
200 Mrs Brown pastel $15
201 A French child pastel $15
1939 228 Peonies $75
229 Portrait of a little girl $50
230 A little Negro boy $25
1943 137 Little girl in pink $45
1944 96 Flower study $150
1946 177 Portrait study $50
1947 192 Portrait $50

MACKINNON, MALCOLM
addr: Merville, B.C.
1936 271 Appleyard's farm, Island Highway, Vancouver Island wc

MACKINNON-PEARSON, CECILIA (m Ian MacKinnon-Pearson)
1889, St Catharines, Ont M
addr: St Hilaire, Que, 1940-2
1940 185 Le petit port wc $25
1941 240 Muskoka cedar etch $20
1942 205 Monreale dry pt

MACKINNON-PEARSON, IAN
21 Mar 1896, Bearsden, Glasgow M WWA53
addr: St Hilaire, Que, 1940-9
1940 378 Plantains dans le Square de la Marine, Vichy etch $6
378A Le Café des Arts, Vichy etch $6
1941 241 Watch and ward dry pt $10
242 Rift in the fog dry pt
1942 206 Half a tanker limps home dry pt $20
207 Percé Rock from the south etch $10
1943 Pearson, Ian MacKinnon, 1943-4
234 Sunset, Quebec roadstead dry pt $15
235 Couvent des Ursulines, Quebec dry pt $15
236 Rue de la Montagne dry pt $15
1944 143 Summer moonlight, Quebec etch & aqua $20
1945 262 L'entrée du Vieux Séminaire, Québec dry pt $15
1947 313 Approaching fog, Mont St Pierre dry pt $9.50
314 Shining waters, Ste Anne des Monts, Gaspé dry pt $9.50
1948 101 The road to the Shick-Shocks, Ste Anne des Monts, Gaspé dry pt (UG)
1949 162 Quebec rooftops by moonlight mezz $15

MACKLEM, KATHERINE B. (Mrs)
addr: Kingston, Ont, 18 Barrie St
1946 169 The young artist

MCLAREN, J. W.
(may be mispr for Thomas McLaren, q.v.)
addr: Montreal, 264 Beaver Hall Hill
1922 369 Addition to a Montreal college

MCLAREN, NORMAN
11 Apr 1914, Stirling, Scot 26 Jan 1987, Montreal CCl CWW84 M WWA84
addr: Montreal, 3590 Ridgewood Ave
1960 81 The backward look
82 Mangoes

MACLAREN, ROBERT N.
addr: Montreal, 3543 Northcliffe Ave
1940 186 Old meeting house, Brookline, New Hampshire pastel $50

MACLAREN, THOMAS
22 Jul 1879, Perth, Scot 11 Apr 1967, Montreal
addr: Montreal: 20 St Alexis St, 1909; 264 Beaver Hall Hill, 1923-7; 1096 Beaver Hall Hill, 1928-37
1909 429 Sketches in Italy nm
1923 272 Cottages
273 Hockey rink
1925 307 Cottage, Montreal West
308 Residence
1927 224 Building, River Road, Chambly Canton
225 Studio, Chambly Canton
1928 251 Study for bank building, Winnipeg

252 Canorasset Lodge
253-4 Memorial archway, bridge, City of Hamilton competition
1929 263 Residence, Montreal West
1930 225 Sport pavilion photo
226 Studio photo
1931 316 Residence, Hampstead, Que
317 Residence
318 Church, study
1937 357 Residence, Madison Ave
358 Country residence
see also Peden, Frank, 1908-15; McLaren, J.W, 1922

MCLARREN, DOROTHY HARRIS (Mrs)
addr: Westmount, 4848 Westmount Ave
1950 29 Old Halifax, Nova Scotia

MCLAUGHLIN, ISABEL GRACE
10 Oct 1903, Oshawa, Ont AGO CWW84 M BGC TB3
addr: Toronto, 150 Balmoral Ave
1939 231 Stan White's, White Fish Falls $100

MCLAUGHLIN, NELLIE
addr: Montreal, 268A St Antoine St, 1905-12
1905 85 Still life $25
1912 249 Cap à l'Aigle $25

MCLEAN, MARY
b 1924
addr: Toronto, 39 Castle Frank Rd,
1957 134 The singing trees nm $85

MCLEAN, N. (addr list Miss M.)
addr: Oshawa, Ont, Albert St
1906 356 Mr Edward Carswell min
357 Portrait of a lady min

MACLEAN, SARAH JEAN MUNRO (m Lachlan A. Maclean)
9 Dec 1873, Pictou, N.S. 21 Feb 1952 Montreal CNS36 M NGC TB3
addr: Montreal: 233 Old Orchard Ave, 1920-3; 425 Beaconsfield Ave, 1924-5; 154 McKenna Ave, 1927-30; 5306 McKenna Ave, 1932-6. Drummondville, Que, 774 Lafontaine St, 1939. Montreal, 4346 Beaconsfield Ave, 1945-7
1920 171 Still life wc
1921 156 Old courtyard, St Vincent Street $50 (NGC)
1922 178 Old house, Carrière Street, Montreal $35
1923 144 Micmac basket seller, Pictou wc $150
1924 162 Eileen
163 Indian houses, Cacouna $50
1925 170 Portrait
171 Birthplace of Sir William Dawson, Pictou, N.S, sketch $25
1927 108 Montreal harbour, sketch $50
109 Phlox and marigolds $150
1928 116 Elevators, Montreal harbour $35
1929 139 Old house, Lachine $35
1930 140 Contentment $125
1932 182 La coiffure $150
183 Phlox and delphinium $50
1933 204 Delphinium and calendula $100
205 Portrait
1934 195 A street in Pictou, N.S. $50
1935 201 Peonies $150
1936 272 Emily Post's doorway, Martha's Vineyard $100
273 The end of the village $75
274 Snapdragon $100
1939 208 Lady's slipper $40
1945 153 A Canadian school girl $300
1947 171 A bit of Grand Manan $75

MACLEAY, ROSANNA MACLEAY STEWART (m Stewart Macleay)
26 Sep 1887, Wakarusa, Kans M
addr: Danville, Que: RR No 4, 1940; Grove St, 1941-5; no addr 1967
1940 187 Hazardous harvest
1941 128 A giant of the earth
1943 132 The coming storm $80 (1967-39A, listed Jessie Dow prize)
1945 154 Will I get there? $150

MCLEISH, ANNIE
addr: Montreal: 1908; 565 St Catherine St, 1909-10
1908 234 A la fête crayon $25
235 Le pierrot pastel
1909 237 The reading lesson pastel
238 Bernard Sheridan, Esq pastel
239 A knight and lady pastel
1910 229 Illustration to Shakespeare song wc
230 Illustration b&w

MCLEISH, JOHN FRASER
addr: Montreal, 3638 Durocher St
1937 202 Clown caprice gouache $35

203 Hurmouresque $25

MCLEISH, MINNIE
addr: Montreal, 1016 St Urbain St
1910 231 Miss Muriel Castle pastel
232 Campbell, portrait pastel
233 Madonna with wounded bird pastel

MACLELLAN, MORNA ISABELLA
21 Nov 1905, Pictou, N.S.
addr: Montreal, 2309 Wilson Ave
1940 188 Nocturne $35

MACLENNAN, DOROTHY see DUNCAN, DOROTHY

MCLENNAN, K.
addr: Montreal, 3480 Ontario Ave
1928 121 Still life $50

MCLENNAN, LOUISE RUGGLES BRADLEY (m John S. McLennan)
Aug 1860, Chicago 1912, Sydney, Cape Breton, N.S. H
addr: Sydney, 1891-2. Boston, 9 Louisburg Sq, 1894. Sydney, Petersfield, 1906-8. Montreal, 776 Dorchester St, 1911
1891 177 Five o'clock wc
1892 185 Winter, Cape Breton wc
186 Brookdale, October wc
187 Morning lessons wc
1894 203 A grey day wc
204 Tower Hill, Dec '92 wc
1906 253 Michael Angelo's cypress wc
254 Vesuvius from Sorrento wc
255 Castel dell'Ovo, Naples wc
256 Borghese gardens wc
257 In Perugia wc
258 The black cat, Rome wc
1908 236 Portrait wc
237 The golden screen wc
238 Old cottages at Vire, Normandy wc
239 Hayfield at Deadham wc
240 Moonlight, Bavarian Tyrol wc
241 Palazzo Publico, Siena wc
242 Oberammergau wc
1911 195 Notre Dame wc
196 La maison de Balzac, Sache wc
197 Portrait wc
198-200 Valley of the Margaree, three sketches wc
201 Steel works, Sydney wc
1894 Assoc 2nd prize 1892, wc

MCLEOD, DONALD IVAN
20 Sep 1886, Owen Sound, Ont d 1967
CWW64 M WWC40
addr: Toronto: Metropolitan Bldg, 1940; 43 Glenayr Rd, 1941-5. Montreal, 1548 Pine Ave W, 1946-9
1940 200 Habitant house
201 Summer morning
1941 137 Busy fishermen
1942 113 Small fry
1943 138 Back from the Banks
1944 97 The outdoor oven
1945 162 Midsummer morning
1946 178 Florida sunshine
1949 72 The old fish house

MCLEOD, ELIZABETH
1875, Pointe du Bute, N.B. 14 Nov 1963, Sackville, N.B.
addr: Sackville: 1920-9; Mount Allison, 1932-3; Ladies College, 1935
1920 172 Zinnias $25
1926 88 Peonies and larkspur $40
1927 121 Hollyhocks $50
122 Bluebells and zinnias $35
1928 122 Flowers
1929 143 Orange lilies
1932 193 Canterbury bells
1933 216 Flowers $35
217 Phlox $25
1935 Elizabeth Fraser McLeod
427 The camp block pr $3

MACLEOD, HAZEL A. PARKS (m D.J. MacLeod)
b Napanee, Ont M
addr: Fredicton, N.B: Dominion Experimental Station, 1944-7
1944 93 Winter, at Experimental Station, Fredericton, N.B. $25
1945 155 Gathering Irish moss, Prince Edward Island $75
1947 172 Woodcock $35

MACLEOD, PEGI NICOL see NICOL, PEGI

MCMAHON, GERTRUDE
addr: Montreal, 2660 Mance St
1923 147 Dragon des wc $50

MACMILLAN, DUNCAN PARK
Jul 1873, Cornwall, Ont 18 Apr 1908. H
addr: Montreal: 807 Dorchester St,

1891-4; 9 Hanover St, 1895; 2 Brunswick St, 1905; 2256 St Catherine St, 1906; Montreal, 1908
1891 82 Spanish girl $50
83 Old woman's head $30
84 Dying day $25
1892 98 Dawn
99 Montreal from the river $20
1894 103 The dreamer $25
1895 79 Death of Abel $400
1905 81 What's the use? $150
82 Percita $100
83 September afternoon, Mount Royal $35
84 Belvedere Road, Westmount $25
173 Helena wc $40
1906 107 St Catherines Road, Outremount $45
108 September afternoon, Mount Royal $40
109 Belvedere Road, Westmount $80
252 July afternoon wc $40
1908 100 The Chinese lantern $500
101 September afternoon $100

MCMILLAN, FRED
addr: Brockville, Ont: 47 King St, 1921-4; 19 Perth St, 1929
1921 175 The edge of the woods $50
1924 172 Summer $10
1929 144 Rock and ice $75

MCMILLAN, W.
addr: Montreal, 456 Clarke St
1914 442 Sculpture, scale model for Houses of Parliament, Regina

MACNAB, FREDERICK JOHN
24 Mar 1885, Dundee, Scot 12 Jun 1961, Ayr, Scot
addr: Montreal, 1050 Beaver Hall Hill, 1931-3
1931 Bell Telephone Co, 1931-3
304 New building, Goyeau St, Windsor, Ont, perspective pencil drwg
305 Baker Exchange, Hamilton, Ont, perspective, elevation, and detail pen & ink drwg
1933 396 Wilbank Exchange, Montreal, and recent addition
397 Hyland Exchange, Toronto
398 Rural Quebec exchange, suggestion

MCNALLY, LORNE WILLIAM
30 Apr 1942, Port Colborne, Ont M
addr: Port Colborne, 98 Wellington St
1964 100 October nm $65

MACNAMARA, GORDON ROBERTSON
14 Dec 1910, Toronto M WWA62
addr: Toronto, 25 Severn St, 1956-60
1956 117 View of San Miguel nm $75
1960 192 Town and sky, Mexico nm $90

MCNAUGHT, EUPHEMIA (BETTY)
8 Oct 1901, Glenmorris, Ont
addr: Calgary, Mount Royal College
1931 171 Before the storm temp $50
172 Indian ponies wc $50

MCNAUGHTON, ETHEL P. (m Jack Ingham)
addr: Westmount, 4565 Sherbrooke St W. 1940-52
1940 204 Madame B's kitchen $20
205 Ste Adèle en Bas wc $8
1941 138 Lac Mercier, Que $20
139 Solitude $20
1943 139 Lac Mercier village, Que wc $20
140 Mr S.
1944 98 Q.M.Stores, St Sulpice Barracks wc $30
99 Ste Adèle, Que $35
144 CWAC Barracks pen drwg $15
145 Ruth charcl
1945 264 Morning, Laurentians pen & ink $30
1946 179 Room 418 wc $30
264 Wharf, Gloucester Mass pen & ink $20
265 A l'auberge pen & ink $20
1947 193 Ski house, St Sauveur $40
317 Corridor drwg $25
1948 103 Ski house, St Sauveur pen drwg $25
1950 153 Ste Marguerite, Que pen & ink $25
1951 139 Summer hotel pen & ink $25
1952 137 Alpine Club camp, B.C. pen & ink $40

MACNAUGHTON, JOHN H.
fl 1876-99 H
addr: Montreal, 27 Rosemount Ave, 1895-7
1895 80 Old woman spinning $35
179 The old trappeur wc $16
1897 176 Haymaking wc $35

177 Old St Germain's house, Côte St Antoine wc $25

MCNICOLL, HELEN GALLOWAY
14 Dec 1879, Toronto 27 Jun 1915, Swanage, Eng CCI M NGC TB3 W78
addr: Montreal: 9 University St, 1906; Montreal, 1908. Westmount, Braeleigh, 2 Forden Ave, 1909-15 (1922, 1925)
1906 114 Betty Brierly
115 In the sun $40
116 Old street, St Ives $75
117 High tide $50
118 Street in sunlight $40
119 The brown hat $125
1908 102 A field of flowers $125
103 Fishing $125
104 Through the orchard $150
105 September evening $250 (1967, 27 3/4 x 24 illus, listed Jessie Dow prize) (Mr and Mrs H.B. McNally, Montreal)
106 The farm yard $85
1909 240 Washerwomen on the Loing $225
241 The gleaner $200
242 Reflections $90
243 A September morning $100
1910 234 In a Surrey orchard $125
235 In the farmyard $150
236 Fishing $225
237 Midsummer $100
1911 202 Gathering apples $250
203 A sunny morning $75
204 Study of a child $75 (MBAM)
205 A country road $60
1912 250 The bean harvest $125
251 Stubble fields $150 (NGC)
252 A sunny morning $110
253 Sketch $50
1914 279 In the shadow of the tent $160 (MBAM)
1915 247 Sunny September $175
248 The white umbrella $50
1922 late Miss McNicoll, 1922-5
195 The Victorian dress
196 The open door
1925 186 Sunny days
187 Memories
188 Reflections

MCPHEE, IVA HAISMAN (Mrs)
addr: Dixie, Que: 125 53rd Ave, 1931; 135 53rd Ave, 1932. Montreal, 251 Milton St, 1933
1931 389 Habitant dance wd engr $8
390 The Chinese lioness wd engr $12
391 Mocking angels wd engr $10
1932 412 Summer wd engr $18
413 Winged horse lino cut $12.50
1933 468 The sailor's wooing wd engr $7
469 La poulette grise wd engr $7
470 Market stall wd engr $9

MACPHERSON, ANNIE A. H. (m D.B. MacPherson)
fl 1887-96 H
addr: Montreal, 1283 Dorchester St, 1894
1888 49 A study
1889 143 Portrait
144 Study of a head
1894 201 Atlantic City wc
202 Boardwalk, Atlantic City wc

MACPHERSON, JESSIE
addr: Montreal, 4995 Earnscliffe Ave
1932 472 Isobel plaster

MACPHERSON, KENNETH ROSE
19 Feb 1861 - 26 Apr 1916, Montreal H
addr: Montreal: 211 Stanley St, 1894-5; 119 Shuter St, 1897-1903; 229 Stanley St, 1906-13
1894 104 Landscape
1895 81 Evening at La Malbaie
1897 89 Portrait
90 Portrait study
1898 77 Solitude $25
1900 72 Landscape
1901 68 A pool in the woods $40
69 The Elm Tree Hole, Dixie $20
1903 83 An old barn $40
1906 110 The red farm $125
111 The old trout pond $75
112 A good place for a links, lower St Lawrence $75
113 The seventh hole, Dixie $50
1910 238 At the edge of the woods
239 The farm by the river
1913 262 The bar, St Anne's Bay, Cape Breton $125
263 From an upper window $75
264 The frog pool under the old willow tree $50
265 Old cottages at Metis $100
266 From St Gabriel to St James

Street wc $50
267 Early September moon wc $50
268 Rainy day, Sydney, Cape Breton wc $25

MACPHERSON, PHYLLIS
addr: Sackville, N.B, Allison Hall
1940 189 Still life $75

MCQUEEN, ISABEL
addr: Montreal, 220 Mance St, 1906-11
1906 435 Punch bowl $15
436 Cup & saucer, 3 $6
1908 412 Plaque, scene $15
413 Plaque, head $15
414 Plaque, Dutch scene
415 Vase, sunset
416 Vase, chestnuts
417 Stein, hops
418 Small stein, monk
1909 70 Vase $5
71 Biscuit jar $8
72 Plaque, scene $15
73 Plaque, head $18
1911 339 Tea set, 3 pieces $15

MACVICAR, ANNIE
addr: Montreal, 69 McTavish St, 1895-1900
1895 180 Gladiolus wc
1900 145 A souvenir of Bic wc $8

MACVICAR, DONALD NORMAN
17 Aug 1869 - 26 Mar 1929, Montreal
PMC
addr: Montreal: 69 McTavish St, 1892; Temple Bldg, 1903-6; Montreal, 1908; 104 Union Ave, 1909-16: 628 Union Ave, 1917-20. Westmount, 4335 Montrose Ave, 1914 (residence)
1892 224 Campanile arch drwg
1903 MacVicar & Heriot, 1903-20
271 Proposed apartment house
272 Chesterville Public School
273 Houses, Weredale Park
274-5 Residence, Westmount (2)
1905 254 The New Sherboooke
255 New museum building
256 Residence, Montreal
257 Residence, Westmount
1906 337 Residence, J.W. Tatley, Esq
338 MacVicar's Memorial Church, Montreal Annex
1908 320 Proposed apartment house, Sherbrooke St
321 Residence, Montreal West
322 Residence, Vaudreuil
323 Municipal building, sketch
1909 430 New school, Verdun, Que
1910 390 Residence, John Fair, Esq
391 New school, Verdun
392 GTR building, Seattle Exposition
393 Bungalow, Vaudreuil
1913 431 Johnston Brothers, building
1914 454 Residence. A.L. Carson, Esq
455 Residence, A. Goff, Esq
456 Garage, C.A. Barnard, Esq
1915 390 Hermitage Country Club, Lake Memphremagog
391 Residence, St Andrews, Que
1916 336 Entrance hall, country residence
1917 377 Country residence
378 Farm building, John Fair, Esq, St Andrews, Que
379 Residence, Windsor Mills, Que
1918 395-6 Country house, vestibule
397 Christ Church Cathedral
1919 389-90 Residence, Three Rivers, Que study, a and b
391 Proposed residence, Westmount
392 Country cottage, Lake Memphremagog, Que
1920 318 Hermitage Country Club
319 Caron Building
1903 269 S. Sisto, Italy wc
270 Ravenna, Italy wc
1908 229 La Torre, Verona wc
1914 260 Ravenna wc
1919 199 Sand dunes, Ogunquit, Me wc

MACVICAR, ELIZABETH M.
addr: Montreal, 22 McTavish St
1927 110 Case of miniatures. A. Miss Joan Dawes, Montreal, B. Master Tony MacTier, Montreal. C. Miss Louise Phillips, Winnipeg. D. Master Bunnie Cameron, Winnipeg

MADDEN, ORVAL CLINTON
2 Feb 1892, Napanee, Ont 15 Dec 1971, Toronto M
addr: Toronto, 179 Delaware Ave, 1933-9
1933 208 Running water $150
467 Harbour reflections litho $10
1934 196 Barnyard $200
1936 275 Fishing dock, Port Burwell $200

1937 180 Autumn winds $225
1939 210 The sheepfold $250

MAGEE, PHOEBE A.
addr: Kitchener, Ont, 33 Margaret Ave
1955 57 The white dory

MAHIAS, ROBERT
12 Oct 1890, Brussels B TB2
addr: Montreal, 678 St Urbain St, 1924-5
1924 167 Sérenité $800
168 Illusion $175
169 Venise batik $75
1925 174 Femme au Cypres $200
175 Femme au Chapleau jaune wc $250
176 Le manteau brun wc $80
177 Derrière l'église wc $50
178 Orage dans le midi de France wc $50

MAHON, CHARLES AUGUSTUS
30 Sep 1867, Montreal H
addr: Westmount, 1215 Greene Ave
1914 261 Portraits on ivory
262 Marsh, twilight wc $25

MAILLARD, CHARLES
8 Feb 1887, Tiaret, Algeria 1973, Montreal M Juror
addr: Montreal: 768 Marie Anne St E, 1912-13; 144 Bureau Ave, 1914-15; Montreal, 1918; 1158 St Denis St, 1921. Outremont, 527 Côte Ste Catherine Rd, 1922. Montreal, 2178 Hutchison St, 1923-4
1912 254 Peint part lui-même
255 Etude de tête
1913 269 Les étages triptyque $700
270 M F.J. Bisaillon, batonnier
271 Portrait de l'auteur
272 Etude
1914 263 Bébé R. Dion
1915 234 N. Faribault
235 La critique
236 Cuivres, nature morte $75
237 Les tours de Notre Dame de Paris $50
1918 223 Mdlle Helene McM.
224 Mdlle Françoise McM.
1921 157 Madame O'B.
158 Lois
159 Etude, tête de fillette
160 Portrait du peintre
1922 179 Madame M, et petite Lily
180 Pat O'B.
181 Poupèe de Clerval
182 Madame Dulude
1923 148 Claire and Andrée de G-B
1924 164 Portrait
165 Subaltern 13th Battalion
166 Pomone $300

MAILLET, CORINNE DUPUIS (Mrs. signs Rhobena Dippy, and Colin Martel)
1895, Montreal M
addr: Montreal: 87 Cherrier St, 1921; 1455 Drummond St, 1935
1921 161 Portrait sketch pastel
1935 425-6 Portrait sketch drwg

MAITLAND, E. J. F.
addr: Montreal, 2370 Mance St
1915 embroidery
466 Twinkle, twinkle little star $75
467 Fan $25

MAITLAND, JAMES S.
addr: 2370 Mance St, 1913-15
1913 432 University of British Columbia des
1914 457 The twin towers
1915 392 The piazza

MAJOR, GERALDINE (m Baron Wrangle. m H. Chisholm)
fl 1922-50 DBA
addr: Montreal: 100 Crescent St, 1925; 7 Chelsea Pl, 1927; Ritz Carlton Hotel, 1941; 900 Sherbrooke St W, Apt 53, 1943-50
1925 pen & ink
357 In the market, Nice $25
358 In the market, Mentone
359 A Cotswold village $25
360 Shepheard's Hill, Haslemere $25
1927 111 Chapel of St Nicholas, Westminster Abbey wc
112 Old bridge on the Firth, Stirling wc
113 Back of the Mermaid Inn, Rye wc
114 Old house, Rye wc
283 Cotswold cottage b&w $15
284 Stirling Castle b&w $25
285 King's House, Tower Green b&w $25

1941 Wrangle, 1941-5
215 Child reading wc $25
1943 218 Tête exotique $100
1944 132 First ball $75
1945 247 Marischa $75
1946 170 Farm yard scene wc $35
1947 Major, Geraldine (Mrs H. Chisholm)
173 Charmain, daughter of Lieut Gen E.W. Sanson, CB DSO
174 Caughnawaga wc
1949 137 Monday morning, Pointe au Pic wc $40
1950 70 Montreal wc $75

MAJOR, LAURE
1930, Montreal M
addr: Westmount, 52 Academy Rd
1960 193 Guerre des divinités nm $35

MAJOR, RICHARD WALTER
20 Nov 1899, Toronto M
addr: Toronto, 18 Grenville St, 1934-5. Montreal: 7782 Champagneur Ave, 1938; 2076 Union Ave, 1939; 2057 Victoria St, 1940; 2041 Victoria St, 1941
1934 197 Yvonne $300
198 The green bottle $250
1935 202 Norma $250
203 Ripening grain wc $25
1938 83 The croaking frog dec panel $250
1939 211 Late afternoon pastel $85
212 Smelter at Copper Cliff, Ont $75
212A Near Georgeville, Que $25
1940 190 Doreen $100
1941 129 Constance wc $150

MAKSOLLY, MAXIMILIAN
addr: Montreal, 2171 Dorchester St W
1937 181 Mrs G. Stoecker pastel
182 Gladioli $300
183 Peonies $250
184 Mme Glikeria Taiga

MALAMUD, ISRAEL
b 1904
addr: Outremont, 1336 Lajoie Ave, Apt 3 1939-47
1939 213-14 A scene in the Laurentians wc $100, np
215 Woods and rocks wc $100
1940 191 August afternoon wc $75
192 A rock wc $35
1941 130 Trees wc $85
1942 109 The cocoanut $25
1944 94 A boy with a green book
1945 156 Mildred
1946 171 Rhoda
172 Italian girl
1947 175 Shacks $100

MALCHI, BEZALEL
26 Nov 1902, Simno, Lithuania CNS36 M
addr: Montreal: 4571 Clarke St, 1934; 209 Villeneuve St W, 1935; 2824 Esplanade Ave, 1936-7; 117 Fairmount Ave W, 1943-7
1934 199 Self portrait ivory
200 The harp player ivory $45
201 The Spanish poet ivory $25
202 The bread winner ivory $50
509 The mulatto plaster $250
1935 471 J.J. Segal, poet plaster $250
472 The two sisters clay $200
473 Rabbi H.J. Stern bust clay
1936 600 Homeless plaster $175
601 A sweet dream plaster $175
602 Mr Small (Shmulevich) bust plaster $150
603 Portrait study plaster $45
1937 425 Portrait study drwg $35
465 Meditation plaster $250
466 Unemployed plaster $300
1943 258 Self portrait wd
1946 290 Esther Segal, poetess plaster $250
1947 176 Winter $50
340 V. Packer, head plaster

MALCOURONNE, KATHLEEN DELACOUR
7 Oct 1885 - 6 Jul 1951, Montreal M
addr: Westmount, 114 Abbott Ave, 1934-41
1934 203 Black billed cuckoo wc $30
1935 204 Notre Dame, city sky line wc $30
1936 276 A solitary sandpiper wc $40
277 An autumn reflection wc $40
1939 216 Signs of spring $45
1940 193 Windy day wc $40
194 Harvest evening wc $40
1941 131 Little old houses wc $25

MALCZEWSKI, RAFAL
24 Oct 1892, Krakow, Poland M
addr: Ste Adèle en Haut, Que, 1945. Montreal, 9 Braeside Pl, 1946. Ste Adèle en Haut, Que, 1949
1945 157 The first snow, Saskatchewan wc $80

1946 173 Lagoa Rodigues Freitas, Rio de Janeiro $500
1949 138 Winter landscape wc $80

MALLET, GASTON
addr: Outremont, 1290 Bernard Ave
1946 174 Génèse $200

MALLOCH, STIRLING
addr: Montreal, 961 Dorchester St
1901 70 Maple leaves $300
71 Riddling potatoes, Tullibardine $300
72 November evening $150
73 November

MALTAIS, MARCELLE
9 Oct 1933, Chicoutimi, Que M
addr: Montréal: 3660 rue de Mentana, 1958; 1415 rue Chomedey, Apt 4, 1960; 2080 rue Crescent, 1961; 1151 ave Seymour, Apr 3, 1963; Galerie Camille Hébert, 2075 rue Bishop, 1964
1958 32 Painting No 100 $130
1960 78 Ubu $200
1961 36 Horizon vertical $225
1963 39 Sourkénac $800
1964 50 Kaminia $800

MALTBY, BEATRICE J. (Mrs)
addr: Toronto, 18 Grenville St, 1934. Town of Mount Royal, Que, 1615 Canora Rd, 1947
1934 204 Rue Capette, Lannion, Brittany $150
1947 177 Negress in white blouse $200
178 Still life $150

MANGOLD, CARL
6 Mar 1901, Trimbach, Switz M
addr: Montreal, 1231 St Catherine St W
1933 209 Sunday in harbour, Santa Margherita $350
210 Drying sails, Santa Margherita $300
211 Clouds $150

MANLY, CHARLES MACDONALD
Sep 1855, Englefield Green, Eng 3 Apr 1924, Toronto AGO CC2 CE EC H M Mo12 NGC TB3 W78
addr: Toronto: 75 Adelaide St, 1892-5; Court Chambers, Adelaide St, 1897; York Chambers, Toronto St, 1898-1900; Yonge St Arcade, 1901-12; Sproat & Rolph, North St, 1913; Toronto, 1918; 36 North St, 1912
1889 145 Cold Creek, Bolton, Canada wc $120
146 A Canadian Sleepy Hollow wc $100
147 The sparkling Teign, Dartmouth wc $120
148 Midsummer day wc $45
1892 100 Over the hills and far away $350
188 Now leafy June a summering comes wc $100
189 A street in Point Levis, Quebec wc $100
190 Spring stirred and broke wc $75
1894 106 Under the greenwood tree $65
205 In old Champlain, Que wc $200
206 The coming of the leaves wc $100
207 The winds of spring are out at play wc $100
1895 181 A sunlit stream wc $150
182 Flowers of the field wc $100
183 Wayside gold wc $45
1897 178 Britford Vale, Wiltshire wc $125
179 The heart of the hills wc $125
180 Spring stirred and broke wc $60
181 Hampshire hedges wc $70
1898 177 The Stour flowing through Canterbury wc $100
1900 146 Sunlit meads, Wiltshire wc $75
147 St David's Pool wc $25
148 A heavy rain wc $30
149 The hills of Glenear wc $60
1901 144 By the stream wc $35
145 Changing weather wc $35
146 Summer breezes wc $30
147 Sunshine of the morning wc $35
1903 200 The glory of the year wc $100
201 Upland and sky wc $50
202 The dewy dusk comes down wc $50
1905 174 Misty morning sun wc $50
175 Haven under the hill wc $30
176 The dark valley wc $20
177 A windflogged sea wc $35
178 Field flowers wc $15
1906 259 Before the gloaming wc $60
260 Lift of the fog wc $60
261 Bear River, N.S. wc $60
262 Spring stirred and broke wc $50

1908 106A Evening on the Conestogo
$250 (NGC)
230 The last gleam pastel $35
231 October in Nova Scotia wc $35
232 October aflame wc $35
1909 247 Afternoon sun wc $35
248 The glory of the year wc $50
249 Noon wc $35
1910 240 Lingering light pastel $50
241 Autumn, Nova Scotia hills wc $35
242 Yard of Monument House, Queenstown wc $100
1911 206 Rennyle Sands wc $60
207 Dartmoor wc $60 (listed 1967, Jessie Dow prize)
208 The sun went down wc $60
1912 256 Rain and flood, Dartmoor $200
257 On the Gatineau wc $100
1913 273 The West Ockment Valley, Dartmoor wc $150
1918 225 The latchstring is out wc $200
226 Waters meet, Conestogo wc $200
1922 183 Mid-September $75
184 Lower Town, Quebec $150
185 Mowing oats pastel $75
1894-7 Assoc, Hon mention 1892 wc

MANN, HARRINGTON Scot
7 Oct 1864, Glasgow 28 Feb 1937, New York B DBA DVP G RA TB1/2 WBA WWB34
addr: New York, 80 W 40th St
1914 264 Mrs Herbert M. Marler

MANN, OLIVE
addr: Montreal, 56 Sherbrooke St W, 1922. Quebec: Château St Louis, Grande Allée, 1936; 305 Grande Allée, 1937
1922 186 Gatherine clouds wc $25
(title crossed out) A summer day wc $50 (rubber stamped)
381 Cherry bowl, luna moth des $15
382 Muffin dish, freesia motif $15
383 Conserve box enamels $10
1936 278 Day in late summer, Quebec $50
1937 185 Lily pool wc $35

MANSON, MARIE ROBERTA
31 Jul 1933, New Westminster, B.C.
addr: Montreal, 1208 St Mark St
1954 125 Women dressing etch $10

MARCHAND, SUZANNE
addr: Hampstead, Que, 29 Northcote Rd
1955 58 St Hilaire

MARCOGLIESE, GIOVANTE
addr: Montreal, 1379 Sherbrooke St W
1936 604 Mussolini, head plaster

MARCUSE, MARGARET
addr: Westmount, 407 Metcalfe Ave
1910 394 Jewelry designs

MARICH, GEZA (GORDON)
1913, Budapest M
addr: Montreal, 6288 Deacon Rd
1961 89 Montreal street scene nm $300

MARION, GILBERT
11 Mar 1933, Montreal AGO M
addr: Montreal, 4253 Esplanade Ave, 1960. Outremont, 1581 Ducharme St, 1965
1960 194 Floraison royale nm $50
1965 26 Plein jaune 3/8 nm $70

MARKELL, JACK HAROLD
14 May 1919, Winnipeg 12 Apr 1979, North Vancouver, B.C. M NGC WWA62
addr: Winnipeg, 9 St Johns Ave, 1947-58
1947 temp & oil, 179-81
179 Mother and child $150
180 Displaced persons
181 Refugees $200
1950 124 Street scene $95
1956 39 Reclining figure $200
1958 33 Horse and rider $300

MARKGRAF, WALTRAUD ERNA ELSE LISA
(m Gerhard Doerrie)
1937, Hanover, Germ AGO M
addr: Toronto, Gallery Moos, 138 Yorkville St
1963 Margraf, mispr
86 Aruns nm $300

MARKLE, ROBERT
25 Aug 1936, Hamilton, Ont AGO IO M
addr: Toronto, Isaacs Gallery, 832 Yonge St
1963 40 All blues: landscape $350

MARLER, ADELAIDE
addr: Montreal, 15 Redpath Cr
1922 188 Still life wc $7

MARLER, AUDREY E. (Mrs)
addr: Montreal, 3764 Côte des Neiges Rd, 1940-1

1940 195 Still life $50
1941 132 Still life $50

MARLIN, BRIDGET see OAKLEY, BRIDGET

MARLING, J. W. (Mrs)
addr: Montreal, 2740 St Catherine St
1900 247 Desert basket, china

MARQUETTE, HILDA SOPHIA (m Alfred Ruston)
22 Sep 1908, Kitchener, Ont
addr: Kitchener: 393 Queen St, 1948; 5 St Ledger St, 1952
1948 30 Mennonite escorts $100
1952 Ruston (Rustan, mispr)
46 Mennonite market $200
47 Tin roofs #200

MARQUIS, M.
addr: Montreal, 347 Garnier St
1921 162 Langage d'une rose b&w $25

MARROTTE, EDGAR SAMUEL
addr: Montreal: 620 Cathcart St, 1931-3; 1190 University St, 1937
1931 306 Residence, Paul E. Barden, Esq
307 The St Lawrence River, 1775 overmantel dec map
1932 409 Santa Maria della Salute, Venezia unfr wd cut $5
1933 399 Lake St Louis Golf and Country Club, Lachine clubhouse
1937 350 W.M. Tomkin's cabin, Seigniory Club drwg

MARSHALL, MARGUERITE
addr: Montreal, 1374 Sherbrooke St W
1943 233 Bobby charcl

MARTEL, A. E.
addr: Montreal, 4277 Des Erables St
1934 205 An old cock $50

MARTEL, LUC (LUCYL)
addr: Montreal, 6793 Christophe Colomb St, 1947-52
1947 315 Portrait drwg $20
1948 31 Nature morte, pommes $60
32 Gilles $85
1952 99 Nature morte $100
100 Le filet $135 Jury II prize 1967-40 24 x 30

MARTEL, MARGO
addr: Montreal, 6793 Christophe Colomb St, 1946-7
1946 175 Nature morte sur le sol $80
1947 182 Poissons rouges $80

MARTIAL, LUCIEN RAOUL JEAN
17 Nov 1892, Paris, France B M TB2
addr: Quebec, 298 Laurier Ave
1931 163 Place de la Concorde, Paris wc $60
164 Les quais, Paris wc $60
165 Ajaccio, le port wc $60
166 Ajaccio, vieux quartiers wc $60

MARTIN, ALFRED
addr: Montreal, 2054 Marlowe Ave
1947 316 Two weavers dry brush ink drwg

MARTIN, BLANCHE
addr: Montreal, 12 St Luke St
1921 163 George b&w
164 Lorraine b&w
165 Alice b&w

MARTIN, EMMA MAY
3 Jan 1865, Toronto 10 Feb 1957, Montreal CNS36 H M
addr: Toronto: North Drive, Rosedale, 1892; 110 Crescent Rd, 1897-1901; 225 Cottingham St, 1905-15; 135 Erskine Ave, 1943
1888 74 Muskoka birches wc $50
1889 149 The meadow path wc $30
1892 191 Late twilight wc $60
1897 182 Farm lane at Eglinton wc $25
183 A September evening wc $25
1898 178 Bala Falla, Muskoka wc $25
1901 148 Cascapedia Bay, Que wc $50
1905 86 Cyripedium $25
179 On the road to Como wc $35
1906 263 Evening on Lake Joseph, Muskoka wc $60
264 A clover field wc $25
1908 233 A summer afternoon wc $50
1909 250 On Montreal mountain wc $35
1910 243 Muskoka woodland wc $50
1912 258 Rideau River, near Ottawa $15
259 Rhodendron, Kew Gardens wc $10
1913 274 Azaleas, Kew Gardens wc $10
275 Lake Memphremagog wc $20
1914 265 Lake Memphremagog wc $20

266 Rosedale Ravine wc $10
1915 238 Chrysanthemums
1943 132A Peonies wc $100

MARTIN, HENRY (HY)
c 1832, Painswick, Eng 20 May 1902, Toronto H
addr: Toronto, 123 Scollard St
1901 149 Church of St Jacques, Dieppe wc $100
150 Chancel and north transept, St Marks, Venice wc $100

MARTIN, HOMER DODGE Amer
28 Oct 1836, Albany, N.Y. 12 Feb 1897, St Paul, Minn B F Gr TB1
1889 39 Westchester hills $100

MARTIN, JOHN (JACK)
1 Aug 1904, Nuneaton, Eng 6 Nov 1965, Ayr, Ont CWW61 M WWA70
addr: Toronto, 31 Winston Ave
1939 217 The boat yard $250
218 The far hills $200
415 My lane, No 2 drypt $15
416 Look thy last on all things lovely drypt $15

MARTIN, RONALD ALBERT
28 Apr 1943, London, Ont CE IO M WWA84
addr: London,
1968 165 Conclusion and transfer, dedicated to Anne Brodzky coll & enamel on plywd 24 x 24 each part, 48 3/8 x 48 3/8 each part $1,500

MARTIN, THERESE
addr: Montreal, 186 Mance St
1901 151 Corbeille de chrysanthèmes wc $30

MARTIN, THOMAS MOWER
5 Oct 1838, Inner Temple, London, Eng 15 Mar 1934, Toronto AGO CC1 CWW10 EC H M Mo98/12 NGC TB3 W78
addr: Toronto: 1880; North Drive, Rosedale, 1891-4; 110 Crescent Rd, 1897-1901; 108 Hazelton Ave, 1903; 225 Cottingham St, 1905-17; 115 Erskine Ave, 1921-2; 135 Erskine Ave, 1929
1880 4 On guard
28 Threatening rain, Dundas Valley
32 Morning in Muskoka
59 Moonrise on the prairies
62 A summer afternoon, Nipegon
73 Setter's head
154 A crow in trouble wc
167 Phloxes wc
187 Beech trees, study wc
1881 7 Peonies
13 Cushing's Island, Maine
15 Untrodden wilds of Canada
18 Morning on the Kaministiquia
20 First day of Indian summer
22 A river bank
24 Nearly through, washing day
26 In the spring time
38, 42 Grapes
53 Phlox wc
63 On the Peabody River, White Mountains wc
1883 16 Rocks at Niagara wc
34 A glimpse of Niagara wc
87 A balmy morning, early spring
88 When the snow has gone
93 A wet day in Muskoka
94 At Port Credit
100 Logging
105 Crossing the ford
106 Near Meaford
111 Deer hunt on White Trout Lake, Ottawa
112 Where the lilies grow
113 Shadow Pool, Muskoka
124 Not lost, but gone before
1885 102 Showery weather wc
104 Oxtongue Lake wc
123 On Muskoka River wc
148 Ravine at Waterdown wc
152 Indian summer, Georgian Bay etch
153 Upper Muskoka etch
154 The settler's home etch
155 Belvidere, Central Park, New York etch
156 Evening, Central Park, New York etch
1886 90 Indian summer
94 And mixes a wi admonition due
110 Sunset north of Lake Superior
1888 6 Bacchus $50
12 Mount Stephen from Kicking Horse Pass $350
35 Mt Sir Donald from Glacier Road $350

43 Hermes $50
80 The glacier of the Selkirks wc $100
108 Van Horne Range wc $50
122 Mount Field, B.C. wc $75
1889 40 In the Don meadows $125
41 After the winter $40
42 Waiting for the spring $40
150 Canadian woodlands wc $150
151 Summer afternoon wc $40
179 Untouched forest etch $10
180 Twilight in the backwoods etch $10
181 Indian camp on Georgian Bay etch $8
182 Settler's home in Muskoka etch $8
183 A farm yard etch $8
1891 85 The portage $500
1892 101 In charge $1,000
102 Disturbed $150
1894 107 The flock at rest $400
108 Woodcock at home $50
109 Toronto Bay $125
1897 91 A pair of mallards $30
1898 79 Otter disturbed at dinner $100
80 Where the woodcock fly $40
81 The approach of the enemy $50
82 An old pioneer's story $75
1901 74 The Golden Gate, California $150
1903 203 Canvas backs wc $45
1905 87 The lost trail $300
180 In the moose country wc $200
1906 265 The moorland road wc $35
266 St Martin's de Tours, Canterbury, where St Augustine preached wc $30
1908 107 Is it a trap? $150
108 Wild goose, duck and grouse $100
1909 251 A warm day in September $350
252 Indian camp, Lake Superior $75
1910 244 Stopping for a rest $200
245 In the moose country wc $60
1911 209 In a Devon barn wc $60
210 Beech woods, York Mills $100
1912 260 Caveat emptor $800
261 Burnham beeches wc $50
1913 276 Near Lineboro', Quebec $40
277 A bit of Ontario $50
1914 267 The farm on the bill wc $20
268 Indian camp, Lake Superior wc $30
269 Burnham beeches wc $25
270 In the moose country wc $50
1915 239 Shore of Lake Memphremagog wc $25
240 Seneca Indians, Georgian Bay $45
1917 222 Mount Sir Donald wc $30
223 Wild Canada in autumn wc $35
224 Trout fishing in northern Quebec wc $15
225 Showery weather $35
226 A hillside in autumn $25
227 A beech stump $15
1921 166 North shore of Lake Superior $350
167 Looking east at sunset $125
168 An early morning breakfast $150
1922 189 Near Jervis Straits, coast of British Columbia $75
1929 141 Indian camp, Georgian Bay wc $100
142 Peonies wc $100

MARTUCCI, CARMEN WILLIAM
5 Feb 1922, Montreal M
addr: Montreal: 4737 Resther St, 1947; 3431 Durocher St, Apt 9, 1950; 3921 Linton Ave, Apt 5, 1952; 9950 St Hubert St, 1953; 3478 Park Ave, Apt 4, 1954-5; 5562 St Denis St, 1957-60
1947 183 Street scene, Belgium $40
184 Interior
1950 125 Still life $50
1952 101 Alley $50
1953 86 The black table $100
1954 60 Still life $50
1955 59 Alley $50
1957 130 Street scene nm $30
1960 195 Drawing $35

MARUSAN, JULIUS
addr: Toronto, 19 Dacre Cr
1961 37 Blue forms $400

MASSE, GEORGES SEVERE
10 Aug 1918, Montreal WWA76
addr: Hampstead, Que, 5655 Côte St Luc Rd, 1942-4. Westmount, 4823 St Catherine St W, 1946-55
1942 208 Formes pen drwg $20
1944 95 L'Université de Montréal $200
1946 263 Contours, à la plume drwg $20
1947 185 Scène Gaspésienne $250

1955 60 Pantomime $400

MASSELOTTE, ANTONIO
addr: Quebec, P.O.Box 91
1937 186 Les Ramparts de Québec $300

MASSON, HENRI LEOPOLD
10 Jan 1907, Namur, Belg AGO B CC2 CE M NGC TB2 WWA80 Juror
addr: Ottawa, 351 Slater St, 1934-40
1934 206 A cold day $100
207 The first snow $50
1935 205 Butcher shop $75
206 November $35
207 Clearing wc $35
1940 196 The ice house $150
197 Spring flood $150 (LPL)
198 La procession wc $75
379 Montreal landscape charcl $35

MASSON, RAYMOND
addr: Boston, 27 Tremont Row
1898 233 Study sculp
234 Miss Ellena B. sculp

MATHER, JEAN
fl 1914-44
addr: Winnipeg, 85 West Gate
1928 117 Lake of the Woods wc $20

MATHESON, RODERICK DAREY
13 Aug 1897, Ottawa M
addr: Ottawa, 69 Russell Ave, 1926-7. Montreal, 3534 Lorne Ave, 1936
1926 82 In the Gatineau Hills $200
1927 115 Cliffs in the Laurentian hills $75
1936 279 Shadows, Mount Royal $300
280 A farm at Youghal $100

MATHEWS, RICHARD GEORGE
16 Jul 1870, Montreal CWW10 MO12 TB2 WWB34
addr: Montreal: 15 Quesnel St, 1898; 2679A St Catherine St, 1900; 25 Sussex Ave, 1901; 2718 St Catherine St, 1903; Star office, 1905; 1217 Dorchester St, 1906; 283 Mountain St, 1927
1898 179 Summer evening wc $15
180 Study wc
1900 174 J.S. Buchan, Esq b&w
175 The lady with the checked skirt b&w
176 Portrait of a lady b&w
1901 191 Rèverie b&w
1903 240 Lady Minto crayon & pastel
241 Lady Eileen Elliot crayon
242 Mark Hambourg crayon $30
243 General Booth crayon $25
244 Miss Katherine Jones crayon $25
245 Mdlle Zelia de Lussan grayon $25
1905 212 Mary Moore pastel $50
213 Sir Charles Wyndham pastel $50
214 Mr Frederick Yorston pastel
215 Mde Lilian Nordica pastel $50
216 David Bispham pastel $30
1906 267-8 Sir William C. Van Horne pastel
269 Mrs George Cantlie pastel
270 Miss Mary Pangman pastel
271 Mrs Charles Davidson pastel
272 Mr John E. Logan pastel
273 Jan Kubelik pastel
274 A study pastel
275 Covenhoven, St Andrew's N.B. pastel
1927 286 Edinburgh Castle etch $45
287 The ballet etch $35
288 The tolbooth etch $30
289 The chess players etch $25

MATHIAS, F. DAVID
see: Spence, D. Jerome, 1938-40

MATHIAS, HARRIETT see MATTHIAS, HARRIETT

MATHIEU, GILLES
addr: Val David, Que
1961 90 Emourie nm $75

MATTE, JACQUES DENYS
13 Aug 1930, Cap Santé, Portneuf, Que M
addr: Quebec, 438 Ste Foy Rd, 1955. Montreal, 1260 Mackay St, 1960-1
1955 61 La ville $100
1960 79 Un buit de noirs $250
1961 138 Nuances des oracles $300

MATTHEWS, MARMADUKE
29 Aug 1837, Barcheston, Eng 24 Sep 1913, Toronto AGO CC1 EC H M Mo98/12 NGC R2 TB3 W78
addr: Toronto, 1880. Bracondale, Ont, 1891-1903. Toronto, 1910

1880 water colour, 1880-1910
152 The Crawford Notch, N.H.
1881 56 View in the White Mountains
62 In the Queen's Park, Toronto
1883 19 The Glen, valley of the Peabudy, N.H.
32 Looking towards Gorham, from Mount Washington
39 Mount Washington from Glen Pond
56 A rainy day in the White Mountains
57 View from Mount Washington, near Tuckerman's Ravine
65 Summer days at home
1886 27 The Androscoggan near Gorham
28 The Mount Washington road
31 The old French fort, Quebec
1889 153 Evening on the Pipestone River, at Laggan, N.W.T. $50
154 Eight thousand feet above the sea, Rocky Mountains $50
1891 178 Mount Macdonald, Roger's Pass $175
179 Restful eve $75
180 The old willow bed $75
1892 192 Lake Louise, the gem of the Rockies $250
193 The old house at home $60
194 Pleasant it was when the woods were green $100
195 Van Horne Range, from Field station $150
196 The old board fence $30
1894 110 Canadian wonderland (oil) $1,000
208 Greenwood $150
209 A woodland pasture $40
1895 184 A Muskoka rendez-vous $40
185 A saucy tenant $40
186 Under the shade of the oak $30
187 Mount Washington from the Glen $30
1901 152 Looking down the Goat Pass $40
153 Main range of the Selkirks $40
154 Mount Washington, New Hampshire $50
155 Evening, Marion Lake $50
1903 204 Flats of Kicking Horse $75
205 Bow River Pass $75
206 After rain on the prairie $50
1910 246 The western waves of the ebbing day $200
247 First discovery of gold in Porcupine Lands $50

MATTHEWS, PETER ALLAN
16 Apr 1931, Montreal M
addr: Montreal: 173 Prince Arthur St W, 1956; 1548 Stanley St, 1957
1956 118 Morning, Ibiza nm
1957 63 Bottles, brushes and rectangles $100

MATTHEWS, VERA see IRVING, VERA

MATTHIAS, HARRIET F. M.
addr: Westmount, 21 Gordon Cr, 1936-8
1936 281 Portrait
1938 Mathias
84 Portrait study

MATTICE, HORTENSE see GORDON, HORTENSE

MATTICE, MARION EVE
b 1878, d 1956
addr: Hamilton
1912 262 The child's prayer $250

MAUDSLAY, GUY ARCHIBALD
addr: Montreal, 842 Dorchester St
1906 120 Warnham Court
121 Warnham Park $40

MAUPAS, EMILE M.
addr: Montreal, 334 Sherbrooke St E, 1909. Manchester, N.H, 1910-11. Montreal: 208 Sherrier St, 1913; 202 Mentana St, 1918-22
1909 401 Epave plaster
1910 373 Mgr Georges Albert Grandin, Eveque de Manchester sculp
374 An all round athelete sculp
375 Groupe de lutteurs sculp
1911 293 Mdlle Eva D. sculp
294 Le tourbillon sculp
1913 415 Quiétude clay $10
416 La princesse plaster $7
417 Porte bonheur clay, in brass $18
1918 373 Femme inconnue sculp
374 Idylle antique sculp
1921 301 Madame H.B. plaster rel
1922 342 Groupe de lutteurs sculp

MAURY, LOUISE M.
addr: Westmount, 168 Côte St Antoine Rd
1914 271 Venetian sails wc $75

MAW, KATHERINE BEATRICE (BETTY) (m Gerard Brett)
26 Jun 1910, Hull, Eng CWW84
addr: Toronto, 148 Glencairn Ave, 1932-6
1932 186 The dance wc $35
1933 212 Pilgrims $60
1934 208 Pilgrims $75
209 Procession $75
210 Fishing shacke, Percé $25
211 Barachois, Gaspé, Que $25
1935 208 Fishing $25
209 St Tite des Caps, Que $25
210 Old houses, Les Eboulements, Que $25
1936 282 The Tun and Oyster $25
283 Head

MAW, SAMUEL HERBERT
12 Sep 1881, Needham Market, Eng 19 Aug 1952, Toronto AGO M PMC
addr: Halifax, Royal Bank Chambers, 1923. Montreal: 274 Beaver Hall Hill, 1924-7; 172A Bishop St, 1927. Toronto, 148 Glencairn Ave, 1932-9. Westmount, 439 Grosvenor Ave, 1942
1923 Maw, L.A. mispr, 1923-4
231 North aisle of choir, Ely Cathedral etch $15
232 Rio del Carmini, Venice etch $12.50
233 An East Anglican village etch $12.50
234 The old lock etch $750
1924 287 The landing place etch $17.50
288 The dock side etch $15
289 Murano, Venice etch $15
1925 304 The Sun Life Building
361 St James Street, Montreal etch $17.50
362 Sun Life Building, Montreal etch
363 The Arts Building, McGill University etch $10
364 The fish wharf etch $10
1926 83 Dominion Square, Montreal wc $75
206 San Giorgio, Venice etch $11.50
207 The Lagoon, Venice etch $11.50
208 Tower Bridge etch $11.50
1927 Mace, S.H, no 219, mispr
219 House in suburbs
290 Canadian Nurses War Memorial etch $25
1932 410 Wharf at Barachois, Que etch $17.50
1939 417 Tower entrance, Parliament Buildings, Ottawa etch $17.50
1942 209 Tercentenary map of Montreal col ink drwg
see also Turner, Philip John, 1926

MAXFIELD, JAMES E. Amer
1848, Detroit B H TB Y
1889 43 Juliet $30
44 All about the 'lection $15

MAXWELL, EDWARD
31 Dec 1867 - 14 Nov 1923, Montreal CE Co Mo12 NGC
addr: Montreal: 1760 Notre Dame St, 1898; 180 Côte St Antoine Rd, 1900; 6 Beaver Hall Sq, 1905-17; 360 Beaver Hall Sq, 1918-26
1898 221 Canadian Pacific Railway, station, Vancouver
222 CPR station and hotel, Moose Jaw, N.W.T.
223 CPR station and hotel, McAdam Junction, N.B.
224 Residence, Mr J.H. Birks
1900 73 The day's work
1909 431 Legislative and Executive Building, Regina
432 Residence, Mr C.F. Smith
433 Residence, Mr C.R. Hosmer, St Andrews, N.B.
see also Maxwell, Edward and William Sutherland

MAXWELL, EDWARD and WILLIAM SUTHERLAND
1905 258 CPR station, Winnipeg
259 Bank of Montreal, Westmount
260 Royal Bank, Westmount
261 Alexandra Hospital, Montreal
262 CPR station, Winnipeg, general waiting room
1906 339 Nurses home, Royal Victoria Hospital
1908 324 Legislative and Administrative buildings, Regina
325-6 Proposed Justice building, Ottawa, elevation
1911 298-300 New gallery, Sherbrooke St, front elevation, ground plan 1st floor plan
1912 415 Office building drwg

1913 433 Executive building, Winnipeg des
434 CPR hotel, Calgary
1917 380-1 House, Sir Thomas Tait, St Andrews, N.B, entrance front, elevation facing golf links wc
1918 398 Bronze memorial tablet, Church of the Messiah
1925 Maxwell, Edward and William S, and Pitts, 1925-6
305-6 Château Frontenac, Quebec additions
1926 148-51 Château Frontenac, view from Lower Town (in foreground old portion by Bruce Price, architect), view from main courtyard, view from St Louis Street, interior of rotunda, private dining room and rotunda

MAXWELL, WILLIAM SUTHERLAND
14 Nov 1874 - 25 Mar 1952, Montreal CE CNS36 CO CWW52 Mo12 NGC PMC TB3
addr: Montreal: Bell Telephone Bldg, 1901; 6 Beaver Hall Sq, 1905-6; 360 Beaver Hall Sq, 1918-27; 1158 Beaver Hall Sq, 1928-39
1901 156 Autumn in Brittany wc
201-4 Salle des Fêtes, proposed plan, front, side elevation
205 State barge, sketch
1905 181 Brittany coast, off St Briac wc
1918 227 Near Florence, Italy pastel $35
1927 Maxwell and Pitts, 1927-39
220 McDougall & Cowans, Montreal private office
221 Living room, residence, Mrs G. Boyer
222 Living room, residence, Percy P. Cowans, Esq
1928 247-8 Residence, Dr W.W. Chipman, sunroom photos
249-50 Residence, P.P. Cowans, drawingroom photos
1931 308-9 Residence, Sir Thomas Tait, St Andrews, N.B. photos
310 Entrance, Westmount property photo
311 Kanawaki Gold Club photo
1937 351 Country House, Mr X. wc
351 Ephraim Scott Presbyterian Church wc
1939 359 Canadian Building, New York World's Fair competition des
see also Maxwell, Edward and William Sutherland

MAY, A. E.
addr: Montreal West, 107 Westminster Ave, 1945-7
1945 158 Lower St Lawrence $150
1947 186 Snow flurries $250

MAY, BETTE (Mrs Thomas)
addr: Westmount, 630 Victoria Ave, 1941. Montreal, 5633 Côte des Neiges Rd, 1942-5
1941 265 Louis XVI mantel
266 Modern bedroom
267 Modern foyer
1942 Thomas, Bette May
226 Modern living room, New York apartment
1943 247 Early American interior
1944 152 Modern interior
1945 271 Country house living room

MAY, CHRISTIANE KLITGAARD (Mrs)
addr: Montreal, Salisbury Flats, 1903. St John, N.B, Clifton House, 1905. Montreal, 1158 Beaver Hall Sq, 1931
1903 84 By lamplight
85 Portrait study
207 Seashore, Denmark wc $30
208 Danish landscape wc $30
310 Miniatures (2)
1905 88 Portrait of a lady
89 Mrs Wilson
1931 167 Maud min

MAY, DEREK JOHN
16 Sep 1932, London, Eng TB3
addr: Montreal: 3557 Hutcheson St, 1956; 1576 Summerhill Ave, 1957; Waddington Galleries, 1456 Sherbrooke St W, 1959-62; Galerie Agnes Lefort, 1504 Sherbrooke St W, 1963
1956 119 Frozen harbour nm $60
1957 64 Landscape I $150
131 Corner of a city nm $150
1959 32 Fountains of the earth nm $150
1962 50-1 Brush drawing $75, $50
1963 41 Number twenty-three $175 (MBAM)

MAY, ELSA
addr: Montreal: 1915; 175 Drummond St, 1916; 278 Stanley St, 1921; 1 View-

mount Ave, 1922
1915 241 Portrait
1916 192 Portrait
1921 169 Master Melville Bell
170 Master Sidney Johnson
1922 190 The outcast $500

MAY, HENRIETTA MABEL
1884, Westmount, Que 8 Oct 1971, Vancouver AGO CC1 CWW67 M NGC TB2/3 WWA70
addr: Westmount, 434 Elm Ave, 1910-43. Vancouver, 1967
1910 248 Moonlight
249-50 Study of a head pastel
1911 211 On the beach $50
212 Study in grey $25
213 Portrait
1912 263 The white boat $50
264 The daisy field $40
265 The dredge $30
266 Fishing boats $30
267 Sketch $25
268 Windy day $30
269 At Cartierville $30
1913 278 Portrait
279 The market $100 (NGC)
280 Dans les jardins $50
281 Autumn $60
282 Sketch, autumn trees wc $15
283 Sketch, interior wc $15
1914 272 The station $200
273 The garden $150
274 On the Seine $125
275 Over the teacups $100
276 Sketch wc $35 (listed 1967, Jessie Dow prize)
277-8 Sketch wc $25 each
1915 242 The story $175
243 Watching the regatta $150 (NGC)
244 Grain elevators, canal scene $125
1916 193 A warm October day $125
194 Spring afternoon $200
195 Edge of the lake $200
196 The white house $200
197 Winter $150
198 Doris and Ruth
1917 228 Autumn in the mountains $500
229 Clearing after rain $250
230 Trees, autumn $250
231 Across the canal $60
232-3 Sketch $35 each
1918 228 Sunny afternoon $500
229 Miss Darrell Morrisey
230 Going to the station $350 (listed 1967, Jessie Dow prize)
231 Blue barges $75
232 The canal
233 The pier $250
1919 200 The ferry $250
201 Saturday afternoon $250
202 Sunny afternoon $250
203 Landing, Peake's Island $35
204-5 Sketch $25, $20
1921 171 Autumn $500
172 In the Laurentian Mountains $250 (AGO)
173 Canal bank, late afternoon $250
174 Winter sketch $40
1922 191 Summer afternoon $500
192 Winter $300
193 Early spring $250
194 Knowlton, early spring $125
1923 149 March $250
150 Farm House, Ste Marguerite $150
1924 224 Early settlers to the bank of the St Lawrence. Shown RCA 1923 exhibit, mural competition
1925 179 Autumn trees $250
180 Melting snow, Knowlton $250
181 Early spring $100
1926 84 Winter in the hills $500
85 Pine trees $400
86 Winter afternoon $200
87 The lake $75
1934 212 Late winter $300
213 A village street $300
214 The sunlit valley $250
1935 211 Castle of industry $300
212 Melting snow $300
213 Early spring $300
214 Study in rose and green $100
1936 284 High water $250
285 Melting snow $500
286 Ski trails $250
287 Autumn $250
1937 187 Beyond the shadows $250
188 Winter landscape $250
1939 220 Blue and silver $250
221 The farm $300
222 Old house by the roadside $200
1941 133 Early June $250
1943 133 In the garden $500
134 The lake $250

1967 41 The pink balloon, 1919 33 X 45
(Miss Lillian R. May, Vancouver)

MAY, PERCY MORELAND
4 Apr 1886, Birkenhead, Eng CNS36
CWW49
addr: Montreal, 5031 Grosvenor Ave, 1936. Westmount: 630 Victoria Ave, 1937-41; 4330 Sherbrooke St W, Apt 6, 1945-7
1936 288 Laurentian pattern $150
289 Cloudy day, St Jovite $50
1937 189 Laurentian harvest $250
190 The port of Montreal $150
1939 233 Laurentian valley $150
1940 199 The red barn $125
1941 134 Winter farmyard $100
135 Near Glacier, B.C. $100
1945 159 Morning at Otter Lake $200
160 Bishop Court, Montreal wc $50
1947 187 Central Park, New York wc $50
188 Peonies wc $65

MAYEROVITCH, HARRY
16 Apr 1910, Montreal M
addr: Montreal: 409 Mount Royal Ave, 1936; 1430 Bleury St, 1937; 1178 Phillips Pl, 1939-43; 1001 Mount Royal Blvd, 1949. Westmount, 4840 Westmount Avenue, 1951-9
1936 290 Street car scene $40
489 Small summer cottage (arch)
553 View of Montreal from Bell Telephone Building etch $15
1937 Mayerovitch & Bernstein, 353-5
353 Residence, Dr Simon Kirsch, Outremont, Que
354 Hungarian Recreational and Cultural Centre, Montreal
355 Residence, Robert Lafleur
426 Portrait of Lily drwg
1939 418 Mr Norman Lee nm
419 Lois Ann nm
420 David nm
421 Miss Esther Tamarin nm
1940 380 Mexican girl nitro cellulose lacquer $75
381 Mexican girl litho $15
382 Mexican peasant litho $15
1941 136 String quarter $100
243 Chana, portrait drwg
1942 110 Home front
1943 135 The defeatists $200
1949 139 Recorder's Court casein
1951 30 Boy and girl $250
1952 34 News vender
74 Casualty lino pr $20
1953 25 Nina
David
1954 61 Mother and child $100
126 Portrait drwg
1959 54 Figure wd

MAYMAN, BERNARD
addr: Montreal: 150B Drolet St, 1927; 3914 Drolet St, 1931; 3445 City Hall Ave, 1939
1927 116 Still life $45
1931 430 Head, study plaster
1939 219 Riverside, Bordeaux $75

MAYRS, CHARLES ALEXANDER
18 Apr 1940, Winnipeg M
addr: Vancouver, 5507 Larch St
1960 196 The sea and I nm $100

MAYRS, FRANK BLACK
7 Jan 1934, Winnipeg M
addr: Ottawa, 338 Somerset St E
1961 39 Low tide $200

MAYRS, WILLIAM JOHN BLACK (BILL)
27 May 1932, Winnipeg M
addr : Vancouver, New Design Gallery, 1157 W Pender St, 1960. Winnipeg, 359 Lanark St, 1963
1960 80 Base of the mountain $250
1963 42 Pandora's box $500

MEAGHER, AILEEN ALETHEA
26 Nov 1910, Edmonton CC2 M
addr: Halifax, 83 Seymour St
1957 135 Bridge nm $35

MEAGHER, GEORGE ALFRED
6 Dec 1867, Kingston, Ont H
addr: Montreal, 14 De Brésoles St, 1900, 1905, 1911. Toronto, 338 Jarvis St, 1901. Ottawa, 113 Daly Ave, 1909
1900 74 Gananoque by moonlight
1901 75 Cupid on the ice $25
1905 90 Indian Lake outlet $100
1909 253 Moonlight, Niagara on Lake, (sic) Niagara on the Lake $50
1911 214 Becalmed $50
215 View, St Lawrence River $75

MEARES, HERMINA (INA)
12 Oct 1921, Greys, Essex, Eng M
addr: Picton, Ont, 19 Johnson St, 1963. Toronto, 28 Astley Ave, 1964
1963 46 Yon twelve-winded sky $350
1964 Neares, mispr
52 Realm of gold $450

MEASE, RUTH T. Eng
fl 1905-13 DBA RA
addr: London, Eng, 26 Christchurch Rd, Streathem Hill
1913 284 An old gateway wc $25
285 Thurlstone Bay, Devonshire wc $15

MEDWIN, ALEC
addr: Montreal, 1671 Sherbrooke St (sic)
1939 232 Autumn wind, Kent wc

MEEKER, JOSEPH RUSLING Amer
21 Apr 1827, Newark, N.J. 1887 St Louis, Mo B F Gr TB
1886 91 Near Bayou Têche, Louisianna

MEIKLE, ELLA
addr: Montreal, 916 St Catherine St W, 1924-6
1924 366 Jardiniere, Market day $75
367 Vase, The bath $60
368 Bowl, Canadian butterfly $25
369 Ring plate $20
1925 321-2 Bowl $35, $25
1926 170 Waterlily tray $18
171 The damsel, vase $40
172 The dancer, vase $50

MEISTER, PAUL ALFRED ERNEST see ALFRED, PAUL

MELIS, JOHANNES EDUARD (HANS)
3 Jun 1925, Tilburg, Nethld d 1978 M
addr: St John's: c/o Newfoundland Academy of Art, 1958; 2 Devon Row, 1959; St John's, 1968
1958 80 Reclining figure ter cot $100 Hon mention
81 Torso ter cot $100
1959 55 Reclining figure ter cot $100
1968 169 MO No 1 ter cot 9 x 14 1/2 x 4 1/2 $150
170 MO No 2 ter cot 14 x 12 x 8 $150

MELOCHE, FRANCOIS XAVIER EDOUARD
1858/59 - 15 Aug 1914, Montreal
addr: Montreal, 43 German St
1892 225 For church, Joliette dec sketch

MELOCHE, SUZANNE (m Christian Marcel Barbeau)
10 Apr 1926, Ottawa M TB3
addr: Montreal: 4541 rue St Hubert, 1946-7; 1631 St Luke St, Apt 5, 1959-1960. Brookline Village, Mass, 22 Washington St, Apt 4, 1961
1946 Barbeau, 1946-7
14 Ténèbreuse, étrange, inattendue $125
1947 18 Vol incrusté des quasi feuilles sensibles $275
19 Cavernane $150
1959 33 La nuit blanche nm
1960 197 Les mains libre nm $150
1961 92 Metronome illus nm Purchase award (MBAM)

MELVILLE, CLARE GLADYS
12 Oct 1897, Ottawa M
addr: Ottawa, 61 Cartier St
1956 120 Landscape nm $35

MENDEL, CHARLES M.
addr: Montreal: 1121 St Urbain St, 1911; 1131 St Urbain St, 1912-18; 4833 Park Ave, 1932-41; 1002 Bleury St, 1946
1911 Mendel, 1911-18
216 Mr C.M.M.
1912 270 Portrait
1914 280 Horace Traubel
281 Mr S. Schwartz, study
282 Lamplight $75
1917 234 Dubby, portrait $50
235 Widow $250
1918 238 The forge $250
239 Jim $150
1932 194 Mrs O.
1933 471 Child's head, study charcl $50
472 Dr Frank Mendel charcl
473 Lithuanian study charcl $75
474 Mrs Louis Cohen charcl
1940 206 An old habitant $200
1941 140 A. Taylor, Esq
244 W.T. Leach, Esq crayon
1946 180 Avery $200
181 Study in red $200
port: by E. Valderrama, 1914-408 (Chas M. Mendel)

MENSES, JAN
28 Apr 1933, Rotterdam CWW84 M WWA84
addr: Montreal: 3265 Goyer Ave, Apt 1, 1961; 2461 Maplewood Ave, Apt 5, 1964; Montreal, 1968
1961 93 1940-45 (V) nm $150
1964 101 The death of Joseph K nm $600
1968 Kaddish series
171 No 30 32 x 24 $750
172 No 36 32 x 24 $750
Klippath series
173 No 18 temp 30 x 22 $750
174 No 24 temp 30 x 22 $750

MERCIER, LISE
18 Aug 1941, Montreal
addr: Montreal, 5618 Phillips Ave
1957 65 Marie-Noelle $85

MERCIER, MADELEINE
19 Nov 1930, Ham Nord, Que M
addr: Québec, 127 rue Ste Anne, 1956. Montréal, 3434 rue St Hubert, 1957
1956 40 Paysage ensoleillé $125
1957 66 Le pont $75

MEREDITH, JOHN (b John Meredith Smith)
24 Jul 1933, Fergus, Ont AGO B CC2 CE CWW84 M TB3 WWA84
addr: Brampton, Ont, 53 Woodward Ave
1960 83 The bridge $650

MEREDITH, MARGARET F.
addr: Pointe Claire, Que
1914 283 Crypt, Gloucester Cathedral wc $40
284 Portico, S Maria della Salute, Venice wc $35
285 Rouen Cathedral and market wc $35

MEROLA, MARIO VIRGILIO
31 Mar 1931, Montreal CC1 CWW84 M TB3
addr: Montreal: 3663 rue Ste Famille, 1963; 3854 rue St Hubert, 1965
1963 107 Dové va wd $3,000
1965 27 Olsen from Oslo nm $150

MERS, WALDYNE DE
addr: Montreal, 2648 Wurtele Ave
1941 284 Infant, study plaster $100

MESNARD, ALBERT
1847, St Lin, Que 6 Sep 1909, Montreal
see Perrault, Maurice, 1894

MEUNIER, CLAIRE
1928, St Denis-sur-Richelieu, Que
addr: Montreal: 217 Gouin Blvd E, 206 St Joseph Blvd E, 1957
1952 102 Moise $85
1957 67 Femme au collier No 2 $100

MEUNIER, JEANNETTE
addr: Montreal, 2039 Peel St
1934 405 Suggested furniture decoration
406 Interior, Westmount
407 Intérieur chez Mde J.B. Woodyatt
port: by Marjorie Smith, 1928-327

MEUX, GWENDOLYN
WWA40
addr: Sackville, N.B, 1920-1. Norman, Okla, University of Oklahoma, Faculty Exchange, 1922
1920 Mews, 1920-1
173 Nasturtiums $25
174 The white house $40
1921 176 The Tantramar Marshes $50
1922 198 Autumn hillside $75
199 The Wichitaw Mountains $85

MEYER, BETTY (Mrs)
addr: Westmount: 4643 Sherbrooke St W, 1939; 4831 Sherbrooke St W, Apt 4, 1940
1939 233 Head of Lois
1940 207 Peonies

MICHAEL, PAUL
addr: Montreal, McGill University, Medical Bldg, 1926-8
1926 etching
209 The Equinox, Berkeley Hills $35
210 Fishing village, California coast $20
211 The oaks, Mills College $20
212 Carmel dunes $15
1927 291 Old fish house, Morro $15
292 Eucalyptus at night $10
293 The whalers dry pt $20
1928 308 Fading skies dry pt $10
309 The poplar dry pt $10
310 The old barn $12

MICHOTTE, JO

addr: Montreal, 3441 Côte des Neiges Rd, 1944-45
1944 146 Quebec India ink $175
1945 263 Lac Louise India ink $200

MICKLE, ALFRED ERNEST
26 Feb 1869, Guelph, Ont 5 Sep 1966, Hamilton, Ont CWW52 M NGC TB3
addr: Toronto: 32 Adelaide St E, 1912-26; 121 Walker Ave, 1927-36
1912 271 Old church and mill, Dorset $175
272 A field of poppies $150
273 In old Dorsetshire $225
274 Harvest field, Hants $70
1913 286 The crest of the hill $175
1914 286 Dyke lands, Grand Pré $500
287 Wild iris meadow, N,B. $375
288 Oxen, land of Evangeline $50
289 Harvest field, Wolfville $250
1915 249 Harvest, land of Evangeline $150
1919 206 Old church, Boxford $90
207 Storm passing over $35
1920 175 Harvesters threatened by rain, Grand Pré, N.S. $225
176 A quaint Hampshire village $76
1921 177 The elms, Meadowvale, Ont $235
1922 200 Showery weather, Grand Pré $60
1923 151 Near North Hatley, Que $230
1924 173 Garden, Sherborne, Dorset pastel $150
174 Old alm houses, Sherborne, Dorset pastel $30
1925 189 Very early snow, Compton, Que $400
190 Ancient alm house, Dorsetshire pastel $175
1926 89 Quebec $300
1927 123 The Citadel of Quebec $500
1928 123 Devil's paint brush flowers, west Shefford, Que $200
1929 145 Quebec from a north-west field $500
146 Wayside poetry, Eastern Townships $250
1930 143 Harvest at Cap à l'Aigle $35
1931 173 Lake Maskinonge, Que $400
1932 195 Old Scotch kirk, Quebec $400
1933 218 Glorious October on the St Lawrence $500
1934 224 A fine day, Charlevoix Co, Quebec $500
1935 223 The village of Rock Island $80
224 Harvest near Murray Bay $50
1936 300 October glory, Carleton, Gaspé $80
301 White house, Portneuf Co, Quebec $80

MICKUNAS, IRENE (m Osvald Mickunas)
1931, Lithuania
addr; Sarnia, Ont
1968 acry collage 175-7
175 Celebration No 2 36 x 36 $500
176 Configuration No 4 42 x 42 $500
177 Celebration No 8 44 x 44 $500
178 Organic landscape No 9 ink 17 1/2 x 21 1/2 $200

MIDDLETON, JANET HOLLY BLENCH (m J. M. Churchill)
15 May 1922, Vernon, B.C. M
addr: West Calgary, Alta, 1116 8th Ave
1952 75 Below Gordon Glacier, B.C. pr

MIEGE, HENRY
addr: Montreal, 448A Guy St, 1925-6
1925 365 Batik $35
1926 213 Hibou st gl $30
214 Chimère batik $30
215 Imprimé à la main, sur velours $30

MIGUEL, ROBERT
addr: Montreal, 3465 Ridgewood Ave
1959 56 Setif plaster

MIKUSKA, FRANK PETER
4 Oct 1930, Winnipeg M
addr: Winnipeg: 656 Asburn St, 1957; Winnipeg, 1968
1957 136 Semblance of spring nm $75
1968 179 Evolution 11 blue perspex & printer's ink 48 x 44 $500
180 Evolution 10 stage 2 perspex & printers ink 48 x 45 $500
181 Expansion printer's ink 45 x 48 $500
182 Vintage 50 printer's ink 45 x 48 $500

MILES, JOHN CHRISTOPHER
17 Mar 1837 - 2 Dec 1911, Saint John, N.B. EC H M Mo12 W78 WWA.06
addr: Saint John: 74 Germain St, 1891; Pugsley Bldg, 1892-5; Saint John, 1908
1881 1 View on Nerepis River, N.B.

30 Duck and partridges
47 Partridges
49 Malaga grapes
1883 67 Old water boats, Mary Island, N.B. wc
68 Glen Tree River, Saint John wc
69 Squaw's Cap, Restigouche River wc
70 View on the Saint John River wc
71 Oak Point, Saint John River wc
72 Wood boats, Saint John River wc
73 Ashore, Navy Island Bar, Saint John wc
74 Red Beach, Deer Island, N.B. wc
75 Flat lands, Restigouche River wc
76 A coaster wc
77 Lobster boats wc
78 Athol farm, Restigouche River wc
79 Bishop's Rock, Grand Manan wc
129 Sport of the waves
134 Lily pond, Sheffield, N.B.
1885 73 On the bay shore
1891 86 'Tween the gloamin and the mirk, when the kye come hame $250
87 After the showers $50
1892 103 Beacon lights, Saint John harbour $75
1894 111 Fisherman's camp, Bay of Fundy $500
112 The Interval Road, River Saint John $150
1895 84 An old bridge in Acadie $50
1908 109 Negro Head, Bay of Fundy

MILES, VICTOR
2 Mar 1929, London, Eng M
addr: West Vancouver, 2696 Palmerston Ave
1964 53 The emergence $350

MILLAR, Alex
addr: Montreal, 538 Lazard Ave
1952 103 The hulk

MILLAR, J. A.
addr: Montreal: 260 Christopher Columbus St, 1918–19; 1193 Phillips Sq, 1931
1918 240 Portrait of a lady
1919 208 Portrait of a girl
209 Autumn tints $25
210 A misty day $25
211 Fishing boat at Gaspé $40
212 Among the birches, Mount Royal $75
1931 174 Memories $400

MILLARD, CHARLES STUART
22 Jun 1837, n Weston, Ont 7 Nov 1917, Cheltenham, Eng B H M NGC
addr: Cheltenham, Eng, Wyastone
1913 287 Barmouth Sands, N.W. England wc $60
288 On the Snowdon moors, N.W. England wc $70 (listed, 1967, Jessie Dow prize)

MILLEN, CHARLOTTE G.
addr: Quebec, 47 Ste Ursule St, 1937. Westmount, 184 Côte St Antoine Rd, 1940
1937 427 S.B.M. drwg
1940 208 First spring day

MILLEN, S. B. (Mrs)
addr: Westmount, 184 Côte St Antoine Rd
1939 234 Valley farm, Montebello

MILLER, ARCHIBALD MCARTHUR (ARCHIE)
18 Feb 1930, Shawinigan Falls, Que M
addr: La Tuque, Que, La Tuque High School, 1958. Bloomfield Hill, Mich, Cranbrook Academy of Art, 1960. Rochester, N.Y: 30 Strathallan Park, 1961; University of Rochester, Dept of Fine Arts, 1963; Rochester, 1970
1958 82 Form wd $175
83 Bird ter cot
1960 248 Seascape bronze $450
1961 117 Green girls bronze $800
1963 108 Snowy landscape conc $450
1970 49 Greek islands polyester resin & glass 50 x 20 x 42 (2 sections) 36 x 20 x 42 (2 sections)

MILLER, CECILIA J.
addr: Montreal: 109 St George St, 1892; 286 St Denis St, 1897. Clarenceville, Que, 1905. Montreal, 132 Mansfield St, 1909
1892 197 Chrysanthemums wc $7
1897 92 Wild roses $8
1905 182 A grey day wc $15
183 Three friends from old Bonsecours wc $20
1909 254 High tide, lower St Lawrence wc $25
255 Waiting for the tide wc

MILLER, E. CHESEBRO (Miss)
addr: Toronto, c/o Mackenzie & Co, 1906. no addr 1908
1906 122 Folly $50
123 Twilight on the Thames
124 Off Rye
1908 110 Going to sea
111 Evening

MILLER, HERBERT MCRAE
3 Nov 1895, Montreal 26 May 1981, Ste Agathe, Que CWW84 M NGC TB3 WWA78
addr: Montreal: 2049 McGill College Ave, 1921-3; 3514 Park Ave, 1934; 3511 Hutchison St, 1938-41. Westmount, 24 Chesterfield Ave, 1945-53
1932 sculpture, plaster, 1932-53
473-4 Portrait bust (2)
1933 522 Carmencita
523 La sourire $60
524 Jeune indienne $60
525 Sally
1934 510 Cécile $75
1938 197 Retrospect
1939 457 Margot
458 Negress
1940 412 Helen $100
413 Ginger $100
1941 285 Miss Sally Ryan
286 Miss Margaret Yuen
1945 281 Lieutenant
1947 341 Malinche $250
1949 175 Helen $150
1950 90 Charlotte $100
1953 64 Gypsy $300

MILLER, JOHN MELVILLE
15 Jun 1875 - 17 Sep 1948, Montreal M NGC PMC
addr: Montreal: 1908; 648 Dorchester St W, 1931; 4749 Roslyn Ave, 1932, 1936-7; 630 Dorchester St W, 1933
1908 243 Street in Lisieaux wc
1931 319 Residence, Knowlton
320 City church, study
321 Country club, study
322 Mountain winter and summer club house, study
1932 196 Winter morning wc $25
197 Winter afternoon wc $25
1932 198 Twilight wc $25
1933 219 Winter scene wc $20
404 Country house wc (arch)
1936 302 Landscape, the pool wc $35
303 Landscape, the brook wc $45
1937 204 Winter afternoon wc $50
359 Private residence wc (arch)
see also Hutchison, Alexander Cowper, 1906-16

MILLER, MARGARET L. (m Henry Miller)
addr: Montreal: 41 Shuter St, 1897; 442 Guy St, 1900-3
1897 271 Tray
272 Bread tray
273 Cup & saucer
1900 248 Tankard and stand $85
249 Cupid dancing $18
250 Fruit plate $10
251 Plaque, roses $15
252 Chocolate pot $12
1901 157 Early spring, Muskoka wc $15
1903 209 On the mountain wc $10

MILLER, MARY ELIZAHETH PALMER (m Otto V.B. Miller)
14 Sep 1903, Saint John, N.B.
addr: Fredericton, N.B, 240 University Ave
1956 41 Whither? $75

MILLER, RUTH
addr: Lachine, Que, 357 Broadway Ave, 1923-32. Charlottetown, P.E.I, 249 Euston St, 1933. Westmount, 252 Kensington Ave, 1944
1923 257 Study ivory $30
258 Study sculp $25
1928 124 Yemenite Jew pastel $10
311 Yemenite girl charcl $10
1929 332 Study charcl
1932 199 Study pastel
1933 475 St Peter's Chapel, Charlettown lino block $4
476 Ice harvesting lino block $5
1944 147 Ernest Neuman, sketch dwrg

MILLET, FRANCIS DAVIS Amer
3 Nov 1846, Mattapoisett, Mass 15 Apr 1912, SS Titanic AAA28 B DBA F TB WWW Y
1883 116 Turkish café

MILLETTE, MARGUERITE THERESE (m Powell Trudeau)
15 Oct 1921, Toronto
addr: Montreal: 3860 St Hubert St, 1951-6; 7421 Outremont Ave, 1957

1951 111 Grain elevators $90
1956 Trudeau
73 Night fire $100
1957 97 Dominion Square $80

MILLIARD, YVON
addr: Québec
1968 183 Formes dans l'espace sculp 62h $600
184 Untitled dessin 46 3/4 x 35 3/4 $200

MILLS, GRAY HOYE
22 Feb 1929, Cleveland, Ohio M
addr: Don Mills, Ont, 6 Tottenham Rd, 1959-60; Ont, RR2 Mono Rd (sic)
1959 13 Bog $200
1960 84 Saugeen shore $200
198 The wall nm $100
1964 54 Xoanon $400

MILNE, DAVID BROWN
8 Jan 1882, n Paisley, Ont 26 Dec 1953, Toronto AGO B CCI CE EC M NGC TB1/2 W 78 WWA53
addr: Palgrave, Ont, 1931-2. Toronto, c/o Douglas Duncan, 3 Charles St W, 1939-40
1931 175 Window $175
392 Waterfall drypt $25 (RM)
1932 200 Lilies from the bush $200
1939 235 Trilliums and trilliums $150
236 Six Mile Lake
1940 209 Trilliums and columbine $140
210 Landing place wc $90

MIRCK, JAN PETER
5 Jun 1920, Shoten, n Antwerp, Belg M
addr: Terrebonne, Que, 23 Ouimet St
1962 66 Pastoral nm $250

MIRO, ALFRED
addr: Montreal: 233 St André St, 1916; 130 Park Lafontaine, 1917; 84 Mentana St, 1918
1916 199 A la grande air $50
200 Effet de neige, Parc Mont Royal $25
201 Etude, Parc Mont Royal $25
1917 236 Premiére neige sur le bord du Lac St Louis $25
1918 241 Vieux souvenir de Viauville, soleil couchant $10

MISCHPETER, META E.
addr: Montreal, 554 Milton St
1934 225 Dignity pastel $3

MITCHELL, BRUCE
addr: Westmount, 393 Kensington Ave
1939 237 Sunlight and shadow $125

MITCHELL, C. GORDON
addr: Montreal: 51 McGill College Ave, 1912; 4 Beaver Hall Sq, 1914-16
1912 275 Autumn reflections, Lake Edward wc $100
1914 450 The Riding Academy of Montreal
1916 337 CNR terminal sub-station at Model City, Montreal

MITCHELL, CHARLES ALEXANDER
b 1877 21 Mar 1953, Montreal
addr: Montreal: 1908; Bank of Toronto Bldg, 1909-10
1908 Charles R, mispr
244 Window, San Jose pen & ink
245 Chinatown, San Francisco wc
1909 Mitchell & Raine
434 Baronial mansion
435 Church des
436-7 House, Westmount des (2)
1910 395 House, Montreal West, E.A. Robertson, Esq

MITCHELL, ELIZABETH
addr: Montreal, 2177 Lincoln Ave
1935 225 A porcelain candlestick wc
226 Roses wc

MITCHELL, HUTTON
1872, Dundee, Scot 1935, Braintree, Essex, Eng DBA
addr: Montreal: 1535 Crescent St, 1928; 1494 Mackay St, 1929; 258 Grey Ave, 1930; 4048 Grey Ave, 1931; 1407 Crescent St, 1932
1928 125 Afterglow, lower Townships $400
126 Gossips $350
1929 147 Fall glory, near Montreal $175
148 Devil's River, near St Jovite $300
149 Near St Margaret's, winter $125
150 Laurentian majesty $600

1930 144 On the Mulet, near Val Morin $700
145 Dutch mussel gatherers $500
146 Val Morin Heights $250
1931 176 Dimanche au soir $500
177 Waiting for the boats, Dutch coast $225
1932 201 Tour d'horlage, Vire, France $300

MITCHELL, JAMES
addr: Montreal, 36 Lorne Ave
1906 340 North transept, Melrose Abbey nm $20
341 South transept and choir, Melrose Abbey nm

MITCHELL, THOMAS WILBERFORCE
14 May 1879, Clarksburg, Ont 18 Dec 1958, Barrie, Ont CWW55 M NGC TB2/3 WWA62
addr: Toronto, 192 Glencairn Ave
1927 124 Hudson's Bay Point, Mattawa $500

MITCHELL, WILLARD MORSE
1881, Saint John, N.B. 1953, Montreal M
addr: Montreal, 907 Keefer Bldg, 1927-8
1927 294 Santa Maria della Salute drwg $450
1928 127 Amherst, Nova Scotia wc $20
312 A Greek temple pen & ink $10

MOIR, DAVID JAMES
1885, Perth, Scot 17 Feb 1957, Montreal
addr: Montreal: 192 Mance St, 1914; 14 Phillips Sq, 1915-24. Outremont, 1220 Bernard Ave, 1927
1914 459 East Yorkshire studies
460 Palazzo Pollini, Siena
1915 393 Santa Maria della Salute, Venice
394 Architectural studies
1916 202 Windsor Street, Montreal wc
1918 399 The Porta Palio, Verona
1921 178 Near Cartierville
1923 152 Hôtel Dieu, Montreal wc $10
1924 339 Patrington Church, E. Yorks, Eng wc
1927 226 War memorial des

MOL, LEO (b Leonid Molodoshanin, or Molodizhanyn)
15 Jan 1915, Ukraine AGO M WWA78
addr: Norwood, Man, 104 Claremont Ave, 1957-9
1957 163 Negro girl bronze
164 Torso ter cot $80 Hon mention
1958 84 Nude ter cot
85 Torso ter cot
1959 57 Negro girl bronze

MOLINA, VALENTINO Amer
1880, Savannah, Georgia AAA41 TB2
addr: Lennoxville, Que, 1914-46
1914 290 Mrs Gustavus Lucke
1915 250 Bermuda
1916 203 Ogunquit Beach, Maine $350

MOLINARI, GUIDO
12 Oct 1933, Montreal AGO B CC2 CE M TB3 WWA84
addr: Montréal: 310 blvd St Joseph E, 1958-61; 2067 rue Filion, 1962-3; 2065 rue Filion, 1964-5; Montreal, 1967-8
1958 70 Dessin linéaire nm $50
1959 34 Calligraphie nm $70
1960 199 Verticale orangée nm $125
1961 42 Equilibre $250
1962 23 Opposition rectangulaire $300 illus (listed 1967, acry latex, Jessie Dow prize)
24 Rectangles et lines jaunes $300 Purchase award (MBAM)
1963 47 Espace rouge No 2 $1,200
48 Espace bleu No 2 $1,200
1964 55 Espace bleu-vert $1,500
1965 12 Mutation brun-rouge illus $2,000. Albert H. Robinson prize $500. 1967-43, latex acry 68 x 81
1968 185 Systêmie sérial 81 x 96 $4,500

MOLNAR, FRANK
1936, Budapest
addr: Vancouver
1970 50 #6 View from Mission Abbey 40 x 42
51 #7 Kalamalka Lake 30 x 30 illus (David Denbigh, Ottawa)
52 #8 The slough 30 x 33 (A. Parker, West Vancouver)

MOLSON, CATHERINE D.
addr: Montreal, 384 Sherbrooke St W
1921 179 View in the Laurentians wc
180 The edge of the wood wc

MONETTE, ANTOINE
20 Apr 1899, Montreal
addr: Montreal, 60 St James St
1931 323 Eglise, façade

MONETTE, GEORGES ALPHONSE
13 Mar 1870 - 16 Jul 1941, Montreal
addr: Montreal, Power Bldg
1915 395 Académie Bourget, Mountain St, Montreal
396 School, Notre Dame de Grace, Montreal

MONGEAU, JEAN-GUY
9 May 1931, Verdun, Que M
addr: Verdun, 1537 Rolland Ave
1960 200 Paysage No 5 nm $125

MONK, BENEDICTA see HEWTON, BENEDICTA

MONTEFIORE, NANCY SEBAG (Mrs)
1 Jul 1920, Montreal
addr: Westmount, 4331 Western Ave, 1942-7
1942 Sebag-Montefiore
160 Laurentian landscape $5
1947 194 Landscape $35
195 Laurentian landscape $35
318 Nude charcl $25

MONTGOMERY, CLAUDE
addr: Town of Mount Royal, Que, 539 Stanstead St
1953 27 Mrs Claude Montgomery

MONTIGNY-GIGUERE, E. LOUISE DE (Mde Giguère)
28 Apr 1878, La Prairie, Que M
addr: Montreal: 3400 Champlain St, 1916; 142 Laurier Ave, 1917; 1294A St Denis St, 1918; 354 Garnier St, 1919; 67 Ste Famille St, 1920-22; 717 Shuter St, 1923-4; Montreal, 1935; 4638B Park Ave, 1926; 6013 Boyer St, 1928-9; 8248A St Denis St, 1930-2; 763 Mistral St, 1933; 7944 St Denis St, 1934-5; 8137 Gaspé St, 1936. Ottawa, House of Commons, Room 131, 1937. Laval des Rapides, 372 blvd des Prairies, 1942-6
Giguère, 1917-23, 1932.
de Montigny-Giguère, 1916, 1933-7, 1946
1916 82 Portrait de genre pastel $50
83 Study pastel $25
1917 155 A study
1918 145 Gaby pastel
1919 142 Portrait
1920 109 Portrait de ma soeur
1921 100 Jeannette Desaulniers
101 Miss Harriet Nelson
102 Study $35
293 Mrs Alphonse Thibodeau plaster
1922 124 Promenade $100
335 Mr Gustave Drolet-Massue plaster
1923 250 Alice Nolin sculp
251 L'epave sculp $50
1924 317 Les pas de trois sculp $25
318 Les misereux sculp $20
319 Esmeralda sculp $25
1925 397 The spirit of the sea (poem) sculp $50
398 Jacqueline sculp $75
1926 249 Nymphe à la flûte sculp $25
250 Menuet de chez nous sculp $25
1928 351 Les deux fleurs clay
352 Son rêve clay
353 Mons A.T. Brassard, de l'Association Chorale Brassard Inc plaster
1929 387 Raymond ter cot
388 Les délaissés ter cot
389 Seule, magnifiquement seule ter cot
390 La neige ter cot
1930 313 Hortense plaster $100
314 Madone plaster $50
315 M.T.G. plaster $50
1931 431 Geo J. Lepine, Esq plaster $150
432 Thérèse et Paul plaster $150
433 Au vent plaster $75
434 Danse champêtre bas-relief $35
1932 463 Hon Cairine Mackay Wilson, first woman appointed to Senate of Canada plaster $200, bronze $500
464 Miss M. Denis plaster $150
465 Maternité ter cot $50
466 Madone ter cot $50
1933 511 Rev Mère St Thomas d'Aquin plaster $150
512 L'attente plaster $150
1934 495 Yamilé sous les cèdres plaster $50
496 La vigne plaster $40

497 Monique plaster $150
1935 463 Debuts biscuit $50
1936 592 La fuite plaster $50 ter cot $150
593 Printemps plaster $10
1937 456 Pierrot dane le cité morte plaster $50
1942 239 The fugitives unbaked clay $75
1944 162 Penché sur l'humanité plaster $150
1945 276 Le repentir plaster $100
1946 277 La robe de laine raw clay

MONTIGNY, MARGUERITE see LAFONTAINE, MARGUERITE

MONTIZAMBERT, BEATRICE BLANCH
24 Feb 1874, Quebec AAA19 B M TB
addr: Montreal: The Sherbrooke, 1918; 319 Prince Arthur St, 1921-2; 73 Ste Famille St, 1924; 3680 St Urbain St, 1927
1918 242 Mrs Hansen min
243 Miss Charlotte Spooner min
244 Rev Father Duffy, SDC min $500
245 Sir William Peterson min $300
246 Orange marigolds min $75
247 Miss Alexander min
248 Maurice min $300
249 Susannah min
1919 213 Summer morning $60
214 I hear the song of birds $75
1921 181 Grandmère $750
182 Children of George H. Montgomery, Esq wc
183 Son of Frank W. Ross, Esq, Quebec min
1922 202 Marion, daughter of Lorne Webster, Esq min
203 Eric, son of Lorne Webster, Esq min
204 HRH the Prince of Wales min $500
205 Portrait of a gentleman
1924 182 Percival, son of C.K. Russell, Esq min
1927 129 Joan, daughter of Dr Guy Johnson min

MONTPETIT, GUY
23 Aug 1938, Montreal M
addr: Montreal
1969 6 Deux cultures, une nation (série C No 4) acry 60 x 48 (MBAM)

MOODIE, CAMPBELLINE R.
addr: Ottawa, 7 Clarey Ave, 1935-6
1935 227 Tulips and daffodils wc $10
228 Study in red wc
1936 304 Backyard in Harlem $75
305 Angular puss wc $50
306 Fish quay wc $100

MOORE, ANNIE E.
addr: Montreal: 328 St Urbain St, 1895; 123 Crescent St, 1897
1895 188 Study of a pet dog wc $25
1897 184 White roses wc $25

MOORE, RICHARD WILLIAM
29 Dec 1893, Glechein, Alta M
addr: Calgary, 1336 11th Ave E, 1931-2
1931 393 Reconstruction of Waterloo Bridge litho $20
394 A roadside smithy etch $10
1932 414 Ancient cottonwoods etch $10
415 Interior of a warehouse etch $5
416 Summer day etch $12.50

MOREAU, PAULINE
1 Feb 1930, Montreal
addr: Outremont, 60 Maplewood Ave, 1955. Pont Viau, Que, 212 Prévost St, 1957
1955 63 Nature morte
1957 68 Femme et tulipes $75

MORENCY, ANDRE
10 Sep 1910, Montreal CNS36 M
addr: Montreal: 6815 Garnier St, 1932-3; 1425 St Hubert St, 1934-6; 3862 Mentana St, 1941
1932 202 Etude wc $50
203 Matinée d'automne wc $35
1933 220 Maison à Caughnawaga $60
1934 226 Matinée, Mont Royal $100
1936 307 Le Vieux Pont, Mont Rolland $125
308 Sous le feuillage wc $40
1941 141 L'auteur de 'Menaud Maître-Draveur'
142 La route de Clermont $100

MORIN, DONALD D'E.
addr: Westmount, 4635 Sherbrooke St W, 1936-41

1936 554 The cloud ink drwg
1937 205 White mice wc $10
422 Head nm $25
1940 384 Head drwg on wd $30
385 Portrait, sketch pencil
386 The Pratt's drwg $50
1941 Lt, RCNVR
245 Fawn pen & ink

MORIN, LAURENT
Sherbrooke, Que
addr: Montreal: 8501 Foucher St, 1939;
8395 Henri Julien St, 1942
1939 238 La sieste $400
1942 114 Espièglerie $300

MORIN, LUCIEN
11 Feb 1918, Montreal M
addr: Montreal, 1697 Dézéry St,
1945 163 Jaillissement magique $100

MORISSET, DENYS
8 Aug 1930, Paris, France M
addr: Quebec, 1180 St Cyrille W, 1957.
Montreal, 964 des Erables Ave, 1960
1957 137 Portrait de Mathilde nm $50
1960 249 Mathilde bronze $250

MORKILL, A. B.
addr: Sherbrooke, Que
1910 251 In the wood, autumn $20

MORRICE, JAMES WILSON
10 Aug 1865, Montreal 23 Jan 1924, Tunis AGO B CC2 CE DBA EC H L M Mo12 NGC R1 TB W78
addr: London, 87 Gloucester Rd, Regents Park, 1891. Paris, 8 rue Campagne-Première, 1892. Montreal, 10 Redpath St, 1897. Paris: 1900-9; Quai des Grands Augustins, 1911-13; Paris, 1914; 45 rue des Grands Augustins, 1916
1889 155 Old farm house wc
156 Landscape wc $45
1891 88 Afternoon $100
1892 104 Evening, Barbizon $150
1897 93 Winter, Ste Anne de Beaupré $100 (MBAM)
94 Evening, Paris
1900 75 Peasants washing clothes, France $150
1903 Morrice, E, mispr (addr Paris)
86 Marine
1906 125 The Public Gardens, Venice
1909 256 Regatta, St Malo $800 (listed 1967, Jessie Dow prize)
257 Port of Venice (sold)
258 Morning, Brittany $800 (MBAM)
259 Venetian fête (sold)
260 Nocturn, Venice $500
261 Circus, Montmarte $500 (NGC) Arcus, Montmartre, mispr
262 Quai des Grands Augustins, Paris (sold) (NGC)
263 The Citadel, Quebec (MQ)
264 St Malo
265 Winter, Montreal $500
266 Snow, Ste Anne de Beaupré $800
1910 252 The Fort, St Malo
253 The bathing place, St Malo
254 Near the Fort, St Malo
255 The yacht race
1911 217 Venice
218 A Dieppe $400
219 Snow, Quebec $400
220 On the beach
221 One day at St Eustache
1912 276 Palazzo Doria $750 (listed 1967, Jessie Dow prize)
277 La nuit à Venise $750 (NGC)
278 Sketches 4 $125 each
1913 289 The woodpile, Ste Anne de Beaupré $500
290 The old Holton house (where the new Galleries now stand) (MBAM)
291 The beach near Pouldhu (NGC)
1914 291 Une Parisienne $500
292 The surf, Dieppe $600
293 The old town, Concarneau
294 On the beach Paramé $150
1916 204 Nude, reading $200
205 Doge's Palace, Venice $500
206 Ruined château, Capri $500

MORRIS, EDMUND MONTAGUE
18 Dec 1871, Perth, Ont 21 Aug 1913, n Portneuf, Que AGO CC1 CWW10 H Mo12 NGC TB3 W78
addr: Toronto: 471 Jarvis St, 1897; Imperial Bldg, 32 Adelaide St, 1898-1903; 9 Toronto St, 1906; Toronto, 1910; 43 Victoria St, 1913
1897 95 Girls in a poppy field $200
96 Man in black $75
1898 83 French Canadian interior $200
84 Woman and child $75
1900 76 Autumn $100

1901 76 Apple orchard, Quebec $50
1903 87 Old Scotch mills $200
88 A Scotch valley
89 A gray day, Haddingtonshire $200
1906 276 Gaspé schooners pastel $30
277 Young sailors aboard the Snow Queen pastel $30
278 The little cook pastel $25
279 A Gaspé schooner pastel $25
1910 256 Old buffalo corral, Porcupine Hills $500
257 Little Shield, a Blackfoot pastel $200
258 The mill $30
1913 292 Coming storm, the country of the Crees $1,000
293 Saskatchewan landscape $800
294 Redpath Castle $50
295 The shore of Ile d'Orléams $50

MORRIS, KATHLEEN MOIR
2 Dec 1893, Montreal 20 Dec 1986, Rawdon, Que CC2 CNS36 CWW81 M NGC TB2 WWA82
addr: Montreal: 31 Lorne Ave, 1914-17; 657 Melrose Ave, 1918; 686 Sherbrooke St W, 1919; Hampton Court Apts, Moun- St, 1920, 1922. Berthier-en-haut, Que, 1921. Montreal, 15 Parkside Pl, 1923. Ottawa, 172 O'Connor St, 1924-9. Montreal: 57 Mountain Slope, 1930-1; 3745 Mountain Slope, 1932; 3745 ave de l' Oratoire, 1933-47; 3745 Coronet Ave, 1951-7
1914 295 Sketch $10
296 Nic
1915 251 Nic $10
252 Chat Lake $15
1916 207 Sketch $5
1917 237 Skaddles $15
1918 250 Billy $15
251 Notre Dame de Grace $15
1919 215 Sunlight and shadow $20
216 A grey day $20
217 Kildare Bim $25
218 Up the lake $20
1920 177 Village street $20
178 Winter, Berthier $25
179 Ogunquit, Me $25 Ogunguit, mispr
1921 184 Winter $25
185 Berthier-en-haut $25
186 Old barn, Berthier-en-haut $25
187 A sketch $25
1922 210 A Saturday morning market $20
211 A corner of the market, Berthier $20
1923 153 Grand mass, Berthier (MBAM)
154 Hitching posts, Sunday morning
1924 175 The fruit stall $40
176 Market day, Ottawa $40
177 Waiting $40 (NGC)
178 The Wood Market, Ottawa $40
1925 191 A bit of old Quebec $70
192 St Stanilas Street, Quebec $50
193 Old city wall, Quebec
194 Nuns, Quebec $50
1926 90 The fruit shop, Ottawa $100
91 The snow carts, Quebec $100
92 Byward Market, Ottawa $150
93 A grey day $50
1927 125 Market day, Ottawa $150
126 St Roch's Market, Quebec $95
127 McGill cab stand, Montreal $150
128 Maison Montcalm, and Garden Street, Quebec $100
1928 128 Awaiting the train, Berthier $150
129 Old Quebec $60
130 Cab stand, Quebec $100
131 Champlain Market $100
1929 151 Market day, Berthier, Que $90
152 Cuthbert Chapel, at Berthierville, Que $50
153 Old shop, Mountain Hill, Quebec $50
154 Old saddler's shop, Ottawa $50
1930 147 A snowy day $200
148 Street scene, Ottawa $75
149 McGill Gates, Montreal $50
1931 178 St Joseph's Oratory, Montreal $150
179 Maison Montcalm, Quebec $175
180 From Côte des Neige $50
181 Old house, Côte des Neige $50
1932 204 Old house, Ottawa $150
205 Mill, St Sauveur, Que $100
206 The market square $150
207 An old timer $50
1933 221 The Shrine, Montreal $100
222 Dominion Square, Montreal $40
223 Chickens $50
224 Saturday market $90

1934 227 St Cecile St, Montreal $85
228-9 Sketch $35 each
1936 309 Lower Town, Quebec $100 (AGH)
310 Beauport, Que $80
311 House on the hill $100
1937 206 Bing
207 Old mill, Morin Heights, Que $75
208 Marshall's Bay, Ont $35
209 At the farm $35
1938 85 Morin Heights $100
1939 239 Craig Street district, Montreal $125
240 Rural Quebec $125
1940 211 Resting $75
212 Mother and son $75
1941 143 In pasture $75
144 Sheep $75
1942 115 Horses $75
116 St Cecile St, Montreal $100
1943 141 At Morin Heights, Que $100
1944 100 Old cab, Mount Royal $100
1945 164 Snow carts, Quebec City $150
1947 196 March in the Laurentians $150
197 Cows $100
1951 32 Old house, Côte des Neiges $150
1953 28 Birds feeding $150
29 Summer $150
1957 69 The Laurentians $175

MORRIS, LINCOLN GODFREY
10 Dec 1887, Newport, Eng M
addr: Montreal, 3025 Sherbrooke St W, 1943-51
1943 142 Early spring, St Laurent, Que wc $30
1951 33 Snow at the Mother House $150

MORRIS, MICHAEL WILLIAM
16 May 1942, Saltdean, Eng M
addr: Vancouver, 1968-70
1968 186 Pacific nation gouache 59 x 39 $550
1969 7 New York letter mirror, plexiglass, photo-reproduction 72 x 288 (MBAM)
see also Lewis, Glenn, 1970-38

MORRIS, PETER J.
addr: Ville St Laurent, Que, 1580 Ouimet St, Apt 29
1957 70 Back street, South Wales $50

MORRISEY, DARRELL
addr: Westmount, 85 Churchill Ave, 1916-23. Montreal: 102 Chomedy St, 1924; 872 Sherbrooke St W, 1928
1916 208 Portrait
1917 238 Sketch pastel $10
239 Edith pastel $5
1918 252 The return $10
253 Children with fruit, sketch $15
254 On the swing $10
255 Sketch $10
1919 219 Farm at Calumet
220 Jean Elizabeth
221 Illustration from the Arabian Nights $15
222 In the garden $15
223 A gentleman, sketch $15
224 On the hill $25
1920 180 Metis Beach $15
181 The creek, Sweetsburg $15
182 The sawdust pile $20
183 The red tam
1921 188 The girl in the middy
189 The red house $25
1923 155 At St Ives $35
156 In Venice $75
1924 179 Monastery at Fiesole, Italy $50
180 Eglise St Julien-la-Pauvre, Paris $25
181 Canal in Venice $25
1928 132 Saint Ives $50
133 Canal bank temp $10
313 At the back of St Patrick's Church red chalk $5
314 Sketch pencil $5

MORRISON, JULIA
addr: Montreal: 164 University St, 1910; 269 University St, 1911
1910 447 Cup & saucer (6)
448 Cologne bottle
1911 340 Game plates (6)

MORSE, SUSAN MARY PETERS (m Charles Morse)
10 Nov 1862, Saint John, N.B. c 1939. H M
addr: Ottawa, 44 McLeod St
1915 253 Sketch, Liverpool, N.S.

MORTON, DOUGLAS GIBB
26 Nov 1926, Winnipeg CWW84 IO M

addr: Regina: 2526 Edward St, 1960-2; Regina, 1968
1960 85 Blue temple $310
1962 25 605 $300
26 January collage $450
1968 187 Aqua II acry 79 x 72 $1,150
188 Blue divide acry 78 x 78 $1,275
189 Tourist acry 70 x 76 $1.050

MORTON, EDITH see POWER, EDITH

MORTON, H. (m George Morton)
H
1886 117 Still life
119 The River Thames at Chatham
120 A study
132 Cut flowers
1889 45 A study

MOSCOVITCH, EDNA (Mrs)
addr: Montreal, 2040 Vendome St
1941 145 Still life

MOSS, CHARLES EUGENE
10 Nov 1860, Pawnee City, Nebr 25 Jan 1901, Ottawa H M NGC W78
addr: Orange, N.J, 1894. New York, 116 W 41st St, 1895. Ottawa: Daly Ave, 1897; 445 Daly Ave, 1898-1900
1894 210 Lachine wc
211 A pastoral wc
1895 189 Mistress Prue wc $75
1897 97 Noontime $75
98 The harvesters $20
185 Roses wc $25
186 Evening in port, Murray Bay wc $25
187 The old pilot at home wc $25
188 Between snowy banks wc $25
189 Sunshine among the birches wc $15
190 Autumnal landscape wc $30
1898 85 William Kingsford, LLD
86 The goose girl $150
87 Melodies of the forest $250
181 The basin, Bonsecours Market wc $40
1900 150 Mending the net wc $75
151 At low tide wc $30
152 Montreal harbour wc $20
1901 deceased
158 Village in Cheshire wc $75
159 Red Brook mill wc $75
160 Under English skies wc $50
161 Over the bar wc $50
162 Milking time wc $35
163 Gardener's cottage wc $35
164 Banff wc $25
165 Landscape wc $12
1903 Moss estate, Ottawa
210 By the chestnut woods wc $25
211 Homeward wc $35
212 Reflections wc $50

MOUNCY, ALLAN J.
addr: Montreal
1908 112 Eventide $25

MOUNT, RITA
7 Feb 1885, or 1888 - 22 Jan 1967, Montreal CWW 64 M NGC TB3 WWA66
addr: Montreal: 1903; 360 Dorchester St, 1905-6; 416 Dorchester St E, 1910-28; 832 Dorchester St E, 1929-49; 8005 Outremont Ave, 1950-3
1903 90 Still life $30
1905 91 Rue Sous le Cap $10
1906 126 Lilas $30
1910 259 Rivière Bleu $40
260 Vieux bateaux $50
1911 222 Portrait
223 Maison de la Reine, Versailles
1912 279 A la montagne $15
280 Etude d'arbres $20
281 La potiche $20
1913 296 Madame Ladouceur $50
297 A lonely road $35
298 The willows $35
299 In the autumn $20
1914 297 Summer $10
298 Road, Phillipsburg $10
299 Sketch, St Eustache $10
1915 254 Carillon $30
1916 209 The spinning wheel $35
210 The market $20
211 The haymaker $35
1917 240 The farm $25
241 Les ballons $10
242 The market $10
1918 256 Autumn, St Eustache $50
257 Gray day $50
258 Rest $25
259-61 St Eustache, sketch $15, $10 $10
1919 225 Victoria Glaciers, Lake Louise $50
226 Near the market, St Lawrence Street $50

227 Sulphur Mountain, Banff $40
228 The newspaper boys $25
1920 184-6 Portrait
187 Landscape, Cartelin, Baie des Chaleurs $60
1921 190 Madame H.L. de Hernandez
191 Effet de brune, Carleton $60
1922 206 Spanish woman $150
207 Grey day $75
208 Autumn $50
209 St Andrew, sketch $30
1923 157 Marie Montante $75
158 Malbaie $50
1924 183 Percé Rock and village $200
184 Fisherman's quarters $100 (NGC)
185 Mt St Anne, Percé $35
186 Le Rocher, Percé $30
1925 195 Unloading, Les Eboulements $250
196 Wild tobacco, Les Eboulements $100
1927 130 Cap Barré, Percé $300
131 Sunflowers $100
132 Les Falaises, Les Eboulements $100
1928 134 At noon, Port Daniel $400
135 Quand la brume de dissippe $125
136 Village, Port Daniel $150
1929 155 Fishing boats, Gaspé coast $300
156 Splitting cod fish $125
1930 150 Noon, Gaspé coast $350
151 Au quai $125
152 Sails drying in the wind $100
153 Country store $75
1931 182 Sunset, Newport, Gaspé $125
183 Fishing boats, Gaspé coast $200
1932 208 The sawmill, Ste Geneviève $250
209 Late winter, Ste Geneviève $225
210 Lowtide, Gaspé coast $225
211 Old St Mathias Church $75
1933 225 Market day, Place Jacques Cartier $325
226 At the mill, Terrebonne $225
1934 230 Petite Rivière aux Renards, Gaspé $350
231 The winding road, Petit Cap $350
1935 229 Cap Des Rosiers $225
230 Three Sisters, L'Echouerie $125
231 Winter day $75
1936 312 Corner of the beach $200
313 L'anse du griffon $75
314 Sunny day $75
1937 210 Late afternoon, Glace Bay $150
211 Harbour scene, Cape Breton $125 (MBAM)
212 Village scene, Gaspé $75
1939 241 Percé Rock $200
242 On the Gaspé coast $125
1940 213 Lunch time $300
214 After the storm $200
1941 146 Victorian days $200
1942 117 Mr de Calvet's house $175
1944 101 Harbour scene, Isle Madame, Cape Breton $125
1945 165 Harbour scene $250
1946 182 Abandoned, Cap des Rosiers $150
183 Village road, Rivière aux Renards $125
1947 198 L'anse aux Gascons, Gaspé $300
199 L'anse Chapados, Gaspé $250
1948 33 L'anse aux Gascons, Gaspé $175
1949 66 Fishing boats, Grande Rivière $175
1950 30 Rainy day, Anse à Beaufils $150
1953 30 Grand Rivière village $150

MOUSSEAU, JEAN-PAUL ARMAND
1 Jan 1927, Montreal CC2 CE DMS M NGC Juror
addr: Montreal: 1482A Champlain St, 1945-49; 975 Chaumont Ave, 1963-4
1945 166 Le Christ se livre $35
1946 184 Appareil d'aération $90
1947 200 Paléontologie quotidienne wc $75
201 Hécatombe wc $75
1949 67 Marchant sur toi, eau nette $300
68 Jet fuligineaux sur noir torturé $300
1963 109 Vibrations plastic rel $2,000
1964 56 Diagonales mauves vibratoires $900

MUELLER, ERNEST see MULLER, ERNEST

MUHLSTOCK, LOUIS
23 Apr 1904, Narajow, Poland AGO CC1 CE M NGC WWA82 Juror
addr: Montreal: 1171 St Dominique St, 1925; 3997 St Dominique St, 1927-35; 3414 Ste Famille St, 1936-58; 3555 Ste Famille St, 1960
1925 366 A smile charcl
367 Head of a blind man charcl

1927 295 Libby charcl
296 Sketch charcl
1928 315 An inmate at the Old People's Home charcl $25
316 Solly charcl
317 Mahriiz-Alis-Hamid charcl $25
1932 417 Study of a head charcl $30
418 Patrick Buttler charcl $30
419 One who suffers charcl $30
1933 477 Marvin Duchow charcl
1934 459 War! charcl $75
460 Ukranian drwg $40
1935 232 Coloured man $100
1936 315 Winter $50
316 La Zone, Paris $75
555 Portrait charcl $50
1938 173 Nude drwg $75
1939 243 View from a window $150
423 Nude sepia drwg $75
1940 215 Autumn, stormy sky wc $50
216 Wet autumn day $75
217 Empty rooms $125
1941 147 Plant in empty room $100
246 Girl at a window crayon $50
247 Nude with lowered head crayon $75
1942 118 The open door $150
119 View from a window $150
1945 167-8 Welder at U.S.L. pastel $75 each
1946 185 Basement with tailor's dummy $150
266 William O'Brien drwg $100
267 Nude sepia drwg $100
1947 202 Autumn on Mount Royal $250
319 The janitor's child drwg $100
1948 34 At Ste Famille and Sherbrooke Streets, 1947 $250
35 Eva, spring 1947 $350
104 Reclining nude 18 x 23 charcl, conté, crayon $50
1949 69 Trees, rocks and moss, Isola, 1947 $300
164 Reclining nude drwg $150
1950 127 View from a Ste Famille window $250
1951 140 Seated nude sepia drwg $150
1952 104 Autumn on Mount Royal $300
1953 87 Groubert Lane $250
1957 71 Spring landscape $400
1958 71 Seated nude, 1955 nm $300
1960 201 Nude No 1 nm $500
port: by Lilias Torrance Newton, 1937-217

MUIR, FRANCIS REED
30 Jun 1898, London, Eng M
addr: Montreal: 3700 St, 1932; 4319 Montrose Ave, 1933-6
1932 212 Bonsecours Church, Montreal wc $45
1933 227 Christ Church Cathedral, Montreal wc $65
1936 317 Christ Church Cathedral, Montreal wc $45
318 Church of St Andrew and St Paul, Montreal wc $45

MUIR, HENRIETTA see EDWARDS, HENRIETTA

MULCASTER, WYNONA CROFT
10 Apr 1915, Prince Albert, Sask
addr: Saskatoon, Saskatoon Normal School
1947 203 Woodland $25

MULHOLLAND, A.J. (Mrs)
addr: Montreal, 29 Durocher St
1894 258 Plate, with Watteau scene

MULLALLY, MARY E.
addr: Montreal, 2021 Union Ave
1936 319 Peonies $60
320 The dreamer $100

MULLER, ERNEST (Ernst Müller/Mueller)
fl 1876-96 H
addr: Montreal, 6 University St, 1892
1889 Mueller, Ernest
46 Still life $30
1892 226 Ceiling decoration
227 Hall decoration

MULLIGAN, LOUIS
addr: Montreal, 1498 Drummond St, 1935-9
1935 365-7 Residence, J.B. Woodyatt, Esq, Westmount, sunroom photos
1936 490 Living room, residence, H.R. Trenholms, Esq 3 photos
1939 360-1 Debutante's bedroom photos
362 Powder room photo

MULOCK, AMY E. (Mrs)
addr: Brockville, 32 St Andrew St, 1914. Montreal, 242 Mountain St, 1917. Brockville, 1918
1914 300 Old church, Rye wc $25
1917 243 Still life $15
1918 262 Still life $15

MUNDY, SARAH ANNIS
addr: Montreal: 6 McGill College Ave, 1905-6; Montreal, 1908; 61A Victoria St, 1910
1905 337 Vase, stork $30
338 Vase, iris $25
339 Vase, geranium $20
340 Vase, dragon $12
341 Cider jug $15
342 Teapot, enamel $20
343 Smoker's set $15
344 Plate, landscape $8
345 Plate, enamel $8
346 Vase, roses $20
347 Mug, geese $3
348 Mug, rabbits $3
1906 437 Lamp $35
438 Gypsy pot $15
439 Plate $5
440 Plate, rarebit $5
441 Tile $3.50
442 Bowl $20
443 Vase, trumpet vine $20
444 Vase, roses $12
445 Rose jar $20
446 Plates, six $12
447 Tobacco jar $10
448 Stein $4
449 Olive dish $2.50
450 Vase, lustre $3
451 Pitcher, lustre $3
452 Nut bowl $10
453 Cups & saucers (3) $3 each
454 Box $15
1908 419 Vase, poplars $25
420 Vase, birds lustre $25
421 Vase, bubbles $10
422 Vase, boats $10
423 Vase, white birds $10
424 Vase, chrysanthemums
425 Stein, grapes
426 Stein, corn $5
427 Stein, crab apples $5
428 Stein, trees $5
429 Tile, conventional $2.50
430 Bonbon (dish), peacock $10
1910 449-50 Vase $15 each
451 Chocolate jug $12
452 Cider jug $12
453 Tray $8

MUNN, ADELAIDE
addr: Montreal: 3465 Côte des Neiges Rd, 1934; 1020 Seaforth Ave, 1936; 2096 Northcliffe Ave, 1937; 2325 St Luke St, Apt 24, 1939-40; 1455 Drummond St, Apt 1013, 1943-5
1934 232 Nasturtiums wc $25
1936 321 October on the Ottawa $65
322 In the Thousand Islands $65
1937 213 Evening on the Ottawa $100
1939 244 The frog and lizard $125
1940 218 Red trilliums $140
1943 143 Marsh marigolds $150
1944 102 Tulips $125
1945 169 Skunk cabbage $125

MUNN, KATHLEEN JEAN
28 Aug 1887, Toronto AGO M
addr: Toronto, 800 Yonge St, 1909-10
1909 267 Girl's head $50
1910 261 The forge $100

MUNRO, JEAN ELIZABETH COCKBURN (m Gordon Munro)
2 Aug 1869, Orillia, Ont d 1945
CNS36 M
addr: Westmount, 222 Redfern Ave, 1927-39
1927 133 Vimy arising from its ruins, 1920 $200
134 Springtime on the Loing $200
1928 137 A port in Brittany $250
1929 157 Sunday on the beach $250
158 A farm by the sea $180
1930 154 Ebbing tide, Brittany $180
155 Winter landscape, Quebec
1932 213 Spring, lower Montreal $250
214 Winding street, La Malbaie $50
1933 228 Baie St Paul, Que $250
229 Canal Del Oro, Venice $40
1934 233 The city in winter $200
234 The road to Mont Tremblant $200
1935 233 Cloud shadows, Cap à l'Aigle, Que $200
234 Birch fringes, Lac Tremblant, Que $400
1936 323 Springtime in a park $200
324 Bay of Islands, Newfoundland $200
1937 214 A sheltered harbour, Newfoundland $150
215 Fishing station, N.S. $125
1939 245 Early spring, Quebec $150
246 Lunenburg, N.S. $150

MUNRO, M. BELLE
addr: Montreal, 634 Dorchester St W
1910 454 Rose $30
455 Figure $40
456 Peacock $40
457 Blue jay $25
458 Punch bowl, tray $70
459 Plate flat enamel $15

MUNTZ, LAURA ADELINE (m C.W.B. Lyall)
18 Jun 1860, Radford, Eng 9 Dec 1930, Toronto AGO B CC1 H M Mo12 NGC TB3 W78
addr: Toronto: 1903; Yonge St Arcade, 1905. Montreal, 6 Beaver Hall Sq, 1906-13. Westmount: 4205 Dorchester St W, 1914; 310 Grosvenor Ave, 1915. Toronto, 24 Bernard Ave, 1925-31
1903 91 Portrait of a child
92 Kitty
1905 184 Motherhood wc $150
185 A head, study wc $35
186 The orphan wc $35
187 Mother and child wc
188 April wc
1906 127 Spring $500
128 Anita $250
129 The passing dream $250
130 A study $50
131 Miss Alice Graham
132 G. Godfrey
133 M. Godfrey
134 The mother $125
1909 268 Stephen, son of George Cantlie
269 Beatrice, daughter of George Cantlie
270 Gilbert, son of Eugene Lafleur, KC
271 Betty, daughter of Harold Redpath, Esq
1910 262 Miss Jean Cantlie
263 Margaret Parker
264 The brothers $800
265 The short story $500
266 In the wood wc $85
1911 224 Day dreams $125
225 In an old garden $125
1912 282 The botanist $250
283 Portrait of a lady
284 Mary, daughter of Dr Colby
285 In a doorway $800
286 Girl in white wc $75
287 Child in a garden wc $75
288 Mother and child wc $75
1913 300 The mandolin player
301 A Florentine $550
302 A madonna $350
303 Miss Margaret Campbell
1914 301 Madonna with children $550
302 Madonna adoring $350
1915 255 Oriental poppies $950
256 The lullabye $950
257 A madonna $800
1925 Lyall
167 A madonna $350
168 At twilight wc $50
169 A babe in the wood wc $75
1928 110 Mother and children $350
111 A madonna pastel & wc $500
1931 Lyall, the late Laura Muntz
154 Mary Scott Fry

MURPHY, CECIL see BULLER, CECIL

MURPHY, J. HERBERT
addr: Westmount, 356 Côte St Antoine Rd
1939 459 A. McA. Murphy plaster

MURPHY, JOHN FRANCIS Amer
11 Dec 1853, Oswego, N.Y. 21 Jan 1921, New York B F H TB WWW
addr: New York, The Chelsea, 222 W 23rd St, 1891. Montreal: 2301 St Catherine St, 1892; Montreal, 1914
1889 47 October morning $350
1891 89 Autumn afternoon $300
1892 105 Study of pineapple
1914 303 Fisherman's haunt, Maine wc $25

MURRAY, GRETA P.
addr: Montreal: 20 McTavish St, 1911-17; 92 St Mark St, 1922
1911 pastel
226 Solitude $20
227 The gardner's daughter
1912 289 A grey day $30
290 A quiet spot $35
291 Landscape $40
292 Study of a young girl $35
1913 304 Sketch of E.C.M.
305 A coming shower $40
306 The cloud $30
307 A changing day $30
1914 304 A breezy day $50
305 Still life $40
1915 258 Summer afternoon $30
1917 244 A changing day $25

1922 212 Approaching storm $50

MURRAY, ROBERT GRAY
2 Mar 1936, Vancouver AGO B CC1 CE IO M
addr: New York, 138 E 22nd St, 1963-4
1963 110 Charybdis bronze $800 illus Hon mention (MBAM)
1964 127 Pointe au Baril II painted steel $4,800 (listed, but not exhibited)

MURRAY, W. A. DOUGLAS
addr: Montreal, 2068 Sherbrooke St W
1956 42 Italian market in winter

MUSGROVE, ALEXANDER JOHNSTON
22 Nov 1882, Edinburgh 31 Jan 1952, Winnipeg CC2 M
addr: Winnipeg, 310 Assiniboine Ave, 1928-47
1928 138 A new Canadian $200
139 The little dock wc $50
1929 159 A study in black $125
1931 395 Summer peace col pr $17
396 The small store col pr $5
1932 215 Harvest wc $25
216 A fall day wc $25
1935 235 October wc $60
1937 428 Mona drwg $10
429 Fish houses, Lake Winnipeg wd cut $10
1947 204 Manitoba River farm $450

MUSTARD, VERNON R.
addr: Montreal: Lower Canada College, 4090 Royal Ave, 1942; 6184 Notre Dame de Grace Ave, 1945; Lower Canada College 1947
1942 120 Notre Dame de Grace, Montreal $60
1945 170 Winter study $150
1947 205 Gladoli $150

MYERS, JOSEPH
addr: Outremont, 516 Hutchison St
1936 556 Douglas drwg

MYLES see BANTING, BEATRICE

MYRAN, FREDA
addr: Montreal, 5694 Esplanade Ave
1944 103 Spring day, Ste Marguerite, Que wc $20

N

N.E.THING CO, LTD see BAXTER, JOSEPH WILSON IAIN

NAKAMURA, KAZUO
13 Oct 1926, Vancouver AGO CC2 CE CWW84 M NGC TB3 WWA84
addr: Toronto, 30 Old Mill Dr, 1961-4
1961 43 Green inlet $750
1963 49 Core waves 2 $675
1964 57 Curved horizon $775

NAPIER, LOUISA N.
addr: Montreal, 248 Prince Arthur St W, 1922-3
1922 213 Sketch pastel $10
1923 159 Autumn $15
160 The home of the habitant pastel $15

NAPIER-SMITH, CONSTANCE see SMITH, CONSTANCE

NASH, BERENICE K. (Mrs)
addr: Vaudreuil, Que, 1909. Westmount, 4480 Western Ave, 1915-17
1909 272 Woodland road $20
1915 455 Satsuma rose jar $20
1916 380 Vase $35
381 Bowl $25
382 Tray $35
1916 383 Small bowl $6
1917 419 Coffee cups & saucers (6) enamels

NAVAY, JULIEN
addr: Chomedey, Que, 188 de l'Elysee
1965 41 Bicycle iron $500

NAYSMITH, J.
1883 81 In Wimbledon Park, Surrey

NEALE, W. O. (Mrs)
addr: Montreal, 9 Buckingham Ave
1919 229 The violin

NEAULT, ARTHUR
addr: Montreal, 709 des Seigneurs St
1949 73 Enfin la paix de l'homme $140

NEDDEAU, DONALD FREDERICK PRICE
28 Jan 1913, Toronto CWW84 IO M WWA84
addr: Toronto, 21 Sherwood Ave
1961 94 Conglomerate nm $200

NEEL, ELLEN NEWMAN (m Edward (Ted) Neel)
14 Nov 1916, Alert Bay, B.C. Feb 1966, Vancouver M
addr: Vancouver, 770 Denman St
1950 91 The frog yellow cedar $30
92 Grizzly bear mask red cedar $37.50

NEHLS, EGON
1927, Rostock, Germ
addr: Montreal, 2158 Crescent St
1960 85 Autumn $300

NEILSON, HENRY IVAN
27 Jun 1865, Cap Rouge, Que 26 Apr 1931, Quebec AGO H M Mo12 NGC PMC TB3
addr: Valcartier, Que, 1913. Cap Rouge, Que, 1916-18
1913 308 Autumn woodlands $350
309 Quebec, from Beauport wc $75
310 In harbour etch $12
1916 212 Sandy Point, lower St Lawrence $400
213 Wayside gossips $200
214 Timber ship, Quebec harbour etch $30
215 French Canadian village etch $25
216 Les Eboulements from l'Islet etch $25
1917 245 The tow, estuary Cap Rouge River etch $25
246 Old mill, St Nicholas etch $20
247 Diamond harbour, Quebec etch $30
248 Fishermen's huts, Origneau Point etch $20
249 Ice carters, Cap Rouge etch $20
250 Le pont, Rivière au Pin wc $50
1918 264 An October day wc $125
265 Dawn, Cap Santé, Que wc $40

NELSON, CECILIA
addr: Montreal, 35 Lincoln Ave, Apt 7
1921 192 Col Noch
193 Bonsecours Market $100

NELSON, DOROTHEA S, (Mrs)
addr: Hudson, Que, 1944-9
1944 104 Tulips $50
1945 171 Lilies $15
1949 74 Summer blooms $50

NELSON, GEORGE
addr: Hamilton, Ont, 121 Park St S
1941 249-50 Lithograph

NELSON, MARION HOPE (m Frank W. Hooker)
27 Mar 1866, Richmond Va 29 May 1946, St Catharines, Ont AGO H
addr: St Catharines
1905 92 Market at Crecy $100
93 Death of Minnehaha $100
94 Heather hills $60

NELSON, ROBERT ALLEN Amer
1 Aug 1925, Milwaukee WWA66
addr: Winnipeg, 952 Dorchester Ave
1956 43 Still life $75

NELSON, W. B. (Mrs)
addr: Montreal, 35 Lincoln Ave
1920 189 Lumber boat
190 Harbour at Sydney, N.S. wc
191 Tor Bay, Newfoundland wc

NESBITT, MATTHEW JOHN
7 Oct 1928, Montreal M
addr: Montreal: 673 Vitre St, 1958; 2625 Albert St, 1963; 6695 Sherbrooke St W, 1964; Agnes Lefort Gallery, 1504 Sherbrooke St W, 1965
1958 M.J.
34 Wild rice $110
1963 111 Phallus metal & stone $800
1964 128 Untitled nickel, steel & steatite $250
1965 42 Untitled bronze & stone illus $800 1967-44 20"h Ladies Comm prize (MBAM)

NESS, JEAN (m John A. Findlay)
1901, Montreal M
addr: Montreal, 243 Mackay St, 1925-7
1925 197 The old Mawr house
1927 135 Moorings $50

NEUFELD, WOLDEMAR
1909, Ukraine
addr: Waterloo, Ont, 35 Church St
1935 428 Monday on the roofs block pr $7

429 Hall's Lane block pr $5

NEUHOF, A. C.
addr: Montreal, 3440 Ridgewood Ave
1960 87 Still life $175

NEUMANN, ERNST
27 May 1907, Budapest Mar 1956, Venice M NGC TB3
addr: Montreal: 757 Bloomfield Ave, 1926-30; 2105 Decarie Blvd, 1932; 1070 Bleury St, 1934; 2040 Union Ave, 1935; 1178 Phillips Pl, 1936. Westmount, 1215 Greene Ave, 1937-48
1926 Newman, Ernest, 1926-30
94 Cyrano de Bergerac (illus to play by Rostand) $15
216 Study of a head litho
217 Pavement menders wash drwg $20
218 Hymn singers and the mockers litho $8 per proof
1928 318 Study of a head pencil
1930 289 Drawing class wd cut $8
1932 217 Self portrait
420 Study of a Jew drwg $75
1934 461 Portrait of a young girl drwg
462 Study of a head drwg
511 Male head in repose plaster $75
1935 430 The nuns lino cut $10
431 Studio scene, the rest period litho $12
432 Unemployed No 6 litho $12
474 Head of a girl plaster
1936 557 St Sauveur etch $10
558 Montreal from the Guard Pier etch $12
559 Seated nude etch $8
560 St Sulpice etch $8
1937 430 Erna Colle drwg
431 Mrs Norman Herschorn drwg
432 Edward Cleghorn drwg
433 Nude etch
1938 174 H. Heimlich, Esq drwg
175 The canal drwg $75
1939 247 Miss Beatrice Day
424 Mrs D.W. Stewart nm
1940 220 Miss Betty Bannantyne
221 Miss Sophia Cohen
222 Miss Sybil Cohen
223 Westmount Station $100
1941 148 Mrs Max Strean
149 Alexander Solomon, Esq
150 Fletcher's Field, Montreal wc $75
1942 121 Morin Heights, summer $150
122 Miss Olive Gibbons
1943 144 Portrait of a girl
1945 172 Nude
1948 36 Portrait study $150
105 Back study etch $20
port: by Ruth Miller, 1944-147

NEWCOMBE, WILLIAM JOHN BERTRAM
18 Jul 1907, Victoria Aug 1969, London, Eng M TB3 WWA59
addr: Vancouver, 4535 Rupert St
1933 230 In the tops wc $50

NEWELL, BEATRICE
addr: Farnham, Que
1950 128 Across the tracks $50

NEWLANDS, ALEX F.
addr: Ottawa, 29 1st Ave
1916 338 Wistaria nm
339 Arrowhead nm
340 Grapevine nm
port: by Ernest Fosbery, 1912-143

NEWTON, ALISON HOUSTON LOCKERBIE (m Stanley Newton)
23 Jan 1890, Edinburgh Leith, Scot, 1967 M
addr: Winnipeg, 130 Helmsdale Ave, 1930-48
1930 156 Harvest, Manitoba wc
1931 184 Mount Robson wc $50
397 Athabaska Valley wd block $12.50
1932 218 Lake of the Woods wc $15
219 Winter wc $20
220 Stagnant pool wc $20
1933 231 Old barn, St Norbert wc $20
232 Farm yard, Gonar wc $20
1935 325 Elevator, St Boniface wc $30
326 Main Street Market, Winnipeg wc $30
1940 224 The wharfside $50
1947 206 Mountain cloud wc $65
1948 84 Catching minnows at Lockport wc $75

NEWTON, LILIAS TORRANCE (m Francis G. Newton)
3 Nov 1896, Montreal 10 Jan 1980, Cowansville, Que AGO CC1 CE CNS36 CWW73 EC M NGC TB2 WWA76 Juror

addr: Lachine, Que, 1616 St Joseph St, 1920-1. Montreal: 32 Lincoln Ave, 1922; 119 St Matthew St, 1925; 1802 University Tower, 1934; 1320 Sherbrooke St W, 1935; 522 Pine Ave, 1937-53
1920 Torrance, 1920-1
270 French Canadian woman $150
271 Portrait of a young man $150
272 Donald in the dinghy
1921 270 Mrs Sidney Johnson
271 Mrs Warwick Chipman
272 Nonnie $200 (NGC)
1922 214 Mrs Sydney Ritchie
215 Miss Betty Dawes
216 The little sister (National Gallery of Canada)
217 The crimson scarf $300
1925 198 Stewart Torrance, Esq
1934 235 Portrait of Frada
236 Still life, lilies and roses
237 Still life, white roses $150
463 Portrait drwg
1935 236 F.E. Meredith, Esq, KC LLD
237 George Hogg, Esq, ex-Mayor of Westmount
1937 216 D.W. Hamilton Fyfe, former Principal, Queen's University
217 Louis Muhlstock (NGC)
218 Sleeping girl, sketch
1939 248 Rt Rev J.C. Farthing, DD, Lord Bishop of Montreal
249 A.Y. Jackson (NGC)
250 Mrs Alan B. Plaunt, Ottawa
251 Young girl $300
1940 225 Mrs Brooke Claxton
1941 151 Miss Maud Edgar
152 Miss Mary Cramp
153 Model resting
1942 123 R.A. Laidlaw, Esq
1943 145 Warwick Fielding Chipman, KC DDL
146 Wing Commander A.H.S. Gillson, OBE (MBAM)
147 Canadian soldier No 1
148 Little boy
1947 207 Margaret Morrison
208 Peter Dobell
209 Nick
1948 37 Dr Jaya Chandy
1949 75 William Dobell
1950 31 C.G. Heward, Esq, KC
1951 34 Shirley Dixon, KC
1952 35 R.A. Laidlaw, Esq
1953 31 Direk and Hildy $500

NEYLAND, HARRY A, Amer
9 Aug 1877, McKean, Pa 23 Oct 1958, New Bedford, Mass B TB WWA40
addr: Hamilton, Ont: 1908; Art School, 1909
1908 113 Breakfast time $125
1909 273 December $150
274 The holm of the elms $175

NICHOL, PEGI see NICOL, PEGI

NICHOLS, EDITH
addr: Montreal, 17 St Mark St, 1912-13
1912 461 Cream jug, sugar bowl
462 Vase
1913 493 Jardiniere

NICHOLS, JACK
16 Mar 1921, Montreal AGO CE CWW70 M NGC TB3 WWA53
addr: Ottawa, 253 York St, Apt 100
1939 252 Portrait of a friend
253 Sleeping men $125
254 Movement and dance $300
425 Labourer drwg $25

NICHOLSON, DONALD
addr: Town of Mount Royal, Que, 417 Laird Blvd
1941 154 The Most Worshipful John Wright

NICHOLSON, MARGARET
addr: Sydney, N.S.
1911 228-30 Studies of China ducks $10 each

NICHOLSON, MARGARET EUNICE (Mrs)
addr: Halifax, 243 Robie St, 1939-41
1939 255 Portrait of my Grandmother wc
1940 226 The cutting, railway terminals wc $5
1942 155 Birch wood, Fleming Park, Northwest Arm, Halifax wc $15

NICOL, PEGI (MARGARET KATHLEEN NICHOL) (m Norman MacLeod)
17 Jan 1904, Listowel, Ont 12 Feb 1949, New York AGO CC1 CE EC M NGC TB2 WWA47
addr: Ottawa, 356 2nd Ave, 1927-29
1927 136 The tree and the fence $25
1929 160 Bia-nint-nen, Indian woman of Hagwelget Canyon $200

NICOLET, FRANK LUCIEN
b 1887
addr: Montreal: 384 Vitre St, 1933;
1441 Drummond St, 1934
1933 233 Northern lights, Labelle, Que wc $150
234 Passing storm, St Jovite, Que wc $150
1934 238 Portrait, Kay wc
239 Last leaves wc $200
240 April thaw wc $100

NICOLETTI, RODOLFO (RUDI)
10 May 1914, Toronto M
addr: Ottawa, 160 Laurier Ave W
1945 V-27356 Naval artist
173 Still life, mural pieces wc $100

NICOLL, MARION FLORENCE S. MACKAY
(m James McLaren Nicoll)
11 Apr 1909, Calgary CC1 CWW83 M
addr: Calgary
1968 190 Guaycura I: red rock, black rock 42 x 54 $500
191 Calgary III: 4 a.m. 45 x 54 $600

NIELSEN, E.
addr: Montreal, 1170 Mountain St
1943 149 Old Hudson's Bay Company, Lachine Post wc $45

NIEMANN, E. J.
1885 13 Richmond, Yorkshire

NIESSEN, WOLFRAM F.
15 Apr 1923, Krefeld, Germ M
addr: Duluth, Minn, 235 1/2 W St Marie St
1964 129 Constellation alabaster, with base $2,500

NIJENHUIS, KOENRAAD
addr: Montreal, 1818 Sherbrooke St W
1932 421 Professor Vanderpoll pencil
422 Mr L.T. pencil

NIVERVILLE, GEORGES-HECTOR DE
29 Aug 1928, Ottawa M
addr: Outremount, 251 Querbes Ave, 1947-52. Ottawa, 351 Island Park Dr, 1963-4; Ottawa, 1968
1947 210 Nature morte $70
320 Nocturne etch $15
1948 38 Femme à l'oiseau $200
1949 76 Femme avec nature morte $175
77 Intérieur $200
1950 129 Intérieur No 2 $200
1951 112 Numéro 6 $350
1952 105 Legend
1963 19 Nu $800
1964 23 Self portrait
1968 62 The school inspector acry 30 x 24 $300
63 Portrait of Aunt Alice posing as Mata Hari acry 30 x 24 $300

NIVERVILLE, LOUIS DE
7 Jun 1933, Andover, Eng CC1 CE Co IO M TB3
addr: Toronto, 36 Langley Ave, 1963; Toronto, 1970
1963 20 The banquet $750
1970 17 Landscape coll 48 x 48
18 Pique-nique coll 48 x 72

NOBBS, PERCY ERSKINE
11 Aug 1875, Haddington, Scot 5 Nov 1964, Montreal CE CNS27 CWW61 Mo12 NGC PMC TB3 WWC21
addr: Montreal: McGill University, 1905; 10 Phillips Pl, 1906; Montreal, 1908; 117 University St, 1910, 157 St James St, 1911; 14 Phillips Sq, 1915-29; old Birks Bldg, 1240 Phillips Sq, 1932-41.(residence) Westmount, 38 Belvedere Rd, 1915-31
1905 263 McGill University Union, prelim study
264 Mosaic decoration 'Majesty' des approx 1/2 actual size
1906 342 McGill Union, lounging room
343 Dr Colby's home, Pine Ave
344 Dr Adami, proposed cottage, Windemere
345 L. Rutherford, Esq, hillside cottage
1908 327 Macdonald Engineering Bldg, McGill University, Montreal
328 Medical Bldg, McGill University, proposed front
1910 396 House, Belvedere Rd, Westmount
397-8 Proposed church, Brandon, Man exterior, interior
399 Remodelling hall, stair, 30 Ontario Ave
1915 259 In Haytian waters wc

260 Twilight, St Thomas wc
261 Thunder clouds, Porto Rico wc
262 Sunrise on Cuba wc
1918 400 Proposed students' residence, at Macdonald
401 McGill University $200
1919 374 Victory from the air sculp
393 The Kremlin of Moscow illum $80
1923 274 Bibliotheca Osleriana $50
275 Proposed McGill University gymnasium $200
1925 399 Catholic Sailors' Home, monument, 'Mary, Star of the Sea' finial, model
400 Jason, sketches, P.E. Nobbs, Sciortinio, F, sculp col plaster
1927 301 Stained glass cart
1928 140 Corneille River wc
141 Esquimaux Point wc
1929 161 A Quebec salmon river wc
162 A gulf barge wc
163 Near Murray Bay wc
1931 185 Nuns' Island, from Westmount wc
186 The garden, Greenwood, Como wc
1932 221 The church, Verchères, Que wc
222 East end of church, Boucherville, Que wc
1937 219 Mixed geraniums wc $25
360 The Abbott Arms champlevé enamel des drwg
361 Proposed George V memorial drwg
1911 Nobbs & Hyde
301 Proposed building, Phillips Sq
1915 397 University of Alberta, Edmonton
398 Proposed residency block
399 Proposed McGill gymnasium, Pine Ave
400 Proposed house, Belvedere Rd
1919 394 Faculty room, Arts Bldg, University of Alberta
395 St James Church, Three Rivers, restoration photo
396 A memorial of the Great War
1920 320 War Memorial Museum, Regina Britania Fountain
321 Strathcona, Peace Centennial, Bancroft Schools, Montreal 3 photos
322 School of Medicine, University of Alberta wc
1925 368 Heraldic tablet for the old mill, Mount Bruno des executed by C.W. Kelsey
1927 227 Medical Bldg, University of Alberta
228 House, F.C. Wilson, Esq, Westmount drwg
229 Craft work photos
230 Canadian Battlefields Monuments Association, memorial stone model
1928 255 Miscellaneous details
256 Proposed school, Verdun
257 Residence, Redpath Cr
1929 264 Pulp & Paper Research Institute, McGill
265 Proposed chancel, St George's Church, Lennoxville
266 Premises, Henry Birks & Sons, Calgary
267 An entrance hall
1931 324 Royal Victoria College, new wing
325 Drummond Medical Building, Montreal
326 St George st gl cart
327 Chateau Richelieu Church, Que memorial altar rail
1932 356 Royal Victoria College, new wing
1939 363 Erskine and American United Church remodelled interior
364 Christ Church Cathedral, proposed chapel
1941 268 Christ Church Cathedral, Chapel of St John of Jerusalem photo executed work

NOBLE, HAROLD
addr: Toronto, 1067 Yonge St
1950 32 Crucifixion

NOLIN, ALICE
addr: Montreal: 2330 Park Ave, 1921-2 266 Sherbrooke St E, 1923-4; 432 Sherbrooke St E, 1927-8; 860 Sherbrooke St E, 1929-35
1921 302 Mon père plaster bust
1922 343 Edouard Monpetit bust
344 Alfred Laliberté, sculpteur bust
1923 259 L'amour et la dorleur sculp $90
1924 Betty sculp $100

321 Tête d'homme sculp
1927 315 Tête de jeune fille sculp $60
1928 354 Modèle au repos plaster $25
1929 391 Dr Dubeau, Dean of Dentistry, University of Montreal bronze
392 Statuette plaster $50
1930 316 Sir William Logan plaster
317 Sir Hippolyte La Fontaine, memorial tablet bronze
318 Camille Bernard bas rel
1931 435 Tête de jeune fille, permission of the Cercle Musicale bronze
436 Head, study plaster $50
437 Charles Gill plaster $75
1935 475 Portrait bas rel
port: by E.L. de Montigny-Giguere, 1923-250

NOORDHOEK, HARRY CECIL
10 Feb 1909, Moers, Ger CWW84 M
addr: Verdun, Que, 1306 Crawford Bridge Ave
1952 36 Windmill Point, Montreal $200

NORMANDEAU, PIERRE AIME
5 Nov 1906, Outremont 3 Nov 1965, Montreal M
addr: Montreal: 801 Bloomfield Ave, 1928-31; 251 Milton St, 1937; 3660 Hutchison St, 1939
1928 355 Portrait, bust plaster
1931 438 Etude, jeune homme sculp
439 Jeune négresse plaster, bronze $250
1937 467 Un jeune sculpteur plaster, bronze $250
1939 460 Madame G.N. plaster
461 Mademoiselle F.G. plaster
462 Martine plaster

NORRIS, GWENDOLYN see FULLER, GWENDOLYN

NORTON, WILLIAM EDWARD Amer
28 Feb 1843, Boston 1916, New York
B F TB WWW
1885 71 Coast view

NORWELL, GRAHAM NOBLE
11 Dec 1901, Edinburgh 20 Jun 1967, Val David, Que AGO M NGC TB2
addr: Ottawa: 15 Truro Apts, 1922; 197 Sparks St, Butterworth Bldg, 1923-4. Montreal: 1516 Mountain St, 1934; 123 Commissioner St, 1925; 2055 Mansfield St, 1937; 148 St Catherine St W,1938; 1478 St Catherine St W, 1943
1922 218 Deserted mill $50
219 Red barn $50
220 Dominion Church, tower wc $50
221 Chelsea Falls $75
1923 161 Winter stream wc $50
162 Moonlight, Ottawa valley $75
163 Early winter $50
1924 187 Thaw $200
188 Autumn, Ottawa valley $100 (NGC)
189 Gatineau, autumn $100
190 Moonlight $100
1934 241 Autumn, Ottawa River $200
242 Northern lights $60
1935 238 Farm house, Laurentians wc $125
239 Champagne Hill wc $95
1937 220 Lake Nipissing 1967-45 25 1/2 x 31 1/2 (Jessie Dow prize) (R.A. MacLeod, New Hartford, Conn)
221 Dead trees conté
222 Northern lights pastel $100
223 Laurentian winter wc $100
1938 86 Temiskaming wc $150
87 Winter pastel
88 Thunder and lighting conté
1943 150 Valley of the Ottawa $300

NOTT, MINA
addr: Winnipeg, 17 St Elmo Apts, Colony St
1932 223 Old boathouses, Lake of the Woods wc $25
224 Bridge at St Norbert, Man wc $20

NOWELL, BEATRICE
addr: Montreal, 191 Belgrave Ave, 1923-4
1923 280 Satsuma vase enamels
281 Mayonnaise bowl enamels
1924 370 Satsuma lamp enamels

NULITIS, ARNOLDS
30 Jul 1896, Latvia M TB2
addr: Toronto, 442 Brock Ave
1956 44 Night $240

NUTT, ELIZABETH STYRING
5 Sep 1870, Ouchan, Isle of Man c 25 Mar 1946, Sheffield, Eng CWW38 DBA M NGC RA TB2
addr: Halifax: Nova Scotia College of Art, 1928-37; 24 George St, 1940

1928 142 Where sunshine falls $1,000
1929 164 A south Yorkshire cottage $750
1931 187 The village shop $750
1932 225 Autumn on the North West Arm, Halifax, N.S. $550
226 Feeding time $150
1933 235 The moorland bridge $450
1934 243 A moorland stream $400
1935 240 Sanctuary $340
1936 327 The edge of the wood $150
1937 224 Street scene, Lymington, Eng
1940 227 Spring on the North West Arm, Halifax, $200

O

OAKLEY, BRIGID MARLIN (Mrs)
addr: Westmount, 419 Lansdowne Ave
1960 88 Mexican boy $150

OBERMAN, TULLY
addr: Outremont, 425 Edward Charles St
1960 89 Seated woman $70

O'BRIEN, LUCIUS RICHARD
15 Aug 1832, Shanty Bay, Ont 13 Dec 1899, Toronto AGO B CE EC H M Mo98 NGC TB W78
addr: Toronto: 1880; 20 College St, 1891-8
1880 18 Sunrise on the Saguenay, Cape Trinity
41 Moonlight at Bishop's Rock, Grand Manan
42 Cape Trinity and Eternity, Saguenay
101 Near Château Richer, on the road to Quebec wc
108 Cap Rouge from Isle aux Fleurs wc
116 A bit of the Ramparts, Quebec wc
117 On the Missisquoi River wc
121 A glimpse of Lake Ontario wc
127 Cap Tourment in an easterly gale wc
145 In the gloaming wc
151 Study of a hulk on the beach, St Andrews, N.B. wc
155 The lifting of the fog, Grand Manan wc
159 At the Château Richer, bateau drying sails wc
160 Off the Laurentian range, Isle aux Fleurs wc
168 At the harbour's mouth wc
169 First tint of autumn wc
176 Landscape wc
1881 50A A cottage in Somersetshire wc
57 Falls on the Chaudière River wc
59 A fog on the banks wc
60 On the road to Sillery Cove, Que wc
61 A sketch in New Forest, near Lyndhurst wc
64 The glen at Château Richer wc
68 St Andrews, Argenteuil wc
71 The wharves at Montreal wc
75 In the Prince's bastion, Citadel, Quebec wc
1883 1 Mackerel fishing in Gaspé Bay wc
7 Percé fishermen beaching their boats in a gale wc
13 Fraser Falls, Murray Bay wc
14 On Percé beach wc
17 Mount St Anne, Percé wc
31 Cap Bon Ami, Gaspé wc
33 Mount Eboulement wc
45 An impression - logging wc
51 Murray Bay wc
53 Salmon fishing on the Restigouche wc
55 The valley of the Restigouche wc
59 A colloquay on the beach wc
61 The elms wc
64 Manor House, at Rivière Ouelle wc
1885 100 De Kews Falls, near St Catharines wc
106 Windsor Castle wc
114 A Gaspé fishing station wc
126 Grand-Mère, St Maurice wc
130 Weathering, Hartland Point, north Devon wc
138 Voyageurs on the St Maurice wc
142 Early morning in Bideford Bay, north Devon wc
149 The Thames at Ousley wc
150 A tributary of the St Maurice wc
1886 12 A summer afternoon on Lake Huron wc

15 Lowtide, Northern Head of Grand Manan wc
17 A Devonshire farm lane wc
18 Off Devonport dockyard wc
20 At Point Levis, Quebec wc
24 A bastion of Fort Chambly, before the restoration wc
36 Off Tadousac wc
39 Fishing boats on north shore, Lake Huron wc
42 In the gulf, deep sea fisherman wc
44 On the Georgian Bay wc
46 A nook in Dartmoor wc
85 Split Rock, Lake Superior
1888 73 Yale, British Columbia wc $200
81 Rail, road and river, in the Fraser Canyon wc $150
84 The perils of the Banks, wc $300
87 On the Caribou Road wc $175
94 The gate of the canyon, Fraser River wc $150
96 In the National Park wc $300
125 Vancouver harbour wc $75
135 An October day on the lower Fraser wc $80
1889 157 Mountains of the Coast Range wc $250
158 A nook on the coast wc $35
159 The lagoon wc $120
1891 181 Windsor wc $300
182 The River of Canada wc $225
183 The Stour, and West Gate, Canterbury wc $150
184 A street in Rye, Sussex wc $150
185 September equinox wc $150
186 Canterbury wc $150
187 Cinque Port, Rye, Sussex wc $150
188 Montmorenci wc $150
189 The valley of the Montmorenci wc $150
190 A channel pilot wc $30
191 Romney Marsh wc $20
1892 198 August wc $200
199 Grand Falls, Saint John River, N.B. wc $125
200 The mill pond at Blair wc $120
1894 212 Wind and water wc $200
213 Salt marsh and sand dunes wc $130
214 A bend of Shadow River wc $50
215 A reminiscence of Rosseau wc $40
1895 85 Eventide (AGO)
86 Cape Gaspé $400
87 Morning mists, Bay of Fundy $150
88 Lifting of the fog, Grand Manan $150
89 The beach, Grand Manan $150
90 Darkening $140
91 The bridge, Clementsport, N.S. $140
92 Sunrise, Clementsport $140
93 Acadian meadows, N.S. $140
94 Off Saint John, Bay of Fundy $50
1897 99 Morning in the harbour, Saint John, N.B. $150
100 Montmorency Falls $75
191 The mouth of the Humber, Toronto wc $40
192 Evening on the Saint John River wc $35
193 Fishing boats on Bay Chaleur wc $25
194 Meadows by the sea wc $35
195 November weather wc $40
196 Evening on the Georgian Bay wc $30
197 Chrysanthemums wc $30
1898 182 On Lake Tadenac wc $250
183 Falls of the Moon River wc $150
184 Toronto from Scarboro Heights wc $100
185 The heart of Niagara wc $100
1900 deceased
77-78 Marine $175, $100
79 Harbour of Saint John $50
80 The landing cove, Grand Manan $120
81 Darkening $80
153 Heart of Muskoka wc $175
154 The Valley of the Don wc $80
155 On the Reservoir Creek, Don Valley wc $60
1892-7 Assoc prize, 1891, water colour port: bust, by Hamilton T.C.P. MacCarthy, 1891-218

O'BRIEN, PATRICIA DOROTHY GUNN (PADDY) (Mrs)
13 Oct 1929, Surrey, Eng IO M
addr: London, Ont, 235 Queens Ave
1958 35 Undertow No 1 $200

O'CONNELL, MICHAEL
addr: Montreal, 1672 Lincoln Ave, Apt 2
1961 44 Constriction $350

O'DONNELL, MARGUERITE see SCOTT, MARGUERITE

OESTERLE, LEONHARD FRIEDRICH
3 Mar 1915, Bietigheim, Germ CWW84 IO M WWA84
addr: Toronto: 575 Oakwood Ave, 1958; 43 Woodlawn Ave W, 1961; 1162 Yonge St, 1962
1958 86 Anna stone $550
1961 118 Penelope bronze $260
1962 75 Mother and child bronze $225

OGDEN, FANNIE G.
addr: Montreal: 507 Guy St, 1921-22; 478 Guy St, 1926
1921 194 Portrait wc
1922 222 Rev John Williams Ogden wc
223 Miss Jessie G. Stevenson wc
1926 95 Rev. J. Williams Ogden

OGDEN, G. S.
addr: Sackville, N.B, Ladies College
1924 371 Stone ware bowl $20

OGILVIE, LILLY
addr: Montreal, 305 Stanley St
1900 253 Fruit plate Dresden des

OGILVIE, WILLA MARGARET
9 Feb 1933, Montreal M
addr: Saraguay, Que
1954 64 Still life with jug

OGILVIE, WILLIAM ABERNETHY
30 Mar 1901, Stutterheim, S Africa
AGO CC2 CE CWW84 M NGC WWA84 Juror
addr: Toronto, 210 Dundas St W, No 602
1931 188 Beyond the time wc $150

OGILVY, ISABELLA EWAN LAURIE (m John Ogilvy)
1863, Montreal CNS36 H
addr: Montreal West, 53 Ballantyne Ave N, 1933-6
1933 236 Sail boat on the Nile, Egypt $25
237 Moonlight on the Mediterranean $50
1934 244 Interior morning-room $75
245 Daffodils $65
1935 241 Still life and roses $45
1936 328 Green Gables, Woodlands $60
329 Tulips and still life $75

O'GORMAN, MABEL (m Constantine A. O'Gorman)
CNS36
addr: St Laurent, Que, 1914. Walkerton, Ont, 1920. Montreal, 4690 Victoria Ave, 1936
1914 306 Old habitant house, Beaupré $20
307 Sketch of child $15
1920 192 The old apple tree $25
1936 330-2 Stetch pastel

O'HENLY, JOHN DONALD
15 Mar 1923, Toronto M
addr: London, Ont
1968 192 Landscape black 28 1/2 x 22 1/2 $250
193 Beach yellow wc 16 x 20 $125
194 Garden detail 20 x 16 $185

OLASSON, B.
1885 65 Moonlight, winter

OLSANSKY, KLEMENT
1909, Brno, Czecho M
addr: Montreal, 3849 St Urbain St
1949 78 Mme Isabella Kotchner $600

OMANSKY, HELEN (Mrs Gross)
addr: Montreal, 40 Merton Cr, 1942, 1951-7. Philadelphia: 3817 Poplar Ave, 1941, 1943; 2022 N Park Ave, 1944
1941 156 Self portrait
157 The prophet pastel
1942 124 The girl in a straw hat
125 Lilies
126 Portrait in the sun
1943 152 Mrs Hugh Chambers
1943 152 Dr P. Beregoff-Gillow
153 Picnic
1944 105 Girl with a yellow jabot
1951 Gross, 1951-4
12 Mother and child
1954 41 Baptism $500
1957 Omansky-Gross
72 Nude $300
73 Grandma's table $200

ONDAATJE, BETTY JANE KIMBARK JONES (m Michael Ondaatje)
2 Oct 1928, Toronto IO M
addr: London, Ont
1970 from house on Piccadilly St series
58 Hall acry 72 x 40 illus

59 Bedroom acry 60 x 48 (MBAM)

ONLEY, NORMAN ANTONIO (TONI)
20 Nov 1928, Douglas, Isle of Man
AGO B CC1 CE CWW84 M TB3 WWA84
addr: Vancouver: New Design Gallery, 1157 W Pender St, 1960-1; 1315 Bute St, Apt 503, 1962. Toronto, Dorothy Cameron Gallery, 840 Yonge St, 1964. Vancouver, 1968-70
1960 202 Coeur d'Alene coll illus $300
1967-46 36 x 45 Jessie Dow Prize
203 Jean nm $275
1961 45 Paysage jaune $250
1962 27 Aleutian No 2 $300
28 Polar No 8 illus Purchase award (MBAM)
1964 58 Zone I $600
1968 195 Silent coast acry on wood panel 20 x 25 3/4 $275
196 Silent land acry on canvas 35 1/4 x 40 3/4 $500
197 Silent rocks acry on canvas 37 1/4 x 40 7/8 $600
198 Silent road oil on acry on chipboard 22 1/2 x 27 7/8 $325
1970 60 Rock pool oil on wood panel 20 x 25 3/4
acry on wood panel 20 x 25 3/4
61 White bush
62 Point Grey
63 Two clouds
64 Oasis
65 Headland

ORCHARD, FREDERICK
addr: Montreal, 2091 St Urbain St
1956 45 Queen Street, Toronto $75

OSBORNE, DENNIS HENRY
23 Dec 1919, Portsmouth, Eng M RA WBA WWB72
addr: St Catharines, Ont, 184 St Paul St
1957 74 The stone crusher $100
75 The bus stop $50

OSBORNE, ROSALYNDE FULLER
b Hamilton M
addr: Hamilton, 7 Turner Ave, 1928-30
1928 143 Honfleur, France wc $25
144 Henri IV Inn, Caudebec wc $25
145 Fifteenth century fireplace wc $25
146 In the Forum Romanum wc $25
1929 165 Silvermoon roses wc $65
166 Ketchopolus Market wc $65
167 Little Theatre, Gloucester wc $65
168 Ravello wc $25
1930 157 Rock pool wc $45
158 White daisies wc $65
159 Gertrude wc $75

OSHWEETUK, A E7-932
1918, Cape Dorset, NWT ED
addr: Baffin Island, NWT
1955 150 Mother and child stone

OSLER, CLARA DU BOIS (m Frederick William Gerald Fitzgerald)
fl 1890-7 H
addr: Toronto: 35 Avenue St, 1894; 102 St Vincent St, 1897
1894 216 Near Roche's Point, Lake Simcoe wc $15
217 A quiet corner wc $15
1897 Fitzgerald
155 On the Silver Creek, Kiononta, Collingwood wc $25

OSTER, JOHN
addr: Montreal: 126 St Hubert St, 1919; 1961 Gouin Blvd, 1920
1919 230 Still life $100
231 Study $45
397 War inspiration
398 Wall decoration for farm house
1920 193 Group of fowl wc $100
194 Panel for music room wc $50

OSTIGUY, JEAN P.
addr: Montreal, 5725 Plantagenet St, 1951-2
1951 113 Nature morte au livre $80
1952 122 Composition aux oiseaux gouache $35

O'SULLIVAN, MARGARET
addr: Montreal, 3587 Notre Dame St E
1940 228 Peonies $40

OSWALD, GRAHAM GREENSHIELDS (m William Robert Oswald)
addr: Montreal, 209 Drummond St
1898 186 Landscape

OUELLET, HORACE
addr: Montreal, 6637 de Gaspé St

1928 147 Nature morte #125

OUTHET, RICKSON A.
addr: Montreal: 151 St James St, 1906; Montreal, 1908; 3 Beaver Hall Sq, 1909; 54 Beaver Hall Hill, 1910-12; 264 Beaver Hall Hill, 1922-5; 1096 Beaver Hall Hill, 1928-9
1906 346 Garden in Tuxedo Park
347 Garden at Weatmount
1908 329 Gardens, Seattle
330 Villa Lanti
331 Villa Aldobrandi
1909 438 Grantham Hall, Drummondville
1910 400 Villa d'Este, Italy
1912 416 A Westmount garden
1922 370 Garden at Breakeyville
371 House project at Cornwall
1924 191 Lac Masson road wc
192 Lac Tremblant wc
1925 199 Villa Borghese, Rome wc
200 Piazza Barbarini, Rome
201 French Canada wc
1928 258-9 Garden, Arthur H. Campbell photos
260 City of Hamilton, competition, park entrance pencil
261 City of Birmingham, civic centre, competition monoc
1929 268-71 Garden in Westmount photos

OUTRAM, OLGA see BELL, OLGA

OVEREND, NORMA
addr: Hamilton, 211 Sherman Ave S, 1932-6
1932 227 Childhood solitude $75
228 Nature symphony $150
1935 242 Light breaking through $35
1936 561 Saturday morning pen & ink $10

OWENS, NINA M. (m Owen E. Owens)
addr: Montreal: 26 Summerhill Ave, 1910-1920; 1015 Sherbrooke St W, 1927
1910 267 Evening
268 The manor
1911 231 Apple trees and elms wc
232 Edmonton
1913 311 A study
1914 308 After the rain $30
309 At Knowlton $35
310 M.
1915 263 Sketch, 2 $25
1916 217-18 Sketch $30 each
1917 251 Smoky day $30
252 Knowlton hills $50
253 At Montebello $50
1918 266 Knowlton Pond $50
267 Coldbrook valley $50
268 Where mullein grows $50
mullen, mispr
269-70 Sketch $15 each
1919 232 Brome Lake $60
233 Sheep pasture $60
234 Spring evening $60
235 Bolton hills $60
236 Autumn $30
237 Canal bridge $30
1920 195 Harbour scene $75
1927 316 O. plaster

P

PAGE, WALTER GILMAN Amer
13 Oct 1862, Boston 24 Mar 1934, Nantucket, Mass B F TB1/2
addr: Boston, 90 Westland Ave, 1900; Boston, 1903-18
1900 82 The soul's awakening $450
1903 93 Hon Charles Hamlin
94 Mrs John Craig
1918 271 Virginia Stuart Reynolds, niece of Mrs H.R. Drummond

PAGINTON, GEORGE ALFRED
1904, Swindon, Eng M
addr: Toronto, Toronto Star, 1940. New Toronto, 30 4th St, 1942
1940 229 Evening, summer $75
230 Afternoon, fall $75
1942 210-11 Circus pencil $20 each
212 Toronto Street pencil

PAGNUELO, FRANCOISE
4 Mar 1918, Westmount d 1957 M
addr: Westmount, 26 Arlington Ave, 1940-53
1940 231 On the way to Chanteclere, Ste Adèle $50
232 View from Ste Adèle $50
1941 158 Hooked rugs $125
159 Originality $75
1942 127 Carré Philippe $100
1943 154 Dans les Laurentides $100
1944 106 Polyanthus $75
1953 32 Begonia $100

PAINE, ARTHUR JAMES CARMAN

21 Aug 1886, Trinity, Nfld 8 Jul 1965, Montreal
addr: Montreal, Sun Life Assurance Co.
1928 262 Sun Life Assurance Company of Canada, head office perspective

PALARDY, JOSEPH JEAN ALBERT
23 Sep 1905, Fitchburg, Mass M
addr: Montreal: 1154 Beaver Hall Sq, 1930; 295 Maplewood Ave, 1931; 546 Milton St, 1932; 2180 St Luke St, 1933
1930 160 Ste Anne de Chicoutimi $125
161 The Arch, Percé
1931 189 The skating rink $50
190 The butcher $50
1932 229 Repose $35
1933 238 Skiers, Chicoutimi $50

PALETTE see PARKER, JOHN FREDERICK DELISLE

PALFREEMAN, ELIZABETH PATRICIA MARY
20 Jan 1929, Braintree, Essex, Eng M
addr: Dorval, Que, 193 St Joseph Blvd, 1955-7; Dorval, 1967
1955 151 Barbara Roet, head plaster
1957 165 David, portrait head plaster $45. 1967-47 21h Ladies Comm prize (Mr Robert M. Boright, Jr, Toronto)

PALM, OTTILLE E. (m Josef Jost)
13 Feb 1878, Hamilton, Ont March 1961, Munich, Germ B M TB
addr: Toronto, 1908. Hamilton, Ont, 19 Bold St, 1909
1908 113A Portrait
1909 275 John S. Gordon
276 Bertha C. Palm

PALMA, ARMAND DE
addr: Montreal, 1425 Panet St, 1942-3
1942 233 Signor Conte F. Pazzi plaster $300
1943 254 Ma Mère plaster $150

PALMER, FRANK see PALMER, HERBERT FRANKLIN

PALMER, FREDERICK E.
addr: Montreal, 4124 Van Horne Ave, 1939. Longueuil, Que, 121 Victoria Ave, 1940
1939 256 Meditation $175
1940 233 St Faustin, Que $75

PALMER, HERBERT FRANKLIN (FRANK)
24 Nov 1921, Calgary AGO CC2 M TB3
addr: Calgary: 1444 28th St SW, 1955-8; Calgary, 1967
1955 123 Docking place wc $85 1967-48 24 x 18 Jessie Dow prize
1958 36 Waterfall $250

PALMER, HERBERT SIDNEY
15 Jun 1881 - 30 Nov 1970, Toronto
AGO CC2 CNS36 CWW64 M NGC TB2 WWA47
addr: Toronto: 322 College St, 1917-8; 170 St Clements Ave, 1927
1917 254 Sheep in sunlight $45
255 Sheep and lambs $35
1918 272 Homeward $40
1927 137 The fairy month of May $250

PALMER, MARY see MILLER, MARY

PANABAKER, FRANK SHIRLEY
16 Aug 1904, Hespeler, Ont CWW84 M PMC WWA80
addr: Hespeler, 1930, 1933-4. Burlington, Ont, 59 Locust St, 1931-2. Hamilton: 94 Duke St, 1935; 33 Forest Ave, 1936; 166 Charlton Ave W, 1937. Ancaster, Ont, 1945, 1967
1930 162 A moonlit lane $200 1967-49 25 x 30 (Jessie Dow prize) (Prof and Mrs Percy Tacon, Toronto)
163 Spray River and Goat Mountain, Banff $250
164 The banquet $60
165 The sun bath $60
1931 191 Along the Grand River $500
192 Down from the pass $350
193 Covered bridge, and Gaspé village $300
1932 230 The Long Sault $500
231 August evening, Haldiman Hills $500
1933 239 Windswept $450
1934 246 The kite $250
247 On the beach $175
1935 243 Wood for a mountain camp $250
244 A squaw of the foothills $100
1936 334 Summer showers, Percé $250
335 Dappled sunlight $200
1937 225 Laurentian lake $250
226 Evening, Laurentians $65
227 Haying $65
228 Repairing the fence $135
1945 174 Fall storm $500

PANGMAN, MABEL
addr: Montreal, 22 Ontario Ave
1912 293 The old quary wc

PANNETON, LOUIS PHILIPPE
10 Jan 1906, Three Rivers, Que M
addr: Montreal: 2025 Victoria St, 1945;
1944 Dorchester St W, 1946-8
1945 175 Gunner Duncan Carter
176 Self portrait
1946 186 Snookie
1947 211 Jeannine Doiron
1948 39 Audrey

PAPINEAU, RENEE L. WESTCOTT (Mrs Christie)
addr: Westmount, 491 Argyle Ave, 1941-2. Montreal, 2165 Lincoln Ave, 1945
1941 160 Piedmont $50
1942 128 Back stream
129 Etude
1945 Papineau-Christie
177 Composition temp oil

PAPP, JOSEPH SULYOK DE
20 Sep 1897, Saujhely, Hungary CNS36
addr: Montreal: 3458 Jeanne Mance St, 1932-3; 3446 Ste Famille St, 1935-6; 3470 St Urbain St, Apt 11, 1940
1932 309 Sister
1933 307 Bonsecours Street $80
1935 245 Calvary $120
246 Dancing peasant girls $60
1936 336 Notre Dame Street $120
337 Sunday afternoon $200
338 Pilgrimage in Abos $250
1940 234 Pilgrimage, Slovakia $160
235 Landscape in Michigan wc $100

PAQUETTE, H.
addr: Montreal, 1145 St Viateur St
1926 251 Carmen sculp

PAQUETTE, JOY
19 Sep 1922, Ottawa M
addr: Ottawa, 1367 Wellington St
1954 65 Still life $100

PAQUETTE, MARGUERITE see FAINMEL, MARGUERITE

PAQUETTE, MAURICE
addr: Montreal, 4251 Delorimier Ave, 1943-6
1943 155 Still life pastel $50
1946 187 Capricho Mejicano pastel

PARADIS, JOBSON EMILIAN HENRI
22 Feb 1871, St Johns, Que 11 May 1926, Guelph, Ont H W78
addr: Montreal: 808 St Urbain St. 1903; 458 Berri St, 1905-6. Westmount, 1908. Montreal: 458 Berri St, 1909-13. Ottawa: 252 Somerset St E, 1914-16; 342 Somerset St E, 1917-24
1903 246 Study red chalk $20
247 Melancholy crayon $5
248 Siesta in Public Gardens, Paris crayon
249 The Pont Marie, Paris crayon $20
250 An old friend crayon $5
1905 95 Le Chemin de l'Eglise, Verres l'Abbaye $60
96 Reading $40
239 Portrait sketch drwg $25
1906 311 A study b&w $15
312 Paris street types b&w $20
313 Young lady reading b&w $15
1908 246 Notre Dame, Paris wc $25
247 Study of a head crayon $10
248 Study in black chalk $10
1909 277 Still life $60
278 Pont Marie, Paris wc $30
279 Old house, St Eustache wc $25
1910 269 The brook wc $35
270 Oat field wc $25
271 Evening wc $35
272 The Great Oak, St Eustache wc $25
1911 233 In the woods $60
234 Rivière du Chene $60
235 St Eustache
235A The old mill wc $25
1912 294 Autumn $30
295 Evening $40
296 The deserted house $30
297 Oat field $25
1913 312 The old mill wc $25
313 Snow scene wc $20
314 St Eustache wc $25
1914 311 The driveway, Rideau Canal $30
312 Autumn effect on the Rideau $25
313 Twilight $20
1916 219 On the Ottawa $25
220 Summer evening $40
221 Twilight $50

222 Victoria Museum tower, Ottawa $50
1917 256 Etudes de chats b&w $30
257 Notre Dame de Paris b&w $25
258 Brodeuse b&w $20
259 Dormeuse b&w $20
260 Rèveuse b&w $20
261 Jacqueline b&w $25
1919 238 Sunset on the Ottawa $50
239 The old mill, St Eustache $50
240 Mid-day $50
241 Evening $75
242 On the river side $75
243 The creek at Iberville $50
1924 193 Scenes d'hiver, Buckingham pastel $40
194 Le gros arme wc $35

PARE, ALICE O.
addr: Montreal, 4450 Kent Ave
1951 61 A man's place gouache $125

PARE, ANNE
4 Oct 1938, Quebec M
addr: Quebec
1968 119 Aucun dessin 24 x 24 $250

PARE, ROGER
b.1929
addr: Montreal, c/o Radio Canada, Dept Graphic Arts, 1625 St Luke St
1960 204 Nord nm $100

PARENT, LOUIS JOSEPH
b 1908 M
addr: Ahuntsic, Que, 10886 Clarke St
1934 248 Evangéline $125

PARENT, LOUISE
18 Apr 1930, St Jerome, Que M
addr: St Jerome, 389 Melançon Blvd
1952 76 Eau-forte etch $25

PARENT, LUCIEN see PARENT, PIERRE

PARENT, MICHEL
31 Dec 1938, Charlesbourg, Que M
addr: Quebec
1968 307 Flottant doucement 30 x 30 $300
308 Relief brun classique peinture avec relief 30 x 20 $250
309 Gros bloc peinture avec relief 30 x 40 $300

PARENT, MIMI
8 Sep 1924, Outremont M
addr: Town of Mount Royal, Que, 39 Cornwall Ave
1948 40 Nature morte $80
106 Jeune fille au collier crayon $45

PARENT, OMER
7 Apr 1907, Quebec CWW84 M
addr: Quebec
1968 200 Liriope 16 x 18 $225
201 Germine 33 x 45 $650
202 The world's a stage 48 x 66 $1,200

PARENT, PIERRE OVIDE LUCIEN
29 Apr 1893 - 27 Mar 1956, Montreal
addr: Montreal: 5300 Park Ave, 1927; 620 Cathcart St, 1929-33; 1051 St James St W, 1941
1927 231 Eglise, Château Richer, Que
232 Eglise de la Visitation, Sault aux Recollets
1929 Parent & Labelle, 1929-31
272 Une résidence d'été
273 Une auberge pour touristes
274 Project d'église à Montréal
1930 227 Résidence, Col J.T. Ostell
228 Collège St Césaire
229 The Parisian Laundry
230 Entrée de taverne
1931 328 Maison d'été (Parent)
328-9 College de St Laurent. nouvelle chapelle plan élévation
1932 357 Noviciat à Ste Geneviève de Pierrefonds
1933 405 The cloister
406 Detail of porch
1941 269 Le chantier à l'Oratoire St Joseph wc
see also Brain, Siméon, 1928-9; Tourville, René Rodolphe, 1940

PARKER, ARTHUR HENRY
1874, Newcastle-under-Lyme, Eng
addr: Montreal, Mount Royal Hotel
1924 195 The windstorm wc $30

PARKER, CHARLES
addr: Halifax, Nova Scotia College of Art
1933 478 Self portrait etch $10

PARKER, HARLEY WALTER BLAIT
13 Apr 1917, Fort William, Ont M
addr: Willowdale, Ont, 255 Dunview Ave,
1954 111 Yellow swamp wc $50
112 Abandoned farm wc $150

PARKER, JESSIE CECILIA ALWARD (m Benjamin Cronyn Parker)
13 Jul 1891, Courtland, Ont M
addr: Winnipeg, 744 McMillan Ave
1933 240 On Kenora Road wc $20

PARKER, JOHN ALLEN
addr: Montreal, 6879 Monkland Ave
1949 140 Pavement reflections wc $65

PARKER, JOHN FREDERICK DELISLE (PALETTE)
16 May 1884, New York 29 Sep 1962, Vancouver M
addr: Vancouver, 1895 W 14th Ave
1947 212 Sawmill $100

PARKER, SEYMOUR D.
addr: Montreal, 492 St Denis St
1910 273 The Canadian Rockies $500
274 The brook $80

PARRISH, CLARA WEAVER (m William P. Parrish) Amer
Selma, Ala 1925 New York AAA28 B DBA F RA TB
addr: New York, 939 8th Ave
1912 298 Natalie etch $12.50
299 Beatrice etch $12.50
300 An old fashioned lady etch $20
301 Lady in black etch $15
302 An old world corner etch $10
303 On the Riviera etch $10
304 The sisters etch $25
305 Old mill, Quimperlé $8

PARSONS, HELEN see SHEPHERD, HELEN

PARSONS, WILLIAM BRUCE
14 May 1937, Montreal M
addr: Regina: 11 Bartleman Apts, Cornwall St, 1964; Regina, 1968
1964 130 Relic No 4 wd $200
1968 203 End run for Allah acry 2 panels each 78 x 132 $1,500
204 Bridge acry 2 panels each 78 x 52 $1,000

PARTOUS, DANIEL
c 1885, Belgium
addr: Montreal, 1638 Bennett Ave
1949 141 The Tetons, Colorado intarsia $50

PARTRIDGE, DAVID GERRY
5 Oct 1919, Akron, Ohio AGO CC1 CWW84 M TB3 WWA84
addr: St Catharines, Ont: 125 Page St, 1947; 12 York St, 1949. Ottawa: 126 Stanley St, 1959; 500 Roxborough Ave, 1961-2. London, Eng, 20 Old Church St, 1963. Montreal, Galerie Agnes Lefort, 1504 Sherbrooke St W, 1964
1947 214 Know thyself oil & temp on masonite $75
1949 165 Poverty litho $10
1959 14 Arctic sun $300
1960 205 Solitude I nm $350
206 Solitude II nm $400
1962 29 Vertebrate form No 1 $400
76 Standing configuration No 9 wd & nails illus 1967-50 43h Ladies Comm award. Purchase award (MBAM)
1963 50 Yellow orb $600
112 Silver and black, nail configuration $500
1964 102 Nucleus nm $100

PARTRIDGE, DONALD WARREN
5 Feb 1900, Cincinnati, Ohio CWW64
addr: Dorval, Que, 100 St Joseph Blvd
1957 76 Kennebunk Beach, Maine

PARTRIDGE, RICHARD B.
addr: Montreal, 1104 Beaver Hall Hill
1935 247 Interior $300
433 Pat drwg $35

PATENAUDE, P. WILLIAM
addr: Montreal, 4176 Hampton Ave, 1936. St Joseph Village, Que, 17 St Peter St, 1942
1936 339 An old homestead near Durham, Que $70
1942 130 Near Georgeville, Que $75 (Patnaud, 1936, misprint)

PATERSON, GEORGE
addr: Winnipeg, 61 Braemar Ave
1947 213 Portrait study

PATERSON, SAMUEL T.
addr: Montreal, 4474 Old Orchard Ave
1937 434 The Clyde, evening drwg $17.50
435 White cottage drwg $20
436 The barge drwg $15
437 Black gondola $17.50

PATON, DAVID
9 Jul 1921, Fernie, B.C. M
addr: Halifax
1968 205 Battle scene lith 19 x 15 $50
207 Misery aqua etch 19 x 15 $50
207 Reclining etch mm 21 x 20 $65

PATON, JOSEPH NOEL, Sir Eng
13 Dec 1821, Dumferline, Scot 25 Dec 1901, Edinburgh B DBA DVP G TB
1883 136 Silenas singing the song of creation to woodland deities

PATRIC, RUTH (Mrs McPherson)
30 Mar 1897, Winnipeg M
addr: Vancouver, 3490 Cedar Cr
1949 79 Luke 10:v 41-42 $100

PATRICIA, HRH PRINCESS VICTORIA PATRICIA HELENA ELIZABETH (d Duke of Connaught) (Lady Patricia Ramsay. m Hon Alexander R.M. Ramsay)
17 Mar 1886, Buckingham Palace 12 Jan 1974, Windlesham, Surrey, Eng
1912 1 In the Public Park, Stockholm
2 At Drottingholm, Sweden
3 In the park at Drottingholm
4 View from Government House, Ottawa
5 A cottage in Sweden
6 A snowstorm

PATTERSON, ANDREW DICKSON
30 June 1854, Picton, Ont 31 Jul 1930, Montreal AGO EC H M Mo12 NGC TB3 W78
addr: Ottawa, 1891. Toronto, 10 Elmsley Pl, 1897. Montreal, Linton Apts, 1909. Westmount, 4160 Sherbrooke St W, 1910-14. Montreal, 241 Beaver Hall Hill, 1918-21; 451 Sherbrooke St W, 1922-8
1891 90 Hon Sir Wm Ritchie, Chief Justice of Supreme Court. painted for Dept of Justice
91 Portrait of my Mother
1897 101 The late Sir Daniel Wilson
102 Prof Chapman, PhD
103 Hon Sir Frank Smith
104 Portrait of a lady, period 1870
1898 88 James Aikenhead, Esq
89 Study in red $200
90 It's not the coat that makes the man $175
91 Prince Krapotkin $100
1900 83 Rev Dr Blackstock
84 Homer Watson, RCA $200 (NGC)
1909 280 Portrait of a lady
281 Isabel, daughter of Dr Robertson, Ste Anné
282 Portrait of a senator
283 Miss E.M.
284 Tennyson, after Watts b&w
285 My Mother b&w
1910 275-7 Chalk portrait
278 Stella, chalk study $25
279 Portrait charcl pastel
1914 314 After painting by Valasquez crayon $55
315 After painting by Sir Joshua Reynolds crayon $50
316 After painting by Sir Thomas Lawrence crayon $40
1918 273 Lady Van Horne, at 17 pastel
274 Countess of Waldegrave, after Hoppner $35
275 A Florentine lady pastel
276 Portrait of Rembrandt pastel
277 Ethelbert Nevin pastel $75
278 Late James Ross, Esq pastel $75
1921 211 Late Sir William Osler, Bart (courtesy Montreal General Hospital)
212 Late Hon C.C. Colby
213 Mrs C.C. Colby
214 Samuel Gerrard, Pres Bank of Montreal, 1820-1826 chalk
1922 224 John S. Sargent, RA $100
225 A brunette $400
226 Sidney Carter
227 Head of old man $150
1923 235 Sir Francis Johnson crayon $150
236 Capt Henry Morgan, MC crayon
237 John Gray, 1st Pres Bank of Montreal crayon $200
238 Miss Margaret Molson crayon
1924 290 Francis J. Shepherd, MD LLD crayon
291 George Iles crayon
292 Countess of Haddington crayon

293 Great-grandparents crayon
1925 202 John W. Cook, Esq, KC, Battonier 1924-1925
203 Alfred Joyce, Esq, at 89
204 Portrait of a child pastel
369 Stephen Leacock crayon
370 Rex Battle crayon
371 Self portrait crayon
1926 219 Dr Simon S, Sperber chalk
220 Mrs Sperber chalk
221 Dr Ruttan chalk
222 Late Mrs G.L. Marler chalk
1927 297 E.L. Stewart Patterson, Esq, Sherbrooke crayon
298 Portrait of a lady crayon
299 Catherine, daughter of W.G. MacKenzie crayon
300 John, son of W.G. MacKenzie crayon
1928 319 Dr A.A. Bruère charcl
320 Late Hon Thomas White crayon
321 Miss Kathleen Stewart crayon
322 Taking a rest crayon $50

PATTERSON, EDITH LALANDE RAVENSHAW (m Andrew Dickson Patterson)
b East Sheen, Surrey, Eng DBA G
addr: Toronto, 10 Elmsley Pl, 1903. Montreal, c/o Scott & Sons, 1905. London, Eng: The Mall Studios, Parkhill Rd, 1914-15; 17 Cathcart Studios, 34 Redcliffe Rd, 1917-22
1903 251 A teasel field nm $25
252 Early morning nm $25
253 Evening nm $25
1905 217 Evening, Rye, Sussex pastel $125
218 Morning, Rye, Sussex pastel $125
1914 etching, 1914-22
317 The black mill, Winchelsea $15
318 The old mill, Winchelsea $15
319 Portsmouth harbour $15
320 Caracalla's Baths, Rome $15
1915 264 Home Office, St James Park $25
265 Victory $15
266 Lincoln Cathedral $15
1917 Lalande, 1917-18
196 Lincoln Cathedral etch aqua $25
197 Lincoln $18
198 Brayford Pool, Lincoln $18
199 Silver peacocks $18
1918 201 The Longwater, Hampton C $20
1919 244 The Victoria Monument, St James Park $30
245 The Gimlet Rock, Prohelli, Wales $20
1922 228 Evening $30
229 A backwater $30
230 Phlox and butterfly $40
231 Waxwings $40

PATTERSON, I. M.
addr: Montreal, 249 Girouard Ave
1924 372 Fruit bowl enamels
373 Sandwich tray

PATTISON, ALBERT MEAD
1887, Clarenceville, Que 26 Nov 1957, Hudson, Que M
addr: Montreal: 44 Lorne Ave, 1911; 96 Durocher St, 1912-14. Clarenceville, Que, 1915. Montreal: 57 McGill College Ave, 1916; 223 Sherbrooke St W, 1919. Town of Mount Royal, Que, 202 Lazard Rd S, 1921-37
1911 236-7 Sketch b&w $10 each
1912 306 The harbour $50
307 Late afternoon $25
308 Portrait sketch
1913 316 Place d'Armes Square wc $25
317 Sketch, Ste Céneviève wc $25
318 Old houses, Jacques Cartier Square wc $20
1914 321 Toll house, Cartierville wc $20
322 The coal barge wc $20
461 Pen rendering
1915 267 Dominion Square, Montreal $75
268 Block house, St Helen's Island $75
269 An old stable $50
1916 223 Beaver Hall Square wc $75
224 The birches wc $20
225 Old sugar shanty $25
1919 246 Duck hunting $150
1921 195 The Basin, Montreal harbour pastel $75
1925 205 Trees and sunshine wc $35
206 A glimpse of the Cathedral, Rouen wc $50
1928 323 Haymarket Square, Montreal pencil $15
324 Uncles, St Antoine Street, Montreal pencil $15
1929 333 Place Royale, Montreal crayon $30
334 Farmhouse, St Lambert crayon $30
1931 194 Sun, snow and a house $100

1932 232 Chaboillez Sq, Montreal wc $100
1933 479 Place d'Armes Hill, Montreal etch $10
480 Arts Building, McGill University etch $8
481 Cathredral St, Montreal etch $8
482 St George's Church, Montreal etch $8
1934 464 St George and Vitre Streets, Montreal etch $10
465 Place d'Armes Sq, Montreal etch $8
466 Old fort at Chambly, Que crayon $20
1937 229 Old bake house, Seigniory of St Luc, Que $25

PATTULLO, MARY FRANCES (m W.D. Gregory)
fl 1889-90 H
1889 48 Students' table $100

PAVITT, D. A. J.
addr: Montreal, 1441 Drummond St, 1932. Westmount, 220 Elm Ave, 1935
1932 233 Autumn corner pastel $15
234 Evening glow pastel $15
1935 248 Winter $200

PAVLYCHENKO, LARISA
addr: Toronto, 235 Spadina Ave
1958 37 Lovers $150

PAYETTE, EUGENE
13 Feb 1874 - 22 Jan 1959, Montreal CWW36
addr: Montreal, 103 St François Xavier St, 1917-19
1917 382 City of Montreal Library perspective
383 Bibliothèque Saint Suplice 6 photos
1918 402 City of Montreal Public Library 2 frames of photos

PAYNE-JOHNSON, JEANNE (m Louis C. Johnson) Amer
14 Apr 1887, n Danville, Ohio 4 Oct 1958 WWA58
addr: New York, 92 5th Ave
1916 226 Little Simone min
227 Japanese lady min
228 Dr Jacques Lazoosky min

PAYZANT, CHARLES ST GEORGE
addr: Santa Monica, Cal, 1023 4th St
1931 195 In Santa Monica wc $30
196 In Sonoratown wc $30
197 Chinatown, Los Angeles wc $50
198 The lake in the park wc $50

PEACE, JANET
addr: Montreal, 2254 Dorchester St W
1965 30 Blue circle nm

PEACOCK, WILBUR KELLS
23 Sep 1898, Canton, Ont M
addr: Toronto, 222 Bedford Park Ave, 1941-2
1941 251 Place of Remembrance, 1914-18, University of Toronto etch $8
1942 213 Abandoned home, Haliburton etch $8

PEARL, HAROLD A.
addr: Montreal, 1501 St Catherine St W
1939 426 The fruit market, Montreal dry pt $15
427 A corner of the market, Montreal dry pt $15
428 The dome of St James, Montreal dry pt $15

PEARSON, FREDA CANELLAKOS (Mrs)
1902, Ottawa M
addr: Ottawa, 486 Albert St
1940 236 Medusa wc $35
237 Promenade, Orphelina St Joseph, Ottawa wc $35

PECK, HUGH A.
5 Dec 1888 - 1 Jun 1945, Montreal M
addr: Westmount, 1 Belvedere Rd, 1931-7. Montreal, 1190 University St 1931 (office)
1931 199 Village of Sandy Bay
331-3 Residence, Cap St Jacques
334 Proposed residence, Isle Bizard, Que
1934 249 Portrait study of a young man
1936 340 Yoshida
341 A Metis afternoon $60
1927 230 A Quebec by-way $125
231-2 On the Gaspé higheay II and III $75, $100

PECK, PAMELA MERRILL (m Esmond H. Peck) signs Merrill M

addr: Westmount, 575 Lansdowne Ave
1952 37 Wagon on Clarke St $225

PEDEN, FRANK
8 Sep 1877, Dalhousie, N.B. 11 Jul 1969, Montreal
addr: Montreal, 20 St Alexis St, 1908-15
1908 Peden & McLaren, 1908-15
332 Cottages, Montreal West
333 Bank, Charlottetown, P.E.I.
334 Bank, Lunenburg, N.S.
335 Various buildings photos
1910 401 City church
402 Bank, sketch
403 Illustration of work executed 3 frames
1911 302 Bank building, perspective
303 Public Library, Port Arthur, sketch
304 Architectural photos
1913 435 Residence, Westmount
1915 401 Loyola College, Notre Dame de Grace

PEEL, MILDRED (Lady, m Sir George William Ross)
1856, London, Ont c 1920 H Mo98/12 M
1889 49 Le déjeuner pour Marie $100

PEEL, PAUL
7 Nov 1960, London, Ont 3 Oct 1892, Paris AGO B CE EC H M NGC TB W78
1883 96 Papa's boat, off Cape Finisterre
167 The spinner (MBAM)
1885 31 The anxious moment
45 Only a bubble
70 Good-bye
1886 75 A peasant mother
1888 22 Papa will return $300
1889 50 The young gleaner $100
51 The Arab $200
52 Young botanist $200
53 Fisherman's wife at home $300
54 Two friends $75
55 Mother's little help $75

PELL, AUGUSTUS J.
fl 1859-85 H
1883 25 Spring wc
54 Autumn wc
1885 128 A Canadian landscape wc

PELLAN, ALFRED (b Pelland)
16 May 1906, Quebec AGO B CC2 CE CWW84 M NGC TB2 WWA84
addr: Limoilou, Que, 211 3rd Ave, 1923. Montreal, 3714 Jeanne Mance St, 1948-9. Auteuil, Que, 1967
1923 Pelland
164 Coin du vieux Québec $200 (NGC)
1948 41 3 êtres $350
42 Pot à tabac automatique $500
1967-51 32 x 39 Jury II prize (National Gallery of Canada)
85 Créophagie omnicolore wc
1949 80 Le petit avion $1,000

PELLETIER, DENISE
addr: Montreal, 1247 Wolfe St
1960 207 Rythme I nm $100

PELLETIER, ROBERT
M
addr: Montreal: 4409 Christophe Colomb St, 1938-40; 5166 Marquette St, 1941; 4407 Christophe Colombe St, 1944
1938 198 Lt Col J. Pelletier, MD, mon grand-père plaster
1939 463 The old fisherman plaster $75
1940 414 Beethoven plaster $150
1941 287 Louis Cyr plaster $200
288 Remords d'Adam plaster $75
1944 163 An officer of the RCASC plaster
164 Indian plaster $350

PELLUS, RAYMOND
addr: Montreal, 2016 Sherbrooke St E
1941 161 Portrait de jeune fille

PELOQUIN, CYRILLE
addr: Montreal, 4519 St Denis St
1929 393 Etude, Frère André, CSC plaster (droits réservés. 1929)

PELTIER, LOUIS
addr: Montreal
1968 208 Fuite litho 16 x 21 $35
209 Jeu gravure burin sur cuivre 5 x 5 $30
210 Coupe graveur sur bois 4 x 5 $30
211 Lutte gravure pointe sèche 5 x 6 $25

PEMBERTON, SOPHIE THERESA (m Arthur Beanlands. m Deane Drummond)
15 Feb 1869 - 31 Oct 1959, Victoria

CC1 DBA DVP G M Mo12
addr: Victoria, Gonzales, 1895. no address 1910
1895 95 Sweet seventeen $25
96 A Normandy peasant $25
1910 Beanlands
280 The Chelsea pensioner $500

PENDLETON, S. R.
addr: Saint John, N.B, 51 Summer St, 1909-10
1909 286 Cascade, Rockwood Park, Saint John wc $25
287 In October $25
1910 281 The brook wc $15
282 Evening wc $15
283 Fog and surf wc $15

PENFOLD, CATHERINE S.
fl 1892-5 H
addr: Paris, 1892. Côte St Antoine, (Westmount), 1894; Clarke Ave, 1895
1892 106 Evening task
1894 113 An unwilling captive $75
114 A sketch $25
1895 97 In an old garden $30
1894-5 Assoc, 2nd student's prize, 1892, 1st student's prize, 1894

PENMAN, EDITH
London, Eng 14 Jan 1929, Woodstock, N.Y. F WWW Y
addr: New York, 939 8th Ave
1912 309 June in the hills $100
310 Moonlight in Devon $20

PENNINGTON, M. J. (Mrs)
addr: Montreal, 387 Sherbrooke St
1905 189 A bit of old St Augustine wc

PENTZ, DONALD ROBERT
18 Sep 1940, Bridgewater, N.S. CWW84 M WWA84
addr: Sackville, N.S.
1968 India ink on mating board, 212-13
212 Snow water 21 x 28 $175
213 Frenchmen's fence 21 x 28 $175
214 Ink banners No 2 India ink on canvas 40 x 54 $250
215 Ink bar India ink, and acry glaze on canvas 50 x 66 $300

PEPPER, GEORGE DOUGLAS
25 Feb 1903, Ottawa 1 Oct 1962, Toronto
AGO CC1 CE CWW58 M NGC TB2 WWA62
addr: Ottawa: 234 Frank St, 1928; 16 Torrington Pl, 1930-2. Toronto: 441 Walmer Rd, 1935; 25 Severn St, 1939
1928 148 The Laurentians, evening $150
1930 290 The sketcher ink drwg $12
291 Winter lino cut $5
1932 235 Storm $30
236 Surf, grey day $25
1935 249 Lighthouse $250
250 Tobacco patch, St Urbain $100 (AGO)
1939 257 An old Indian $50

PEPPER, KATHLEEN see DALY, KATHLEEN

PERCIVAL, GERTRUDE F.
addr: Montreal, 328 Mackay St, 1918-24
1918 279 Sketch pastel
1920 196 News
197 The purchase
198 Homeless
1921 196 Sailing boats $60
197 Miss Lillian Percival
198-9 Sketch
1922 232 Miss Muriel Percival
233 Bord-à-Plouffe
345 Annie plaster
1923 260 Joseph W. Percival sculp
1924 197 The edge of the forest
198 At North Hatley, sketch
322 A gust of wind sculp

PERCIVAL, PHYLLIS M. REYNOLDS (m Albert C. Percival)
b U.S.A. CNS40
addr: Montreal West: 220 Percival Ave, 1928-35; 252 Ballantyne Ave N, 1936-44
1928 149 River St Pierre $10
1929 169 Study of coloured man $50
170 Boats at Lachine $30
1931 200 House by the road, Ste Geneviève, Que $50
201 Ste Geneviève, Que $50
1932 237 The dusky maid $50
238 The road to the ferry $50
239 The old bakery, Quebec $50
1933 241 Monastery garden, Oka $80
1934 250 Edith Bradburn, Cree Indian $50
251 Celery field, St Martin $75
252 St Patrick Street, Montreal $50
253 Old houses, St Catherine Street $40

1935 251 Shadows, Victoria Street $50
252 Tug at anchor, Lachine $50
253 The beach, Ogunquit $100
1936 342 Coming storm $150
343 Old house, Mayor Street $50
1937 233 Noella $300
234 Margot $200
1939 258 Old Montreal, Common Street $150
1943 156 September day $75
1944 107 Portrait of Miss Pause $50

PERDRIAU, ETHEL S.
addr: Outremont, 810 Durocher St
1914 323-4 Case of ivory miniatures

PEREHUDOFF, DOROTHY see KNOWLES, DOROTHY

PEREHUDOFF, WILLIAM W.
21 Apr 1919, Langham, Sask CE M WWA84
addr: Saksatoon: 1131 2nd Street E, 1963-5; Saskatoon, 1968
1963 51 Color intervals $500
1964 59 Templum No 2 $1,000
1965 13 Templum No 3 $500
1968 acrylic
216 Zephrus No 7 64 x 70 $700
217 Zephrus No 8 64 3/4 x 84 3/4 $900
218 Zephrus No 9 64 3/4 x 88 1/4 $1,000
219 Zephrus No 11 69 x 70 3/4 $900

PERELMA, OSSIP (Ossy de)
RIAFA, Russia. Salon des Beaux Arts, Paris B
addr: Montreal, 384 Claremont Ave
1925 207 Bartholmey, French sculptor $2,000
208 Inondation, Paris $100
209 Breton fishermen $500
210 Street scene wc $50

PERRAULT, JEAN JULIEN
11 Dec 1893 - 13 Jan 1970, Montreal
addr: Montreal: 5300 Park Ave, 1927; 10 St James St W, 1929
1927 233 Themis Bldg, St James & St Lawrence Streets
234 Proposed apartment house
235 Proposed garage
1929 275 Railway Exchange Bldg photo
276 Themis Bldg photo
277 Victoria Sq office bldg photo

PERRAULT, MAURICE
12 Jun 1857 - 11 Feb 1909, Montreal
CWW10
addr: Montreal, Place d'Armes Hill
1894 Perrault, Mesnard & Venne
266 Laval University perspective
267 Monument National
268 Banque du Peuple

PERRAULT, SUZANNE PARENT (Mrs)
28 Mar 1924, Montreal M
addr: Ste Dorothée, Qué, 4 blvd Union
1962 67 Assisi nm $75

PERRE, HENRI
1824, or 1825, Strasbourg 17 Jun 1890, Toronto AGO DCB EC H M NGC W78
addr: Toronto, 1880
1880 60 Pennsylvania landscape
135 On the Wissipeckon wc
143 Wild flowers wc
156 On the Schuylkill wc
161 Group of swamp oaks wc
191 Willows, on the Schuylkill wc
1883 22 A natural mountain path, near Intercolonial Railroad wc
24 Near the St Lawrence, Quebec wc
29 Boulders on the St Lawrence wc
35 Near the Intercolonial Railroad wc
38 A little French Canadian village, morning wc
43 Group of spruce trees wc

PERREAULT, GABRIEL HENRI JOSEPH
2 May 1932, Ste Sophie, Que M
addr: Montreal: 723 Walnut St, 1957; 2774 Cadillac St, 1961
1957 138 Figure nm $15
1961 95 Midi d'étë nm $60

PERRET, MERY
addr: Paris, 83 ave Victor Hugo
1903 311 J.J.M. Pangman, Esq min
312 Duchesse Bourgogne min $10
313 Duchesse de Berry min $10

PERRIGARD, HAL ROSS
3 Jan 1891 - 23 Apr 1960, Montreal M
NGC PMC TB2
addr: Montreal: 571 Sherbrooke St W, 1913-15; 747 St Catherine St W, 1916-23; 269 Old Orchard Ave, 1924; 220 Mountain St, 1925. Westmount, 418

Claremont Ave, 1927-52
1913 319 Poster wc $35
1914 325-6 Poster wc $75, $35
1915 270 Poster, decorative scheme wc $75
271 Up beyond the city, poster wc $60
272 Poster wc $50
1916 229 On Lachine Canal $225
230 Pontoon bridge $175
231 At Outremont, sketch $25
232 Summer, sketch $30
1917 262 Fantasy, fairyland $250
263 Sentinels $125
264 On Lachine Canal wc $100
265 Lone pine, Sherbrooke $100
266 Winter, sketch $50
267 Windsor Station $250
1918 280 The coal trestle $150
281 Seven o'clock pastel $150
282 Landscape $150
283 The stone house pastel $150
284 The gorge $50
285 Winter on the gorge $50
1919 247 The elm guard, valley of St Francis $500
248 Sun glow and winter velvet pastel $300
249 Cloud drifts pastel $200
250 Wild growth, sketch $25
251 Quaryman's shack $200
252 Mountain house $50
1920 199 April $250
200 The silent hour pastel $110
201 Tower of Babel, Valley of the Ten Peaks, Canadian Rockies pastel $350
202 The stage of the Gods wc $250
1921 200 Path of gold, near Banff $150
201 Snowpeak Avenue, Emerald Lake, Canadian Rockies $300
202 Old news vender $350
203 Three buildings on the Magog wc $100 (listed 1967, Jessie Dow prize)
1922 234 The gown from Grandmother's trunk $200
235 In brown $150
1923 165 Lalage $250 (NGC)
166 Vere $250
167 The green mill $150
168 Lake Agnes, Canadian Rockies $300
1924 199 Sea $200
200 September's valley $325
201 Sand dunes of Annisquam $250
202 An old mill and its friends, the trees $300
1925 211 Cathetral, Canadian Rockies $600
212 Mums $500
213 Sun play $500
214 Rock-bound shore $100
215 Winter silence pastel $250
1927 138 The chasm $500
139 Grandfather's place $100
140 Silence $300
141 Dark sails wc $160
142 Reflections pastel $250
1928 150 Playtime $150
151 Hell's Gate, Canadian Rockies $450
152 Among the Canadian Rockies pastel $115
153 The last light pastel $250
1929 171 The lobster shop $160
172 Late summer $250
173 Winter pastel $250
174 Resting time $225
1931 202 Silhouette on the St Francis $300
203 End of day $380
1932 240 Sun play $375
1933 242 The busy shore $175
243 A village street $250
1934 254 Country homestead $350
255 Castle Mountain $400
256 Montcalm's Headquarters, Quebec $200
257 Sun peak $300
1935 254 Grist mill, wayside inn, Sudbury, Mass $350
255 Old Hay Market, Montreal $350
256 Doorway, Sea Fencibles' Barracks wc $125
1936 344 On River St Francis $150
345 Old houses at Oka $100
346 Steve'e house $300
1939 259 Remnant of old days $300
1940 238 Stone houses, Quebec (demolished) $200
1943 158 Canadian winter day $275
1945 178 Springtime in the country $500
179 By the North River $225
1946 188 Shoreline points $350
1947 215 Snow blanket $400
216 Near the docks, Gloucester $450
1949 81 Ruins of Fort Cuillerier $500
1950 35 Abandoned barns $375

1951 35 Abandoned barns $375
1952 38 Pattern in the gorge $400

PERROCHET, CHARLES
addr: Montreal, 920 Castle Bldg, 1934-5
1934 258 St Lawrence shore at Metis wc $75
259 Percé wc $75
1935 257 The water hole wc $60
see also Ernest Isbell Barott, 1934-369; Robert Findlay, 1934-392

PERRON, GERMAIN (signs Germain)
15 Aug 1943, Montreal M
addr: Montreal, 3559 University St
1961 Germain
17 1° $275

PERRON, J. EUGENE
1900 - 19 Jan 1969, Montreal
addr: Montreal, 4258 St Hubert St
1933 407 Office building

PERRY, ALFRED LESLIE
30 Sep 1896, Lachine, Que 13 Jun 1982, Montreal
addr: Montreal: 14 Phillips Sq, 1926-7; 1190 University St, 1928-9; 620 Cathcart St, 1930-2; New Birks Bldg, 1933-5; 1405 Bishop St, 1937-9; Montreal, 1947. (residence) Montreal, 340 Oxford Ave, 1921-2. Westmount: 341 Côte St Antoine Rd, 1925; 721 Grosvenor Ave, 1930. Montreal, 4647 Grosvenor Ave, 1935-7. Westmount, 972 Belmont Ave, 1945
1926 152 Residence, Westmount, Que
1927 236 Residence, Mrs James Wilson, Westmount
237 Residence, E.J. Thompson, Esq, Westmount
1928 Perry & Luke, 1928-37
263 Residence, Laval-sur-le-Lac
264 Residence, Outremont, Que
265 Residence, Westmount, Que
266 Apartment house, Montreal
1929 278 Hermitage Country Club, Magog
279 Westmount Park Melville Church
280 Residence, St Andrews East
281 Residence, The Boulevard, Westmount
1930 231 Residence, F.W. Sharp, Esq
232 Proposed clubhouse, Quebec Golf Club
1931 335 Residence, Sherbrooke, Que
336 Substation, Montreal
337 Residence, E.J. Clark, Esq
1932 358 Residence, Dr H.S. Evans, Hudson Heights
359 Residence, Westmount
1933 408 Residence, J.A. Wales, Esq, Westmount
409 Proposed residence, Westmount
1935 368 Transfer depot
369 Verdun High School
1937 362 Residence, Dr Victor Jekill, Westmount
363 Residence, Mr Edward Renouf, Westmount
364 United Church, St Lambert, Que
365 Astor Theatre, St Lambert, Que
1939 Perry, Luke & Little, 1939
365 Chantecler Hotel, Ste Adèle
366 Proposed, St Peter's Church, Mount Royal
367 Proposed, Queen Mary Road United Church
368 Residence, Dr F.N.K. Falls, Westmount
1945 270 Three Rivers High School
1947 331A Office building
1921 204 Redpath Crescent wc $15
205 McGill University wc $10
1922 236 St Paul St, Montreal wc
237 St James Cathedral, Montreal wc $15
1925 216 Duomo Florence, from Boboli Gardens wc $40
1930 292 Old street, Quebec City drwg $35
293 Farmhouse, Quebec drwg $35
1933 244 Farmhouse near Ste Marguerite, Que $20
245 Mont Rolland, Que $20
1934 260 Stream at Morin Heights $45
261 North River, Mont Rolland $50
262 Sundown, Val Morin $35
1935 258 Spring on the North River $45
1937 235 Early spring, Ste Marguerite, Que $50
1945 180 Spring reflections $200

PERRY, ELEANOR
addr: Montreal, 121 Bayle St, 1909. Westmount, 121 Irvine Ave, 1911-12. Montreal, 287 Oxford Ave, 1914-26
1909 74 Tankard, grapes

75 Plate, fruit
76 Plate
77 Bouillon cup & saucer
1911 341 Small punchbowl $18
342 Tea strainer $6
1912 466 Candlestick $4
467 Satsuma vase $12
468 Satsuma teapot
469 Stud box
1914 522 Stein $20
523 Fruit compote enamel $12
524 Vase $8
1922 384 Satsuma vase, enamels $35
385 Teapot & stand, enamels $15
386 Sugar bowl, cream set flat enamel $18
1923 283 Satsuma lamp enamels $50
1924 374 Satsuma bowl enamels
375 French coffee pot enamels
1925 323 Lemonade pitcher $18
324 Jug $8
325 Satsuma lamp base vase $45
326 Chocolate pot
1926 173 Satsuma bowl $75
174 Luster bowl $50
175 Vase, dancing girl $75

PERRY, FRANK
15 Jan 1923, Vancouver CWW84 M WWA84
addr: Vancouver, 4671 Slocan St, 1958. London, Eng, c/o J.C. Cain, 63 Park Rd, Chicwick, 1959. North Vancouver, 1967
1958 87 Bird form bronze $150. Ladies Comm prize
1959 58 Bird form metal $125
1967 52 Untitled treated copper 7 1/2h (Douglas Gallery, Vancouver)

PERRY, LEILA H.
addr: Westmount, 89 Arlington Ave
1913 494 Jardiniere
495 Cake plate
496 Radish dish

PERRY-HAMILTON, RUTH
addr; Montreal, 4915 Côte Ste Catherine Rd
1950 85 Nandi Warrier pastel

PETEL, PIERRE
21 Apr 1920, Montreal M
addr: Montreal, 6526 de Lorimier Ave, 1940-1. Hull, Que, 74 Jeanne d'Arc St, 1948-50. Montreal, 4071 Decarie Blvd, 1951
1940 239 Cimetière d'hiver $25
1941 162 L'adolescente au coussin d'or $100
1948 43 Le pinacle de Baldwin Mills $70
1949 82 Baigneur aux Iles Mingan, Que
1950 34 Excursion dans les Isles Mingan $250. Jessie Dow prize
1951 36 Chasse au loup-marin, Isles Mingan $250

PETERS, KENNETH M.
3 Aug 1939, Regina M
addr: Regina: 525 Pasqua St, 1963; 2740 Retallack St, 1964; 2206 Cornwall St, Apt 11, 1965; Regina, 1968
1963 52 Silence $400
1964 60 A yellow sun $600
1965 14 Ring around the rosy $450
1968 220 Please, sweet Adeline, do not sing again acry emulsion 79 x 100 $970
221 Molly Brown is ahead acry emulsion 79 x 100 $970

PETERS, L. J.
no addr
1912 423 Box with modelled panels
424 Gerfalcon, study in metal colours
425 Humming bird and nest

PETERS, LLOYD A.
b c 1912 M
addr: Toronto: 2096 Danforth Ave, 1939; 40 Westlake Ave, 1941
1939 dry point 1939-41
429 Hay for sale $18
430 Apple pickers $18
431 Barn's broad open door $18
432 Life passed by $18
1941 252 Time out $8
253 February snow $8
254 Winter haven $8
255 Life o' Rieley $8

PETERSON, MARGARET S. (m Howard O'Hagan)
3 Jun 1902, Seattle, Wash M WWA66
addr: St Lambert, Que, 139 Edison Ave
1934 263 Apple cider $15

PETRIK, NATHALIE (Petrik-Pervushina)
b Paris

addr: Montreal, 3240 Sherbrooke St E
1950 130 Le juge $250

PETTIE, JOHN Eng
17 Mar 1839, Edinburgh 30 Feb 1893, Hastings, Eng B DBA DVP G TB
1883 108 Halbert Clendinning's vision of the White Lady, Scott's Monastery

PFEIFER, BODO
15 May 1936, Dusseldorf, Germ M WWA78
addr: Vancouver
1968 222 Untitled No 80 mm 80 x 47 $800
223 Untitled No 81 mm 80 x 72 $1,000 (MBAM)

PFEIFFER, GORDON EDWARD
10 Oct 1899, Quebec 25 May 1983 Rosemère, Que CNS36 M
addr: Quebec: 208 Bougainville Ave, 1928-32; c/o 4 McMahon St, 1933-42; 55 Casot Ave, 1943. Westmount, 693 Victoria Ave, 1945-7. Montreal: 4064 Wilson Ave, 1950-1; 3330 Ridgewood Ave, 1952-4
1928 154 Ice floe at Quebec $150
1930 166 Château Richelieu, Quebec $100
1931 204 Dimanche matin $50
1932 241 Le four abandonné $300
242 Basilica, Quebec $250
243 November ploughing, Laval $250
244 Hôtel Dieu Chapel
1933 246 Pumpkin season $50
1934 264 Cape Trinity $350
265 Grand Lac Jacques Cartier $175
1935 259 October wind, upper Saguenay $200
1936 347 Sillery Hill $150
348 April, Lac Beauport $90
1937 236 A virgin island $150
1939 261 The cabbage patch $100
262 The mill, Les Eboulements $100
1940 240 The lime kiln $300
1942 131 Barley harvest $600
132 Moonlight ballet $250
1943 159 Winter road to St Urbain $100
1945 181 House on a hilltop $200
1946 189 Little Champlain Street $175
190 Old grist mill $175
1947 217 Hauling shore grass, Island of Orleans
1950 35 Red, white and blue $300
1951 37 Looking north, Island of Orleans $250
1952 39 Jay Peak from Masonville $300
1954 66 Summer, Baie des Chaleurs $300

PFEIFFER, HAROLD SAMSON
4 Apr 1908, Quebec IO M
addr: Quebec: c/o 4 McMahon St, 1933-40; 1 Ste Geneviève Ave, 1941. Montreal, 1441 Drummond St, 1942. Toronto: 40 College St, 1944; 25 Severn St, 1945. Westmount, 693 Victoria Ave, 1946. Ste Anne de Bellvue, Que, Macdonald College, 1947. Montreal, 4064 Wilson Ave, 1950. St Johns, Que, RCAF School of English, 1952. Sillery, Que, 1750 Sheppard Ave, 1955. Ottawa, 167 Waverley St, 1964
1933 526 T.M. Forsyth, Esq, American Vice-Consul, Quebec plaster
1940 415 Jacqueline, daughter of Mr & Mrs C.V. Darveau sculp
1941 289 Arthur LeBlanc, violinist plaster
1942 241 Peter and Pamela, war guests plaster $100
1944 165 Ross Pratt, pianist plaster $150
166 Hon Charlach Mackintosh plaster
167 War worker plaster $250
1945 282 Mrs Lees Playfair Reazin of Limberlost tinted plaster
1946 291 Taiwa Solarin, RAF. Lagos, Nigeria plaster $200
1947 342 Judy plaster $300
1950 93 Lt Col Patrick Baird plaster, bronze $800
1952 82 Young David plaster $100
1955 152 Elia, Cape Dorset, Baffinland Eskimo art stone $100 bronze $200
1964 131 Youth bronze $300

PFLUG, CHRISTIANE SYBILLE SCHUTT (m Michael Pflug)
20 Jun 1936, Berlin 4 Apr 1972, Hanlan's Point, Toronto Island M
addr: Toronto, Isaacs Gallery, 832 Yonge St
1965 15 At the kitchen door

PFLUG, MICHAEL
27 Jun 1929, Kassel, Germ M
addr: Toronto: Gallery Moos, 169 Avenue Rd, 1962; Gallery Moos, 138

Yorkville St, 1963
1962 30 Divertissement du matin $180
31 Terre rocheuse $180
1963 53 Winter landscape $250

PHELAN, I. L.
addr: Montreal, 126 Stanley St
1912 463 Peacock vase
464 Japanese vase
465 Cracker jar

PHELPS, HELEN WATSON Amer
1859, Attleboro, Mass 6 Feb 1944, New York TB1/3 WWA40/47
addr: New York, 58 W 57th St, 1909-12
1909 288 A young girl $100
1912 311 The dreamer $400
312 The letter $100

PHENIX, LOUIS SERGE
12 Apr 1924, Outremont M
addr: Montreal: 371 ave Edouard Charles, 1949; Montreal, 1967
1949 142 Marionettes wc $15. Jessie Dow prize
143 Aérolithe wc $15
1967 53 Tapis dans l'antre. 1948 encres 16 x 14

PHILLIPS, MARY MARTHA
1856, Montreal d 1937 H Mo12
addr: Montreal: 2274 St Catherine St, 1891, 1894-5; Victoria School of Art, 1892; 2278 St Catherine St, 1897-1901; 138 Metcalfe St, 1903; The Old Sherbrooke, 1909
1891 92 A quiet spot $25
192 The last of the summer wc $16
193 Old windmill, Lachine wc $18
194 Roses wc $10
1892 201 Yellow daisies wc $25
202 A whittler wc $20
203 Virginie $18
1894 218 Early morning, Lac des Sables wc
219 Sketch in the Laurentians wc $10
1895 190 Idleness wc
191 Roses wc $40
192 Spring wc $8
1897 198 Laval court yard, Quebec wc $35
199 Under the cliff, Quebec wc $35
1898 187 An oyster boat wc $10
188 Laprairie houses wc $10
189 White house wc $8
1900 156 The tide creeping in wc $20
1901 166 Through the wood wc $8
167 A cool retrest wc $8
1903 213 Near Port Daniel wc $25
214 A sunny day wc
254 A hay field by the sea pastel $25
1909 289 Winter afternoon wc $25
290 Annisquam wc $20

PHILLIPS, WALTER JOSEPH
25 Oct 1884, Burton-on-Humber, Eng 5 Jul 1963, Victoria AGO B CC1 CE CWW61 EC M NGC PMC TB2 W78 WWA53
addr: Winnipeg: 110 Bannerman Ave, 1916; 32 Bannerman Ave, 1917-22. Ottawa, 135 Rideau Terr, 1926. Winnipeg, 501 River Ave, 1938. Calgary, 1711 12th St W, 1942-8. Banff, Alta, 222 St Julian Rd, 1954
1916 233 Evening on the Red River wc $40
234 Winter night wc $40
235 The river bank wc $30
1917 268 Christmas morning wc $100
269 Spring wc $75
270 A stream in Manitoba wc $75
271 The reader etch $25
272 A derelict, Lake of the Woods etch $15
273 Winnipeg River No 3 etch $10
1918 286 Lake of the Woods, sketch wc $50
287 Young poplars wc $50
288 Whitefish Bay, Lake of the Woods $12
col pr from wd blocks 289-91
289 Rosie wood $7
290 The Golden Horn $10
291 Dying pines $8
1919 253 The island $10
254 Summer afternoon $10
255 The path of gold $10
256 Margaret $5
257 The lake $10
1920 209 Christmas morning wc $100
210 Veil of mist wc $150
211 Crow's Island, Lake of the Woods col pr $17.50
212 The Little Saskatchewan col pr $15
1922 238 Margaret wc $50
239 Marry wc $50
240 Two lakes b&w $30

241 Norman Bay b&w $25
1926 col pr from wd blocks 223-4
223 Flying Island $21.50 unfr $20
224 The field barn $21.50 unfr $20
1938 176 The vapours round the mountain curled col wd cut $25
1942 133 Mount Rundle, Banff wc $250
134 Herbert Lake wc $175
1947 218 Columbia Ice Fields wc $250
219 Sulphur Mountain wc $180
220 Johnson's Canyon wc $210
1948 86 Mount Rundle wc $175 (NGC)
1954 113 Lake Minnewanka wc $250

PICARD, FRANCOISE
17 Apr 1923, West Sheffield, Que M NGC TB3
addr: Granby, Que: 74 Main St, 1947; 74 Principale St, 1949
1947 221 Nature morte $70
222 Route No 1, Grandby gouache $45
1949 144 Les marronniers, Paris, 1948 gouache $40
145 La Seine, Paris. 1948 gouache $45

PICHE, ALPHONSE
18 Jan 1874 - 10 Nov 1938, Montreal CWW38
addr: Montreal, 33 Belmont St
1928 267 Loyola College
268 Montreal West Presbyterian Church
269 College Jean de Brébeuf

PICHE, FRANCIS (Françoise Godin. m Paul Emile Piché)
addr: Outremont, 700 de l'Epée Ave, 1961. Montreal, 5907 Hutchison St, 1963
1961 96 Tree forms nm $35
1963 54 Quest $255

PICHER, CLAUDE
30 May 1927, Quebec AGO CC2 M NGC TB3 WWA84
addr: Québec: 893 ave Bougainville, 1956; 580 Grande Allée e, 1960; Québec, 1967
1956 46 L'hiver $200. Jessie Dow prize
1967-54 Le port de Québec en hiver 24 x 54 (M Clermont Pepin, Montréal)
47 Le neige $200
1960 90 The impenetrable forest $450

PICHET, ROLAND (b Pichette)
4 Jul 1936, Verdun, Que M
addr: Outremont, 733B de l'Epée Ave, 1962-4
1962 52 Le chemin de Damas nm $55
1963 87 Printemps noir nm $50
1964 103 Contrepoint nm $40

PIDDINGTON, HELEN M.
addr: Montreal, 456 Mackay St
1911 238 Catalogue

PIERCE, JEAN (m Sydney Pierce)
addr: Westmount, 709 Roslyn Ave, 1938-40
1938 90 Flowers
1939 260 Calla lilies $100
1940 241 Cyclamen $35

PIERCE, JOHN GREENE
addr: Westmount, 1 Albert Pl
1932 423 Marshall Joffre pen & ink $10
424 On the Spanish Main pen & ink $12.50

PIGOTT, MARJORIE
6 Jan 1904, Yokohama CWW84 IO M WWA84
addr: Toronto, 300 Claire Ave W
1964 104 Ballet of the birches nm $200

PIKE, PATRICIA C.
addr: Montreal, 4065 Côte des Neiges Rd
1943 160 Barns at St Sauveur wc $25

PILOT, ROBERT WAKEHAM
9 Oct 1898, St John's, Nfld 17 Dec 1967, Montreal CC1 CE CNS36 CWW64 EC M NGC TB2 W78 WWA53 WWB54 Juror
addr: Montreal: 3 Beaver Hall Sq, 1914-17; 2540 Park Ave, 1919-20; 2540A Park Ave, 1921; 67 St Famille St, 1923-5, 1927; c/o Watson Art Gallery, 679 St Catherine St W, 1926, 1928; 3531 St Famille St, 1930-8; 2049 McGill College Ave, 1946-7; 1519 Pine Ave, 1948, 1950-4; 3416 Peel St, 1949, 1952; Montreal, 1967
1914 327 Winter sunset $15
328 Winter sketch $15
1915 273 Sunset $25
274 Winter $15
275 Autumn day $100
276 Old mill $100
1916 237 The bridge, winter $20

238 Winter morning $20
239 St Patrick's Church, evening $150
1917 274 Near Netley Camp, Surrey, England, sketch wc
275-7 Sketch wc
1919 258 Shell burst wc $75
259 Prisoners of war wc $75
260 Impressions of a strafe at night wc $50
261 Cemetry near Cambrai wc $30
262 Trenches at night wc $30
263 Grain elevators $100
1920 203 From the Ramparts, Quebec $350
204 Quebec, from Lévis $350
205 The red house, sunglow $100
206 Old lower town, Quebec $100
1921 207 Evening $150
1923 169 Fishing port, Brittany $300
170 Le Pont du Change, Paris $350
171 View at Larriec wc $60
172 Pont Aven wc $60
173 View of Chartres wc $40
174 Brittany wc $60
175 Residence of the late Andrew Robertson b&w
1924 203 Breton funeral $1,000
294 House, Quimperle etch $25
1925 217 Snow carts $110
218 The sun glow $175
371 Richelieu Church, and dam etch $20 (UG)
1926 98 Schooner in winter quarters, Quebec $150
99 Snowshoe parade st Lévis $350
225 View from Lévis etch
225A Quebec from Lévis etch
1927 143 Sunset, Peggy's Cove, N.S. pastel $250
1928 155 Indian summer, Lunenburg, N.S. $200
156 Winter sunset, Nova Scotia $200
157 Moorish walls, Tetuan $200
158 Drying sails, Lunenburg $200
1930 167 Autumn afternoon, Quebec $700
168 The Seminary, Lévis, Que pastel $150
294 Bonsecours Market etch $25
1932 245 Indian summer, Quebec $600 (listed 1967, Jessie Dow prize)
246 View of Percé, Que $400
247 Melting snow, Grand Manan, N.B. $400
1933 247 St Patrick's Church, Montreal $250
248 The ice breaker, Quebec $200
1934 266 House at Chambly, Que $400 (listed 1967, Jessie Dow prize)
267 Midwinter, Beaupré, Que $500
268 Church at Sault-aux-Recollets, Que $250
1935 260 Low tide, Château Richer, Que $400
261 March thaw, Beaupré, Que $400
1936 349 Mont Tremblant from Grey Rocks Inn $500
350 Winter stream, St Jovite $250
351 Champagne Hill, St Jovite $250
1937 237 Low tide, Murray Bay, Que $275
1938 91 October plowing, St Agnes, Que (Quebec Museum)
1946 191 Autumn, St Sauveur $500
192 Tumbling waters, Quebec $300
193 Laurentian lake, October $300
1947 223 Falling snow, Piedmont, Que
224 Spring break-up, Piedmont $600
1948 44 The Saguenay, autumn $1,000
1949 83 The Lévis ferry, Quebec $900
1950 36 Cape Diamond, Quebec $900
37 Still life, flowers $200
1951 38 Twilight, Dufferin Terrace
1952 40 Winter, Dufferin Terrace, Quebec $800
41 Schooner in the ice, Baie St Paul $600
1954 67 Old Quebec, winter $600
1967 55 The blue house, Chambly. 1934 24 x 32 (MBAM, 1940)

PINE, JOHN MICHAEL
1928, Wolverhampton, Eng M
addr: Ottawa, 325 Besserer St
1958 88 Construction wire $150

PINHEY, JOHN CHARLES
24 Aug 1860, Ottawa 7 Sep 1912, Montreal CWW10 EC H M Mo12 NGC TB3 W78
addr: Montreal, 174 Mance St, 1891-2. Hudson, Que, 1894-1907. Hudson Heights, 1908-10
1885 36 Portrait
1889 56 The lost children $98
57 The village belle $60
58 In the Midi, road to the Mountain of the Winds $200
59 A spring morning in the Forest of Fontainebleau $30

60 A silk weaver in the Midi $17
61-3 Portrait
64 Afternoon tea in a studio $275
1891 93 A Christian martyr $200
94 A trysting place $50
95 A farewell $50
96 The fisherman's daughter $50
97 Fancy head $25
1892 107 The sister arts $250
108 Christ in the wilderness $75
109 Faith $15
1894 115 The picture book $200
116 A sunset $20
117 Iris $15
118 Felicia $30
119 Wild flowers $30
120 An old barge $10
1895 98 A man mowing hay $225
99 Clio $65
100 Vivian $25
101 Stella $25
1897 105 La Penserosa $500
1898 92 With driftwood beached in past spring tides, we light our sullen fires $125
1900 85 Gilliatt, from 'Toilers of the sea' by Victor Hugo $225
1901 77 A father in Israel $125
168 A sunset, Lake of Two Mountains wc $23
169 Evening, Lake of Two Mountains wc $23
170 A summer's day, Mount Victoria wc $23
171 A symphony in grey wc $15
1903 95 Olivia $75
96 A Roman maiden $75
1906 135 The prodigal's return $150
136 Oaks in September $150
1908 114 A woodland glade $100
115 Old mill $50
116 An old sluice gate $75
117 An old bridge $65
1909 291 Melody $150
292 Storm and sunshine $125
293 An old bridge $125
294 Landscape, early summer $115
1910 284 The old mill dam $125
285 The haunted mill $125
286 Pine trees $125
287 An upland $125
1895-7 Assoc Hon men 1892, figure

PINKERTON, CONSTANCE C.
addr: Montreal: 55 Trafalgar Ave, 1911; 10 Phillips Pl, 1912-17; 251 Hampton Ave, 1918
1911 239 Landscape and sheep $100
240 After sunset $40
241 Sketch in New Glasgow $25
242 Sketch in Brome County $10
1912 313 Village road, Beaupré $100
314 Winter sketch, Beaupré $30
315 Winter evening $35
316 Autumn pasture $35
317 October sketch $30
318 Small sketches 6, $10 each
1913 320 Landscape, Berthier $100
321-3 Sketch, Berthier $15 each
1914 329 Morning breeze $40
330 Landscape, Knowlton $40
331 Afternoon $30
1917 278 October $30
279 On the Côte St Luke Road $25
1918 292 One frame small pictures $15 each
293 Under the willows $30
294 The hayfield $25

PINKERTON, E. M. (Miss)
addr: Montreal, 55 Trafalgar Ave
1911 243 Landscape wc $13
244 Masts of gold wc $13

PINKERTON, HARRIET JANE TAYLOR (m Robert Pinkerton)
1852, Toronto d 1936 H
addr: Montreal: Côte St Antoine, 1892. 55 Trafalgar Ave, 1912-13; 34 St Matthew St, 1914; Notre Dame de Grace, 1915; 251 Hampton Ave, 1917-19; 407 Northcliffe Ave, 1920-4
1892 110 Chrysanthemums
1912 319 Cape Tourment $20
320 Road to St Joachim $12
321 Sketch below Quebec $12
322 View on Grand River $12
1913 324 Beaupré $18
325 Rivière des Prairies $18
326 Sketch on Back River $12
1914 332 The close of day $18
333 The edge of the field $15
334 The trout stream wc $13
335 The storm cloud wc $13
1915 277 At Morin Heights $12
278 Notre Dame de Grace $12
1917 280 Coming storm, Dart's Lane $15
281 Coogin's Rocks, Old Orchard $15

282 Mount Royal from Notre Dame de Grace $14
283 Still life study wc $25
1918 295 The picnic $15
296 Still life wc $15
297 At Old Orchard wc $12
1919 264 Path through the woods $20
265 Autumn $18
1920 207 Prouts Neck, Old Orchard $22
208 Monklands $22
1921 206 Notre Dame de Grace, sketch $20
1922 242 Summer $25
243 The old farm $18
1923 176 Old quarry, Westmount wc
1924 204 Morin Heights, sketch $25
205 The edge of the wood $25

PINNEO, GEORGIANA PAIGE
26 Mar 1896, Waterville, N.S. M
addr; Montreal: 3610 Lorne Cr, 1939; 1442 Sherbrooke St W, 1941-6
1939 263 Cape Breton, sketch $25
1941 163 Still life wc $35
164 Grey day, Rockport wc $35
1942 135 End of the road wc $45
1943 161 Old homestead wc $50
162 Memphremagog barns wc $40
163 Wood interior wc $50
1944 108 Falls, Bic River, Bic, Que wc $50
1946 194 Amaryllis in window wc $50

PINSKY, ALFRED
31 Mar 1921, Montreal M WWA82
addr: Montreal: 3816 St Lawrence Blvd, 1941; 433 St Joseph Blvd W, 1945; 3504 Colonial Ave, 1946; 643 Milton St, 1951-5. Westmount, 353 Kensington Ave, 1957. Montreal: 2101 University St, 1960; 3475 Stanley St, 1963
1941 165 Red chair $100
1945 182 Lunchtime $150
1946 195 Strike $125
1951 130 Street scene casein $150
1952 138 Newstand litho $20
1953 99 Storefront casein $75
1954 68 Summit $100
1955 124 Street scene nm $250
1957 77 Underpass $175
1960 91 Landscape $225
1963 55 Painting $450

PINSKY, CLAIRE see HOGENKAMP, CLAIRE

PINSKY, GHITTA see CAISERMAN, GHITTA

PIPON, FLORENCE MACDONALD (Mrs)
addr: Halifax, 2 Oakland Rd,
1931 205 Peggy's Cove, N.S. $150
206 Main Street, Herring Cove $100

PITTS, GORDON MCLEOD
10 Mar 1886 - 1 Mar 1954, Montreal
see Edward & William S. Maxwell, 1925-6; William S. Maxwell, 1927-39

PLANTA, ETHEL ANN CARSON COPELAND (m Clive Planta)
27 Mar 1896, Newcastle, N.B. M
addr: St John's, Nfld, 1 Atlantic Ave, 1952. Hull, Que, 28 Tache Blvd, 1956
1952 42 A man's raincoat $250
1956 48 Croten leaves, British Guiana $200

PLATT, ALETHA HILL Amer
1861, Scarsdale, N.Y. 24 May 1932, White Plains, N.Y. AAA31/32 B F TB
addr: New York, 939 8th Ave
1912 Alethra, mispr
323 Old English workshop $500

PLATTS, ELSIE MAUD
addr: Montreal, 15 Church St
1920 213 Sunlit hills $30
214 At the bend of the road $30

PLAYFAIR, CHARLES GREGORY PAUL
19 Apr 1917, Hagersville, Ont M TB3
addr: Hamilton, 11 McNab St,N, 1947-52
1947 321 The personality drwg $100
1948 45 Dancers resting $250
1952 106 Two-part invention $250

PLETZER, GEORGE ARNOLD
1 May 1907, Orangeville, Ont
addr: Toronto, 2 Failsworth Ave
1934 269 Winter fuel $200

PLIMSOLL, ELLEN J.
addr: Montreal, 464 Guy St
1892 205 Chambly Fort wc $30
206 A bit of Mount Royal wc $25

PLIMSOLL, FANNY GRACE Eng
b London, Eng DBA H

addr: Montreal, 404 Guy St, 1891. Brook Green, S.C, 1892. Montreal, YMCA Bldg, 1894. Paris: 17 rue Hégésippe-Moreau, 1897; 9 rue Washington, 1906. London, Eng: 36 Queen's Rd, 1909; 161 Cromwell Rd, 1912, 1914. Paris, 1913. London, Eng, 17 Earl's Court Sq, 1916
1891 98 Old Nan $55
99 End of day on the St Francis River $40
195 The hawthorne bush wc $25
196 Old sugar house wc $25
197 Mother Katie wc
1892 111 Morning in the buttercup field $75
112 A Piccaniny $75
204 Ready for the quilting bee wc $40
1894 121 En bas Canada, novène pour la pluie $125
122 A studio interior $75
220 The poplars wc
221 On the sands wc $27
1897 106 Alchia, a toiler by the sea $250
1906 137 The milking hour $250
1909 295 Solitude, dunes of Bergen nm
1912 324 Dutch milkmaid $100
325-7 Scene in north Holland $100 each
328 Miniatures on ivory $100
1913 327 La dentellière de Bruges $500
1914 336 Le moment tranquille $375
337 Dutch girl knitting $250
1916 240 Dutch canal and bridge wc $35
241 Woman at spring, Holland wc $35

POGGI, VINCENT
M
addr: Montreal, 4058 Ontario St E, 1941-4
1941 210 Miss Janette
211 Reflection
1944 148 Prisoner of war drwg

POIRIER, NARCISSE
19 Mar 1883, St Felix de Valois, Que
fl 1983 M
addr: Montreal: 1301A Berri St, 1912-13; 1354 Berri St, 1914-20; 1352 St Denis St, 1922-5; 4908 St Denis St, 1927-37
1912 329 Nature morte
1913 328 Nature morte $25
1914 338 Paysage, Isle Ste Helène $100
1915 279 Vieille maison, Varennes $30
1916 242 Etude $10
243 Grand-père
244 Maison blanche $100
1917 284 Nature morte $50
285 Tête d'enfant
1918 298 Nature morte $75
1919 266 Nature morte $40
267 Etude $10
1920 215 Bouquet de fleurs $20
1922 244 Petite grange $75
245-6 Etude à Paris, France, 1921 $30 each
247 Nature morte $20
1923 177 Maison Henri IV, Montmartre, Paris $200
1924 210 Vieille église de Tadousac $150
1925 219 Nature morte $200
1927 144 Maison Mimi Pinson, Montmartre, Paris $250
1928 159 Eglise Notre Dame de Paris $250
160 Etude de fraise $75
161 Nature morte $50
1929 175 Coin de village à Lorette, indienne $150
176 Nature morte $125
1930 169 Nature morte
1931 207 Coin à Montmartre, Paris $400
208 Nature morte $100
1932 248 La temps des sucres $300
1933 149 Ruine canadienne $100
1934 270 Premiers beaux jours $100
1935 262 Coin de ferme $200
263 Nature morte $100
1936 352 Le vieux moulin $250
1937 238 Les sucres dans le nord $300
239 Etude de framboise $50

POITVIN, RACHEL
addr: Montreal, 604 De La Salle Ave
1937 240 Life like $48

POKLEN, JEFFREY ERVIN
24 Jul 1934, Carmel, Cal M
addr: Regina, University of Saskatchewan, School of Art, 1964. Sackville, N.B, 1968
1964 Descent $550 (MBAM)
1968 latex on masonite, 224-5
224 Origin 20 48 x 48 $450
225 Origin 11 48 x 48 $450
226 Mandala 1 tissue paper & latex on masonite 48 x 48 $450

POLLOCK, DAVID RAYMOND
14 Jun 1926, Toronto M
addr: Westmount, 4757 Grosvenor Ave, 1946-50
1946 196 Night club $60
1947 225 My Grandfather oil & temp
322 Old house, Sherbrooke St etch $5
1948 46 Self portrait $60
1950 154 Standing figure charcl $20

POMEROY, MARY A.
addr: Montreal, 14 Tower Ave, 1912-14
1906 280 Future dreams wc $150
358-9 Miniatures 2 cases
1914 339 Morning hour in the forest wc $75
340 Dancing sunshine on the pine trees wc $75
341 The lecture pine, Green Acre wc $100

POPE, MAUD MARY
1867?, Watertown, N.Y. H
addr: Quebec: 1908; 10 de Salaberry St, 1909; 556 St John St, 1911; 552 St John St, 1916
1908 118 Willows by the lake
1909 296 Over the hill $20
297 Gedling Valley, Notts $20
1911 245 A country road wc $10
1914 342 Le chemin d'enfer wc $15
1916 245 Moonlight pastel $35

PORTEOUS, CHARLES E.
fl 1880-96 H
1886 4 Can the story be true? wc
21 Cinderella wc
25 The oleander wc
26 Suspicious wc
32 In the maremma wc
34 In doubt wc

PORTEOUS, E.
addr: Montreal, 826 Dorchester St W
1924 206 Harbour, St Ives, Cornwall, Eng wc $15
207 Fishing boats, St Ives, Cornwall, Eng wc $20
208 Farm, Hove, Eng wc $25
209 Old houses, Hove, Eng wc $10

PORTEOUS, FRANCES ESTHER DUDLEY
10 Sep 1896, Ste Petronille, Que Sep 1946, Montreal M
addr: Montreal: The Maxwelton, Sherbrooke St W, 1916; 1509 Sherbrooke St W, Apt 24, 1936-41. Ste Petronille, Island of Orleans, Que, 1942. Montreal, 1227 Sherbrooke St W, 1943; Ste Petronille, 1944. Montreal, 1509 Sherbrooke St W, Apt 76, 1945
1916 246 From the window
1936 353 A farm house pastel $25
354 White hyacinth pastel $10
355 Flower study pastel $25
1941 256 Bruce in his Sunday suit ink drwg $15
257 A darkie ink drwg $15
1942 136 Village houses, Ste Petronille wc $35
1943 164 High land wc $35
1944 109 Field flower wc $75
1945 183 Unloading ice wc $50

PORTEOUS, HELEN M.
addr: Island of Orleans, Que
1910 288 South shore, from the Island

PORTEOUS, JANET
addr: Westmount, 48 Holton Ave
1940 328 Plan, and elevations, dining-room

PORTEOUS, PIERCEY EVELYN FRANCES (m George Robert Younger)
25 Feb 1907, Montreal M
addr: Montreal, 25 Redpath St, 1925. Ottawa, 450 Wilbrod St, 1945-8
1925 220 Habitant house, Island of Orleans wc
221 Studies on the harbour front, St Ives wc
222 The Sloop Inn, St Ives wc
1945 Younger
248 David
1948 46 Robin

PORTEOUS, R. A.
addr: Town of Mount Royal, Que, 47 Wicksteed Rd, 1934-6
1934 271 Landing the catch wc $50
1936 356 Jack-o-lanterns wc $35

PORTER, MARY see ZWICKER, MARY

POTTER, DULCIE see CRANSTON, DULCIE

POWE, LAWRENCE WILFRED

b Montreal M
addr: St Lambert, Que, 92 Murray Ave, Greenfield Park, 1936-7. Montreal, 544 Ville Marie St, 1947
1936 358 Making port $50
359 Unsettled weather, Châteauguay River $100
1937 242 Time and tide, Maine coast $50
1947 226 The inlet, Prince Edward Island wc $60

POWELL, E. (Miss)
addr: England
1897 200 Boy's head pastel

POWER, EDITH ALICE MORTON (m Joseph William Power)
1854, Brockville, Ont H
addr: Kingston, Ont, 72 Sydenham St, 1905-9
1905 190 Making hay wc $10
1909 298 Gananoque Road wc $20
299 Navy Bay wc $15
300 Woods near Rice Lake wc $15

POWER, FLORENCE
addr: Montreal, 23 Milton St
1892 113 A bit of Chambly
114 Path on the mountain

POWER, GEOFFREY
addr: Waterloo, Ont, 254 Sunview St
1964 105 Sturgeon nm $150

PREFONTAINE, ALFRED
addr: Montreal: 55 St François Xavier St, 1912; 182 St Catherine St E, 1915-17
1912 Prefontaine & Drouin
417-18 Maison pour M C.R. façade, foyer
1915 402-3 Eglise
1916 341-2 Eglise, St Rédempteur, projet perspective, plan
343 Une chapelle, façade
1917 384 Maison à Verchères

PRENDERGAST, MURRAY
addr: Montreal: 7 Hanover St, 1894-5; 997 Dorchester St, 1898
1894 242 Portrait study pastel
1895 102 Chaumière canadienne $125
103 L'approche de l'orage $30
1898 190-2 Portrait

193 Fantaisie wc
194 Petit coin de Venice wc
195 Paysage italien wc

PRENT, MARK GEORGE
23 Dec 1947, Montreal CE CWW84 M WWA84
addr: Montreal
1970 fiberglass & polyester resin 66-7
66 Hit and run 77 1/2 x 36 x 5 illus
68 Untitled 1/5 15 x 10 x 9
68 Rotisserie 1/3 mm kinetic 65 x 20 x 12
69 Untitled 1/5 epoxy & fibreglass 64 1/2 x 13 1/4 x 5 1/2

PREVOT, MARIE
addr: Montreal, 1880 Clarke St, 1916-17
1916 247-8 Sketch $25, np
1917 286 Around the church, Magog, Que $75
287 Le livre d'heures b&w $15
288 Sketch $15

PREZAMENT, JOSEPH
3 Jan 1923, Winnipeg M WWA80
addr: Montreal: 4611 Park Ave, 1950; 5823 Jeanne Mance St, Apt 5, 1952; 2650 Goyer St, Apt 12A, 1956-8
1950 131 Park walk $80
1952 139 First step linocut $15
1956 121 Tavern nm $50
1957 139 Portrait nm $150
1958 72 Birds in the rain nm $35

PREZAMENT, RITA see BRIANSKY, RITA

PRICE, A. VICTOR COVERLY see COVERLY-PRICE, A. VICTOR

PRICE, ARTHUR DONALD
22 May 1918, Edmonton IO M WWA66
Juror
addr: Cyrville, Ont, RR 1, 1954-61
1954 139 Sublime sculp $125
1955 153 Ascension bronze $275
154 Fish bronze $185
1958 89 Birds on sidewalk bronze $300
1960 250 Angel with trumpet bronze $150
1961 119 The masked Venus bronze $1,500

PRICE, LAURA M. (Mrs Dare)
addr: Montreal: 43 St Mark St, 1921; 1419 Drummond St, 1939; 7545 Sher-

brooke St W, 1940; 2054 Victoria St, 1941; 4860 Dornal Ave, 1942
1921 208 Top of the mountain, composition $15
209 Near North Hatley $15
1939 Dare
93-4 Decoration for a modern room $40, $75
95 Majorcan peasants $100
1940 318 Murals, ballroom of A Bronfman, Esq photo
319 Doors in card room photo
320 Entrance doors, ballroom of S. Bronfman, Esq photo
321 Decorative panels, grillroom, Mont Tremblant Lodge photo
1941 50 Old fashioned bedroom temp $20
51 Bedroom decoration temp $25
219 Murals, Saguenay Inn, Arvida, Que photo
1942 38-9 Decorative piece temp $15 each

PRIESTMAN, BERTRAM Eng
1868, Bradford, Eng 19 Mar 1951, Woodbridge, Eng B DBA DVP G RA TB1/2 WWB50
addr: London, Eng
1913 329 A Yorkshire hillside, Upper Wharfedale $450
330 Suffolk floods, August 1912 $300

PRINGLE, ANNIE WHITE GREIVE (James B. Pringle)
6 Mar 1867, Leith, Scot 12 Dec 1945, Smith Falls, Ont CNS36 H M
addr: Montreal: 167 Rozel St, 1919; 16 Sussex Ave, 1925-7; 196 Harvard Ave, 1929. Westmount, 13 Brooke Ave, 1933. Montreal, 2080 Marlowe Ave, 1935-6
1919 268 At the turn of the road $45
1925 223 Head study, Roumanian woman $25
1927 146 A quiet spot $30
1929 177 Fall, Laurentians $25
1933 251 Miss B.R.
1935 264 Head, study $25
1936 360 Autumn tints $100

PRIVETT, MOLLY
19 Dec 1905, Streatham, Eng M
addr: Victoria, Royal Roads, 1956-7
1956 122 In the studio nm $95
1957 140 Near Campbell River nm $125

PROCTOR, FLORENCE EVELYN KEMP (Mrs)
17 Jan 1886, Montreal M
addr: Toronto, 111 Glen Road
1928 162 The Chinese cabinet $300

PRODNUK, FRANK GREGORY (also signs Salmon Harris)
20 Dec 1948, Vancouver
addr: Vancouver
1970 70 Dairy landscape acry polymer on canvas 74 1/2 x 50 1/4
71 Ford script polyester resin, acry oplymer on canvas 71 3/4 x 71 3/4
71 Pigskin preview acry polymer 50 1/2 x 50 1/2

PROULX, JOSEPH ONESIME
b 1890
addr: Montreal: 2721 Bordeaux St, 1917-22; 6645 Bordeaux St, 1926; 6641 Bordeaux St, 1929
O.J, 1917, P.O, 1922, mispr
1917 289 Sketch $5
1919 269-70 Etude $20 each
1921 210 Drawing charcl
1922 248-9 Drawing b&w
1926 100 Tempête de neige $100
101 Effet de soleil $50
226 Portrait de jeune femme drwg
1929 178 The old Ogilvie home on Cremazie Road $175

PROVINCE OF QUEBEC ASSOCIATION OF ARCHITECTS
1909 Improvements of Montreal
439 Fletcher's Field
440 Atwater Avenue
441 Avenue de la Confederation, Lafontaine Park
442 River front
443 Prince Arthur Drive, new park entrance

PULLON, BERTRAM
addr: Montreal, 300 St James St
1910 289 Across Solway Firth from England $50

PURCELL, JOSEPH DOUGLAS
21 Oct 1927, Halifax M
addr: Halifax, 58 Russell St, 1945-8. Montreal: Continental Galleries, 1949; 1450 Drummond St, 1950-2
1945 184 From a needle to an anchor wc $30

1948 47 Mahone Bay, N.S.
1949 84 January day, Herring Cove, N.S. $350
146 Fishing shacks at New Harbour, N.S. wc $200
1950 38 Street in Dartmouth, N.S. $300
73 Winter day, Nova Scotia wc $150
1951 39 Fishing stand, Blue Rocks, N.S. $350
62 Winter port, Nova Scotia wc $150
1951 65 Pasture in spring wc $150

Q

QUEBEC ASSOCIATION OF ARCHITECTS see PROVINCE OF QUEBEC

QUENTIN, RENE EMILE
1860, Paris 1914, Providence, R.I.
H
1889 65 Dr Lachapelle
66 Portrait of the artist
177 Veteran de la Maine crayon
186 Dessin pour illustration

QUINN, HUGH SUMMERVILLE
c 1876 - 25 Aug 1948, Ottawa M
addr: Ottawa: 205 Daly Ave, 1917-18; 116 Osgoode St, 1928
1917 290 A little bit of nature $35
291 Early morning $35
1918 299 Summer, near Ottawa $25
1928 163 Early winter $50
164 In the Gatineau hills wc $35
165 The pool wc $30

R

RACKUS, GEORGE KESTUTIS
1927, Lithuania AGO IO M
addr: Clarkson, Ont, Box 401
1960 92 Le soleil noir $600

RAILLAND, RENE
addr: Montreal, 752A Cartier St
1925 373 Box wd carv

RALTON, RICHARD REGINALD
12 May 1895, Croyden, Surrey, Eng
addr: Brockville, Ont, 1918-20. St Catharines, Ont, 85 St Paul St, 1923
1918 300 A misty morning wc $10
1920 216 The village wc $15
217 The road thro' the meadow wc $25
218 The last gleam wc
219 Winter sunshine wc $15
1923 178 Evening, Lake Penage pastel $7
239 The ice harvest wd cut $7
240 Winter night col pr $5

RAINE, HERBERT
2 Dec 1375, Sunderland, Eng 24 May 1951, Montreal AGO M NGC TB2
addr: Montreal: 1908; New Birks Bldg, Cathcart St & Union Ave, 1913-33; 1321 Sherbrooke St W, 1943-5
1908 249 Santa Maria della Salute wc
250 St Faustin wc
336 J. Raine, house, Bainbridge, Yorks
337 Wayside cottage des
1913 436 W.G.M. Shepers, Esq, house, West Crescent Heights, Westmount
1915 etchings, to 1923
280 The Pazzi Chapel, Santa Croce, Florence $50
281 The Archbishop's Palace, Evreux $25
282 Siena, Italy $20
283 Louviers $20
1916 249 Biddeford Pool, Maine $18
250 From the heights of Phillips Square $20
251 Santa Maria della Salute, Venice $35
252 Bonsecours Market, 1915 $35
1917 292 Interior of St Ouen, Rouen $35
293 Old houses on the hill, Beaupré, Que $20
294 On the road to St Joachim $20
295 Old house near Kamouraska, Que $20
196 The wharf, Kamouraska $20
1918 301 The wayside Cross, St Joachim, Que $26
302 Bank of Montreal, Montreal $27
303 St Paul Street, Montreal $21
304 Old houses, St Vincent St, Montreal $21
305 Place Jacques Cartier, Montreal $21
306 Craig Street, Montreal $26
1919 271 St Vincent St, Montreal $21

272 The pilgrims, St Anne de Beaupré, Que $21
273 From the barn, St Joachim $21
274 A farmyard, St Joachim $26
275 The hillside, Beaupr. $26
1920 220 Château Richer, Que, the church $35
221 On the St Joachim road $25
222 Haycarts on the road to St Joachim, Que $25
223 The little old house, Cap Tourmente, Que $25
1921 215 The Grove, Beaconsfield, Que $30
216 Pigs and a house, St Fercot, Que $25
217 The ferry, Quebec $25
218 The wharf, Les Eboulements $25
1922 250 Château de Ramezay, Montreal b&w $30
251 Schooners, Quebec b&w $25
252 A farmhouse, St Joachim $30
253 The Ramparts, Quebec $30
1923 241 Lobster pots, Gloucester, Mass $30
242 Rockport, Mass $40
drawing, to 1925
243 Boats, Gloucester, Mass $35
244 Sheds, Gloucester, Mass $35
1924 295 Albi Cathedral $100
296 Faded palaces, Albi $100
297 Old bridge, Albu $60
298 Market place, Carcassonne $50
1925 374 Commissioners Street, looking west, Montreal $29
375 Old bridge, Carcassonne, France $29
376 Notre Dame, Montreal, front $34
377 Notre Dame, Montreal, from the rear $34
1926 etching, to 1931
227 Notre Dame, Lamballe, Brittany $30
228 Auray, Brittany $23
229 Dol, Brittany $23
230 Tréguier, Brittany $18
1929 335 A farmyard at St Joachim $20
336 An old wharf near Quebec $20
337 Dol, Brittany $30
338 Corner of West Street and Stepcote Hill, Exeter $30
1931 398 Corner of Hébert and Ste Famille Streets, Quebec $25
399 Notre Dames des Victoires, Quebec $35
400 The Basilica, Quebec $40
401 The church at Heule, Belgium dry pt $40
1933 252 Boule Rocks, Metis Beach wc $100
253 A blue sea, Metis, Que wc $100
254 Metis Beach with Boule Rocks in distance wc $100
255 Metis Beach with lighthouse wc $100
1943 165 North Hatley, Que wc $75
166 Nicolet, Que wc $60
237 The Piggery, Gloucester etch $25
238 Street scene, Albi, France etch $25
1945 265 St Anne Mountain, Que ink drwg $75
266 Cathedral Mountain, Rockies ink drwg $75

RAJOTTE, YVES
11 Aug 1932, Montreal M
addr: Montreal: 8330 Ontario St E, 1960; Montreal, 1968
1960 93 Poursuite $150
1968 acry sur toile
227 Sans titre No 9 32 x 32 $175
228 Sans titre No 10 34 x 34 $190
229 Sans titre No 15 34 x 34 $190
230 Sans titre No 17 32 x 32 $175

RAKINE, MARTHE DE (m Boris de Rakine)
20 Nov c 1906, Moscow AGO B CC2 M NGC TB2
addr: Toronto, 30 Prince Arthur Ave
1954 69 The yellow blouse $450
70 The vase and the chair $450

RAMAUT, LOUIS
23 Nov 1917, Ottawa
addr: Montreal, 62A Jean Talon St E,
1951 40 Victoria Pier $150

RAND, PAUL (b Otto Schellenberger)
27 Nov 1896, Bonn, Germ 27 Jan 1970, Vancouver
addr: Vancouver, 3820 Cambie St, 1947-52
1947 227 Driftwood $150
1952 43 Timberman $650

RANEY, SUZANNE BRYANT (Mrs)
7 Oct 1918, London, Eng WWA66
addr: Dunnville, Ont, RR 7

1955 125 Laikos penicillium nm $12

RAPHAEL, WILLIAM
1833, Prussia 15 Mar 1914, Montreal
CE EC H Mo98/12 NGC W78
addr: Montreal: 1880; 2204 St Catherine St, 1891-1901
1880 9 Indian encampment, lower St Lawrence (NGC)
15 Point au Pic, Murray Bay
20 Morning at Murray Bay
43 Tandem, Montreal
1881 37 In maiden meditation
39 Woodcock and snipe
41 A rise in molasses
43 Plover and teal
44 Natures own beauties
1883 132 A sketch from nature
1885 26 The path through the woods
64 A sketch from life
76 Potatoes in bloom
1888 25 L'enfant du sol $40
33 Autumn $40
50 In the Adirondacks $40
1889 67 Woodland scene $40
68 Homeward bound $60
1891 100 Ruins, St Hilaire $250
101 The mill $75
102 Two friends $100
103 The village pet $100
1892 115 Harvest time $100
116 Mill dam $60
117 The oat field $60
1895 104 A peep through the woods $60
105 In for a swim on Lake St Louis $50
1900 86 Yorkshire terrier $50
87 A smoke before starting $40
1901 78 The creek, Dorval $40
79 The pond $50

RATHE, THOMAS IGNACE
addr: Montreal: 4078 Northcliffe Ave, 1958-62
1958 38 Quartette $100
1962 68 Northern lights, Tadoussac nm $200

RATTRAY, DAWN AMELIA McCRACKEN
10 Jun 1935, Fredericton, N.B.
addr: Montreal: 406 Pine Ave, Apt 53, 1959; 456 Pine Ave, Apt 33, 1960
1959 15 Summer morning $100
1960 94 Paris hotel room $100
95 Wintry day $200

RATZKA, ARTHUR LUDWIG Amer
24 Sep 1869, Andrejowa, Hungary
B TB WWA59/62
addr: New York, 140 W 69th St
1933 256 Hon Dr Charles Winter pastel
257 Self portrait

RAVENSHAW, EDITH see PATTERSON, EDITH

RAWSON, MAURICE
addr: Montreal, 299 Sanguinet St, 1921-2
1921 219 Sketch b&w
1922 254 Head of a faun b&w $45

RAY, JESSIE F.
addr: Westmount, 495 Lansdowne Ave, 1915-16
1915 456 Box $350
1916 384 Sandwich tray
385 Tea pot stand
386 Hair receiver

RAYCROFT, JESSIE (Mrs)
1886 98 Solitude

RAYMOND, JEAN (Mrs) see RAYMOND, SUZANNE

RAYMOND, MAURICE
23 Jul 1912, Montreal NGC WWA62
addr: Montreal, 410 Beaubien St E
1943 167 Jeune femme reveuse $100
168 La chaise jaune $90

RAYMOND, MEDARD
addr: Montreal: 2219 Beaudry St, 1935; 3536 Dorion St, 1936
1935 265 Negro pastel $75
1936 361 Late October $75

RAYMOND, SUZANNE MORIN (m Jean Raymond)
addr: Montreal, 4959 Victoria Ave, 1939-41
1939 Mrs Jean
264 La croix de l'école $30
1940 242 Vieille maison, Verchêres $40
1941 166 Madame D.

RAYNER, GORDON
14 June 1935, Toronto AGO CC1 CE IO WWA84
addr: Toronto, 9 Beaumont Rd

1960 96 Still life with sculpture $300

RAYNSFORD, LOUIE K. (Mrs)
addr: Westmount: 35 Barat Rd. 1934-5; 65 Springfield Ave, 1939-40
1934 miniatures
273 C.G. Heward, Esq
274 Jas. G. Knap, Esq
1935 266 Mme Arthur Surveyer
267 Helen
268 James Eliot Scott
269 R.P.R. Jr
1939 265 Ian
266 Joan
1940 243 Heather Doig
244 Mrs Henry Newell Bate, Ottawa

REA, KENNETH GUSCOTTE
24 Jun 1878 - 6 Nov 1941, Montreal
CWW36 WWC21
addr: Montreal: 1908; 3 Beaver Hall Sq, 1909; 54A Beaver Hall Hill, 1910-13; 285 Beaver Hall Hill, 1921; 1111 Beaver Hall Hill, 1928-30; 1429 Chomedy St, 1933; 1529 McGregor St, 1936
1908 338 Residence, Westmount, Duncan McEachran, Ormstown
1909 444 Royal Bank, Montreal Annex
1910 404 Royal Bank, Lethbridge
405 Cottage, Mrs Yuile, Little Metis
406 Houses, Mr J.E. Hanna, and Mrs Spencer, Westmount
1913 437 Uptown residence
438 Lewis Building
439 Royal Bank, Edmonton
440 Guarantee Company Building
1921 312 Lennoxville doorways
313 Bank of Montreal, branch des
314 Merchant's Bank, St James St, proposed building
1928 270-2 Bank of Montreal, Notre Dame de Grace, Halifax, Hamilton
273 Montreal Badminton and Squash Club
1930 233 Bank of Montreal, Hamilton
234 Residence, A.B. Purvis Esq, St Margaret
1933 410 Bank of Montreal, Calgary
1936 494 Canadian Legation, Tokyo, Japan photo

READ, GEORGIA B. (m George Barton)
b Summerside, P.E.I. WWA84
addr: Sackville, N.B, Mt Allison Ladies College, 1927. Borden, P.E.I, 1929
1927 147 Still life $35
1929 339 The residence block pr $15

RECKNAGEL, JOHN H.
addr: Brooklyn, N.Y, 83 Monroe St
1891 198 Sketch wc $35

REDFERN, BARBARA
addr: Montreal, 768 Sherbrooke St W
1955 64 Soft tones $100

REDINGER, WALTER FRED
6 Jan 1940, Wallacetown, Ont B WWA84
addr: West Lorne, Ont
1968 fiberglass & epoxy
231 Spermatogenesis No 1 36 x 132 x 36 $350
231 Spermatogenesis No 2 36 x 126 x 36 $350

REDSELL, PAULINE HAZEL DAISY (m William Fediow)
13 Jan 1908 - 10 Mar 1980, Toronto
addr: Toronto: 481 Shaw St, 1934; 32 St Joseph St, 1936
1934 275 La magasin de Monsieur Beaudoin $20
276 Snow $20
1936 562 A Cumberland mountainside wash drwg $40

REED, TORQUIL ARNOLD SARGENT
31 Oct 1920, Quebec
addr: Montreal, 1944 Dorchester St W, 1945-7
1945 185 Street scene, St James Street wc $50
1946 197 Unloading in Montreal harbour $125
198 Street scene, Quebec City $75
199 Fishing village, Newfoundland $125
1947 228 Pouche Cove, Newfoundland $150

REHN, FRANK KNOX MORTON Amer
12 Apr 1848, Philadelphia 6 Jul 1914, Magnolia, Mass B H TB WWW
1883 91 Fishing boats, Cape Elizabeth, Me
1889 69 A lowery day $250
160 Evening wc $200

REICHERT, DONALD KARL

11 Jan 1932, Libau, Man AGO CWW84 WWA84
addr: Winnipeg
1968 233 Daria enamels, fluorescent paint 28 x 22 $175
234 Moria lacq 28 x 22 $175
235 Passage I acry 60 x 70 $750
236 Passage II acry 60 x 70 $750

REID, ALISON
addr: Town of Mount Royal, Que, 102 Vivian Ave
1940 329 Interior, English period des
330 Interior, Louis XVI period des

REID, GEORGE AGNEW
25 Jul 1860, n Wingham, Ont 23 Aug 1947, Toronto AGO B CC1 CE CWW36 EC H Mo98/12 NGC PM TB1/2 W78 WWA47
addr: Toronto: Yonge Street Arcade, 1891-1900; 435 Indian Rd, 1901-6; Toronto, 1908; Wychwood Park, 1909-15
1888 1 Gossip $500 (AGO)
42 At sunset $35
56 November $40
59 Study of a head $50
1889 70 Logging $400
71 A cabbage patch $60
72 A brigand $75
73 Study of a head $50
74 The lake, Montsouris Park $35
75 A corner of a courtyard $30
1891 104 Family prayer $800
105 The crow's homeward flight $200
106 The clover field $100
107 A colloquy $75
108 A pasture $25
109 Spring sunshine $20
1892 118 The foreclosure of the mortgage $3,000
119 The berry pickers $1,000
207 Afterglow wc $100
1894 123 A story
124 Hon Edward Blake
125 Tristesse $75
126 Summer sunshine $40
127 A grey day $30
128 Mist $25
238 Landscape, evening pastel $30
239 Winter pastel $30
240 Autumn sunlight pastel $25
1895 106 Portrait
107 A modern madonna $1,000
108 City and country $300
109 Rest dec panel $200
110 Among the daisies $125
111 In the orchard $100
112 A gray evening $30
193 Landscape wc $25
214 Day dreams pastel $50
1897 107 Court of Lions, Alhambra $150
108 Aqueduct of the Alhambra $150
109 Old musician $50
110 Twilight $100
1898 93 The foot bridge
196 Twilight and the new moon pastel $75
1900 88 The cloud $100
89 Nightfall $100
1901 80 Interior of carpenter's shop $40
81 The pines $40
172 Music, study dec panel pastel $50 (AGO)
1903 255 Autumn nm $100
256 Child's head nm $50
1905 97 Spring dec panel $500
1906 138 A study in green $300
139 Spring $1,000
281 Reading pastel $200
1908 119 Glow at twilight $500
120 On the verandah $400
251 Nocturne wc $150
252 Where the cranes feed wc $150
1909 301 Woodland at sunset $50
302 Brown and gold $500
1910 290 The woodcutter $800
291 Summer clouds $150
292 Solitude wc $150
1915 284 A breezy morning $300
285 The coming of the white man pastel $200
1892-7 Assoc extra prize 1891, genre/figure. Medal, Chicago, 1893

REID, ISOBELLE CHESTNUT (Mrs)
27 May 1903, Fredericton, N.B. AGO
addr: Toronto: 82 Montgomery Ave, 1937; 207 Elizabeth St, 1940
1937 267 Houses wc $30
1940 245 Tritoma wc $50
246 Shoppers wc $25

REID, LORNA FYFE
8 Jul 1887, London, Ont NGC TB2
addr: Toronto: Studio Bldg, 25 Severn St, 1917; Toronto, 1918

1917 297 Wayside cottage $50
298 The winding road $50
1918 307 Market day $50

REID, MARY AUGUSTA HIESTER (m George Agnew Reid)
10 Apr 1854, Reading, Pa 4 Oct 1921, Toronto AGO B CC2 EC H Mo12 NGC TB3 W78
addr: Toronto: Yonge Street Arcade, 1891-1900; 435 Indian Rd, 1901-6; Toronto, 1908; Wychwood Park, 1909-15
1888 32 Roses $15
62 The guitar player $55
1889 76 From my window $35
77 In the cloisters $20
78 Roses $15
1891 110 A panel $75
111 A roadside cottage $60
112 Violets and mignonette $50
1892 120 Roses and still life $100
121 Chrysanthemums $35 (NGC)
122 Roses and antique vase $25
123 Carnations $15
124 Still life $75
1894 129 Mermet roses $80
130 First autumn leaves $50
131 Pansies $25
132 Yellow roses
1895 113 In the harvest field $200
114 An idle hour $150
115 Field daisies $35
116 A studio corner $35
1895 117 Pansies $20
1897 111 The gate of the Alhambra $50
112 Towers of the Alhambra $50
113 Roses in jar $40
114 Roses in antique vase $30
1898 94 Roses $100
95 Moonrise in June $10
1900 90 Chrysanthemums $80
91 Full moon, July $40
92 Interior $35
1901 82 Looking east $125 (NGC)
83 A verandah $75
1903 97 Autumn morning $50
98 Roses $75
1905 98 Spring evening $50
99 Autumn $75
1906 140 Afternoon sunlight $100
141 Last traces of snow $75
142 Spring twilight $75
1908 121 A grey day, early spring $125
122 Indian summer $125
123 Interior $50
1909 303 Lowlands $250
304 A misty evening, October $125
305 An arrangement $75
306 Pines at sunset $250
1910 293 Misty evening, October $125
294 Nasturtiums $60
1915 286 Chrysanthemums $15
1894-7 Assoc prize, 1892, still life
port: by Mary Evelyn Wrinch, 1906-360 min

REID, MARY EVELYN see WRINCH, MARY

REILLY, NELSON GERALD
28 Feb 1931, Port Huron, Mich
addr: Toronto, 30 Holborne Ave
1956 123 Cell block 69 nm $150

REINBLATT, MOSES MARTIN (MOE)
20 Jun 1917 - 24 Aug 1979, Montreal
AGO CC1 NGC TB1 WWA53
addr: Montreal: 266 St Joseph Blvd W, 1936-43, and Mont Joli, Que, No 9 B & G School, 1943. Montreal: 5657 Park Ave, Apt 6, 1946-50; 4577 De La Patrie St, 1952-5; 4520 Rosedale Ave, 1957-70
1936 362 Back lane $60
1937 243 Apples and pussywillows $40
1939 268 Jeanne Mance Street $50
1940 247 Windowsill $75
248 Gay day $100
1941 167 Joe
168 Winter day temp $75
1942 137 Mayor Street gouache $65
138 Lilly
1943 169 Still life $150
239 Hangars at night brush drwg $75
240 Daily inspection, night brush drwg $75
1946 200 The market $125
1947 323 The beggar dry pt $15
1948 48 Rearing horses $500
49 Riders $175
1950 132 Still life $125
1952 107 The resevoir $150
1954 71 View of the university $150
1955 65 View of the city $250
1957 78 Flowers on a blue cloth $200
1959 16 Reclining figure $400
1960 97 Winter fields $550

RENAUD, PIERRE
22 May 1928, Montreal
addr: Montreal, 4613 Marcil Ave, 1961-3
1961 46 Nature morte au compotier bleu
1963 56 Vestige Aztèque $300

RENAUD, TOUSSAINT-XENOPHON
fl 1895-1930 H
addr: Montreal, 5564 Esplanade Ave
1928 166 Ferme sur la Rivière Ottawa, prè Grandville $40

REPPEN, JOHN RICHARD
17 Jul 1933 - 2 Jun 1964, Toronto AGO CC2 CE W78
addr: Don Mills, Ont, 1960-2. Toronto, 140 Farnham Ave, 1963-4
1960 98 The beauty contest $270
1961 47 Evolution $360
1962 32 San Miguel at night illus Purchase award (MBAM)
33 Outside Pueblo $425
1963 57 Lush temple $485
1964 62 On ancient grounds $485

REVEL, LAURENT
addr: Montreal, 1062 Park Ave
1909 307 Basse Cour, Savoie $150

REVELL, WILLIAM
1830-1902 H
addr: Toronto: 1880; 618 Ontario St, 1892
1880 126 Pickings wc
1881 58 Foxglove wc
66 Fruit and flowers wc
1892 208 A bit of the old homestead wc $40
209 Crossed, by shades and sunny gleams wc $100

REYNOLDS, EDWIN BARRIE
22 Oct 1880 - 18 Jan 1960, Ottawa
addr: Ottawa, 263 Clemow Ave
1955 66 Wheat harvest, Pelican Lake $65

REYNOLDS, JOHN MCCOMBE
8 May 1916, Toronto
addr: Westmount, 512 Argyle Ave
1950 133 Dovecote $200

REYNOLDS, PHYLLIS
addr: Westmount, 48 Chesterfield Ave, 1918. Montreal, 168 Harvard Ave, 1919
1918 308 Bowl of roses $15
1919 276 Window seat $10

RHEAUME, JEANNE see LEBLANC, JEANNE

RHIND, H. NANCY GREENLEES (m J.M. Rhind)
addr: Montreal, 14 Oldfield Ave, 1937-9
1937 244 Still life $25
1938 92 Peonies $75
93 Zinnias $50
1939 269 Tulips and narcissus $50
270 Zinnias and calendulas $20

RHO, JOSEPH ADOLPHE (or Rheau)
1 Apr 1835, Gentilly, Que 6 Aug 1905, Bécancourt, Que H W78
1886 66 Canadian pilgrims at the River Jordan, 1884

RHODES, CATHERINE L. J.
addr: Quebec, St Louis Rd, 1925-6
1925 224 Still life $75 (MBAM)
1926 102 Still life

RICHARD, JULIE see SZABLOWSKI, JULIE

RICHARD, RENE JEAN
1 Dec 1895, Chaux de Fonds, Switz
31 Mar 1982, Baie St Paul Que WWA53
addr: Montreal, 370 Laurier Ave W, 1948-50
1948 107 Maison de mon maître charcl $70
1949 86 La Bature, Baie St Paul $250
1950 39 Scène de Baie St Paul $200

RICHARDS, CECIL CLARENCE
5 Jan 1907, Rinsey, Eng AGO
addr: Winnipeg, University of Manitoba, School of Art, 1952-5
1952 149 Two women marble $500
1955 155 Woman in the sun marble $300

RICHARDS, FRANCES see ROWLEY, FRANCES

RICHARDS, PHYLLIS see HARVEY, PHYLLIS

RICHARDSON, EFFIE G. (m J.H. Richardson)
addr: Westmount: 49 Bruce Ave, 1921-2; 457 Mt Stephen Ave, 1930-6
1921 220 Ian
1922 255 Charlotte

1930 171 Chinese woman, study
1931 209 Mrs H.
1934 277 Mrs W. Williamson pastel
1936 363 Study $25

RICHARDSON, MARGARET W. (Mrs)
addr: Lennoxville, Que, Bishop's College, 1934-9
1934 278 Peonies
1935 270 Peggy min
271 John, son of Dr J.B. Winder, Lennoxville min
272 Donald and John, sons of Prof Kuehner, Bishop's College min
1936 364 Peonies
365 Anne Elizabeth, daughter of Cecil Teakle, Esq min
366 Margaret Jean, daughter of Prof Home min
367 Baby, eight months old min
1939 271 Boyhood min
272 Catherine Anne min

RICHMOND, AGNES M. (m Winthrop Turney)
b Alton, Ill F WWA62 Amer
addr: New York, 122 E 59th St
1912 330 Under the trees $200
331 Summer pastel $100

RICHMOND, EVELYN
addr: Sydney, N.S, 38 Rigby Rd
1938 273 Still life $30
274 Over the rooftops $20
275 Fog over the Trantbamar marshes $15

RICHMOND, JOHN RUSSELL
25 Oct 1926, Toronto CWW84 IO
addr: Port Credit, Ont, 1370 Holleyrood Ave, 1955-6
1955 126 Fish, fowl and foliage nm $450
1956 49 The Fifth Station $300

RICHMOND, LEONARD
1874, Somerset, Eng d May 1965. B DBA RA TB1/2 WBA WWB29
addr: Ottawa, National Gallery of Canada
1925 225 Early morning, Le Puy, France wc $70
226 River Doubs, Besançon, France wc $70
227 Afternoon, Besançon, France wc $70

RICHSTONE, BELLE C.
addr: Montreal, 2085 Decarie Blvd, 1930. Rawdon, Que, Mount Loyal, 1934-5. Montreal, 5255 Côte St Luc Rd, 1936
1930 172 Peonies $45
1934 279 Flowers
1935 273 White flowers $100
1936 368 Flowers $35

RICKETTS, HARRY E. G.
b 1901
addr: Verdun, Que, 444 Moffat Ave, 1932-5. Town of Mount Royal, Que, 212 Kindersley Rd, 1936-52
1932 water colour
249 A bunch of red roses $65
250 White roses $65
1933 258 Morning sunshine, Ottawa River, Carillon $35
259 A study in scarlet $30
1934 280 Winter landscape, Morin Heights $65
281 Wind-rippled drifts $65
282 End o' day $25
283 Nature's blanket $30
1935 274 Mid-winter brightness, Morin Heights $85
1936 369 Snow road $35
370 Suburban woodyard $85
371 Quietude unexcelled $40
372 Truck farm $85
1937 245 The sun peeps through $85
246 After sundown $85
1938 94 Roadside farm $85
1939 276 Autumn, roadside, sketch $35
1941 169 Canopy $75
170 Coming snow $35
1947 229 Wind patterns $100
1951 63 Lonely road $100
1952 66 Shade trees, Rockport $100

RIDDEL, JAMES Scot
1857, Glasgow 14 Mar 1928 B DBA DVP G RA TB WBA WWB29
addr: Balronie, Balerno, Scot
1927 148 A.F. Riddel, Esq
149 J.B. Trudeau wc

RIDDELL, OLGA M.
addr: Westmount: 379 Olivier Ave, 1901-3; 364 Olivier Ave, 1905
1901 263 Fruit plate set of 6
1903 314 Fancy head, vase $10
315 Child's head, vase $7

316 Forget-me-not, cup & saucer
317 Forget-me-not, cream & sugar $4
318 Jonquil, tray $4
319 Enamel bonbon box $4.50
320 Nut bowl, gold & rose
321 Cup & saucer
322 Plate $4.50
1905 349 Jardiniere and stand, rose $40
350 Plate, underglaze blue $20
351 Salad bowl, nasturtiums $20
352 Bouillon cups, roses and violets $20
353 The awakening plaque $20

RIECKER, ALBERT
addr: Verdun, Que, 4506 Verdun Ave, 1931; Verdun, 1932
1931 210 Jobless $250
1932 251 Dancer $350

RIGG, WILLIAM
3 Apr 1877, Barhead, n Glasgow, Scot 1942 Glasgow
addr: Montreal, 479 Guy St, 1921. Westmount, 221 Clarke Ave, 1932-5
1921 221 North River, near St Margaret, Laurentians $150
222 Norrent Fontes, Vimy front, 3rd Canadian Division $80
223 Woodland scene, near Hermiene, north France $50
224 Evening glow in the woods $50
1932 425 The old Mint House, Edinburgh drwg $75
426 The White Horse Inn, Edinburgh drwg $75
1935 275 Laurentian river wc $100

RIOPELLE, JEAN-PAUL
7 Oct 1923, Montreal AGO B CC1 CE CWW84 L NGC TB2
addr: Montreal: 4089 Delormier Ave, 1944-6; 75 Sherbrooke St W, 1949
1944 110 Paysage wc $30
1945 188 Après-midi, d'hiver, carré St Louis $45
1946 202 Création d'un monde $150
203 Graphomancie léthiférique wc $65
204 Tête wc
1949 87 Propagation de Zarathoustra $200

RIORDON, JOHN ERIC BENSON
5 Dec 1906, St Catharines, Ont 23 Dec 1948, Montreal CNS36 CWW48
addr: Montreal: 4084 Côtes des Neiges Rd, 1931-7; 4801 Grosvenor Ave, 1938-40. Piedmont, Que, 1946. Ste Adèle en Bas, Que, 1947
1931 211 October morning pastel $40
212 Laurentian foothills, winter pastel $35
1932 252 October on Caché Lake pastel $50
253 Shady winter road pastel $40
254 Open water pastel $40
1934 284 Tranquility, Haute Savoie $75
1935 276 Peaceful valley, Switzerland $300
277 On top of the world, Austrian Tyrol $150
434 Portrait du Château d'Ussé pencil $15
1936 373 The still hour of evening $150
374 The joyous song of the sea $150
375 Afternoon sun, Laurentians $100
1937 246A Evening, upper North River $135
247 The Atlantic, west coast, France $175
1938 95 Afternoon sun, near Ste Adèle $75
1939 277 Peace (motif from l'anse à valleau Gaspé) $275
1940 249 The eternal breakers, New England coast $225
1946 205 The far hills $400
206 Running free $275
1947 230 Evening in March $400
231 January afternoon, St Sauveur $300

RIORDON, MARY KATHLEEN (m Gordon R. Forbes)
addr: Montreal: 4084 Côtes des Neiges Rd, 1934-5; 4048 Côtes des Neiges Rd, 1939-40. Rivers, Man, c/o E.E. Grant, 1941. Val d'Or, Que, P O Box 408, 1946
1934 285 Oriental $75
286 Portrait
1935 278 Petite vallée $150
1939 Forbes, 1939-41
134 Hardrock Mine $85

135 McLeod Cockshutt Mine $85
136 Prospector $100
398 Child's head charcl $35
1940 113 Five shaft hoist, Noranda wc $75
355 Shatfman drwg $35
1941 68 Air Force $300
1946 207 Paul Croteau

RIOUX, YOLANDE see ROUSSEAU, YOLANDE

RITCHIE, JAMES EDWARD
5 Dec 1929, Montreal
addr: Montreal, 1651 Sherbrooke St W
1959 61 Madonne bronze $175

RITCHIE, PERCIVAL MOLSON MACKENZIE (Mrs)
7 Jul 1917, Pointe à Pic, Que
addr: Montreal, 3335 Ridgewood Rd
1946 208 The big hill at Porte au Persil $75

RITCHIE, SAMUEL DOUGLAS
20 Jan 1887, Three Rivers, Que 20 Nov 1959, Montreal
addr: Westmount: 357 Greene Ave, 1909; 475 Prince Albert Ave, 1917-18
1909 444 Museum des
1917 385 House, Ste Anne de Bellevue
386 House, Grand'Mère
1918 403 Mr W.B. Baptise house, Three Rivers
404 Westmount house
see also Shorey, Harold Edgar, 1922-1941

RIVARD, HARVEY
20 Aug 1913, Trois Rivières, Que
addr: Trois Rivières, 478 Des Forges St
1954 73 Canard et pigeons

RIXKENS, CARL
28 Jun 1881, Suchteln, Germ TB
addr: Montreal, 5165 Côte St Antoine Rd
1931 213 A study in blue, Fraulein Hildegarde Agethen $1,250

ROACH, GERALD
30 Jul 1933, Windsor, N.S.
addr: Halifax, 31 South St, Apt 5
1960 99 Rock face with snow $180

ROBB, CHARLES see BUSH, CHARLES ROBERT

ROBB, FREDERICK G.
25 Sep 1881 - 22 Apr 1936, Montreal
addr: Montreal, 462 Mackay St
1927 238 Proposed new Engineering Building, McGill University

ROBERGE, AGNES
addr: Montreal, 534 Prince Arthur St
1936 563 Operating scene wd engr $8

ROBERTS, GOODRIDGE see ROBERTS, WILLIAM GOODRIDGE

ROBERTS, GRACE
addr: Montreal, 103 University St
1898 197 Snow balls wc $15

ROBERTS, THOMAS KEITH
22 Dec 1909, Toronto CNS40 CWW84 10 WWA84
addr: Toronto: 663 Oriole Parkway, 1932; 82 Bedford Rd, 1933; 18 Grenville St, 1934-8. Port Credit, Ont, 1312 Stavebank Rd, 1950-61
1932 255 The water lily pool wc $35
256 Georgian Bay sunshine wc $35
427 Early evening col lino cut $10
1933 260 Tree trunks col lino cut $10
1934 287 Waiting for spring wc $50
288 Wheel repairing shop wc $50
467 The back way lino cut $15
1935 279 Mountainside, Baie Fine wc $35
280 Moonlight in the courtyard wc $50
281 Village shops wc $20
282 Afternoon reflections wc $25
1936 376 Winter moon $75
377 Maple sugar shanty, October $40
378 Morning solitude wc $35
564 Dawn, Killarney Mountains col pr $15
1938 98 October mist, Ottawa wc $30
1950 40 Below Streetsville $300
41 March, Mt Nemo $375
1951 41 Winter in the town $400
42 Quebec school children $400
1952 44 Chez Yvan $300
1956 51 November, Cobalt $400
1957 82 Coppermine Point, Lake Superior $450
1960 101 Noon $500

1961 48 Scattered showers, Quebec $650

ROBERTS, WILLIAM GOODRIDGE
24 Sep 1904, Barbados 28 Jan 1974, Montreal AGO B CC2 CE CWW70 NGC TB2 W78 WWA76 WWB56 Juror
addr: Kingston, Ont 123 King St, 1935. Montreal: 1843 Dorchester St W, Apt 8, 1937-39; 1628 Lincoln Ave, 1941; 3520 Shuter St, Apt 1, 1942-7; c/o Dominion Gallery, 1438 Sherbrooke St W, 1948-9, 1952; 1448 St Catherine St W, 1950; 107 Mount Royal Ave W, 1951; 1301 Pine Ave, Apt 7, 1953; 1102 Elgin Ter, Apt 201, 1956. Westmount, 460 Grosvenor Ave, 1957-9. Fredericton, N.B, 7 Hawthorne Ter, 1960. Westmount, 355 Lansdowne Ave, 1962-4. Montreal, 1967
1935 435 Gatineau River wash drwg $15
1937 438 Young woman drwg $25
1938 96 Road in sunlight wc $40
97 Standing nude $150
179 Seated nude drwg $75
1939 278 Seated figure $75
279 Gatineau hills wc (listed 1967, Jessie Dow prize)
1941 171-2 Still life $150 $75
173 Street scene $75
174 Landscape $100
1942 142 Youth $150
143 Laurentian road $100
144 Laurentian lake $150
1945 189-90 Nursery fantasy col drwg $75 each
1947 232 Still life $400 (NGC)
233 Lynched man and mourners $600
1948 51 Lake Orford $400 (NGC)
52 Seated boy $375 (NGC)
87 Clouds over Georgian Bay wc $75 (listed 1967 Jury II prize)
1949 88 Passing clouds $450
89 Still life $450
1950 135 Toward evening $475
145 Young fir trees wc $145
1951 114 The Gouffre River $700
1952 108 Studio in the country $650
1953 35 Trees and path $700
36 Still life $375
1956 50 Gray day, Georgian Bay $750
1957 81 From a back window in winter $700
141 Georgian Bay wc Jessie Dow Prize, 1967-56, 21 x 28 1/2
1958 39 Seated nude $800
1959 17 Still life with easle and daffodils $700
18 Seated nude $750
1960 100 Reclining nude $1,000
1962 34 Dark landscape $800
1964 63 Still life with pears $1,400

ROBERTS, WILLIAM GRIFFITH
25 Jul 1921, Nelson, B.C. AGO NGC TB2 WWA82
addr: Roxdale, Ont, 29 Hardisty Dr, 1955-61
1955 127 Panchia nm $50
1957 142 Store fronts of a small Ontario town nm $85
1958 75 The house that looks out to the sea nm $200
1960 102 Atlantic rocks $300
1961 97 Atlantic rock nm $100

ROBERTSON, AGNES MUIR (Mrs)
addr; Toronto
1919 277 Cap à l'Aigle wc

ROBERTSON, BEATRICE HAGARTY (m Percy Robertson)
17 Dec 1879, Toronto
addr: Toronto, 2 Oaklands Ave,
1936 379 Marsh marigolds $65

ROBERTSON, DORIS
addr: Montreal: 1509 Bishop St, 1933; 3555 University St, 1935-6; 1461 Mountain St, 1938-46
1933 484 Moving in wd cut $3.50
485 Whither lino cut $4
486 Supplication wd cut $4
1935 436 Native carrying fruit wd cut $6
1936 565 Camp Otoreke, Laurentians lino block $7
566 Heavyweight wd cut $6
1938 177 Indian and totem lino cut $7
1946 209 Laurentian window $100

ROBERTSON, HAZEL M.
addr: Montreal, 12 Phillips Pl
1906 314 Marguerite b&w
315 Ada b&w

ROBERTSON, HUGH DOUGLAS
11 Jan 1900, Hamilton, Ont IO
addr: Hamilton, 46 Herkimer St, 1933-40. Ottawa, 226 Augusta St, 1943. Hamilton, 1967

1933 261 Pine tree, Georgian Bay wc $55
1934 289 Dormer window wc
290 Horizon wc $50
291 Solitary bather wc $50
292 Willows wc $50
1937 248 Hill at Fox River, Que wc $40
249 Rough weather, Georgian Bay wc $60
250 Boat time, Go Home Bay, Georgian Bay wc $30
1938 99 Trees in November wc $50
1940 250 Church tower, Nassau wc $100
251 Courtyard, Nassau wc $100
252 Nassau boatman wc $100
1943 171 Threshing wc $70 1967-58, 15 x 20 (Jessie Dow prize) (Mr Lewis W. Lawson, Toronto)
172 Georgian Bay wc $40
173 Oak tree in autumn wc $75

ROBERTSON, MADGE
addr: Montreal, The Grosvenor
1910 295 The quiet pond wc
296 The azalea swamp wc $18
297 A Charleston garden wc $25

ROBERTSON, MARION E.
addr: Montreal: 417 Laurier Ave, 1911; 738 Shuter St, 1915; 284 Mackay St, 1920-4; 1470 Fort St, 1928-39
1911 246 The pergola $15
1915 287 The sleeping beauty b&w $10
288 The companion b&w $10
289 King Lear wc $10
1920 224 The lantern wc $15
225 The rehearsal wc $10
1923 184 Grey Nuns wc $25
1924 211 Tremblay farm wc $25
212 Blocks ink
213 Secrets ink $10
1928 167 Convent pupils wc $25
168 Spring wild flowers wc $20
1929 179 Summer sands wc $10
180 Winter snow wc $15
181 Champ Elysées wc $30
1931 214 Children in Murray Park wc $25
1936 380 Frog and water lily wc $12
381 Autumn berries wc $12
1937 439-40 Illustration drwg $10 each
1938 178 Lilies lino block $12
1939 433 Interior, Vermont lino cut $3
434 West Branch Road lino cut $3
435 Four Winds farm lino cut $3

ROBERTSON, SAMUEL
1868, Montreal 24 Mar 1943 (in the Laurentians, Que)
addr: Montreal: 43 Victoria St, 1895-7; Montreal, 1908; 333 Guy St, 1909
1895 118 A rain cloud $15
119 In the garden $10
120 Country road $10
1897 115 Wheat field $20
116 Winter $20
117 St James Methodist Church, Montreal $70
1908 124 Landscape $20
125 Landscape, St Eustache $20
1909 308 Landscape $25

ROBERTSON, SARAH MARGARET ARMOUR
16 Jun 1891 - 6 Dec 1948, Montreal AGO CCI NGC TB2/3 WWA47
addr: Montreal: 46 Shuter St, 1912; 738 Shuter St, 1913-16; 284 Mackay St, 1919-27; 1470 Fort St, 1928-45
1912 332 Sketch, Birk's Building $15
1913 331 Old fort, Chambly $15
1914 343 Sketch, autumn $20
1915 290 The goode girl $30
291 The retreat $15
292 A winter morning $15
1916 253 Late afternoon, sketch $15
254 Grey day, sketch $15
255 The fair, composition $15
256 Composition $15
1919 278 A winter day $15
279 In the garden $15
280 The celebration $15
281 The little house $15
1920 226 Portrait
227 The fountain, composition $20
1921 225 La vendeuse $75
226 Monday morning $50
227 Hôtel Dieu $20
228 Spring $20
1922 256 Portrait
257 Portrait, sketch
258 On the mountain $20
259 Hôtel Dieu $20
1923 185 Portrait
186 The blue sleigh $20
1924 214 Mont St Anne wc $35
215 Murray Bay village, Que $200
216 Sketch $30
1925 228 Grey Nunnery, sketch $15
229 Sketch $15
230 On the canal wc $15

231 Legatt's Point wc $15
1926 103 Convent from Atwater Avenue, sketch $25
104 Les Soeurs Grises $40
105 Near Little Metis $100
1927 150 Sketch $25
151 Ice cutting, Lake of Two Mountains $150
1928 169 Near Waterloo, Que $250
170 Malbaie $30
171 Hudson, sketch $25
172 Thousand Islands, sketch $25
1929 182 March snow $100
183 The Needle's Eye $50
184 The village road $20
1932 257 McGill College cab stand $100
258 Lake of Two Mountains $75
428-9 Design wc $6 each
1935 283 The white house $100
284 Late September $250
1936 382 Pink tulips $35
383 White tulips $35
1937 251 Afternoon in March $100
1938 100 Lac Manitou, Que $100
101 Petunias, sketch $25
1939 280 Ontario farm in September $200
281 Lilies $50
1940 253 Fort of Suplician Seminary $150 (MBAM)
1941 175 Moss Glen Falls $150
1942 145 Pink tulips $30
146 Fantasia $20
1945 191 Sulpician Seminary in September wc $50
192 Flower decoration wc $50

ROBERTSON, SYBIL OCTAVIA (m Francis Curzon Dobell)
addr: Westmount, 4156 Dorchester St W, 1920-3. Montreal, 1537 St Matthew St, Apt 13, 1945-7
1920 228 Miss Benedicta Caverhill
1921 Robinson, error
229 Mrs Monk
230 Miss Katherine Stewart $100
1922 260 Miss Margareth Williamson $500
261 Miss Dorothy Acer $150
1923 187 Jean
188 Study of my sister $400
1945 Dobell, 1945-7
70 Lilies $75
70A Margot McDougall
1946 72 Mrs Benedicta Innes Ker $350
73 Mrs Robert H. Craig, Jr
1947 67 My daughter Sally
68 Mrs C.E. Ford Jones

ROBIDEAU, RICHARD
addr: Malone, N.Y, 46Morton St
1958 90 Female figure wd $20

ROBINSON, ALBERT HENRY
2 Jan 1881, Hamilton, Ont 7 Oct 1956, Montreal AGO CC1 CWW52 EC Mo12 NGC TB3 W78 WWA59 Juror
addr: Hamilton, 1908. Montreal: 10 Phillips Pl, 1910-12, 1914-15; Johnson Copping, 1913; Main St, Mercier Ward, 1919; 158 Vendome Ave, 1920-24, 1928-30; Watson Art Galleries, 679 St Catherine St W, 1926; 3568 Vendome Ave, 1932-7
1908 126 Sunset $200
127 Ste Agathe des Monts $200
128 Snow scene $60
129 Villa Gisele $200
1909 309 Montreal from St Helen's Isle $200
310 Autumn landscape $50
311 Old house, Paris, Ont $60
312 Evening, Dieppe harbour $50
1910 298 Night effect, Montreal harbour $150
299 Jacques Cartier Market $125
300 The hay barge $75
301 In the locks $75
302 Effect of steam, CPR station $100
1911 247 Sunday afternoon on the Ottawa $150
248 Montreal, from St Helen's Island $100
249 Landing at Carillon $75
250 Street scene $50
251 Evening, Dominion Park $50
252 On the St Lawrence $50
1912 333 The sea, St Malo $300
334 Leaving port, night effect $200
335 Fishing boats $75
336 Night, St Servain $100
337 High tide $50
338 Low tide $50
339 Sunset over Dinard $50
340 Red light and moonlight $50
1913 332 Fishing boats $75
333 Coast scene $50
334 Village street $225

335 Village gossip $150
1914 344 Evening lights $300
345 Sunset on the Thames $200
346 The carter $100
347 A cottage in Carhaix $75
1915 293-4 Winter sunrise $500 each
295-6 Snow scene $300 each
1919 282 Ice bridge, evening $500
283 Winter industry $500
284 Retournant à Boucherville $500
285 The parish church $500
286 Marchand de fruits $250
287 The lodge $40
1920 229 Noontime, Longue Pointe village $500
1921 231-2 Snow scene $250 each
1922 262 Snow patched hills $500
263 The green house $300
264 Corner on the St Lawrence $300
1923 179 Québec $500
180 St Joseph $500
181 Snow storm $500
182 Return from Easter mass $500
1924 217 The open stream $500
218 Sunlit hills $500
219 A church in Westmount $150
1926 105A Bridge below Quebec $300
1928 173 Murray River valley $500
174 Sunny day, La Malbaie $300 (listed 1967, Jessie Dow prize)
175 Boys at play, La Malbaie $300
1929 185 Spring freshet $500
1930 173 St Fidele $500
174 On the way to church $300
1932 259 Down from the Gatineau $300
260 Summer landscape $250
1933 262 Sun-clad hills $500
263 Village in the valley $500
264 The old pink house, Baie St Paul $300
265 Cap Tourmente $200
1934 293 Boats in ice $500
1935 285 Winter, La Malbaie $300
1937 252 Laurentian village
253 A March day, lower St Lawrence
The Albert Henry Robinson Grand Award inaugurated 1963 from funds bequeathed by Mrs Mary E. Davis

ROBINSON, MADELYN D. (or Madalyn)
addr: Westmount 418 Mt Stephen, 1923-4; 4357 Montrose Ave, 1942-7
1923 183 Drawing b&w $15
1924 220 Marigolds wc $20
221 Incoming tide, Bic wc
1942 141 Sketch wc
1947 234 Old houses, Provincetown wc $20

ROBITAILLE, LUDGER
6 Dec 1885 - 19 Nov 1946, Quebec CNS29
addr: Quebec, 22 St Jean St
1929 Rotibaille & Desmeules
282 Appartements La Fontaine, Québec

ROCHELEAU, ALICE
addr: St Pie, Bagot, Que
1914 525 Berry dish $12.50

RODGER, Z. LOUISE
addr: Montreal West, 144 Strathern Ave
1921 338 Fruit bowl

ROGERS, OTTO DONALD
19 Nov 1935, Kerrobert, Sask CC2 CE WWA84
addr: Saskatoon, 438 8th St E, 1961; University of Saskatchewan, 1965
1961 49 Still life $250
1965 43 Everything about to change wld steel $600

ROHUSSAR, RAOUL
b Estonia
addr: Montreal, 6900 Sherbrooke St W
1964 132 Smiling woman hydrastone $150

ROLLIT-GODARD, E (m Harlow Godard)
addr: Montreal, 4327 Wilson Ave
1939 282 Autumn in the Berkshires, Mass $35
283 White birches at Back River, Cartierville $35
284 Chambly, trees $35
285 An old habitant house $15

ROLPH, JOSEPH THOMAS
8 Sep 1831, London, Eng 13 Jun 1916, Toronto H
addr: Toronto, 158 St George St, 1892-1905
1888 70 Bay of Quinte, Adolphus Town wc $30
95 Road through High Park, Toronto wc $35
114 After the shower, Lake of the Mountain wc $20

117 Dusty lane, early spring, near Deer Park, Toronto wc $40
118 Late November new cutting, High Park, Toronto wc $35
1892 210 Old Canadian cottage, Lake Simcoe wc $50
211 The old Baldwin homestead, Spadina Avenue, Toronto wc $50
1894 222 November morning, near Toronto wc $35
223 Fall day, near Deer Park, Toronto wc $35
1897 201 Beddington, Kent, England wc $50
202 River Wandle, Wadden, Kent, England wc $50
1905 191 Digby Heights, N.S. wc $35
192 Mouth of the Kennebunkport, Maine wc $35

ROMBACH, JESSIE
Addr: Montreal: 531 Canning St, 1942; 1422 Pierce St, Apt 7, 1944-5; 1468 Bishop St, 1946
1942 147 Thru' the window $35
1944 111 Back street $40
1945 193 Cajun homestead $250
1946 210 Across the street $100

ROMER, ANNA DE
addr: Westmount, 6 Park Place, 1950. St Elzear de Laval, Que, 1954
1950 74 Mrs Don Oland wc
1954 96 Return from the fair wc

ROMER, SOPHIE DE
addr: Montreal, 1474 Fort St, 1953-5
1953 15 Anna
1955 98 Bill nm

ROOKE, ALICE CONSTANCE (Mrs)
1886, n Brandon, Man
addr: Barrie, Ont: 28 Theresa St, 1932-5; 28 Dundonald St, 1942
1932 261 Phlox pastel $60
262 Lily pond, Temagami forest pastel $50
1935 286 Down from the glacier $85
1942 148 Open water, Kempenfeldt Bay $150

ROSAIRE, ARTHUR DOMINIQUE (Rozaire in 1900, mispr)
17 Jan 1879, Montreal Feb 1922, Los Angeles NGC W78
addr: Montreal, 433 St Antoine St, 1900-5. Westmount, 4302 St Catherine St, 1906-9; Montreal, 1908. Westmount, 4323 Montrose Ave, 1910-14. Montreal, 296 Mountain St, 1915-17
1900 Rozaire, 1900
93 A sunless day $15
1901 84 Old house, Côte des Neiges $15
1905 100 Evening $75
101 Winter sunset $75
1906 143 Early snow $100
144 Evening, Laurentian Mountains $100
145 Sunset, autumn $100
1908 130 Night $150
131 The sugar bush $150
1909 313 Coal barges
314 Night effect
315 Street scene
1910 303 Sand hills $100
304 Glen Bridge $125
1911 253 Snow drifting, morning $150
254 Part of Westmount $150
255 As the moon rises $75
256 A change of route $50
1912 341 In the Laurentians $200
342 Mostly in shadow $150
1913 336 Old Mount Royal $200
337 The stray calf $200
338 Between sunset and moonrise $400
1914 348 Early morning $400
349 Mulet River, Laurentians $300
350 Spring time $500
351 Fall sunlight, mid-day $300
1915 297 Evening visit $200
298 Canal mud barges $300
299 Grey Nunnery Church $300
300 Convent play yard $300
301 St Margaret, Laurentian Mountains wc $150
1916 257 Sap buckets $250
258 Spruce trees $250
259 The novitiate $800
260 Hillside, Laurentian Mountains pastel $75
261 Gully, Laurentian Mountains pastel $75
262 Cordwood sleigh $400
263 On the benches wc $70
1917 299 The garden of light $1,000
300 Going home $500
301 The doctor's visit $400

302 Over the hill $300
303 Desolation $400
304 Farm house $75

ROSAMOND, MARY
addr: Montreal: 3500 Shuter St, 1940; 3615 Lorne Cr, Apt 3, 1942
1940 254 Road to Tatlock $60
255 Pine woods, Almonte $60
1942 149 Sonya under banana tree

ROSE, BERYL
addr: Westmount, 486 Argyle Ave
1919 288 Head of a cat

ROSE, JOYCE ESTHER DANGOOR (m Alan Henry Rose)
22 Nov 1927, Shanghai
addr: Montreal, 1555 Summerhill Ave, Apt 104, 1959-63
1959 enamel on copper, 1959-63
62 Springbok $90
1963 113 The lions $225

ROSEMARIN, R.
addr: Montreal, 5222 Esplanade Ave
1947 235 Harbour scene

ROSENBERG, HENRY MORTIKAR
28 Feb 1858, New Brunswick, N.J. 24 Dec 1947, Dartmouth, N.S. DBA F H WWA40
addr: Halifax, N.S.
1906 146 The birch and the brook $150

ROSENGARTEN, ANN J.
addr: Montreal, 3315 Ridgewood Ave
1950 136 Jamaican landscape $105

ROSENGARTEN, GEORGE J.
addr: Montreal: 6202 Sherbrooke St W, 1950; 422 McGill St, 1951
1950 137 Jamaican cemetry
1951 115 Sacré Coeur, Paris '51

ROSENGARTEN, MORTON
1933, Montreal
addr: Montreal, 2135 Mackay St, 1960-1
1960 251 Reclining figure bronze $200
1961 120 Aviva bronze $350

ROSEWARNE, FRANCES see JONES, FRANCES

ROSEWARNE, ROBERT VICTOR
31 Oct 1925 - 2 Jan 1974, Ottawa
addr: Ottawa, 233 Argyle Ave
1960 210 Autumnal mycology nm $60
211 Regal cathedral nm $45

ROSS, DORIS EVANS
addr: Montreal, 791 University St, 1920; 2090 Sherbrooke St W, 1932
1920 230 Sketch of a dog
1932 263 Dinty $150

ROSS, ELEANOR M. Eng
fl 1880-1919 DBA RA
addr: Montreal, 212 Mountain St
1897 203 Miss Nicolson pastel miniature on ivory 225-8
225 HRH the late Duke of Clarence
226 Miss Martha Montagu Allan
227 Mrs Gillespie
228 The late Prof Blackie

ROSS, FREDERICK JOSEPH
12 May 1927, Saint John, N.B. TB2 WWA84
addr: Saint John
1968 237 Harlequin rel sculp nm 8 circle 13 x 11 box $100
238 The yellow dress temp 31 x 31 $400
239 Musician No 1 chalk & temp 33 x 24 $200
240 Musician No 2 chalk & temp 42 x 31 $250

ROSS, GEORGE ALLEN
24 Oct 1878 - 21 Jan 1946, Montreal CNS27 CWW38 PMC WWC30
addr: Montreal: 51 Bank of Ottawa Bldg, St James St, 1905-6; Beaver Hall Hill, 1909-16; 1 Belmont St, 1927-9; Architects Bldg, 1933
1905 265 Palais du Petit Trianon nm
1906 Ross & Macfarlane (D.H.) 1906-9
348 Dominion Guarantee Co, new office building
349 New library, Bishop's College School, Lennoxville
1909 446,448 Central Union Passenger Station, Ottawa Terminal Railway Co, and waiting room
447 Hotel, Ottawa Terminal Railway Co
449 St Matthias Church, Westmount
1916 Ross & Macdonald (R.H.) 1916-33

H.G. Jones, J.M. Lyle, assoc, 1916
344-5 Toronto Union Station, exterior, interior
1927 H.L. Fetherstonhaugh, assoc, 1927
239 The Château, Montreal photos
1929 283 Royal York Hotel, Toronto
284 Dominion Square Bldg, Montreal
1933 411 Price Brothers Bldg, Quebec drwg
412 Terminal Bldg, Montreal drwg
413 Architects Bldg, Montreal drwg
414 Neurological Bldg, McGill University, Montreal drwg
415-18 Price Brothers Bldg, Quebec, plaster models for wood carvings
see also Archibald, John S, 1931-253

ROSS, GRAEME H.
c 1930, La Tuque, Que
addr: Westmount: 116 Arlington Ave, 1949-52; 5 Park Place, Apt 9, 1956; 241 Clarke Ave, 1960
1949 90 Back country of Cacouna $125
91 Spring in Piedmont $75
1951 116 Corner house, Montreal $70
1952 140 Girl with pig-tail charcl $25
1956 52 Fishing boats, Majorca $200
1960 212 Lower St Lawrence nm $225
213 Boats, Cacouna nm $100

ROSS, J. J.
addr: Montreal, 873 Wellington St
1913 418 Late Dr Craik bust
419 Late Dr J. Chalmers Cameron bust

ROSS, JOHN FENWICK (JACK)
addr: Montreal, 3497 Holton Ave, 1938-49
1938 102 Calendulas
1939 286 Isle Bizard, Que $150
1942 150 Ballet dancer
1946 211 Still life $35
1949 92 Betty $35

ROSS, PHYLLIS G.
addr: Montreal, 355 Mountain St
1922 346 Aileen plaster
347 Jean plaster
348 Fountain, sketch wax

ROSS, ROBERT
29 Dec 1902, Toronto AGO
addr: Toronto, 68 Grenville St
1939 436-7 Drawing of a head charcl $40 each

ROSS, STUART (Miss)
addr: Westmount, 753 Lansdowne Ave
1941 176 Amanda

ROSS, V.
addr: Hawkesbury, Ont
1930 175 Black Bay, Laurentian Mountains $125

ROSSI, ALBERTO Ital
8 Aug 1858, Turin, Italy B TB
addr: Cairo
1894 133 Cottage interior, Italian Alps $60

ROTT, MARGARET (MARGRIT)
18 Jun 1898, Budapest
addr: Westmount, 4059 Dorchester St W, 1952. Montreal: 4780 Côte des Neiges Rd, Apt 19, 1953-5; 5205 Earnscliffe Ave, 1960
1952 45 Child with fruit $250
1953 37 Village in Hungary $250
38 Still life $100
1955 67 Spring in Rougemont $200
1960 103 Hungarian girl $120

ROUEN, JACQUELINE DE
addr: Montreal, 4457 Earnscliffe Ave
1936 527 W.W. Grant, Esq charcl

ROUGERON, MARCEL JULES Amer
6 Oct 1875, Paris B F TB2 WWA40
addr: New York
1918 309 Jacques Laflamme pastel

ROULEAU, JACQUES
b 1932
addr: Montreal, 9370 Chateaubriand St, 1960-3
1960 104 Machine de notre epoque $120
1963 58 Peinture, novembre 1962 $150

ROUSSEAU, ALBERT
17 Oct 1908, Charny, Que
addr: Quebec, 9 Laval St, 1930-48. Lévis, Que 1967
1930 295 Moulin Vincennes etch $15

1939 287 La havre, Québec $175
1940 256 L'Université Laval $40
1941 177 M.G.
178 Côte à Coton, Québec $50
1944 112 Des Ramparts $75
112A Vieille maison à Quebec $75
1946 212 Une vieille maison de la rue Sous le Cap, à Quebec $50
213 Une vieille maison à Québec $50
1948 53 Portrait, Roland Chenail (listed 1967, Jessie Dow prize)
1967 59 Formes bleues. 1966 60 x 48

ROUSSEAU, YOLANDE (Mme Rioux)
12 Jul 1910, Trois Pistoles, Que
addr: St, Laurent, Que, 830 Buchanan St, 1959. Montreal, 4485 Marcil Ave, 1964
1959 Rioux, 1959
59 Portes sur l'horizon tile $50
60 Fille à la mouette mosaic $50
1964 133 Promenade, Place Ville Marie sculp (divers) $100

ROUSSEL, CLAUDE
6 Jul 1930, Edmundston, N.B. CWW84 WWA84
addr: Moncton, N.B, St Anselme
1968 huile sur contre-plaque 241-3
241 Relief No 10 15 x 30 $190
242 Relief No 20 28 x 24 $190
243 Relief No 30 29 1/2 x 23 $190
244 Le prisonnier métal et plastique 64 x 12 x 11 $350

ROUSSIL, ROBERT
18 Aug 1925, Montreal B CE DMS
addr: Montreal, 2721 Hochelage St, 1947. Verdun, Que: 434 3rd Ave, 1949; 7460 Champlain Blvd, 1952-5; Montreal, Galerie Dresdnere, 2170 Crescent St, 1961
1947 343 Self portrait plaster
1949 176 Embrace stone $300
1952 150 Canada wd
151 Paix wd
1954 140 Structure de paix sculp
1955 156 Espoir de paix wd
1961 121 Oiseau d'antan ter cot $400

ROWAT, EVELYN E.
addr: Town of Mount Royal, 15 Dobie Ave
1940 387 Portrait drwg

ROWAT, RUSKE LLOYD
addr: Montreal, 4228 Royal Ave
1947 236 Barn, Côte St Luc Road wc $150
237 Players' Theatre, Cape Cod wc $90
238 The bridge, Montfort wc

ROWLES, GEORGE A.
addr: Ottawa, 355 McLaren St, 1927-9
1927 154 Carrousel Bridge, Paris $45
1928 176 Seascape, Mediterranean $50
1929 186 The old granary $150

ROWLEY, FRANCES ELWOOD RICHARDS (m William Edwin Rowley)
1852, Brockville, Ont 1934 Glassonby, Eng B DBA H
1889 161 Study of a head wc $50
174A By the sea wc $60
174B Esmeralda wc $45

ROY, ELAYNE (Mme Mailhot)
17 Jul 1931, Nicolet, Que NGC
addr: Quebec, 53 1/2 St Louis St
1956 Elyane, mispr
53 Appréhension $85
54 Sur nappe blanche $65

ROY, J. ANTOINE
addr: Montreal: Ecole des Beaux Arts, 1928-9; 750 Sherbrooke St W, Studio 3, 1943
1928 356 Sports d'hiver statuette plaster
1929 394 Le sentiment qui renâit à l'antique plaster
1943 174 Nocturne pastel $100

ROYDS, MABEL ALINGTON (m Ernest Stephen Lumsden) Eng
fl 1899-1940 DBA
addr: Toronto, Havergal College, Jarvis St
1906 147 Louise $28
148 The fat girl $25

ROYLE, STANLEY
12 Dec 1888, Stalybridge, Eng 27 Apr 1961, n Sheffield, Eng CCI CWW38 DBA NGC RA TB2 WBA WWB41 Juror
addr: Halifax: Nova Scotia College of Art, 1932-3; 77 Queen St, 1934. Sackville, N.B, Mount Allison University, 1936-45

1932 264 Quarry face pattern $525
265 Jerry $250
266 The coast near Halifax, N.S. wc $60
1933 266 Calm evening, Peggy's Cove, N.S. $60
1934 294 Willows $200
1936 384 Sally $200
385 Corfe Castle, Dorset wc $40
1937 254 Tantramar marshes, Sackville, N.B. $200
1938 103 Dr George J. Trueman, Pres Mount Allison University
1939 288 Lumber wharf, Halifax, N.S. $300 (MBAM)
289 Moonlight on snow, Corfe Castle, England $300
1940 257 Meditation
258 Coastline, Peggy's Cove $100
259 Grey morning, Peggy's Cove $60
1941 179 Carolyn $250
180 Blue and gold, Prospect, N.S. $125
1942 151 Evening light, Prospect $1,000
1943 175 Fisherman and girl $1,000
176 Peggy $200
177 Rock pool, Peggy's Cove $200
1945 194 Myself
195 Harvest time, Cape Tormentine, N.B. $250

ROZYNSKI, STANLEY
1931, Montreal
addr: Montreal, 1443 Mansfield St
1964 134 Figure ter cot $300

RUDDICK, DOROTHY COLE
1925, Chicago
addr: Montreal, 1290 Pine Ave W
1955 128 Heads nm $50

RUDDICK, ERNESTINE S.
addr: Montreal, 43 Mark St
1920 335 Lamp base and shade (made by artist) Hon mention

RUEL, WILLIAM H.
fl 1880-94 H
addr: Halifax, 1880
1880 78 Halifax harbour
1883 148 First on the ground
1885 4 Waiting for the tide
18 Lowery weather
20 Getting a tow
66 A friendly race
90 On the banks
1886 73 Marine sketch

RUHMAN, WALTER
1899, Germany
addr: Westmount, 4549 Sherbrooke St W
1956 55 Unnamed vision

RUSSELL, ANDREA ELIZABETH
30 Nov 1932, Dryden, Ont
addr: Westmount, 510 Victoria Ave, 1952. Montreal, 1585 Pine Ave W, 1953
1952 123 The morning nets wc $15
1953 100 Dry distillation one temp $60

RUSSELL, GEORGE HORNE
18 Apr 1861, Banff, Scot 25 Jun 1933, St Stephen, N.B. AGO B CC2 EC H Mo12 NGC PMC R2 TB1/3 W78
addr: Montreal: 55 Church St, 1895-1900; 25 Durocher St, 1901-6; 6 Beaver Hall Sq, 1908-17; 360 Beaver Hall Sq, 1918-27; 1158 Beaver Hall Sq, 1928-33
1895 194 The old La Salle homestead wc $75
1898 198 Lizzie wc
1900 94 Moonrise, Herring Cove, N.S. $130
95 Portrait
1901 85 Low tide, St Andrews, N.B. $150
86 Captain of the lifeboat crew
87 Mrs Russell
1903 99 Rt Hon Lord Strathcona and Mount Royal
100 Under the willows $125 (NGC)
101 A Scotch moorland $275
1905 102 An October day $275
103 A marsh meadow $80
1906 149 Ploughing $140
150 In shallow water $75
282 Their native heath wc $75
283 An ancient home wc $20
284 An autumn landscape wc $25
1908 133 W.R. Baker, Esq
134 Sighted $175
135 In the shade $75
136 Fishin' Jimmy, Jr $75
1909 316 Lt Col Carson
317 Miss Russell
318 Milking time $175
319 At the well $80
1910 305 Mrs W.C. Hodgson
306 H.W. Ashby, Esq

1911 257 Sir Robert Ashton Lister
1912 343 Sir Wilfrid Laurier
344 Miss Russell
345 Mount Robson, Canadian Rockies $400
1913 339 Madeleine
340 Albert J. Brown, KC
341 McDuff Lamb, Esq
1914 352 The foster mother $150
353 A Scotch moorland $600
354 Miss C.
355 Master Horace McAuley Murphy
1915 302 E. Alexander, Esq
303 Early spring $250 (NGC)
304 Evening on the canal $500
305 Old benignity $150 (MBAM)
1916 264 Mrs Russell
265 Noonday $250
266 Fishing boats, St Andrews, N.B. $200
267 Calves $150
1917 305 Windmill Point $300
306 An old pensioner $300
1918 310 Ralph, son of Norman Wilson, Esq
311 Cairne, daughter of Norman Wilson, Esq
312 Boys on the beach
313 Digging clams $400
1919 289 Flight Commdr J. Roy Allan, DSO, RNAS (deceased)
290 A silvery sea $350
291 Duck pond $200
292 Line fishers $100
293 Low tide, St Andrews $100
294 Evening, St Andrews $100
1920 231 Sir Thomas Tait
232 Rev George Adam
233 Scotch firs (MBAM)
1921 234 Robert Harvie, Esq
235 Miss Marjorie Annable
236 Scotch firs $800
237 Old town, Stonehaven, Scotland $500
1922 267 Charles Gurd, Esq
268 A calm sea $250
269 A fresh breeze $425
1923 189 Miss Livingston
190 The duck pond $350
191 On the Heads, St Andrews $700
192 Silver mists, St Andrews $1,000 (listed 1967, Jessie Dow prize)
1924 228 Hugh Paton, Esq
229 In Monhegan harbour $600
230 Surf, Monhegan $800
1925 232 Dr Frank D. Adams, PhD, late Dean, faculty of Applied Sciences, McGill University
233 Lumber schooners, St Andrews $750
234 Boats at Eastport $450
235 Evening, St Croix River, N.B. $200
236 Washing clams, St Andrews wc (listed 1967, Jessie Dow prize)
237 Passamaquoddy Bay, N.B. wc $120
1926 106 John Hamilton, Esq, DCL, Chancellor, Bishop University, presentation portrait
107 The late James Carruthers
108 On the coast of Maine at Monhegan $850
109 The duck pond $350
1927 152 Marine at Monhegan $850
153 Incoming tide $550
1928 177 After the storm $850
178 Marine $350
1929 187 John Watson, MA, LLD, DD
188 Howard Smith, Esq
189 The Louisburgh lights $750
1930 176 Dr F.C. Harrison, FRSC, Dean, Graduate Faculty, McGill University
177 Monhegan harbour $650
1931 215 Surf, $1,000
216 George A. Campbell, KC
1932 267 Mrs Horne Russell
268 On the Cape Breton coast $500
269 Seal Harbour, N.B. $400
270 A sheltered port $375
1933 267 The sea $1,000
268 Moonlight, St Andrews $800
269 Hugh Paton, Esq
270 Marjorie, daughter of Dr & Mrs J. McK. Wathen

RUSSELL, GYRTH
30 Apr 1892, Dartmouth, N.S. 8 Dec 1970, Wales AGO B CWW67 DBA NGC TB1/2 WHC WWB34
addr: Halifax, N.S, 17 Wright Ave, 1912; Halifax, 1913. Paris, 74 rue d'Alleray, 1914
1912 346 The snowstorm etch $7
347 The shipyard etch $7
348 The snowstorm aqua $5
1913 342 Fish houses etch $10

343 The hilltop etch $10
344 Old courtyard, Halifax etch $10
345 Old street, Halifax etch $10
346 Old courtyard, Halifax $50
347 Harbour scene, Halifax $50
1914 356 Sketch, Charenton $15
357 Sketch, Bas Meudon $15

RUSSELL, LILLIAN E.
addr: Quebec: 1908; 59 d'Antigny St, 1910; 45 Esplanade, 1913; 53 St Louis St, 1914; 24 Lafrance St, 1916-17; 24 Fraser St, 1918-23
1908 132 The close of the year $25
1910 307 The misty city $25
1913 348 Les bateaux $30
349 Early evening on the Saguenay $30
1914 358 The Citadel city $35
359 Early evening $35
360 St Louis Gate, rainy evening $30
1916 264 Late afternoon $35
1917 307 Quebec from the Lévis shore $35
308 The Citadel, Quebec $35
314 On the St Lawrence $20
1919 295 Mount St Anne de Beaupré $100
1921 233 The Citadel, Quebec $50
1922 265 Quebec $100
266 St Louis Gate, Quebec $75
1923 193 Quebec $75

RUSTON, HILDA see MARQUETTE, HILDA

RYALL, SUSAN
addr: Montreal
1901 264 Tankard
265 Fern pot
266 Bonbon box
267 Small vase
268-9 Tray $7, $6
270 Vase, chrysanthemum $4
271 Plate, poppies $4
272-3 Plate $4 each
274 Vase, geranium $2.75
275 Bonbon dish $2.50

RYAN, JOSEPH B.
addr: Mont Tremblant, Que, 1947-9
1947 239 Beauvallon
1949 93 Stevie $100

RYCHOR, A.
addr: Montreal, 4416 Christophe Colomb
1929 190 Stage of erection $1,200

RYSHPAN, DAISY SHIEF LEFSON (m Meyer Ryshpan)
addr: Montreal: 5205 Durocher St, 1934; 417 St Joseph Blvd W, 1935; 5180 Esplanade Ave, 1937; 117 Mount Royal Ave W, 1942
1934 295-6 Still life $75, $50
1935 287 Wild flowers $50
1937 255 Still life $50
1942 214 The old pipe drwg

RYSHPAN, MEYER
1898, Poland
addr: Montreal: 5205 Durocher St, 1934; 5180 Esplanade Ave, 1936-7; 5346 St Urbain St, 1939; 395 Dowd St, 1940-7
1934 297 Music store wc $15
298 Flowers $20
1936 386 Men of leisure wc $20
387 Skating scene wc $30
567 Old man etch $10
568 The afflicted one drypt $15
1937 256 The unemployed wc $50
257 Tired wc $25
258 New snow wc $25
259 The gambling spirit $50
1939 290 Waiting for trolley wc $50
291 Cold day wc $25
292 Gossip wc $25
438 Sleepy drwg $20
1940 260 Girl reading wc $50
261 Political discussion wc $75
1942 152 Fresh snow wc $50
153 Mount Royal in March wc $50
215 Barnyard scene col etch $15
1947 240 Mount Royal in April wc $75
241 Joan practising

S

SADOWSKA, KRYSTYNA KOPCERYNASKA (m Konrad Sadowski. m Stefan Siwinski)
2 Jun 1918, Lublin, Poland CWW84 IO TB2
addr: Indian Harbour, N.S, 1953. Aurora, Ont, 75 Ross St, 1955. Toronto, 561 Spadina Rd, 1956-63

1953 39 Composition $150
60 Drawing Chinese ink $20
1955 129 Susanne & the elders nm $100
1956 124 Spring nm $100
1963 114 Abstract form metal $400
115 Christ metal $1,300

SAETHER, BJORN EVEN
25 Feb 1917, Oslo
addr: Winnipeg, 170 Langside St
1953 88 From Caddy Lake

SAGER, PETER WINCHELL
23 Feb 1920, Vancouver TB2
addr: Montreal, Dominion Gallery, 1438 Sherbrooke St W
1964 135 Fort Huron bronze $1,100

SAINT CHARLES, JOSEPH
10 Jun 1868 - 26 Oct 1956, Montreal
CC2 CE CNS36 Mo12 PMC TB2
addr: Paris, 117 Notre Dame des Champs, 1891. Montreal: YMCA Bldg, 1895; 34 Labelle St, 1900-1; 14 Phillips Sq, 1903; 15A Bleury St, 1905; 473 St Hubert St, 1906; Montreal, 1908; 17 Bleury St, 1909; 182 St Denis St, 1910; 314 St Catherine St W, 1911; 519 St Catherine St W, 1912-13; Montreal, 1918; 801 St Hubert St, 1920-2, 1924-5; 706 St Catherine St E, 1923; 3703 St Hubert St, 1927; 3764 St Hubert St, 1933
1891 116 Portrait of my Mother (MBAM)
117 Venus of Milo $50
118 Old man $100
119 Dr J.L. Auger
1895 125 Mon portrait
126 Rémouleur
127 Tête de jeune fille
128 Portrait d'homme
129 Portrait de femme
1900 100 Portrait of the artist
101 Corner of studio
177-8 Study of a head b&w
1901 92 Mons Laroque
93 Camerière, Rome $75
94 The mandolin player $100
175 Mrs B. crayon
176 Miss S. crayon $40
177 Portrait crayon $25
1903 107 Philippe Hébert, sculptor (MQ)
108 Maj J. Pelletier, 1st CMR
109 Expectative $40
257 Henri Hébert crayon
1905 104 Mon frère, F.X. St Charles
105 Une convalescente $50
106-7 Tête de jeune fille $50, $125
240 Quelques croquis de Montréal drwg $75
241-2 Croquis du port de Montréal drwg $12 each
1906 151 Lt Col Mackay
316 Recolte de foin b&w $15
317 Sous les grands arbres b&w $15
318 Un coin à la Côte des Neiges b&w $15
319 Sur la Petite Rivière b&w $15
1908 137 Tête de Zouave
253 Tête pastel
254 Etude pastel
1909 320 Portrait
321 Italienne en priere $150
322 Femme en plein air (MQ)
323 Tête d'italienne
324 Tête de jeune fille
1910 308 Habitant $100
309 Emprisonné $60
310 Tête de forgeron $45
311 Cabane à sucre $40
312 Tête de jeune fille crayon
1911 254 Portrait of the artist
1912 349 Hon T. Berthiaume
350 Portrait of a woman pastel
351 Portrait of a woman $200
352 Study of a head $75.20 (sic)
353 Woman reading $60
1913 350-2 Pastel
353-4 Drawing
355 Home where Jacques Cartier was born
356-7 Head of a girl
1918 315 Young lady pastel
316 Young lady
317 Portrait
318 Old barn $75
1920 234 Modesty $250
235 J. Saint Charles, painted by himself
236 Young girl pastel $200
1921 238 Jeune fille fusain $125
239 Tête fusain
240 Mr J.M. Dupuis
1922 270 Head of a woman b&w
271-2 Charcoal $100 each
273 Interior effect $300
1923 212 Tête de jeune fille $300

1924 244 Mr Ernest Pellessier, KC, Battonier du Barreau de Montréal
1925 262 Dr L.J. Lemieux, Sheriff of Montreal. Presented to the Sheriff by Montreal Council of the Bar, for the Court House
1927 166 Maréchal Nantel, Esq, KC
167 Paul St Germain, Esq, President of the Bar of Montreal
302A Young girl reading b&w $75
1933 271 Dr J.A. Mureault

SAINT JEAN, J.
addr: Montreal, 2666 St Denis St
1919 296 Maisonnettes $75
297 Le vieux moulin $50

SAINT JEAN, MICHEL
17 Jul 1937, Montreal
addr: Montreal, 1247 Wolfe St
1962 69 Journée future nm $125

SAINT PIERRE, F.
addr: Montreal: 1906 Prefontaine St, 1932; 1797 St Hubert St, 1937
1932 360 Arms, Earl of Bessborough st gl
1937 260 The Annunciation wc

SAIT, GWENDOLYN L.
addr: Montreal, 4134 Old Orchard Ave, 1935-8
1935 288 Lengthening shadows $75
1937 468 Laddie plaster $12
469 Carroll plaster
1938 199 Joan Mary plaster

SALETTE, LOUIS
16 Nov 1932, Montreal
addr: Montreal South, 662 Dollard Ave
1960 105 Tempête $100
106 Souvenirs $150

SALMON, PETER
addr: Saint John, N.B.
1968 310 Clara 20 1/2 x 16 $125
311 Judith oil on Donnaconna board 30 x 29 1/2 $250
312 Drawing of Saint John, N.B. pencil & gouache on brown paper 24 1/4 x 18 1/2 $100
313 Raquel Welch 16 1/4 x 18 $150

SALTMARCHE, KENNETH CHARLES
29 Sep 1920, Cardiff, Wales WWA84
addr: Windsor, Ont, Willistead Art Gallery
1951 43 Judy reading

SAMILA, DAVID JOHN
26 Mar 1941, Winnipeg IO
addr: London, Eng, 117 Marlborough Flats, Walton St, 1965. Sackville, N.B.
1965 28 London nm $140
1968 acrylic
245 Love Tormentine 48 x 72 1/4 $800
246 Marsh 48 x 72 1/4 $800
247 Sage 48 1/4 x 96 3/8 $800
248 Martha's place 60 1/4 x 85 1/4 $1,000

SAMPSON, JOSEPH ERNEST
11 Jul 1887, Liverpool, Eng 29 Oct 1946, York Mills, Ont AGO CNS36 CWW36 NGC
addr: Toronto, 72 St Leonard Ave
1927 155 Foam $500

SAMUEL, CHARLES E.
1883 92 Perplexed
103 The empty cradle

SAMUELLEE (SAMUELLIE) E 1004
1920, Cape Dorset, NWT ED
addr: Cape Dorset
1955 157 Pair of musk oxen franite

SANBORN, MARGARET JANE
26 Jul 1861 10 Apr 1949, Montreal H
addr: Montreal: 5 Closse St, 1892; 5 Essex Ave, 1894-8. Westmount: 119 Belmont Pl, 1900-11; 566 Roslyn Ave, 1912-33; 4253 Dorchester St W, 1934; 359 Victoria Ave, 1935
1892 125 Portrait
126 Don't wake me up $50
1894 134 A July day $10
1895 195 Worn out wc $5
1897 204 At Black's Bridge wc $10
205 Old apple tree wc $10
206 Dolls and dandelions wc $8
207 Sketches $8 each
1898 199 An old Westmount landmark wc $15
200 The pines, Mount Royal Park wc $8
1900 157 Old St Germain house, Montreal wc $15

1901 173 Old Lachine Canal wc $15
1903 215 Old Hudson's Bay House, Lachine wc $6 (Hudson Bay, mispr)
216 Old house, lower Lachine wc $10
217 In June wc $6
218 A hillside wc
1905 193 The Pinnacle wc $18
1906 285 Evening mist rising wc $12
286 Beach, Hudson Heights wc $10
1908 255 Sunset wc $10
299 Miniatures on ivory (4)
1909 325 Wading $35
326 The Pinnacle, Eastern Townships wc $15
1910 313 Hofkirche, Lucerne
314 Lake Lucerne
315 Mr Titlis, Lucerne $15
316 Old H.B. House, Lachine
1911 259 An old elm $25
1912 354 River and Library, Ottawa wc $25
355 Pasture land, Bolton wc $15
356 Hillside, October $15
357 Old mill, sunset wc $15
1913 358 Jane Hester, wife of Capt Michael Holliday min, ivory
359 After the rain wc $20
360 Canadian village wc $20
361 Road across Westmount Golf Links wc $40
1914 361 Bend in the river $20
362 Watson's Pond, Dunham $20
363 Sunset in harvest time wc $20
1915 306 Major and Mrs Sweeny (parents of late Col Sweeny) min
307 Mrs McLaughlin min
308 Range of hills in the Eastern Townships $15
1916 269 On the way to Oka, from St Eustache $25
270 Shakespeare Lane, Côte des Neiges wc $10
1917 309 Miss Marion Slack wc min, ivory
310-11 Portrait study pastel
312 The mill stream wc $10
1918 319 Lieut James Harvie, RFA min, ivory
320 The distant village wc $15
1919 298 Trillium time wc $15
299-300 Miniature on ivory
1920 237 Miss Margery Birch, Ottawa wc min
238 Napierville roses wc $10
1921 242 Canterbury bells wc $20
243 Case of miniatures
1922 274 Portrait on ivory min
275 Chancel window, Church of the Good Shepherd, Buffalo wc $20
276 Capt Bennett's boat, Great Chebeque Island, Maine wc $20
1925 238 At work wc $25
239 Girl's head wc $15
240 Portrait, on ivory
1927 156 Old house near Lachine Rapids wc $25
1928 179 Col R.C.L. Sweeny, DSO, OBE, MC wc
1933 272 Joan Wight min
273 Mr Strachan Bethune min
274 View from St Helen's School, Dunham $20
1934 299 Shirley Wight min
300 Canterbury bells wc $12
1935 289 Portrait on ivory min
290 Norma Wight min

SANDERS, WILLIAM
addr: Ville Emard, Que, 6048 Hurteau St
1936 388 Anglican Church, Worcester, Eng wc $20

SANDHAM, HENRY
24 May 1842, Montreal 21 Jun 1910, London, Eng AGO B CWW10 DBA EC H Mo98 NGC TB W78 WHC
addr: Montreal, 1880. Boston: 1891; 152 Boylston St, 1894
1880 21 Thos Coats, Esq, Paisley
35 Beacon Light, Saint John harbour (NGC)
36 Cattle
53 Fish nets, Bay of Fundy
56 View on the St Lawrence
61 Portraits, the Misses Coats, Paisley
71 Sketch in Mount Royal Park
100 Study of rock wc
147 Gulf of St Lawrence wc
170 Montreal harbour, sketch wc
177 Low tide, Indian Cove wc
1881 52 Where are they gone? Chiswick Churchyard wc
54 Happy moments wc
74 Low tide on the Thames wc
1883 20 The meadows of St Anne, lower St Lawrence wc

36 Scoop her up! wc
47 A timely warning wc
886 10 At Murray Bay, St Lawrence wc
67 The Le Salle homestead
79 A Canadian oven
102 On the western plains
1889 79 All for fun $200
1891 113 The village mill $100
114 Alla Stella confidente $1,000
115 In the potato field
199 Maiden meditations wc $200
200 The ferry wc $200
201 The water babies wc $250
1894 135 Portrait of an ancestor $500
136 Self satisfaction $150
224 The fall of the leaf wc $125
225 Château Frontenac, Quebec wc $50

SARGENT, SONIA see CROSSEN, SONIA

SARNER, SAMUEL
addr: Montreal, 8554 Stuart Ave
1950 138 First snow

SARTONI, GIULIA
addr: Montreal, 487 Sherbrooke St W
1929 191 Portrait

SASAKI, TOMIYO
23 Dec 1943, Vernon, B.C.
addr: New York
1970 73 Great American pastime
7 figures and other fixtures, papier mâche plus mixed media life size illus

SATOK, RONALD MAURICE
22 Feb 1932, Simcoe, Ont
addr: Toronto, 1016 Eglinton Ave W
1961 98 Man's inability to understand himself nm $300

SAUNDERS, LOIS
H
addr: Kingston, Ont 244 King St
1894 137 Guelder roses $50
138 Horse chestnuts $40

SAUNDERS, V. G. (Mrs F. W.)
addr: Montreal, 103 Closse St, 1923-5
1923 282 Cocoa jug flat enamels
1925 327 Muffin dish
328 Cheese and cracker dish
329 Vase

SAURIOL, ANDREE
addr: Dorion, Vaudreuil, Que, 31 ave Brodeur
1958 40 Nature morte $90

SAVAGE, ADELE
addr: Montreal, 1832 Bayle St, Apt 6
1940 263 Blue Monday wc $25
264 Passin' de time of day wc $25
388 Handmaiden conté drwg $15
389 Lovella conté drwg $15

SAVAGE, ANNE DOUGLAS
27 Jul 1896 - 25 Mar 1971, Montreal
AGO CC1 CE CNS40 NGC TB2 WWA62 Juror
addr: Montreal: 52 Trafalgar Ave, 1917-18; 20 Highland Ave, 1919-31; 4090 Highland Ave, 1933-61
1917 313-5 Sketch
316 Sketch b&w
1918 321 Wonish Hills
322 Kilmarnock
323 The snow sprites $15
324 Transportation $15
1919 301 Over the hills and far away
302 The cut, Côte des Neiges
303 The meeting
304 Spring
305 Sketch
1920 239 The park $35
240 Sketch $35
241 A windy say $35
1921 244 Nursery decoration
245 March
1922 277 Sketch $25
278 Birches $100
279 The rink
1923 194 Beaver Hall Square $150
195 Winter $100
196 Lake Placid $100
1924 225 Fortis et veritas. Shown RCA 1923 exhibit, mural competition
1925 241 Northland spring
242-3 Brittany sketch
1926 110 The woods, March
111 Concarneau
1929 192 John
1931 217 July in the Laurentians $50
1933 275 Pines, Metis
1934 301 The plough $150 (MBAM)
1935 291 Little balsam $50
292 The still pond, Georgian Bay $150

1936 389 St Sauveur $150 (NGC)
390 The wood $100 (AGO)
1937 261 Laurentian lake
262 The poppy
1938 104 La petite niche $150
1939 293 Autumn $150
1940 262 April in the Laurentians $150
1941 181 Spring, Seize Isles
182 After rain, Cap à l'Aigle (NGC)
1942 154 Le presbytaire
1944 113 From the studio $100
1946 214 Mary
1947 242 Canoe fantasy $150
1948 54 Des framboises $150
1949 94 Twilight $150
1956 56 Autumn bouquet $125
1959 19 Twilight, Laurentians $250
1960 109 April evening $275
1961 50 Laurentian landscape ill Purchase award (MBAM)

SAVAGE, ELEANOR MCK.
addr: Montreal
1908 431 Muffin dish

SAVAGE, GLADYS
addr: Montreal, 4920 Côte des Neiges Rd, 1951-2
1951 67 Sorrowing trees wd engr $15
68 The source wd engr $10
1952 77 The quiet stream wd engr $20

SAVAGE, HARRY
1938, Camrose, Alta
addr: Edmonton
1968 249 Simon says acry construction 20 1/2 x 26 1/4 x 3 1/2 $300
250 View from our window sergph 20 x 24 $50

SAVAGE, RAPHAEL
addr: Toronto, c/o 31 Alexander St, Apt 917
1961 99 Still life nm $185

SAVARD, JEAN N.
addr: Montreal, 5355 Hutchison St, 1929. Town of Mount Royal, 47 Cornwall Ave, 1932-5
1929 N. Savard
340 Le Glengarnorck crayon $25
1932 361 Small house, Ste Dorothée, Que
1934 408 Rural cottages erected near St Eustache, Que
409 Suburban residence, Van Horne Ave
1935 N.J. Savard
370 Maison de campagne
371 Ancienne maison, agrandie et restaurée

SAVOIE, GERALD
addr: Outremont, 63 Côte Ste Catherine Rd
1963 88 Ariane et Axos nm $125

SAWATSKY, N. J.
addr: Saskatoon
1970 58 Autochthonic landscape re-entry without Lem services acry 44 x 66 (MBAM)

SAWCHUK, GEORGE
1927, Kenora, Ont
addr: Vancouver
1970 75 Five pieces 2" x 12" random lengths. 1969 wd 84 illus
76 Sunconcious. 1968 wd, shell, metal 47

SAWYER, JOSEPH
1 Dec 1874, Three Rivers, Que 1 Mar 1965, Montreal CNS44 Mo12
addr: Montreal, 407 Guy St
1927 240 Women's General Hospital
241 Eglise Ste Catherine

SAWYER, WILLIAM
9 Nov 1820, Montreal 9 Dec 1889, Kingston, Ont DCB H NGC W78
1881 46 Sherbrooke

SAXE, CHARLES JEWETT
21 May 1970, St Albans, Vt 4 Feb 1943, Montreal PMC
addr: Montreal: Imperial Bldg, 107 St James St, 1897-1903; 59 Beaver Hall Hill, 1905-12; 314 Dorchester St W, 1915; no addr 1918; 1673 St Luke St, 1932-7
1897 Saxe & Archibald
233 Two houses, Rosemount Ave study
234 Royal St Lawrence Yacht Club premeditated des
235 Dominion Rifle Association of Canada Bldg, Bisley, Eng
1898 225-6 Residence, Mr Thomas A.

Lynch, Grosvenor Ave, dining room, hall
227 Mr Charles Manhire residence, Grosvenor Ave
228 Block of houses, Greene Ave, for Mr M.S Foley alternative des
1900 184 Residence, S.S. Bain, Verdun
185 Montmorenci Cotton Mills Co, workmen's houses des
186 M.S. Foley, Bellevue Apts, entrance hall des
1903 276 Residence, James Shearer, Esq 4 views
1905 266 Bishops Court Apts, Montreal
1906 350-1 Emmnauel Congregational Church, front, side elevation
352 Messrs Robinson & Co, store
1908 339 Residence, A. Falconer, KC
340 Emmanuel Church, Drummont St, interior
341 Residence, J.H. Plummer, Esq, Sydney, Cape Breton
1910 407 Residence, J.M. Wilson Esq
408 Dominion Bridge Co, office building, Lachine
409 Yorkshire Insurance Co, bldg
410 Montreal Technical School
1911 305 Office building, Winnipeg
1912 419 La Sauvegarde Assurance Co, building
420 Kaniwaki Club, club house
1915 404 Residence, Geo Rabinovitch
405 Residence, C.I. De Sola
1918 325 St Charles Road, Beaupré, Que $25
1932 271 Bermuda $50
1937 263 Old bridge at Ste Marguerite, Que $100
see also Amos, Louis A, 1927-179; Fetherstonhaugh, Harold L, 1927-203

SAXE, HENRY
24 Sep 1937, Montreal B WWA84
addr: Montreal: 4806 St Lawrence Blvd Apt 2, 1964; Montreal, 1969
1964 64 2nd cartel $200
1969 9 X-tree link vinyl coated steel pipe 2' to 5' (MBAM)

SCHACTER, WILLIAM M.
addr: Montreal, 1521 Van Horne Ave, Apt 12
1952 124 Sunlife wc

SCHAEFER, CARL FELLMAN
30 Apr 1903, Hanover, Ont AGO CC2 CE CWW84 NGC TB2 WWA84
addr: Toronto, 157 St Clements Ave
1955 130 Wheatfield nm $500

SCHALK, LESLIE (LADISLAS, LASZLO)
4 May 1900, Budapest
addr: Montreal: 5276 Queen Mary Rd, 1953; 4800 Clanranald Ave, 1954-6; 4729 Fulton St, No 3, 1960
1953 40 In the studio $500
41 Blue jar $200
1954 74 The blue bottle $250
75 In the studio $300
1955 68 Still life $200
1956 57 In the bush $260
1960 214 Composition I nm $500

SCHEEPERS, MALVINA see COBURN, MALVINA

SCHEFFER, D.
addr: Montreal: Pensionnat de l'Ange Gardien, 1907 St Jacques St, 1919; 470 St Antoine St, 1922
1919 312 L'habitant $50
1922 387 Vase $40
388 Plate, cherries $15

SCHELL, JAMES EDGAR
b 1877
addr: Toronto, 5 Maxwell Apts, Harbord St, 1917. Montreal, 358 Beaver Hall Sq, 1921
1917 317 Portrait of an artist friend $250
318 The artist's Mother
1921 246 Country home $75

SCHELL, MARY HALLMAN (Mrs)
addr: Montreal, 3488 Northcliffe Ave
1947 243 Early spring along highway, Beaconsfield pastel $20

SCHELLENBERGER, OTTO see RAND, PAUL

SCHINTZ, JANET D. (m Theodore Marie Schintz)
addr: High River, Alta, RR 2
1942 155 The elf wc $15

SCHINTZ, THEODORE MARIE
19 May 1904, Almelo, Holland
addr: Montreal, 463 Sherbrooke St W,

1932; 3548 Hutchison St, 1933. High River, Alta, RR 2, 1942
1932 272 Pinto Kid $175
273 Chuck wagon race $150
274 Steer decorating $120
275 Bucking horse $80
430-2 Bucking horse charcl $50 each
1933 276 The bronco busters $175
277 Fall branding $60
278 The artist's wife
1942 156 Mountain trail $75

SCHLEEH, HANS MARTIN
9 Oct 1928, Koenigsfeld, Germ CWW84 WWA84
addr; Montreal: 4360 Decarie Blvd
1956 152 Spring and summer Queensten marble

SCHMIDT, W. EDWARD
addr: Westmount, 565A Victoria Ave, 1933-4. Morin Heights, Que, 1937
1933 283 Flying wild swans $200
284 Wild ducks $60
1934 468 Love pen drwg $12
469 Young fox pen drwg $8
470 Squirrel pen drwg $7
471 Angry lion pen drwg $15
1937 366 Mural painting, Norwegian Room, Laurentide Inn, Ste Agathe des Monts, Que photo

SCHNEIDER, C. H. (Mrs)
addr: Montreal, 148 Vendome Ave
1922 389 Marmalade jar $8
390 Butter tub $8
391 Jewel box $5
392 Decanter enamels

SCHOFIELD, JOHN
15 Mar 1883, Monaghan, Ire 16 Nov 1971 Barbados
see Archibald, John S, 1929-223, 1930-209-10

SCHOFIELD, RUTH (Mrs)
addr: Montreal, 4516 Girouard Ave, 1945-6
1945 196 Portrait study
1946 215 The woodpiler, Georgeville, Que
268 Gloucester drwg

SCHRECK, MICHAEL H.
addr: Montreal, Dominion Gallery, 1438 Sherbrooke St W
1954 77 Composition with fruit $210

SHOULDS, MAX see SCHULZ, MAX

SCHREIBER, CHARLOTTE MOUNT BROCK MORRELL (m Weymouth George Schreiber)
1834 Woodham, Essex, Eng 1922 Paignton, Devon, Eng CE EC H Mo98 NGC W78
addr: Toronto, 1880
1880 12 Of what is she thinking? (port)
19 Christabel
22 Joan of Arc before battle
30 Dear old nurse's teachings
31 The croppy boy (NGC)
66 Lie still, sweet
1883 137 A wash-up after tea
158 A trial of patience

SCHULZ, MAX (JULIUS JOSEPH MARIA) (MAX SHOULDS)
21 Mar 1889, Coblenz, Germ
addr: Montreal, 6037 Hutchison St, 1930. Outremont, 1156 Lajoie St, 1933. Montreal: 3669 De Bullion St, 1937-8; 3574 Jeanne Mance St, 1942
1930 178 Old homes $100
1933 279 The golden fleece $250
1937 264 Emden $200
1938 105 Mr De Lall, portrait sketch
1942 157 Sugar camp $80

SCIORTINO, FRANCESCO SAVERIO
12 Nov 1875, Citta Rohan, Malta 1 Sep 1958, Oka, Que PMC
addr: Montreal: 75 Sherbrooke St W, 1915-16; 428 Bleury St, 1918; 210 St James St, 1920-5; 1218 Notre Dame de Lourdes St, 1927
1915 381 Dame de L'ile de Malte sculp
382 Fountain detail sculp
383 Fountain, sketch
1916 323 His late Lordship, Mgr Archambeault sculp
324 His Majesty Edward VII sculp $100
1918 375 Montréal à Adam des Ormeaux sculp. International competition postponed on account of the war
1920 307 Aurora plaster
308 Portrait bas rel plaster
1921 315-6 Cemetry monuments to Sir Wilfrid Laurier front, side views

317 Plain pencil drawings
1922 349 Sacrifice d'Aaron rel
350 Cain et Abel sculp
1923 261 At the sepulchre rel panel
262 Contemplation of the Cross rel panel
263 Towards Jerusalem rel panel
264 Consolations rel panel
1924 323 Fragment of a church memorial sculp $50
1925 400 Jason, from sketches by Percy E. Nobbs col plaster
1927 317 Tabernacle, St Catherine's Church sculp

SCLATER, GILBERT TURNBULL
9 Dec 1908, Edinburgh Mar 1939, Toronto
addr: Toronto: 128 Park Rd, 1934-8; 23 Elm Ave, 1939
1934 302 Clouds $125
1935 293 The land of Lorne $25
1936 391 The north shore wc $25
569 St Octave, Que lino cut $5.50
1938 180 Eilean Donan Castle, Loch Duich wd engr $5
181 Pigeons wd engr $5
182-3 Illustration wd engr $5, $7.50
1939 439 Merchiston Castle School, Edinburgh lino cut $3.50
440 Farm, Hogg's Hollow wd engr $10
441 Head of a man wd engr $5
442 Sound of Jura, Scotland wd engr $5

SCLATER, MABEL
addr: Montreal, 229 Mountain St, 1901-3
1901 88 Head, sketch
1903 102 Sketch $10

SCOTT, ADAM SHERRIFF
18 Jul 1887, Galashields, Scot 23 Oct 1980, St Anne de Bellevue, Que CNS36 NGC TB2
addr: Montreal: 364 Dorchester St W, 1920-5; 725 St Catherine St W, 1927; 3531 Ste Famille St, 1932-4; 3615 Lorne Cr, 1935-8; 1536 Bishop St, 1940-6. Westmount, 4480 Western Ave, 1947-53
1920 246 Alfred Norton Francis, son of A.E. Francis
1921 251 Lands End $250
252 The green hat $200 (NGC)
253 Decorative panel pastel $75 (NGC)
1923 197 The locket $250
1925 244 Mrs Sydney Carter
1927 157 Miss Young, Superintendent, Montreal General Hospital
1932 276 Sheila
277 Late Ven Archdeacon J.G. Norton, MA DD
1933 280 Arrangement in black and grey $400
281 Portrait sketch
1934 303 The artist's daughter $500
304 Paul
305 Alan Macnaughton
1935 294 Frontenac at Cataraqui, c/o Mr John Irwin (AE, gift of Mrs John Irwin)
295 The studio visitor $750
296 Mrs L. Shklar
1936 392 Harmony in brown and grey $750 (MBAM)
1937 265 Stillness before snow $750
266 Quebecois, portrait study $500
267 The green boat, sketch $150
1938 106 Anne $2,000
107 W. M. Birks, Esq
1940 265 Flower study $250
1941 183 Mrs R.W. Steele
1942 158 Lieut Robert Sharps, RCNVR
1944 114 C.A. de Lotbinière-Harwood
1945 197 Maj Paul Tricquet, V.C. c/o Dept of National Defence, Ottawa
198 Old time sugaring party $750
1946 216 Corporal John Reford, sketch portrait
217 Sketch portrait
1947 244 Geo. G. Hodges, Esq
245 Brigadier H.M. Elder, CBE, DSO, ED, MD, CM, FACS
1950 42 Portrait of Monica
1951 44 Mrs David Cape
1952 48 Mrs R.W. Steele
49 Crest of the hill $500
1953 42 Laurentian winter $500

SCOTT, ARLENE C. (Mrs)
addr: Montreal, 200 Beaconsfield Ave, 1921; 252 Wilson Ave, 1922
1921 339 Plate blue glaze $5
340 Fern dish $15
1922 393 Jardiniere glaze $50

SCOTT, CAMPBELL
5 Oct 1930, Milngavie, Scot IO WWA84
addr: St Catharines, Ont

1968 251 Sand dunes wd cut 25 x 15 $125
251A Mystery No 1 wd cut 22 x 34 $200

SCOTT, CHARLES HEPBURN
29 Nov 1886, Newmilns, Scot 28 Jun 1964, Vancouver CC1 CWW61 EC TB2 WWA62
addr: Vancouver, 6212 Balaclava St
1947 246 Penticton valley, B.C. wc $75

SCOTT, COLIN ALEXANDER
Oct 1861, Pakenham, Ont H Mo98/12
1889 162 Casco Bay wc $20

SCOTT, EMILY MARIA SPAFORD Amer
27 Aug 1832, Springwater, N.Y. 9 Apr 1915, New York AAA15 F TB
1881 33 Bethel, White Mountains
94 Portland harbour, sunset wc

SCOTT, IVAN ESMOND
5 Aug 1892, Morton, Ont 19 May 1975, Kingston, Ont
addr: Gananoque, Ont RR 3
1956 58 Harbour, evening $150

SCOTT, LOUISE
1936, New York
addr: Montreal, Galerie Libre, 2100 Crescent St
1964 65 Sunday afternoon $350

SCOTT, MARGUERITE (Mrs O'Donnell)
addr: Quebec, 80 St Louis St, 1938-9
1938 108 A corner of Lower Town, Quebec wc $25
184-5 Study drwg
1939 296 The Ursulines, Quebec wc $25
297 Market horses wc $25

SCOTT, MARION MILDRED DALE (m Francis Reginald Scott)
26 Jun 1906, Montreal AGO B CE CWW84 NGC TB2 WWA84 WWB58 Juror
addr: Montreal: 552 Pine Ave W, 1918-25; 22 Highland Ave, 1929-31; 3651 Oxenden Ave, 1933-7. Westmount: 50 Summit Circle, 1939; 451 Clarke Ave, 1945-55
1918 Dale, 1918-29
74 The beach
1920 60 Early morning
1924 55 The madonna
56 Gruyère, Switzerland
1925 83 Street in Stressa
340 Poster des
1929 46 View from apartment $50
47 Wharf road $40
1931 218 Cliff path $70
219 Flowers $20
402 Lake Deslauriers lino cut $10
403 Resevoir lino cut $10
1933 282 Lorne Crescent $30
1934 306 Head
307 Flower $30
308 Rhubarb $50
309 Harbour bridge $30
1936 393 Portrait $50
394 Backyard $30
1937 268 Gorge $25
269 North River $25
1939 294 Bulb $40
295 Tulip $40
1945 199 Cell dividing $100
200 Cell and crystal $75
1948 55 Figures, two $150
1950 139 Field $100
1951 141 Drawing (into oil on paper) $35
1952 109 Group 3 $40
1953 89 Group V $175 (MBAM)
1955 69 Apostles No 5 $225

SCOTT, MARY S.
1889 80 Lemons $40

SCOTT, NORMAN M.
addr: Westmount, 456 Mount Stephen Ave, 1948-53
1948 56 Hills at Ste Marguerite $175
1953 43 Hills, Baie St Paul $150

SCOTT, W. P.
H
1885 23 Chambly Basin
63 Montmorency Falls
1886 125 On the river bank at Bord à Plouffe
127 Low tide, Kamaraska
136 Split Rock Falls
1888 65A La chute de bien, Murray Bay $50
1889 81 A cold morning, Pointe à Pic $25
82 Under the bluff $25
83 A mountain stream $25
84 On the shore $25

SEALE, NELSON C.

addr: Westmount: 360 Kensington Ave, 1934; 4823 Western Ave, 1935
1934 310 Autumn on the Richelieu $150
311 Collation $100
1935 297 Mill stream wc $30

SEATH, ETHEL
1879 - 10 Apr 1963, Montreal AGO NGC TB2 WWA53
addr: Montreal: 2690 St Catherine St, 1905-6; Montreal, 1908; 870 St Catherine St W, 1909-1911. Westmount, 329 Victoria Ave, 1912-26. Montreal: 9 Seaforth Ave, 1927-30; 3570 Côte des Neiges Rd, 1932-7; 1536 Bishop St, 1938. Westmount, 361 Melville Ave, 1939-56
1905 Edith, mispr
243 Among the sparrows nm $12
244 Interior, St John the Evangelist, Montreal nm $10
1906 320 Interior, Christ Church Cathedral b&w $50
321 Chapel, St John the Evangelist b&w $20
1908 256 Book plates pen & ink
257 Street in Murray Bay etch $5
258 Sous-le-Cap etch $7
1909 327 Chancel, Christ Church Cathedral wc $40
328 Side alter, Notre Dame wc $15
329 French Canadian house, Murray Bay b&w $10
330 St James' Cathedral, Montreal b&w $10
1910 317 St Patrick's Church $50
318 Christ Church Cathedral $50
319 The pulpit, St Patrick's Church etch $8
320 Courtyard, Laval, Quebec etch $6
1911 260 Harvest, Cushing $15
261 French houses, Phillipsburg wc $15
1912 358 Autumn sunlight, Phillips Square $35
359 Grande Rivière, Beaupré $20
360 etchings in one frame
The harbour, Montreal $6
Side altar, St James' Cathedral $6
Cab stand, Phillips Square $6
1913 362 Cab stand, Grey Nun's Convent wc $15
363 Abbot's Hill, St Andrew's, Quebec wc $15
1914 364 Patience $15
365 Bonsecours Market, frame of etchings $10 each
366 Ferry landing, Gloucester, Mass pastel $20
1915 309 Night effect, Glen Bridge $75
310 Baby Bunting wc $15
1916 271 Awakening the pussy willows b&w $15
1917 319 A tempting morsel b&w $15
320 Snow elves b&w $15
1918 328 The green fountain $30
1919 313 Balloons $35
314 Gold $45
1920 247 Purple cineraria $40
248 Birch trees, Laurentians $25
1922 280 The music man wc $30
281 The fronzen lake wc $30
282 A bit of China $100
283 On the canal, Montreal $150
1923 198 Sunny afternoon $75
199 Schoolroom decoration
1924 231 The canal, Montreal $100
232 A cab stand, Montreal wc $25
233 The train wc $25
1925 245 A stream in winter $75
1926 112 The farmer's house $50
1927 158 Hilltop, winter $50
159 Kent Gate, from the market, Quebec pastel $40
160 Cab stands, St John's Gate, Quebec pastel $40
1929 193 Old house, Côtes des Neiges
194 Corner of the garden
1930 179 The gardener's house (NGC)
1932 278 Street corner $80
1934 312 The pink fruit dish
1935 298 Sunflowers $75
1937 270 The mast $150
1938 109 Shell pattern No 2 $50
1939 299 Pink fruit dish $100
300 Studio table $150
1941 184 White barn, Quebec $125 (NGC)
185 Street scene, 1940 $100
186 Still life $75
1942 159 Fisherman's luck
1956 125 Avocada plant nm $50

SEBAG, NANCY see MONTEFIORE, NANCY

SEELEY-SMITH, DOROTHY see SMITH, DOROTHY

SEFEROVIC, A. V.

addr: Gaspé Co, Que, Corner of the beach
1943 178 After the catch wc $75

SEGAL, A. J.
addr: Montreal: 3668 Durocher Ave, 1933-6; 3755 Côte St Catherine Rd, 1939
1933 plaster, 1933-9
527 Renée
1934 512 A brunette, portrait study
1935 476 Portrait study
1936 605 Self portrait
1939 465 Renée

SEGUER, ROGER
addr: Montreal, 3250 Barclay Ave
1956 59 Provence $70

SEGUIN, TUTZI see HASPEL, TUTZI

SEIDEN, REGINA (m Eric Goldberg)
4 Jul 1897, Rigaud, Que NGC WWA59
addr: Montreal: 1113 Marie Anne St, 1915; 169 Park Ave, 1916-18; 152 Park Ave, 1919; 27A McGill College Ave, 1923-4; 257 Peel St, 1925-6; 682 St Catherine St W, 1928. Westmount, 496 Mountain Ave, 1930
1915 311 Sketch $15
1916 272-3 Portrait
274 Sketch $15
1917 321 Portrait
322 Girl in white $75
323 Dancing girls $15
324 The promenade $15
325-25A Sketch $10 each
1918 329 The blue sock $100
330 Fantasy $20
331 Dance in a garden $20
332 Vanity $20
333 Phillipsburg, sketch $15
1919 315 Girl in blue $75
316 Out buildings, Calumet $25
317 Nymphs $60
318 September $15
319 Grenville $15
1920 249 Portrait
250 The magic wood $75
251 Cowansville $50
252 Fantasy $30
1921 254 The jade necklace $250
255 The immigrant $250
256 Decoration $40
257 Pierrot et Pierrette $30
1923 200 Raizel $300
201 Nude $400
202 Old palace, Venice $40
203 Vegetable stall, Florence $40
1924 234 Dinner, French Canadian farm $125
235 Lace makers, Chioggia $50
236 The paisley shawl $400
237 Buddy
1925 246 Halina $400
247 A pierrette $450
248 Dancers $40
249 A passage, Florence $50
1926 113 Two sisters from Kiev $600
114 Habitabt, Oka $300
115 Blue boat, Gloucester $40
1928 180 Mrs B. Joseph
181 Port St Tropez wc $50
182 Old houses, St Tropez wc $40
1930 180 A Palestinian

SEJNOHA, JAROSLAV
24 Aug 1889, Sebroinice, Bohemia, Czech
addr: Toronto, 559 St Clements Ave
1957 83 Lake of Two Rivers, Algonquin Park $100

SEMPLE, MARGARET HUNTER DOTY (m Howard Mitchell Semple)
3 Mar 1900, Yarmouth, N.S.
addr: Halifax: 7 Cartaret St, 1940-3; 210 Inglis St, 1945
1940 266 Still life
1943 179 Rock formation wc
1945 201 Gray morning wc
202 House at Prospect $45

SENECAL, ANNETTE see BELLEFEUILLE, ANNETTE

SENECAL, GERARD
addr: Montreal, 4336 St Denis St
1940 267 Back houses wc $30
268 A corner of Verdun wc $30

SENITT, CATHY (m Glen Harbison)
18 May 1945, Rochester, N.Y. M
addr: Fergus, Ont
1970 Senitt-Harbison
77 BWBOP 48 x 48
78 MVAAD 48 x 48

SETON-THOMPSON see THOMPSON, ERNEST

SEWELL, C. M. (Miss)
addr: Quebec, 114 St Augustine St, 1910-11
1910 321 On the road to Aber Falls, N. Wales wc $15
1911 262 On the road to the mill $25

SEWELL, M. (Miss)
addr: Quebec, 68 St Louis St
1910 322 Lake Beauport wc $5

SEWELL, RICHARD G.
1942, St Louis, Mo
addr: Toronto
1970 vinyl on vinyl
79 Still with chair life 48 x 54 illus
80 Interior 52 x 54

SEYBOLD (Miss)
addr: Montreal, 2 Weredale Park
1900 254 Service plate, Indo-Persian des

SEYMOUR, MUNSEY
1837, Mint, Calcutta 1912, Barton, Vt
H NGC WHC
addr: Montreal, 1891-4. St Paul, Minn, 1897. Montreal, Scott & Sons, 1739 Notre Dame St, 1900
1888 34 'Twixt the gloaming and the dusk, when the kye come home
39 A misty morning $75
45 Here, where the world is quiet, Here, where all trouble seems, Dear winds and spent waves riot, A sleepy world of streams $300
1891 120 Morning mists, Cascapedia Bay
121 Marine
122 Lights and shadows, Charlo, N.B. $80
123 An autumn glow
124 Lachine Rapids
202 October twilight wc $65
203 Along the beach, Bay of Chaleur wc $65
1892 127 Missing at Lloyd's
212 Percé Rock from the east wc
213 An Atlantic voyage wc $15
214 First impressions, Liverpool & London wc $15
1894 139 Ruined woodlands
140 Quebec
226 Glimpse of Percé Rock wc $30
227 On the Richelieu, near St Johns, Que wc $30
228 A prairie slugh wc $20
229 Fog, early morning, Bay of Chaleur wc $20
230 The old mill, Lachine wc $20
1897 208 Highland cottage wc
1900 158 Loch Achray wc $125
159 Tantallon Hold wc $125
1892-4 Assoc prize, 1891, seasacpe

SHABAEFF, VALENTIN
1899, Russia AGO TB2
addr: Montreal: 3531 Ste Famille St, 1932; 4491A Queen Mary Rd, 1947
1932 Shebaeff, 1932-47
1932 284 The spinner $75
285 Approaching storm $85
286 The miner $125
1947 253 Troika temp & wc
324 Madonna and child cer plaque $500

SHACKLETON, KATHLEEN
5 Feb 1884, Dublin DBA
addr: Montreal: 1913; 275 Mance St, 1914; 400 Overdale Ave, 1915; c/o Mrs Hugh Walkem, 448 Mackay St, 1927; 188 Phillips Pl, 1932; 1610 Sherbrooke St W, 1933. Westmount, c/o Mrs E. H. Brietzcke, 315 Springfield Ave, 1934-47
1913 364 Set of bookplates, and a headpiece
1914 367 Huntley Drummond, Esq b&w
368 Miss Eugenie Clements b&w
369 Kathlenn, Countess of Desmond etch after Rembrandt
1915 312 Miss A. Coghlin pastel
1927 161 Abner Kingman, Esq
162 An islander, Aran Isles, Ireland $50
163 Teddie Knatchbull-Hugessen
1932 pastel, 1932-44
279 Miss Diana Walker
280 Mrs F.P.J.
1933 285 Hugh Simpson Garland, Esq, a sportsman
286 Edward, son of Allan Bronfman, Esq
287 Mrs M. Magill Tait
288 W.B. Converse, Esq
1934 313 Lt Col Walter Ray
314 Theodora
315 Percé Rock, from North Beach $100

1941 187 Dan McCowan, naturalist, author
1944 115 Sub Lt D. Atkinson, RCNVR

SHADBOLT, JACK LEONARD
4 Feb 1909, Shoeburyness, Eng AGO CC2 CE CWW84 NGC TB2 WWA84
addr: Vancouver, 885 Thurlow St, 1947-8. Burnaby, B.C, 461 N Glynde St, 1952-68
1947 247 The beast $80
1948 88 Tank in bomb crater wc $100
1952 125 Presence after fire ink & casein on paper $175. Jury II prize. 1967-60, 26 1/4 x 36 1/4 (National Gallery of Canada)
1955 131 Autumn façade nm $150
1963 59 Winter theme No 7 $500
1968 258 Northern emblem (Silence) oil & lucite 79 x 60 $1,000

SHADLOCK, FRANK
addr: Hamilton, Ont: 46 Balmoral Ave N, 1932-33; 83 Sanford Ave S, 1935
1932 281 Miss Lenna Mae Lea
282 Brazen laughter; still life wc $75
283 Laughter of the gods; still life $120
433-5 Russian dance, original costume des wc $10 each
1933 289 Still life $35
1935 299 Meadow, Belfountaine, Ont wc $25
300 Old barn, Belfountaine, Ont wc $25
301 Brayford wharf, Lincoln, Eng wc $25

SHADLOCK, LOUISE
addr: Hamilton, Ont, 83 Sanford Ave S
1937 271 The house at the end of the road wc $15

SHAPIRO, HELEN FLORA TARSHIS (m Herbert Shapiro)
4 Jan 1922, Montreal
addr: Westmount, 648 Belmont Ave
1964 66 Young boy with shells $110

SHARP, DOROTHEA
addr: Westmount, Braeleigh, Forden Ave
1914 370 Ducks $75

SHARP, GEORGE LISTER THORNTON
1880 2 Jul 1974, Chemainus, B.C.
addr: Vancouver, 626 W Pender St
1936 395 Goblin tree, Vancouver Island wc $40
396 Evening cove wc $40

SHARP, HELEN
addr: Westmount: 341 Côte St Antoine Rd, 1924-5; 430 Côte St Antoine Rd. 1926
1924 376 Fruit bowl $20
377 Vase $10
378 Silver vase $8
379 Salt & pepper shakers $3
1925 330 Lamp
331 Bonbon dish $7
332 Olive dish $8
333 Macaroon dish $8
1926 Sharpe
176 Luster vase $80
177 Bonbon dish $10

SHARPS, ROBERT G.
addr: Montreal: 3622 Lorne Cr, 1936-7; 1540 Crescent St, 1938-41. Westmount, 323 Selby St, 1947
1936 397 Habitant $150
398 Waterfront, Cape Cod $75
1937 272 Self portrait
1938 110 Margaret $100
1940 269 Corner of McGill Campus wc $25
1941 188 Self portrait
1947 248 Midge $150
port, by Adam A. Scott, 1942-158

SHARRER, HONORE (m Perez Zagorin)
1920, USA WWA70
addr: Westmount, 496 Lansdowne Ave, 1963-4
1963 60 Reception II $2,000
1964 67 Leda and the folks illus $5,000 Hon mention

SHAVER, IRENE (m H.S. Shaver)
24 Aug 1897, East Williamsburg, Ont
addr: Montreal, 4445 Wilson Ave
1955 70 Montreal harbour $100

SHAW, AUSTIN
addr: Montreal, Windsor Hotel
1917 327 The nurse $250
328 Portrait of my son

SHAW, AVERY MAYNARD
27 May 1907, St Martin, DWI 17 Feb 1957, Saint John, N.B.
addr: Halifax, 66 South Park St, 1935-7. Montreal, Lower Canada College, Royal Ave, 1939
1935 302 Still life $25
303 Flower study wc $25
304 Flower piece $40
305 Petunia wc $20
1937 273 Squash and drape $50
274 Green squash $50
275 Flower temp $50
1939 301 Halifax landscape
302 Prospect shore wc
303 Man with accordian coll $200

SHAW, CARILL JOHN HAY
addr: Montreal, 3450 St Urbain St
1931 221 A gay trio, Holland $20

SHAW, HILDA M.
addr: Westmount: 259 Metcalfe Ave, 1936; 4493 Sherbrooke St W, 1939
1936 606 Jeannette plaster $75
1939 466 Prof W.G. McBride plaster

SHAW, JANE BRUMM (m Charles Anthony Law)
1917, Philadelphia
addr: Quebec: 125 Ste Anne St, 1940; 127 Ste Anne St, 1942
1940 270 Lobster pot floats wc
1942 161 Fête Dieu $75

SHAW, PEGGY
addr: Montreal, 1272 Redpath Cr, 1935-41
1935 306 A winter afternoon from the mountain wc $25
1936 399 Market day wc $15
1937 276 The Chalet, 1937 wc $25
1938 111 Der Haufbram, Munich wc $25
1941 189 The making of Canada wc $100

SHEA, FELIX JAMES
13 Feb 1896, Montreal
addr: Montreal: 1188 Phillips Pl, 1933; 1104 Beaver Hall Hill, 1934; 4082 Tupper St, 1936
1933 487 Nude study lino cut $20
488 Gulls wd cut $8
489 Dawn wd cut $8
1934 472 Duck in flight 3 block lino $15
473 Feeding 3 block lino $15
474 Pitching in wd cut $8
1936 400 Red heads feeding $75

SHEARER, JAMES BRODIE
19 May 1911, Montreal IO
addr: Westmount, 636 Roslyn Ave, 1934-42. Ste Agathe, Que, P.O. Box 145, 1945-8. Ottawa, 1967
1934 316 Mud Creek $150
1936 401 When the whipporwill sings
1937 277 Champlain, Que $150
1940 271 Golden rod $75
272 Third range $75
1942 162 Ecole $150
1945 203 Still life & chains $150
1946 218 The wedding $175
1947 249 Valley near St Faustin $200
250 Still life and rug $150
251 Rock and cliff $175
252 Light Mill Road wc $40 (1967-61, 13 1/2 x 17 1/2. Jury II prize)
1948 57 Quel caprice $175

SHEBAEFF, VALENTIN see SHABAEFF, VALENTIN

SHEEHAN, D. R.
addr: Montreal, 720 Berri St, 1919-20
1919 320 Bay of Fundy
1920 253 Evening, St Andrews-by-the-Sea $135
254 Lubec, Maine, sketch $40

SHEINFELD, ROSLYN see SWARTZMAN, ROSLYN

SHENNAN, DAVID
Jan 1880, Dumfries, Scot 27 May 1968, Montreal
see, Archibald, John S, 1927-84

SHEPHERD, HELEN SOMERTON PARSONS (m Reginald Shirley Moore Shepherd)
16 Jan 1923, St Catharines, Ont
CWW84
addr: St John's, Nfld
1968 252 Damnation 36 x 48 $1,000
253 Cabbage 20 x 24 $200

SHEPHERD, REGINALD SHIRLEY MOORE
28 Mar 1924, Portugal Cove, Nfld
CWW84 TB3

addr: St John's, Nfld
1968 254 Giant squid No 1 monoscreen 17 x 22 1/2 $170
255-7 The whale, Nos 2, 4, 6 monoscreen 17 x 22 1/2 $170 each

SHEPPARD, PETER CLAPHAM
21 Oct 1882, Toronto 24 Apr 1965, Newmarket, Ont AGO CWW61 NGC TB2 W78 WWA62
addr: Montreal, 63 Summerhill Ave, 1916. Toronto: 70 Oakwood Ave, 1925-8; 48 Oakwood Ave, 1931-4; 68 Kendall Ave, 1935-6; 48 Oakwood Ave, 1937-9; 35 Northumberland St, 1940-50
1916 275 Portrait $50
276 Cossack sentry $75
1925 250 The tramp $400
251 Old store, Craig Street $275
1928 183 Lower town $250
184 The express stand $275
1931 222 The storm $250
223 The bridge $180
1932 287 Cab stand $250
288 The market, winter $125
1933 290 Three old houses, Louisa Street, Toronto $300
291 The green boat $250
1934 317 Early spring, Toronto waterfront $450
318 The market, November $450
1935 307 Low tide, Bay of Fundy $300
308 Laid up $300
1936 402 The ferry $250
403 Autumn $140
1937 278 Farmer $200
279 Portrait study $200
1939 304 The fair $300
1940 273 Fisherman $250
1941 190 Forgotten $300
191 Cattlemen $250
1945 204 Quebec market $250
205 Ice bound $250
1946 219 Credit River, Alton, Ont $100
220 Frosty morning $175
1949 95 Mill town $350
1950 43 Coming storm $300

SHER, JOSEPH
b Russia
addr: Montreal: 789 Henri Julien Ave, 1923; 4612 Clarke St, 1929; 4843 Clarke St, 1933; 1379 Sherbrooke St W, 1939
1923 204 Sketch of a man
205 Sketch of an old lady b&w
1929 195 Portrait of a gentlemen
196 Head of a young man
1933 292 Lionais Street, Montreal $40
1939 305 Self portrait

SHERWOOD, WILLIAM ALBERT
1 Aug 1855, Omemee, Ont 5 Dec 1919, Toronto AGO H CWW10 Mo98/12 W78
addr: Toronto: 54 Yonge Street Arcade, 1891-8; 2 Queen St E, 1905-9
1891 125 Winter evening, Omemee $20
126 Major W.H. Orchards
127 W.A. Sherwood
128 F.M. Bell-Smith
1892 128 An Alpine warder $75
1894 141 Miss May Paterson
243 Portrait of a lady pastel
1895 121 Mr Julius Scriver
1897 118 The little news boy $75
119 Strayed or stolen $35
1898 201 St Bernard pastel $75
1905 108 Inspector Stark
1909 331 The mirror of the forest $200
332 Stolen fruit $35

SHKLAR, LOUIS
addr: Montreal, 3575 St Lawrence Blvd, 1932; Outrement, 512 Champagne St, 1936
1932 289 Early spring in the Laurentian Mountains $200
1936 607 Self portrait plaster

SHOEBRIDGE, JOHN
addr: Montreal, 4266 Old Orchard Ave, 1960-1
1960 110 Composition No 2, singing the blues
1961 51 Interloper $180

SHONIKER, CLAIRE MARIE (m Viktoras Brickus)
12 Sep 1931, Toronto IO
addr: Toronto, 105 Isabella St
1960 111 Bus stop $250

SHORE, HENRIETTA MARY
b Toronto B NGC TB2 WWA53
addr: Toronto: 1908; Yonge Street Arcade, 1909-12. Los Angeles, The Stratford, 1914
1908 138 Girl in brown $75
1909 333 Sisters $100
1911 263 Miss Phyllis Sanford
264 Ready for fun $75
265 Grey and black wc $25

1912 361 Sisters $500
362 Dahlias $100
363 Lady in white waist $150
364 In the park $100
1914 children of Alan Sullivan, Esq
371 Kathleen
372 Nathalie
373 D'Arcy

SHOREY, HAROLD EDGAR
1885 - 17 Jun 1971, Montreal CNS51
addr: Montreal: 56 Beaver Hall Hill, 1914; 207 St James St, 1919-22; 360 Beaver Hall Sq, 1924-7; 1158 Beaver Hall Sq, 1928-9; 2040 Union Ave, 1930-41
1914 462 Registry office, competition drwg
463 Proposed indoor tennis court
464 A Masonic temple, competive des
1919 399 Proposed residence, Mrs W.H. Drummond, Lake Manitou
1920 323 Proposed apartment house
1922 Shorey & Ritchie, 1922-41
372A Harold Reynolds, house, Winnipeg
372B Proposed house, Senneville, Que
372C Canadian Battlefields Memorials, competitive des
1924 340 Residence, Belvedere Rd, Westmount wc
341 Proposed residence, Redpath Cr
342 Residence, Edgehill Rd, Westmount
343 House, Campbell Humphrey, Esq, Choisy, Que
1925 309 House, Ernest Whitley, Esq, Westmount
310 House, Fred Peverley, Esq, Clarke Ave, Westmount
1926 153 House development, Outremont
154 Residence, Mr H. Newman, Westmount
155 Residence, Mr A.J. Nesbitt, Westmount
1927 242 Proposed country house, Beaurepaire, Que
243 Shawinigan High School, Shawinigan Falls, Que
244 Residence, Allan Boswell, Esq, Quebec
245 House, C.J. Brown, Esq, Clarke Ave, Westmount
246 House, model
1928 274 Residence, Mr D. Forbes Angus, Senneville, Que
275 Houses, Redpath St
276 Proposed apartment house, Westmount
277 Residence, Mr A.J. Nesbitt, Forden Cr, Westmount
1929 285 Black River, power house
286 Cedar Avenue development
287 St John County Hospital, children's ward
288 Houses, Edgehill Rd
1930 235 Design for a church photo
236 Housing development, Priest's Farm photo
1931 339 Proposed development, Cap St Jacques, Lake of Two Mountains
340 Anglican Church, Shawinigan Falls
341 Residence, H.R. Cockfield, Edgehill Rd
342 Seven Sisters, power development, Winnipeg
1932 362 Residence, Harold Crabtree, Esq
363 Iona Avenue School, Montreal
364 Houses, L.A. Ogilvie, Esq, Westmount
365 Residence, G. Lamartine, Esq, Lakeside
1933 419 Residence, Mr Irving Tarshis, Ramezay Rd, Westmount drwg
1934 410 Proposed office building
411 House, Westmount
412 Iona School
1936 492 Development, Charlottetown
493 Country house, sketch
494 Proposed house, Town of Mount Royal
1937 367 Iona Avenue School, completed
368 Country house
1941 270 House, A.W. Browne, Hudson wc
271 House, Cecil Nelson, Hudson wc
272 House, Miss N. Howlett, Como wc
273 House, Mr George Muir, Pointe Claire wc

SHOUB, LISA (Mrs)
addr: Montreal, 7280 Querbes Ave
1946 221 Still life wc

SHOULDS, MAX see SCHULZ, MAX

SHRAPNEL, EDWARD SCROPE
c 1847, Gosport, Hants, Eng 25 Sep 1920, Oak Bay, Victoria, B.C. H
1881 86 Muskrat trapper wc
87 Deer hunting wc
91 Fishing nets on the St Sawrence wc
92 Whaling off the Bermudas wc
1888 51 Speckled beauties $25
82 Travelling in a jumper wc $10
88 Deer hunting bivouac wc $15
121 Cutting ice wc $15

SHRECK, MICHAEL HENRY
b 1901
addr: Outremont, 1503 Lajoie Ave, 1953. Montreal, Dominion Galleries, 1438 Sherbrooke St W, 1954-6
1953 90 Manitou Lake $150
1954 77 Composition with fruit $210
1955 72 Flowers and fruit $175
1956 61 Field flowers $175
62 After the rain, Lake Placid $125

SIEBNER, HERBERT JOHANNES JOSEF (VOM SIEBENSTEIN)
16 Apr 1925, Stettia, Germ CCI CWW84 WWA84
addr: Victoria: 1038 Hillside Ave, 1956; 2078 Goldesmith St, 1965
1956 63 Two brothers $200
1965 17 Etruscan family $850

SILVER, BEN
addr: Toronto, 333 Harbord St
1943 180 Winter pastel $20
241 Blackout, eastern Canadian port drwg $20

SILVERBERG, DAVID
19 Jan 1936, Montreal AGO
addr: Montreal, 2740 Goyer St, 1960-1. Kyoto, Japan, 1968
1960 216 Nuit en forêt nm $50
1961 100 The prophet nm $45
1968 steel engraving, 259-62
259 Barrage 21 x 14 1/2 $95
260 Thoughts and women IV 18 x 13 $85
261 Artery 18 x 13 $85
262 Sea and desert 21 x 14 1/2 $95

SILVERMAN, BEN
addr: Montreal, 3993 Clarke St
1928 325 Barges, a dull day red chalk

SILVERSLETH, MARGRETHE see SIVERSLETH, MARGRETHE

SIMARD, JEAN (SIM)
17 Aug 1916, Quebec CCI WWA62
addr: Montreal, 3651 Durocher Ave, 1944-5
1944 116 Suzanne et les vieillards $200
1945 206 Sisina

SIMARD, TOMI
addr: Montreal, 1215 Drummond St
1946 222 Guerre (War) gouache

SIMCOE, DAVID
addr: Outremont, 763 Bloomfield Ave
1946 292 Mask bronze $300
293 Raymonde plaster $250

SIMISTER, WARREN
addr: Montreal, 108 Durocher St
1909 334 Storm clouds $60
335 After the storm $50
336 Montreal harbour, evening $30

SIMON, BEH
addr: Verdun, Que, 820 Verdun Ave, 1916. Montreal, 173 Marcil Ave, 1917
1916 346 Hall and stairway
347 Dining room, in white enamel
348 Dining room, fresco border
349 Vestibule in a town house
350 Music hall, in Pompeian style
351 Garden room in a country house, old fashion
1917 387 Hans Christian Andersen's birthplace
Old rooms from Denmark,
388 Common room, 1712 drwg
389 Dining room, 1665 drwg
390 Farmer's 'proud room', 1620 drwg

SIMONS, LUCIE
b London, Eng
addr: Lachine, Que, 730 47th Ave, 1956-61. Pointe Claire, Que, 32 Golf Ave, 1962-4
1956 64 Interior with doorway $150
1957 84 Florist's counter $100
1958 41 Quebec farm $125
1961 52 Hen house $100
1962 70 Church bazaar nm $125
71 Children playing with horse nm $125

1964 68 Beach picnic $200

SIMPKINS, HENRY JOHN
16 Jan 1906, Winnipeg CNS40 WWA80
addr: Montreal, 1549 Mackay St, 1931-2. Verdun, Que, 848 6th Ave, 1933. Montreal: 1481 Sherbrooke St W, 1934; 3534 University St, 1935-6; 5206 Decarie Blvd, 1939; 5538 Trans Island Ave, 1940; 5902 McLynn Ave, 1945-8; Dorval, Que: 87 Pine Beach Blvd, 1950-5; Dorval, 1967
1931 224 The valley $40
225 Sous le Cap wc $50
226 Sherbrooke Street wc $40
1932 290 Bonsecours Market wc $75
1967-62, 19 x 28 (Mr and Mrs C.L. Brownlee, Montreal)
291 In dry dock wc $35
292 The fish man wc $30
293 Spring morning wc $30
1933 293 The swimming hole $275
294 The logging river wc $100
295 Lake Labelle wc $40
296 Afternoon $200
1934 319 At break of day wc $100
320 Early morning wc $75
321 Near Morin Heights wc $100
(listed 1967, Jessie Dow prize)
322 Winter's mid-day wc $100
1935 309 Evening shadows wc $125
310 Winter blanket wc $150
311 Changing weather wc $125
1936 404 Where the red deer roam wc $125
405 Peggy's Cove, N.S. wc $50
406 Afternoon sunlight wc $50
1939 306 In a Laurentian valley wc $50
307 In the locks wc $150
1940 274 The City Hall, Montreal wc $125
1945 207 Bates' sugar camp $250
1946 223 Winter shadows wc $200
224 The blacksmith shop wc $100
1947 254 The Gorge, Rouge River wc $150
255 Night workers wc $100
1948 89 Clear morning wc $125
1950 75 A wet day wc $125
1951 64 Relic of the past wc $100
1952 67 Arundel station wc $200
1955 132 Arundel valley nm $200

SIMPSON, CHARLES WALTER
16 Apr 1878 - 16 Sep 1942, Montreal
CC2 CNS36 EC NGC PMC TB2 W78
addr: Montreal: 305 Pine Ave, 1909-10, 1916-19; 214 Park Ave, 1911-15; 65 McGill College Ave, 1921-5; 2049 McGill College Ave, 1928-34
1909 337 Spring
338 The brook
1910 323 Coal barges $100
324 The cottage $100
325 Hollyhocks $50
326 Before the ice breaks $40
1911 266 Winter sunshine $100
267 Stormy day $35
268 Study of a young girl
269 The snow dump $100
1912 365 Quebec from Beauport $125
366 The day returns $125
Quebec series, 367-8, etch
367 Sous le Cap $15
The King's Bastion $10
Sous le Fort $15
368 Cape Diamond $15
Chapel of the Grey Nuns $12
Sous le Cap, No 2 $15
369 Coal barges, Montreal harbour etch $15
370 Notre dame de Bonsecours etch $12
1913 365 At the nets $250 (NGC)
366 The clam diggers $250
367 The derrick $150
368 A March thaw $50
369 The tollgate, Cartierville etch $18
370 On the Cow Bay Road, Halifax etch $5
1914 374 Sunlight and shadow $300
375 Tail race $40
376 In Evangeline's land, sketch $40
377 Outremont, sketch $40
1915 313 On the canal $500
314 Indian summer $500
315 The flat rocks $250
316 The breaker $100
317 Sous le Fort, Quebec etch $20
318 An oratory, Notre Dame etch $20
319 The eastern passage etch $4
320 The farm house etch $4
1916 277 The water gate $300
278 On the Côte des Neiges Road $300
1917 329 The tow path $300
330 Manitoba wheat fields $300
1919 321 The city $500
1921 241 The end of the season,

Montreal harbour $500 (listed 1967 Jessie Dow Prize)
1922 284 The wayside shrine $800
285 Low tide, Gloucester $250
1923 206 The white schooner $500
206A Roofs $500
1924 238 The blue shawl $600 (NGC)
239 The white fan $600
240 Autumn leaves decoration $1,200
1925 252 Miss Margaret Coughlin
253 Miss Olga Guilaroff
254 Sixteen, decorative study
1928 185 The yellow gown $750
1930 181 Golden October $750
1932 294 Ice in the harbour $200
295 Broken ice $500
296 Sunlight and shadow $200
1933 297 The hillside $350
298 Early spring $200
1934 323 Sherbrooke Street $600
324 The first snow, Montreal River $150
325 Evening $75
326 The rocks $75
1936 407 Gaspé fishermen wc $60
408 Gaspé schooners wc $60
409 Evening, the Grand Canyon wc $60
410 Mid-day, the Grand Canyon wc $75
1937 280 The face of the cliff, Ogunquit $500
281 Blue and gold day, Ogunquit $75
282 Winter afternoon, Ste Genevieve, Que $75
1938 112 Thin ice $750
113 The frozen pool $750

SIMPSON, GEORGE SHIRLEY
addr: Westmount, 355 Melville Ave, 1935-40
1935 312 The old dresser $40
1939 308 Lannacombe Cove, south Devon $50
1940 275 Old treasures $75

SIMPSON, GRACE
addr: Montreal, 1463 Bishop St
1949 96 Late afternoon, Gloucester, Mass $35

SIMPSON, J. C.
addr: Montreal: 25 The Linton, 1910; 45 Union Ave, 1911
1910 327 Nurnberg b&w
328 The canal, Volendam
329 Volendam
330 The Castle, Brueneck
1911 270 La Trappe, Oka wc $10

SIMPSON, MINNIE R.
H
1888 58 Study of onions $30
60 Still life study $30

SIMPSON, THOMAS (Mrs)
addr: Montreal, 3095 Linton Ave
1946 325 Our pup charcl

SINCLAIR, DON
addr: Toronto, 211 Marlborough Pl
1964 69 Section of a cycle $80

SINDON, GERARD (signs Gécin)
24 Dec 1907, Montreal AGO M
addr: Montreal: 7518 Casgrain St, 1960; Galerie Dresdnère, 2170 Crescent St, 1962
1960 217 Pieta nm
218 Nature morte à la lampe II nm $150
1962 Gécin
58 Après une promenade nm $175

SINGER, SYLVIA ROBERTS (b Weininger)
26 Mar 1930, Montreal IO
addr: Hamilton
1968 M31 series, mm two-sided print, size, diameter of circle
263 No 3 12 $70
264 No 4 14 1/2 $80
265 No 6 15 3/4 $90
266 No 8 15 3/4 $90

SISSONS, LYNN (LILLIAN)
13 Sep 1898, Portage la Prairie, Man
1932 297 Dunraven farm, Manitoba wc $20
298 Old barns at Delta, Manitoba wc $15

SITWELL, GRACE (Mrs)
addr: Westmount, 636 Murray Hill
1941 192 Kifabakazi, Uganda wc
193 Lilaea Cattleya, Uganda wc $40

SIVERSLETH, MARGRETHE

23 Jul 1897, Christiansholm, Den
addr: Montreal, 2050 Victoria St, 1931-2
textile des drwg $200 each
1931 404-6 Silk, cotton, wool
1932 436-8 Wool, cotton, silk

SKAIFE, GERTRUDE
addr: Westmount, 88 Church Hill Ave
1916 279 Sugar house
280-1 Portrait, sketch b&w $25, np

SKELTON, LESLIE JAMES
27 Apr 1848, Montreal 10 Jan 1929 Colorado Springs AAA29 B F H NGC TB
addr: Montreal, 138 Metcalfe St, 1891-2. Colorado Springs, 1897. Montreal: 96 St Peter St, 1898; c/o 336 Mountain St, 1905. Colorado Springs, 1225 N Tejon, 1913-23
1891 129 Adirondack birches
130 Sunset
1892 129 In the Adirondack wilderness
1897 120 Peach blossom and adobe $40
121 Afterglow, Mount Lafayette, White Mountains $50
122 Winter in Colorado $25
123 The day slow dying in the west $45
124 Quiet waters $35
1898 96 Prairie sunset $150
97 Twilight shadows $50
98 Peach blossoms in Archbishop's garden, Sante Fé $75
1905 109 A Venetian afternoon $650
1913 371 The storm cloud $1,350
372 Sunset on the Lagoon, Venice $200
1923 207 Air and space, St Vaast, la Hogue, France $750 (MBAM)

SLABIEV, VASSIA
c 1928, Belgrade
addr: Montreal: 3453 Hôtel de Ville Ave, 1955; 3449 Hôtel de Ville Ave, 1956; 3451 Laval Ave, 1957
1955 73 Etude
1956 126 Portrait nm $20
127 Tête nm $12
1957 143 Dance nm $35
144 Drawing np

SLACK, CRAWFORD C.
addr: Montreal
1908 139 Season of grey and gales $25

SLACK, HELEN see WICKENDEN, HELEN

SLATER, RUTH see WAINWRIGHT, RUTH

SLIPPER, GARY PETER
27 Apr 1934, Calgary
addr: Hamilton, 316 St James St S
1963 61 The blind singing to the deaf $300

SLOAN, JOHN
29 Apr 1891, Aberdeen, Scot 31 Dec 1970, Hamilton Ont
addr: Hamilton: 80 Graham Ave S, 1932-6; 39 Sherman Ave A, 1937-43
1932 475 Bessie, head plaster $100
1933 528 Sixty degrees below plaster $100
1934 513 Flute player plaster $200
1935 477 Judgement of Phryne plaster $250
1936 608 A hewer of wood and a drawer of water plaster $200, stone $500
1937 470 There is no truth more true than death plaster $350, stone $750
1938 200 Valerie plaster $100, stone $300
1940 416 Late Homer Watson, RCA sculp (MBAM)
1943 260 Late J.W. Beatty, RCA sculp $150

SMARDON, KATE I.
H
addr: Montreal, 1894
1888 Kate J, mispr
72 Study of pansies wc
98 Study of sun flowers wc
136 View of the Thames wc
1894 231 Sunflower wc
232 View of Hochelaga wc $20

SMART, EDMUND HODGSON Eng
12 Mar 1873, Alnwick, Eng 14 Nov 1942 DBA TB WBA WWB34
addr: Montreal, 29 Bank of Toronto Bldg, 444 Guy St, 1912-15
1912 B. Hodgson, mispr
371 A lady in black
372 F.W. Ancott, Esq
373 Geo Durnford, Esq
374 My Mother

1913 373 Lt Col Renouf
374 W.D. Lighthall, KC
375 Miss Augusta Schmidt
377 Harmony, Frau Werner Selbach (377 mispr for 376 in catalogue)
1914 378 T.R. Wilson, Esq, BA, MD, DPH
379 Mrs T.R. Wilson
380 A Hungarian lady
381 Mrs David Wilson, Ottawa
1915 321 Au revoir, portrait of an English lady
322 T.A. Trenholms, Esq
323 Mrs H.A. Stewart
324 Miss Waller, of Haarlem

SMELLIE, SYLVIA
addr: Ottawa, 459 Laurier Ave E
1933 299 Dahlias $25

SMILEY, S. J.
addr: Montreal: 132 St James St, 1941; 5422 Brodeur Ave, 1945-53
1941 194 Bernie
1945 208 Still life $250
1953 46 Portrait of a child

SMILY, ELIZABETH MARION WOLF (m O. Powell Smily)
15 Jun 1918, Shipley, Eng
addr: Montreal, 3315 Ridgewood Ave
1953 47 Portrait of a girl $350

SMITH, A. HARRIS (Miss)
addr: Toronto, 569 Broadview Ave
1936 411 Autumn reflections $50

SMITH, ADALBERT
addr: Montreal, 29 Notre Dame de Lourdes St
1926 252 Bust, a study plaster $50
253 Vision bas rel plaster $30

SMITH, CECIL G. (Mrs)
addr: Montreal, 3422 Stanley St, 1930-4
1930 182 Group of miniatures
1934 327 The bird bath min
328 Mrs Valentine Macy min
329 Janie min
330 Dr A. Lapthorn Smith min

SMITH, CHARLES ALEXANDER see ALEXANDER, CHARLES

SMITH, CONSTANCE NAPIER
addr: Montreal: 7282 Sherbrooke St W, 1937; 1433 Bishop St, 1939; 1961 Tupper St, 1940-1
1937 290 Napier-Smith, of Montreal
291 Majorcan girl
1939 309 Still life
444 Portrait of a man drwg
1940 Napier-Smith, 1940-1
219 Anne Smith, portrait
1941 248 Marie-Thérèse Bodson, evacuée de Luxembourg chalk

SMITH, DONALD APPELBE
18 Jul 1917, London, Eng IO
addr: Winnipeg, 765 Broadway Ave
1937 283 Red River scene, Winnipeg wc $35
284 Shadows 'neath the pier wc $35
285 Prelude to the fishing season wc

SMITH, DOROTHY SEELY (m Edward Smith)
d 27 Jul 1961, Victoria, B.C.
addr: Montreal, Lincoln Ave, 3/21 Grove Apts. London, Ont, 536 Queen's Ave, 1931
1920 255 Case of miniatures wc $300
1931 Seely-Smith
220 Sawkill $100

SMITH, E. MAY
1886 61 In the orchard

SMITH, EDITH AGNESS (m Kenneth Smith)
2 Oct 1867, Halifax d 1954 H
addr: Halifax: Halifax Ladies' College, 1934; 117 Henry St, 1941
1934 331 Gray day, Blue Rocks, N.S. wc $35
1941 195 An eastern Canadian coast $150

SMITH, EDITH G.
addr: Montreal, 3850 Harvard Ave
1957 85 Everglades, Florida $100

SMITH, EVELYN R.
addr: Montreal, 3422 Stanley St, 1933-5
1933 300 Lyn min
1935 313 Shirley-Anne min
314 Barbara min
315 Two portraits min

SMITH, CHARLOTTE FLORENCE PENNINGTON
(m Robert Cooper Smith)
addr: Westmount, 4280 Dorchester St
1903 219 The Lees, Folkstone wc
220 Salisbury Cathedral wc

SMITH, FRANCIS HOPKINSON Amer
23 Oct 1838, Baltimore, Md 7 Apr 1915, New York AAA13 B Gr H
1883 30 Ponte di Sarpi, Venice wc
44 The Sand Market, Seine, France wc

SMITH, FREDA PEMBERTON
2 Apr 1902, Montreal
addr: Westmount, 42 Windsor Ave, 1922-47, 1950-3. Dunham, Que, St Helen's School 1949
1922 291 Miss R. pastel
1923 208 The late George Durnford, Esq
209 Study of a boy pastel $35
1927 302 Johnny Boker charcl $25
1929 197 The balloon man pastel $50
1930 183 A man's head in profile $50
1932 299 The lady-chair $50
1933 301 The playground $50
1934 332 Alice in the garden $75
333 March morning, Côte St Antoine Road $50
334 Lake l'Achigan, Que $35
475 Portrait charcl
1935 437 Alice drwg $25
438 Celia drwg $25
1936 412 Flowers on the kitchen shelf $25
570 Portrait drwg
571 A child drwg $25
1937 286 Willow and water $150
1938 114 Elizabeth reads in bed $75
1939 310 West wind, Choisy $75
1940 276 On the Georgeville wharf $25
277 Blue water over the Elephant $150
278 Looking over Lake Memphramagog $50
1941 258 Alice M. charcl
1943 181 Celia wears blue $150
182 Lt Col C.M. Benett
1946 225 The green glasses $100
1947 256 Young Celia $75
1949 97 A sketch of Joyce $100
1950 44 Maureen $150
1953 48 In an 1870 frock $350

SMITH, GORDON APPELBE
18 Jun 1919, Hove, Eng AGO CC1 CE CWW84 NGC TB2 WWA84
addr: West Vancouver, 4590 Keith Rd, 1961; (West) Vancouver, 1968
1961 53 Blue landscape $300
1968 267 Violet over grey screen pr 18 x 18
268 Compulsive purple acry 55 x 55 $700 (MBAM)

SMITH, GORDON HAMMOND
8 Oct 1937, Montreal CC2 CWW84 IO WWA82
addr: Montreal, Waddington Galleries, 1456 Sherbrooke St W, 1959-61
1959 63 Infinity bronze $175
1961 122 Apprehension metal $525

SMITH, HARRY LESLIE
26 May 1900, Montreal
addr: Montreal: 255A Mance St, 1923; 40 Overdale Ave, 1924-6; 83 Sherbrooke St W, 1928; 1207 Bleury St, 1932; 426 Sherbrooke St W, 1933; 1104 Beaver Hall Hill, 1934-8; 1074 Beaver Hall Hill, 1940-2; 1096 Beaver Hall Hill, 1943; 1178 Phillips Pl, 1944-7; 1506 McGregor St, 1949-57; Montreal , 1967
1923 210 Portrait b&w
1924 246 Notre Dame, Montreal $100
247 Morning sunlight $75
1926 116 Portrait of L.
1928 186 Self portrait
1932 300 J.A. Akin, Esq
301 The artist $150
302 Cloudy sky $100
303 Sketch $35
1933 302 Roof tops $25
490 T.R. Macdonald, sketch chalk
1934 335 Studio interior $500
336 Barns $75
1935 316 Self portrait $150
317 Charlesbourg Church $100
1936 413 The Russian blouse wc $50
414 The derby wc $25
415 The immigrant wc $25
416 Lady in green $150
1937 287 Laurentian landscape wc $35
288 Bonsecours Church wc $35
289 Farm yard $100
1938 115 Immigrant girl $150
116 The pink barn wc $50
117 Tea room wc $75
1940 279 Over the roof tops wc $50

280 Heavy snow wc $50 1967-63 11 x 15 (The Arts Club, Montreal)
1941 196 Old church at la Tuque wc $50
197 Laurentian farm house wc $50
198 Snow on the roofs wc $25
258 Alice M. charcl
1942 163 Green tanks wc $75
164 Cafe scene wc $75
1943 183 Bleak farm wc $50
184 Hazy day wc $50
185 Farm on hill wc $50
186 Primitive barns wc $50
1944 117 Hôtel Commerciale wc $50
118 Rue Principale wc $50
1945 209 Winter haze wc $75
210 Vernon's house wc $75
1946 226 The reaper wc $100
227 Town hall wc $100
228 Grey day wc $100
1947 257 Country road wc $75 (listed 1967, Jessie Dow prize)
258 Studio interior wc $75
1949 98 Interior $150
1950 45 Bleak house $150
1952 51 Notre Dame Street, Montreal
1953 49 David $100
1957 86 Landscape $150

SMITH, HENRY PEMBER Amer
20 Feb 1854, Waterford, Conn 16 Oct 1907, Asbury Park, N.J. B F TB WWW
1885 77 On Cape Ann coast
112 Lowery day on the New Jersey coast wc

SMITH, HENRY WALTER
16 May 1917, Hamilton, Ont NGC TB2
addr: Hamilton, 43 Bold St
1949 147 The subway, Hamilton wc $85

SMITH, JAMES AVON
22 Apr 1832, Macduff, Scot 10 May 1918, Toronto H NGC W78
addr: Toronto, 80 Summerhill Ave, 1894
1889 85 A spanking breeze $30
1894 142 Parliament Buildings, London $125

SMITH, JOHN IVOR
28 Jan 1927, London Eng AGO CC2 IO WWA82
addr: Montreal: 3435 Grey Ave, 1956-7; 4650A Vezina St, 1960. 7370 Somerled Ave, 1961-5. Piedmont, Que, 1967-70
1956 128 Pigeons in flight nm
153 Family wd
1957 166 Figure wd $150
167 Head metal $300
1960 252 Smiling head No 1 cast stone $300
253 Smiling head No 2 cast stone illus $300. Centenary grand prize (listed 1967) (UG)
1961 123 Head cast stone $350
1962 77 Figure I cast stone $350
78 Figure II cast stone $1,250
1963 116 Sleeping family cast stone
117 Head cast stone $350
1964 136 Horizontal figure cast stone $1,800 with base
1965 44 Torso with hose wd $2,250
1967 64 Sphinx. 1965 bronze 40 1/2h (Mr & Mrs Eldon Grier, Montreal)
1970 fibreglass reinforced epoxy
81 Burgundian head 25h illus
82 Chelsea micro 48h
83 Sea figure 65h

SMITH, JOHN ROXBURGH
10 Aug 1883, Greenock, Scot 12 Jul 1975, Montreal CNS51 CWW73 NGC
addr: Montreal: 6 Beaver Hall Sq, 1909-11; 235 Dorchester St, 1912. Outremont, 20 Querbes Ave, 1914. Montreal: 190 Laurier Ave, 1915; 1 Belmont St, 1916; Montreal, 1918; 210 Hutchison St, 1919-24; 85 Osborne St, 1929; 1221 Osborne St, 1930-7
1909 339 Montcalm house, Quebec
340 Quebec Bank, Quebec
1910 411 Architectural perspective
1911 306-7 A plan problem
308 An order problem
309 A Christmas card
1912 421 Lake Shore Club House (arch)
1914 382 Temple of Vesta wc
383 Fiesole wc
384 Venetian sketch wc
384 Campanile, Siena b&w
1915 325 Fleet Street, Sunday morning pastel $10
326 Souvenir wc $10
327 Study from the Louvre wc
1916 282 Villa d'Este, Tivoli wc $35
1918 334 In Venice
1919 322 The valley wc
400 Palazzo Bevilacqua, Bologna b&w
401 Siena Cathedral b&w
402 Christmas card des
403 Magazine illustrations pen & ink

1920 256 Northern landscape wc
257 Sketch at Rosemere, Que drwg
324 Norman staircase, Canterbury
1921 258 Street scene, Quebec wc $20
259 Mountain top, Argenteuil Co, Que wc $20
260 Old house, Quebec wc $20
261 Venetian quay wc $20
1922 286 The green vase, Versailles wc $20
287 Notre Dame de Recouvrance, Orleans wc $20
1923 245-6 Wood cut $5 each
1924 241 Chateau de Ramezay, Montreal wc $25
242 Old grist mill, Chambly Canton wc $25
299 New Year's card des
1929 198 An alley in Quebec
199 Chateau de Ramezay, Montreal
289 Proposed residence (arch)
341 Book plate des
1930 237 Proposed residence (arch)
1933 420 St Leonard's Golf and Country Club (arch)
1937 441-2 Winter at St Joseph du Lac, Que crayon $40 each

SMITH, JORI see SMITH, MARJORIE

SMITH, KATE ADELINE (m Frank Hoole)
10 May 1878, Rotherham, Eng
addr: Vancouver, 7626 Heather St
1922 288 Old farm at Missenden, England $100
289 Milking time wc $25
290 The Lions, Vancouver, B.C. wc $15

SMITH, LESLIE VICTOR
1880, Simcoe, Ont 23 Mar 1952, Toronto
addr: Toronto, 341 Sherbourne St
1910 331 Old Mermaid Inn, Rye $65
332 The Beguinage, Bruges $30

SMITH, LEWIS EDWARD
1 Aug 1871, Halifax d 1926
addr: Halifax: 1912; 376 Robie St, 1924
1912 375 Edinburgh Castle, from the Vennel etch $5
376 Notre Dame de Paris aqua $5
377 Pont Neuf aqua $7
1924 243 Golden rod $150

SMITH, MABEL F.
addr: Westmount, 59 Arlington Ave
1906 455 Cider jug $15
456 Cream jug, sugar bowl

SMITH, MARIANNE see LEE-SMITH, MARIANNE

SMITH, MARJORIE THURSTON (JORI) (m Jean Palardy)
1 Jan 1907, Montreal NGC Juror
addr: Montreal: 129 Mayfair Ave, 1928-30; 295 Maplewood Ave, 1931; 546 Milton St, 1932; 2180 St Luke St, 1933. Westmount, 728 Roslyn Ave, 1934. Montreal, 3531 Ste Famille St, 1945-56. Senneville, Que, 1967
1928 187 Barbara Richardson
326 Paul Lemieux charcl
327 Jeanette Meunire charcl
1929 201 Lili Charlebois pastel
1930 184 Portrait d'une bébé pastel
1931 227 Madame G.
1932 304 Suzanne $75
305 François Langlois, pêcheur $75
439 Ben Zilch charcl $25
1933 303 Portrait
304 Still life $75
491 Drawing
1934 337 Maternity $45
338 Childhood $45
1945 Jori, 1945-67
211 Nude (Dr A. Jutras)
212 Communiate $200
1948 58 Jeune française, France, 1947 $150
59 Petite française, France, 1947 $200
1951 117 Flowers
1955 Still life with green apples. Jessie Dow Prize. 1967-65, 19 x 22 1/2 (Philip Surrey)
1956 65 Child with daisies

SMITH, VELMA B.
addr: Trenton, Ont, 15 Sutcliffe Blvd
1957 87 Sky and water $75
88 Landscape $75

SMITH, W.
addr: Verdun, Que, 6403 Beurling Ave
1956 66 Snow on roof $125

SMITH, WILLIAM SAINT THOMAS
30 Mar 1862, Belfast 18 Feb 1947, St Thomas, Ont CWW36 H Mo12 NGC PMC TB2
addr: St Thomas
1905 194 Surf and reef wc $200

SMOOR, E. C.
addr: Montreal, 1820 McGregor St
1955 133 Curaçao shells & coral nm $100

SMYTH, NORAH L.
addr: Westmount, 433 Lansdowne Ave, 1936-43
1936 417 Ann $35
1938 118 Little Jean, portrait $25
1943 178 Old Montreal, Marguerite de Bourgeoys' house $75

SNELLING, N.
addr: Montreal, 751 Shuter St
1925 255 Sick $100
256 The Saguenay River $125
257 Reval wc $35
258 Montreal wc $50
378 Mrs Z. drwg

SNIDER, H. (Mrs)
addr: Westmount, 4832 Sherbrooke St W
1915 384 M. Fleury, Esq, of Switzerland bust

SNOW, JOHN HAROLD THOMAS
12 Dec 1911, Vancouver AGO CC2 WWA84
addr: Calgary; 915 18th Ave W, 1956-62; Calgary, 1967
1956 129 Summer scene nm $75
130 Jugs nm $25
1957 145 Theatre nm $18
146 Woman reading nm $14
1958 76 Flowers and fruit nm $30
1959 36 Woman in a green dress nm $35
1960 219 Road over the hills nm $35
1961 101 Night nm $35
1962 53 Still life, 1961 nm illus $42 Jessie Dow prize. 1967-66 litho col 18 x 14 (private collection)

SNOW, MICHAEL JAMES ALECK
10 Dec 1929, Toronto AGO B CC1 CE CWW84 DMS IO TB3 WWA84
addr: Paris, Maison Canadienne, Cité Universitaire, 29 bd Jourdan, 1954. Toronto: 70 Sharles St E, 1959-60; Isaacs Gallery, 736 Bay St, 1961; Issacs Gallery, 832 Yonge St, 1964. New York, 1970
1954 114 La femme et le diamant gouache $40
1959 20 Off minor $350
1960 112 Night way $400
113 News $400 (AE)
1961 54 Train $400
1964 70 Flash $800 (MBAM)
1970 84 Sink color photo photo mounted on plastic 11 x 14

SOHNS, G. FREDERICK Scot
fl 1868-1901 DBA H
1881 81 View of Strathearn, Perthshire wc
85 On the River Earn, near Comrie wc

SOLOMON, DANIEL
13 Jul 1945, Topeka, Kans IO
addr: Toronto
1969 10 The grass is greener acry on canvas with grass, wd box and sand 72 x 24, 72 x 72, 24 x 24

SOLOMON, DAVID
addr: Montreal, 1575 Summerhill Ave
1956 67 Character study No 3 $100

SORBONNE, NOEL
addr: Montreal, 5940 Sherbrooke St W
1932 440 Tête de femme des

SORGE, WALTER FELIX
25 Oct 1931, Forestburg, Alta
addr: Dawson Creek, B.C, 9613 8th St
1959 37 Christ crucified nm $75

SOUCY, CLEOPHAS
d 21 Jun 1950, Ottawa
addr; Montreal
1908 276 Hand carved frame, Louis XV $25

SOUCY, DONAT
addr: Montreal, 1199 Bleury St
1936 609 Portrait of a child plaster

SOUCY, JEAN BAPTISTE
1 Jul 1899, St Antonin, Que WWA62
addr: Montreal, 7448 St Denis St
1930 185 Eglise St Germain des Pres, Paris wc $150

186 Le Château St Honorat, Cannes wc $100
187 La Citadelle de Corte, Corse wc $100
188 Le Pont St Benézet, Avignon, France wc $100

SOUCY, JOSEPH ALFRED ELZEAR
10 Nov 1876, Onémisme, Que d Feb 1970
addr: Montreal: 1908; 255 Bleury St, 1916-22; 1999 Bleury St, 1928-39
1908 277 L'hiver wd carv $35
1916 325 La Croix Rouge sculp
1917 369 Louis XVI dec panel $60
370 Francis I dec panel $40
1918 376 J.J. Olier maq sculp
1920 309 Monument to the soldiers maq
1921 303 Miss P. Cye, portrait bust
304 Jeanne, portrait bust
1922 351 Sir L.H. Lafontaine sculp
1928 358 St Jean Baptiste plaster $100
359 Rêverie plaster $25
1929 395 La recherche anxieuse plaster $500
1930 319 La pipe wd $100
1931 440 D'Iberville bronze $200
1932 476 Alderman H. Auger bronze
477 Monseigneur Lafleche bronze $500
478 Mr H. Gleroux plaque
1933 529 Tonkourou plaster
1934 514 Mr A. Brassard plaque
1935 478 Madonna and child walnut $250
1936 610 Tonkouru walnut (Mr C.E. Duquette)
1937 471 Winter walnut
1939 467 Robert Burns walnut $100

SPENCE, DAVID JEROME
18 Oct 1875, Louisville, Ky 22 Mar 1955, Montreal
addr: Montreal: 246 Beaver Hall Hill, 1927; 2063 Union Ave, 1938-40
1927 247 Garden mansion
248 Proposed office building
1938 Spence & Mathias
144 Modern residence drwg
1940 Spence, Mathias & Burge
331 Residence, J.M. Cape, Esq
see also Finley, Samuel Arnold, 1903-9

SPENCE, JOHN C. & Sons
d 1891 H
1885 158 Memorial window, Disputation in the Temple st gl
1889 191 Panels: music, painting, architecture, sculpture in H. Wallis, Esq, Montreal residence

SPENCER, ARTHUR
addr: Montreal, 3515 University St
1956 131 Polywog paradise nm $100

SPENCER, F. MURIEL
addr: Westmount, 47 Argyle Ave
1914 386 Green Mountains, Vermont $15
387 The elms $15

SPENDLOVE, SADIE F.
addr: Montreal: 905 St Catherine St, 1910-12; 111 Laporte St, 1914; Westmount, 3 Gladstone Ave, 1917-18
1910 333 Study red chalk
1911 271 Rob Roy and Heatherbell wc
1912 Saidai, 1912, 1918
378 A pair of collies $25
379 Louise min
380 Portrait of a young girl min $50
1914 388 Nan
389 Roses $10
390 Portrait
1917 331 Sketch wc $15
1918 335 Hollyhocks $15

SPERBER, MAURICE
addr: Montreal, 630 Prince Arthur St W
1948 108 Portrait of an artist conté crayon $100

SPICKETT, RONALD JOHN
11 Apr 1926, Regina AGO CC1 CWW84 TB3 WWA84
addr: Banff, Alta, P O Box 973
1957 89 Repentant armor $300

SPOONER, LESLIE G.
addr: Montreal: 3469 Ste Famille St, 1936; 5255 Saranac Ave, 1937
1936 611 Betty plaster
1937 472 Bust of a man plaster

SPOONER, RUBY YOUNG (Mrs)
fl 1891-7 H
addr: Montreal, 146 Peel St

1891 131 Still life, vegetables $25

SPRINGLE, EVELYN
addr: Montreal: 55 Fort St, 1922; 756 Sherbrooke St W, 1923-4
1922 352 Joy clay $6
1923 211 The dryad wc $8
265 The find sculp $8
266 The enchantress sculp $50
1924 324 Before twilight book rests, sculp $25 set

SPURR, GERTRUDE see CUTTS, GERTRUDE

SQUIRES, GERALD LEOPOLD
17 Nov 1937, Change Island, Nfld
WWA84
addr: Willowdale, Ont, 26 Claybourn Rd
1965 29 Look with thy face upon the mountains nm $125

STAGG, HELEN
25 Jan 1919, Kingston, Ont
addr: Kingston, 74 Colborne St
1964 106 Shrine of Enya nm $40

STANFORD, J. HENRY
addr: Montreal: 721A Sherbrooke St, 1903; Montreal, 1908; Engineers' Club, 1910
1903 Stanford-Szewlinski
105 Camp fire in the forest $60
106 Bleak December, dunes $60
1908 143 The Rideau River, panel for Engineers' Club
144 The mill pond $75
1910 334 Fountain Medici $75
335 Versailles $125
336 Pont St Michel $100
337 Old Paris $75

STANTON, FERN (m Alex Stanton)
addr: Montreal, 4541 Royal Ave
1947 259 Old French Canadian houses, Westmount $50

STAPLES, OWEN
3 Sep 1866, Stoke-sub-Hamdon, Eng
5 Dec 1949, Toronto AGO CNS36 CWW48 H Mo12 NGC PMC TB2 WWA47-53
addr: Toronto: 39 McGill St, 1894; 7 Maitland Pl, 1897; 67 Hogarth Ave, 1906-36
1894 144 The log barns $40
145 The love song $40
1897 125 Tom $30
1906 155 Rapids $50
287 Light at eventide wc $150
1908 145 Spreading flax $100
146 Winter $40
1909 343 Quay at Clovelly wc $75
344 Allan Line docks, Havre wc $50
345 Old house, Clovelly wc $75
346 St Paul from Waterloo Bridge wc $100
1924 252 St Louis Street, Quebec wc $40
253 A street in old Quebec wc $40
1925 259 The Town Hall, Yorkville wc $100
260 The prairie, Saskatchewan wc $50
261 Loading grain, Saskatchewan wc $35
1927 164 Trinity Street wc $75
165 The coal boat wc $80
1929 342 Steel construction etch $12
343 Quadrangle, Hart House, University of Toronto etch $12
344 Convocation Hall, University of Toronto etch $12
1932 306 Autumn wc $100
307 Toronto, from Hanlan's Point wc $100
1936 418 Killarney Mountain, Georgian Bay wc $85
419 Tiger lilies wc $75

STARR, RUTH
addr: Montreal, 1805 St Luke St, 1936. Saint John, N.B, 51 Carieton St, 1947
1936 420 Pears $35
1947 260 Remnant counter $30

STEAD, HAY
addr: Winnipeg, The Telegram
1917 332 The blizzard wc $30
333 Winter sunshine wc
334 The unbroken road wc $50
335 Poplars wc $15
336 Prairie winter wc

STEEGMAN, JOHN
10 Dec 1899, London, Eng 22 Apr 1966, Coffinswell, Eng CWW55 TB2 WWB34
addr: Montreal, 3430 Ontario Ave

1955 134 Wales: how green was my valley nm $35
port, by Robin Watt, 1956-77

STEELE, SYDNEY HAZEL RUSE (m Robert Wilson Steele)
addr: Westmount, 65 Forden Ave, 1939-45
1939 311 Tulips $35
1941 199 The milk-house, August afternoon wc $50
1945 213 Still life $100

STEGEMAN, FRANCOISE see ANDRE, FRANCOISE

STEIGER, FREDERIC
21 Oct 1899, Solwutz, Romania CWW84 TB2 WWA84
addr: Saskatoon, D-C Block, 2nd ave
1940 281 Batchelor button $300

STEINHOUSE, TOBIE THELMA DAVIS (m Herbert Steinhouse)
1 Apr 1925, Montreal B WWA84
addr: Westmount, 10 Springfield Ave
1963 89 Subterranean - ancient nm illus $50 Jessie Dow prize.
1967-67 col etch 12 3/8 x 15 3/8 (MBAM)

STEINMETZ, GEORGE
29 Jun 1908, Austria
addr: Montreal, 1429 Bishop St
1957 90 Low tide

STEINS, ILGVARS
1925, Riga, Latvia
addr: Halifax, 172 Henry St
1961 102 Night games nm $60

STENHOUSE, WALTER
1883, Montreal d 1962
addr: Montreal: 314 Belmore Ave, 1918; 84 St François Xavier St, 1919-20; 2288 Regent Ave, 1936
1918 336 Bonsecours Market $100
1919 323 Clam gatherer's return, St Andrews, N.B. $50
324 Chaboillez Square $125
1920 258 Dredge boat in fog $40
259 Sunrise
1936 421 Dominion Square pastel $50
422 The ice gleaners $50

STENNETT, H. G.
addr: Toronto
1892 130 Chrysanthemums

STEPHENS, BARBARA
addr: Quebec, 52 Ste Genevieve Ave
1930 296 Old houses on Marche Champlain etch $10
297 Corner of Palace Hill and St Paul, Quebec etch $10

STEPHENS, GEORGE
addr: Montreal, 4333 Beaconsfield Ave
1933 305 The little farm, Hogg's Hollow, Toronto $75

STEVENS, DOROTHY (m Reginald de Bruno Austin)
2 Sep 1888, Toronto 5 Jun 1966, Toronto AGO CE CWW64 NGC TB2 W78 WWA62
addr: Toronto, 168 Bay St, 1913-14
1913 etching, 1913-14
378 St Jacques Cathetral, Dieppe $20
379 Hotel de Ville, Bruges $20
380 The merry-go-round $15
381 St Nicola, Ghent $20
1914 391 Sortie de l'église $20
392 On the canal, Chartres $15
393 Autumn in Bruges $13
394 A windy day $13

STEVENS, DOROTHY WALPOLE see COPE, DOROTHY WALPOLE

STEVENSON, ALICE HAMILTON (m H. Stevenson)
26 Aug 1910, Santa Monica, Cal
addr: Montreal, 4100 Côte des Neiges Rd
1953 50 Reflections $50

STEVENSON, EDITH P.
1885, Youngstown, Ohio Mo12
addr: Thornhill, Ont
1910 338 An old fashioned girl $300

STEVENSON, ERNEST H.
addr: Montreal: 85 Brewster St, 1909; 46 Coursol St, 1912
1909 347 Still life nm
1912 381 Nun's Island $25

STEVENSON, MARJORIE S.
addr: Montreal, 1545 Drummond St
1932 470 Come and listen plaster $75

STEVENSON, WILLIAM LEWY LEROY
22 May 1905, Guelph, Ont 1966 Calgary
addr: Calgary: 117 14th Ave E, 1932;
212 17th Ave W, 1955
1932 308 Landscape with figure wc $25
1955 75 Landscape with old house $150

STEWART, CHRISTINE
Westmount, 69 Clandeboye Ave, 1910-15
1910 460 Tray, roses
461 Cup & saucer, violets
462 Jardiniere, roses $15
1911 Christina
343 Vase, iris
1915 457 Tea pot stand
458 Bonbon dishes (2)

STEWART, DOROTHY LINTON
9 Sep 1928, Montreal
addr: Montreal, 3438 Stanley St
1959 21 December 1958 $400

STEWART, GEORGE M.
addr: Montreal: 232 Mance St, 1916-17;
1188 Phillips place, 1937
1916 352 Haddon Hall, Derbyshire sketches
1917 391 Monk Bar, York
1937 369 Study of tower col drwg
370 Parliament of South Africs col drwg

STEWART, HILDA JOYCE POCOCK (m John Hutchison Stewart. m H.J. Bell)
12 Jul 1892, London, Eng CWW70 DBA
addr: Luseland, Sask
1933 306 Case of miniatures $600

STEWART, JOHN E.
27 Aug 1926, Port Washington, N.Y.
addr: Montreal: 4726 Lacombe Ave, 1953;
1447 Metcalfe St, 1954; 3583 University St, 1957; Waddington Gallery, 1456 Sherbrooke St W, 1960
1953 91 Studio interior $160
1954 115 Muddy Branch Falls casein $50
1955 135 Château de Ramezay nm $75
1957 91 Late afternoon $85
147 Twilight nm $60
1960 114 Halcyon days $300

STEWART, MARJORIE V.
addr; Montreal: 242 Mountain St, 1916-18; 748 Dorchester St W, 1919
1916 387 Vase, pine cone $8
388 Dinner set, 3 of 96 pieces $150
389 Lemonade jug $8
1917 430 Vase $7
431 Electric table lamp $35
432 Cigarette set $7
433 Belleek loving cup $6
434 Salad bowl $7
1918 437 Electric table lamp $20
438 Hexagonal vase $10
439 Muffin dish $9
440 Jug $7.50
441 Butter dish, covered $7.50
442 Bread tray $7.50
1919 428 Muffin dish, covered $12
429 Hexagonal vase $11
430 Bread tray $8
431 Coffee pot $8

STEWART, PAMELA DAWES
addr: Montreal, 1519 Pine Ave W, 1954-5
1954 78 The big four! np
1955 76 Boy on a bicycle np

STEWART, ROSANNA see MACLEAY, ROSANNA

STIKEMAN, ANNIE Eng
fl 1880-1911 DBA DVP H
addr: Montreal: 949 Dorchester St W, 1896-1903; 216 Drummond St, 1906-11
1896 water colour, 1896-1911
197 Bushy Island $25
1897 212 The Willows, Prout's Neck
213 The bay, Prout's Neck
1898 202 The old harbour, Folkestone $25
1900 160 A summer afternoon $15
1901 178 An old street in Whitby, England $25
179 Fishing boats, Whitby, England $20
1903 221 Lake Thun, Switzerland
1906 288 A summer's day on Lake Thun $30
289 Pointe Banquette, Sark $30
1908 259 A field of vetch $25
260 Murray Bay village $20
261 Low tide, Point à Pic $15
1909 348 Habitant cottage $25
349 Backs woods, Saguenay $25
1911 272 Le Lac de Trois Truites $25
273 A peep at our camp $25

STOECKER, BRUCE
addr: Montreal, 3877 Draper Ave, 1945-7. Morin Heights, Que 1948
1945 214 Tanning of the nets wc

1946 229 Church ruins, Nijmegen, Holland wc
1947 261 The Pook, Almelo, Holland wc
1948 90 The waterfall, Morin Heights wc $85

STONE, AMY BLANCHE
18 May 1887, Bristol, Eng CNS40
addr: Westmount, 18 Severn Ave, 1936-7; 355 Kensington Ave, 1939
1936 423 Trilliums wc $50
424 Tulips wc $40
1937 292 Cyclamen in pot wc $100
293 Calla lilies wc $75
294 Laurentian hills wc $60
1939 312 Maine coast wc $40

STONE, FRANK FREDERICK
28 March 1860, London, Eng AAA33 F TB WWA36
addr: Montreal: 973 Cadieux St, 1894; 5 Forfar St, 1895; 83 1/2 Rushbrooke St, 1898
1894 269 Cardinal Manning bust
270 Group, Oliver Twist and the Dodger sculp
271 The late Lord Tennyson medln
272 Cardinal Manning medln
273 Rev C.H. Spurgeon medln
274 Lord Salisbury sculp
275 Mr Gladstone sculp
276 Louise Michel sculp
1895 198 A cloudy morning wc $7.50
199 The canal basin, Montreal wc $8
230 Rt Hon W.E. Gladstone bust
231 Henry M Stanley medln $12
232 John Ruskin medln $15
1898 203 Tower Bridge, London, England wc $10
204 Egypt House, Cowes, Isle of Wight wc $10

STONE, MARY A. (Mrs)
addr: Montreal, 5 Forfar St
1895 200 Steephill Castle gates, Ventnor, Isle of Weight wc $7

STRANGE, DONALD E.
addr: Westmount, 4282 Dorchester St W
1956 132 Still life nm $30

STRANKS, GORDON E.
addr: Ottawa, 458 Melbourne Ave, 1945-9
1945 RCNVR
215 The flats oil on paper $75
1947 262 Wood interior $50
1949 99 St Dunstan's in the east $125

STRATHY, MARGUERITE
addr: Westmount, 8 Selkirk Ave, 1913-14
1913 382 September wc
1914 395 Under the pines wc $5

STRATTON, MAY
b Peterborough, Ont 1 Oct 1940, Peterborough
addr: Ottawa, 224 Cooper St
1903 110 Iris $25

STRICKLAND, WALTER REGINALD
Aug 1841 - 6 Feb 1915, Lakefield, Ont
1889 Strickland & Symons
187 House in Rosedale, Toronto
188 Church of St Simons, Toronto

STUART, ETHEL M.
addr: Montreal, 480 Guy St, 1914-19
1914 526 Salad bowl
527 Salad plates
1915 459 Tray
460 Coffee cups
461 Cup & saucer
1916 390 Bowl, Algonquin
391 Cup & saucer 6
1919 432 Tray
433 Cup & saucer 6 Women's Art Society prize
434 Bowl

STURDY, KENNETH GORDON
19 Apr 1920, Pen-y-lan, Wales CWW84
addr: Montreal, 4516 Decarie Blvd
1964 71 Enigma $500

SULLIVAN, FRANCOISE (m William Paterson Ewen)
10 Jun 1925, Montreal
addr: Montreal, 4127 Wilson Ave, 1962-3
1962 79 Fer gaufre metal $250
80 Flute 'X' metal $200
1963 Ewen
98 Construction iron $325
99 Cluster of angle beams iron $300

SULYOK-PAPP, JOSEPH see PAPP, JOSEPH

SUMNER, Miss
addr: Montreal, 865 Dorchester St
1895 273 Toilet tray

SUNNIER, O.
1885 103 Evening wc
133 Sunshine wc
135 Old farm hard wc
145 A misty morning wc

SURES, JACK
20 Nov 1935, Winnipeg
addr: Winnipeg, 645 Niagara St
1957 148 In the beginning nm $45

SURREY, PHILIP HENRY HOWARD
8 Oct 1910, Calgary AGO B CC2 CE CWW84 NGC WWA84
addr: Montreal: 1016 Keefer Bldg, 1938; 1488 Bishop St, 1939; 3434 Ste Famille St, 1940; 1830 Lincoln Ave, 1945-8. Westmount, 478 Grosvenor Ave, 1950-63. Montreal, 1967
1938 119 Noumenal construction $125
1939 313 The board walk $125 (MQ)
314 Sunday afternoon $75
1940 282 Girl in grey $125
1945 216 Composition $125
1948 60 Summer dresses $125
1950 155 Street fight pen & wash $20
1952 110 Pedestrians $800
1953 92 Softball players $300 Jury II prize. 1967-68, 20 x 24 (M. Gilles Corbeil, Montreal)
1954 79 Dominion Square $400
1957 92 Business men
1959 22 Westmount Park $250
1960 220 Plaza Café nm $175
221 Bus travellers nm $125
1963 62 The underpass

SUTHERLAND, ELIZABETH (BETTY)
14 May 1920, Liverpool, N.S.
addr: Montreal: 1190 University St, 1945-6; 5391 Sherbrooke St W, 1949; 8035 Kildare St, 1958
1945 217 Mother and blind son $50
218 Saturday night $50
219 Between the lines gouache
1946 231 Composition $50
1949 100 The outdoor clinic $150
1958 42 Patient $100

SUTHERLAND, MARGARET D.
addr: Montreal, 314 Sherbrooke St W
1916 283 Sketch wc $10

SUTHERLAND, VIVA
addr: Montreal, 1528 Mance St
1916 392 Bowl

SUZOR-COTE, MARC AURELE DE FOY
5 Apr 1869, Arthabaska, Que 27 Jan 1937, Daytona Beach, Fa AGO B CC1 CE CWW36 EC Mo12 NGC TB2
addr: Paris: 131 rue Vaugirard, 1892; 11 imp Roussin, 1894. Montreal: YMCA Bldg, 1895; 153 St Denis St, 1897. Paris: 37 bd Montparnasse, 1898-1900; 11 imp Roussin, 1903. Montreal: 125 Berri St, 1906; 81 St Hubert St, 1909-10. Arthabaska, Que, 1911. Montreal: 222 Berri St, 1912-15; 26A Victoria St, 1916-18; 67 Ste Famille St, 1919-26; 3531 Ste Famille St, 1928; 445 Querbes Ave, 1929; 1490 Drummond St, 1931-5
1892 Coté, 1892-1903, 1910-13
26 Les coteaux de Senlis $125
27 Coucher de soleil à Cernay $75
28 Sentier pres de Chaville $25
29 Tête de vieillard $25
30 Vaches au pasturage $15
1894 35 Effet de soleil, village de Foucherolles $75 (MQ)
36 Vieux fumeur $50
37 Paysanne Normande $50
38 Interieur de ferme $40
39 La Seine à Choisy, fin de journée $40
40 Route déserte, environs de Paris $40
1895 27 Miss B.
28 Study of geese
29 Old street at Champigny, France
212-13 Study of a head pastel $75 each
1897 21 Un ravin sur la Colline $125
22 Entrée du bois St Michel $75
23 Un chemin montant $65
24 Le mirage soir d'été $50
1898 15 Onions
16 Lilacs
17 Wild duck, whistler
18 Landscape, evening
1900 20 Pastourelle
21 L'amateur

22 Solitude
23 Portrait d'un vieux paralysé
24 Portrait d'un vieux Breton
1903 29 Dans les landes du Cap Frébel, Bretagne $150
1906 156 Un coin de Cernay, sous la neige $125
157 Village de Cernay, sous la neige $125
158 Baie de Margot, après midi $75
159 Oignons, nature morte $75
160 Village de la Galonnière, tombé de la nuit $100
1909 350 Brittany woman praying $500
351 Old cottage, Normandy $300
352 Pasture, cloud effect $200
353 Bohemian girl $300
354 The brook, November $150
355 Winter scene, Arthabaska $300 (NGC)
356-8 Study of a head b&w $25 each
402 Peasant in furs plaster $100
1910 93 Hauling wood $600
94 Primitive sugar camp $400
95 Autumn ploughing
96 The road to the sawmill $300
97 The little Nicolet River $200
98-9 Portrait b&w
100 Enjoying a good smoke b&w
101 One of Arthabaska's settlers b&w
102 Sketch for a portrait b&w
355 Returning home sculp
1911 73-7 Drawings b&w
289 Bust plaster
1912 91 Sketches 6, a-f nm
92-3 Portrait pastel
94 Drawings 6, a-f
1913 84 Mauve et or $300
85 Sunny winter afternoon $350
86 The pond, morning $400
87 Radiant September afternoon $450
401 Le vieux pionnier canadien statuette plaster (MBAM NGC US, bronze)
1914 396 Après la débâcle $600
397 Les fumées $500 (listed 1967 Jessie Dow prize)
398 Isolement $300
399 Trois dessins b&w
1915 328 Douleur $1,000
329 Onotaha
330 La vallée de Senlis, France $800
331 La font de la glace, Riviere Nicolet 2 des fusian $300
332-3 Type canadien b&w
1916 284 Ferme, Bretonne, soir $40
285 Soir d'octobre $30
286 La clairière, soir $60
287 Après midi, octobre $75
288 Jour d'automme $60
289 Jour sombre, octobre $75
1918 337 Le vieux pommier $500
338 Une rue à Trois Rivières $400
339 Vieille cabane à sucre $500
340 Matinee de septembre $300
341 Type canadien, étude $500
377 Statuette plâtre
378 La compagnon du vieux pionnier canadian, to be cast in bronze $150 (MBAM US bronze)
1919 325 Harmonie du soir panneau déc
326 Jeunes paysans canadiens
327 Etude pour une décoration pastel
328 Etude, porteur d'eau pastel
329 Etude, mon neveu pastel
330 Tricotteuse canadienne b&w
1920 260 Après-midi d'avril $500
261 Fin de poudrerie $500
262 Dégel, avril $150 (MQ)
263 Le soir, Lac Nicolet, Que $200
1921 262 Magdalena $2,000
263 Vieillard de chez nous $1,500
264 Maisons anciennes $1,000
265 Dégel $1,000
1922 from Louis Hémon book, 353-4
353 Maria Chapdelaine plaster
354 Les epoux Chapdelaine plaster
355 Le remmancheur d'Arthabaska plaster
356 Le portageur plaster (NGC US, bronze)
1923 212A Young Canadian peasant
212B Rougette, nude study
266A The pianist, Geo M. Brewer sculp
266B The nun sculp
1924 248 The old willow $1,500 (UG)
249-51 Nude study pastel $500 each (one in MQ, one in NGC)
325 Bacchante sculp
326 Indian women sculp (same sculpture as 1925-402)
327 Roland Poisson, violinist sculp
328 Dr R. Boulet sculp

1925 263 Passing shadows, winter afternoon $1,500 (listed 1967, Jessie Dow prize)
264 Jean Baptiste Cholette $1,000
265 Boy from my village $800
266 Dutch-Canadian girl $800
267 Saint Ange du Planty $800
268-270 Nude study wc $300 each
379 November wind charcl $200
380 Balthazar Paradis praying charcl $200
381 Balthazar Paradis charcl $200
382 Lucie Moreau charcl $200
401 Hauling logs, Quebec bronze $600 (NGC)
402 Caughnawaga women bronze $500 (AGH AGO MBAM NGC VAG)
403 A man of sorrows bronze $300
404 Bacchante bronze $250
1926 117 Marine, Little Metis $600
118 The model pastel $250
119 Drinking at a spring pastel $250
120 The sun bath pastel $250
231 November evening in the brulé charcl $250
232 The meaning of the winds charcl $150
233 Young girl charcl $150
234 A woman's head, study charcl $150
254 Démangeaison plaster, in bronze $200
255 Harry Norton, Esq bust
256 Miss J.B. bust
257 Miss A.F. Nation bust
1928 188 March snow in the gully $500
189 Old habitant pastel $125
190 The flax worker pastel $125
328 Study of a head charcl $125
360 Louis Joliet, Canadian explorer bronze $450
1929 202 Fisherman's house, Brittany $400
203 Landscape, Arthabaska $300
204 At the spring $475
204 Nude study pastel $450
396 Le trappeur bronze $250
1931 441 Old pioneer bronze $450
442 The bishop bronze $450
443 Louis Graveure bronze $150
1933 308 Indien chassant à l'arc
309 Golden September $650
310 Habitant pastel
311 Symphonie pathetique pastel
492 Man with a hoe charcl $125
530 La glaneuse bronze $200
1935 318 La pastourelle pastel $250
479 The village tanner bronze $165
480-1 Mrs S.C. bust (2) bronze
port: by Alfred Laliberte, 1938-196

SWARTZ, BURRELL
18 Jan 1925, Vancouver
addr: Ottawa, 7 4th Ave
1964 72 Early Ontario Landscape $600

SWARTZMAN, ROSLYN SHEINFELD (m Monte Swartzman)
17 Aug 1931, Montreal WWA84
addr: Montreal: 4186 Girouard Ave, 1952-3; 4840 Plamondon Ave, 1954-6. L'Abbord à Plouffe, Que, 4596 2nd St, 1961. Chomedey, Que, 4596 2nd St, 1964
1952 Sheinfeld, 1952-6
50 Still life with potatoes $45
1953 44 Phillips Square $50
45 Two girls on Mount Royal $55
1954 76 Vegetables $75
1955 71 Mount Royal $65
1956 60 Laurentian landscape $75
1961 103 Birds nm $30
1964 107 Japanese tree nm $40

SWEENY, FRANCES BEATRICE
b Montreal CNS36
addr: Westmount, 337 Kensington Ave, 1934-43
1934 339 Crown Derby and Waterford glass wc $15
340 Gladioli wc $35
341 A vanished landmark wc $20
1935 319 Spring flowers wc $40
1936 425 Rowan berries wc $100
426 Darwin tulips wc $60
1937 295 Hollyhocks wc $75
1943 188 Old houses in Varennes wc $75

SWEENY, KATHLEEN see LIEBICH, KATHLEEN

SWEEZEY, HARRIET WATSON (m Robert Oliver Sweezey)

addr: Westmount, 48 Belvedere Rd, 1929-30
1929 206 Clouds at sea wc $25
207 Montego Bay, Jamaica pastel
1930 189 Mr Morgan's beach, Bermuda pastel $25

SWINTON, GEORGE
17 Apr 1917, Vienna CC1 IO WWA84
addr: Northampton, Mass, 13 Belmont Ave, 1952. Winnipeg: School of Art, University of Manitoba, 1955-58; 191 Yale Ave, 1964; Winnipeg, 1968
1952 141 Holy Family rel etch $30
142 Inquisition soft ground etch $20
1955 77 Quartet $250
1958 43 White still life $250
1964 108 Lake song: shore after the rain nm $125
1968 ink and gouache, 269-71
269 Prairie song (67-1) 20 1/2 x 28 1/2 $150
270 Prairie song (67-4) 21 x 29 $150
271 Northern song (68-1) 21 x 29 $150
272 Prairie song (Sunset) gouache 21 1/2 x 29 1/2 $150

SYMONS, NANCY M.
addr: Montreal, 6012 Sherbrooke St W, 1951-2
1951 142 Still life pastel $75
1952 143 Still life with rhubarb pastel $50

SYMONS, WILLIAM LIMBERY
1870, Stoke Gabriel, Eng 17 Feb 1931, New York
see Strickland, Walter Reginald, 1889-187-8

SYVERSON, TERRENCE
24 Jun 1939, Kincaid, Sask
addr: New York, 144 E 22nd St, Apt 52
1963 63 Untitled $950

SZABLOWSKI, JULIE ANNE RICHARD (m George J. Szablowski)
1932, Sackville, N.B. IO
addr: Montreal, 3565 Durocher St
1964 137 Waiting soapstone $350

T

TACON, PAUL
addr: Dundas, Ont, Highway 9A RR3
1961 55 Composition in yellow and green $175

TACON, PERCY HENRY
2, or 18 Jul 1902, London, Eng
addr: Hamilton, 352 Aberdeen Ave, 1935-6. Toronto, 21 Edgar Ave, 1948
1935 320 The tulip
321 A little bit of Mexico $100
1936 427 Canterbury hells $35
1948 91 Congo wc $75

TAIGA, GLIKERIA (Mrs)
addr: Montreal, 2171 Dorchester St W
1937 296 The Bermuda madonna $2,000
443-4 prices for copies from the original
443 Queen of the sea charcl & pastel $200
444 Escaped Siberian convict charcl & pastel $40

TAIT, FRANCES DAVIDSON (Mrs)
addr: Westmount, 15 Springfield Ave
1946 269 Isle Cadieux, Que etch

TAIT, SYLVIA (m Eldon B. Grier)
20 Mar 1932, Montreal
addr: Montreal, 6644 Monkland Ave, 1950-2. Town of Mount Royal, 221 Dresden Ave, 1957. San Miguel de Allende, Mexico, Pila Seca 11, 1960. Montreal, 4060 Madison Ave, 1961
1950 156 Still life pastel $30
1952 111 Still life with bottle $60
1957 93 Still life with fruit and branches $200
1960 115 Still life with almond jar $175
1961 56 Vallauris vase $175

TANABE, TAKAO
16 Sep 1926, Prince Rupert, B.C. AGO CC2 CE NGC TB2
addr: Winnipeg, 683 Furby St, 1951. West Vancouver, 3939 Viewridge, 1965
1951 118 Ebonat $100

1965 18 Intersection $700

TANCREDE, ROBERT ALBERT RENE
16 Aug 1906, Paris
addr: Montreal, 5120 Côte des Neiges Rd, 1935-8
1935 322 Pont d'Entrevaux, France $70
1936 428 St Martin's Bridge, Toledo, Spain wc $100
429 Alcantara Bridge, Toledo, Spain wc $100
430 Quai de l'Hôtel de Ville, Paris $100
431 Les Martigues, France $100
1938 120 Besse, Auvergne, France $100

TANSLEY, PAMELA
addr: Hampstead, Que, 5 Holmdale Rd, 1930-3
1930 190 Clare pastel
1932 441 Portrait sketch drwg
1933 312 On the ice $30

TAPANILA, JACK
addr: Montreal
1970 85 Untitled sculp 1/2 fiberglass, & polyester resin 48 x 43 x 32
86 The rack sculp 1/2 fiberglass, wood, metal 98 x 72 x 36 illus

TAPLIN, BEN
addr: Montreal: c/o Johnson & Copping, 1913; 913 New Borks Bldg, 1914
1913 383 A breezy morning $200
1914 400 Warwick, Bermuda wc $100
401 Pembroke, Bermuda wc $100
402 Southport, P.E.I. wc $100

TARDIF, J. HERVE
fl 1926-67
addr: Montreal, 5053 Christophe Colomb St, 1927-31
1927 249 Proposed war memorial, Regina, Sask drwg
250 Residence, sketch model
1930 238 Apartment house, perspective drwg
1931 343 Proposed terminal building

TARDIF, THERESE see COTE, THERESE

TARSHIS, HELEN see SHAPIRO, HELEN

TASCONA, ANTONIO (TONY)
16 Mar 1926, St Boniface, Man AGO CWW84 WWA84
addr: Norwood, Man: 71 Horace St, 1956-7; 46 Gauvin St, 1960-1. Montreal, 11789 Depatie St, 1964. St Boniface, 1968
1956 68 Untitled abstraction $75
1957 94 Jeremiah $200
1960 116 The combine $250
222 Centipede (single edition) nm $75
1961 57 The deluge $400
1964 73 The Rosary $700
1968 lacquer
273 Time cycle structure 48 x 42 $700
274 Compressed variations 48 x 42 $700
275 Structure 48 x 72 $1,200
276 Space variations 72 x 48 $1,200

TATE, JAMES RICHARD
18 May 1882, Buxton, Eng 21 May 1960, Toronto
addr: Toronto, 88 Quebec Ave, 1930-41
1930 191 Vegetables
1931 228 A.J. Rostance, portrait sketch
1933 313 Quebec market $150
1935 323 East port $100
1936 432 Atlantic coast
1939 315 F. Rostance as the Guardsman
316 Still life
1941 200 Air raid

TAYLOR, ALICE
addr: Montreal, 18 Lorne Ave
1895 201 Le Grand Ruisseau, Murray Bay wc $25
202 Montreal harbour wc $25
203 Thatched barn, Murray Bay wc $20

TAYLOR, ANDREW THOMAS, Sir
Oct 1850, Edinburgh 5 Dec 1937, London, Eng CWW36 H Mo98/12 NGC TB1/3
addr: Montreal, 43 St Francis Xavier St, 1891-1901
1885 134 Street scenes, Louvain, Belgium wc
151 View in Perugia, Italy wc
157 Semi-detached residence arch drwg
158 Terrace houses arch drwg

1891 204 View in Ghent, Belgium wc
214 Macdonald Technical Building, McGill College
1901 206 Merchants Bank, Winnipeg, in course of erection
207 Bank of Montreal, Sydney, N.S, in course of erection
208 McGill University, Medical Faculty, proposed new façade and other additions, views

TAYLOR, ANNE
1886 93 A study

TAYLOR, FREDERICK BOURCHIER
27 Jul 1906, Ottawa AGO B NGC TB2 WWA84 Juror
addr: Ottawa, 451 Wellington St, 1933-5. Westmount, 4136 Dorchester St W, 1938. Montreal: 3633 Oxenden Ave, 1939-45; 3025 Trafalgar Ave, 1947-51; 3552 Mountain St, 1952-7; 3690 Mountain St, 1959. San Miguel de Allende, Mexico, Diez de Sollano, 43, 1960
1933 493 The race etch $5.50
494 Ski jump No 1 drypt $9.50
1935 439 Tandem jump etch $10 unfr
440 In Kitzbuhel, Austria etch $10 unfr
1938 186 Head of a Chinaman pencil drwg $25 unfr
1939 317 Central Montreal, from the Lachine Canal $75
318 Miriam $250
445 H. Smith Johannsen, Esq pencil drwg $38, unfr $35
446 Dredging flotilla, Montreal harbour etch $12, unfr $10
1940 283 Mr Allen Snowdon, Master of Beagle Hounds
390 Lt Col D. Stuart Forbes, MC charcl $75
1941 201 Mrs James Alvin Bohannon
202 Self portrait $500
1942 165 Miss Eugenia Watts $250
166 Canada's reaction to war, 1939-1942 $500
167 McGill undergraduate $500
1943 189 Munitions inspector $150
190 Charging the cupola, iron foundry, Dominion Engineering Works, Lachine, Que $150
191 Teamwork, drilling in the armoured steel nose casting for a Valentine tank, Angus Shops, Montreal, $100
1944 119 Mlle Jeanne Melchers $150
1945 220 Welding kiln sections $250
1947 263 Back galleries, St Antoine Street, Montreal $350
1948 61 Rubby dub drinkers $150 (MBAM)
109 Early winter, Montreal aqua etch $15
1949 101 Wind, Hull, Que $250
1950 46 Côte Labadie, Lévis, Que $350
47 On Westmount, Que $250
1951 45 Current suspense $450
1952 52 Rooftops from Dufferin Terrace, Quebec (MBAM)
1957 95 Champlain Street, Montreal $450
1959 23 Mexican woman $300
1960 117 Overlooking San Miguel de Allende, Mexico $400

TAYLOR, IRVING A. (Mrs)
addr: Montreal
1908 432 Tankard, grapes $35
433 Plaque, Ophelia $50
434 Plaque, strawberry $10
435 Stein, sunset, conventional $10
436 Stein, moonlight $10
437 Vase, conventional, lustre $35
438 Vase, storks $15
439 Dish, conventional $12
440 Vases, roses, geraniums

TAYLOR, JOHN BENJAMIN
12 Jun 1917, Charlottetown, P.E.I, 15 Sep 1970, Edmonton
addr: Edmonton, University of Alberta, Fine Arts Dept
1960 118 Forum Romanum $400
119 Lake McArthur $350

TAYLOR, LILA see KNOWLES, LILA

TAYLOR, M. P.
fl 1890-1903 H
addr: Edinburgh, 1891. Montreal, 19 Essex Ave, 1903
1881 76 Abbey of Lindesfarne wc
82 Belfry of Bruges wc
83 In a quaint old Flemish city wc
88 Porte de Gand, Bruges wc
1891 205 Loenvand, Nord Fjord, Norway wc
1903 223 The Field of Bannockburn wc $35

TAYLOR, MABEL G.
addr: Montreal, 2816 St Catherine St
1903 222 Anstey's Cove, Torquay wc $10

TAYLOR, MARY I. (Mrs)
addr: Halifax, 89 Inglis St
1941 203 Ultima Thule wc $50

TAYLOR, NOVA HECHT (m Frederick Bourchier Taylor)
16 Sep 1918, Saluda, N.C.
addr: San Miguel de Allende, Mexico, Diez de Sollano, 43
1960 223 Floral fantasy nm $150

TAYLOR, WILLIAM HUGHES
23 Dec 1891, Port Stanley, Falkland Islands NGC TB3
addr: Montreal: 5286 Western Ave, 1918-19; 185 Oxford Ave, 1920-22; 30 Benoit St, 1923; 211 Girouard Ave, 1925; 597 Harvard Ave, 1930; 4439 Harvard Ave, 1931
1918 342 Hillside $15
343 Chateauguay $15
1919 331 Spring sunset, Notre Dame de Grace $250
332 Pte Geo. Wilcox
333 Evening, Notre Dame de Grace pastel $50
334 Dominion Square, Montreal pastel $100
335 The light of day b&w $30
1920 264 Caughnawaga $400
265 On Mount Royal pastel $100
1921 266 Contemplation $200
267 The black dress
268 Carting snow, Craig Street, Montreal $200
269 The gypsy costume $100
1922 292 Drying sails, schooners, Quebec $250
293 Portrait
294 Whistling boy $200
1923 213 Alfred
214 Keeper of the locks, Lachine Canal wc $50
1925 271 The Lion d'Or, Quimper $35
272 Courtyard, Lion d'Or, Quimper $35
273 Old bridge, Rapallo $100
274 Bateaux, Thonniers, Concarneau wc $75
383-4 Etching $15, $25
1930 192 A bit of Lunenburg, N.S. pastel $160
193 Peggy's Cove, N.S. $75
194 Lifting fog, Peggy's Cove $50
1931 230 Old sloop, Rockport, Mass pastel $100

TEDESCHI, EDNA SANTINA
13 Aug 1910, Keewatin, Ont
addr: Montreal: 1260 Mackay St, 1953; 1325 St Catherine St W, Studio 9, 1956
1953 101 Fish temp $35
1956 133 Crucifixion nm $75
134 Sans souci nm $75

TEITELBAUM, MASHEL ALEXANDER
2 Feb 1921, Saskatoon d Aug 1985
AGO CC1 IO
addr: Vancouver, 3212 W 32nd St, 1949. Toronto: Gallery Moos, 138 Yorkville Ave, 1963; 52 Rosehill Ave, 1964
1949 148 Wintry race gouache
1963 64 White jazz $800
1964 74 Red heraldic $600

TELFER, HENRI
addr: Verdun, Que, 135 3rd Ave
1950 160 Head plaster

TELFER, MARY see WARDROPE, MARY

TELFER, W. W.
addr: Montreal, c/o The Linton Apts
1946 F/O RAF
232 Still life wc $20

TEMPLE, KATHLEEN E.
addr: Toronto, Havergall College
1909 359 Venice from S Maria della Salute wc $25
360 St Paul's from south side wc $25
361 An old fashioned corner

TERROUX, R. DE V.
addr: Montreal, 797 University St
1920 266 Buildings, Three Rivers drwg
267 Houses, Three Rivers, Que drwg

TETLEY, CHARLES REGINALD
16 Apr 1886, England 21 Jul 1960, Montreal CNS27
addr: Montreal: 78 Crescent St, 1914; 1074 Beaver Hall Hill, 1931; Archi-

tects Building, 1935; 630 Dorchester St W, 1938
1914 Tetley & Doggart
465 Registry office, competitive des
466 Residence, Lachine, sketch
467 Drawing, by A.R. Doggart
1931 344 St Matthias Church, Westmount extensions and rectory
345 Railway station, Lacolle, Que
346 Proposed residence, Westmount
347 Senneville Country Club, proposed club house
1935 372 House, Mrs R. Rolf Struthers, Mount Bruno, Que
373 St Matthias, Parish Hall
374 Argyle School, Westmount
375 Cottage, Lac Brule, Que
1938 145 Residence, W.B. Converse, Esq Queen Mary Rd

TEUSCHER, ANNE MARIE
addr: Montreal, 3280 Ridgewood Ave, 1955-6
1955 136 Temptation of Saint Anthony nm $50
1956 135 Dean nm $50

THACKER, ALFRED DENNIS
12 Jan 1879, Walsall, Eng 26 Sep 1938, Montreal CNS29
addr: Montreal: 104 Union Ave, 1914; 405 Guarantee Bldg, 1926; 1111, or 1100 Beaver Hall Hill, 1927-8; 1178 Phillips Pl, 1931
1914 104 Fire-hose tower des
1926 156 Central United Church, Rosemount
1927 251 First Church of Christ Scientist, Montreal
1928 278 First Church of Christ Scientist
279 Tyre and gas service station, Notre Dame de Grace
1931 348 House, Chambly
349 Village church des
350 United Church, Caughnawaga

THATCHER, FREDERICK S.
addr: Ottawa, 1312 Lexington St
1955 78 Perkins Mills, Gatineau $60

THEBERGE, CLAUDE
4 Sep 1934, Edmundston, N.B.
addr: Montreal, 3375 Maplewood Ave
1961 58 Ombres et lumières $200

THEPOT, ROGER FRANCOIS
18 Feb 1925, Landeleau, France B CWW 84 IO TB3 WWA82
addr: Toronto
1968 277 Echec au carré série de 5 différentes sergph 27 x 28 chaque $60 chaqun

THERRIEN, GAETAN
20 Apr 1927, Drummondville, Que
addr: Ste Rose, Que, 46 ave Parc
1951 72 Maternité stone $200

THOMAS, ALICE BLAIR POLLARD (m Adolphus George Thomas)
fl 1897- 1916 d c 1945, Los Angeles H
addr: Toronto, 33 Avenue Rd
1903 224 The thunder storm wc $30
225 Marine, the return wc $35
258 Moonlight on the coast monotone $40

THOMAS, BETTE see MAY, BETTE

THOMAS, LIONEL ARTHUR JOHN
3 Apr 1915, Toronto AGO CC2 CWW84 NGC TB2 WWA84
addr: Vancouver, Firebreak Rd, Capilano, 1949; 1004 Canyon Blvd, Capilano, 1951-2
1949 102 Red tongues $175
1951 119 Wind in the trees $225
1952 112 Ominious feelings $300

THOMAS, MAURICE G.
addr: Montreal: 4932 Coolbrook Ave, 1938; 6185 Hudson Rd, 1947
1938 121 Etude $75
1947 264 Farm near Mt Gabriel wc $75

THOMPSON, BERNICE see DRUMMOND, BERNICE

THOMPSON, ERNEST EVAN SETON
14 Aug 1860, South Shields, Eng 23 Oct 1946, Seton Village, Sante Fe, N.M. AGO B CC2 CE CWW36 EC H Mo98/12 TB W78
addr: Toronto, 86 Howard St
1894 146 The siege
233 Study of a lion's head wc

THOMPSON, GRATTAN D.
2 Jan 1895, Toronto 18 Sep 1971, Montreal
addr: Montreal: Côte des Neiges Rd, 1920-1; 304 University St, 1922-4; 65 McGill College Ave, 1925-7; 2049 McGill College Ave, 1929-44
1920 268 The rose terrace wc $25
1921 318 South tower, Chartres Cathedral $25
319 Figure of saint $25
320 The Chain Gate, Wells, Somerset $25
321 Christmas card des wc
1922 373 De Bleury Seigneury, St Vincent de Paul b&w $15
374 John Smyth, Esq, Montreal West, bungalow
1924 344 Residence, Dr W.G. Turner photo
345-6 Roddick Memorial Gates, McGill University, preliminary study, alternative des
347 Residence, Ross Emmans, Esq
1925 311 Residence, G.R. Cooper, Esq, Dixie
385 Pencil sketch
1926 157 Proposed hotel, Senneville
1927 252 Residence, A.A. Bowman, Esq
253 Office building
1928 280-1 Mount Stephen Club
1930 239 Residence, Lac Brule
240 Residence, Westmount
1933 421 Church of Raphael the Archangel 1934-414-15
1934 413 Residence, Hampstead
1935 376 Residence, Laurentians
1936 495-7 Residence, Westmount
1937 371 Reaidence, St Andrews East
372 Residence, Westmount
373 Interior, residence, Westmount
374 Post office, Brownsburg, Que
1940 332 Residence, Lachute
333 Residence, St Andrews East
334 Pepsi-Cola Company of Canada, Ltd
1944 152 Franke Levasseur Co Ltd
see also Gordon, Donald M, 1931-3

THOMPSON, MARGARET COLLINS DUNCAN (m R.R. Thompson)
10 Dec 1884, Brooklyn N.Y.
addr: Westmount, 487 Argyle Ave, 1931-9
1931 231 Mist in the valley, Lake Memphremagog wc
1933 316 Before the storm, Lake Memphremagog wc $15
317 Georgeville Bay, Lake Memphremagog wc $15
1934 343 A breezy day, Firth of Clyde, Scotland wc $25
344 In the Auvergne Mountains, France wc $35
1936 433 On the coast, Carmel, California wc $40
434 Ocean Point, Maine wc $50
1937 297 Lifting clouds wc $15
1939 319 A cleft in the rocks $18

THOMSON, GEORGE
10 Feb 1868, n Claremont, Ont 21 Jul 1965, Owen Sound, Ont AGO CWW61 NGC WWA62
addr: Owen Sound, 591 8th St E, 1929-39. Toronto, 759 Yonge St
1929 208 A breeze from the south $400
209 An old beech $300
210 Bay at Owen Sound $200
1930 195 Nature's decoration $400
1931 232 A summer night $400
1933 314 A country road $400
315 Breeze from the south $400
1934 342 April in Muskoka $400
1935 324 Reflected sunlight
1936 435 Spring in the Caledon Hills $300
1937 298 A Georgian Bay cliff $400
1939 320 Spring in La Cloche Mountains $325
1940 284 A breeze from the north $325 (Mellors Gallery)

THOMSON, MARY HELEN (m J.H. Thomson)
28 Nov 1915, Montreal
addr: Upper Woodlands, Que, 410 Lac St Louis Rd
1956 69 Early spring $75

THOMSON, THOMAS JOHN (TOM)
4 Aug 1877, n Claremont, Ont 8 Jul 1917, Canoe Lake, Ont AGO B CC1 CE EC NGC R1 TB W78
1922 deceased
294A Landscape

THOMSON, WILLIAM JAMES

28 May 1858, Guelph 25 May 1927, Toronto AGO EC H W78
addr: Toronto, 11 Bleecker St, 1912-15
1912 etching, 1912-15
382 Muggy night, Lake Ontario $22
383 Zero weather $18
384 42nd Street, N.Y. $12 (AGO)
385 Riverside, N.Y. $12 (AGO)
1914 403 Fisherman's harvest, Vancouver $20
404 Madison Street, Chicago $15
405 River at Edmonton $15
406 Two views of Vancouver from False Creek $15
1915 334 Winter wash day in the suburbs $15
335 Market day, Toronto $15
336 The top of the grade $10
337 The brick mill $10

THORNTON, MILDRED VALLEY STINSON (m John Henry Thornton)
7 May 1890, Dresden, Ont 27 Jul 1967, Vancouver
addr: Regina, 1955 Robinson St
1933 318 Sir Frederick Haultain, Chief Justice of Saskatchewan $1,000

TIBBLES, LESLIE G.
b 1916
addr: Ottawa: 497 Clarence St, 1945; 193 Carling Ave, 1946-7
1945 221 Blackstone Lake, Parry Sound $100
221A Our place $75
1946 234 Black Lake, Gatineau Park $150 (MBAM)
235 Early spring, Wrightville $150
1947 265 Winter shadows $250

TIESSEN, GEORGE
1935, Leamington, Ont
addr: Sackville, N.B.
1968 intaglio print
278 Unknown precinct 13 3/4 x 16 5/8 $40
279 Section north 13 1/4 x 13 3/8 $35
280 Untitled 21 1/2 x 16 7/8 $45
281 Rime 16 5/8 x 13 3/4 $40

TIFFANY, GEORGE (Mrs)
addr: Outremont, 703 B Bloomfield Ave
1926 121 Petite bretonne
122 An elf maid

TILEY, JAMES HENRY
22 Sep 1933, London, Eng
addr: Toronto, 310 High Park Ave, 1963-5
1963 65 Rock column $300 (LPL)
1964 75 Monolith No 8 $500
1965 19 Statement 7 $650

TILLEY, ELIZABETH S. (Mrs)
addr: Saint John, N.B, 215 Germain St
1906 290 A stitch in time wc $50

TIMMERMAN, GRANT
addr: Montreal, 3552 Shuter St
1940 285 Maggie, portrait $400

TINNING, GEORGE CAMPBELL
25 Feb 1910, Saskatoon CWW84 NGC TB2 WWA84
addr: Montreal: Sidney Carter Galleries, 2025 Victoria St, 1939-41; 1536 Summerhill Ave, 1942. Halifax, H.Q. 2nd Br, Black Watch, RHR, 1943. Montreal; 1178 Phillips Pl, 1948-1957; Montreal, 1967
1939 water colours, 1939-54
321 Sea rhythm, Prout's Neck $40
322 The last of the four masters, Wisscaset $40
323 Victoria Street, Montreal $40
324 Old houses, Biddeford, Maine
1940 286 Flowers $75
287 Sherbrooke St, 4 o'clock $50
1941 204 Emperor tulips $50
205 Piedmont $50
206 Cranes and tanks $50
1942 168 Suggested by Tchaikowsky's 'Romeo and Juliette' $30
169 Suggested by the waltz movement, Tchaikowsky's 5th Symphony $50
170 March, the Basilica of St James $75
171 Runway at Trenton, Ontario, Air Station $75 (listed 1967, Jessie Dow prize)
1943 L/Cpl
192 Suggested by Shoenberg's 'Transfigured night' $50
193 Suggested by Beethoven's piano concerto in C sharp minor $35
194 Waterford, N.B, October 1942 $50

195 Mountains at Field, B.C, June 1942 $250
1948 92 November, Sherbrooke Street, Montreal
93 San Giovanni in Romanga $125 1967-69, 15 x 21
1954 116 Sketch at the rehearsal of the London Festival Ballet $150
117 Naramata, B.C. $200
1956 136 House in New Orleans, La nm
1957 149 Round Hill, Jamaica, B.W.I. nm $250

TODD, FREDERICK G.
11 Mar 1876, Concord, N.H. CWW48 Mo12
addr: Montreal; 801 New Birks Bldg, 1913; 920 Castle Bldg, 1934-5
1913 441 Bowering Park, St John's, Nfld
442 Coldbrook Garden City, Saint John, N.B.
443 National Battlefields Park, Quebec
444 Garden and pergola, Senneville
1934 416 Sewell Garden, Seigniory Club
417 Proposed Montreal Protestant Memorial Park, Chinese tower
418 Proposed Montreal Memorial Park
1935 377 The lily pond
378 The chimes tower
see also Barott, Ernest I, 1934-369

TOLGESY, VICTOR
22 Aug 1928, Miskolc, Hungary 6 Jan 1980, Ottawa CC1 TB3 WWA78
addr: Ottawa: 157 Stanley Ave, 1957; 84 Bradford St, 1960
1957 168 Stone age cast stone $200
1960 254 Christ figure wc $300

TOMMEV, FOTO SPIRO
c 1899, Zhelevo, Greece
addr: Toronto, 855 Lansdowne Ave
1933 319 Beech trees, winter $10

TONDINO, GENTILE
3 Sep 1923, Montreal CC2 NGC TB2
addr: Montreal: 523 Faillon St, 1947; 4100 Côte St Catherine Rd, 1949; 3653 Durocher St, 1950-1; 523 Faillon St, 1954; 3435 Barclay St, 1956; 5905 Côte des Neiges Rd, 1957-61
1947 266 Studio corner $100
267 Self portrait $100
1949 103 The artist $75
1950 48 Boats $75
1951 120 Still life $75
1954 80 Still life $125
81 Young boy
1956 70 Woman and still life $300
71 Still life $150
1957 96 Head $75
1958 24 Trees $500
1960 120 Nude with drapery $200
1961 59 Still life $400

TONNANCOUR, JACQUES GODEFROY DE
3 Jan 1917, Montreal AGO B CC2 CE NGC TB2 WWA76 Juror
addr: Montreal, 3058 Lacombe Ave, 1948-50. St Lambert, Que, 211 Walnut Ave, 1953-4
1948 62 Head $300
1949 104 La Dame de Pique $350
105 Nature morte au bégonia $275
1950 140 Femme accoudée $475
157 Nu assis mine de plomb
1953 72 Nature morte $350
1959 5 Paysage d'hiver No 1
6 Paysage d'hiter No 2
1960 24 Présence d'un pin $900 (MBAM)
1961 11 Composition $850
1964 24 Les retombées $475

TOPHAM, WILLIAM THURSTON
23 Jul 1888, Spondon, Eng 11 Mar 1966, Montreal
addr: Montreal: 2574 Esplanade Ave, 1913-15; Arts Club, 1918, 1920; 84 St François Xavier St, 1919; 305 Beaver Hall Hill, 1922; 358 Beaver Hall Sq, 1923-4; 533 Phillips Sq, 1929-37; 2047 Victoria St, 1938-40; Arts Club, 1941-3; 2049 McGill College Ave, 1945-7
1913 384 Lamplight, drawing-room, Neues Palais, Potsdam wc $60
385 Summer afternoon, Cotswolds wc $55
1914 407 Early October morning, Dominion Square $200
469 Hall interior des 1915-406
1915 338 Sketch, Notre Dame, Montreal $25
339 A courtyard, Bavaria wc $35
340 Sketch, Victoria Square wc $12
341 Fishing boats pastel $60
1918 Gunner

344 Who died for us (The Crucifix on the Fricourt-Contalmaison Road, night of July 8th 1916) $250
345 The Fricourt Road, July 1916 $35
1919 336 Night bombardment, Fricourt, first Battle of the Somme, 1916 $250
337 Edgar Allan Poe poem illus $75
338 The dancer in green $60
339 Child with chickens $25
340 Haddon Hall, Derbyshire $25
1920 269 Old houses, St Vincent Street, Montreal $75
1922 295 Moonlight, rue Cardinal, Paris $200
1923 215 Old houses, winter, Notre Dame Street wc $50
216 Lincoln, Brayford Pool pastel $50
1924 254 Gypsy girl, study wc $35
255 The House of Usher wc $120
256 Arc de Triomphe, Paris $100
257 The hay wagon $35
1925 275 Moonlight, Seminaire de St Sulpice, Notre Dame Street, Montreal $250
276 The turquoise necklace wc $40
1926 123 Silver winter, Black Lake $150
124 Thundering weather, Tulworth Cove $150 (125 not in catalogue)
126 Doorway, Amiens wc $25
127 The excavation, Eaton's new building wc $40
1927 168 The moonlit portal, Maison Mère des Soeurs de la Congregation, Montreal $350
1929 211 Moonlight, Ypres $250
1930 196 Northern lights $250
197 Winter night, North River pastel $100
1931 233 Rock pool in the bush $250
234 La Barrière, Que $300
1932 310 Moonlight and clouds, old mill near Boucherville $400
311 Sunlight after rain, Green Lake $150
1933 320 Full moon, full flood, North River $250
321 Half-Moon Lake $100
1934 345 Winter moonlight, Sous le Cap, Quebec $300
346 Laurentian fall over-mantel dec $150
1935 325 Rue Sous le Cap, Quebec wc $100
326 Lost River at Fraser Lake wc $75
327 Moonlight, Montreal from La Prairie $300
1936 436 Vieille rue, nocturne $400
437 Sunlight in the bush, early October wc $200
438 Sunrise, Mont Tremblant, study wc $50
1937 299 Grey day, Montreal from University Tower wc $250 (listed 1967, Jessie Dow prize) (MBAM)
300 Above the falls near Macdonald Lake, Que wc $200
301 Moonlight, September, North River wc $75
1938 122 Evening, Lac Croche, Chapleau Club $200
1939 325 Castle in the sky, Sun Life Building from Victoria Street, night wc $250
1940 288 October, North River $150
289 North River Rapids wc $150
1941 207 Wild water, early spring, North River $150
208 Rapids near Ste Marguerite, North River wc $150
1942 172 Laurentian farm, Val David $300 (listed 1967, Jessie Dow prize)
173 Winter landscape, Shawbridge, Que wc $75
1943 196 Take-off, Saint Johns training school, seen from control tower
1945 222 Last of the snow $200
1947 268 Shadows in the bush $350

TOPPINGS, MURRAY GLENN
8 Dec 1930, Kipling, Sask 3 Mar 1972, Vancouver
addr: Vancouver, 2646 West 10th Ave, 1961. Sunshine Falls, Burrard Inlet, (n Vancouver) 1963
1961 60 Mid-light $125
1963 66 QA $350

TORRANCE, ELIZABETH M.
addr: Châteauguay Basin, Que
1895 130 Jacqueminot rose

274 Tea caddy
275 Plates
276 Bouillon cup & saucer

TORRANCE, LILIAS see NEWTON, LILIAS

TOUCHETTE, DENISE (m Jacques Vincent)
14 Jul 1930, Howick, Que
addr: Ste Dorothée, Que, 27 rue Lawson
1957 150 Tête nm $50

TOUPIN, FERNAND
12 Nov 1930, Montreal CWW84
addr: Montréal, 1316 rue St Zotique
1960 121 Envol $120

TOURVILLE, RENE RODOLPHE
24 Aug 1897, Louiseville, Que 7 Oct 1962, Montreal CNS36
address: Montreal, 10 St James St W
1940 Tourville & Parent
335 Intérieur d'églish, étude
336 Petite église à Ferme-Neuve, Que
337 Eglise St Jean, Berchmans, intérieur
338 Un monastère, étude

TOUSIGNANT, CLAUDE
23 Dec 1932, Montreal B CCI CE CWW84 WWA84
addr: Montréal; 1247 rue Wolfe, 1960-1. Fort Chambly, Que, 53 rueRichelieu, 1962-3. Montréal: 3811 rue St André, 1964-5; Montréal, 1968
1960 224 La ligne jaune nm $250
1961 61 Multiligne $350
1962 35 Poème electronique $500
1963 67 Asti spumante $500
68 Pouilly-Fuissé $500
1964 76 Boule d'hum $550
1965 20 141 $2,000
1968 liquitex sur toile
282 Transformateur chromatique 89d $2,550
283 Gong 80 80d $2,250

TOUSIGNANT, SERGE
28 May 1942, Montreal B CC2 CE
addr: Montréal, 1681 rue Sicard
1964 77 Sillages $150

TOWLE, G.
addr: St Sauveur-des-Monts, Que
1957 151 Montagne, St Sauveur nm

TOWN, HAROLD BARLING
13 Jun 1924, Toronto AGO B CC2 CE CWW84 NGC TB2 WWA84
addr: Toronto: 9 Castle Frank Cr, 1960-3; Toronto, 1968
1960 122 The spectre No 3 illus Purchase award (MBAM)
225 Gateway to Atlantis single autographic print $290
1962 36 The culture wall $1,900
1963 69 Decline of the tyranny of the corner nm illus $2,200 A.H. Robinson prize. 1967-70, oil & lucite 44 on canvas 70 x 81 (Mr Livio Muresan, Montreal)
70 Welders set $1,900
1968 284 Persia oil & lucite on canvas 81 x 64 $4,200
285 Thurber's O smoke & fixative, ink & brush on illustrated board 60 x 40 $1,200
286 Vinyl vor smoke & fixative, ink, pen, brush & tape 60 x 40 $1.900
287 Enigma ink brush, ink & pen on coloured stock 25 5/8 x 19 3/4 $1,500

TOZER, MARJORIE HUGHSON
24 Jul 1900, Halifax
addr: Halifax, 35 Fenwick St, 1928-35. Montreal, 2028 Victoria St, 1936
1928 191 Quidi Vidi, Nfld pastel $35
192 Cockles Cove, Nfld pastel $25
1930 198 Cape Rouge, Cape Breton pastel $35
199 Cheticamp, Cape Breton pastel $35
1931 235 Wind swept $500
1932 312 Sanctuary $500
1934 347 Polperro $200
1935 328 A Cornish fishing village $150
1936 439 Across the street pastel $75

TRAQUAIR, RAMSAY
29 Mar 1874, Edinburgh 26 Aug 1952, Guysborough, N.S. CWW49 PMC
addr: Montreal, McGill University, Dept of Architecture, 1918-33
1918 405 Cottage in Nova Scotia
1920 273 Perseus' flight wc $50
274 The city gate wc $50

1922 296 Scotch firs wc $25
297 Fort Point, Guysborough, N.S. wdcut $10
1933 322 Halfway Cove, N.S. wc $25
323 The barrens, N.S. wc $25

TRAVERS, GWYNETH MABEL GWILLIM (m C.H. Travers) IO WWA82
6 Apr 1911 - 28 Jan 1982, Kingston, Ont
addr: Kingston
1968 288 Solar flare etch 8 1/2 x 12 $40
289 Archaic forms etch 12 x 16 $50
290 Clock tower metal gr 12 x 16 $50

TREACY, MARION CRAWFORD
addr: Toronto, 1 Cheritan Ave, 1955-6
1955 79 Holiday $85
1956 72 Outing $100

TREMBLAY, CONRAD
addr: Wrightville, Que, 30 7th Ave, 1951. Ottawa, 60 Henderson Ave, 1952
1951 143 L'envoi des rhizomes ink $20
1952 126 Oiselets, marins wc & drwg

TREMBLAY, GEORGES E.
addr: Iberville, Que, 113 9th Ave, 1933-6
1933 531 Béatrice plaster
532 Georgette plaster
533 Chamoine J. Chas. Cormier bronze
534 Ma Mère plaster
1934 515 Dr Alexis Bouthillier, MPP bronze
516 Melle Cécile Coderre, Farnham, Que plaster
517 Mr S. Deschatelets, Montreal plaster
518 Projet de monument funéraire wd & plasticine
1935 482 Mme Geo E. Tremblay, et sa fille Georgette d'Iberville plaster
483 Prof J.B. Dubois, violincelliste, de Montréal plaster
1936 612 Mlle Frances Bianco plaster
613 Mr James Bianco and family plaster
614 Mde G. Racicot, Trois Rivières Plaster
615 M Jacques Dery, Montreal plaster

TREMBLAY, GERARD
3 Sep 1928, Les Eboulements, Que
addr: Montreal: 6280 Iberville St, 1951-2; 8233 Lajeunesse St, 1954; 6215 2nd Ave, 1956; 3507 Van Horne Ave, 1961; Montreal, 1967
1951 131 Les sémaphores gouache $100
132 Les jouets innocents gouache $100 Jury II prize
1952 113 Les cristaux des planètes $125
114 La faune de la nuit $200
1954 118 La mer c'est une forêt wc $75
119 Les oiseaux ont peur de tout wc $75
1956 137 Les douelles nm $75
1961 62 Le petit moulin des mères $225
1967 71 Sans titre. 1961. 38 1/2 x 58 (M Bernard Jasmin, Montreal)

TREMBLAY, JACQUES
10 Feb 1935, Ile Perrot, Que
addr: Montreal, 5518 Lafond St
1951 46 Côte de la Place d'Armes $200

TREMBLE, G. EDWARD
addr: Montreal, 1390 Sherbrooke St W, 1946-7
1946 233 Early spring
1947 269 The spring break-up $125

TRENHOLME, FLORENCE THOMPSON (m Frederick Minden Cole)
addr: Montreal: Rosemount, 1897; 215 Stanley St, 1905
1897 214 Quebec wc $12
1905 Cole
145 Gloucester harbour wc $25

TREPANIER, RACHEL
addr: Verdun, Que, 4060 Ethel St, 1943. Montreal, 3458 Laval Ave, 1943-8
1943 plaster, 1943-8
261 M François Desmarais
1945 283 My Father
1946 294 Léon, portrait
1948 118 Etude, portrait

TREWEEK, G. E.
addr: Plymouth, Eng
1908 262 Early morning, Alderney wc $40
263 Near St Agnes, Cornwall wc $40

TRIM, KATHLEEN
addr: Montreal, 780 Belmont Ave
1936 572 Isabel drwg

TRIMINGHAM, RUTH K.
addr: Montreal, 3539 Shuter St, 1936; 2069 St Luke St, 1937
1936 440 Austin $35
1937 301 Colonial door, Georgeville, Que $15

TROTTIER, GERALD MATHEW
9 Sep 1925, Ottawa AGO CC2 IO NGC TB2
addr: Ottawa: 36 Newton St, 1950; 291 Crichton St, 1951; Ottawa, 1968
1950 76 Shore line, Ottawa River wc $70
77 Stillman's Gym, New York wc $70
1951 65 The jetty wc $60
1968 liquitex on canvas
291 Self portrait in overcoat 84 x 60 $1,500
292 The masons 72 x 84 $2,000
293 Shrine banner 72 x 70 $1,500

TRUCHON, ROLAND SEVERIN
21 Sep 1920, La Malbaie, Que d 1961
addr: Montreal, 3404 de Bullion St, 1951. Roxboro, Que, 10451 Gouin Blvd, 1952
1951 133 Prudents comme les serpents wc $20
1952 115 Là dans un bosquet entourré de fleurs $200

TRUDEAU, POWELL
29 Jan 1910, Montreal
addr: Montreal, 3860 St Hubert St, 1953. Town of Mount Royal, 485 Ellerton Ave, 1961
1953 61 Study charcl
1961 104 Evolution nm $100

TRUDEAU, YVES
3 Dec 1930, Montreal CC2 CE DMS WWA84
addr: Outremont, 183 Querbes Ave
1964 138 Script sculpture bronze $600

TUCKER, LILLIAN
d 1939 H
addr: Montreal, Côte St Antoine, 1894. Westmount: 4211 Dorchester St, 1897-8; 4203 St Catherine St, 1900; 4203 St Catherine St, 1901
1894 147 A study $35
1897 126 Old mill at La Tortu $15
127 A solitary oak $12
128 Un ouvrier $20
1898 100 N. Tucker, Esq
101 Early morning, St Ann's Market $20
102 Sous le Cap, Quebec $18
103 River St Pierre $15
1900 102 Miss M. Nellis
161 A bit of Montreal wharf wc $12
162 On the brow of a hill wc $10
1901 95 Kennebunk River $13
96 Indian summer $12

TULLEY, CHARLES
27 Aug 1885, London, Eng 16 Aug 1950, Montreal CNS36
addr: Verdun, Que, 197 Egan Ave, 1921. St Hubert, Que, 1922. Verdun, 63 Argyle Ave, 1924; 655 Argyle Ave, 1929-37. St Hubert, Que, 1945
1921 322 Town Hall, Oudenarde $15
323 Town Hall, Bruges $15
324 Guild Hall, London
1922 298 Amiens Cathedral b&w
299 Rheims Cathedral b&w
300 Westminster Abbey b&w
301 Old belfry, Bordeaux b&w
1924 300 Elgin Cathedral b&w
301 Maison San Luis Ry b&w
302 Canford Manor b&w
1929 345 Three races drwg
1932 313 Courtyard wc
1933 324 Antwerp Cathedral wc
325 Victory wc
326 School days wc
1934 348 Bonsecours
476 St Bartholomews, London pencil
1935 329 Old houses, Benoit Street, Montreal wc $15
1936 441 The Ostende mail paquet wc
1937 303 Man's humble servant
304 The rest
305 An impression of old Montreal wc
306 The thinker wc
1945 223 The Fleming Mill at La Salle, Que $150

TULLEY, EDWARD
addr: Verdun, Que, 655 Argyle Ave
1932 314 Bordeaux wc

TULLY, SYDNEY STRICKLAND
10 Mar 1860 - 18 Jul 1911, Toronto AGO

CC1 CWW10 H Mo12 NGC W78
addr: Toronto: Yonge St Arcade, 1892; 61 Prince Arthur Ave, 1894-5; 176 Roxborough St E, 1898-1901; 27 Wellington St, 1903; Argyle Studios, 36 Toronto St, 1905-9
1892 131 Oysters and lemons $50
132 An acolyte painting $50
133 Sketching $60
134 Mr Kivas Tully
1894 148 Within sound of the sea $50
244 Beatrice pastel $75
1895 131 Memories $100
132 Lullaby $50
215 A wind came up out of the sea, and said O mists make room for me pastel $85
1898 104 Shipping, Rye, Sussex $85
105 Jeanne, a study $100
205 Phoebe pastel $95
1901 97 Etretat, Normandy $75
180 Portrait of a lady pastel $200
1903 111 Cloud effect, Cap à l'Aigle $50
112 Landscape $50
259 Portrait of a lady pastel $200
260 The sisters pastel $200
1905 113 Twilight $75
114 The coming of spring $350
219 The enchanted forest pastel $450 (AGO)
1906 161 The gateway of the forest dec panel $175
162 Sunset, Portneuf $60
163 After rain, Portneuf $50
291 A study pastel $30
1909 362 Peasblossom dec study
363 Midsummer night's dream pastel $150
364 Misty morning, Holland wc $60
365 Dutch interior wc $40
366 Evening, Holland wc $35

TURCOTTE, EDWARD J.
1894, Percy, N.H, 12 Oct 1975, Montreal
addr: Montreal: 459 Dorchester St E, 1921; 1158 Beaver Hall Hill, 1928; 1135 Beaver Hall Hill, 1934
1921 273 Le ruisseau $20
1928 284 Church of the Ascension, Westmount
1934 419 St Ignatius School
420 Church, study
see also Archibald, John S, 1933-345

TURNBULL, ANDREW WATSON Eng
Apr, 1874, England DBA DVP G RA TB2 WWB50
addr: Westmount, c/o Mrs J.B. Blodon, 85 Holton Ave, 1927-9, 1931. Richmond, Surrey, Eng, 21 Sheen Rd, 1930, 1933
1927 303 Bristol University, England etch $20 unfr
304 Salisbury Cathedral, England dry pt $17.50 unfr
1928 329 West of St Paul's, London etch $30
330 The glory of St Paul's, London etch $30
331 St Mary-le-Strand, London etch $30
332 Cataluna, Spain etch $30
1929 346 St Martin's Church, London etch $50
347 Edinburgh, from the Calton Hill dry pt $20
348 Donegal, Lough Belshade dry
1930 298 Wadham College, Oxford col pr
1931 Academy of Art Ltd, Birmingham, copyright 407-9 etch
407 London University
408 Royal Edinburgh
409 The old tolbooth, Edinburgh
1933 495 Sir Arthur Keith, facile princeps among anthropologists dry pt $10
496 White Lodge, Richmond Park, birthplace of the Prince of Wales etch $10
497 Loch Duich, Rosshire dry pt $5.50
498 On the River Garry, Perthshire dry pt $5.50

TURNBULL, MAY L'ESTRANGE
addr: Montreal, 18 The Metcalfe Apt
1910 413-4 Repoussée brass frame $15 each

TURNER, PHILIP JOHN
1876, Stowmarket, Eng 13 Aug 1943, Montreal CNS36 CWW38 Mo12 PMC
addr: Montreal: Coristine Bldg, 1909; Board of Trade Bldg, 1910-14; 49 Beaver Hall Hill, 1915-16; 274 Beaver Hall Hill, 1923-27; 1100 Beaver Hall Hill, 1928-39
1909 450 Houses, Grosvenor Ave, Westmount

1910 412 Ice Palace 1910 des
1911 310 Building for Anglican Mission to the Jews
311 St Alban's Memorial Church, Montreal
1912 422 Molson's Bank
1913 445 Molson's Bank, Drummondville
446 Residence, Elm Ave, Westmount
447 Proposed residence, Lincoln St, Montreal
448 Moose Jaw, City Hall des
1914 Turner & Carless, 1914-15
470 House, Montrose Ave, Westmount
471 House, Comte and Chomedey Sts
472 House, Pointe Claire, Que
1915 407 Molson's Bank Bldg, St Lawrence and Ontario Sts
1916 353 Molson's Bank, Sorel, Que
354 Molson's Bank, Norwich, Ont
355 Residence, Carleton Ave, Westmount
1923 276 Summer residence, Point Cavagnol, Como
277 Office building, Montreal des
278 Bethanie Presbyterian Church
1925 312 Crown Trust Company, offices, Montreal
313 Residence, Avenue Road, Westmount
1926 Turner & Maw
158 National War Memorial, Ottawa des
159 Suburban residence
1927 254 Bishop's University, Lennoxville, Que, proposed Convocation Hall, Gymnasium, Dormitory Bldgs
1928 282 Extension to banking room, 200 St James St
283 Crown Trust Co, office bldg
1929 290-2 Church of St Columba, Parish Hall, Montreal, exterior, interior, guild room
1930 241-5 St Philips Church, Montreal, West, general view from SE, view from Connaught Ave, view from Brock Ave, interior, interior of chapel photos
1936 498-9 St Paul's Church, Côte des Neiges, Montreal
500 Christ Church Cathedral, Montreal, children's corner
1937 375-6 Memorial chapel, Montreal interior, narthex
1939 369-71 Chapel, YMCA, Drummond St, Montreal, interior, detail of sanctuary, corridor of honour, entrance

TURNER, STANLEY FRANCIS
1 Aug 1883, Aylesbury, Eng 3 Jun 1953, Toronto AGO CNS36 CWW49 TB3
addr: Toronto, 150 Redpath Ave
1924 226 Western pioneers shown RCA 1923 exhibit, mural competition

TURQUAND, HELEN ELIZABETH
17 Jun 1885, Hamilton, Ont AAA32
addr: Toronto, 123 Cottingham St, 1912-22
1912 386 The orange shawl pastel $40
387 Old houses, Volendam pastel $25
388 Dutch peasant girl pastel $30
1922 302-3 On the Atlantic coast $60 each

TWEEDIE, C. D. (Mrs)
addr: Outremont, 25 St Catherine Rd
1916 393 Tea set, Dutch $25

TWEEDIE, LILIAN A.
addr: Montreal, 5567 Darlington Ave, 1936-7
1936 442 Mixed flowers $35
1937 307 Lily of the valley $20

TYLER, GERALD HALL
25 Jul 1897, Birmingham, Eng
addr: Vancouver, 1103 Robson St
1935 330 Near Ruskin, B.C. $35

U

UNDERHILL, ERNEST HENRY
11 Jul 1922, Winnipeg
addr: Montreal, 1490 Mountain St, 1951. Charleswood, Man, 31 Dieppe Rd, 1955
1951 134 The organ grinder gouache $60
1955 80 Noel $85

UPJOHN, ANNA MILO
addr: Westmount, 4295 Montrose Ave
1928 193 Elizabeth

URATA, SUNAO

addr: Toronto, 35 Britain St
1964 78 Violet murmur $250

U'REN JOHN CLARKSON Eng
fl 1880-1920 DBA DBW DVP G
addr: Plymouth, Eng
1908 264 Stormy weather Kynance wc $100
265 Lizard Head wc $75

URQUHART, ANTHONY MORSE (TONY)
9 Apr 1934, Niagara Falls, Ont AGO B CCI CE IO NGC TB2 WWA84
addr: Niagara Falls, 1923 Main St, 1960. London, Ont, 21 Grand Ave, 1961. c/o Isaacs Gallery, 832 Yonge St, 1962, 1964. London, Ont, 51 Royal Rd, 1963. Toronto, 1968-70
1960 123 Landscape on a tapestry I $350
1961 105 C-note nm $250
1962 37 Grand hero!
1963 90 In admiration of Fan Kuan nm $350
1964 109 Caulfield rain forest III nm $125
1968 294 Broken (2nd version) acry, masonite, plywood 66h $1,000
295 The great view oil on masonite & acry 60 x 36 1/2 $750
296 Grotto box plywood, acry & resin glue 42h $500
1970 87 The Roman line oil on wood veneer on plywood 36 x 13 3/4 (Michael Ondaatje)
88 Temple I plywood & mm 32 1/4 x 14

URQUHART, KATHERINE
addr: Sackville, N.B, Ladies College
1935 441 Reflections block pr $3

URSENBACH, JESSIE REDD (m Octave W. Ursenbach)
15 Aug 1895, New Harmony, Utah
addr: Lethbridge, Alta, 1259 6th Ave 'A', 1943. Toronto, 133 Lyndhurst Ave, 1944-46
1943 197 Ruffled petunias wc $25
1944 120 Forty Mile Creek, Alta wc $50
1945 224 Baby mums wc $75
225 Shady Lyndhurst wc $75
1946 236 Banff poppies wc $75

V

VACHELL, DESMONG see HARVEY, DESMOND

VAILLANCOURT, ARMAND
4 Sep 1932, Black Lake, Que CE DMS
addr: Montreal: 502 Prefontaine St, 1958-9; 1199 Bleury St, 1961-2; 1051 Champlain St, 1963; 3724 St André, 1964. Montreal, 1967
1958 91 Volonté iron $150
1959 64-5 Nos 1 and 2 wd
1961 124 Sculpture No 1 metal illus $900. Ladies Comm prize. 1967-72, wld steel 18 x 88 1/2 (Jean-Pierre Labreque, Montreal)
1962 81 The Holy Trinity steel $3,000
82 The F...bird bronze $2,100
1963 118 Architecture of to-day bronze illus. Ladies Comm prize (listed 1967)
1964 140 Le rideau de fer fonte $5,000

VAILLANCOURT, JOHN A.
addr: Montreal, 4591 St André St
1932 480 Marcelle plaster

VAILLANCOURT, JOSETTE
addr: Outremont, 141 Pagnuelo Ave, 1939-40
1939 326 Lois
1940 290 Peggy

VALDERRAMA, E.
addr: Paris
1914 408, Peintre, Chas M. Mendel

VALENTINE, HUGH ALLEN INGLIS
1 May 1904, Dundee, Scot 16 Feb 1978, Port Hope, Ont
addr: Montreal: 1539 Bishop St, 1933. 1671 Sherbrooke St W, 1936; Beaver Hall Bldg, 1939-41
1933 499 Carcassonne, France drwg $10
500 The walls of Carcasonne drwg $15
1936 443 Maison de la Congrégation du Notre Dame, Montreal wc
573 Chartres Cathedral, France pencil
1939 372-4 Bell Telephone Company of Canada, buildings, Ste Anne de

Bellevue, Que, Bracebridge, Ont, Gananoque, Ont, St Johns, Que
1940 339-42 Bell Telephone Company, buildings, London, Ont, Kitchener-Waterloo, Ont, Clairval dial office, Montreal, Sudbury, Ont
1941 274-6 Bell Telephone Company, buildings, Port Colborne, Ont, Kingston, Ont, two

VALIUS, TELESFORAS
10 Jul 1914, Riga, Latvia 1 Dec 1977, Toronto IO WWA80
addr: Toronto, 84 Pine Cr Rd, 1954-64
1954 127 Country linocut $50
1957 152 Golgota nm $150
1964 110 Post morning nm $60

VALLANCE, HUGH A.
Dec 1866, Hamilton, Ont 14 Mar 1947, Montreal NGC
see Brown, David R, 1909-406, 1910-380-3

VALLANCE, WILLIAM F.
addr: Hamilton, 74 West Ave S, 1936-7
1936 444 Russian holiday, still life $50
1937 308 Spring, still life $50

VAN BUSKIRK, CAROLINE RUTH
17 Oct 1868, St Thomas, Ont
addr: St Thomas, 108 Gravel Rd, 1916. Montreal, 32 Ste Famille St, 1920
1916 290-2 North Wales, wc $15 each
293 Corn field, autumn wc $10
1920 275 Heathery hilltop, north Wales wc $20

VAN DALEN, ANTON
13 Jul 1938, Amsterdam
addr: Toronto, 620 Church St, 1963. New York, 1970
1963 71 The face of the deep $325
1970 89 Leaves - Time magazine 80 x 60
90 Leaves - computer card 65 x 135 (Graham Gallery, New York, 89-90)

VAN DEN BROECK, CLEMENCE see BROECK, CLEMENCE

VAN DER LINDE, LOUISE
addr: Peterborough, Ont, Box 659
1892 miniatures on ivory
219 Ethel $50
220 Portrait $60
221 Portrait of a lady $60

VANDERPOEL, EMILY NOYES (m John A. Vanderpoel) Amer
1843 - 1939, New York F WWA38
1888 69 Family jars wc $50
78 Tulips wc $35
106 Rosita wc $25

VANDERPOLL, GERALD
1882, Amsterdam CNS36
addr: Westmount, 4100 Western Ave, 1939. Montreal, 1818 Sherbrooke St W, 1932-3. Westmount, 1215 Greene Ave, 1939. Montreal, 4310 Decarie Blvd, 1943
1931 410 Cloister at Roermond, Holland etch $25
411 Old alley, 16th century, Amsterdam drwg $50
412 Market entrance, Amsterdam drwg $15
1932 etching, 1932-39
442 Trader Horn $10
443 The Motherhouse by moonlight $15
444 Old Amsterdam $15
445 Nocturne $15
1933 501 Mary-Ann Vanderpoll col etch
1939 468 Sherbrooke Street, Montreal $12
469 Sundown, Montreal $12
470 Beaver Hall Hill, Montreal $12
1943 198 Early fall pastel
242 Mrs H.J. Barrie col etch
port: by Koenraad Nijenhuis, 1932-421

VAN DER VOSSEN, ANN (m Joannes Van der Vossen)
addr: Ottawa, 382 Ashbury Rd
1957 98 Refuge $65

VAN EVERY, JANE (m Hugh Van Every)
addr: Kitchener, Ont, 538 Park St, 1949-50
1949 149 Childhood memory of the kitchen wc
150 Let's go to the hill around wc $50
1950 78 Beach at Provincetown wc $50

VANIER, BERNARD

4 Apr 1927, Quebec
addr: Paris, 9 rue Faiguière
1961 106 Terre ancienne nm $33

VANSIER, BORIS
7 Jun 1928, Russia
addr: Montreal, 4870 Côte des Neiges Rd
1954 82 Sur la plage

VAN STOCKUM, HILDA (m Erwin Marlin)
9 Feb 1908, Rotterdam WWA53
addr: Westmount: 520 Argyle Ave, 1950; 419 Lansdowne Ave, 1961
1950 49 Autumn still life $250
50 The professor of French $300
1961 63 Sheila $250

VANSTONE, ZORA SHARP
addr: Brantford, Ont, 151 St Paul Ave
1934 350 Farm house $25

VAN TUYL, CATHERINE H. (m L.G. Van Tuyl)
addr: Montreal: 1450 Mountain St, 1930; 4918 Piedmont Ave, 1932-3; Westmount, 456 Elm Ave, 1935
1930 miniatures, 1930-5
200 Master John Norris
201 Miss Lucille Collins
1932 316 Mrs H.M. Kennedy (A) Herbert (B) Max (C) Tommy
1933 327 Capt Nelson Young
328 Max
329 Mrs Ernest Bolton
330 Betty Stewart
1935 331 Miss Ruth Elizabeth Dettmers
332 Miss Shirley Anne Hyde
333 Master John Gilmour
334 Master Peter Lighthall

VARLEY, FREDERICK HORSMAN
2 Jan 1881, Sheffield, Eng 8 Sep 1969, Toronto AGO B CC1 CE CWW67 EC NGC TB2 WWA53
addr: Toronto, 70 Lombard St, 1924. Ottawa, 145 O'Connor St, 1940. Montreal, 1419 Drummond St, 1943
1924 227 Immigrants. Shown RCA 1923 exhibit, mural competition 2nd prize
1940 291 Northern lights, B.C. $50
292 Dawn, Lynn Valley, B.C. $50
293 Arctic nights $50
294 Ice $50
1943 199 Trooper X, 1943 $600
200 A soldier $600

VART, LEON
addr: Montreal, 4216 Northcliffe Ave
1950 79 Purgatory gouache $100

VARVARAND, ROBERT EMILE
2 Jan 1922, Lyond, France AGO CC1 TB2
addr: Toronto, 1449 Dundas Highway E, Islington, 1957; Greenwich Gallery, 736 Bay St, 1958-9; Issac Gallery, 736 Bay St, 1960
1957 99 Nature morte au vase noir $175
1958 44 Les tournesols $120
1959 25 Nature morte $175 (MBAM)
1960 124 Interior with table I $225

VASS, IDA M. (Mrs)
addr: Montreal, 1595 Macgregor St, 1937-9
1937 309 Still life $50
1939 327 Autumn afternoon $100

VAUTELET, RENEE
addr: Montreal, 3488 Durocher St, 1934-45
1934 351 Autumn afternoon, Côte de Liesse $50
352 Autumn morning, Côte de Liesse $50
353 Afternoon, Percé, Que $50
354 Bonaventure Island, Percé
1935 335 Summer seas, Ogunquit, Maine $100
336 Drowsy waters, near Percé $70
1936 445 Sunrise, Ogunquit $125
1937 310 Day's end, Ogunquit $130
1945 226 Restless sea $125

VAUTIER, BORIS
addr: Outremont, 622 McEachran Ave
1949 151 Conversation avec un modèle gouache $100

VAUX, EMMA PLIMSALL
b Brockville, Ont
addr: Toronto
1908 147 Portrait study $60
266 Tête de femme. Litho Salon, 1906 $25

VAZAN, WILLIAM JOSEPH
18 Nov 1933, Toronto WWA82
addr: Montreal, 1969-70

1969 11 Untitled cloth tape 140h
1970 91 Subway rides photos, subway transfers, map, documentation 2 parts 34 x 84 each illus

VENNE, EMILE
10 Jul 1896, Montreal CNS51
addr: Montreal, 402 Plessis St
1920 drawing
276 Le secret du paon
277 Le secret des fauvettes
278 Le secret de l'albatros $25
279 Le secret que je garde

VENNE, JOSEPH
14 Jun 1859 - 9 May 1925, Montreal
addr: Montreal: Place d'Armes Hill, 1905; Montreal, 1908; 5 Beaver Hall Sq, 1913
1908 342 Church, perspective
1905 Venne & Labelle, 1905, 1913
267 St Michel de Percé, Gaspesie, perspective view
1913 449 St Catherine Roman Catholic Church, Amherst St, Montreal perspective study
see also Perrault, Maurice, 1894. Viau, Joseph D, 1916

VENNE, LUDGER
1891, Quebec Province 24 Apr 1973, St Lin, Que
addr: Montreal, 698 St Catherine St W
1927 258 Eglise catholique, Jackman, Maine
see also Viau, Joseph D, 1927-255-7

VENOR, ROBERT GEORGE
12 Jan 1931, Montreal WWA78
addr: Montreal: 649 Vitre St, 1961; Montreal, 1970
1961 64 Quebec carnival $150
1970 92 Dream No 1 epoxy styrofoam 48h

VERNER, FREDERICK ARTHUR
26 Feb 1836, Sheridan, Ont 6 May 1928, London, Eng AGO CE EC H Mo12 NGC TB3 W78
addr: Toronto, 1880. Windsor, Ont, c/o Dr Coventry, 1891. Toronto, 79 King St W, 1892-4. London, Eng, 16 Edith Villas, W Kensington, 1895-8. Montreal, c/o Johnson & Copping, 1900, 1903, 1913. London, Eng, 39 Palace Terrace, 1901. London, 1905; 417 Fulham Palace Rd, 1906-22
1880 54 Sioux tepees on the Assineboine
77 Ojibway Indians gambling
79 Canadian fruit
138 Ojibway pow-wow, moonlight wc
141 Lac des Mille Lacs wc
164 On the look out wc
173 Camp, Lake of the Woods wc
178 Twilight, Lake of the Woods wc
1881 3 Solitude, Scarborough
4 Twilight on the Humber
28 Old windmill near Montreal
29 Eagle Lake
31 White Head, near Portland
89 Twilight on the Humber wc
90 After sunset, High Park wc
1883 3 Pig Street, Lynton, north Devon wc
23 The adjutant wc
50 Crossing the marsh wc
1885 105 Ojibbawa (sic) Indians crossing Nipigon Lake wc
117 Grimston, Dorset wc
143 A rocky bed wc
147 Wigwams on Nipigon River wc
1886 96 The upper Ottawa
1889 163 Group of buffalo wc $200
164 Buffalo in moonlight wc $75
165 Head of Lake Shebandowan wc $75
166 Ojibbewa (sic) Indianc wc $75
167 Bison by moonlight wc $75
168 Muskoka Lake wc $40
1891 206 Canadian elk wc $150
207 Misty morning, Nipigon Lake wc $60
1892 135 Jersey cows $250
215 Sunset on the prairie wc $60
216 Ice flow, Detroit River wc $50
1894 234 Druidical remains, Salisbury Plain wc $100
1895 204 Harvest time, Stratford-on-Avon wc $35
205 Thatched cottages, Warwick wc $35
206 Group of buffalo, evening wc $30
207 Wigwams, Nipigon River wc $30
208 Ojibbewa (sic) camp wc $30

209 Sunset, Norfolk wc $20
1897 215 Buffalo, hazy morning wc $100
216 Red cedar, afterglow, Point Pelee wc $110
217 Group of Canadian elk, wapiti, morning wc $100
218 Round wigwam, north shore, Lake Huron wc $50
219 Near Sandwich, Ontario wc $40
220 Beech trees by the brook wc $40
1898 106 Buffalo, winter evening $300
206 Group of birches wc $60
207 Round wigwam, Rainy River wc $35
208 Mick-Mack camp, White Mountains wc $40
209 The portage wc $35
1900 163 Birch woods wc $40
164 Sandy Point, Lake Erie wc $35
165 At even, ere the sun has set wc $30
166 An autumn impression wc $30
167 Woodland wc $30
168 A shady pool wc $30
1901 181 Bison, morning wc $50
182 Sunset, near Sandwich wc $40
183 Birch woods, autumn wc $40
184 Sunset wc $25
185 Twilight wc $25
1903 226 A winter evening wc $35
227 St Clair marsh wc $30
228 Burnham Common wc $35
229 Birch woods wc $35
1905 195 Old church at Chingford wc $50
196 Twilight effect wc $25
197 Return from market wc $25
198 Tower of London wc $35
199 Lone Wolfe, Indian chief wc $50
200 Gumming a canoe wc $50
1906 292 Birchwood wc $50
293 West Angle, Lake of the Woods wc $50
294 Bison crossing frozen stream wc $75
295 French River wc $50
296 Evening wc $25
1908 148 A Sioux encampment $300
267 Bison, misty morning wc $125
268 Autumn, birch woods wc $50
1909 367 Sunset, Fulham wc $50
368 Bison in the snow wc $200
369 Camp, Blackfeet Indians wc $250
1910 339 Bison, misty moon $200
340 Advocate's Close, Edinburgh b&w $100
341 Bison, evening $50
1911 274 Bison, autumn evening wc $200
275 Buffalo, evening wc $75
276 Lake Superior wc $60
1912 389 Group of bison wc $75
390 Bison, evening wc $100
1913 386 Advocate's Close, Edinburgh wc $75
387 Bison, mid-day $200
388 Twilight wc $35
389 Lion's Head, Jersey wc $35
1914 409 Bison resting by lake $250
410 Stag Inn, Burnham wc $50
411 Dutch fishing folk wc $50
412 Indian alone in marsh wc $50
1915 342 Buffalo, winter evening $250
343 Bison alone on prairie wc $75
1916 294 November evening $50
295 Birch woods wc $40
296 Beech tree wc $40
297 Tintern Abbey wc $40
1917 337 Round wigwam, Rainy River wc $75
338 North shore, Lake Superior wc $75
339 Buffalo bull and cow wc $50
1918 346 Bison $300
347 Pevensey Church $75
348 Beech woodlands $75
1919 341 The lone buffalo wc $60
342 Winter, Wimbledon Common wc $50
1921 274 Beechwoods $50
275 Twilight $50
1922 304 Advocate's Close wc $75

VERREAULT-LAPOINTE, GISELE (m P.M. Lapointe)
addr: Montreal, 655 Bloomfield Ave
1961 65 "= 1/2 mv" $175

VEZINA, EMILE
6 Jan 1876, Cap St Ignace, Que 16 Jul 1942, Montreal
addr: Montreal: 22 Notre Dame St E, 1906; 203 Montgomery St, 1915; 318 St Denis St, 1916; 338 Ontario St E. 1920
1906 164 Portrait de l'artiste
1915 344 Study
1916 298 Sketch
1920 338 Mademoiselle E. Giroux

VIAU, GUY
7 Aug 1920, Montreal 6 Nov 1971,

Paris Juror
addr: Montreal: 4001 Northcliffe Ave, 1945; 3821 Harvard Ave, 1957
1945 227 Nature morte aux citrons $50
1957 100 L'atelier St Colomban
153 Françoise nm $30

VIAU, JOSEPH D.
29 Sep 1881, Ste Anne de Bellevue 24 Aug 1938, Quebec
addr: Montreal: 76 St Gabriel St, 1916; 99 St James St E, 1927
1916 Viau & Venne, Joseph
356 Noviciat des Frères des Ecoles Chrétiennes, Laval des Rapides
357 Oratoire St Joseph du Mont Royal, Montreal 1927-256
358 Fire and police station, Tétreauville
359 Municipal building, Lachine
1927 Viau & Venne, Ludger
255 Residence, J.S. Durocher, Esq, Dunlop Ave, Outremont
257 Hôpital du Sacre Coeur, Cartierville, Que

VIAU, ROGER
11 May 1906, Montreal
Montreal, 1160 Laurier Ave W, 1932. Outremont: 19 Vimy Rd, 1939-41; 254 St Catherine Rd, 1943
1932 317 Nature morte $25
318 Rue Union, Montreal $75
1939 328 Mrs V.F.
329 Self-portrait, winter
330 Rue des Carrieres, Montréal $100
332 La chaise rouge $75
1940 295 Mme R.V.
296 La délaissée $100
297 Poires et pommes $75
1941 209 City limits $80
1943 201 Cyclamen $100
202 Nature morte $80

VICAJI, DOROTHY E. Eng
d 13 Feb 1945 DBA F RA WBA
addr: London, Eng, The Studio, 17 Holly Mount, 1925. New York, St Regis Hotel, 1926-7
1925 277 Mrs Noman Stines
1926 128 Mrs R. Magor
129 Robert Magor, Esq
1927 169 Margit $2,000

VICAJI, RUSTON Eng
fl 1918-27 DBA
addr: London, Eng, The Studio 17 Holly Mount
1925 278 Venice wc $200
279 Ducal palace wc $200
280 Thames at twilight wc $200

VICKERS, HENRIETTA MOODIE
AAA1900
addr: Toronto, 172 Adelaide St W
1903 230 The last match wc $35
323 Japan jug $10
324 Old man of the sea (china) $4
325 Cup & saucer, water lily $6
326 Jardiniere $3.50
327 Vase
port: by Mary Evelyn Wrinch, 1903-328 (min)

VICKERS, R. H.
addr: Montreal, 274 Union Ave
1922 305 H.E. the Duchess of Devonshire min (Lady Meredith)
306 Mrs Bowman min
307 Miss Joan Riddell min

VIGNEAU, MARGUERITE (MARGO)
addr: Montreal, 3660 Hutchison St, 1944-9
1944 Margo
168 Negrillonne ter cot
1949 177 Fleur de chine ter cot

VINANTE, DONATO
addr: Montreal, 428 Bleury St
1918 379 Electric fixture $150

VINCELETTE, ROMEO
b Verdun, Que
addr: Montreal: 4480 Des Erables, 1943; 1178 Phillips Place, 1945-7
1943 203 Piedmont, early March $100
1945 228 North River, Piedmont $300
1947 270 Lac Millette Road pastel $200

VINCENT, POGGI see POGGI, VINCENT

VINEBERG, LOUISE (m Henry Charles Vineberg) (signs Louvin)
1924, Montreal M

addr:Montreal, Galerie Agnes Lefort, 1504 Sherbrooke St W
1963 38 Cityscape $200

VINEBERG, SIMA GEFTER
addr: Montreal, 5565 Trans-Island Ave
1956 74 Paris hotel room

VOCE, FRED
addr: St Lambert, Que, 103 Pine Ave
1929 212 Ilfracombe harbour, England wc $75

VOGT, ADOLPHE Amer
1843, Liebenstein, Thuringia, Germ
1871 New York B H NGC TB
1880 deceased
8 Cow
24 Breath of morning air
34 View on the Mississipi, valley of the Ottawa, by Otto R. Jacobi, animals by Vogt
40 Cattle piece
63 When the kye comes home

VON GONTARD, LUDWIG see GONTARD, LUDWIG VON

VOYER, MONIQUE
25 Jul 1928, Magog, Que
addr: Montreal, 3420 Hutchison St, 1955-6. Duvernay; Que, 655 Franchere St, 1960; 515 Hocquart St, 1964
1955 137 Jeune fille et les fleurs nm $10
1956 75 Composition $60
76 Nature morte $65
1960 125 Vestiges orientals $200
1964 79 L'oiseau chimère $350

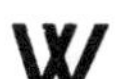

WADDELL, E.
addr: Toronto, 340 Bloor St
1910 342 A corner of the farm $50

WAGNER, HERBERT WILLIAM
1889, Galt, Ont Nov 1948, Toronto
addr: Weston, Ont, 22 Sykes Ave
1928 194 Breezy autumn, Muskoka $160

WAINWRIGHT, RUTH SLATER (m Inglis Lough Wainwright)
2 May 1902, North Sydney, N.S. TB2
addr: Halifax, 77 1/2 Larch St
1937 311 Margaree Harbour, Cape Breton wc

WAITE, EMILY BURLING (m Arthur William Manchester) Amer
12 Jul 1887, Worcester, Mass B F TB1/2 WWA62
addr: Boston
1918 349 Mrs Fenwick Williams
350 Near T wharf etch
351 Mr Irving Tomlinson etch $15
352 Mrs James Weaver etch $10
353 Miss Amelia Muir Baldwin etch $10
354 Elizabeth

WAKEFIELD, CHARLES COLE
c 1897-1959
addr: Toronto, 321 Birchmount Rd, 1945-53
1945 229 Spring blizzard $300
1946 237 Back yard $95
1947 271 The butternut tree $75
1953 56 Feeding time wc $35

WALES, JEANNETTE
addr: Montreal, 3592 Durocher St, 1936. St Andrews East, Que, 1937
1936 446 Old houses, St Andrews East wc $20
1937 312 Constance pastel $5

WALES, PHILIP
1866, Port Louis, Mauritius H
addr: Ottawa, 437 Gilmour St
1898 107 In the bush $25

WALES, SHIRLEY (m S.J. de Jong)
24 Jul 1931, Montreal AGO
addr: Aspremont, Alpes Maritime, France, 1963. Montreal, Galerie Agnes Lefort, 1504 Sherbrooke St W,1964
1963 91 Cathedral nm $50
92 Cascade nm $60 (AGO)
1964 111 Papillon de nuit nm $75

WALKER, ELIZABETH (Mrs)
addr: Montreal: 1908; 15 Lorne Ave, 1909. Outremont, 768 St Catherine Rd, 1911
1908 269 Among the Monadhliah Hills wc

1909 370 Between the sand dunes wc
1911 277 The western waves of ebbing day rolled o'er the glen their level way wc $20

WALKER, HORATIO
12 May 1858, Listowel, Ont 27 Sep 1938, Ste Pétronille, Que AGO B CC2 CE EC H Mo98/12 NGC TB WWA38
addr: L'Ile d'Orleans, Que
1901 98 The lime kiln, moonlight
99 Spring ploughing

WALKER, JESSIE see AITCHISON-WALKER, JESSIE

WALKER, JOLIFFE
addr: Montreal; 1908; 100 Metcalfe St, 1909-10
1908 149 Sir Thomas Shaughnessy, KCVO
150 Sir George A. Drummond, KCMG
1909 371 Sir George Drummond
372 Miss Maud Hanson Walker
1910 343 The late Sir George Drummond
344 Mrs H.R.D, study

WALKER, VIVIAN (Mrs)
addr: Montreal, 2075 Lincoln Ave, 1943-50
1943 204 Back yards, Rodgerdale, Que $100
1945 230 The old canal, Lachine, Que $75
1946 238 Still life $60
1947 272 What to do $75
1948 63 Calendulas $75
1949 106 Petunias $65
1950 51 The old quarry, Ile Perrot, Que $75
1952 53 Eighty summers $100

WALLACE, GEORGE BURTON
7 Jun 1920, Sandy Cove, Dublin Co, Ire AGO IO
addr: Dundas, Ont
1968 297 The dead Christ wld steel 15h x 84 long $2,600
298 Death with flowers wd steel 72h $2,600

WALLACE, IAN
25 Aug 1943, Shoreham, Eng
addr: Vancouver
1969 12 Untitled wd & vinyl 72 x 168 x 10

WALLIS, Constance C. (Mrs)
addr: Westmount, 4278 Sherbrooke St W, 1944-6
1944 121 Flower piece
1946 239 Zinnias

WALLIS, KATHERINE ELIZABETH
1861, Peterborough, Ont 15 Dec 1957, Santa Cruz, Cal B H Mo12 NGC TB1/2
addr: Paris, 54 ave de Maine, 1910. Peterborough, 309 Park St, 1922. Paris, 27 rue des Fleurs, 1931-5
1910 376 Dog, dachshund sculp $12
377 Rat sculp $85
378 De repos $35
379 Mrs H.L. Haultain bas rel
1922 357 Symbol of Prince Edward Island low rel $40
358 Dolly, daughter of Robert Ross, Esq, D Sc low rel
1931 444 La lutte pour la vie mahogany $4,000 (NGC)
1935 484 A Canadian girl marble $250

WALSH, JOHN STANLEY
16 Aug 1907, Brighton Eng AGO WWA80
addr: Montreal, 1112 Elgin Ter, 1945-7. Beaconsfield, Que, 8 Kirkwood Ave, 1948. Lachine, Que: 675 44th Ave, 1952-4; 142 52nd Ave, 1960; Lachine, 1967
1945 231 Alley, Montreal gouache $60
232 Lagauchetière Street, Montreal wc $60 (Jury II prize, listed 1967)
1946 240 Lorne Crescent wc $60
1947 273 Montreal lane wc $65
274 Night study, Montreal wc $45
1948 110 Street in Paris charcl $45
111 Market scene, Ghent charcl $45
1952 68 Winding street wc $180
1954 83 Quebec No 1 $130
1960 226 Taxco at night nm $200
1967 73 Two churches at night, 1966 wc 24 x 20

WARD, WILLIAM DUDLEY BURNETT
19 Apr 1879, Graveley Bank, Staffs, Eng Feb 1935, Toronto AGO
addr: Toronto, 110 Scarborough Rd, 1915. Outremont, 1310 Lajoie Ave, 1925-6. Montreal: 750 Bloomfield Ave, 1931; 2241 Maplewood Ave, 1933; 2089 Ile Visitation St, 1935

1915 Dingbat-land
345 Bubbles wc $50
346 Fright wc $85
347 No 3 wc $40
1925 281 Fairy light wc $150
282 In Dingbat-land wc $75
283 Surprise wc $150
386 Leap frog drwg $7
1926 130 Vanity wc $80
131 Modern Mother Goose wc $75
132 Friend or foe wc $50
1931 237 The rumble seat wc $20
238 'Midsummer night's dream' illus wc $50
1933 331 Vanity wc $75
332 None but the brave deserve the fair wc $75
333 The bogey-man 'll get you if you don't watch out wc $75
502 Eskimo, Coronation Gulf charcl
1935 deceased
337 Gossip wc
338 Fright wc $50
339 Secutiry? wc

WARDELL, DOROTHY WILMA
5 Dec 1910, Hamilton, Ont
addr: Toronto, 59 Kendal Ave, 1942-5
1942 174 Miss Alice McCarthy pastel $100
175 McCaul Street, Toronto pastel $40
176 Sugar camp, Lafontaine wc $35
1943 205 Artist's brother pastel
206 Fishermen's shacks wc $50
207 Wharf, Penetanguishene wc $50
1944 122 Shipyard wc $60
123 Fishermen's Point wc $45
1945 233 Portrait pastel
234 Back yards wc $40

WARDROPE, MARY JANE (Mrs Telfer)
addr: Montreal, 6410 Sherbrooke St W
1954 129 The talking bird wd cut $15

WARE, L. GRAEME (Miss)
addr: Toronto
1892 136 Knitting $25

WARING, HENRY FRANKS Eng
b Birkenhead, Eng, fl 1900-40 DBA G WBA
addr: Chiswick, Eng, 1912. Montreal, 116 Board of Trade Bldg, 1913
1912 water colour, 1912-13
391 The moated grange, Groombridge, Kent $75
392 One summer day $65
393 Evening on the Mold, Dorking $55
394 Fordwick, Kent $35
395 In a Sussex village $35
1913 390 The village of Wingham, Kent $50
391 The village of Groombridge, Kent $50
392 Old mill near Wingham $75
393 Dorking Church $75

WARKOV, ESTHER (m Frank Visscher)
12 Oct 1941, Winnipeg WWA84
addr: Winnipeg, 1968-70
1968 pencil, 1968
299 A bird in the ear is worth 2 in the nose 11 x 13 $140
300 The technology of love 10 x 12 $140
301 Dalton Camp having a medieval vision 15 x 13 $140
302 Noon hour target practice at the Funny Farm 48 x 164 $2,500
1970 93 Memories of a dead love 68 x 120

WARREN, AGNES VERONICA KETTER (m C.T. Warren)
addr: Saskatoon: 218 11th St E, 1934; 218 1st St E, 1936
1934 355 Girl in brown $225
356 Mlle Philo St Denis
1936 447 Portrait of May $150
448 San Toy pastel $50

WARREN, B. ALEXANDRIA
addr: Sackville, N.B, Lodge, Mount Allison University
1940 298-9 Still life $75, $60

WARREN, E. L. (Mrs)
addr: Montreal, 4811 St Catherine St W
1936 449 Miss Phyllis Wills pastel

WARREN, EMILY MARY BIBBENS
20 Oct 1869, Exeter, Devon, Eng 28 Jun 1956, Dunrobin, n Ottawa DBA WWB39
addr: Ottawa, Ottawa Ladies' College, 1928-9. Montreal, 1340 St Catherine St W 1928-34

1928 195 Rouen from St Catherine's Hill wc $45
1929 213 The Thames from Tower Bridge wc $20
1932 319 St George's Chapel, Windsor wc $150
1934 357 Cathedral of St Gudule, Brussels wc $100

WARREN, FRANK CHICKERING
addr: Montreal, 492 Melrose Ave
1926 133 Moonlight, Capri $200

WARWICK, SEPTIMUS
1881, England 27 Oct 1953, St Leonards, Eng DBA G RA
addr: Montreal: 696 Sherbrooke St W, 1914; 59 Beaver Hall Hill, 1915; 390 Sherbrooke St W, 1917-19
1914 473 Berkshire country house, England
474 Holborn Town Hall, London, England
475 Country house, Meath, Ireland
476 Manchester Free Library, London, Eng competition des
1915 408 London County Hall final competition des
409 Lambeth Town Hall, principal entrance
410 Council chambers, Holborn Town Hall
411 St George's House, Perth, W Australia
1917 392 Domestic work, Turnbridge Wells, for late Marquess of Abergavenny, K.G. centre illus, alterations to house at Brighton
393 Gosport Gas & Coke Co, main office
394 Proposed civic centre, Vancouver competitive des
395 Proposed hotel preliminary study
1918 406-7 House, garage, garden, Edgehill Rd, Westmount, and interior views
408 Cottage, Laurentians
409 House, Westmount Blvd
1919 404 J.J. McGill, Esq, residence, Dorval
405 A.J. Wood, Esq, residence, Westmount, interior views
406 Victory loan arch, Montreal
407 St James Methodist Church, Montreal, interior dec
408 Church and Sunday school, Notre Dame de Grace

WATKINS, A. N.
addr: Montreal, 453 Sherbrooke St W
1920 281 Richmond in Yorkshire wc
282 Scene near Bath, Eng wc $75
283 Old fortress near Boulogne wc $40
284 Sand dunes north of Boulogne wc $40

WATKINS, B. (Professor)
addr: Montreal, 453 Sherbrooke St W, 1922
1889 169 A monring on the moors wc $30
170 Tombs of the Kings, Westminster Abbey wc $25
171 The old dock abandoned, Bristol wc $25
1922 312 Iceberg wc $40
313 Pangbourne wc $35
314 Pointe Claire, Lake St Louis wc

WATLING, H. Edward
addr: Westmount, 4380 Montrose Ave
1936 452 Interior

WATSON, ALEXANDER
17 Oct 1858 - 1923, Saint John, N.B. H
addr: Saint John: 5 King St, 1900-5; 105 Wentworth St, 1915-22
1900 103 Waiting for the tea to draw
104 An evening sky $100
105 Landscape $75
1901 100 Memories $150
186 In Saint John harbour wc $50
187 Old fish houses wc $50
188 Girl with a violin wc $50
1905 201 The watering place wc $60
202 Evening at the chalet wc $60
1915 348 Bay of Funday packet $100
349 Harbour light, St Martins, N.B. wc $60
1916 299 A friendly chat $100
300 The old shed wc $75
1917 340 September in New Brunswick $100
341 Old willow at Westfield $100
342 Grey day, Nerepis River wc $30
343 The old shed wc $25
1918 355 Summer afternoon $75

356 Beach at Smith's Cove, N.S. $30
357 Shady pool
1919 343 Old Well house at Westfield, N.B. wc $50
344 White birches wc $30
345 Small craft, Saint John wc $50
346 Coal barge and schooner wc $50
1922 308 Showery weather, South Bay, N.B. wc $60
309 Summer afternoon, Digby, N.S. wc $40
310 Fog in the offing, Lorneville, N.B. wc $40
311 The three birches, Saint John River wc $40

WATSON, HOMER RANSFORD
14 Jan 1855 - 30 May 1936, Doon, Ont
AGO B CC1 CE EC G H Mo98/12 NGC TB1/2 W78
addr: Doon, 1880-1936
1880 29 Approaching storm, Adirondacks
1881 10 The stone road, Dundas
25 Clearing up
1883 97 Down the ravine
110 The day has been wet and weary
144 A land of thrift
1885 16 Evening
1888 61 His head towards home $45
1889 86 Evening $100
87 A lowland burn $100
88 Departing shower $100
1891 132 When mists have rolled away
133 A March day $150
1892 137 Stream by the woods $150
138 From shelter to pasture $500
139 After the mists have lifted $400
140 October
1894 149 The woodcutters (MBAM)
150 October day
151 Path under the oaks
152 Woodland
153 Wood gatherers in the oak glade $300
154 Hillside road $200
155 The wayfarer $200
156 Among the beeches, November morning $250
157 At work among the ricks $75
158 The swineheard $75
159 The forest lane $75
1895 133 An old sheep barn
134 The farm in the wood $100
1897 129 The old mill $250
1898 108 The mill ford
109 After the storm
110 The village under the hill
111 Grand River woodlands $300
112 Squally weather, fishing boats running to harbour $300
1900 106 The dry watercourse $550
107 Memory of a Scotch town $500
108 The well in the forest $500
109 The limestone ridge $500
110 November in the clearing $500
111 River meadow lands $500
112 Moonrise
1903 113 Below the mill (MBAM)
114 A hayfield
1908 151 A March morning at Pine Hill
1910 345 Approaching storm $250
346 The old sawmill $250
1913 394 Rolling surf, Louisburg $2,000
395 Stumpers at night fall $2,000
396 Sunset $150
397 The timber wagon $150
1921 276 The red oak $1,000
277 The brae village $1,000
1924 260 Gleaning the wood lot
261 November at the pit $700
262 The wayside inn
263 Moonlight, waning winter $500 (NGC)
1927 170 Early winter in the wood lot
171 December moonrise, sketch $500
172 River forest $500
1928 196 Glacial stream, B.C.
1929 214 The cabin in the lane
215 Oak of the banks, Grand River
1933 334 Drouth at Boulder Creek, B.C.
335 The book oak
336 March ice break, Grand River
1934 358 Woodland ford
1935 340 Storm drift at the Pitt
341 Under the trees at Caledon
1935 450 High water, Pine Bend, Grand River $1,500
451 Near twilight, B.C. $1,400
1894-7 Assoc 2nd prize landscape, 1892; 1st prize landscape, 1894
port: by Andrew Dickson Patterson, 1900-84; sculp by John Sloan, 1940-416 (MBAM)

WATSON, THOMAS

addr: Nelson, B.C, c/o W.J. Biker, Esq
1927 173 Near Painswick, Glos, England wc $45
174 Cotswold cottages, Glos, England wc $45

WATT, HENRY ROBERTSON (ROBIN)
26 Sep 1896, Victoria 11 Sep 1964, Cowansville, Que Juror
addr: Montreal: Coronation Bldg, 1405 Bishop St, 1928; 1509 Sherbrooke St W, 1929-31. Westmount, 439 Mount Pleasant Ave, 1949-50. Montreal: 3489A Drummond St, 1951-6; 1200 McGregor St, 1957-60
1928 197 Portrait of the artist's wife
198 Ralph Hobday, Esq
199 Sholto Watt, Esq
200 The convalescent
201 Miss Jane Cory pastel
202 Portrait sketch pastel
1929 349 Miss Jane Holt chalk
350 Miss Lucille Molson chalk
351 Miss Orian Stewart chalk
352 Master Anthony Dobell chalk
1930 202 Beatrice Mary Angus pastel
299 Master Ian Hyde chalk
1931 239 Miss Lucille Molson pastel
240 Miss Yvonne Sutherland pastel
1949 107 Donnie Yuile, Esq
108 J.P. Lewis, Esq
1950 52 Geoffrey Hedges, Esq
53 Still life
1951 47 Frances Doble, Lady Lindsay-Hogg
1952 54 James Muir, Esq
1953 51 Mrs John Bourne
1954 84 David Walker, Esq
1955 82 Royden, son of J.G. McConnell, Esq
1956 77 John Steegman, Esq, OBE MA FSA
1957 101 John, son of Richard F. Angus, Esq
1960 126 Isaiah Gavin illus Purchase award (MBAM)

WATTERSON, GRACE MARGARET VICTORIA WILSON (m J.C. Watterson)
22 Apr 1905, or 1906
addr: Montreal, 1525 St Mark St, 1932-7. Westmount, 168 Metcalfe Ave, 1939
1932 320 Spring flowers pastel
1937 313 Mrs H.M. Bolger min
1939 332 Laurentian village $75

WATTS, ETTA (m W.H.Watts)
fl 1895-1900 H
addr: Montreal, 610 St Denis St, 1895. Westmount: 459 Clarke Ave, 1898; 538 Grosvenor Ave, 1900
1895 135 A garden in Bavaria $500
136 A blacksmith's shop, Fyfe, Scotland $150
137 In mischief $100
138 A gleam of sunshine $100
139 In doubt $100
1898 113 Vieilles maisons aux environs de Paris
114 Early Autumn, Berthier, Que
1900 113 Lumber boats, Beaupré, Que $50

WATTS, JOHN WILLIAM HURRELL
16 Sep 1850, Teignmouth, Eng 26 Aug 1917, Ottawa H Mo98 NGC
addr: Ottawa: 1891-5; c/o Wilson & Co, 1897
1891 134 Woodland pool $18
208 Autumn hillside wc $35
1894 160 Fall ploughing $25
161 Spring time $25
1895 140 An uphill road $20
141 A misty morning $15
1897 221 The last of the leaves wc $40
222 Chill October wc $40

WATTS. L. MONTAGUE
addr: Montreal, 2570 Esplanade Ave
1922 315 The Priory, landscape, Hampshire, England b&w
316 Iford village, Hampshire b&w
317 Ringwood, Dorset, Eng b&w

WAY, ANNIE M.
fl 1899-1915 H
addr: Montreal, 9 University St, 1900. Lausanne, Switz, 31 ave de Rumine, 1914
1900 114 In the harvest field $5
169 Elm trees wc $5
1914 417 At Orta wc $10

WAY, CHARLES JONES
25 Jul 1835, Dartmouth, Eng 13 Feb 1919, Lausanne, Switz B DBA H Mo98/12 NGC TB W78
addr: Lausanne, Switz: 1880-89; 1894; 1908-9; 31 ave Rumine, 1910-17; Florence, Italy, 1892. Montreal, 9 University St, 1900

1880 27 The valley of Champery, Canton Valais
105 Landscape, Switzerland wc
111 The morning catch wc
122 High pastures, Dent du Midi wc
124 Storm clearing off Devonshire coast wc
125 Old bridge at Champery, Switzerland wc
127A Cap Rosier, Gulf of St Lawrence wc
171 A la fontaine, Suisse chalk
172 The birth of a torrent chalk
185 Near Murray Bay wc
1881 23 An Alpine torrent
1883 21 The Besso Zinal, Switzerland wc
1885 107 Alpine bridge wc
111 Swiss mountains wc
132 A solitude, Mount Desert, Maine wc
1886 23 Church of Santa Maria della Salute, Venice wc
30 Market landing, Grand Canal, Venice wc
69 The valley of Champrey, Switzerland
1889 174D A winter's morning at the foot of the Wetterhorn wc $300
174E A Devonshire fishing village, sea fog coming in wc $200
174F A veteran wc $30
1892 217 A fisherman's house at Capri wc $30
1894 235 Ave Maria wc
236 Children of the Appenines wc
1900 115 Birch trees, Cap à l'Aigle $50
170 Rapids on Grand Rivière wc $75
171 A windy day at Capri wc $100
172 Unloading charcoal, Venice wc $20
1908 270 Lakes Como and Lecco wc $20
271 Autumn evening, Tremezzo wc $50
272 Summer morning, Ependes wc $75
1909 373 Court of Mermaid Inn, Rye wc $20
374 The Land Gate, Rye wc $15
375 Where John Wesley preached his last sermon wc $40
376 Chestnut trees, Tremezzo, Como wc $50
1910 347 A road in Sussex wc $50
348 Mountain village, Sunday morning wc $20
349 Winchelsea Church wc $20
1911 278 The Matterhorn, evening wc $50
279 The Church Terrace, Brissago wc $30
280 Afterglow on the mountains wc $15
1912 396 The Arno, Florence, evening wc $50
1913 398 In the Fraser Canyon, morning, noon and evening wc $400
399 In a Sussex village wc $20
400 The Barbican Gate, Sandwich wc $20
1914 418 A street in Sandwich, Kent wc $15
419 Entrance to old house, Orta wc $20
420 Meadows and streams, Sandwich wc $25
421 Near Kilmalcolm, Renfrewshire wc $30
1915 350 The road to the convent wc $30
351 At Orta, Italy wc $30
352 In Renfrewshire wc $30
1917 344 Gate to an old farm wc $30
345 Old house and garden wc $20
346 Rocks of the Fereboni, Capri wc $150

WAY, EVELYN
addr: Montreal, 951 Tupper St
1923 284 Vase enamels on Satsuma
285 Vase glazes and enamels
286 Vase, Chinese boy, enamels
287 Bowl raised enamel
288 Bowl lustre

WEAGANT, ALLEN (Mrs)
addr: Smith's Falls, Ont, 1900-01
1900 255 Lustre dish mother of pearl effect $12
256 Lustre nut dish shell effect $10
257 Dresden china dish old ivory effect $40
258 Bonbon box $20
259 Lustre frame $3
260 Rose plaque $40
1901 276 Doulton cake plate
277 Bowl $12
278 Violet vase $10
279 Glass vase $4

WEAVER, C.
addr: Montreal, 1474 Mansfield St
1937 314 Security pastel $30
315 Quick sketches pastel $20

WEBBER, GORDON MCKINLEY
12 Mar 1909, Sault Ste Marie, Ont 17 Nov 1965, Montreal AGO CC2 TB2 WWA62
Juror
addr: Montreal: 1494 Mackay St, 1944; 1102 Elgin Ter, 1946-55
1944 124 A three party line temp & wc $50
125 Changing relationships temp $50
1946 241-3 Design Nos 1-3, 1946 wc $75 each
1947 275-77 Design Nos 1-3, Vermont, 1946 temp $100 each
1948 64 Design No 12, Vermont, 1947 temp $100
1952 127 Design No 1, 1952 temp $100
1955 138 Abstract composition No 3, Mexico nm $85

WEBSTER, ADELAIDE (m George H. Donald)
addr: Montreal: 131 Crescent St, 1926-7; 1523 Crescent St, 1930-50
1926 134 In a carpenter's shop, Paris $1,000
135 Georgina Winnifred, daughter of Mr & Mrs George W. Grier pastel
136 Elizabeth pastel
1927 175 Mrs G. Ross Sims
1930 203 George Arthur Donald wc
204 James Robert MacGregor Donald wc
205 Black tulle
1932 321 The scarf
1933 337 Jean, portrait sketch
1934 Donald, 1934-6
92 Miss Margot Dorken
93 Jean in brown
1936 137 Margot
1939 333 Fresh from the garden $150
1947 278 Portrait of a lady in black
1948 65 Mother and daughter
1950 54 Mrs J. Willis Jones

WEBSTER, CHARLOTTE B.
addr: Montreal
1908 miniatures
300 Mr B.
301 Mrs B.
302 Miss A.B.
303 Miss Madeline Biggar
304 My Mother
305 Mrs Wentworth Buchanan
306 Mr Wentworth Buchanan
307 Miniature after Boucher $75

WEBSTER, DANIEL T.
1886-1952
see Barott, Ernest I, 1915

WEBSTER, HERBERT HENRY
28 Nov 1909, Windsor, Ont
addr: La Salle, Ont, 150 Lafferty St
1957 102 Clown $150

WEBSTER, JEFFREY C.
addr: Westmount, 57 Hallowell St, 1928-9. Montreal: 3636 Decarie Blvd, 1936; 5530 Côte St Luc Rd, 1941-3
1928 pen & ink, 1928-9
333 Christ Church Cathedral, Montreal
1929 353 Arch of Triumph, Paris
354 St Bartholmew the Great, Smithfield
355 Church of St John the Evangelist, Montreal
356 St Matthias Church, Westmount
1936 574 The Seminary clock, St Sulpice, Montreal pen & ink
575 Marika dry pt
1941 dry point, 1941-43
259 Christ Church Cathedral, Montreal $10
260 Arts Building, McGill University $10
261 Nude $10
1942 216 Church of St Columba, Montreal $10
1943 243 Depth charge $12

WEDIN, PETER
addr: Montreal: 908 St James St W, 1930; 2075 Dorchester St W, 1931
1930 carved panels, 1930-1
320 Morning in the fishing cabin $50
321 Pulling off Grandpa's boots $50
1931 351 In the fishing cabin $45
352 By the fireplace $45
353 Preparing the supper $45
354 To the train $55

WEIHS, KURT
addr: Montreal, 3469 Hutchison St
1945 235 Erika
236 Two girls
237 Acrobats $200

WEININGER, SYLVIA see SINGER, SYLVIA

WEIR, ALDEN JULIEN Amer
30 Aug 1852, West Point, N.Y. 8 Dec 1919, New York B F TB
addr: New York, 11 E 12th St
1892 141 The open book $2,000

WEIR, WINNIFRED
addr: Westmount, 94 Westmount Blvd
1915 353 Waiting pastel $15

WELDON, R. L. (Mrs)
addr: Westmount, 381 Claremont Ave
1918 358 A winter sketch $20

WELLS, CHRISTOPHER
b Summerside, P.E.I.
addr: Ottawa, 135 Riverdale Ave
1964 80 The proxy $350

WESBROOM, WILLIAM N.
1889 172 At Portneuf wc $75

WESTON, ELOISE
fl 1880-1 H
1881 93 Flowers wc

WESTON, JAMES L.
c 1815 d 1896 H
addr: Montreal, 1880. New York; 110 E 23rd St, 1894; 106 E 23rd St, 1895
1880 49 Study of grapes
133 Market scene, Dieppe wc
1881 11 The young Home Ruler
21 Little sunshine and shadow
27 Habitants killing time on a frosty night
1888 55 School days $35
110 Evening, Montreal harbour wc $25
137 On the coast, Nahant, Mass wc $40
1889 89 Near Marblehead, Mas $35
90 Daybreak $45
173 On the Richelieu wc $25
1894 237 Study wc $85
1895 210 Country road, Long Island wc $65

WESTON, JULIA
fl 1880-1 H
1881 73 Fruit wc

WESTON, WILLIAM PERCY
3 Nov 1879, London, Eng 20 Dec 1967, Vancouver CC2 CWW67 NGC TB2 WWA62
addr: Vancouver: 1045 West 15th Ave, 1930-9; 1419 Dogwood Ave, 1947
1930 206 Evening, Coast Range, B.C. $400
300 Winter, Grouse Mountain, B.C. drwg $25
1931 241 Crown Mountain $225
242 Autumn, Mount Cheam $225
413 Totems drwg $30
1932 322 A winter trail, Grouse Mountain $250
323 Forest spires $250
1933 338 Pines, Vancouver Island $250
1938 123 Gleneagles $350
1939 334 Winds wept $350
1947 279 The white church $300

WEYMAN, RONALD CHARLES TOSHACH
13 Dec 1915, Erith, Kent, Eng
addr: Toronto, 217 Glen Rd
1945 Lt Cdr RCNVR
238 Music makers $75

WHALLEY, PETER GRAHAM
20 Feb 1921, Brockville, Ont
addr: Halifax, 402 Tower Rd, 1940. Westmount, 4142 Dorchester St W, 1947-8. Morin Heights, Que, 1956
1940 391 End of the street $5
392 Cargo etch block pr $15
1947 280 Still life $75
1948 94 Still life with hat box gouache $50
1956 138 Mont Rolland nm $50

WHEELER, LEONARD A.
addr: Westmount, 326 Selby St
1921 278 Portrait b&w

WHEELER, ORSON SHOREY
17 Sep 1907, Barnston, Que CWW84 NGC TB2 WWA84 Juror
addr: Montreal: 3485 McTavish St, 1928; 1490 Drummond St, 1931; 1441 Drummond St, 1932-57
1928 361 Jeanne plaster
1931 445 Canon Scott plaster

1932 481 Dr F. Owen Stredder plaster
1933 535 Male figure, study plaster
536 Female plaster
1934 519 Negro plaster
1935 485 Sheila plaster
486 The dancer plaster $50
bronze $350
1936 616 Louise plaster
617 St Giles Indiana lime stone
1937 473 Dean F.M.G. Johnson head
plaster 1939-471 bronze
1938 201 Late Mrs Charles Carroll
Colby bronze
202 Warwich Chipman, KC plaster
1939 472 Archdeacon F.G. Scott bust
bronze
1940 417 Abdul plaster
418 Nude plaster
1941 290 Miss Jessie M. Colby, OBE
plaster
291 Robert J. Meekren, Esq plaster
292 Nude plaster
1942 242 Alex Ross plaster
1943 262 Dean H.F. Hall head plaster
1944 169 Harry A Norton, Esq plaster
(MBAM)
1945 284 Prof Claude Willett Thompson
plaster
1946 295 Loana plaster
1948 119 Pauline Johnson plaster
1949 178 Hon Pierre Basile Mignault
bronze
1952 83 Professor John Bland plaster
1957 169 Dr W.P. Percival plaster

WHILLIER, WAYNE KENNETH
23 Dec 1940, Winnipeg
addr: Bowness, Alta, 5923 Bow Cr
1961 66 Figures in red $155

WHIPPLE, JOHN Eng
fl 1873-1919 DBA DVP G
1889 93 Streathy on the Thames $200
94 Windsor Castle on a summer
morning $100
95 The old church and loch at
Stratford-on-Avon $100

WHITE, GEORGE HARLOW Eng
c 1817, London, Eng 18 Dec 1887,
Charter House, London, Eng AGO B DBA
DCB G H NGC TB W78
1883 water colour, 1883-6
52 Conway Castle, north Wales
60 Rye, south coast, England
63 Port of Llede, north Wales
66 The Conway River, north Wales
1885 124 Hastings, England
125 The River Wye, England
127 The old Hollyhead road
140 Fisherman's quarters, Hastings
1886 2 Creceth Castle
6 Eaton on the Thames
11 Windsor Castle

WHITE, JOSEPHINE H. J.
addr: Montreal, c/o Johnson's Art
Galleries, 634 St Catherine St W,
1926. Westmount, 38 Anworth Rd, 1934
1926 137 St Jean de Luz, France, in
an old square $300
138 A stormy day on Lake Rosseau,
Muskoka $70
1934 359 Old houses in Dinkelsbuhl,
Bavaria pastel $20
360 Street in Dinkelsbuhl,
Bavaria pastel $20

WHITE, LYN
addr: Montreal, 3345 Barclay Ave,
1949-50
1949 109 Self portrait $55
1950 141 Study

WHITE, MARGARET E. (Mrs)
addr: Westmount, 475 Argyle Ave
1940 300 Back yard $30
301 Still life $30

WHITE, RAY (Miss)
Addr: Montreal, 89 Mackay St
1895 277 Tea pot stand, tile

WHITEHEAD, ALFRED ERNEST
10 Jul 1887, Peterborough, Eng 1 Apr
1974, Amherst, N.S. CWW70 WWA73
addr: Montreal: 1544 Mackay St, 1942-5;
1463 Bishop St, 1946-7
1942 177 Grey day, Gatineau Hills $80
1943 208 Sherbrooke Street, winter $50
209 New Hampshire coast $45
1944 126 Rainy day, Montreal $40
127 Springtime, the Laurentians
$40
1945 239 La Have, River, Nova Scotia
$30
1946 244 Winter noon $65
245 Factories $65

1947 281 Bonsecours Church, Montreal
$75

WHITEHEAD, AMY MOSHER (m Alfred Ernest Whitehead)
addr: Montreal, 276 Pine Ave
1926 178 Satsuma lamp $200

WHITEHEAD, JEAN VALERIE ELIZABETH (BETTY) (m Robert P. Lang)
addr: Montreal, 1544 Mackay St
1943 210 Summer flowers
211 Dahlias $55

WHITNEY, ELIZABETH
fl 1876-98 H
addr: Montreal: 2274 St Catherine St, 1895; 2278 St Catherine St, 1897-8
1895 278 Punch bowl $75
279, 281-2 Vase, $20, $5, $3
280 Tray $8
283 Small bowl $2
284 Fish plate (12) $30
285 Dessert plates (6) $15
286 Finger bowls (6) $15
287 Tray
288 Tea caddy
289 Cup & saucer
290 Bowl
1897 274 Large vase $20
275 Small plates (6) $10
276 Tiles for freize $5
277 Game plates (6) $30
278 Cup & saucer $2.50
279 Lamp globe $4
1898 269 Punch bowl $50
270 Cream jug $6
271 Plate $3
272 Glass vase $3
273 Photo frame $2.50

WHITZMAN, DAVID
15 Jul 1915, Halifax
addr: Halifax: 9 1/2 Black St, 1942; 41 Newton Ave, 1943
1942 178 Self portrait
1943 212 Cecilia

WHYTE, PETER
22 Jan 1905, Banff, Alta d 1966
addr: Banff, Alta: 1932; Bow Ave, 1947
1932 324 Lake O'Hara
325 Yoho Valley $50
326 A lake in the Rockies $50
1947 282 Stonies $300
283 Mountain solitude $300

WICKENDEN, HELEN SLACK (m Alfred Ahier Wickenden)
Wickenden)
27 Dec 1887, Bethel, Conn CNS36
addr: Westmount, 265 Melville Ave
1946 246 October day $35

WICKENDEN, MARGARET ROBERTSON (m Horace Watson Wickenden)
3 Jun 1915, Winnipeg
addr: Saskatoon, 335 6th Ave N
1957 154 City nocturne nm $50

WICKENDEN, ROBERT JOHN Amer
8 Jul 1861, Rochester, Eng 28 Nov 1931, Brooklyn, N.Y. B H Mo12 TB2 WWW
addr: Montreal: YMCA, 1901; 5 Beaver Hall Sq, 1905; 219 University St, 1915-16; 207 Mansfield St, 1921-5
1901 101 The Canadian woodman $1,000
102 The late Philip Gilbert Hamerton
1905 115 The exiled poet: 'Je regarderai l'ocean' $1,000
116 Miss W.
117 The lake, Ste Adele $100
118 A woodland path, Ste Adele $75
119 An autumn field $75
120 Gathering the flock, Anvers-sur-Oise $50
121 The old shepherd $50
245 J. George Adami, MD drwg
1915 354 Sir William Van Horne, KCMG
1916 301 His late Majesty King Edward VII
302 Hon A.W. Atwater, KC, Batonnier of the Montreal Bar
1921 279 Avida wc
1922 318 Autumn trophies $250
1925 284 Laurentian maples $150
285 Pine Point, Lake St Joseph wc $50

WICKSON, PAUL GIOVANNI
1860, Toronto 2 Sep 1922, Paris, Ont
CWW10 H Mo12 R1 TB W78
addr: Paris, Ont, 1891-2
1885 57 Sound on the Goose
61 The end of the week
1889 91 The rose and the thorn $100

92 La belle canadienne $80
1891 135 Bensville smithy $150
1892 142 Professional opinion $250

WIELAND, JOYCE (m Michael Snow)
30 Jun 1931, Toronto AGO B CC1 CE CO IO WWA84
addr: New York
1970 cotton
94 J'aime Canada 49 x 49 illus
95 I love Canada 49 x 49 illus

WIESENBERG, LOUIS
12 Sep 1893, Russia
addr: Montreal: 636 St Lawrence Blvd, 1916; 752 St Lawrence Blvd, 1920; 39 Crescent St, 1926
1916 Wisenberg, 1916-20, mispr
303 A longing soul b&w
1920 286 Mr W, portrait sketch
1926 235 Harold Anderson, Esq charcl

WIGGS, HENRY ROSS
28 Dec 1895, Quebec 16 Mar 1986, Hamilton, Ont CNS47 CWW84 PMC
addr: Montreal: 1111 Beaver Hall Hill, 1927; 1110 Castle Bldg, 1928; 4065 Côte des Neiges Rd, 1933; 1135 Beaver Hall Hill, 1935; 630 Dorchester St W, 1936-7; 1221 Osborne St, 1939
1927 176 The plowman wc
258A A suburban residence
258B-C A chauffeur's cottage, front and rear views
258D Small house, a study
1928 285 Residence, W.J.S. Evans, Esq, Ottawa
286 Six room cottage, Ottawa
287 Group of houses, Ottawa
288 Country house, rendering
1933 422 Suburban residence
423-4 Proposed house, Westmount, street and garden views
425 Stone house, rendering
1935 379 House, Summit Cr, Westmount
380 House, Armand Collet, Esq, Westmount 1936-501-2
381 House, Daulac Rd, Westmount
382 Small cottage
1936 503 Proposed residence, Westmount
504 House, Sillery, Que
1937 377 Small house, study
378 Proposed residence, Outremont
379 Proposed house, Oakland Ave, Westmount
1939 376-7 Mountain lodge, Mont Tremblant, Que
378 Mackerel fleet, Gloucester, Mass wc

WIGHT, ISOBEL
addr: Westmount, 221 Elm Ave
1922 319 Composition

WILCOX, GEORGIE M. CRAWFORD (m Howard Buell Wilcox)
1889, Winnipeg
addr: Winnipeg, 9 Middle Gate
1947 284 The town square $250

WILKES, BARBARA F. (Mrs Adams)
addr: Westmount, 202 Côte St Antoine Rd, 1940-3
1940 302 Dynamite in sepia $50
1941 212 Lights and shadows wc $30
1943 Adams
1 The bay $50

WILKINSON, ALAN LEIGHTON
1915, Montreal
addr: Montreal: 4168 West Hill Ave, 1940-2; 1239 Sussex Ave, 1950
1940 303 The sulks wc $25
393 Waiting brush, India ink $30
1942 218 The joke charcl
219 Heartbreak pencil
1950 55 Waiting for the tide $200

WILKINSON, CAROLINE see ARMINGTON, CAROLINE

WILLAR, FRED
1939, Saint John, N.B.
addr: Renforth, N.B.
1968 303 Light tower wd figerglass, electric light 85h $500
304 Completed rainbow wd enamel 96 x 96 x 132 $600

WILLER, JAMES SIDNEY HAROLD
25 Feb 1921, Fulham, Eng WWA82
addr: Winnipeg, 200 Lanark St
1956 78 Façade, San Moise, Venice $250

WILLIAMS, DOROTHY MAY BENTLEY (m George R. Williams)
b Brooklyn Corner, N.S.
addr: Kamloops, B.C, 662 Pine St

1943 213 Roundhouse wc $20

WILLIAMS, EVA see DONLY, EVA

WILLIAMS, JOHN C.
addr: Verdun, Que, 3534 Joseph St
1956 139 The forest nm $100

WILLIAMS, MARY see DIGNAM, MARY

WILLIAMS, RICHARD EMERSON
5 Sep 1921, Pittsburgh, Pa TB2
addr: Winnipeg, University of Manitoba, School of Art, Old Law Courts Bldg, Kennedy St
1955 139 Concert hall nm $35

WILLIAMS, SARAH H.
addr: Westmount, 4150 Sherbrooke St W, 1918-19
1918 359 Low tide, Scarborough, Maine wc $10
1919 347 An Italian hill village wc
348 The Scarborough marshes wc $10
349 Scarborough beaches, Maine wc $5

WILLIAMS, YVONNE
9 Sep 1901, Port of Spain, Trinidad TB2
addr: Toronto, 81A Wellesley St
1936 577-80 The ancient mariner st gl des $50 each, in glass

WILLIAMSON, CATHARINE M. (Mrs)
addr: Montreal, 4829 Grosvenor Ave, 1947-51
1947 285 Interior pastel
1951 144 November day pastel $100

WILLIAMSON, EFFIE G.
addr: Westmount: 1908; 4126 Dorchester St, 1909-12
1908 273 The boy pastel $10
274 Sketch pastel
1909 377 A southern type $25
378 Our baby $15
1910 350 Gretchen
351-2 Sketch
1911 281 Baby Jean
282 Study of a child
283 Portrait study
1912 397 Mary Courtney $50
398 Mary $50
399 R.B, portrait
400 Study

WILLIAMSON, ELEANOR (Mrs)
addr: Ottawa, 243 McLeod St, 1943-6
1943 214 Oriental pastel $50
215 The buckskin jacket pastel $50
1946 247 Grandma's Easter bonnet pastel $75

WILLIAMSON, FRANCIBEL
address not listed
1912 411 Study sculp

WILLIS, DOROTHY GWENDOLYN HENZELL (Mrs)
4 Sep 1899, England
addr: Edmonton, 11504 96th St E, 1937-40
1937 316 A gay bouquet wc $15
1939 335 Thompson River country, B.C. wc $20
336 Old graveyard, Alert Bay, B.C. wc $25
1940 304 Torn asunder, cypress trees, Point Lobos wc

WILLIS, RALPH TROTH Amer
1 Mar 1876, Leesylvania, Freestone Point, Va F WWA40
addr: Brooklyn, N.Y.
1909 mural proofs for decoration
451 Church of the Salute, Venice $45
452 Walls of Nuremberg $30

WILLIS, ROSE MACDONALD (m William Arthur Willis)
1885, or 86, Scotland 1960, Victoria
addr: Westmount, 2 Albert Pl, 1909-12
1909 78 Tankard $15
79 Berry bowl $10
80 Water pitcher $10
81 Cream & sugar $5
1912 470 Vase
471 Freda, portrait

WILLS, I. A. D.
addr: Westmount, c/o I.H. Wardleworth
1914 422 The bridle track $125

WILSON, ARTHUR G.
addr: Montreal, 1 Belmont St, 1920-1
1920 285 Bazaar, Tangier $50
1921 280 Old house, Back River, Que $35
281 Beach scene $25

WILSON, DOROTHY E,
addr: Sackville, N.B, Mount Allison University, 1940-2
1940 305 Still life $50
1941 179 Preparing for the dance $50

WILSON, FRANK HOWARD
14 Nov 1908, Montreal CWW58
addr: Westmount, 250 Kensington Ave
1962 72 Autumn nm $125

WILSON, GEORGE EVERETT
26 Dec 1909, Montreal CWW70
addr: Montreal: 4210 Wilson Ave, 1935, 1940; 1050 Beaver Hall Hill, 1936-8
1935 442 The Town Hall, Stockholm drwg $20
1936 Wilson & Auld, 1936-40
505 Residence, F.T. Parker, Esq, Westmount
506 Residence, Pointe Claire
1937 380-1 House, Carillon, Que, before and after restoration
1938 146 Stable and groom's house, Ste Geneviéve, Que
147 Residence, L.C. McQuat, Esq, Ste Marie, Que
1940 343 Factory project
344 Residence, Mr & Mrs McConnell, Ste Marguerite, Que
345 Residence, Messrs J.H. Hutcheson & F.G. McArthur, Ste Marguerite, Que

WILSON, JAMES
1852, Montreal 31 Aug 1932, Pickanock, Que H
addr: Ottawa: 1891; Sparks St, 1892-4; 123 Sparks St, 1895-1919; Ottawa, 1923; 108 Sparks St, 1924-9
1885 34 A calm lakeside
50 Winds in the leafless trees complain
72 A headland, lower St Lawrence
78 Autumn, Canadian hillside
1886 86 Still night on the River Seine
87 A woodland brook
89 A sketch, early spring
1889 174 Off South Harpswell wc $20
1891 136 On the banks of the Ottawa $15
209 The brook, autumn wc $12
1892 143 When the tide is low $75
218 Wild woodland stream wc $100
1894 162 The Pangan on the Gatineau $20
1895 142 Spring on the Ottawa $20
1903 115 Off Bicquette $25
231 Woodland pool wc $35
1906 165 Trout pool, Algonquin Park $50
166 On the edge of the sea $50
167 After a nor'easter $30
1914 423 After the storm $25
424 Rough weather off Bonaventure $20
1915 355 Pyramid at sunset, Jasper Park $12
1917 347 Percé, from Bonaventure Island $20
348 Off Percé $20
1918 360 Baie de Chaleur $35
361 Rough weather, south west point, Bonaventure Island $25
1919 350 Headland, Island of Bonaventure $20
351 Out of the fog, Mount Robinson $25
1923 217 From green to gold $35
218 Rough day off Percé $15
1924 258 Clearing weather, Percé $75
1925 286 After a northeaster, Baie des Chaleurs $75
1926 139 Rock goddess, under the new moon $30
1928 203 Baie des Chaleurs $100
1929 216 Low tide, Percé, under a misty moon $50
port: by Ernest Fosberry, 1931-90 (NGC)

WILSON, PAUL
addr: Outremont, 899 Outremond Ave
1947 286 Paysage wc $35
287 L'Ange Gardien wc $35

WILSON, PERCY ROY
19 May 1900, Birmingham, Eng Juror
addr: Montreal, 348 Sherbrooke St W, 1922-4. Westmount, 58 Belvedere Rd, 1928, 1932-3. Montreal: 616 Castle Bldg, 1929; 1434 St Catherine St W, 1930-1; 1839 Lincoln Ave, 1934-5; 5021 Sherbrooke St W, 1936. Westmount, 42 Sunnyside Ave, 1937-50
1922 359 Battlefield Memorial, Competition; plan, elevation & section des. Rec'd one of 4 final $1,000 prizes
1928 289 Proposed country house, R.O. Sweezey, Esq, Thousand Islands

1929 294 'Meadowsedge', country house, R.O. Sweezey, Esq
1930 246 Power house, study
247 House, Alan D. McCall, Esq
248 House, E.A. Sherrard, Esq
249 Wrought-iron house grills, R.O. Sweezey house photo
250 Wrought-iron fire screen photo
301 Stained glass window des
322 Newel post top, R.O. Sweezey house sketch model, plaster
1931 355 House, Mr Jones
356 Power house, façade model
357 House, Wm Taylor May
358 St Lawrence st gl panel
1933 426-9 R.O. Sweezey house, general view, garage, dining room, main stair, hall photos
430-2 A.D. McCall house, Westmount, south front, gable and terrace photos
1934 421 House, G.R. McCall, Esq, Lachute, Que
1935 383 Welland War Memorial, Competition, 2nd prize
1936 507 Cabin, M.R. Chipman, Esq
1937 382 House, Charles E. Frosst, Esq, Westmount
383 Small brick house des
1938 148 Own house, Westmount
1939 379 Semi-detached house, to cost $7,000, in a mill town
1943 248 A stone house
249 House on a hillside
1944 154 Replanning a Montreal block
1945 272 Farm house, Bevans Lake model
1924 259 Sunset in the Coliseum wc
303 Abbaye de Lessay b&w $35
304 Gable of the Lygon Anus Broadway, Worcestershire b&w $25
1928 334 Demolition of high bridge, New York etch $6
335 Aqua Morta, Verona pencil
1930 207 The mote house, Ightham pastel
1932 327 Maidstone pastel $18
446 Durham Cathedral etch $5
447 Doorway to the Cathedral, Verona etch $5
448 Stanton in the Cotswold etch $5
449 The village funeral etch $5
1934 361 In the foothills wc $10
362 Alpine snowdrift wc $10
363 Late Laurentian afternoon wc $15
477 San Felix, Gerona etch $8
478 Notre Dame, Montreal etch $6
1935 342 Gun'les awash wc
443 Moorish bridgehead, Cordova etch $10
1936 453 Bridge of the Three Arches, Venice wc $20
454 Cross country wc $20
581 Pont Valentré, Cahors etch $10
1937 317 The Gothic bridge wc $10
318 Church of San Pedro, Avila, Spain wc $30
1938 124 Pont Valentré, Cahors wc $50
1939 338 In the tall timbers wc $50
1945 240 Rounding the bend wc $75
241 ...and all I ask is a windy day wc $30
1947 288 Temple of the snow Gods wc $90
289 Soft, undulating counterpane of snow wc $70
1950 80 'Thione' homeward bound wc $100

WILSON, PETER E.
addr: Skokie, Ill, 9257 Leclaire Ave
1963 93 Study for a diptych nm $100

WILSON, RONALD YORK
6 Dec 1907 – 10 Feb 1984, Toronto AGO CCl CE CWW84 IO NGC TB2 WWA84
addr: Toronto, 117 Mackay Ave, 1931. Willowdale, Ont, 76 Owen Bldv, 1955. Toronto, 41 Alcina Ave, 1956-60. Montreal, Galerie Agnes Lefort, 1504 Sherbrooke St W, 1963
1931 243 The Ward wc $45
244 Richmond and York, Toronto wc $40
1955 83 Montmartre $600
1956 140 Thou preparest a table nm $500
1957 103 Moroccans $600
1960 127 Gondola mobile $1,000
1963 72 Dragozzi $1,800

WILSON, RUTH T. (Mrs)
addr: Montreal, 5549 Queen Mary Rd, 1939. Hampstead, Que, 122 Dufferin Rd, 1947
1939 339 November afternoon wc
340 Sugar house near Orford wc
1947 290 Late sunlight, Lac Marois $85

WILSON, STANLEY B.
18 Mar 1881 d Jan 1960

addr: Montreal, 6 Durocher St, 1910-11. Westmount, 231 Elm Ave, 1914-45
1910 353 The canal $20
1911 284 The tollgate $25
285 In the canal wc $5
286 Old house, Lower Lachine Road wc $15
1914 425 Farm, Montreal West wc $25
426 Sketch of a mill wc $10
1917 349 Old house, Lachine wc $15
350 On the Lower Lachine Road wc $15
1918 361 Lachine convent wc $15
1934 364 Rough water wc $10
1945 242 Time to rest wc $40

WILSON, STUART ANDREW
18 Oct 1912, Montreal
addr: Montreal, 2282 Belgrave Ave, 1939-48
1939 447 Canal bank scene ink & wc $5
448 Scott cabin, Sixteen Island Lake lino cut $5
1940 394 T.G.B.X 102 wc & ink $15
1942 180 Quarry edge wc & ink $20
217 Chimneys col lino cut
1947 344 Doodle box balsa wd
1948 112 Boating club ink $25

WINDEAT, EMMA S.
b Brockville, Ont d 1926 H
addr: Toronto, 46 Cecil St, 1897-8
1897 130 A great day $30
223 Cloud effect wc $35
224 Interior wc
1898 115 Willows and pool $50
116 On the St Lawrence, near Berthier $25

WINDEYER, RICHARD CUNNINGHAM
1830 Fort Amherst, Chatham, Eng 24 Mar 1900, Toronto
1889 189 Church of St Alban the Martyr, Toronto (arch)

WING, THERESA
addr: Montreal, 23 Victoria St
1895 211 Miniatures on ivory wc

WINKLER, FRIEDRICH (FRED)
5 Sep 1894, Weimar 27 Nov 1974, Toronto
addr: Toronto, 316 Glen Rd
1933 537 Mrs F.W. bust
538 Black panther plaster, bronze $450
539 The cardinal sins plaster, bronze $120
540 Eve plaster, bronze $250

WINSLOW, MARJORIE SCARTH (Mrs)
10 Dec 1907, Montreal
addr: Lachine, Que, 22 Riverside Dr, 1936-9. Portsmouth, Ont, RR1, 1942-4. Westmount, 3061 Westmount Blvd, 1945-7. Châteauguay, Que, RR1, 1959
1936 618 Portrait sketches plaster $15
619 Katharine and Garry plaque $10
1937 319 Ethel Goodwin $20
474 G.H. Duggan, Esq plaster
465 E.P. Winslow, Esq plaster
476 The storm plaster $15
1939 337 Run down
473 Admonition plaster
1942 181 The wake of the storm wc $12
182 March wc $12
1943 216 In back wc $15
263 Bob and Daphne plaster plaque
1944 170 André Bieler ter cot
171 Daphne plaster
1945 285 Madame Haenni plaster
1946 296 Mr E. Lemieux plaster
297 The snow ball plaster $25
1947 345 The cue plaster $25
1959 38 Concentration nm $35
66 R.E. Powell, Esq, Chancellor, McGill University plaster

WISE, ROLAND
19 Jun 1923, San Francisco
addr: Winnipeg, University of Manitoba, School of Art
1954 85 Forest image

WISELBERG, FANNY
addr: Westmount, 43 Holton Ave, 1931-45
1931 245 Old Italian woman, a study $150
414 Drawing charcl $40
415 Young Arabian girl drwg $40
1935 444 Still life drwg $20
1936 455 Still life
1937 320 Portrait
321 Still life $35
1938 125 Stella $60
1939 341 Young woman $75
1941 213 Beatrice $75
1942 183 Seated nude $75
184 Girl in blue $100

1944 128 Head of a girl $100
1945 243 Model resting $150

WISELBERG, LINA
addr: Westmount: 3 Holton Ave, 1923-6; 43 Holton Ave, 1935
1923 Line, mispr
219 A hanging batik $100
220 Cerberus batik $75
221 Slave batik $100
1925 387 Batik
1926 236-7 Batik $25, $35
1935 343 Rococo room, Royal Palace, Genoa wc
344 Room, Borghese Palace, Rome wc
345 Room, Caserta, Rome wc
346 Bathroon, Pitti Palace, Florence wc

WISELBERG, ROSE
6 Jan 1908, Montreal
addr: Westmount, 43 Holton Ave, 1932-60
1932 450-1 Drawing charcl $20 each
1941 214 Miss L. $100
1942 185 Landscape $75
1944 129 Jacques Cartier Square, Montreal $150
1945 244 Landscape, Lachine $85
245 Portrait study $100
1946 248 Montreal harbour $100
1960 128 Still life $225

WISENBERG, LOUIS see WIESENBERG, LOUIS

WOLINSKY, EVA
20 Apr 1925, Budapest
addr: Winnipeg, 57 Middle Gate
1959 67 The night is long wd

WONG, PAUL C.
19 Oct 1933, Hong Kong
addr: Vancouver, 123C Pender St E
1965 21 Between illus $700 Jessie Dow prize 1967-74, 69 x 72

WOOD, CANDACE
1883 131 Little Bo-Peep

WOOD, FAITH (m Mel Breen)
21 Sep 1917, Devon, Eng IO
addr: Sackville, N.B, York St, 1939-47. Toronto, 3 Heathbridge Park, 1954
1939 342 Audrey $100
1942 186 Miss Joan Steele $25
1943 217 Dorothy
1947 291 Self portrait
1954 130 Mushroom gatherers nm $65

WOOD, GEORGE MELVILLE
3 Jun 1932, Regina
addr: Calgary: 2820 Morley Trail, NW, 1962; 25 Kirby Pl, 1964
1962 38 Ptg A.1.7.61 $200
1964 81 Ptg A.4.6.63 $500

WOOD, GEORGE W.
1863 - 27 Sep 1941, Montreal
addr: Montreal, 50 Royal Insurance Bldg
1916 304 Notre Dame Street, Montreal wc
see also Hutchison, Alexander Cowper, 1900-33

WOOD, MARY E.
addr: Peterborough, Ont, Monaghan Rd. Westmount, 267 Olivier Ave, 1939-40
1936 456 Jessie
1939 474 John plaster
1940 306 Irene $100

WOOD, THOMAS CHARLES
2 May 1913, Westboro, Ont AGO
addr: Ottawa: 342 Kenwood Ave, 1944-9; 280 Claremont Ave, 1952; Ottawa, 1967
1944 130 Cécile de Masham, Que $50 Jessie Dow prize (listed 1967)
131 Town Hall, Almonte $40
1947 292 Road in the bush $70
293 Mandolin player $70
1948 66 Les Eboulements, Que $85
1949 110 Fall landscape $90
1952 55 Derelict $90

WOOD, VIRGINIA H. W.
addr: Montreal, 620 Dorchester St W
1929 217 Portrait of a gentleman
218 Portrait of two girls pastel

WOOD, WILLIAM JOHN
26 May 1877, Ottawa 4 Jan 1954, Midland, Ont AGO CC2 CE NGC TB2
addr: Midland, 275 1st St, 1931-51
1931 246 Margaret $100
1932 452 Summer airs etch $5
1933 503 Axe-men etch $5
1936 457 Daybreak $100

576 Sparrow Lake etch $3
1938 187 Summer morn etch $5
188 Etcher and wife etch $5
1940 395 Elevator etch $5
396 Music etch $5
397 Willows etch $5
398 Squared timber etch $5
1942 220 March etch $5
221 Lullaby etch $5
222 Eastertime etch $5
1944 149 Shipyard etch $5
150 Bayview etch $5
1946 270 Hillside farm etch $5
271 January thaw lino engr $5
272 New tug etch $5
1947 326 Lake Shore Road copper etch $7
327 Mid-winter zinc etch $5
328 A telegram zinc etch $5
329 Ironing zinc etch $5
1949 166 Scotty zinc etch $10
1950 86 Axe-men zinc etch $5
1951 69 Dreamland zinc etch $5

WOODALL, RONALD
5 Jul 1935, Montreal
addr: Montreal West, 136 Strathearn Ave, 1960-1
1960 129 Boat hoist $200
1961 67 Hulk $200

WOODCOCK, PERCY FRANKLIN
17 Aug 1855, Athens, Ont 11 Feb 1936, Montreal B CC1 H Mo98/12 NGC PMC TB1/2
addr: Brockville, Ont, Waterniche, 1891-2. New York, 162 E 48th St, 1894. Brockville, 1903. Montreal, Scott & Sons, 99 Notre Dame St, 1914-28
1883 126 The late return
127 Cottage at Cerney-la-ville, France
1885 17 The last in
22 Forbidden ground
38 Portrait
51 Abandoned nest
55 Returning from the well (NGC)
80 Working homeward
85 Sunlight and shadow
1886 57 The reaper
68 Spring time
71 Working homeward
1888 11 Theodosia $200
1891 137 The approaching storm $120
138 Canadian farm $120
139 Indian camp $55
140 Camp by the river $55
141 Indians on the move $60
1892 144 Canadian farm, St Eustache (MBAM)
145 Il m'aime $300
146 Autumn tints $150
147 The mail carrier $150
148 Cabbage garden $150
149 A windy day, the Grand Nord $75
1894 163 The approaching storm
164 Clearing up, old house at Lachine
165 Sunset on the St Lawrence
166 Farm at Berthier
1903 116 Winter evening $350
117 Summer evening $350
118 Cabbage garden $125
119 Water Lily Bay $125
120 Old house, St Geneviève $125
121 Canadian winter evening $125
122 Thistledown $125
123 Golden rod $125
1914 427 Autumn, Lake Memphremagog $300
428 Early morning mists $150
429 Jones' Creek, Brockville $300
430 Canadian landscape $300
1915 356 Near Châteauguay, Que $1,000
357 25 miles from Paris, on the Seine, St Germaine $1,000
1916 305 Sunset $150
306 Morning, 10 below zero $150
307 A grey day $150
308 An Ontario farm $300 (listed 1967, Jessie Dow prize) (NGC)
1917 351-3 Landscape near Montreal $900, $300, $150 (one, MBAM)
354 Canadian winter landscape $250
355 Canadian autumn landscape $150
356 The creek $200
1918 363 Landscape, Montreal $150
364 Landscape $200
365 Waterbury, Vermont $350
366 Environs of Montreal $1,000
1919 352-4 Canadian landscape, $500, $500, $150
355 Canadian landscape, winter $150
1920 287 Spring time $600
288 Canadian landscape $500
289 Autumn $450
290 Winter $200

1921 282-3 Canadian landscape $150, $250
284 In the fall of the year $450
285 On the Seine, France $850
1922 320 Canadian landscape $850
321 Spring blossoms $250
322 Early spring $225
1925 287 Landscape, Province of Quebec $150
288 A summer day $150
289 The after glow $550
1928 204 Landscape in the White Mountains $350
205 Winter at Brockville $175
206 Canadian landscape $175
1894 Assoc 1st prize 1892, figure

WOODFORDE, MILLICENT L. (Mrs)
addr: Montreal, 1908. Quebec, 125 Anne St, 1912
1908 152 Mr S. $200
153 Portrait $100
1912 401 The fir wood pastel $30
402 The black bird pastel
403 Stanley Palace, Chester pastel
404 A Cornish stream wc $20

WOODHEAD, DORA KELSEY (m Robert Charles Woodhead)
addr: Montreal West, 328 Ballantyne Ave
1945 246 Wing Comdr R.C. Woodhead

WOODHOUSE, EDITH
fl 1898-9 H
addr: Montreal, 32 Redpath St
1898 117 Portrait
118 Soudanese $50
210 Portrait pastel
211 Deutsch madchen crayon
212 Case of miniatures

WOODHOUSE, H. O.
addr: Lakeside, Que, 20 Lakeside Ave
1933 433-4 Proposed residence, Sydney, Australia, lounge

WOODMAN, FLORENCE
addr: London, Ont, 480 Adelaide St
1906 457 Jardiniere, roses $30
458 Chocolate set $40
459 Punch bowl, peaches $18
460 Orange bowl, raspberries $20
461 Lemonade jug, currants $10
462 Vase, grapes $25
463 Vase, American beauties $20
464 Vase, jonquils $15
465 Vase, lilacs $20
466 Vase, violets $18

WOOLMER, ALFRED
addr: Montreal: 112 Masson St, 1924; 2030 Masson St, 1926
1924 264 A touch of autumn wc $35
265 Foster Lane, Waterloo, Que wc $25
266 Autumn, Outremont wc $25
1926 140 Isle Visitation wc $50

WORK, WILLIAM
addr: Montreal: 6 Beaver Hall Sq, 1914; 256 Fairmont Ave W, 1922. Toronto, 125 Edgewood Ave, 1928
1914 431 Mountain scene wc $30
1922 323 Grey Nun Street, looking south pastel $15
324 Bonsecours Market wc $15
1928 207 Vermilion River, northern Ontario $150

WORLING, VERA see KOCHANSKI, VERA

WRANGEL, GERALDINE see MAJOR, GERALDINE

WRANGEL, NATACHA
5 Apr 1920, Kertch, Russia
addr: Sorel, Que, 29 Bréboeuf St, 1957-64
1957 155 Tranquilité nm $45
1959 39 Little girl nm $100
1964 112 Fillette nm $125

WRIGHT, R. L.
addr: Brockville, Ont, 1918-27; 19 Sherwood St, 1938-36
1918 367 The winding stream $10
1919 356 Early snow $15
357 Rocks and snow $15
1920 291 Path through the woods $10
292 The cottage in the wood $10
293 Snow-clad pines $10
1922 325 The old barge $10
326 The green house $10
327 An old grey pine $10
1924 267 Winter afternoon $15
268 The pines $15

1925 290 Cedars $15
1926 141 The dead pine $15
142 The roadway $15
1927 177 The ravine $25
178 The bridge $75
1928 208 Pine trees $25
1929 219 The break-up $25
220 An Ontario farm yard $25
1931 247 Butler Creek $75
248 Spring freshets $25
249 Winter sunlight $25
1932 328 The last of the snow $125
1934 365 The last of the ice $75
366 Autumn $25
1935 347 After the storm $125
1936 458 Snow banks $75

WRINCH, MARY EVELYN (m George Agnew Reid)
12 May 1877, Kirby-le-Soken, Essex, Eng 19 Sep 1969, Toronto AGO NGC TB2
addr: Toronto: 619 Church St, 1903; 36 Toronto St, 1905-6; Toronto, 1908; 9 Rowanwood Ave, 1909
1903 328 Miss H. Moodie Vickers min
329 A child's head $35
1905 122 Twilight $75
123 The last gleam $50
1906 360 Mrs G.A. Reid min (AGO)
361 Row of elms on a grey day min $60
362 Portrait study min
1908 154 Garden in Muskoka $100
155 Reflections $40
1909 379 Wood interior $200

WUETHRICH, HUGO VIRGILIO
2 Sep 1926, Berne Switz
addr: Montreal, 6695 Fielding Ave
1962 39 Composition $250

WYANT, ALEXANDER HELWIG Amer
11 Jan 1836, Evans Creek, Ohio 29 Nov 1892, New York B Gr H TB
1889 96 Summer afternoon $600

WYER, RAYMOND
addr: Montreal: 1908; 17 Chomedy St, 1909
1908 156 Dutch interior $125
1909 380 Field worker $200
381 Interior
382 Ruth $75

WYERS, JAN GERRIT
20 Jul 1888, Steendersen, Neth 1973, Belg CC2
addr: Windthorst, Sask
1960 130 Winter passage $100

WYKE, GEORGE
5 Jul 1892, Liverpool, Eng
addr: Montreal: 793 Querbes St, 1918-19; 3168 Clarke St, 1921. Lachine, Que, 30 10th Ave, 1922
1918 368 Woolworth Building b&w $25
369 Grain elevators, Montreal b&w $25
1919 358 Wash day b&w $25
359 On Phillips Square b&w $25
1921 286 Between December clouds $175
287 Decorative b&w $100
1922 328 The barn $25
329 On the water front wc $75
330 Prohibition b&w $35

WYLE, FLORENCE
27 Nov 1881, Trenton, Ill 14 Jan 1968, Newmarket, Ont AGO CC2 CE CWW64 EC NGC TB2 W78 WWA62
addr: Toronto, 110 Glen Rose Ave
1922 360 The rimmer bronze $500

WYNNE-CLARKE, A.
addr: Toronto, 163 Wolverleigh Blvd
1928 209 Blue, black and gold pastel $125

Y

YAMAMOTO, JOHN N.
addr: Montreal, 5115 Bordeaux St
1947 294 Lifting storm, Ste Anne wc $50

YANE, LILLIE
addr: Montreal, 5236 Jeanne Mance St
1938 126 Shirley pastel $75
127 Rae pastel $75

YARWOOD, WALTER HAWLEY
19 Sep 1917, Toronto AGO CC2 TB2 Juror
addr: Toronto, 39 McMurrich St
1964 139 Hiding place wld bronze $750

YELLIN, MERVIN

29 Sep 1928, Montreal
addr: Montreal, 5315 St Urbain St, 1915-8
1951 48 Ruelle Leduc
1952 144 Street dance ink $20
1953 108 The circus posters block lino cut $40
1954 128 The pigeons lino cut $35
1958 77 The black rooster nm $75

YEWDALE, GERRIE (m A.A. Pheely)
addr: West Vancouver, 641 Kenwood Rd
1964 113 Arrested motion nm

YIP, CHUCK WING
3 Sep 1923, Vancouver
addr: Vancouver, 51 E Pender St
1954 120 Nocturne mm $100

YOUNG, ETTA N.
addr: Montreal, 2338A Mance St, 1915-6
1915 462 Satsuma bowl enamels $8
1916 394 Lustre vase, Japanese $5
395 Matt vase, blue $3
396 Pitcher, brown, conventional scenery $4

YOUNG, HELEN
addr: Westmount, 359 Greene Ave, 1900. Montreal: 34 Thornton Park, 1905; 864A Park Ave, 1906. Westmount: 1908; 107 Belmont Pl, 1909-12; 107 Blenheim Pl, 1914-24
1900 261 Ink bottle $3
262 Large plate $7
263 Miniature plate $5
1905 354 Fruit dish
355 Cups & saucers $2.75
356 Vase $5
357 Chocolate pot
358 Jelly dish $3
1906 467 Jug $16
468 Tankard $18
469 Bouillon cup & saucer $4.50
470 Small vase $3.75
471 Bell
1908 441 Bell
442 Dessert plates $5 each
443 Tobacco jar $20
444 Lemonade jug $18
445 Cup & saucer $8
446 Stein, with monk $12
447 Vase $5
448 Tankard $18
449 Match holder $4
450 Jug $16
1909 82 Vase
83 Jardiniere
1910 463 Vase $15
1911 344 Vase $25
345 Side dish $12
1912 472 Teapot
473-4 Jug
475 Cup & saucer
476 Radish dish
1914 528 Tankard
529 Pudding dish
530 Hot water jug $2.75
1915 463 Bowl $15
464 Radish dish $3.25
465 Egg cups and stand (6) $8
1916 397 Satsuma tea pot $12
398 Jug $5
1917 435 Vase $18
1924 380 Rose jar enamels

YOUNG, JACK
1894, Salisbury, Eng 2 Oct 1963, Montreal
addr: Montreal: 6926 Sherbrooke St W, 1932; 6887 Sherbrooke St W, 1951
1932 329 Old house near St Hubert, Que $40
1951 49 Twilight hour $200

YOUNG, MIRMA
addr: Montreal, 584 Walpole Ave
1956 141 Still life nm

YOUNGER, PIERCY see PORTEOUS, PIERCY

Z

ZADOROZNY, ANDREI MYCHAILOVITCK (MICHAEL)
27 May 1921, Borsziv, n Lvov, Ukraine
addr: Montreal, 5040 Barclay Ave, 1959-60
1959 40 Westmount summit nm $180
1960 227 Spring thaw, Westmount nm $175

ZARNOWER, TERESA
addr: Montreal, 3432 Drummong St
1943 264 Canadian soldier sculp

ZELENAK, EDWARD JOHN
9 Nov 1940, St Thomas, Ont B IO WWA84

addr: West Lorne, Ont
1968 305 Untitled No 3 fibreglass
24h $4,000
306 Untitled No 2 fibreglass
48 3/4h $4,500

ZIMMERMAN, IDESSA CAROLINE EICHLER (m Morris Zimmerman)
26 Apr 1913, Bridgeport, Ont
addr: Bridgeport, 64 Woolwich St
1958 45 The village blacksmith, Bridgeport $50

ZIMMERMAN, M.
addr: Montreal, 3653 Henri Julien Ave, 1930-3
1930 plaster, 1930-3
323 Head of a girl $50
324 Head of a young boy $50
1931 446 Head of a young man $75
447 Head of a Negress $75
1932 482 Louise, portrait
483 Young lady bust $75
1933 541 Head of a boy $75
542 Head of a girl $50

ZIMMERMAN, SAMUEL
addr: Toronto, 514 Brunswick Ave
1961 107 Nude study nm $45

ZOLTVANY, BELA
c 1892, Budapest 28 Sep 1956, Montreal
addr: Montreal, 4558 Earnscliffe Ave, 1945-53
1945 286 The bombardier walnut
1946 298 Morning on the lake mahogany $150
1951 73 The model teak $300
1952 84 Gothic teak $300
1953 65 St John the Baptist sculp

ZOLTVANY-SMITH, A.
addr: Montreal: 7406 Henri Julien Ave, 1927-32; 2434 Ste Famille St, 1933; 75 Sherbrooke St W, 1934-6; 3572 Jeanne Mance St, 1937-40
1927 318-19 Portrait bust
1928 Smith, A. Zoltvany
357 Sunbeam plaster
1929 397 My wife plaster
1931 448 The emigrants plaster, bronze $250
1932 484 Vision marble $120
1933 543 War plaster
1934 520 Artemis plaster, bronze $300
1935 487 Mgr Dauray plaster
1936 620 Immaculée Conception plaster
1937 477 Study plaster
478 Canadian veterans of the Great War bas rel bronze $100
1939 475 XIIth Station, the Way of the Cross plaster
1940 419 Sacrifice de Melchisedech (relief pour les stipes d'un autel) plaster

ZUCCA, ALBERTO
addr: Westmount, 4700 Westmount Ave, 1934. Montreal: 2024 McGill College Ave, 1935-7; 1199 St Catherine St W, 1938; 1970 St Catherine St W, 1939; 1968 St Catherine St W, 1944-5
1934 521 Bust plaster
1935 488 Head for stone, plaster $200
1936 621 Negro mahogany $250
1937 479 Ornamental fish wd $75
1938 203 P.J. Niemi plaster
1939 476 Decorative head chestnut $75
1944 172 The nestling teak $75
1945 287 Andrée plaster

ZWERLING, LEON
1906, Halifax
addr: Halifax, 4 Berlin St
1942 187 Berté $75

ZWICKER, LE ROY JUDSON
21 Jul 1906, Halifax TB2 WWA82
addr: Halifax: 120 Granville St, 1932-6. 142 Granville St, 1937, 1948-50; 69 Vernon St, 1938-42
1932 453 Hot air etch $5
1934 479 Fisherman pen & ink $5
1935 348 The Churn, Yarmouth, N.S. $50
1936 459 Figure, study $25
1937 322 The old and the new $100
323 Gas Lane, Halifax $50
1938 128 Brodder Keeler
1939 343 End of the wharf $35
1940 307 Tribute to Van Gogh $100
1942 188 Maritime $50
189 An eastern Canadian port $100
1948 68 Spires and tenements $100
1949 111 Still life $25
1950 56 Indian Harbour $50

ZWICKER, MARY MARGUERITE PORTER (m Le Roy Judson Zwicker)

1904, Yarmouth, N.S.
addr: Halifax, 87 Allan St, 1930. Wolfville, N.S: Highland Ave, 1933; Acadia University, 1934. Yarmouth, N.S, King St, 1936-7. Halifax: 69 Vernon St, 1939; 142 Granville St, 1949

1930 Porter, 1930-7
170 Peggy's Cove pastel $25
1933 250 The old mill $100
483 The breakwater pen & ink $25
1934 272 Herring Cove $30
1936 357 A winter afternoon $50
1937 241 Winter landscape $75
1939 344 Waterfront, Yarmouth, N.S. $75
345 Margaree Harbour, Cape Breton wc $25
1949 152 Sentinels of New Mexico wc $35

Members of Juries

The catalogues listed the jurors from 1938-41, 1934, and 1945-70.

ARTISTS

Arbuckle, George Franklin, 1947, 1950, 1952, 1954, 1961
Arthur, Paul, 1962
Beament, Thomas Harold, 1947, 1949 1951-2
Beauchemin, Micheline, 1963
Beaulieu, Claude, 1960
Beder, Jack, 1952
Bieler, André, 1939, 1959
Bloor, Ronald Langley, 1962, 1969
Borduas, Paul-Emile, 1946-7
Brandtner, Fritz, 1946, 1955
Bush, Jack Hamilton, 1962
Caiserman, Ghitta, 1952, 1958
Casson, Alfred Joseph, 1960
Clark, Paraskeva, 1956
Cloutier, Albert Edward, 1955
Coburn, Frederick Simpson, 1938-41, 1943
Colville, David Alexander, 1958, 1964
Cormier, Ernest, 1950
Cosgrove, Stanley Morel, 1950
Dumouchel, Albert, 1951, 1958, 1964
Earle, Paul Barnard, 1946
Forster, Michael, 1951
Fosbery, Ernest George, 1947
Fox, John Richard, 1962
Gagnon, Charles, 1968
Gagnon, Clarence Alphonse, 1938
Gaucher, Yves, 1965
Goldberg, E. Eric, 1953
Hébert, Adrien, 1940-1, 1945-6, 1949, 1951, 1954
Hébert, Henri, 1938-9, 1946
Hébert, Julien, 1957
Heward, Efa Prudence, 1945
Holgate, Edwin Headley, 1938, 1940
Jack, Richard, 1945
Johnson, Pauline E., 1959
Jongers, Alphonse, 1939, 1943
Kahane, Anne, 1958
Kennedy, Sybil, 1947, 1959
Lefort, Marie Agnes, 1962
Lemieux, Jean-Paul, 1956
Lismer, Arthur, 1941
Lyman, John Goodwin, 1947, 1949, 1953
MacDonald, Thomas Reid, 1959
McEwen, Jean Albert, 1959
McKay, Arthur Fortescue, 1964
Maillard, Charles, 1943
Masson, Henri Leopold, 1955
Mayerovitch, Harry, 1957
Mousseau, Jean-Paul Armand, 1961
Muhlstock, Louis, 1945
Newton, Lilias Torrance, 1938, 1941, 1943, 1953
Ogilvie, William Abernathy, 1939
Pellan, Alfred, 1952, 1960
Pilot, Robert Wakeham, 1938, 1946, 1949, 1953
Price, Arthur Donald, 1956
Roberts, William Goodridge, 1940, 1950, 1963
Robinson, Albert Henry, 1938, 1941
Royle, Stanley, 1939
Savage, Anne Douglas, 1951, 1955, 1963
Scott, Adam Sherriff, 1943, 1945, 1950, 1952
Scott, Marian Mildred Dale, 1946, 1949-50
Smith, Marjorie Thurston (Jori), 1953
Taylor, Frederick Bourchier, 1951
Tonnancour, Jacques Godefroy de, 1950, 1957

Viau, Guy, 1949
Watt, Henry Robertson (Robin), 1953
Webber, Gordon McKinley, 1947, 1954
Wheller, Orson Shorey, 1938, 1940-1, 1943, 1945
Wilson, Percy Roy, 1938-41, 1943
Yarwood, Walter Hawley, 1963

OTHER JURORS

Agee, William, Curator, Whitney Museum of American Art, 1968
Amaya, Mario, Curator, Art Gallery of Ontario, 1970
Ayre, Robert, writer, critic, 1960
Band, Charles Shaw, collector, 1961
Bland, John, architect, 1945, 1947
Boggs, Jean Sutherland, art administrator, 1964
Buchanan, Donald William, art administrator, 1964
Cameron, Dorothy, art consultant, 1968
Corbeil, Maurice, collector, MMFA Council, 1961
Davis, Robert Tyler, Director, AAM, 1948
Gagnon, Maurice, writer, critic, 1948
Harper, J. Russell, Curator, art historian, 1961
Heinrich, Theodore A., art historian, 1965
Hickson, J.W.A., AAM Council, 1945
Jarvis, Alan Hepburn, art administrator, 1960
Lewis, Mostyn, AAM representative, 1945-7
Lippard, Lucy, 1969
McCall, G.R., AAM representative, 1946-7
McCurry, H.O., Director, National Gallery of Canada, 1948
Marcoux-Caillé, Mme C., 1959
Messer, Thomas M., Director, Solomon R. Guggenheim Museum, 1963
Paradis, Andrée, editor, Vie des arts, 1969
Parkin, John Cresswell, architect, 1963
Peers, Gordon F., Rhode Island School of Design, 1965
Rainville, Paul, Curator, Musée du Québec, 1948
Sise, Hazen, architect, 1959

List of Exhibitions

The list shows the number of the exhibition, the year, the number of works, and when the exhibition was held. The Gallery was on Phillips Square from 1880 to 1911. Since 1912 the Museum has been on Sherbrooke Street West. The explanation of the numbering from 1880 to 1892 is in the Preface, p viii.

1	1880	170	Special exhibition of the works of Canadian artists, including Diploma pictures, etc, from the recent exhibition of the Canadian Academy of Arts, Ottawa, 14 Apr
2	1881	95	Special exhibition of the works of Canadian artists, 11 Apr
(3)	1882		Royal Canadian Academy of Arts
4	1883	168	Annual spring exhibition of works by Canadian artists, (no date)
(5)	1884		Royal Canadian Academy of Arts
6	1885	161	Annual spring exhibition of works by Canadian artists, Apr
7	1886	135	Annual spring exhibition of works by Canadian artists, Apr
(8)	1887		Royal Canadian Academy of Arts
9	1888	140	Annual spring exhibition of oil paintings & water colours, drawings, Apr
10	1889	207	Annual spring exhibition of oil paintings, water colour, drawings, statuary, etc, Apr
(11)	1890		Royal Canadian Academy of Arts
12	1891	218	Annual spring exhibition of oil paintings, water colour, drawings, statuary, etc, (no date)
13	1892	232	Annual spring exhibition of oil paintings, water colour, drawings, statuary, &c, 18 Apr-14 May
(14)	1893		Royal Canadian Academy of Arts
15	1894	281	Annual spring exhibition of oil paintings, water colour, drawings, statuary, &c, 23 Apr-19 May
16	1895	299	Annual spring exhibition of oil paintings, water colour, drawings, statuary &c, 6-30 Mar
	1896		Royal Canadian Academy of Arts
17	1897	279	Annual spring exhibition of oil paintings, water colours, sculpture, &c, 1 Apr
18	1898	273	Annual spring exhibition of oil paintings, water colours, sculpture, &c, 4 Apr
	1899		Royal Canadian Academy of Arts
	1900	263	Annual spring exhibition of oil paintings, water colours, sculpture, &c, 16 Mar

20	1901	279	Annual spring exhibition of oil paintings, water colours sculptures, etc, 8-23 Mar
	1902		Royal Canadian Academy of Arts
21	1903	329	Spring exhibition of oils, water colours, etc, 12 Mar-4 Apr
	1904		Royal Canadian Academy of Arts
22	1905	358	Spring exhibition of oils, water colours, etc, 17 Mar-4 Apr
23	1906	471	Spring exhibition of oils, water colours, etc, 23 Mar-14 Apr
	1907		Royal Canadian Academy of Arts
24	1908	458	Spring exhibition of oils, water colours, etc, 24 Mar-11 Apr
25	1909	535	Spring exhibition, 2-24 Apr
26	1910	473	Spring exhibition, 4-23 Apr
27	1911	347	Annual spring exhibition, 9 Mar-1 Apr
			(number 28 was overlooked)
29	1912	377	Spring exhibition of oils, water colours, etc, 14 Mar-6 Apr
30	1913	496	Spring exhibition of oils, water colours, etc, 26 Mar-16 Apr
31	1914	530	Spring exhibition of oils, water colours, &c, 27 Mar-18 Apr
32	1915	478	Spring exhibition of oils, water colours, &c, 26 Mar-17 Apr
33	1916	398	Spring exhibition of oils, water colours, &c, 24 Mar-15 Apr
34	1917	456	Spring exhibition of oils, water colours, &c, 22 Mar-14 Apr
35	1918	444	Spring exhibition of oils, water colours, &c, 4-27 Apr
36	1919	435	Spring exhibition, 20 Mar-12 Apr
37	1920	335	Spring exhibition, 25 Mar-17 Apr
38	1921	340	Spring exhibition, 1-23 Apr
39	1922	404	Spring exhibition, 21 Mar-15 Apr
40	1923	294	Spring exhibition, 16 Mar-14 Apr
41	1924	380	Spring exhibition, 27 Mar-20 Apr
42	1925	404	Spring exhibition, 2-26 Apr
43	1926	257	Spring exhibition, 26 Mar-18 Apr
44	1927	324	Spring exhibition, 24 Mar-18 Apr
45	1928	361	Spring exhibition, 22 Mar-15 Apr
46	1929	397	Spring exhibition, 21 Mar-14 Apr
47	1930	327	Spring exhibition, 21 Mar-21 Apr
48	1931	448	Spring exhibition, 20 Mar-19 Apr
49	1932	484	Spring exhibition, 17 Mar-17 Apr
50	1933	543	Spring exhibition, 16 Mar-16 Apr
51	1934	522	Spring exhibition, 19 Apr-13 May
52	1935	488	Spring exhibition, 21 Mar-14 Apr
53	1936	625	Spring exhibition, 19 Mar-12 Apr
54	1937	480	Spring exhibition, 18 Mar-11 Apr
55	1938	201	Spring exhibition, 17 Mar-10 Apr
56	1939	477	Spring exhibition, 9 Mar-2 Apr
57	1940	420	Spring exhibition, 20 Mar-14 Apr
58	1941	292	Spring exhibition, 20 Mar-13 Apr

59	1942	241	Annual spring exhibition, 1-30 Apr
60	1943	264	Annual spring exhibition, 1-30 Apr
61	1944	174	Annual spring exhibition, 1 Apr-2 May
62	1945	290	Annual spring exhibition, 5-29 Apr
63	1946	299	Annual spring exhibition, 28 Mar-28 Apr
64	1947	348	Annual spring exhibition, 21 Mar-20 Apr
65	1948	119	Annual spring exhibition, 4-31 Mar
66	1949	178	Annual spring exhibition, 20 Apr-15 May
67	1950	160	Annual spring exhibition, 14 Mar-9 Apr. A selection of works exhibited at the Musée de la Province de Québec, (no date)
68	1951	146	Annual spring exhibition, 2-30 May
69	1952	151	Annual spring exhibition, 9 May-18 Jun
70	1953	108	Annual spring exhibition, 14 Mar-19 Apr
71	1954	140	Annual spring exhibition, 17 Mar-18 Apr
72	1955	157	Annual spring exhibition, 2 Apr-1 May
73	1956	153	Annual spring exhibition, 6 Apr-6 May
74	1957	169	Annual spring exhibition, 5 Apr-5 May
75	1958	91	Annual spring exhibition, 28 Mar-27 Apr
76	1959	67	Annual spring exhibition, 3 Apr-3 May
77	1960	254	Annual spring exhibition, 8 Apr-8 May
78	1961	124	Annual spring exhibition, 8 Apr-7 May
79	1962	82	Annual spring exhibition, 7 Apr-6 May
80	1963	118	Annual spring exhibition, 5 Apr-5 May
81	1964	140	Annual spring exhibition, 7 Apr-3 May
82	1965	44	Annual spring exhibition, 9 Apr-9 May
	1966		Museum closed for alterations
	1967	75	Prize award winners 1908-1965 Spring Exhibitions / Lauréats 1908-1965 Salons de Printemps, 30 Mar-30 Apr
	1968	314	Survey 68 / Sondage 68, 8 Mar-7 Apr
	1969	12	Survey 69 / Sondage 69, 16 May-26 Jun
	1970	95	Survey / Sondage 70 Realism(e)s, 8 May-7 Jun. Art Gallery of Ontario, 7 Aug-7 Sep

www.ingramcontent.com/pod-product-compliance
Lightning Source LLC
LaVergne TN
LVHW010447080826
844660LV00027B/1230